Volume I
Student-Centered Mathematics Series

Teaching Student-Centered Mathematics

Developmentally Appropriate Instruction for Grades PreK–2

Third Edition

John A. Van de Walle
Late of Virginia Commonwealth University

LouAnn H. Lovin
James Madison University

Karen S. Karp
Johns Hopkins University

Jennifer M. Bay-Williams
University of Louisville

 Pearson

330 Hudson Street, NY NY 10013

Vice President and Editor in Chief: Kevin M. Davis	**Cover Art:** TongRo/Getty Images
Portfolio Manager: Drew Bennett	**Media Producer:** Linda Bishop
Content Producer: Yagnesh Jani	**Editorial Production and Composition Services:** SPi Global
Portfolio Management Assistant: Maria Feliberty	
Executive Product Marketing Manager: Christopher Barry	**Full-Service Project Manager:** Jason Hammond, SPi Global
Executive Field Marketing Manager: Krista Clark	
Procurement Specialist: Deidra Smith	**Text Font:** 10/13
Cover Designer: Cenveo, Carie Keller	

Library of Congress Cataloging-in-Publication Data:
Names: Van de Walle, John A. | Lovin, LouAnn H. | Karp, Karen S. | Bay-Williams, Jennifer M.
Title: Teaching student-centered mathematics. Developmentally appropriate instruction for grades preK–2.
Other titles: Teaching student-centered mathematics. Grades K-3
Description: Third edition / John A. Van de Walle, late of Virginia
   Commonwealth University, LouAnn H. Lovin, James Madison University, Karen S. Karp, Johns Hopkins
   University, Jennifer M. Bay-Williams, University of Louisville. | New York : Pearson
   Education, [2018] | Series: Student-centered mathematics series ; volume 1 | Includes bibliographical
   references and index.
Identifiers: LCCN 2016051023| ISBN 9780134556437 | ISBN 0134556437
Subjects: LCSH: Mathematics–Study and teaching (Primary) | Mathematics–Study and teaching (Early
   childhood) | Individualized instruction.
Classification: LCC QA13 .V36 2018 | DDC 372.7–dc23
LC record available at **https://lccn.loc.gov/2016051023**

2   17

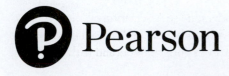

ISBN 10: 0-13-455643-7
ISBN 13: 978-0-13-455643-7

About the Authors

The late **John A. Van de Walle** was a professor emeritus at Virginia Commonwealth University. He was a mathematics education consultant who regularly gave professional development workshops for K–8 teachers in the United States and Canada. He visited and taught in elementary school classrooms and worked with teachers to implement student-centered math lessons. He coauthored the Scott Foresman-Addison Wesley Mathematics K–6 series and contributed to the Pearson School mathematics program, enVisionMATH. In addition, he wrote numerous chapters and articles for the National Council of Teachers of Mathematics (NCTM) books and journals and was very active in NCTM, including serving on the Board of Directors, as the chair of the Educational Materials Committee, and as a frequent speaker at national and regional meetings.

LouAnn H. Lovin is a professor of mathematics education at James Madison University (Virginia). She coauthored the first edition of the *Teaching Student-Centered Mathematics* Professional Development Series with John A. Van de Walle as well as *Teaching Mathematics Meaningfully: Solutions for Reaching Struggling Learners* (2nd ed.) with David Allsopp and Sarah Vaningen. LouAnn taught mathematics to middle and high school students before transitioning to preK–grade 8. For almost twenty years, she has worked in preK through grade 8 classrooms and engaged with teachers in professional development as they implement a student-centered approach to teaching mathematics. She has published articles in *Teaching Children Mathematics*, *Mathematics Teaching in the Middle School*, *Teaching Exceptional Children*, and *Journal of Mathematics Teacher Education* and has served on NCTM's Educational Materials Committee. LouAnn's research on teachers' mathematical knowledge for teaching has focused most recently on the developmental nature of prospective teachers' fraction knowledge.

Karen S. Karp is at the School of Education at Johns Hopkins University in Baltimore (Maryland). Previously, she was a professor of mathematics education at the University of Louisville for more than twenty years. Prior to entering the field of teacher education she was an elementary school teacher in New York. She is also coauthor of *Elementary and Middle School Mathematics: Teaching Developmentally*, *Developing Essential Understanding of Addition and Subtraction for Teaching Mathematics in Pre-K–Grade 2*, and numerous book chapters and articles. She is a former member of the Board of Directors of NCTM and a former president of the Association of Mathematics Teacher Educators (AMTE). She continues to work in classrooms to support teachers of students with disabilities in their mathematics instruction.

Jennifer M. Bay-Williams is a professor of mathematics education at the University of Louisville (Kentucky). Jennifer frequently offers professional development about effective mathematics teaching to K–12 teachers and leaders. She has coauthored numerous books, including *On the Money: Math Activities to Build Financial Literacy*; *Mathematics Coaching: Resources and Tools for Coaches and Leaders, K–12*; *Developing Essential Understanding of Addition and Subtraction for Teaching Mathematics in Pre-K–Grade 2*; *Math and Literature: Grades 6–8*; and *Navigating through Connections in Grades 6–8*. Additionally, she has written dozens of articles on teaching and learning in NCTM journals. Jennifer serves on the NCTM Board of Directors, and has served on the TODOS: Equity for All Board, and president of the Association of Mathematics Teacher Educators (AMTE). Jennifer taught elementary, middle, and high school in Missouri and in Peru, and continues to work in classrooms at all levels with students and with teachers.

Brief Contents

Expanded Table of Contents

Part 2: Teaching Student-Centered Mathematics

Preface

All children can learn mathematics with understanding! We believe that teachers can and must create learning environments in which children have this experience. Effective mathematics instruction involves posing worthwhile tasks that will engage children in the mathematics they are expected to learn. Then, by allowing children to interact with and productively struggle with the mathematics using *their* ideas and *their* strategies—a student-centered approach—children will develop a robust understanding of the mathematics. As they learn to see the connections among mathematical topics and to their world, children will value mathematics and feel empowered to use it. The title of this book, *Teaching Student-Centered Mathematics: Developmentally Appropriate Instruction for Grades PreK–2*, reflects this vision. Part 1 of this book is dedicated to addressing how to build a student-centered environment in which children can become mathematically proficient and Part 2 elaborates on how that environment can be realized across all content in the grades PreK–2 mathematics curriculum.

What Are Our Goals for the Student-Centered Mathematics Series?

Creating a classroom in which children design their solution pathways, engage in productive struggle, and connect mathematical ideas is complex. Questions arise, such as, "How do I get children to wrestle with problems if they just want me to show them how to do it? What kinds of tasks lend themselves to this type of engagement? Where can I learn the mathematics content I need in order to be able to teach in this way?" With these and other questions firmly in mind, we have three main objectives for the third edition of this series:

1. Illustrate what it means to teach mathematics using a student-centered, problem-based approach.

2. Serve as a go-to reference for all of the mathematics content suggested for grades PreK-2 as recommended in the *Common Core State Standards for Mathematics* (CCSSO, 2010) and in other standards used by various states, as well as research-based strategies that depict how children best learn this content.

3. Present a practical resource of robust, problem-based activities and tasks that can engage children in the mathematics that is important for them to learn.

These are also goals of *Elementary and Middle School Mathematics: Teaching Developmentally*, a comprehensive resource for teachers in grades K–8, which has been widely used in universities and in schools. There is overlap between the comprehensive K–8 book and this Student-Centered Mathematics Series; however, we have adapted the Student-Centered Mathematics Series to be more useful for a practicing classroom teacher by addressing the content for specific grade bands (with more activities!), removing content aimed at preservice teachers, and adding additional information more appropriate for practicing teachers. We hope you will find that this is a valuable resource for teaching and learning mathematics!

What's New to the Third Edition of the Student-Centered Mathematics Series?

The most significant change to the third edition is its availability as an Enhanced Pearson eText. Teachers can now take advantage of eText technology, easily accessing downloadable resources to support many of the math activities offered in the text and linking to videos that demonstrate how to teach certain math concepts. Another big change is that the third edition appears in four-color so pedagogical features are more easily found and studied. We are hopeful too that the addition of color helps to enhance and clarify the ideas we have intended to convey. We have also included some new features that we briefly describe here. (More detailed information about the new features can be found in the following section.) We then highlight the most substantial changes we have made to specific chapters to reflect the changing landscape of mathematics education.

What Are the New eText Features?

Each volume in the Student-Centered Mathematics Series is also available as an Enhanced Pearson eText* with the following point-of-use features:

- *Downloadable Activity Pages and Blackline Masters.* Hyperlinks provide access to ready-to-use teaching resources including Activity Pages and Blackline Masters to support students' engagement in a large number of math activities.
- *Videos.* Links to videos allow teachers to observe an interview with a child, watch an idea play out in a classroom, or listen to a more in-depth description of an important math concept.
- *Activities Correspond to CCSS-M.* The numerous problem-based tasks presented in activity boxes are now connected to the appropriate *Common Core State Standards for Mathematics*.
- *Immediate Access to Expanded Lessons.* A custom basket located on the navigation bar links teachers to full and Expanded Lessons and include the Blackline Masters or Activity Pages if needed to execute each lesson. Expanded Lessons are referenced at point-of-use in numbered math activities throughout the eText.

What's New in Part 1?

Part 1 consists of seven chapters that focus on important "hot" topics that address ideas for creating a classroom environment in which all students can succeed. These chapters are, by design, shorter in length than the content chapters in Part 2, but are full of effective strategies and ideas. The intent is that these chapters can be used in professional development workshops, book study, or professional learning community (PLC) discussions. Changes to Part 1 chapters include:

Chapter 1: Setting a Vision for Learning High-Quality Mathematics. Changes to this chapter include a new table that relates CCSS-M's mathematical practices (CCSSO, 2010) to NCTM's process standards (2000), clarification about the difference between modeling mathematics and modeling with mathematics, and an additional emphasis on the characteristics of productive classrooms that promote student understanding.

---

*These features are only available in the Pearson eText, available exclusively from **www.pearsonhighered.com/etextbooks** or by ordering the Pearson eText plus Vol I Book Package (ISBN: 0134090683) or the Pearson eText Access Code Card (ISBN: 0134556453).

Chapter 2: Teaching Mathematics through Problem Solving. The eight mathematics teaching practices from *Principles to Actions* (NCTM, 2014) have been added! In addition, several new sections were added: evaluating and adapting tasks to increase their potential for learning, growth versus fixed mindsets (connected to productive struggle and learning from mistakes); and effective aspects of questioning. Finally, more detail pertaining to the three-phases (before, during, and after) is provided.

Chapter 3: Creating Assessments for Learning. Supported by the recent position statement from professional organizations (NCSM and AMTE) about assessment for learning (AFL), this chapter was revised to be more explicit about how to collect evidence from students on their progress, interpret that evidence, make informed decisions about the next instructional steps and provide actionable feedback to students. There is also an expanded section on using writing to learn mathematics.

Chapter 4: Differentiating Instruction. This chapter was revised to better highlight differentiated tasks for whole-classroom instruction. You will also find new team-building activities to enhance your students' interactions with each other when working in groups.

Chapter 5: Teaching Culturally and Linguistically Diverse Students. In this chapter, significant revisions were made to reflect research in the field (twenty-two new references). Among these changes was increased attention to Culturally Responsive Mathematics Instruction (CRMI), developed around four key aspects and an expanded section on nurturing students' mathematical identities.

Chapter 6: Planning, Teaching, and Assessing Students with Exceptionalities. Several new tools were added to this chapter including a printable set of cards, each with a Strategy for Making Math Accessible for learners who struggle. This tool can be used when planning core instruction modifications or interventions for students with special needs. There is also a Mathematics Integration Plan Template to support planning for gifted students or students with a high interest in exploring mathematical topics in relation to other subject areas or perspectives.

Chapter 7: Collaborating with Families and Other Stakeholders. This chapter was significantly revised to focus on advocacy across stakeholders. This included increased attention to communicating about CCSS Mathematics. Finally, the homework section was expanded, including new activities and games for families.

What's New to Part 2?

In addition to the changes listed previously that are included across all three volumes, there are many changes specific to Volume I, Part 2 to meet the needs of primary learners. Across all content chapters, more activities and many activities pages were added, in particular to address hard-to-teach topics. The list below highlights significant new content in a number of chapters.

Chapter 8: Early Number Concepts and Number Sense. We have included a new learning progression for counting that identifies increasingly sophisticated levels of reasoning. In addition, there are several new activities focused on developing early counting skills. We have also included a new section on thinking about zero. Although zero is one of the most important digits in our base-ten system, we find that too often because early counting often involves touching an object, zero is not included in discussions about numbers and counting. We have tried to be more cognizant of this tendency and have included more tasks, questions, and purposeful discussions about the number zero in this and other chapters.

Chapter 9: Meanings for Operations. We increased the focus on helping children write equations from word problems, using both computational and semantic forms. We also improved the section on helping children analyze contextual problems by detailing strategies that can help children prepare to solve problems. A new section was added about helping children solve multistep problems, including the use of hidden questions to help children progress from one-step to multistep problems.

Chapter 10: Basic Facts. In Chapter 10 there is an increased emphasis on assessing basic facts. We present the risks of using timed tests and share a collection of alternative assessment ideas. There is also a new recommendation to develop fluency with foundational facts first (e.g., +0, +1, +2, Doubles, and Combinations of 10), before working on other basic facts. Finally, as described in the CCSS and related research, there is a shift from a focus on mastery to a focus on fluency. Also included are new activities and games to support basic fact fluency.

Chapter 12: Whole Number Computation Strategies. There is an enhanced section that discusses the connection between place value and addition and subtraction. More examples of the equal additions strategy are provided for clarification. And a new section about computational estimation includes recommendations for instruction and several new activities.

Chapter 16: Geometry. Chapter 16 has been reorganized around the four geometry strands (shapes and properties, location, transformations, visualization) to provide a more cohesive approach to introducing geometry to children. As each level of geometric thinking is introduced, examples of appropriate activities are presented to help clarify each geometric level.

Chapter 17: Data. The new addition of *driving questions* (Hourigan & Leavy, 2015/2016) is introduced as a way to motivate children's involvement in the processes of doing statistics. There is an increased emphasis on helping children consider the shape of the data as they engage in the analysis and interpretation phases of doing statistics. We also share three levels of questions you can ask to help children interpret and reason with data displayed in graphs.

What Special Features Appear in Pearson's Student-Centered Mathematics Series?

Features Found in Parts 1 and 2

- *Teaching Tips.* These brief tips identify practical take-away ideas that can support the teaching and learning of specific chapter content being addressed. These might be an instructional suggestion, a particular point about language use, a common student misconception, or a suggestion about a resource.

- *Stop and Reflect.* Reflective thinking is the key to effective learning. This is true not only for our students but also for ourselves as we continue to learn more about effective mathematics teaching. Keep your eye out for these sections that ask you to pause to solve a problem or reflect on some aspect of what you have read. These Stop and Reflect sections do not signal every important idea, but we have tried to place them where it seemed natural and helpful for you to slow down a bit and think deeply about an idea. In addition, every chapter in Part 1 ends with a Stop and Reflect section. Use these for discussions in professional learning communities or for reflection on your own.

- *New! Downloadable Resources including Activity Pages and Expanded Lessons.* Many activities that previously required cards or recording sheets now include these as ready-to-use, downloadable pages. You will also find a variety of downloadable resources that support teaching activities such as formative assessment and team-building activities. You can access these downloadable pages by clicking the blue text in the eText at point of use.

- *New! Videos.* The book now includes a collection of videos that are positioned right when you need them—when a child's misconception during a diagnostic interview will reinforce a point, when a strategy needs a more in-depth description or when it helps to see a teacher carry out an idea in a classroom of children. When accessing the e-book, you can click on the link to see an idea in action. There is also a video of John Van de Walle sharing some of his insights on how to teach a mathematics topic through the perspective of a student-centered, problem-based approach.

Additional Features Found in Part 2

- *New! NCTM Teaching Practices Appendix.* The *Principles to Actions* (NCTM, 2014) eight teaching practices are provided in Appendix C. These describe the actions that teachers do to support student thinking and provide guidance on how to enact student-centered mathematics.

- *New! Blackline Masters Hyperlinked in Chapters.* Blackline Masters are used in some of the activities and Expanded Lessons. Look for the call outs for the hyperlinks embedded in the activities that alert you to the corresponding print-friendly PDF of the Blackline Master. In Appendix E, you will find a list of the Blackline Masters and a thumbnail version of each.

- *New! Activities Correspond to the CCSS-M.* Numerous problem-based tasks are presented in activity boxes that are connected to the appropriate *Common Core State Standards for Mathematics*. Additional ideas are described directly in the text or in the illustrations. They are designed to engage your children in *doing* mathematics (as described in Chapter 2). Most of these activities are presented in the numbered activity boxes and include adaptation and accommodation suggestions for English language learners and children with special needs denoted with icons for easy reference. In addition, activities that incorporate technology are denoted with a technology icon. In Appendix D, you will find *Activities at a Glance*. This table lists all the named and numbered activities with a short statement about the mathematical content goal for each, the CCSS-M standard(s) and the page number where it can be located.

It is important that you see these activities as an integral part of the text that surrounds them. The activities are inserted as examples to support the development of the mathematics being discussed and how your children can be supported in learning that content. Therefore, we hope that you will not use any activity for instruction without reading carefully the full text in which it is embedded.

- *New! Downloadable Expanded Lessons.* In each chapter, one or more activities have been expanded it into a complete lesson plan, following the *before, during, after* structure described in Chapter 2 and are available by clicking on the link in the eText. These Expanded Lessons provide a model for converting an activity description into a full lesson that can engage children in developing a robust understanding of the related concept. In this new edition, all of the Expanded Lessons are now aligned with CCSSO grade-level recommendations and include adaptation suggestions for English language learners and children with disabilities. Many use the new Activity Pages or Blackline Masters.

- *New! Common Errors and Misconceptions.* Each chapter in Part 2 includes a table with common errors and misconceptions for chapter-related mathematical topics. This table includes examples of student work or verbal responses you should look for when a child is exhibiting these errors and ways to help the child move past these mistaken understandings. Using these tables, you can anticipate how you might support children in confronting common barriers so they can be unearthed and debunked. These lists also help you plan for gathering student assessment data that is targeted to catch areas of confusion or misconceptions prior to formally assessing children on a high-stakes evaluation of their performance. These examples were identified through the research literature and from the voices of teachers like yourself, about the common mistakes their children are making.

- *Formative Assessment Notes.* Assessment should be an integral part of instruction. As you read, we want you to think about what to listen and look for (assess) in different areas of content development. Therefore, you will find Formative Assessment Notes that describe ways to assess your children's developing knowledge and understanding. These Formative Assessment Notes can also help improve your understanding about how to help your children through targeted instruction.

- *Technology Notes.* These notes provide practical information about how technology can be used to help your children learn the content in that section. Descriptions include open-source software, interactive applets, and other Web-based resources—all of which are free.

- *Standards for Mathematical Practice Notes.* Connections to the eight Standards of Mathematical Practice from the *Common Core State Standards* are highlighted in the margins. The location of the note indicates an example of the identified practice in the nearby text.

- *Common Core State Standards Appendices.* The *Common Core State Standards* outline eight Standards for Mathematical Practice (Appendix A) that help children develop and demonstrate a deep understanding of and capacity to do mathematics. We initially describe these practices in Chapter 1 and highlight examples of the mathematical practices throughout the content chapters in Part 2 through margin notes. We used the *Common Core State Standards for Mathematics* (CCSSO, 2010) as a guide to determine the content emphasis in each volume of the series. Appendix B provides a list of the critical content areas for each grade level discussed in this volume.

- *Big Ideas.* Much of the research and literature espousing a developmental approach suggests that teachers plan their instruction around "big ideas" rather than isolated skills or concepts. At the beginning of each chapter, you will find a list of the key mathematical ideas associated with the chapter. These lists of learning targets can provide a snapshot of the mathematics you are teaching.

Acknowledgments

We would like to begin by acknowledging *you:* the reader, the teacher, the leader, and the advocate for your children. The strong commitment of teachers and teacher leaders to always strive to improve how we teach mathematics is the reason this book was written in the first place. And, because of ongoing input and feedback, we endeavored to revise this edition to meet your changing needs. We have received thoughtful input from many teachers and reviewers, and all of it has informed the development of this substantially revised third edition!

In preparing the third edition we benefited from the thoughtful input of the following educators who offered comments on the second edition or on the manuscript for the third: Dr. Lucia M. Flevares, The Ohio State University; Melanie N. Woods, Wright State University. Their comments helped push our thinking on many important topics. Many specific suggestions offered by these reviewers found their way into the pages of this book. We offer our sincere appreciation to these esteemed educators for their valued suggestions and constructive feedback.

As we reviewed standards, research, and teaching articles; visited classrooms; and collected students' work samples, we were continually reminded of the amazing commitment to effective mathematics teaching and learning. From the mathematics educators and mathematicians working on standards documents, to the teachers who facilitate discussions about mathematics in preK–grade 8 classrooms and then share the results with others, we are grateful for the broad and heartfelt commitment to mathematics education for *all* students on the part of so many educators—particularly the teachers with whom we have worked in recent years.

We also want to acknowledge the strong support of our editorial team throughout the process, from the first discussions about what the third edition might include, through the tedious editing at later stages in the development. Without their support, the final product would not be the quality resource we hope you find it to be. Specifically, we thank Meredith Fossil for helping us envision our work, Linda Bishop for seeing this vision through, and both of them for their words of encouragement and wisdom. Working on three volumes of a book simultaneously is quite an undertaking! We are also truly grateful for Miryam Chandler at Pearson and Jason Hammond and the team at SPi Global who helped us wade through the permissions process and the production and editing of our new edition and eText.

Even with the support of so many, researching and writing takes time. Simple words cannot express the gratitude we have to our families for their support, patience, and contributions to the production of these books. Briefly we recognize them by name here: Karen thanks her husband, Bob Ronau, and her children and grandchildren, Matthew, Tammy, Josh, Misty, Matt, Christine, Jeff, Pamela, Jessica, Zane, Madeline, Jack, and Emma. LouAnn thanks her husband, Ramsey, and her two sons, Nathan and Jacob. Jennifer thanks her husband, Mitch, and her children, MacKenna and Nicolas.

The origin of this book began many years ago with the development of *Elementary and Middle School Mathematics: Teaching Developmentally* by John A. Van de Walle. What began as a methods book for preservice teachers spread enthusiastically throughout the teaching community because it offered content support, activities, and up-to-date best practices for teaching mathematics. The three-volume series was developed as a way to focus on and expand the specific grade-level topics. John was adamant that *all* children can learn to reason and make sense of mathematics. We acknowledge his commitment and his significant contributions to the field of mathematics education. His ideas and enduring vision continue to inspire the work you see in this new edition.

The response to the second edition has been amazing. We hope the third edition will be received with as much interest and enthusiasm as the second and continue to be a valuable support to your mathematics teaching and your children's learning.

1

Setting a Vision for Learning High-Quality Mathematics

In his book *The World Is Flat* (2007) Thomas Friedman discusses how globalization through technology has created the need for people to have lasting, adaptable skills so they can survive the ever-changing landscape of available jobs. He points out that in our digital world, lovers and doers of mathematics will always have career options and opportunities. However, no matter their career choice, given the extent to which our world relies on technology and the processing of massive amounts of information, all students need to develop skillsets that will allow them to be successful in our economy and society. Lynn Arthur Steen, a well-known mathematician and educator, stated, "As information becomes ever more quantitative and as society relies increasingly on computers and the data they produce, an innumerate citizen today is as vulnerable as the illiterate peasant of Gutenberg's time" (1997, p. xv).

To prepare students for an ever-changing world, for jobs that possibly do not even exist today, can't we just pay more attention to the high school curriculum? Certainly what students learn in high school is important. However, a growing number of studies points to a strong association between early gains in mathematical ability and later academic achievement (e.g., Claessens, Duncan, & Engel, 2009; Watts, Greg, Duncan, Siegler, & Davis-Kean, 2014). So we need to begin this preparation early in elementary school and continue to build on this foundation throughout the school years.

Understanding and Doing Mathematics

The changing world influences what should be taught in mathematics classrooms, even at the pre-K–2 level. The dialogue on the best ways to prepare students to be successful in this changing world has involved mathematics educators, researchers, teachers, policymakers, and elected officials and has considered the many National Council of Teachers of Mathematics (NCTM) standards documents, international assessments, and research.

One of the influential documents that added to this dialogue is *Adding It Up* (National Research Council [NRC], 2001). Based on a review of the research on how children learn mathematics, this document identified the following five strands of mathematical proficiency that are seen as indicators of someone who understands (and can do) mathematics.

- *Conceptual understanding:* Having a robust web of connections and relationships within and between ideas, interpretations, and representations of mathematical concepts.

- *Procedural fluency:* Being able to flexibly choose and accurately and efficiently perform an appropriate strategy for a particular problem. For more on fluency, go to the NCTM website and search for the 2014 Annual Meeting Webcast "President's Session–Fluency . . . It's More Than Fast and Accurate."

- *Strategic competence:* Being able to make sense of, represent, and determine solutions to mathematical problems.

- *Adaptive reasoning:* Being able to think about, explain, and justify one's ideas using mathematically sensible reasons coupled with the ability to shift strategies when needed.

- *Productive disposition:* Having an ingrained awareness that mathematics makes sense and is useful, valuable, and rewarding along with the belief that one is capable of being successful in learning and doing mathematics through hard work and perseverance.

Figure 1.1

Interrelated and intertwined strands of mathematical proficiency.

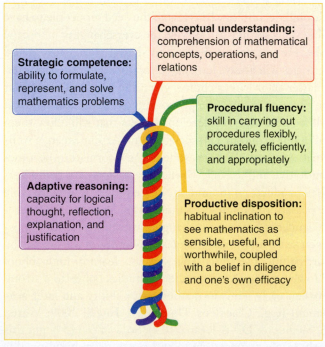

Strategic competence: ability to formulate, represent, and solve mathematics problems

Conceptual understanding: comprehension of mathematical concepts, operations, and relations

Procedural fluency: skill in carrying out procedures flexibly, accurately, efficiently, and appropriately

Adaptive reasoning: capacity for logical thought, reflection, explanation, and justification

Productive disposition: habitual inclination to see mathematics as sensible, useful, and worthwhile, coupled with a belief in diligence and one's own efficacy

Source: From "The Strands of Mathematical Proficiency" in *Adding It Up: Helping Children Learn Mathematics.* Edited by Jeremy Kilpatrick, Jane Swafford, and Bradford Findell. Published by proceedings of the National Academy of Sciences, © 2001.

Figure 1.1 illustrates the interrelated and interwoven nature of the strands of mathematical proficiency: As one strand develops it builds on and builds up other strands, resulting in a strengthened whole. As an example, consider the ineffective practice of teaching procedures in the absence of conceptual understanding. Often this approach yields a lack of retention and increased errors, rigid approaches, and inefficient strategy use. (**Watch a related video at https://www.youtube.com/watch?v=FVKtQwARe6c.**) When children are in classrooms where these strands of proficiency are allowed to develop together, they are able to build a stronger understanding of both mathematical concepts and procedures.

Numerous other reports and standards were developed as part of the effort to improve mathematics teaching and learning and prepare students for the ever-changing world. Among these was NCTM's *Curriculum Focal Points* (2006), which offered guidance in developing a PreK–8 mathematics curriculum that was focused, provided depth, and explicitly showed connections between mathematical ideas. In turn, the *Common Core State Standards* (CCSS-M) (CCSSO, 2010) and other state standards were developed that recognize the need for coherent and rigorous standards that promote college- and career-readiness.

In particular, the CCSS-M articulates an overview of critical areas for each grade from K–8 to provide a coherent curriculum built around big mathematical ideas. At this time, more than 40 states; Washington, D.C.; four territories; and Department of Defense Schools have adopted the CCSS-M. A few states chose to not adopt these standards from the start and others are still deciding their level of participation or re-evaluating their own standards against CCSS-M. Nonetheless, this represents the largest shift of mathematics content in the United States in more than 100 years.

This effort to develop standards that promote college- and career-readiness has resulted in attention to the *processes* of *doing* mathematics, not just the *content*. Notably, NCTM (2000) identifies the process standards of problem solving, reasoning and proof, representation, communication, and connections as ways in which children acquire and use mathematical knowledge. Children engaged in the process of *problem solving* build mathematical knowledge and understanding by grappling with and solving genuine problems, as opposed to completing routine exercises. They use *reasoning and proof* to make sense of mathematical tasks and concepts and to develop, justify, and evaluate mathematical arguments and solutions. Children create and use *representations* (e.g., diagrams, graphs, symbols, and manipulatives) to reason through problems. They also engage in *communication* as they explain their ideas and reasoning verbally, in writing, and through representations. Children develop and use *connections* between mathematical ideas as they learn new mathematical concepts and procedures. They also build *connections* between mathematics and other disciplines by applying mathematics to real world situations. The process standards should not be regarded as separate content or strands in the mathematics curriculum; rather they are integral components of all mathematics teaching and learning. By engaging in these processes, children *learn* mathematics by *doing* mathematics.

The CCSS-M also includes the Standards for Mathematical Practice (CCSSO, 2010), which are ways in which children can develop and demonstrate a deep understanding of and capacity to do mathematics (see Appendix A). Whether your state has adopted the CCSS, the eight Standards of Mathematical Practice are worthy of attention. These mathematical practices are based on the underlying frameworks of the NCTM process standards and the components of mathematical proficiency identified by the National Research Council's document *Adding It Up* (NRC, 2001). Like the NCTM process standards, these practices are not separate, but integral to all mathematics teaching and learning. Here we provide a brief discussion about each mathematical practice.

1. *Make sense of problems and persevere in solving them.* To make sense of problems, children need to learn how to analyze the given information, parameters, and relationships in a problem so that they can understand the situation and identify possible ways to solve it. Encourage younger students to use concrete materials or bar diagrams to investigate and solve the problem. Once children learn strategies for making sense of problems, encourage them to remain committed to solving them. As they learn to monitor and assess their progress and change course as needed, they will solve the problems they set out to solve!

2. *Reason abstractly and quantitatively.* This practice involves children reasoning with quantities and their relationships in problem situations. You can support children's development of this practice by helping them create representations that correspond to the meanings of the quantities, units, and operations involved. When appropriate, children should also learn to represent and manipulate the situation symbolically. Encourage children to find connections between the abstract symbols and the representation that illustrates the quantities and their relationships. For example, when children use drawings to show that 5 bears can be represented with 3 red bears and 2 yellow bears, encourage them to connect their representation to the number sentence $5 = 3 + 2$. Ultimately, children should be able to move flexibly between the symbols and other representations.

3. *Construct viable arguments and critique the reasoning of others.* This practice emphasizes the importance of children using mathematical reasoning to justify their ideas and solutions, including being able to recognize and use counterexamples. Encourage children to examine each others' arguments to determine whether they make sense and to identify ways to clarify or improve the arguments. This practice emphasizes that mathematics is based on reasoning and should be examined in a community—not carried out in isolation. Tips for supporting children as they learn to justify their ideas can be found in Chapter 2.

4. *Model with mathematics.* This practice encourages children to use the mathematics they know to describe, explain, and solve problems from a real-world context. For younger students this could mean writing an addition or a subtraction equation to represent a given situation or using their number sense to determine whether there are enough plates for all the children in their class. Be sure to encourage children to determine whether their mathematical results make sense in the context of the given situation. Note that this practice is different from *modeling mathematics*, which involves using representations such as concrete materials to illustrate mathematical ideas (e.g., base ten materials to show the 10-1 relationship in our number system).

🌱 *Teaching Tip*

Research suggests that children, in particular girls, may tend to continue to use the same tools because they feel comfortable with the tools and are afraid to take risks (Ambrose, 2002). Look for children who tend to use the same tool or strategy every time they work on tasks. Encourage all children to take risks and try new tools and strategies.

5. *Use appropriate tools strategically.* Children should become familiar with a variety of problem-solving tools that can be used to solve a problem and they should learn to choose which ones are most appropriate for a given situation. For example, second graders should experience using the following tools for computation: pencil and paper, manipulatives, calculator, hundreds chart, and a number line. Then in a situation when an estimate is needed for the sum of 23 and 52, some second graders might consider paper and pencil, manipulatives, and a calculator as tools that would slow down the process and would select a hundreds chart to quickly move from 50 down two rows (20 spaces) to get to 70.

6. *Attend to precision.* In communicating ideas to others, it is imperative that children learn to be explicit about their reasoning. For example, they need to be clear about the meanings of the operations and symbols they use, to indicate the units involved in a problem, and to clearly label the diagrams they provide in their explanations. As children share their ideas, make this expectation clear and ask clarifying questions that help make the details of their reasoning more apparent. Teachers can further encourage children's attention to precision by introducing, highlighting, and encouraging the use of accurate mathematical terminology in explanations and diagrams.

7. *Look for and make use of structure.* Children who look for and recognize a pattern or structure can experience a shift in their perspective or understanding. Therefore, set the expectation that children will look for patterns and structure and help them reflect on their significance. For example, look for opportunities to help children notice that the order in which they add two numbers does not change the sum—they can add 4 + 7 or 7 + 4 to get 11. Once they recognize this pattern through several experiences with other examples, they will have a new understanding and the use of a powerful property of our number system, the commutative property of addition.

8. *Look for and express regularity in repeated reasoning.* Encourage children to step back and reflect on any regularity that occurs to help them develop a general idea or method or to identify shortcuts. For example, as children begin adding numbers together, they will encounter situations in which zero is added to a number. Over time, help children reflect

on the results of adding zero to any number. Eventually they should be able to express that when they add or subtract zero to any number, the number is unaffected.

Note that the process standards are embedded in the mathematical practices. Table 1.1 shows one way to think about the relationship between the process standards and the eight mathematical practices. For example, ways to engage children in reasoning and proof involve the mathematical practices of reasoning abstractly and quantitatively, constructing viable arguments and critiquing others' reasoning, modeling with mathematics, and looking for and making use of structure. Bleiler, Baxter, Stephens, and Barlow (2015) provide additional ideas to help teachers further their understanding of the eight mathematical practices. Children who learn to use these processes and practices of *doing* mathematics have a greater chance of becoming mathematically proficient.

Table 1.1. Connections between NCTM's process standards and CCSS-M's mathematical practices.

	MP1	MP2	MP3	MP4	MP5	MP6	MP7	MP8
Problem Solving	■	■		■	■		■	■
Reasoning and Proof		■	■	■		■	■	
Communication		■	■		■	■		
Representation	■	■	■	■				
Connections				■			■	■

MP1: *Make sense of problems and persevere in solving them.*
MP2: *Reason abstractly and quantitatively.*
MP3: *Construct viable arguments and critique the reasoning of others.*
MP4: *Model with mathematics.*
MP5: *Use appropriate tools strategically.*
MP6: *Attend to precision.*
MP7: *Look for and make use of structure.*
MP8: *Look for and express regularity in repeated reasoning.*

How Do Children Learn?

As noted in NCTM's (2014) *Principles to Actions* document, research in mathematics education as well as in cognitive science supports the notion that learning is an active process in which each child, through personal experiences, interactions with others, and reflective thought, develops his or her own mathematical knowledge. The active nature required in developing the NCTM Process Standards and the CCSS-M Mathematical Practices is what makes them such powerful places for students to learn as they engage in doing mathematics.

Two research-based theories about learning, constructivism and sociocultural theory, provide us with specific insights into the active nature of the learning process. Although one theory focuses on the individual learner and the other emphasizes the social and cultural aspects of the classroom, these theories are not competing and are actually compatible (Norton & D'Ambrosio, 2008).

Constructivism

At the heart of constructivism is the notion that learners are not blank slates but rather creators (constructors) of their own learning (Piaget, 1976; von Glasersfeld, 1995). All people, all of the time, construct or give meaning to things they experience or think about. Whether you are listening passively to a lecture or actively engaging in synthesizing findings in a project, your brain uses your existing knowledge to make sense of new information.

Through reflective thought, people connect existing ideas to new information and in this way modify their existing knowledge to incorporate new ideas. Making these connections can happen in either of two ways—*assimilation* or *accommodation*. Assimilation occurs when a new concept "fits" with prior knowledge and the new information expands an existing mental network. Accommodation takes place when the new concept does not "fit" with the existing network, thus creating a cognitive conflict or state of confusion that causes what learning theorists call *disequilibrium*. As an example, consider what happens when children start learning about numbers and counting. They make sense of a number by counting a quantity of objects by ones. With larger numbers, such as two-digit numbers, they continue to use this approach to give meaning to the number (assimilation). Eventually, counting large amounts of objects becomes cumbersome and, at the same time, they are likely learning about grouping in tens. Over time they begin to view two-digit numbers differently—as groups of tens and ones—and they no longer have to count to give a number meaning (accommodation). It is through the struggle to resolve the disequilibrium that the brain modifies or replaces the existing knowledge so that the new concept fits and makes sense, resulting in a revision of thought and a deepening of the learner's understanding.

For an illustration of what it means to construct an idea, consider Figure 1.2. The blue and red dots represent ideas, and the lines joining the ideas represent the logical connections or relationships that develop between ideas. The red dot is an emerging idea, one that is being constructed. Whatever existing ideas (blue dots) are used in the construction are connected to the new idea (red dot) because those are the ideas that give meaning to the new idea. The more existing ideas that are used to give meaning to the new one, the more connections will be made.

Each child's unique collection of ideas is connected in different ways. Some ideas are well understood and well formed (i.e., connected), others less so as they evolve. Children's experiences help them develop connections and ideas about whatever they are learning.

Figure 1.2

How someone constructs a new idea.

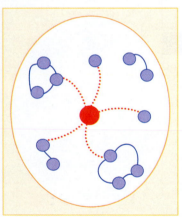

Sociocultural Theory

Like constructivism, sociocultural theory not only positions the learner as actively engaged in seeking meaning during the learning process, but it also suggests that the learner can be assisted by working with others who are "more knowledgeable." Sociocultural theory proposes that learners have their own zone of proximal development, which is a range of knowledge that may be out of reach for individuals to learn on their own but is accessible if learners have the support of peers or more knowledgeable others (Vygotsky, 1978). For example, when young children are learning to measure length, they do not necessarily recognize the significance of placing measurement units end to end. As children measure objects, they may leave gaps between units or overlap units. A more knowledgeable person (a peer or teacher) can draw their attention to this critical idea in measurement.

The most effective learning for any given child occurs when classroom activities are within his or her zone of proximal development. Targeting that zone helps teachers provide children with the right amount of challenge, while avoiding boredom on the one hand and anxiety on the other when the challenge is beyond the child's current capability. Consequently, classroom discussions based on children's own ideas and solutions are absolutely crucial to their learning (Wood & Turner-Vorbeck, 2001).

Teaching for Understanding

Teachers generally agree that teaching for understanding is a good thing. But what do we mean by *understanding*? Understanding is being able to flexibly think about and use a topic or concept. It goes beyond knowing; it is more than a collection of information, facts, or data. It is more than being able to follow steps in a procedure. One hallmark of mathematical understanding is a student's ability to justify why a given mathematical claim or answer is true or why a mathematical rule makes sense (CCSSO, 2010). Although children might *know* their basic addition and subtraction facts and be able to give you quick answers to questions about these facts, they might not *understand*, for example, the different meanings of subtraction. They might not be able to justify how they know an answer is correct or provide an example of when it would make sense to use a particular basic fact. These tasks go beyond simply knowing mathematical facts and procedures. Understanding must be a primary goal for all of the mathematics you teach.

Understanding exists along a continuum (Figure 1.3) from an instrumental understanding—doing or knowing something without meaning—to a relational understanding—knowing what to do and why. These two terms were introduced by Richard Skemp in 1978 and continue to provide an important distinction about what is important for children to know about mathematics. Instrumental understanding, at the left end of the continuum, shows that ideas (e.g., concepts and procedures) are learned, but in isolation (or nearly so) to other ideas. Here you find ideas that have been memorized. Due to their isolation, poorly understood ideas are easily forgotten and are unlikely to be useful for constructing new ideas. At the right end of the continuum is relational understanding. Relational understanding means that each new concept or procedure (red dot) is not only learned, but is also connected to many existing ideas (blue dots), so there is a rich set of connections.

Figure 1.3

Continuum of understanding.

The common notion of quickly "covering the material" and moving on is problematic when trying to help children develop relational understanding. Relational understanding is an end goal—that is, it is developed over time by incorporating active learning through the process standards and mathematical practices and striving toward mathematical proficiency. Therefore, relational understanding must be a goal for both daily and long-term instruction.

Teaching for Relational Understanding

To explore the notion of understanding further, let's look into a learner-centered second-grade classroom. In learner-centered classrooms, teachers begin *where the children are*—with the *children's* ideas. Children are allowed to solve problems or to approach tasks in ways that make sense to them. They develop a robust understanding of mathematics because they are the ones who explain, provide evidence or justification, find or create examples, generalize, analyze, make predictions, apply concepts, represent ideas in different ways, and articulate connections or relationships between the given topic and other ideas.

In this particular second-grade classroom, the children have done numerous activities with the hundreds chart and an open number line. They have counted collections of objects and made many measurements of things in the room. In their counting and measuring, they often count groups of objects instead of counting by ones. Counting by tens has become a popular method for most, but not all, children. The class has taken big numbers apart in different ways to emphasize relationships between numbers and place value. In many of these activities, the children have used combinations of tens to make numbers. The children in the class have not been taught the typical procedures for addition or subtraction.

The teacher sets the following instructional objectives for the students:

1. Use number relationships (e.g., place-value ideas, such as 36 is 3 groups of 10 and 6 ones; 36 is 4 away from 40; etc.) to add two-digit numbers.

2. Apply flexible methods of addition.

As is often the case, this class begins with a story problem and the children set to work.

When Carla was at the zoo, she saw the monkeys eating bananas. She asked the zookeeper how many bananas the monkeys usually ate in one day. The zookeeper said that yesterday they ate 36 bananas but today they ate only 25 bananas. How many bananas did the monkeys eat in those two days?

Stop and Reflect

Before reading further, see how many different ways you can solve this problem (36 + 25). Then check to see if your ways are alike or different from those that follow.

Some children use counters and count by ones. Some use the hundreds chart or base-ten models and others use mental strategies or an open number line. All are expected to use words and numbers and, if they wish, drawings to show what they did and how they thought about the problem. After about 20 minutes of moving about the room, observing and listening to the children's ideas, the teacher begins a discussion by having specific children share their ideas. As the children report, the teacher records their ideas on the board so everyone can see them. Sometimes the teacher asks questions to help clarify ideas but makes no evaluative comments. The teacher asks the children who are listening if they understand or have any questions to ask the presenters. The following solution strategies are common in classrooms where children are regularly asked to generate their own approaches.

Avery: I know that 25 and 25 is 50—like two quarters. And 35 is ten more so that is 60. And then one more is 61.

Teacher: What do you mean when you say "35 is ten more"?

Avery: Well, I used 25 of the 36 and 25 and ten more is 35.

Sasha: I did 30 and 20 is 50 and then 6 + 5 more. Five and five is ten and so 6 + 5 is 11. And then 50 and 11 is 61.

Juan:	I counted on using the hundreds chart. I started at 36 and then I had to go 20 from there and so that was 46 and then 56. And then I went five more: 57, 58, 59, 60, 61.

Marie:	I used an open number to help me. I started at 36 and went up 4 to 40. Then I went up a jump of 20 and then one more to get to 61. (Figure 1.4)
Teacher:	Where is the "25" in your strategy?
Marie:	It's above the jumps. 4 + 20 + 1 is the same as 25.

Figure 1.4

A child uses an open number line to solve 36 + 25 by starting at 36 and then adding 4, 20, and 1. The child wrote the numbers on the number line as the numbers move from 36 to 61.

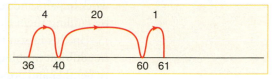

Stop and Reflect

What ideas did you learn from those shared in this example? Try using some of these new ideas to find the sum of 64 and 27.

This vignette illustrates that when children are encouraged to solve a problem in their own way (using their own particular set of blue dots or ideas), they are able to make sense of their solution strategies and explain their reasoning. This is evidence of their development of mathematical proficiency.

During the discussions in classes such as this one, ideas continue to grow. The children may hear and immediately understand a clever strategy that they could have used but that did not occur to them. Others may begin to create new ideas that build from thinking about their classmates' strategies. Some in the class may hear excellent ideas from their peers that do not make sense to them. These children are simply not ready or do not have the prerequisite concepts (blue dots) to understand these new ideas. On subsequent days there will be similar opportunities for all children to grow at their own pace based on what they already understand.

Teaching for Instrumental Understanding

In contrast to the lesson just described, in which children are developing concepts (understanding of place value) and procedures (ability to flexibly add) and building relationships between these ideas, let's consider how a lesson with the same basic objective (addition using place-value concepts) might look if the focus is on instrumental understanding.

In this classroom, the teacher introduces only one way to solve multidigit addition problems—by modeling how to add numbers using base-ten materials. The teacher distributes base-ten blocks so that pairs of children have enough materials to solve any problem. The teacher reads to the class the same monkeys and bananas problem that was used earlier. The class quickly agrees that they need to add the two numbers in the problem. Using a Smart Board to demonstrate, the teacher directs the children to make the two numbers on their place-value mats. Care is taken that the 25 is shown with the base-ten blocks beneath the base-ten blocks for 36. The children are directed to begin combining the pieces in the ones place. A series of questions guides them through each step in the standard algorithm.

1. How many ones are there all together?
2. What do we need to do with the 11 ones? (regroup, make a ten)

3. Where do we put the ten?

4. How many tens are there?

5. What is the answer?

Next, the children are given five similar problems to solve using the base-ten blocks. They work in pairs and record answers on their papers. The teacher helps anyone having difficulty by guiding them through the same steps indicated by the preceding questions.

In this lesson the teacher and children are using manipulatives to illustrate regrouping in addition problems. After engaging in several similar lessons, most children are likely to remember and possibly understand how to add with regrouping using the standard algorithm. It is important to note that this lesson on the standard algorithm, in combination with other lessons that reinforce other approaches, *can* build relational understanding, as it adds to children's repertoire of strategies. But if this lesson represents the sole approach to adding, then children are more likely to develop an instrumental understanding of mathematics because the lesson provides few opportunities to build connections between mathematical concepts. For example, children are not provided opportunities to use mental counting strategies, the hundreds chart, or the number line to add the numbers. Seeing that all of these methods work to reach the same solution helps children build connections between mathematical ideas and across representations—fundamental characteristics of relational understanding.

> **Stop and Reflect**
>
> Before reading further, what similarities and differences did you notice between the two classrooms? How do you think these differences might affect the learning that takes place?

The Importance of Children's Ideas

Let's take a minute to compare these two classrooms. By examining them more closely, you can see several important differences. These differences affect what is learned and who learns. Let's consider the first difference: Who determines the procedure to use?

In the first classroom, the children look at the numbers in the problem, think about the relationships between the numbers, and *then* choose a suitable computational strategy. They have developed several strategies to solve addition problems by exploring numbers and various representations, such as the open number line and the hundreds chart. Consequently, they are relating addition to various representations and employing number relationships in their addition strategies (taking numbers apart and putting them together differently). The children in the first classroom are being taught mathematics for understanding—*relational* understanding—and are developing the kinds of mathematical proficiency described earlier.

In the second classroom, the teacher provides one strategy for how to add—the standard algorithm. Although the standard algorithm is a valid strategy, the entire focus of the lesson is on the steps and procedures that the teacher has outlined. The teacher solicits no ideas from individual children about how to combine the numbers and instead is only able to find out who has and who has not been able to follow directions.

When children have more choice in determining which strategies to use, as in the first classroom, there are more opportunities for learners to interact with each other and with the teacher as they share ideas and results, compare and evaluate strategies, challenge results, determine the validity of answers, and negotiate ideas. As a result, they can learn more content and make more connections. In addition, if teachers do not seek out and value children's ideas, children may come to believe that mathematics is a body of rules and procedures that are learned by waiting for the teacher to tell them what to do. This view of mathematics—and what is involved in learning it—is inconsistent with mathematics as a discipline and with the learning theories described previously.

A second difference between the two classrooms is the learning goals. Both teachers might write "understand two-digit addition" as the objective for the day. However, what is captured in "understand" is very different in each setting. In the first classroom, the teacher's goals are for children to connect addition to what they already know and to see that two numbers can be combined in many different ways. In the second classroom, understanding is connected to being able to carry out the standard algorithm. The learning goals, and more specifically, how the teacher interprets the meaning behind the learning goals, affect what children learned.

These lessons also differ in terms of how accessible they are—and this, in turn, affects *who* learns the mathematics. The first lesson is differentiated in that it meets children where they are in their current understanding. When a task is presented as "solve this in your own way," it has multiple entry points, meaning it can be approached in a variety of ways. Consequently, children with different prior knowledge or learning strategies can figure out a way to solve the problem. This makes the task accessible to more learners. Then, as children observe strategies that are more efficient than their own, they develop new and better ways to solve the problem.

In the second classroom, everyone has to do the problem in the same way. Children do not have the opportunity to apply their own ideas or to see that there are numerous ways to solve the problem. This may deprive children who need to continue working on the development of basic ideas of tens and ones as well as children who could easily find one or more ways to do the problem if only they were asked to do so. The children in the second classroom are also likely to use the same method to add all numbers instead of looking for more efficient ways to add based on the relationships between the numbers. For example, they are likely to add $29 + 29$ using the standard algorithm instead of thinking $30 + 30$ and then take away 2. Recall in the discussion of learning theory the importance of building on prior knowledge and learning from others. Student-generated strategies, multiple approaches, and discussion about the problem in the first classroom represent the kinds of strategies that enhance learning for a range of learners.

Children in both classrooms will eventually succeed at finding sums, but what they learn about addition—and about doing mathematics—is quite different. Understanding and doing mathematics involves generating strategies for solving problems, applying those approaches, seeing if they lead to solutions, and checking to see whether answers make sense. These activities were all present in the first classroom but not in the second. Consequently, children in the first classroom, in addition to successfully finding sums, will develop richer mathematical understanding, become more flexible thinkers and better problem solvers, remain more engaged in learning, and develop more positive attitudes toward learning mathematics.

For more information about relational and instrumental understanding as well as the short-term and the long-term effects of teaching with each type of understanding as your goal, **watch this video: https://www.youtube.com/watch?v=TW_RQXWiCFU**.

Mathematics Classrooms That Promote Understanding

An important part of helping children develop relational understanding and mathematical proficiency is to ensure the children are the ones doing the thinking, talking, and the mathematics, however, there are other factors that play a role. Based on an extensive review of the literature, Schoenfeld and Floden (2014) identified the following five dimensions of "productive classrooms—classrooms that produce powerful mathematical thinkers" (p. 2). We address each of these dimensions throughout the book, but in particular, in Chapters 1–7.

1. *The Mathematics:* We have discussed in this chapter the importance of coherent and rigorous standards that promote college- and career-readiness. This includes developing procedural proficiency in conjunction with conceptual understanding as well as developing productive habits of minds through the mathematical processes and practices.

2. *Cognitive Demand:* Productive struggle is an important part of the process of learning and doing mathematics. We discuss in Chapter 2 the importance of engaging children in appropriate levels of challenge that allow them to productively struggle. Activities throughout Part 2 of the book are designed to be high cognitive demand tasks.

3. *Access to Mathematical Content:* All children must be actively engaged in learning core mathematical ideas. To make this happen for some children, purposeful and appropriate levels of support must be in place. These ideas are addressed in Chapters 4–6.

4. *Agency, Authority, and Identity:* Learning is enhanced when children are engaged with others who are working on the same ideas. Encouraging student-to-student dialogue that involves making conjectures, explaining, justifying, and building on each other's ideas can help children think of themselves as capable of making sense of and doers of mathematics. This goal requires that the teacher create a classroom culture in which children can learn from one another, a topic that is addressed in Chapter 2.

5. *Uses of Assessment:* Eliciting children's ideas and reasoning to inform subsequent instruction has the potential to contribute to everyone's learning, especially when common misunderstandings and mistakes are capitalized on and explored. We discuss assessment that supports instruction and learning in Chapter 3.

Teaching Tip

Listen carefully to children as they talk about what they are thinking and doing as they engage in a mathematical task. If they respond in an unexpected way, try to avoid imposing *your* ideas onto their ideas. Ask clarifying questions to try to make sense of the sense your children are making!

As with most complex phenomena, these dimensions that promote a productive classroom are interrelated. For example, the results of assessment (dimension 5) can help identify an appropriate mathematical task (dimension 1) that can, in turn, affect the potential for cognitive demand (dimension 2). The degree of appropriate support provided (dimension 3) in conjunction with all of the above can influence how a child perceives him or herself as a doer of mathematics (dimension 4). Children have the best chance of becoming powerful mathematical thinkers and doers in classrooms where these five dimensions are implemented well.

Three of the most common types of teaching are direct instruction, facilitative methods (also called a *constructivist approach*), and coaching (Wiggins & McTighe, 2005). With direct instruction, the teacher usually demonstrates or models, lectures, and asks questions that are convergent or closed-ended in nature. With facilitative methods, the teacher might use investigations and inquiry, cooperative learning, discussion, and questions that are more open-ended. In coaching, the teacher provides children with guided practice and feedback that highlight ways to improve their performances. You might wonder, if the goal is to teach mathematics for relational understanding, which type of instructional approach is most appropriate. Unfortunately, there is no definitive answer because there are times when it is appropriate to engage in each of these types of teaching, depending on your instructional goals, the learners, and the situation.

Constructivism, a theory of learning (not a theory of teaching), explains that children learn by developing and modifying ideas and by making connections between these ideas–and each type of instruction can support children's learning when used at the appropriate time. The instructional approach chosen should depend on the ideas and relationships children have already constructed. Assessment can shed light on what and how our children understand, and, in turn, can help us determine which teaching approach may be the most appropriate at a given time. Sometimes children need time to investigate a situation so they can become aware of the different ideas at play and how those ideas relate to one another (facilitative). Sometimes they need to practice a skill and receive feedback on their performance to become more accurate (coaching). Sometimes they are ready to make connections by listening to a lecture (direct instruction). The key to teaching for understanding, no matter which type of teaching you use, is to maintain the expectation for children to reflect on and productively struggle with the situation at hand. In other words, regardless of instructional design, the teacher should not be doing the thinking, reasoning, and connection building—it must be the children who are engaged in these activities.

Most people go into teaching because they want to help children learn. It is hard to think of allowing—much less planning for—the children in your classroom to struggle. Not showing them a solution when they are experiencing difficulty seems almost counterintuitive. If our goal is relational understanding, however, the struggle is part of the learning, and teaching becomes less about the teacher and more about what the children are doing and thinking.

Keep in mind that you too are a learner. Some ideas in this book may make more sense to you than others. Some ideas may even create dissonance for you. Embrace this feeling of disequilibrium and unease as an opportunity to learn—to revise your perspectives on mathematics and on the teaching and learning of mathematics as you deepen your understanding so that you can help your children deepen theirs.

Stop and Reflect

Look back at the chapter and identify any ideas that challenge your current thinking about mathematics or about teaching and learning mathematics or that simply make you uncomfortable. Try to determine why these ideas challenge or raise questions for you. Write these ideas down and revisit them later as you read and reflect further.

2

Teaching Mathematics through Problem Solving

Preparing children to be quantitatively literate so they can function in today's increasingly complex world will allow them to think more logically, work flexibly with numbers, analyze evidence, and communicate their ideas to others effectively. Unfortunately, as Elizabeth Green points out in her article *Why Do Americans Stink at Math?* (2014, February), many Americans of all ages demonstrate quantitative deficiencies. Green argues that to overcome these quantitative deficiencies we must change our view of mathematics from rules to be memorized to sense-making ways of looking at the world around us. Teaching mathematics through problem solving is a method of teaching mathematics that supports children in developing the kinds of skills and understanding that will serve them well in today's world and beyond. In this chapter, we focus on how to teach through problem solving, including how to select worthwhile tasks and facilitate student engagement in those tasks.

Teaching through Problem Solving: An Upside-Down Approach

For many years and continuing today, mathematics has been taught using an "I-we-you" approach: The teacher presents the mathematics (I), the children practice the skill with the teacher (we), and, finally, the children, on their own, continue to practice the skill and solve word problems that require using that skill (you). In this approach—called teaching *for* problem solving—the role of problems is to provide applications for newly learned skills. For example, children learn their basic addition facts and once those are mastered, solve story problems that involve addition. Unfortunately, this "do-as-I-show-you" approach to mathematics teaching has not been successful in helping many children understand mathematics concepts (e.g., Pesek & Kirshner, 2002; Philipp & Vincent, 2003). Here are a few reasons why:

- It requires that all children have the necessary knowledge to understand the teacher's explanations—which is rarely, if ever, the case.
- It communicates that there is only one way to think about and solve the problem, which is a misrepresentation of mathematics and genuine problems.
- It positions the child as a passive learner who is dependent on the teacher to show them ideas, rather than as an independent thinker who is capable and responsible for solving the problem.
- It decreases the likelihood that a child will attempt a novel problem without explicit instructions on how to solve it.

In the past we assumed that walking children through a procedure or showing a step-by-step method for solving a particular type of problem was the most helpful approach to learning. However, this approach can actually make children worse at solving problems and doing mathematics, not better.

Teaching mathematics *through* problem solving means that children work with problems to learn new mathematics and to extend their current understanding. This is sometimes called learning through *inquiry*. With this approach, problem solving is completely interwoven with learning. As children do mathematics—make sense of cognitively demanding tasks, provide evidence or justification for strategies and solutions, find examples and connections, and receive and provide feedback about ideas—they are simultaneously engaged in the activities of problem solving and learning. Children learn mathematics through real contexts, problems, situations, and models that allow them to build meaning for the concepts (Hiebert et al., 1997). Teaching *through* problem solving acknowledges what we now know about learning and doing mathematics (see Chapter 1). Our understanding is always changing, incomplete, situated in context, and interconnected. What we learn becomes part of our expanding and evolving network of ideas—a network without endpoints.

So teaching *through* problem solving might be described as "upside down" from the traditional approach of teaching *for* problem solving because the problem or task is presented at the beginning of a lesson and related knowledge or skills emerge from exploring the problem. An example of teaching *through* problem solving might have children explore the following situation before they are taught the basic facts related to five (e.g., $0 + 5$; $1 + 4$; $2 + 3$, and so on).

Tatyana's mother is decorating a cake for Tatyana's fifth birthday but she only has green and blue candles. If she wants to use exactly 5 candles on the cake, how many green and blue candles could she use?

The teacher would explain to the class that there is more than one correct solution to this problem and that they are to find as many different solutions as they can. As children work on the problem, they may use green and blue counters, they may choose to draw the candles, or they may simply use numbers to capture their ideas.

Stop and Reflect

Find all the possible combinations of blue and green candles. How do you know you have found all the combinations? What is the significance of using two colors of candles?

Through this context and exploration, children could grapple with the commutative property of addition as they compare combinations such as 2 (green) + 3 (blue) and 3 (green) + 2 (blue). This problem also generates opportunities for children to investigate 0 as they consider whether they can have 5 green candles and 0 blue candles or vice versa.

Teaching *through* problem solving positions children to engage with mathematics to learn important mathematical concepts. With this approach, children:

- Ask questions
- Determine solution paths
- Use mathematical tools
- Make conjectures
- Seek out patterns

- Communicate findings
- Make connections to other content
- Make generalizations
- Reflect on results

Hopefully these student behaviors sound familiar. This list reflects the CCSS Standards for Mathematical Practice and the NCTM process standards as well as components of being mathematically proficient that were discussed in Chapter 1.

Mathematics Teaching Practices for Teaching *through* Problem Solving

Teaching *through* problem solving requires a paradigm shift, which means that teachers are doing more than just tweaking a few things about their teaching; they are changing their philosophy about how they think children learn best and how they can best help them learn. At first glance, it may seem that the teacher's role is less demanding because the children are doing the mathematics, but the teacher's role is actually more demanding in such classrooms.

Classrooms where children are engaging with and making sense of mathematics through inquiry do not happen by accident—they happen because the teacher uses practices and establishes expectations that encourage risk taking, reasoning, the generation and sharing of ideas, and so forth. Table 2.1 lists eight research-informed, high-leverage teaching practices, identified in NCTM's (2014) *Principles to Actions*, that support children to develop a robust understanding of mathematics. These teaching practices are designed to address issues of access and equity so that all children can succeed in learning mathematics. We will refer back to these teaching practices throughout this chapter as we consider how to teach mathematics *through* problem solving.

Table 2.1. Eight mathematical teaching practices that support student learning.

Teaching Practice	What Is the Teacher Doing to Enact the Practice?
1. Establish mathematics goals to focus learning	• Articulates clear learning goals that identify the mathematics children will learn in a lesson or lessons. • Identifies how the learning goals relate to a mathematics learning progression. • Helps children understand how the work they are doing relates to the learning goals. • Uses the articulated goals to inform instructional decisions involved in planning and implementation.

2. Implement tasks that promote reasoning and problem solving	• Selects tasks that:
	  • Have maximum potential to build and extend children's current mathematical understanding.
	  • Have multiple entry points.
	  • Require a high level of cognitive demand.
	• Supports children to make sense of and solve tasks using multiple strategies and representations, without doing the thinking for the children.

3. Use and connect mathematical representations	• Supports children to use and make connections between various representations. • Introduces representations when appropriate. • Expects children to use various representations to support their reasoning and explanations. • Allows children to choose which representations to use in their work. • Helps children attend to the essential features of a mathematical idea represented in a variety of ways.
4. Facilitate meaningful mathematical discourse	• Facilitates productive discussions among children by focusing on reasoning and justification. • Strategically selects and sequences children's strategies for whole class discussion. • Makes explicit connections between children's strategies and ideas.

5. Pose purposeful questions	• Asks questions that
	  • Probe children's thinking and that require explanation and justification.
	  • Build on children's ideas and avoids funneling (i.e., directing to one right answer or idea).
	  • Make children's ideas and the mathematics more visible so learners can examine the ideas more closely.
	• Provides appropriate amounts of wait time to allow children to organize their thoughts.

6. Build procedural fluency from conceptual understanding	• Encourages children to make sense of, use, and explain their own reasoning and strategies to solve tasks. • Makes explicit connections between strategies produced by children and conventional strategies and procedures.
7. Support productive struggle in learning mathematics	• Helps children see mistakes, misconceptions, naïve conceptions, and struggles as opportunities for learning. • Anticipates potential difficulties and prepares questions that will help scaffold and support children's thinking. • Allows children time to struggle with problems. • Praises children for their efforts and perseverance in problem solving.
8. Elicit and use evidence of student thinking	• Decides what will count as evidence of children's understanding. • Gathers evidence of children's understanding at key points during lesson. • Interprets children's thinking to gauge understanding and progress toward learning goals. • Decides during the lesson how to respond to children to probe, scaffold, and extend their thinking. • Uses evidence of children's learning to guide subsequent instruction.

Source: Based on *Principles to Actions: Ensuring Mathematical Success For All* (NCTM), © 2014.

Using Worthwhile Tasks

When teachers teach mathematics *through* problem solving, the teacher needs to use worthwhile or rich tasks that promote reasoning and problem solving. Not surprisingly, this is one of the eight mathematics teaching practices identified in *Principles to Actions* (NCTM, 2014) (see practice #2 in Table 2.1). As a teacher you need to know what constitutes a worthwhile task and where to find, adapt, or create such tasks. A worthwhile task is problematic as **this video demonstrates (https://www.youtube.com/watch?v=XI3-52B0V6s**). It poses a question for which (1) the children have no prescribed or memorized rules or methods, and (2) there is no perception that there is a specific "correct" solution method (Hiebert et al., 1997). Because the process or solution method is not obvious, justification is central to the task.

A worthwhile task can take many forms. It might be open-ended or clearly defined; it may involve problem solving or problem posing; it may include words or be purely symbolic; it may develop concepts, procedures, or both; it may take only a few minutes to solve or weeks to investigate; or, it may involve a real-life scenario or be abstract. What makes the task worthwhile is that it is problematic as it engages children in figuring out how to solve it. Here are some tasks to try.

CONCEPTS: CARDINALITY (HOW MANY), DECOMPOSITION OF NUMBERS

Four friends are playing in a playhouse at a park. The playhouse has two floors. Draw a picture to show how many friends might be on each floor. Can you find more than one way? How many ways do you think there are? Why?

CONCEPT: EQUALITY

$$3 + 6 = 1 + \underline{\quad}$$

Find a number for the blank so that the equation is true. Is there more than one number that will make the equation true? Why or why not? Can you find more than one way to find a number for the blank so that the equation is true?

PROCEDURE: SUBTRACTING TWO-DIGIT WHOLE NUMBERS

Solve this problem in two different ways: $32 - 17 = \underline{\quad}$. For each way, explain how you solved it.

Note that a task can be problematic at first and then become routine as a child's knowledge and experience grows. For example, the third example above could be a rich task to explore in grade 1 or 2, but would be "routine" for older or more mathematically advanced children. If the task immediately triggers an approach that the child goes directly to use, the task may be appropriate practice, but it is not a task that is likely to provide the child with new mathematical insights or knowledge.

In thinking about the variety of worthwhile tasks that you can pose, it is important to incorporate tasks that develop both procedural fluency and conceptual understanding. Remember that *procedural fluency* and *conceptual understanding* are two of the five intertwined strands of mathematical proficiency discussed in Chapter 1. Both are equally valuable in children's development toward proficiency—so much so that they are included in one of the teaching practices from *Principles to Action* (NCTM. 2014): *build procedural fluency from conceptual understanding* (see Table 2.1). Using worthwhile tasks where children are able to use a variety of methods and strategies that make sense to them, are expected to explain and justify their approaches, and are encouraged to look for connections among strategies is precisely how children build procedural fluency from conceptual understanding.

High Levels of Cognitive Demand

Engaging children in productive struggle is one of the teaching practices identified in *Principles to Actions* (NCTM, 2014) (see Table 2.1). It is crucial to children's learning mathematics with understanding (Hiebert & Grouws, 2007). Posing worthwhile tasks sets the stage for this productive struggle because such tasks are cognitively demanding, meaning they require higher-level thinking. High-level, cognitively demanding tasks challenge children to make connections, analyze information, and draw conclusions (Smith & Stein, 1998). On the other hand, low-level cognitively demanding tasks (also called *routine problems* or *lower-level tasks*) are straightforward and involve stating facts, following known procedures, and solving routine problems. As an example of different levels of tasks, consider the degree of reasoning required when asking children to find the sum of three given numbers versus asking them to find three numbers whose sum is 35. The first task only requires children to add three numbers. The second task requires them to use number sense to generate three reasonable numbers that will result in a given sum. As a consequence of working on this second task, children have potential opportunities to think about and use number relationships while they work on their computational skills for adding.

Table 2.2 shows a well-known framework that is useful in determining whether a task has the potential to challenge children (Smith & Stein, 1998). As you read through the descriptors for low-level and high-level cognitively demanding tasks, you will notice that the low-level tasks are straightforward and routine, meaning that they do not engage children in productive struggle. Although there are appropriate times to use low-level cognitively demanding tasks, a heavy or sole emphasis on tasks of this type will not lead to a relational understanding of mathematics. When children (even very young children) know that struggle is an expected part of the process of doing mathematics, they embrace the struggle and feel success when they reach a solution (Carter, 2008).

Table 2.2. Levels of cognitive demand.

Low-Level Cognitive Demand Tasks	High-Level Cognitive Demand Tasks
Memorization	**Procedures with Connections**
• Involve either memorizing or producing previously learned facts, rules, formulas, or definitions • Are routine in that they involve exact reproduction of previously learned procedures • Have no connection to related concepts	• Focus children's attention on the use of procedures for the purpose of developing deeper levels of understanding of mathematical concepts and ideas • Suggest general procedures that have close connections to underlying conceptual ideas • Are usually represented in multiple ways (e.g., visuals, manipulatives, symbols, problem situations) • Require that children engage with the conceptual ideas that underlie the procedures in order to successfully complete the task

(Continued)

Table 2.2. Levels of cognitive demand. (continued)

Low-Level Cognitive Demand Tasks	High-Level Cognitive Demand Tasks
Procedures without Connections	***Doing* Mathematics**
• Use procedures specifically called for • Are straightforward with little ambiguity about what needs to be done and how to do it • Have no connection to related concepts • Are focused on producing correct answers rather than developing mathematical understanding • Require no explanations or explanations that focus on the procedure only	• Require complex and nonalgorithmic thinking (i.e., nonroutine—without a predictable, known approach) • Require children to explore and to understand the nature of mathematical concepts, processes, or relationships • Demand self-monitoring or self-regulation of children's own cognitive processes • Require children to access relevant knowledge in working through the task • Require children to analyze the task and actively examine task constraints • Require considerable cognitive effort

Multiple Entry and Exit Points

Your children will likely have a wide range of experiences in mathematics, so it is important to use problems that have multiple entry points, meaning that the problems have varying degrees of challenge or can be approached in a variety of ways. Having multiple entry points can help accommodate the diversity of learners in your classroom because children are encouraged to use a strategy that makes sense to them instead of using a predetermined strategy that they may or may not be ready to use successfully. Having a choice of strategies can also lower the anxiety of children, particularly English Language Learners (Murrey, 2008). Some children may initially use less efficient approaches, such as guess and check or counting, but they will develop more advanced strategies through effective questioning by the teacher and by reflecting on other children's approaches. For example, for the task of finding three numbers whose sum is 35, one child may use a guess-and-check approach, listing three numbers and adding them to see if their sum is 35, whereas another child may use a more systematic approach, such as splitting 35 into 30 and 5 and then splitting 30 or 5 into two addends. Still other children may choose two numbers they estimate will sum to an amount less than 35 and then subtract that sum from 35 to find the third number. Asking children to compare these approaches, and in particular to identify advantages and disadvantages of each, can help children move toward more advanced strategies.

Tasks should also have multiple exit points, or various ways that children can express solutions that reveal a range of mathematical sophistication. For example, children might draw a diagram, write an equation, use manipulatives, or act out a problem to demonstrate their understanding. Even though children might initially select an inefficient or less sophisticated approach, as ideas are exchanged during and after the problem is solved, children will have opportunities to understand and try other approaches. As they discuss ideas, draw visuals, use manipulatives, or act out a problem, defend their strategy, critique the reasoning of others, and write about their reasoning, they engage in higher-level thinking. As an added bonus, the teacher is also able to gather useful formative assessment data about children's mathematical understanding.

Consider the opportunities for multiple entry and exit points in the following tasks. Both tasks use an everyday classroom routine to provide children an opportunity to work on skills related to counting.

TASK 1:

(The teacher places snacks on a table.) Do we have enough snacks for everyone in the class?

TASK 2:

(The teacher gives each child a sheet of paper with a picture of the snack item copied in rows a certain number of times.) Do we have enough snacks for everyone in the class?

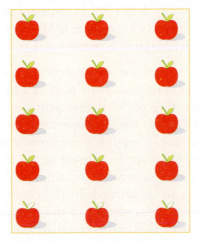

Source: Adapted from *Young Mathematicians at Work: Constructing Number Sense, Addition, and Subtraction* by Catherine Twomey Fostnot and Maarten Dolk. Copyright © 2001 by Catherine Twomey Fosnot and Maarten Dolk. Published by Heinemann, Portsmouth, NH. Reprinted by permission of the publisher. All rights reserved.

Stop and Reflect   500 ⟳ 250   ⌇⚛ 3𝑥   ▱ 𝒔 5° ∞ 𝑛 ⟍ 2.5

To what degree do these tasks offer opportunities for multiple entry and exit points?

If the snacks are readily available, as in the first task, the children will most likely pass them out to see if there are enough snacks and will miss any opportunity to think deeply about the situation. The second task offers more opportunity for children to engage with the task in a variety of ways, which also offers the teacher more information about each child's level of understanding. For example, how children organize their count of the pictured snacks is informative. Do they start at the top and count across the rows? Or do they haphazardly count and miss or double-count? Do they count by ones? Do they count from one or do they count on from a recognized amount? Once they know how many snacks are on the sheet, can they automatically state whether there are enough snacks for everyone, or do they need to represent each child in the class, say, with a counter, and match a counter with a pictured snack? Clearly, the second task offers many more opportunities for all children to engage in the task in a variety of ways.

Relevant and Well-Designed Contexts

One of the most powerful ways to teach mathematics through problem solving is to begin the lesson with a problem that can get children excited about learning mathematics. Compare the following first-grade introductory tasks on counting in groups. Which one do you think would be more exciting to children?

🌿 Teaching Tip

Before giving a selected task to your class, anticipate several possible student responses to the task, including possible misconceptions, and think about how you might address these responses. Anticipating the responses gives you time to consider how you will respond to various ideas and it also helps you to quickly recognize different strategies and misconceptions when children are working on the task.

Classroom A: "Today we are going to use straws to show the day of the month. We will bundle the straws into as many groups of ten as we can and then leave the leftovers loose."

Classroom B: "You all have been busy deciding which kinds of plants we want to put in a garden outside our classroom. The store where I am getting the plants will put them in a plastic container so they will be easier to carry. Each container holds two rows of five plants. If I get 26 plants, how many of these containers will I need?"

Familiar and interesting contexts increase children's engagement. Your goal as a teacher is to design problems using familiar and interesting contexts that provide specific parameters, constraints, or structure that will support the development of the mathematical ideas you want children to learn. Note that in solving a worthwhile problem the problematic or engaging aspect of the problem must be a result of the mathematics that the children are to learn. Any context or external constraints used should not overshadow but highlight the mathematics to be learned. In the context used in Classroom B, the situation involves plants that are arranged in two groups of five. The teacher is aware that some of the children still need to count by ones, but the constraint that each container has two groups of five will require that they group their plants into two groups of five, very likely after drawing and counting by ones. This constraint begins to incrementally move these children toward more efficient ways of counting. For those children who are already counting by fives, the two groups of five move them toward working with groups of ten. For children already working with groups of 10, they might not draw plants at all and instead draw a rectangle to represent each container and label it with "10." By building in such constraints, parameters, or structure, teachers can support children in developing more sophisticated strategies that honor where the children currently are in their understanding (Fosnot & Dolk, 2001).

Children's literature is a rich source for generating high cognitive demand tasks with multiple entry and exit points. For example, the popular children's book *Two of Everything* (Hong, 1993) offers several possibilities for tasks that can be launched from the story. In this Chinese folktale, a couple finds a magic pot that doubles whatever is put into it. In a second-grade class, the children can determine how many children would be in their class if the whole class fell in the magic pot. Children can use various strategies, such as using a hundreds chart, ten frames, or number sense, to solve the problem (multiple entry points). To explain how they figured out the solution, children can verbally share, write out their explanation, or demonstrate their reasoning using a hundreds chart or ten frame (multiple exit points). You can also use the story as a springboard to other problems. For instance, the magic pot can start doing other unexpected things, such as tripling or increasing by 5 what is put into it, and so on (see Suh, 2007a and Wickett, Kharas, & Burns, 2002, for more ideas related to this children's book).

Evaluating and Adapting Tasks

In a great many places you will find suggestions for tasks that *someone* believes are effective for teaching a particular mathematics concept or skill. Unfortunately, many of these readily available tasks fall short of being worthwhile or rich tasks. Table 2.3 provides some reflective questions you can use to evaluate whether a task you are considering has the maximum potential to help your children learn relevant mathematics. These questions are meant to

Table 2.3. Reflective questions to use in selecting worthwhile tasks.

Task Evaluation and Selection Guide	
Task Potential	Try it and ask … ❏ What is problematic about the task? ❏ Is the mathematics interesting? ❏ What mathematical goals does the task address (and are they aligned to what you are seeking)? ❏ What strategies might students use? ❏ What key concepts and/or misconceptions might this task elicit?
Problem-Solving Strategies	Will the task elicit more than one problem-solving strategy ❏ Visualize ❏ Look for patterns ❏ Predict and check for reasonableness ❏ Formulate conjectures and justify claims ❏ Create a list, table, or chart ❏ Simplify or change the problem ❏ Write an equation
Worthwhile Features	To what extent does the task have these key features: ❏ High cognitive demand ❏ Multiple entry and exit points ❏ Relevant contexts
Assessment	In what ways does the task provide opportunities for you to gain insights into student understanding through: ❏ Using tools or models to represent mathematics ❏ Student reflection, justification, and explanation ❏ Multiple ways to demonstrate understanding

help you consider to what extent the task meets these criteria, so all the boxes do not need to be checked off. A task could rate very high on the number of problem solving strategies, but miss the mark for having a relevant context for your children, and therefore you would decide to change the context to something more interesting. Or, the task is complete with worthwhile features and problem-solving strategies but it does not match the mathematical goals for the lesson. You may choose to alter the task to focus on the relevant mathematics or save it for when it is a better match.

You will find many problems in student textbooks, on the Internet, at workshops you attend, and in articles you read that don't quite meet the mark of a worthwhile task. Boaler (2016) offers the following six suggestions for adapting tasks to increase their potential for learning:

1. *Allow multiple ways:* Modify the task so children can use multiple methods, strategies, and representations to solve.

2. *Make it an exploration:* Change the task so that children must do more than complete a procedure and change it so there is potential to learn by doing the task. For example, rather than ask children to add 3 + 5, ask them for various numbers they could add to get the number 8.

3. *Postpone teaching a solution method:* This way children have the opportunity to use their intuition to think about the situation before learning about conventional methods. For example, prior to teaching children about bar graphs, ask them to devise ways to represent their classmates' choice of a favorite book or some other relevant data.

4. *Add a visual requirement:* Visualization can be a powerful tool for enhancing understanding. You can require children to use color coding to show connections or relationships. Or require that they use two different manipulatives to justify their solution.

5. *Increase the number of entry points:* To lower the floor, simply ask children to write down everything they know about the problem or the given concept. To raise the ceiling, once children have completed a task, have them write their own related questions. Challenge them to write questions that are more difficult than the original question and to justify why they are more difficult.

6. *Reason and convince:* Require children to not only provide their reasoning but to be convincing in their mathematical argument and to require others to be as well. Ask learners to be skeptics and to ask clarifying questions of others. You will need to model the expectations for being a skeptic by asking children follow-up questions when they have not been convincing enough.

Additional strategies for modifying tasks to offer differentiated challenges for children can be found in the chapter on differentiating instruction (Chapter 4).

What Do I Do When a Task Doesn't Work?

Sometimes children may not know what to do with a problem you pose, no matter how many hints and suggestions you offer. Do not give in to the temptation to "tell them." When you sense that a task is not moving forward, don't spend days just hoping that something wonderful may happen. You may need to regroup and offer children a simpler but related task that gets them prepared for the one that proved too difficult. If that does not work, set it aside for the moment. Ask yourself why it didn't work well. Did the children have the prior knowledge they needed? Was the task too advanced? Consider what might be a way to step back or step forward in the content in order to support and challenge the class. Nonetheless, trust that teaching mathematics *through* problem solving offers children the productive struggle that will allow them to develop understanding and become mathematically proficient.

Orchestrating Classroom Discourse

Participating in discussions about mathematics contributes to children's understanding in a multitude of ways. Discussions improve children's ability to reason logically as they learn to share their ideas and listen to the ideas of others. Misconceptions and naïve conceptions are also more likely to be revealed in discussions, providing opportunities for teachers to explicitly address them. As children realize they can learn from each other, they are more motivated and interested in what their classmates have to say.

Learning how to orchestrate an effective classroom discussion is quite complex and requires attention to a number of elements. The goal of productive discourse is to keep the cognitive demand high while children are learning and formalizing mathematical concepts (Breyfogle & Williams, 2008/2009; Kilic et al., 2010; Smith, Hughes, Engle, & Stein, 2009). The purpose is not for children to state their answers and get validation from the teacher. The aspects involved in orchestrating classroom discourse are so important, they directly involve three out of the eight teaching practices from

✎ Teaching Tip

What are misconceptions and naïve conceptions? Consider a misconception as a student understanding that is not mathematically accurate, for example, thinking fourths means four parts regardless of the size of the parts. A naïve conception is a partial and typically less powerful, but mathematically accurate understanding—for example, thinking of subtraction in terms of separating or take-away (and not also as comparison and missing part). In either case, these conceptions are important to diagnose so that a deep understanding can be developed.

Principles to Actions (NCTM, 2014): Facilitate meaningful mathematical discourse; Pose purposeful questions; and Elicit and use evidence of student thinking.

Classroom Discussions

The value of student talk throughout a mathematics lesson cannot be overemphasized. As children describe and evaluate solutions to tasks, share approaches, and make conjectures, learning will occur in ways that are otherwise unlikely to take place. Questions such as those that ask children if they would do it differently next time, which strategy made sense to them (and why), and what caused problems for them (and how they overcame them) are critical in developing mathematically proficient children. As they listen to other children's ideas, they come to see the varied approaches in how problems can be solved and see mathematics as something that they can do.

Smith and Stein (2011) identified five teacher actions for orchestrating productive mathematics discussions: anticipating, monitoring, selecting, sequencing, and connecting. The first action, *anticipating* responses to the selected worthwhile task, takes place before the lesson even begins. As children work on the task, the teacher *monitors*, observing children's strategies and asking questions such as:

- How did you decide what to do? Did you use more than one strategy?
- What did you do that helped you make sense of the problem?
- Did you find any numbers or information you didn't need? How did you know that the information was not important?
- Did you try something that didn't work? How did you figure out it was not going to work?

These and similar questions are meant to help children reflect on their strategies and help the teacher determine which strategies to *select* for public discussion in the next part of the lesson. Having selected a range of strategies to be shared, the teacher strategically *sequences* the presentations so that particular mathematical ideas can be emphasized. During the presentations, the teacher generates questions and ideas that *connect* strategies and mathematical concepts. These tend to be questions that are specific to the task, but some general questions include:

- How did [Kathy] represent her solution? What mathematical terms, symbols, or tools did she use? How is this like/different from [Colin's] strategy?
- Was there something in the task that reminded you of another problem we've done?
- What might you do the same or differently the next time you encounter a similar problem?

Notice these questions focus on the problem-solving process as well as the answer, and what worked as well as what didn't work. A balanced discussion helps children learn how to do mathematics.

Because of the important benefits of talking about mathematical ideas, you also need to make sure that everyone participates in the classroom discussion. Finding ways to encourage children to share their ideas and to engage with others about their ideas is essential to productive discussions. You may need to explicitly discuss with children why discussions are important and what it means to actively listen and respond to others' ideas. Wagganer (2015) shares some

🎵 Teaching Tip

To help teach children to pay attention to their peers when they are sharing ideas, create two different kinds of cards, ones with a picture of lips or a mouth and others with a picture of an ear. When a child is speaking, the child holds the card with the picture of the mouth. The other children hold pictures of the ear to indicate they are listening. You can attach the picture of the mouth on the end of a stick to hand to the child whose turn it is to speak.

helpful ideas to explicitly teach children how to engage in active listening. For example, children can demonstrate they are listening by making eye contact with the speaker and through nonverbal cues (e.g., nodding); letting the speaker finish before sharing questions or ideas; and responding appropriately and respectfully by asking questions or summarizing the speaker's ideas. Also, Table 2.4 identifies five "talk moves" that help get everyone talking about mathematics (Chapin, O'Connor, & Anderson, 2009).

Table 2.4. Productive talk moves for supporting classroom discussions.

Talk Moves	What It Means and Why	Example Teacher Prompts
1. Revoicing	This move involves restating the statement as a question in order to clarify, apply appropriate language, and involve more students. It is an important strategy to reinforce language and enhance comprehension for ELLs.	"You used the hundreds chart and counted on?" "So, first you recorded your measurements in a table?"
2. Rephrasing	Asking students to restate someone else's ideas in their own words will ensure that ideas are stated in a variety of ways and encourage students to listen to each other.	"Who can share what Ricardo just said, but using your own words?"
3. Reasoning	Rather than restate, as in talk move 2, this move asks the student what they think of the idea proposed by another student.	"Do you agree or disagree with Johanna? Why?"
4. Elaborating	This is a request for students to challenge, add on, elaborate, or give an example. It is intended to get more participation from students, deepen student understanding, and provide extensions.	"Can you give an example?" "Do you see a connection between Julio's idea and Rhonda's idea?" What if . . . "
5. Waiting	Ironically, one "talk move" is to not talk. Quiet time should not feel uncomfortable, but should feel like thinking time. If it gets awkward, ask students to pair-share, and then try again.	"This question is important. Let's take some time to think about it."

Source: Based on *Classroom Discussions: Using Math Talk to Help Students Learn, Grades K–6,* by Suzanne H. Chapin, Catherine O'Connor, Nancy Canavan Anderson. Published by Math Solutions, © 2009.

Considerable research into how mathematical communities develop and operate provides additional insight into promoting effective classroom discourse (Chapin, O'Connor, & Anderson, 2009; Rasmussen, Yackel, & King, 2003; Stephan & Whitenack, 2003; Wood, Williams, & McNeal, 2006; Yackel & Cobb, 1996). This collection of research offers the following recommendations:

- Encourage student–student dialogue rather than student–teacher conversations that exclude the rest of the class. "Juanita, can you answer Lora's question?" "Devon, can you explain that so that LaToya and Kevin can understand what you are saying?" When children have differing solutions, have them work these ideas out as a class. "George, I noticed that you got a different answer than Tara. What do you think about her explanation?"

- Encourage children to ask questions. "Pete, did you understand how they did that? Do you want to ask Antonio a question?"

- Ask follow-up questions whether the answer is right or wrong. Your role is to understand children's thinking, not to lead children to the correct answer. So follow up with probes to learn more about their answers. Sometimes you will find that what you assumed they were thinking is not correct. And if you only follow up on wrong answers, children quickly figure this out and get nervous when you ask them to explain their thinking.

- Call on children in such a way that, over time, everyone is able to participate. Use time when children are working in small groups to identify interesting solutions that you will highlight during the sharing time. Be intentional about the order in which the solutions are shared; for example, select two that you would like to compare and have children present them back-to-back. All children should be prepared to share their strategies.

- Demonstrate to children that it is okay to be confused and that asking clarifying questions is appropriate. This confusion, or disequilibrium, just means they are engaged in doing real mathematics and indicates that they are learning. Make a point to tell them this!

- Move children to more conceptually based explanations when appropriate. For example, if a child says that he knows 5 + 3 is the same as 3 + 5, ask him (or another child) to explain why this is so.

- Be sure all children are involved in the discussion. ELLs, in particular, need more than vocabulary support; they need support with mathematical discussions (Moschkovich, 1998). For example, use sentence starters or examples to help children know what kinds of responses you are hoping to hear and to reduce the language demands. Sentence starters can also be helpful for children with disabilities because it adds structure. Have children practice their explanations with a peer. Invite children to use illustrations and actual objects to support their explanations. These strategies benefit all children, not just children in the class who struggle with language.

- Pay attention to whether you are taking over children's thinking. Jacobs, Martin, Ambrose, and Philipp (2014) identify warning signs of such behavior—for example, interrupting a child's strategy or explanation, manipulating the tools instead of allowing the child to do so, and asking a string of closed questions (i.e., funneling). Taking over children's thinking sends the message that you do not believe they are capable and can inhibit the discourse you are trying to encourage.

Aspects of Questioning

Questions are important in learning about children's thinking, challenging conclusions, and extending the inquiry to help generalize patterns. Questioning is very complex and something that effective teachers continue to improve on throughout their careers. Here are some major considerations related to questioning that influence children's learning.

1. *The "level" of the question asked.* There are numerous models that identify different levels of questions. For example, the Levels of Cognitive Demand in Table 2.2 include two low-level demand categories and two high-level demand categories. Also, Bloom's Taxonomy Revised includes six levels (knowledge, comprehension, application, analysis, synthesis, evaluation), with each level meant to be more cognitively demanding than the previous (Anderson & Krathwohl, 2001). However, you can still ask a low-level cognitively demanding "create" question on Bloom's Taxonomy Revised. For example, brainstorming ideas would be lower-level than say, designing a model, but both could be categorized as "create." Check out Simpson, Mokalled, Ellenburg, and Che (2015) who share a tool that can help analyze the depth of knowledge that can occur across the categories in Bloom's Taxonomy Revised. Regardless of the taxonomy or specific categories, it is critical to ask higher-level, cognitively demanding questions to support children in developing a robust understanding of mathematics.

2. *The type of understanding that is targeted.* Both procedural and conceptual understanding are important, and questions must target both. If questions are limited to procedural ideas, such as "How did you solve this?" or "What are the steps?" then children will think about procedures, but not about related concepts. Questions focused on conceptual knowledge include, "Will this rule always work?" "How does the equation you wrote connect to the picture?" and "How is your strategy like Caroline's?"

3. *The pattern of questioning.* Some patterns of questioning teachers use do not lead to classroom discussions that encourage all children to think (Herbel-Eisenmann & Breyfogle, 2005). One such common pattern of questioning goes like this: teacher asks a question, student answers the question, teacher confirms or challenges answer (called "initiation-response-feedback"or "IRF" pattern). Another ineffective pattern is "funneling," when a teacher continues to probe children in ways to get them to a particular answer. This is different than a "focusing" pattern, which uses probing questions to negotiate a classroom discussion and help children understand the mathematics. The talk moves described previously are intended to help facilitate a focusing discussion.

4. *Who is doing the thinking.* Make sure your questions engage all children! When you ask a great question, and only one child responds, then children will quickly figure out they don't need to think about the answer and all your effort to ask a great question is wasted. Instead, use strategies to be sure everyone is accountable to think about the questions you pose. For example, ask children to "talk to a partner" about the question. Or have children record their ideas on a whiteboard or index card.

5. *How you respond to an answer.* When you confirm a correct solution rather than use one of the talk moves, you lose an opportunity to engage children in meaningful discussions about mathematics and so limit the learning opportunities. Use children's solutions to find out if others think the conclusions made are correct, whether they can justify why, and if there are other strategies or solutions to the problem and how they are connected.

How Much to Tell and Not to Tell

One of the most perplexing dilemmas for teachers is how much information and direction to provide to children during mathematical inquiry. On one hand, telling can diminish what is learned and lower the level of cognitive demand in a lesson by eliminating the productive struggle that is key to conceptual understanding (Hiebert & Grouws, 2007). On the other hand, telling too little can sometimes leave children floundering. Following are suggestions about three things that you need to tell children (Hiebert et al., 1997):

- *Mathematical conventions:* Symbols, such as + and =, are conventions. Terminology is also a convention. As a rule of thumb, symbolism and terminology should be introduced *after* concepts have been developed, and then specifically as a means of expressing or labeling ideas.

- *Alternative methods:* If an important strategy does not emerge naturally from the children, then you should propose the strategy, being careful to identify it as "another" way, not the only or the preferred way.

- *Clarification or formalization of children's methods:* Help children clarify or interpret their ideas and point out related concepts. A child may add 38 and 5 by noting that 38 and 2 more is 40 with 3 more making 43. This strategy can be related to the Make 10 strategy used to add 8 + 5. The selection of 40 as a temporary target in this child's strategy is an important place-value concept. Drawing everyone's attention to this connection can help other children see the connection while also building the confidence of the child who originally proposed the strategy.

The key is that you can share information as long as it does not solve the problem, remove the need for children to reflect on what they are doing, or prevent them from developing solution methods that make sense to them (Hiebert et al., 1997).

Leveraging Mistakes and Misconceptions to Enhance Learning

Children inevitably will make mistakes and exhibit misconceptions and naïve conceptions—especially when we pose challenging tasks in our classrooms. You may not want to highlight a child's mistake or misconception because you are concerned that it might embarrass the child or confuse the struggling learners in your classroom. How we choose to treat mistakes and misconceptions in the classroom can have a tremendous effect on children's perceptions about learning and themselves as learners.

When mistakes, misconceptions, and naïve conceptions are perceived and used (explicitly or implicitly) to judge how "smart" someone is, children want to hide their mistakes as well as their lack of understanding. Children can develop a fixed mindset in which they believe their intelligence is set and cannot be further developed through effort (Dweck, 2006), which means they are very unlikely to persevere in solving difficult problems that require productive struggle (Boaler, 2013). To them, difficult tasks are not perceived as opportunities to learn and improve, but rather as spotlights that highlight their inadequacies (Boaler, 2016; Dweck, 2006). On the other hand, children who adopt a growth mindset appreciate, take on, and persist with challenges because they perceive these as opportunities to learn. They also view mistakes as a chance to reconsider, revise, and improve their understanding. An online TED talk of Carol Dweck describing mindsets (titled "The power of believing you can improve") is worth watching.

We want children to embrace a growth mind-set—to see mistakes, misconceptions, and struggles as opportunities for learning. In fact, this is a critical part of the teaching practice *support productive struggle in learning mathematics* (see Table 2.1). Publicly valuing a mistake or misconception in class and having children think about why it is a mistake or misconception reinforces the important message that we all make mistakes and have misconceptions and can improve our understanding by examining them more closely. You can even design lessons around tasks that elicit common misconceptions or mistakes (Bray, 2013; Lim, 2014). For example, Bray (2013) chose a task that required children to create thirds rather than halves or fourths because she knew some children would try to use halving to create the fractional parts. The task also elicited misconceptions about whether thirds meant three parts or three *equal* parts.

Flawed ideas, strategies, and solutions can come from either children's work or from the teacher. If the mistakes or misconceptions come from children in the class, Bray (2013) offers some helpful suggestions for ensuring that the error maker is respected. For example, ask the child for permission to publicly share the mistake or misconception, give the child the choice to explain, acknowledge to the class where there is good reasoning involved in the child's flawed thinking, and express appreciation for the opportunity to analyze the mistake or misconception as a way to improve their classmates' mathematical understanding.

Choosing to publicly treat mistakes and misconceptions in a positive light in your classroom will help children be risk takers and to persevere with challenging tasks. Rather than fearing mistakes and misunderstandings they will appreciate the powerful role these can play in learning.

Representations: Tools for Problem Solving, Reasoning, and Communication

One of the teaching practices identified in *Principles to Actions* (2014) is *use and connect mathematical representations*. The fact that representations made the cut on this short list should give you some sense of its importance in teaching for relational understanding.

Build a Web of Representations

Different representations can illuminate different aspects of a mathematical idea. So to help children build their understanding, they should be encouraged to use, explore, and make connections among multiple representations. Figure 2.1 provides a general Web of Representations that can be applied to any mathematical concept and illustrates the various ways mathematical ideas can be represented. Children who have difficulty translating a concept from one representation to another also have difficulty solving problems and understanding computations (Clement, 2004; Lesh, Cramer, Doerr, Post, & Zawojewski, 2003). Strengthening children's ability to move between and among representations improves their understanding and retention of ideas. For any topic you teach, you can give children the **Translation Task** to complete. (More information is given regarding the use of the Translation Task in Chapter 3, Creating Assessments for Learning.) Fill out one box and ask children to insert the other representations, or you can invite a group to work on all four representations for a given topic (e.g., addition).

Figure 2.1

Mathematical understanding can be demonstrated through these different representations of mathematical ideas. Translations between each can help children develop new concepts and demonstrate a richer understanding.

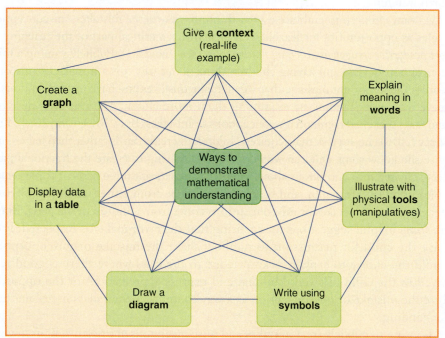

Explore with Tools

A *tool* is any object, picture, or drawing that can be used to explore a concept. CCSS-M includes calculators and manipulatives as tools for doing mathematics (CCSSO, 2010). Manipulatives are physical objects that children and teachers can use to illustrate and explore mathematical concepts. Choices for manipulatives (including virtual manipulatives) are plentiful—from common objects such as lima beans to commercially produced materials such as Pattern Blocks. A range of manipulatives (e.g., geoboards, base-ten blocks, spinners, number lines) are available in a virtual format, for example, on the National Library of Virtual Manipulatives (NLVM) website and the NCTM Illuminations website.

Some research suggests benefits to incorporating both physical and virtual manipulatives in instruction (Hunt, Nipper, & Nash, 2011). Physical manipulatives can build the foundation for conceptual understanding while subsequent use of virtual manipulatives can assist learners in bridging to the abstract. For example, at some websites, such as the NLVM website, a displayed number representing the computerized base-ten blocks changes as the base-ten blocks are modified so that children can see the corresponding results of the changed manipulatives on the numbers.

Note that a tool does not "illustrate" a concept. While the tool is used to visualize a mathematical concept, an individual has to impose the mathematical relationship on the object (Suh, 2007b; Thompson, 1994). In other words, the manipulative is not the concept but offers a testing ground for emerging ideas. Figure 2.2 shows three blocks commonly used to represent ones, tens, and hundreds. If a child is able to identify the rod as the "ten" piece and the large square block as the "hundred" piece, does this mean he has constructed the concepts of ten and hundred? No, all you know for sure is that he has learned the names typically assigned to the manipulatives. The mathematical concept of a ten is that one ten is the same as ten ones. This concept is the relationship between the rod and the small cube. This relationship called "ten" must be created by children in their own minds and imposed on the manipulative or the model used to represent the concept. For a child who does not yet understand the relationship, the model does not illustrate the concept for that individual. Over time, discussions that explicitly focus on the mathematical concepts can help children make the connections between manipulatives and related concepts. When you are considering using particular tools, take time yourself to try to separate the physical tool from the relationship that you must impose on the tool in order to "see" the concept. This insight will help you support your children as they work with the given tool.

Although tools can be used to support the development of relational understanding, used ineffectively, they do not accomplish this goal. The most widespread misuse of manipulatives occurs when teachers tell children, "Do exactly as I do." There is a natural temptation to get out the materials and show children exactly *how to use them*. Children mimic the teacher's directions, and it may even look as if they understand, but they could be just following what they see. A rote procedure with a manipulative is still just that, a rote procedure. The converse is to provide no focus or purpose for using the tools. Neither approach promotes thinking or aids in the development of concepts (Ball, 1992; Stein & Bovalino, 2001).

Drawings are another option for children to represent and illustrate mathematical concepts and are important for a number of reasons. First, when children draw, you learn more about what they do or do not understand. For example, if children show $\frac{1}{2}$ with their own drawings, you can observe whether they understand that each half must be the same size. Second, manipulatives can sometimes restrict how children can model a problem, whereas a drawing allows children to use any strategy they want. Plus, because children enter school with a limited ability to express their ideas in writing, a drawing may be the most appropriate way for them to express their ideas. Figure 2.3 shows an example of one kindergartner's solution for ways to

Figure 2.2

Objects and names of objects are not the same as mathematical ideas and relationships between objects.

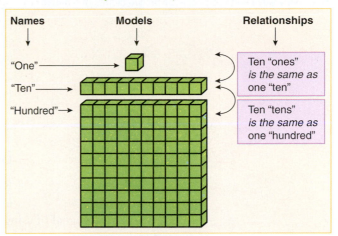

🎵 Teaching Tip

It is incorrect to say that a manipulative or object "illustrates" or shows a concept. Manipulatives can help children visualize the relationships and talk about them, but what they see are the manipulatives, not concepts.

Figure 2.3

A kindergartner shows her thinking about ways to make 5.

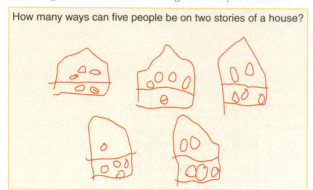

How many ways can five people be on two stories of a house?

make 5. Children should eventually be encouraged to connect their drawings to symbols, but they should not be forced to do so too soon. Some children will take longer than others to make this connection and that difference should be honored. Look for opportunities to use children's representations during classroom discussions to help them make sense of the more abstract mathematical symbols. Furthermore, as children use different representations to solve a problem, have them compare and contrast the various ways to facilitate making connections.

Tips for Using Representations in the Classroom

Representations give learners something with which they can explore, reason, and communicate as they engage in problem-based tasks. The goal of using representations is that children are able to manipulate ideas and make connections in a meaningful manner. The following are rules of thumb for using representations in the classroom:

- Introduce new representations or tools by showing how they can represent *the ideas* for which they are intended. But keep in mind that, because the representations are not the concepts, some children may not "see" what you see.

- Encourage children to create their own representations. Look for opportunities to connect these student-created representations to more conventional representations.

- Allow children (in most instances) the opportunity to choose their own representations to reason through a problem and to communicate their ideas to others (Mathematical Practice 5: Use appropriate tools strategically). The representations that children choose to use can provide valuable insight into their ways of interpreting and thinking about the mathematical ideas at hand. Note that it is appropriate to encourage a child who is having difficulty to use a particular representation when you believe it would be helpful.

- Ask children to use representations, such as diagrams and manipulatives, when they explain their thinking. This will help you gather information about children's understanding of the idea and also their understanding of the representations that have been used in the classroom. It can also be helpful to other children in the classroom who may be struggling with the idea or the explanation being offered.

🌱 *Teaching Tip*

Pay attention to children's choices of representations and use those representations as starting points for dialogues with them about their thinking. What they find important may be surprising and informative at the same time.

- In creating tasks and when facilitating classroom discussions, look for opportunities to make connections among the different representations used (and make sure each is understood). Helping children make these connections is crucial to their learning.

Lessons in the Problem-Based Classroom

Lessons that engage children in problem solving look quite different from traditional lessons that follow the "I-we-you" or "explain, then practice" pattern. Mathematical practices such as modeling mathematics, reasoning quantitatively, and looking for generalizations and structure are not developed in a lecture-style lesson. In contrast, in classrooms where learning is assumed to be a complex process and where inquiry and problem solving are emphasized, worthwhile tasks are posed to challenge children's thinking and children are expected to communicate and justify their ideas. In these kinds of classrooms, preparing a lesson shifts from preparing an agenda of what will happen to creating a "thought experiment" to consider what might happen (Davis, Sumara, & Luce-Kapler, 2008).

The first teaching practice listed in Table 2.1, *establish mathematics goals to focus learning*, is one of the most important. Being clear about the target mathematics that you want children to learn as a result of a particular lesson or lessons helps you to be intentional as you make instructional choices during planning as well as implementation. For example, in planning the lesson, you need to purposefully select a worthwhile task that has maximum potential to illuminate the target learning goals. Without this intentionality, your lesson can lack focus and consequently, not culminate in the desired results. The three-phase lesson format discussed next is intended to support the creation of intentional lessons that support mathematical inquiry.

A Three-Phase Lesson Format

A lesson format that uses the three phases *before*, *during*, and *after* provides a structure for teaching mathematics through inquiry or problem solving. *Before* refers to what happens in the lesson to set up the inquiry, *during* refers to the time during which the children explore the worthwhile problem, and *after* refers to what happens in the lesson after the problem is solved (e.g., discussion, reflection, and making connections). A lesson may take one or more math sessions, but the three-phase structure can also be applied to shorter tasks, resulting in a 10- to 20-minute mini-lesson. Table 2.5 describes appropriate teacher actions and provides some illustrative examples for each phase of the lesson.

Before

The essence of the *before* phase of the lesson is to prepare children to work on the worthwhile task you have purposefully selected. What you do in the *before* phase of the lesson will vary depending on the mathematical goals and the selected task. For example, if your children are familiar with solving story problems and know they are expected to use words, pictures, and numbers to explain their reasoning in writing, all that may be required is to read through the problem together and make sure everyone understands it. On the other hand, if the task requires children to model the situation with a new manipulative, more time may be needed to familiarize them with the tool. Or if vocabulary needs to be revisited, a related but simpler task could be used in the *before* phase as a way to activate prior knowledge to ensure children understand the terms used in the focus task.

As you plan for the *before* part of the lesson, it is important to analyze the problems you will give to children in order to anticipate their approaches and possible misinterpretations or misconceptions (Wallace, 2007). This process can inform what you do to prepare the children to work on the selected task, without giving away how to solve the task. The more questions raised and addressed prior to the task, the more engaged children will be in the *during* phase.

During

In the *during* phase of the lesson children engage in mathematical activity (alone, with partners, or in small groups) to explore, gather, and record information; make and test conjectures; and solve the mathematical task. In this phase of the lesson you should be engaged in "professional noticing"—that is, in the moment, trying to understand what children know, how they are thinking and approaching the task at hand, and how to respond appropriately to extend children's thinking (Jacobs, Lamb, & Philipp, 2010). In making instructional decisions in the *during* phase you must ask yourself, "Does my action lead to deeper thinking or does it remove the need to think?" These decisions are based on carefully listening to children's

Table 2.5. Teaching mathematics through problem solving lends itself to a three-phase structure for lessons.

Lesson Phase	Teacher Actions in a Teaching Mathematics through Problem-Solving Lesson	
Before	Activate prior knowledge.	Begin with a related but simpler task; connect to children's experiences; brainstorm approaches or solution strategies; estimate or predict if tasks involve a single computation or are aimed at the development of a computational procedure.
	Be sure the problem is understood.	Have children explain to you what the problem is asking. Go over vocabulary that may be troubling. Caution: This does *not* mean that you are explaining how to *do* the problem—just that children should understand what the problem is about.
	Establish clear expectations.	Tell children whether they will work individually, in pairs, or in small groups, or if they will have a choice. Tell them how they will share their solutions and reasoning.
During	Let go!	Although it is tempting to want to step in and "help," hold back and enjoy observing and learning from the children.
	Notice children's mathematical thinking.	Base your questions on the children's work and their responses to you. Use questions like "Tell me what you are doing"; "I see you have started to [add] these numbers. Can you tell me why you are [adding]?" [substitute any process/strategy]; "Can you tell me more about . . . ?"; "Why did you . . . ?"; "How does your diagram connect to the problem?"
	Provide appropriate support.	Look for ways to support children's thinking and avoid telling them how to solve the problem. Ensure that the children understand the problem (e.g., "What do you know about the problem?"); ask the children what they have already tried (e.g., "Where did you get stuck?"); suggest to the children that they use a different strategy (e.g., "Can you draw a diagram?"; "What if you used cubes to act out this problem?"; "Is this like another problem we have solved?"); create a parallel problem with simpler values (Jacobs & Ambrose, 2008).
	Provide worthwhile extensions.	Challenge early finishers in some manner that is related to the problem just solved. Possible questions to ask are "I see you found one way to do this. Are there any other solutions?"; "Are any of the solutions different or more interesting than others?" Some good questions for extending thinking are "What if . . . ?" or "Would that same idea work for . . . ?"
After	Promote a community of learners.	You must teach children about your expectations for this time and how to interact respectfully with their peers. Role-play appropriate (and inappropriate) ways of responding to each other. The "Orchestrating Classroom Discourse" section in this chapter provides strategies and recommendations for how to facilitate discussions that help create a community of learners.
	Listen actively without evaluation.	The goal here is noticing children's mathematical thinking and making that thinking visible to other children. Avoid judging the correctness of an answer so that children are more willing to share their ideas. Support children's thinking without evaluation by simply asking what others think about a child's response.
	Summarize main ideas and identify future problems.	Formalize the main ideas of the lesson, helping to highlight connections among strategies or different mathematical ideas. In addition, this is the time to reinforce appropriate terminology, definitions, and symbols. You may also want to lay the groundwork for future tasks and activities.

ideas and knowing the learning goals of the lesson. This is very different from listening for or leading children toward an answer. Don't be afraid to say that you don't understand a child's strategy. When you are open to learning, you help children become more comfortable with engaging in the learning process.

Children will look to you for approval of their results or ideas. This is not the time to evaluate or to tell children how to solve the problem. When asked whether a result or method is correct, respond by asking, "How can you decide?" or "Why do you think that might be right?" Asking questions such as "How can we tell if that makes sense?" reminds children that the correctness of the answer lies in the justification, not in the teacher's brain or answer key.

Letting go, one of the teacher actions in this phase, includes allowing children to make mistakes. Ask children to explain their process or approach when they make mistakes as well as when they are correct. As they explain they may catch their mistake. Also, in the *after* portion of the lesson, children will have the opportunity to explain, justify, defend, and challenge solutions and strategies. This process of uncovering and working through misconceptions and computational errors emphasizes the important notion that mistakes and misconceptions are opportunities for learning (Boaler, 2016; Dweck, 2006).

Use this time in the *during* phase to identify different representations and strategies children used, interesting solutions, and any misconceptions that arise that you will highlight and address during the *after* phase of the lesson. As you notice the range of ideas, consider how they are related and in what order you might sequence the sharing of solutions in the *after* phase of the lesson (Smith & Stein, 2011).

After

In the *after* phase of the lesson your children will work as a community of learners, discussing, justifying, and challenging various solutions to the problem that they have just worked on. The *after* phase is where much of the learning will occur as children reflect individually and collectively on the ideas they have explored. As in the *during* phase of the lesson, the goal here is noticing children's mathematical thinking; but additionally, in the *after* phase we want to make this thinking visible to other children. By strategically sequencing which drawings, notations, and ideas are shared, you can create spaces for children to take up, try on, connect, and expand on the ideas of others. This is also the time to reinforce precise terminology, definitions, or symbols. After children have shared their solutions, strategies, and reasoning, formalize the main ideas of the lesson, highlighting connections between strategies or different mathematical ideas.

Because this is the place in the lesson where much of the learning will occur, it is critical to plan for and save ample time for this part of the lesson. Twenty minutes is not at all unreasonable for a good class discussion and sharing of ideas. It is not necessary to wait for every child to finish the task before moving into the *after* portion of the lesson. The time they have engaged with the task should prepare them to share and compare ideas.

Variations of the Three-Phase Lesson

The basic lesson structure we have been discussing assumes that the lesson is developed around a task given to the whole class. However, not every lesson is structured in this way. The three-phase format can be applied to other lesson structures, such as mini-lessons and learning centers.

Mini-Lessons

A three-phase lesson that capitalizes on the use of routines can be accomplished in as few as 10 minutes. These mini-lessons are not intended to replace the math curriculum or consume most of the instruction time for math, but like in longer lessons, children are expected to use strategies that make sense to them and to explain their thinking. A routine called

Number Talks, already embraced in many elementary classrooms, engages children in using number relationships and the structures of numbers to do mental computations, followed by sharing their various strategies (Humphreys & Parker, 2015; Parrish, 2014). These brief routines are praised for developing children's number sense as well as their enthusiasm for thinking about and sharing their strategies (Parrish, 2011). McCoy, Barnett, and Combs (2013) share seven mathematical routines that can be easily used with a variety of mathematical content and at various grade levels. One routine, *Alike and Different*, requires children to consider how two or more numbers, shapes, properties, and so on are similar and different. Having children explain and justify their reasons for the similarities and differences they identify is valuable experience in constructing mathematical arguments. McCoy, Barnett, and Combs (2013) also identify ways to increase the cognitive demand of tasks as children become familiar with a given routine.

Once the routine is introduced and understood by children, the *before* part of the mini-lesson involves posing the task to the children and ensuring they understand the vocabulary and any context used. In the *during* portion of the mini-lesson, children spend time developing their own ideas about the task. You can then have the children pair with a classmate and discuss each other's strategies. You can also have small groups discuss or go straight to the whole class to share and compare strategies. Just keep in mind that think-pair-share provides an opportunity to test out ideas and to practice articulating them. For ELLs, children with learning disabilities, and children who are reluctant to participate in larger groups, this offers both a nonthreatening chance to speak and an opportunity to practice what they might later say to the whole class. Like in longer lessons, the *after* part of the mini-lesson involves children sharing, justifying, questioning, and looking for connections between ideas.

Learning Centers

Sometimes a mathematical concept or topic can be explored by having children work on different tasks at various classroom locations or *learning centers*. Children can work on concepts or topics in learning centers as an initial introduction, as a midway exploration, or as a follow-up task that provides practice or allows extension. Because you can decide which children will be assigned to which centers, you can differentiate the content at each center. For example, each center can use different manipulatives, situations, or technology, require children to use a different approach to solve a problem, or vary in terms of the difficulty of the task (e.g., different centers can use different numbers that change the level of difficulty). (For more information regarding differentiation see Chapter 4.)

For a given topic, you might prepare four to eight different activities (you can also use the same activity at two different learning centers). However, be sure to keep the centers focused on the same topic or concept so that you can help children build connections across the centers. Using centers that focus on a variety of topics will more likely result in a disconnected learning experience for children.

When using learning centers, it is still important to think about the *before* phase in which you elicit prior knowledge, ensure the task is understood, and establish clear expectations. For example, to ensure greater student success at the centers, model what happens at each center and review any necessary skills and vocabulary. The *during* phase is still the time where children engage in the task, but with learning centers, they stop and rotate to new centers within this phase of the lesson. It is still important to interact with and ask children questions as they engage in tasks from the different centers and even more important to keep track of their strategies, including those you will later highlight. In the *after* phase, you may decide to focus on one particular center, begin with the least challenging center and progress to the most challenging one, or instead of discussing each center, ask children to talk about what they learned about the target topic or concept.

A good task for a learning center is one that can be repeated multiple times during one visit. This allows children to remain engaged until you are ready for them to transition to another center or activity. For example, at one center children might play a "game" in which they take turns covering part of a known number of counters while the other child names the amount in the covered part. Technology-enhanced tasks on the computer or interactive whiteboard that can be repeated can provide the focus of a center, but these tasks must be carefully selected. Among other aspects, you will want to choose technology-based tasks that require children to engage in reflective thought. For example, "Hiding Ladybug" in the National Council of Teachers of Mathematics online resources (search for "NCTM illuminations 4.3.1 hiding ladybug") offers children opportunities to plan and check a path for a ladybug to take so it can hide under a leaf. They can quickly check to see whether their plan works, make changes based on the results, and check the revised plan. As they engage in this interactive environment, they are enhancing their understanding of location and movement in space. Once they have successfully created a path, they can move the leaf and start the challenge again. Even if a learning center, such as this one, is used for independent work, the three-phase model can be implemented by placing a series of reflective questions at the center for children to use as they participate in the tasks.

Life-Long Learning: An Invitation to Learn and Grow

In her book *Building A Better Teacher* (2015), Elizabeth Green attacks the myth of the natural-born teacher—the common notion that good teachers are good because of an innate ability for teaching. Instead she develops the case that teaching is a complex craft that must be taught and developed over time. No matter where you are in your journey as a teacher, there is always more to learn about the content and methodology of teaching mathematics. In fact, the mathematics content and teaching described in this book may not be similar to what you experienced as a student in grades K–8. We know a great deal more about teaching and learning mathematics than we did even five years ago! Just as we would not expect doctors to be using the exact same techniques and medicines that were prevalent when you were a child, teachers' methods should be transformed through the powerful collection of expert knowledge about how to design effective instruction based on such things as how the mind functions and the influence of motivation on learning (Wiggins, 2013).

Planning three-phase inquiry lessons using worthwhile tasks and ensuring that the lesson meets the needs of all children requires intentional and ongoing effort. Questions are likely to surface. You can access responses to seven of the most commonly asked questions about problem-based teaching approaches by **clicking here**. These questions and responses may help as you contemplate how to plan for your children, or consider ways to advocate for teaching through problem solving with other teachers, families, and/or administrators.

The best teachers are always trying to improve their practice through reading the latest article, reading the newest book, attending the most recent conference, or participating in the next series of professional development opportunities. Highly effective teachers never stop learning—they never exhaust the number of new mental connections that they can make. As a result, they never experience teaching as a stale or stagnant profession.

Stop and Reflect   500   250   3x   2.5

Describe in your own words what is (and isn't) meant by "teaching mathematics *through* problem solving." What do you foresee to be opportunities and challenges to implementing problem-based mathematics tasks effectively in your classroom?

3

Creating Assessments for Learning

Assessment That Informs Instruction

When using a problem-based approach, teachers might ask, "How do I assess?" NCTM's position statement on formative assessment (2013), and the joint NCSM/AMTE position statement on formative assessment (n.d.) stress several important ideas: (1) assessment should enhance children's learning, (2) assessment is a valuable tool for making instructional decisions, and (3) feedback should help learners progress. This aligns with the distinction between assessment of learning, where children are only evaluated on what they know at a given moment in an effort to home in on what they don't know, and assessment for learning (AFL), where children are continually evaluated so that instruction can be targeted to gaps and their learning is improved over time (Hattie, 2015; Wiliam & Leahy, 2015).

Assessment is not separate from instruction and should include the critical CCSS mathematical practices and NCTM processes that occur in the course of effective problem-based instructional approaches (Fennell, Kobett, & Wray, 2015). A typical end-of-chapter or end-of-year test of skills may have value, but it rarely reveals the type of data that can fine tune instruction to improve individual children's performance. In fact, Daro, Mosher, and Corcoran (2011) state that "the starting point is the mathematics and thinking the child brings to the lesson, not the deficit of mathematics they do not bring" (p. 48). NCTM's *Principles to Actions* (2014) urges teachers in their mathematical teaching practices to incorporate evidence of child thinking into an ongoing refinement of their instruction.

Assessments usually fall into one of two major categories: summative or formative. *Summative assessments* are cumulative evaluations that take place usually after instruction is completed. They commonly generate a single score, such as an end-of-unit test or a standardized test that is used in your state or school district. Although the scores are important for schools and teachers, used individually they often do not help shape day-to-day teaching decisions.

On the other hand, *formative assessments* are assessments that are used to check children's development during instructional activities, to preassess, or to attempt to identify children's naïve understandings or misconceptions (Hattie, 2009; Popham, 2008; Wiliam & Leahy, 2015). When implemented well, formative assessment is one of the most powerful influences on achievement (Hattie, 2009). It dramatically increases the speed and amount of a child's learning (Nyquist, 2003; Wiliam, 2007; Wilson & Kenney, 2003) by providing targeted feedback to children and using the results and evidence collected to inform your decision making about next steps in the learning progression.

Wiliam (2010) notes three key processes in formative assessment: (1) Identify where learners are; (2) Identify goals for the learners; and (3) Identify paths to reach the goals. Let's look at an example of this process. For example, to see whether first graders can find a missing addend you could use the following word problem: "If Lindy has 6 shells in her collection, how many more shells does she need to get 13?" The teacher observes one child taking out connecting cubes, counting out 6 and then adding more until she reaches 13. Then she goes back to the pile of cubes, takes out 6, and counts the remaining cubes, stating "seven." Another child places her hands on the table with fingers stretched out and, if observed carefully, shows signs that she is "counting on" from 6 by pressing 7 fingers down one at a time until she reaches 13. A different child calls out "7" almost immediately. When asked how he arrived at that answer, he says that $6 + 6 = 12$, so $6 + 7 = 13$. The information gathered from observing these children reveals very different paths for the next steps. This teacher is at the first step in Wiliam's three key processes, noting where children are in their learning. Moving into the second step, the teacher notes that one child should move to more challenging tasks while two children need to move closer to the CCSS standard of using addition and subtraction within 20 to solve a variety of word problems through more targeted instruction.

If summative assessment can be described as a digital snapshot, formative assessment is like streaming video. One is a picture of what a child knows that is captured in a single moment of time; the other is a moving picture that demonstrates active student thinking and reasoning. In the following pages and throughout Part 2 of this book in Formative Assessment Notes, we focus on four basic methods for using of formative assessments to evaluate children's understanding: observations, questions, interviews, and tasks. Here we discuss each method in depth.

Observations

All teachers learn useful bits of information about their children every day. When the three-phase lesson format suggested in Chapter 2 is used, the flow of evidence about children's performance increases dramatically, especially in the *During* and *After* portions of lessons. If you have a systematic plan for gathering this information while observing and listening to children during regular classroom instruction, at least two very valuable results occur. First, information that may have gone unnoticed is suddenly visible and important. Second, observation data gathered systematically can be combined with other data and used in planning lessons, providing feedback to children, conducting parent conferences, and determining grades.

Depending on the information you are trying to gather, several days to two weeks may be required to complete a single observation of how a whole class of children is progressing on a standard. Shorter periods of observation will focus on a particular cluster of concepts or skills or on particular children. Over longer periods, you can note growth in mathematical processes or practices, such as developing problem solving, representation, or reasoning. To use observation effectively, take seriously the following maxim: Only try to collect data on a reasonable number of children in a single class period.

Anecdotal Notes

The act of *professional noticing* is a process where you observe learners through a focus on three phases: (1) attending; (2) interpreting; and (3) deciding (Jacobs, Lamb, & Philipp, 2010). You want to collect anecdotal notes on these phases to help understand learners' strategies and thinking as you plan potential next steps. That means you *attend* to everything such as if the child is nodding his head or if she is using her fingers to count, or if she is creating appropriate models, or if he is using strategies that he can clearly describe and defend. Then *interpret* those children's gestures, comments, drawings and actions by making notes of possible strengths and the level of sophistication of their conceptual understanding. Then you can move to noting *decisions* for subsequent instructional actions.

One system for recording your professional noticing is to write these anecdotal notes on an electronic tablet and store them in a spreadsheet or in a multicolumn table that documents such things as children's use of mathematical practices. In any case, focus your observations on approximately five children a day. The children selected may be members of one or two cooperative groups or a group previously identified as needing additional support.

Figure 3.1

A focused checklist and rubric that can be printed for each child.

NAME: *Sharon V.*	NOT THERE YET	ON TARGET	ABOVE AND BEYOND	COMMENTS
PLACE VALUE				
Skip counts by tens		✓		
Skip counts by hundreds		✓		*Took out hundreds pieces while skip counting*
Understands 100 equals ten tens	✓			
Reads and writes numbers to 1000	✓			
Compares three-digit numbers		✓		*Showing greater reasonableness*
MATHEMATICAL PRACTICES				
Makes sense of problems and perseveres		✓		*Stated problem in own words*
Models with mathematics	✓			*Reluctant to use abstract models*
Uses appropriate tools		✓		

Checklists

To help focus your attention, a checklist with several specific processes, mathematical practices, or content objectives can be devised (see Figure 3.1). As you can see there is a place for comments that should concentrate on big ideas and conceptual understanding. For example you will probably find a note such as "is beginning to see how multiplication facts can be related, such as using 6 + 6 to think about 6 + 16" more useful than "knows easy addition facts but not hard ones."

Another Observation Checklist involves listing all children in a class on one to three pages (see Figure 3.2). Across the top of the page are specific abilities or common misconceptions to look for, possibly based on learning progressions. Pluses and minuses, checks, or codes can be entered in the grid. A full-class checklist is more likely to be used for long-term objectives such as problem-solving processes, strategic use of representations or tools, and such skill areas as basic fact fluency or computational estimation. Dating entries or noting specifics about observed performance is also helpful.

Questions

Probing children's thinking through questioning can provide better data and more insights to inform instructional next steps. As you circulate around the classroom to observe and evaluate children's understanding, your use of questions is one of the

Figure 3.2

A class observation checklist.

Topic: *Addition with sums to 20* **Names**	Not There Yet *Can't do mentally*	On Target *Has at least one strategy*	Above and Beyond *Uses different methods with different numbers*	Comments
Lalie		✓ 3-18-2017 3-21-2017		
Pete	✓ 3-20-2017	✓ 3-24-2017		*Difficulty with addends of 8 and 9*
Sid			✓ + 3-20-2017	*Flexible approaches used*
Lakeshia		✓		*Count up and over ten*
George		✓		
Pam	✓			*Beginning to look for ways to make ten*
Maria		✓ 3-24-2017		*Use a counting on strategy from the highest addend*

most important ways to formatively assess in each lesson phase. Have **Question Probes** on a tablet or in print as you move about the classroom to prompt and probe children's thinking.

To make sure you are asking critical thinking questions you may want to consider videotaping yourself and having a friend score how many high-level or how many recall questions you are asking. Use a matrix such as the Cognitive Rigor Matrix (Simpson, Mokalled, Ellenburg, & Che, 2014/2015) which is a blend of Bloom's Taxonomy and Webb's Depth of Knowledge (2002) for additional information.

Getting children used to responding to these questions (as well as accustomed to asking questions about their thinking and the thinking of others) helps prepare them for the more intensive questioning used in interviews.

Interviews

"An assessment system designed to help steer the instruction system must give good information about direction as well as distance to travel. A system that keeps telling us we are not there yet is like a kid in the back seat whining 'are we there yet?' " (Daro et al., 2011, p. 51). Interviews, particularly diagnostic interviews, are means of getting in-depth information about a child's knowledge of concepts and strategy use to provide needed navigation. The diagnostic interview is usually a one-on-one investigation of a child's thinking about a particular concept, process, or mathematical practice that lasts from three to ten minutes. The challenge of diagnostic interviews is that they are assessment opportunities, not teaching opportunities, making it hard to watch children make errors and not respond immediately. The interviews are used to listen to children's descriptions of their strategies and probe their understanding with the purpose of discovering both strengths and gaps.

To start, select a problem that matches an essential understanding for the topic children are studying and have paper, pencils, and a variety of materials available (particularly manipulatives used during previous instruction). Also, be ready to jot down notes about emerging understandings, common methods you expect children to use, or common misunderstandings that you anticipate. Then ask the child to solve the problem and make sure the child verbalizes his or her thinking at several points. Encourage multiple representations by asking

Teaching Tip

These interviews can be time intensive but they have the potential to provide information that you simply cannot get in any other way. So how can you accomplish this? Think of these interviews as tools to be used for only a few children at a time, not for every child in the class. Briefly interview a single child while others work on a task or are in learning centers. Some teachers work with one child at an interactive whiteboard and record the whole conversation, any written work, or use of virtual manipulatives. Other times a paraprofessional or student teacher can interview.

the child to demonstrate his or her thinking using materials or drawings. Fennell, Kobett, and Wray call this the "show me" approach (2015, p. 56).

Sometimes children self-correct a mistake but, more frequently, you can unearth a child's misunderstanding or reveal what strategies are mastered. When you focus on exploring common errors and pitfalls, you can then build greater sophistication in children's conceptual understanding (Bray & Santagata, 2014). Primary diagnostic interviews might include tasks such as counting a group of objects and writing down the number on paper, or asking children to solve a missing addend problem such as $4 + \square = 12$. Also, see a **Sample Interview for Primary Grades** and/or **Student Observation and Interview: Learning through Problems**.

After examining hundreds of research studies, Hattie (2009) found that feedback that teachers received from children on what they knew and did not know was critical in improving children's performance. That is precisely what diagnostic interviews are designed to do! For example, are you sure that your children have a good understanding of place value, or are they just doing subtraction exercises according to rote procedures? Remediation will be more successful if you can pinpoint why a child is having difficulty before you try to fix the problem.

Let's look at an actual example of a diagnostic interview.

Mr. Dix was working with a child who was displaying difficulty with calculating subtraction problems. To get the child to reveal where her thinking was in terms of what she understood and where some gaps might be, Mr. Dix planned a diagnostic interview. Using an adaptation of a task (Philipp, Cabral, & Schappell, 2012), he showed the child a problem (see Figure 3.3) and asked her to talk about her thinking as she answered. The child said, "Four from zero is four and five from eight is three, so my answer is 34." Although base-ten materials were on the table, they went untouched. As is necessary in these interviews, Mr. Dix resisted the temptation to immediately correct the child, and instead probed further by asking the child if she could show the same problem using base-ten materials. Showing fluency with the values of base-ten materials, the child took out correct amounts and placed them on the table. She used the 54 that she took out as a reference and touched the other materials (in the group of 80) to show how many she would be taking away. This time she arrived at the answer 26. The confusion was evident in her expression, but when asked which answer was correct, she pointed back to her original calculation. She even redid the algorithm and repeated her mistaken "four from zero is four." The child quietly pondered and then pointed again to the answer of 34.

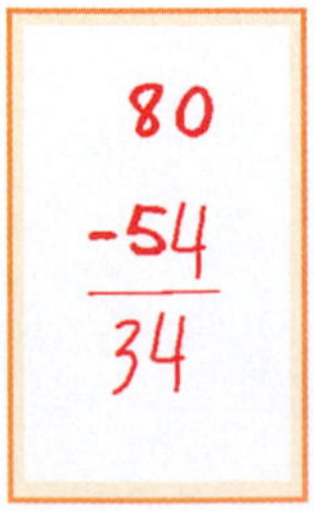

Although this interview revealed that the child had a good grasp of the value of the base-ten materials, it also revealed that the child was not seeing the need to regroup and may not fully understand place-value concepts. The child also referred to the numbers in the tens column as "8" and "5" rather than 80 and 50. Notice that the teacher explicitly linked the assessment to classroom instruction through the use of concrete materials. This connection provided a way for the child to think about the number rather than just the individual digits. In addition, the cognitive dissonance caused by getting two different numerical outcomes, one responding to the procedure alone and the other using the corresponding concrete materials, enabled more connected ideas to emerge. Planning could then begin for future instruction based on actual evidence from the child.

Figure 3.3

A child's work on a diagnostic interview task.

$$\begin{array}{r} 80 \\ -54 \\ \hline 34 \end{array}$$

There is no one right way to plan or structure a diagnostic interview. In fact, flexibility is a key ingredient. You should, however, have an overall plan that includes an easier task and a more challenging task in case you have misjudged your starting point. Also, did you notice that Mr. Dix had appropriate instructional materials ready for the child to use? Be sure you have materials available that have potential to provide insight into children's understanding. Also be prepared to probe children's thinking with question like these:

- Can you explain what you just did?
- How would you explain this to your younger sister?
- Can you draw a picture to help you think about this problem?
- What does this [point to something on the paper] stand for?
- Why did you solve it that way?
- Can you show me what you are thinking with [materials such as counters, hundreds chart, and so on]?
- Why do you think you got two different answers? Which one do you think is correct?

In each case, it is important to explore whether children can use models to connect actions to what he or she wrote or explained earlier.

Consider the following suggestions as you implement your diagnostic interview:

- *Avoid revealing whether the child's answer is right or wrong.* Often facial expressions, tone of voice, or body language can give a child clues. Instead, use a response such as "Can you tell me more?" or "I think I know what you are thinking."

- *Wait silently for the child to give an answer.* Give ample time to allow a child to think and respond. Only then should you move to rephrasing questions or probing for a better understanding of a child's thoughts. After the child gives a response (whether it is accurate or not), wait again! This second wait time is even more important because it encourages the child to elaborate on initial thoughts and provide more information.

- *Avoid interjecting clues or teaching.* The temptation to interrupt is sometimes overwhelming. Watch and listen. Your goal is to use the interview not to teach but to find out where the child is in terms of conceptual understanding and procedural fluency.

- *Give opportunities for children to share their thinking without interruption.* Encourage children to use their own words and ways of writing things down. Correcting language or spelling words can sidetrack the flow of children's explanations.

The benefits of diagnostic interviews become evident as you plan instruction that capitalizes on children's strengths while recognizing possible weaknesses and confusion. Also, unlike large-scale testing, you can always ask another question to find out more when the child is taking an incorrect or unexpected path. You may also discuss results of interviews with colleagues to gain shared insights (Stephan, McManus, & Dehlinger, 2014). These insights are invaluable in moving children to mathematical proficiency, as there is perhaps no better method for developing instruction that supports children's understanding than having them explain their thinking and a team of teachers sharing a conversation about evidence.

Tasks

Tasks refer to products that include performance-based tasks, writing, and children's self-assessments. Good assessment tasks for either instructional or formative assessment purposes should permit every child, regardless of mathematical ability, to demonstrate his or her knowledge, skill, or understanding.

Problem-Based Tasks

Problem-based tasks are tasks that are connected to actual problem-solving activities used in instruction. High-quality tasks permit every child to demonstrate his or her abilities (Rigelman & Petrick, 2014; Smith & Stein, 2011) and include real-world or authentic contexts that interest children or relate to recent classroom events. Of course, be mindful that English language learners may need support with context as challenges with language should not overshadow the attention to their mathematical ability.

Problem-based tasks have several critical components that make them effective. They:

- Focus on an important mathematics concept or skill aligned to valued learning targets.
- Stimulate the connection of children's previous knowledge to new content.
- Allow multiple solution methods or approaches that incorporate a variety of tools.
- Offer opportunities for children to correct themselves along the way.
- Provide occasions for children to confront common misconceptions.
- Encourage children to use reasoning and explain their thinking.
- Create opportunities for observing children' use of mathematical processes and practices.
- Generate data for instructional decision making as you listen to your children's thinking.

Notice that the following examples of problem-based tasks are not elaborate, yet when followed by a discussion, each can engage children for most of a class session (also see **Problem-Based Tasks**). What mathematical ideas and practices are required to successfully respond to each of these tasks?

PARTITIONING (GRADES K–1):

Learning Targets: (1) Decompose numbers in a problem situation. (2) Use reasoning and regularity of patterns to make sense of quantities and the relationships of quantities.

Six bowls of cereal are placed at two different tables. Draw a picture to show a way that six bowls might be placed at two tables. Can you find more than one way? How many ways do you think there are?

SHARES (GRADES K–2):

Learning Targets: (1) Solve problems involving the operations. (2) Use manipulatives and words to describe a solution.

Leila has 6 gumdrops, Darlene has 2, and Melissa has 4. They want to share them equally. How will they do it? Draw a picture to help explain your answer.

At second grade, the numbers in the "Shares" task should be larger. What additional concepts would be involved if the task were about sharing cookies and the total number of cookies, 34, was given?

ONE UP, ONE DOWN (GRADES 1–2):

Learning Targets: (1) Work with addition equations. (2) Look for and make use of structure.

When you add 7 + 7, you get 14. When you make the first number 1 more and the second number 1 less, you get the same answer. Does this work any time the numbers are the same? Does it work when the addends are not the same?

Much can be learned about children's understanding in a discussion that follows children solving the task individually. In particular, it is important for children to compare and make connections between strategies and debate ideas in order to assist them in organizing their thoughts and analyzing the ideas of others.

Translation Tasks

One important assessment option is what we refer to as a *translation task*. Using four possible representations for concepts (see Figure 2.3), children are asked to demonstrate understanding using words, models/materials, and numbers for a single problem. As children move between these representations, there is a better chance that a concept will be formed correctly and integrated into a rich web of ideas.

So what is a good way of structuring a translation task? With use of a template based on a format for assessing concept mastery from Frayer, Fredrick, and Klausmeier (1969) (see Figure 3.4) and the Translation Task Template, you can give children a computational equation and ask them to:

- Tell a story or write a word problem to match an equation.
- Illustrate the equation with materials or drawings.
- Given a story situation, write an equation or draw a picture.

In particular, children's ability to communicate how they solved a problem is critical for open-response questions on many summative assessments (Parker & Breyfogle, 2011).

Translation tasks can be used for whole-class lessons or for individual or small-group diagnosis. For example, second-grade children may be given an equation such as $36 + 49 = ?$ (see Figure 3.4). The task could be for children to draw a model, say, of base ten-materials in "Manipulatives/Illustration" (younger children can show a manipulative), describe a real-world situation in which that addition is used in "Real-World Story or Word Problems," and explain to another person in writing (or scripted or audio recorded for younger children) how they solved the addition in the fourth area labeled "Explain Your Thinking." Think about using translation tasks when you want to find out more about a child's ability to represent ideas and explain how these representations are connected. Depending on the concept, the translation task can start in a different section of the template.

Consider these possible starters.

- Start with this problem in the section "Real-World Story or Word Problem":

Figure 3.4

Translation task template with example task.

Numbers/Equation	Real-World Story or Word Problem
$36 + 49 =$	
Manipulatives/Illustration	**Explain Your Thinking**

Jack was at the pet store. A group of puppies came over and sat on Jack's lap. Two of the puppies jumped off. Now Jack has three puppies on his lap. How many puppies did Jack have on his lap in the beginning?

Then children create the equation that corresponds with the problem, make a matching drawing, and explain how they came to their answer.

- In the "Manipulatives/Illustration" section show two groups of coins in two circles. In one circle show an illustration of 2 quarters and 2 pennies (a coin stamp) and in the other circle show 3 dimes, 1 nickel, and 3 pennies with the question, "How much money do you have?" Then children should write a corresponding equation to show the combining of both groups of coins, write a word problem, and in the last section explain to a friend how to approach this problem.

Writing

As an assessment tool, writing in journals, exit slips for older children, or other formats provide a unique window to children's perceptions and the way they are thinking about an idea. Children can make sense of problems, express early ideas about concepts, unearth confusion, connect representations, or even clarify strategy use (Casa, 2015). When children explain their thinking about their solutions to a task in writing prior to class discussions, the written record serves as a rehearsal for the class conversation. Children who otherwise have difficulty thinking on their feet now have a script to support their contributions. Call on more reluctant talkers first so that their ideas are heard and valued.

If you are working with PreK–1 children, writing in mathematics may sound too advanced as it may be difficult for prewriters and beginning writers to express ideas. To begin the development of the writing-in-mathematics process in these early grades, use a language experience approach. After an activity, you can write the words "Giant Journal" and a topic or prompt on a large chart or interactive whiteboard. As children respond to the prompt verbally, the teacher writes down their thoughts, including the contributor's name and even drawings when appropriate, as in Figure 3.5. All children can draw pictures of some sort to describe what they have done. Dots can represent counters or blocks. Shapes and figures can be cut out from duplicated sheets and pasted onto journal pages.

Figure 3.5

A journal in PreK or kindergarten may be a class product on a chart or whiteboard.

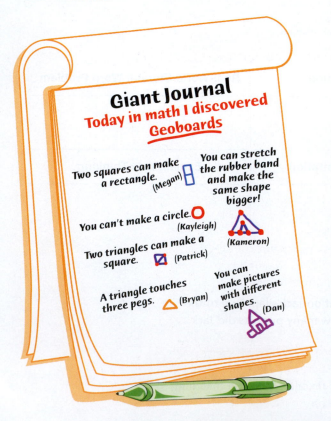

In Mathematical Practice 3, mathematically proficient children are able to "justify their conclusions, communicate them to others, and respond to the arguments of others" (NGA, 2010, pp. 6–7). Helping children pull evidence to show how they answered a problem often requires showing them the work of other children. By showing exemplars and counterexamples from real or "created" peers, children begin to identify elements of a sound argument and cohesive communication (Lepak, 2014).

Children's Self-Assessment and Reflection

Wiliam (2015) stresses that a key strategy in effectively using formative assessment is the activation of children as "owners of their own learning" (p. 169). Stiggins (2009) suggests that children should be informed partners in understanding their progress in learning and how to enhance their growth in understanding concepts. They should use their own assessment results to move forward as learners as they see that "success is always within reach" (p. 420). Children's self-assessments should not be your only measure of children's learning or dispositions, but rather a record of how *children perceive* their strengths and weaknesses as they begin to take responsibility for their learning. You can gather children's self-assessment data in several ways, including preassessments that catch areas of confusion or misconceptions prior to formally assessing children on particular content or by using sticky notes when concluding the lesson. **Watch this video (https:// www.youtube.com/watch?v=1ejQcTTwEtA)** shown with older children that is applicable to any grade to see a "stoplight" approach. Here the teacher uses green, yellow, and red plates to gather children's responses to see how they evaluate where they are.

As you plan for children's self-assessment, consider what you need to know to help you find better instructional strategies and revised learning targets. Convey to your children why you are having them do this activity—they need to grasp that they must play a role in their mastery of mathematics rather than just focus on completing a task.

Although in general, it takes additional time to infuse children's self-assessments and formative assessment into the daily schedule, allowing children to take part in the assessment process is motivating and encourages them to monitor and adapt their approaches to learning. Remember, start the process of incorporating these assessment ideas in this chapter over time building strategy by strategy (Petit & Bouck, 2015) and growing your ability to effectively assess children.

Rubrics and Their Uses

Problem-based tasks tell us a great deal about what children know, but how do we analyze and use this information? These assessments yield an enormous amount of information that must be evaluated by examining more than a simple count of correct answers. A *rubric* is a scale based on predetermined criteria with two important functions: (1) It permits children to see what is central to excellent performance, and (2) it provides you with scoring guidelines that support equitable analysis of children's work.

In a teaching-through-problem-solving approach, you will often want to include criteria and performance indicators on your rubrics such as the following:

- Solved the problem(s) accurately and effectively.
- Persevered and demonstrated resilience when facing a challenging problem.
- Explained strategies they used or justified their answer.
- Used logical reasoning.
- Expressed a grasp of numerical relationships and/or mathematical structure.
- Incorporated multiple representations and/or multiple strategies.
- Demonstrated an ability to appropriately select and use tools and manipulatives.
- Communicated with precise language and accurate units.
- Identified general patterns of ideas that repeat, making connections from one big idea to another.

Generic Rubrics

Generic rubrics identify categories of performance instead of specific criteria for a particular task and therefore can be used for multiple assignments. The generic rubric allows you to score performances by first sorting into two broad categories, as illustrated in the four-point rubric shown in Figure 3.6. Then you to separate each category into two additional levels as shown. A rating of 0 is given for no response, no effort, or for responses that are completely off task. The advantage of this scale is the relatively easy initial sort into "Got It" or "Not There Yet."

Another possibility is to use your three- or four-point generic rubric on a reusable form (see **Four-Point Rubric**), as in Figure 3.6. This method is especially useful for planning purposes. But there are times when generic rubrics do not give enough definition of specific criteria for a particular task. For those instances, try a task-specific rubric.

Figure 3.6

A four-point generic rubric.

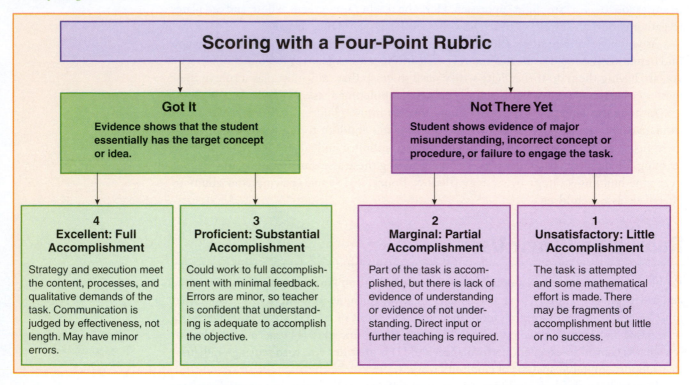

Task-Specific Rubrics

Task-specific rubrics include specific statements, also known as *performance indicators* that describe what children's work should look like at each rubric level and, in so doing, establish criteria for acceptable performance on that particular task (see Figure 3.7 and **Anecdotal Note Rubric**). Initially, it may be difficult to predict what children's performance at different levels will or should look like, but your criteria depend on your knowledge and experience with children at that grade level and your insights about the task or mathematical concept. One important part of setting performance levels is predicting children's common misconceptions or their expected approaches to similar problems.

To facilitate developing performance levels, write out indicators of "proficient" or "on target" performances before using the task. This excellent self-check ensures that the task is likely to accomplish your purpose. If you find yourself writing performance indicators in terms of the number of correct responses, you are most likely looking at drill or practice exercises, not the problem-based tasks for which a rubric is appropriate. Like athletes who continually strive for better performances rather than "good enough," children should always recognize opportunities to excel. When you take into account the total performance (processes, strategies, answers, justifications, extensions, and so on), it is always possible to "go above and beyond."

Early in the year, discuss your rubric (such as Figure 3.7) with the class and post it prominently. Make it a habit to discuss children's performance on tasks in terms of the rubric. For example, if you are using the anecdotal note rubric, rubric language can be used informally: "Tanisha,

Stop and Reflect

Consider the task "Shares" on page 44. Assume you are creating a task-specific four-point rubric to share with your first graders. What task-specific indicators would you use for level 3 and level 4 performances? Start with a level 3 performance, then think about level 4. Try this before reading further.

the rubric states to get an Above and Beyond you need to solve the problem with two different representations and explain your thinking. Is that what you did?" This approach lets children know how well they are doing and encourages them to persevere by giving specific areas for improvement. You might also have children use the rubric to self-assess their work, having them explain reasons for their ratings. Then target follow-up instruction in response to their gaps and misunderstandings building on their identified strengths.

Determining performance indicators is always a subjective process based on professional judgment. Here is one possible set of indicators for the "Share" task:

Level 3: Determines correct answer or uses an approach that would yield a correct answer if not for minor errors. The picture drawn or the explanation does not fully explain the combining and sharing process.

Level 4: Determines the total number of gumdrops and the amount of each equal share using words, pictures, and numbers to explain and justify the result and how it was obtained.

What about level 1 and level 2 performances? Here are suggestions for the same task:

Level 2: Uses only two numbers in the addition instead of three and, therefore, fails to come up with the correct amount to share or adds correctly but does not carry out the division. The child shows some evidence of knowledge of addition but explanations and drawings are not aligned with the situation.

Level 1: Shows some effort but little or no understanding of addition or how to make equal shares.

Unexpected methods and solutions happen. Don't limit children to demonstrating their understanding only as you thought they would when there is evidence that they are accomplishing your objectives in different ways. Such occurrences can help you revise or refine your rubric for future use.

Figure 3.7

Record names in a rubric used during an activity or for a single topic over a period of several days.

Observation Rubric **Partition Regions into Equal Shares** (3/17)		
Above and Beyond Clear understanding. Communicates concept in multiple representations. Shows evidence of using idea without prompting. **Can partition rectangles and circles into two, four, and eight equal shares. Explains that partitioning the same wholes into more shares makes smaller shares.**	Sally Latania Greg	 Zal
On Target Understands or is developing well. Uses designated models. **Can partition regions into equal shares and describes as "halves" and "fourths." May need prompt to compare halves and fourths.**	Lavant Julie George Maria	Tanisha Lee J.B. John H.
Not There Yet Some confusion or misunderstanding. Only models idea with help. **Needs help to do activity. No confidence.**	John S.	Mary

Teaching Tip

When you return papers, especially with second graders, review the indicators with children, including examples of correct answers and successful responses. This will help children understand how they could have done better. Often it is useful to show anonymous children's work. Let children decide on the score for the anonymous child. Importantly, children need to see models of what a level 4 performance looks like.

Stop and Reflect

How can having children assess peers' work (both strong and weak responses) support their ability to generate more in-depth responses?

4

Differentiating Instruction

Every classroom at every grade level contains a range of children with varying abilities and backgrounds. Perhaps the most important work of teachers today is to be able to plan (and teach) lessons that support and challenge *all* children to learn important mathematics. Designing and implementing instruction in ways that best reach each child is the crux of differentiated instruction. We address differentiation first in a general sense in this chapter. Then in the next two chapters, we focus on differentiation with specific learners, English Language Learners and learners with exceptionalities.

Differentiation and Teaching Mathematics through Problem Solving

Teachers have for some time embraced the notion that children vary in reading ability, but the idea that children can and do vary in mathematical development may be new. Mathematics education research reveals a great deal of evidence demonstrating that children can vary in their understanding of specific mathematical ideas. Attending to these differences in children's mathematical development is key to differentiating mathematics instruction for your children.

Interestingly, the problem-based approach to teaching is the best way to teach mathematics while attending to the range of children in your classroom. In a traditional, highly directed lesson, it is often assumed that all children will understand and use the same approach and the same ideas as determined by the teacher. Children not ready to understand the ideas presented by the teacher must focus their attention on following rules or directions without developing a conceptual or relational understanding (Skemp, 1978). This, of course, leads to endless difficulties and can leave children with misunderstandings or in need of significant remediation. In contrast, in a problem-based classroom, children are expected to approach problems in a variety of ways that make sense to *them*, bringing to each problem the skills and ideas that they own. So, with a problem-based approach to teaching mathematics, differentiation is already built in to some degree.

To illustrate, let's consider a first-grade classroom in which the teacher provided the children with a picture of six dogs as shown in Figure 4.1(a). She asked the children to determine how many dogs are in the picture and to be ready to explain how they know. Following are some of the children's explanations:

Carmen: I counted them and got 6. (Points to each dog and counts by ones.)

Sam: I counted them, too. But I counted by twos. (Puts two fingers over two dogs at a time and says, "Two, four, six.")

Edwin: I saw a pattern. I recognized the five, like on a die. I knew one more is six.

Nora: I also saw a pattern. But I saw a group of 3 and 3—that is 6. (See Figure 4.1(b).)

Some children are still counting by ones while others have begun skip counting or even recognizing the number of objects without counting. If the teacher had expected all children to count the dogs by ones, then many of the children might have used less-efficient methods than they would have independently used. Also, the cognitive demand of the task would have been lowered! If the teacher had expected all the children to recognize the number of objects without counting, then some children may have been confused because they still need to count objects by ones to determine how many. Instead, the teacher allowed the children to use their own ideas to determine how many dogs are in the picture. This expectation and the recognition that different children will approach and solve the same problem in various ways honors children's varying mathematical development and sets the stage for differentiated

Figure 4.1

How many dogs are there? Nora's solution: 3 and 3 is 6.

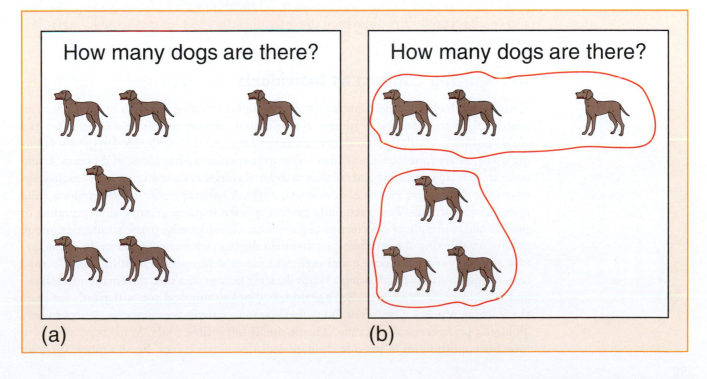

mathematics instruction. In addition, by listening to how different children approach the task, the teacher has acquired important information that can be used to plan subsequent instruction that meets a variety of children's needs.

The Nuts and Bolts of Differentiating Instruction

Differentiation is an instructional approach that requires a shift from focusing on the "middle-of-the-road" child to attending to all children. As overwhelming as this may sound, differentiation does not require a teacher to create individualized lessons for each and every child in the classroom. Rather, it requires emphasizing three basic ideas (Sousa & Tomlinson, 2011):

- Planning lessons around meaningful content, grounded in authenticity.
- Recognizing each child's readiness, interest, and approach to learning.
- Connecting content and learners by modifying content, process, product, and the learning environment.

Planning Meaningful Content, Grounded in Authenticity

Before you begin to think about differentiation, you first need to know where you want your children to "be" at the end of the learning experience. You must be explicitly aware of the content that children should know, understand, and be able to do after engaging in a given lesson or sequence of lessons. This awareness enables you to effectively guide children's learning by varying or differentiating instruction. If you do not have a clear idea about the specific learning outcomes, identifying how and when to differentiate can be difficult. In fact, Tomlinson (1999) claims that "If the 'stuff' [content] is ill conceived, the 'how' [differentiation] is doomed" (p. 16).

Note that the content must be authentic and grounded in important mathematics that emphasizes the big ideas in ways that require children to develop relational understanding. Authentic content engages children with the heart of mathematics by requiring them to be problem solvers and creators of knowledge. Through this kind of engagement, children also develop a productive disposition toward mathematics and see it as sensible, useful, and worthwhile.

Recognizing Children as Individuals

Knowing each child in the context of learning requires finding out who he or she is as an individual on traits such as readiness, interests, and learning profile. *Readiness* refers to a child's proficiency with the knowledge, understanding, and skills embedded in specific learning goals. *Interest* means a child's attraction to particular topics, ideas, and events. Using contexts that are interesting and familiar to children enhances their attention and motivation to engage and achieve (Sousa & Tomlinson, 2011). A *learning profile* identifies how a child approaches learning—how each child prefers to learn (e.g., in groups, alone); prefers to process and reason about information (e.g., by listening, observing, participating, or through talking; by thinking about details first and then the big picture or vice versa; by doing one task at a time or multitasking); and prefers to use or demonstrate what has been learned (e.g., writing, verbalizing, drawing). When deciding how to structure the environment, tasks, and assessments, consider children's preferences for learning and you will greatly facilitate the learning process. This is not to say that you must narrow learning experiences to only children's preferences all the time. That is simply impossible to do. What is possible is to look for opportunities to provide children some learning choices. Furthermore, knowing children's preferences alerts you to when they may need additional supports or guidance when those preferences are not possible to incorporate.

Information about your children's traits can inform how you might modify different elements of the classroom (e.g., Sousa & Tomlinson, 2011; Tomlinson, 2003). You can gather information pertaining to children's readiness by using preassessments several days before a given unit so that you have time to analyze the evidence and assess each child's readiness for the unit. You can also use surveys, typically at the beginning and midpoint of the year, to gather information about children's interests and learning profiles. Interest surveys give children opportunities to share personal interests (e.g., what they like to do after school, on the weekends, and during the summer; what school subjects they find most interesting and why) and information about pets, siblings, and extracurricular activities. Increase your children's motivation and engagement by using their interests to provide contexts for the mathematics they are learning. Learning profile surveys or questionnaires also help children think about what helps them learn and what does not, such as preferring to work in pairs versus alone, being able to work with background noise, and needing to process ideas verbally (Figure 4.2). For younger children, use icons or images on the survey that they can circle to indicate their choice or conduct a quick informal interview using a checklist. Teacher observation can also provide valuable insights. By recording children's information on index cards, you can quickly refresh your memory by looking through the cards as you plan lessons. You can also sort the cards to help you create groups based on interests or learning profiles.

Figure 4.2

Learning profile inventory.

When working on a task, I like to . . .	I like to work . . .	When working, I like the room to be . . .	When working, I like . . .	When learning about new ideas, I like to . . .	When sharing information, I like to . . .
☐ sit at my desk ☐ sit somewhere other than my desk ☐ stand ☐ lie on the floor ☐ other	☐ with a partner ☐ in a small group ☐ alone ☐ other	☐ warm ☐ cool ☐ darker, lights off ☐ bright ☐ other	☐ quiet ☐ noise ☐ music ☐ other	☐ hear about it ☐ read about it ☐ see visuals about it ☐ use materials to explore ☐ talk about it ☐ other	☐ talk ☐ show ☐ write ☐ other

Connecting Content and Learners

A critical component of differentiated lesson planning is determining how to modify four classroom elements to help the learner better connect with the content (Tomlinson, 2003). These four classroom elements are content, process, product, and the learning environment.

Content: What You Want Each Child to Learn

Generally, what is learned (the big ideas) should be relatively the same for all children. However, content can still be differentiated in terms of depth (level of complexity) and breadth (connecting across different topics) (Murray & Jorgensen, 2007; Small, 2012). Children's readiness typically informs the level of complexity or depth at which the content is initially presented for different groups of children. Interest and learning profiles tend to inform differentiation geared toward breadth.

An example of a depth adaptation for developing understanding and skill with organizing, representing, and interpreting data is a mini-lesson in which all children organize and represent data and answer questions based on the data. However, some children may have a smaller set of data to deal with, or they may be asked to answer given questions about the data, while others, who are ready for more sophisticated content, are asked to generate their own questions about the data. An example of a breadth adaptation for the same objective is to allow children a choice in terms of the kind of data with which to work. For example, based on their interests, children might choose to work with data pertaining to sports, books, science, or pets. By working with data from various contexts, children not only learn something about those contexts but also can begin to see the broader applications of organizing, representing, and interpreting data.

Process: How Children Engage in Thinking about Content

Although the big ideas of a learning experience remain relatively stable when differentiating, how children engage with and make sense of the content—the process—changes. Tomlinson (1999) described the process as children "taking different roads to the same destination" (p. 12). You can use different strategies or encourage children to take different "roads" to increase access to the essential information, ideas, and skills embedded in a lesson (Cassone, 2009; Tomlinson, 2003). For example, the use of manipulatives, games, and relevant and interesting contextual problems provides different ways for children to process their ideas while engaging with content.

The mathematical process standards in the *Principles and Standards for School Mathematics* (NCTM, 2000), which served as a basis for the Standards for Mathematical Practice in the *Common Core State Standards* (CCSSO, 2010), lend themselves well to differentiating how children engage with and make sense of content. In particular, the process standard of representation emphasizes the need to think about and use different ways to represent mathematical ideas, which can help children make connections between concepts and skills.

Teaching Tip

Be sure that the differentiated tasks you ask children to do are closely aligned with the learning objectives of the lesson.

With the process standard of communication, children can use verbal or written communication as they share their reasoning, depending on their strengths. In addition, the process standard of problem solving allows for differentiation because of the myriad of strategies that children can use—from drawing a diagram or using manipulatives to solving a simpler problem and looking for patterns.

Due to children's different levels of readiness, it is imperative that they be allowed to use a variety of strategies and representations that are grounded in their own ideas to solve problems. You can facilitate children's engagement in thinking about the content through a variety of methods. For example, teachers may

- Use visuals or graphic organizers to help children connect ideas and build a structure for the information in the lesson.

- Provide manipulatives to support children's development of a concept.

- Provide different manipulatives than those previously used with the same content to expand children's understanding.

- Use an appropriate context that helps children build meaning for the concept and that employs purposeful constraints that can highlight the significant mathematical ideas.

- Share examples and nonexamples to help children develop a better understanding of a concept.

- Gather a small group of children to develop foundational knowledge for a new concept.

- Provide text or supplementary material in a child's native language to aid understanding of materials written or delivered in English.
- Set up learning centers or a tiered lesson (a lesson that offers learners different pathways to reach a specific learning goal).

Product: How Children Demonstrate What They Know, Understand, and Are Able to Do after the Lesson Is Over

The term *product* can refer to what a child produces as a result of completing a single task or a major assessment after an extended learning experience. The products for a single task are similar to the ways children share their ideas in the *After* portion of a lesson, described in Chapter 2, which could include children explaining their ideas with manipulatives, through a drawing, in writing, or simply verbally. The products related to an extended experience can take the form of a project, portfolio, test, write-up of solutions to several problem-based inquiries, and so on. An important feature of any product is that it allows a variety of ways for children to demonstrate their understanding of essential content.

Learning Environment: The Logistics, Physical Configuration, and Tone of the Classroom

Consider how the physical learning environment might be adapted to meet children's needs. Do you have a child who prefers to work alone? Who prefers to work in a group? Who can or cannot work with background noise? Who prefers to work in a setting with brighter or dimmer lighting? Attending to these children's needs can affect the seating arrangement, specific grouping strategies, access to materials, and other aspects of the classroom environment. In addition to the physical learning space, establishing a classroom culture in which children's ideas and solutions are respected as they explain and justify them is an important aspect of a differentiated classroom. Refer to the recommendations provided in Chapter 2, *Teaching Mathematics through Problem Solving*, pertaining to facilitating effective classroom discussions and establishing a supportive and respectful learning environment.

Differentiated Tasks for Whole-Class Instruction

One challenge of differentiation is planning a task focused on a target mathematical concept or skill that can be used for whole-class instruction while meeting a variety of children's needs. Let's consider two different kinds of tasks that can meet this challenge: parallel tasks and open questions (Murray & Jorgensen, 2007; Small, 2012).

Parallel Tasks

Parallel tasks are two or three tasks that focus on the same big idea but offer different levels of difficulty. The tasks should be created so that all children can meaningfully participate in a follow-up discussion with the whole class. You can assign tasks to children based on their readiness, or children can choose which task to work on. If they choose a task that is too difficult, they can always move to another task. Consider how the following parallel tasks emphasize the big idea of subtraction, but at different levels of difficulty.

TASK 1:

There are 38 second graders on the playground; 22 of them come in for lunch. How many children are left on the playground?

TASK 2:

There are 108 second graders in our school; 29 of them leave on a field trip. How many second graders are left in the school?

Stop and Reflect

Which of the two tasks do you think would be more difficult, and why?

Both tasks provide opportunities for children to work with subtraction, but the numbers in the second task increase the level of difficulty regardless of the strategy a child uses. First, the numbers in the second task, 29 and 108, are farther apart than the numbers in the first task, 22 and 38. In the second task, if children use a counting-up strategy to determine the difference, they will need to move across multiple decades while keeping track of the count. Plus, crossing over the 100 mark can also be difficult for children. Even if children use the typical procedure for multidigit subtraction, the second task requires regrouping across a zero whereas the first task does not require regrouping at all.

You can facilitate a whole-class discussion by asking questions that are relevant to both tasks. For example, with respect to the previous two tasks, you could ask the following questions of the whole class:

- How did you determine how many children were left?
- Some of you indicated that you added to find your answer. Why does adding make sense?
- Suppose one more child left. How would that change your answer?
- Suppose there had been one more child to begin with. How would that change your answer?

Although children work on different tasks, because the tasks are focused on the same big idea, these questions allow them to extend their thinking as they hear others' strategies and ideas.

For many problems involving computation, you can simply insert multiple sets of numbers to vary the difficulty. In the following problem, children are permitted to select the first, second, or third number in each set of brackets. Giving a choice increases motivation and helps children become more self-directed learners (Bray, 2009; Gilbert & Musu, 2008).

LEARNING OBJECTIVE: (CCSS-M: 1.OA.A.1)

Use addition and subtraction within 20 to solve word problems involving situations of adding to, taking from, putting together, taking apart, and comparing, with unknowns in all positions, e.g., by using objects, drawings, and equations with a symbol for the unknown number to represent the problem.

Task: Mark had [9, 12, 6] stickers. Natalie gave him [5, 7, 8] more stickers. How many stickers does Mark have now?

The following parallel tasks for kindergarten focus on the big idea of cardinality or counting to tell the number of objects (see Figure 4.3).

With the first task, the teacher provides a task for children who are ready to find ways to organize their count. The parallel task still offers an opportunity for children to count but provides a built-in structure that can help children keep track of their count.

In thinking about how to create parallel tasks, once you have identified the big idea you wish to focus on, consider how children might differ in their reasoning about that idea. The size of the numbers involved, the operations children can use, and the degree of structure inherent in the task are just a few things to consider as you create parallel tasks. Start with a task from your textbook and then modify it to make it suitable for a different developmental level. The original task and the modified task will serve as the parallel tasks offered simultaneously to your children. If you number the parallel tasks and allow children to choose the task they will work on, be sure there are instances in which the more difficult task is the first one. This randomness will ensure that children consider both options before they choose their task.

Figure 4.3

Parallel tasks for telling how many objects.

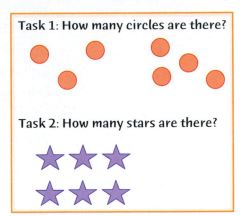

TASK 1:

How many circles are there? (Circles are in a scattered configuration.)

TASK 2:

How many stars are there? (Stars are arranged in a rectangular array.)

Open Questions

Many questions found in textbooks are closed, meaning there is one answer and often only one way to get there. These kinds of questions cannot meet the needs of the range of learners in your classroom. Alternatively, open questions are broad-based questions that can be solved in a variety of ways or that can have different answers. Because these kinds of questions invite meaningful responses from children who are at varying developmental levels, they more readily meet the needs of a range of learners (Small, 2012). Following are two examples of open questions. Both questions can have different answers and can also be solved in a variety of ways.

- I measured an object in the classroom and found that it was 8 inches long. What could the object be?
- The sum of three numbers is 25. What could the three numbers be?

Stop and Reflect

How would you solve each of these tasks? Can you think of at least two different strategies and at least two different answers for each task?

Open questions have a high level of cognitive demand, as described in Chapter 2, because children must use more than recall or do more than merely follow steps in a procedure. As such, there are ample opportunities for them to approach the problems at their own level, which means open questions automatically accommodate for student readiness. Consequently, when given an open question, most children can find something appropriate to contribute, which helps to increase their confidence in doing mathematics and can provide you insight into their level of understanding.

You can use a variety of strategies, such as the following, to create open questions (Small, 2012; Sullivan & Lilburn, 2002):

- Give the answer and ask for the problem.
- Replace a number in a given problem with a blank or a question mark.
- Offer two situations or examples and ask for similarities and differences.
- Create a question in which children have to make choices.

The two previous examples of open questions illustrate the first strategy of giving an answer and asking for the problem. Table 4.1 shows examples of using the three other strategies to convert standard questions to open questions.

Table 4.1 Converting standard questions to open questions.

Strategy	Standard Question	Open Question
Replace a number in a given problem with a blank or a question mark.	23 + 68 = ____	?3 + 6? = ____
Offer two situations or examples and ask for similarities and differences.	Draw a triangle.	How are these triangles the same and how are they different?
Create a question so that children have to make choices.	What number is 10 more than 25?	A number is 10 greater than another number. What could the numbers be?

Facilitating follow-up discussions is also important when you use open questions. While children work on an open question, walk around and observe the strategies they are using and the answers they are finding. During this time, plan which children will share their ideas during the follow-up discussion, ensuring that a variety of strategies and answers are examined. During the discussion, look for opportunities to help children make connections between different ideas that are shared. For example, in the preceding task in which children are finding two numbers that are 10 apart from each other, suppose some children identified 45 and 55 as their two numbers. One child might explain that to find the two numbers she used the hundreds chart, started at 45, and then moved down a row to 55. Another child might say that he started at 45 and counted 10 more using his fingers. Ask the class how the strategy of counting on your fingers could be shown on the hundreds chart or how moving down one row on the hundreds chart is the same as counting 10 on your fingers. Asking questions that help children build connections can support those who need additional help to track on significant ideas and can also challenge children to extend their understanding.

Tiered Lessons

In a tiered lesson, you set the same learning goals for all children, but different pathways are provided to reach those learning goals, thereby creating the various tiers. First, you need to decide which category you wish to tier: content, process, or product. If you are new to preparing tiered lessons, tier only one category until you become more comfortable with the process. Once you decide which category to tier, determine the challenge of each of the defined tiers based on student readiness levels, interests, and learning profiles (Kingore, 2006; Murray & Jorgensen, 2007; Tomlinson, 1999). Murray and Jorgensen (2007) suggest starting by creating three tiers to make the process more manageable: a regular tier or lesson, an extension tier that provides extra challenge, and a scaffolding tier that provides more background or support. Once you have this framework, you can design as many tiers as needed to meet your children's needs. All tiered experiences should have the following characteristics (Sousa & Tomlinson, 2011):

- Address the same learning goals.
- Require children to use reasoning.
- Be equally interesting to children.

We have already considered some ways to tier the content by using parallel tasks and open questions. However, varying the degree of challenge is not just about the content. You can also tier lessons using any of the following four aspects (Kingore, 2006):

- ***Degree of assistance.*** If some children need additional support, you can partner children, provide examples, help them brainstorm ideas, or provide a cue sheet (Figure 4.4).
- ***Structure of the task.*** Some children, such as children with disabilities, benefit from highly structured tasks. However, gifted children often benefit from a more open-ended structure.
- ***Complexity of the task.*** Make tasks more concrete or more abstract and/or include more difficult problems or applications.
- ***Complexity of the process.*** As you think about your learners, ask yourself these questions: How quickly should I pace this lesson? How many instructions should I give at one time? How many higher-level thinking questions are included as part of the task(s)?

Consider in the following examples how the original task is modified to change the level of challenge:

Figure 4.4

Problem-solving cue sheet.

Ways to help me think about the problem	5 + 7 =
	Counting chips
	Ten-frame
	Finger counting
	Drawing
	Other

ORIGINAL TASK:

Elliot had 9 toy cars. Sasha came over to play and brought 8 cars. How many cars do Elliot and Sasha have together? Explain how you know.

The teacher has distributed cubes to children to model the problem and paper and pencil to illustrate and record how they solved the problem. He asks them to model the problem and be ready to explain their solution.

ADAPTED TASK:

Elliott had some toy cars. Sasha came over to play and brought her cars. How many cars do Elliott and Sasha have together? Explain how you know.

The teacher asks children what is happening in this problem, how they might solve the problem, and what tools might help them solve the problem. Then the teacher distributes task cards that tell how many cars Elliot and Sasha have. The teacher has varied the difficulty of the numbers, giving children who are struggling sums that are less than 10 and the more advanced children sums greater than 20.

Card 1 (easier)

Elliot has 5 cars and
Sasha has 3 cars.

Card 2 (middle)

Elliot has 9 cars and
Sasha has 8 cars.

Card 3 (advanced)

Elliot has 17 cars and
Sasha has 16 cars.

In each case, children must use words, pictures, models, or numbers to show how they figured out the solution. Various tools are provided (connecting cubes, counters, number line, and hundreds chart) for children's use.

Stop and Reflect 500 ☽ 250 ◿ ? 3✗ ▱ 5° ∞ ⋂ ↘ 2.5

Which of the four aspects that change the challenge of tiered lessons was addressed in the adapted task?

You would preassess your children to determine the best ways to use these task cards. One option is to give children only one card, based on their current academic readiness (e.g., easy cards to those who have not yet mastered addition of single-digit numbers). A second option is to give out cards 1 and 2 based on readiness, then use card 2 as an extension for those who successfully complete card 1, and card 3 as an extension for those who successfully complete card 2. In each of these cases, you will need to record at the end of the lesson which children were able to model and explain the various levels of the problems so that the next lesson can be planned appropriately. Notice that this tiered lesson addresses both the complexity of the task (difficulty of different cards) and the process (instructions are broken down by starting with the no-numbers scenario).

The following example illustrates how to tier a lesson based on *structure*. Notice that the different tasks vary in how open-ended the work is, yet all tasks focus on the same learning goal of analyzing and comparing two-dimensional shapes.

LEARNING OBJECTIVE: (CCSS-M: K.G.B.4)

Analyze and compare two-dimensional shapes, in different sizes and orientations, using informal language to describe how they are the same and how they are different, or parts (e.g., number of sides and vertices/"corners").

Children are given a collection of two-dimensional shapes (e.g., squares, a variety of triangles, nonsquare rectangles, hexagons). Some children may be given collections that have fewer shapes and fewer varieties of shapes in each category. The tasks are distributed to different groups based on their learning needs and prior knowledge of two-dimensional shapes.

- *Group A:* Explore the set of shapes. For each kind of shape, what do you notice about the shape? Make a list of the ideas that you think are true for each kind of shape. [open-ended]
- *Group B:* Explore the set of shapes. For each kind of shape, what do you notice about the number of sides and the number of corners (vertices)? [slightly structured]
- *Group C:* First, sort the shapes into like shapes. Count the number of sides and the number of corners (vertices) of each shape. Use the following table to record your findings. What do you notice about the number of sides and the number of corners (vertices) for each kind of shape? [most structured]

	Number of Sides	Number of Corners
Triangles		
Squares		
Rectangles		
Hexagons		

The three tiers in this lesson reflect different degrees of difficulty in terms of task structure. However, all children are working on the same learning objective and they all must engage in reasoning about the shapes to complete their tasks.

In Chapter 6 you will read about response to intervention (RtI), a multitier student-support system that offers struggling children increasing levels of intervention. We want to distinguish between the tiers in RtI and tiered lessons used in differentiation. In RtI the tiers refer to the

Teaching Tip

Make sure children understand the vocabulary used in tasks before they begin working independently. For instance, two of the tasks in the tiered lesson example use the words *sides* and *corners*. Before they start the tasks, have a group discussion with children who are assigned these tasks about the meaning of the terms.

different degrees of intervention offered to children as needed—from the first tier, which occurs in a general education setting and involves the core instruction for all children based on high-quality mathematics curriculum and instructional practices, to the upper tier, which could involve one-on-one instruction with a special education teacher. Tiered lessons used in differentiation would be an avenue to offer high-quality core instruction for all children in the first tier or level of RtI.

Flexible Grouping

Allowing children to collaborate on tasks supports and challenges their thinking and increases their opportunities to communicate about mathematics and build understanding. In addition, many children feel that working in groups improves their confidence, engagement, and understanding (Nebesniak & Heaton, 2010). Even children who prefer to work alone need to learn the life skill of collaboration and should be provided opportunities to work with others.

Determining how to place children in groups is an important decision. Avoid grouping by ability. This kind of grouping, although well-intentioned, perpetuates low levels of learning and actually increases the gap between more and less dependent children. **Watch this video** (**https://www.youtube.com/watch?v=R4iAwShVIBE**) that shares some of the negative effects of ability grouping. Instead, consider using *flexible grouping*, in which the size and makeup of small groups vary in a purposeful and strategic manner (Murray & Jorgensen, 2007). When coupled with the use of differentiation strategies, flexible grouping gives all children the chance to work successfully in groups.

Flexible groups can vary based on children's readiness, interests, language proficiency, and learning profiles, as well as the nature of the tasks. For example, sometimes children can work with a partner because the nature of the task best suits two people working together. At other times, flexible groups might be created with four children because their assigned task has enough components or roles to warrant a larger team. Note that although it can be tempting to occasionally place struggling learners with more capable children, consistently pairing struggling learners with more capable children is not helpful for either group. The idea behind flexible grouping is that groups can and do easily change in response to all children's readiness, interests, and learning profiles and the nature of the task they will be doing.

Regardless of how you group your children, the first key to successful grouping is individual accountability. While the group is working together on a product, individuals must be able to explain the content, the process, and the product. Second, and equally important, is building a sense of shared responsibility within a group. At the start of the year, it is important to engage children in **Team-Building Activities** and to set expectations that all group members will participate in the assigned group task(s) and that all group members will be responsible for ensuring that the entire group understands the concept.

Reinforcing individual accountability and shared responsibility may create a shift in your role as the teacher. When a member of a small group asks you a question, pose the question to the whole group to find out what the other members think. Children will soon learn that they must use teammates as their first resource and seek teacher help only when the whole group needs help. Also, when you are observing groups, rather than ask Amanda what she is doing, ask Kyle to explain what Amanda is doing. Having all children participate in the oral report to the whole class also builds individual accountability. Letting children know that you may call on any member to explain what the group did is a good way to ensure that all group members understand what they did. Additionally, having children individually write and record their strategies and solutions is important. Using these techniques will increase the effectiveness of grouping, which in turn will help children learn mathematical concepts more successfully.

Stop and Reflect

Why is teaching mathematics through problem solving (i.e., a problem-based approach) a good way to differentiate instruction and reach all children in a classroom?

5

Teaching Culturally and Linguistically Diverse Children

Culturally and Linguistically Diverse Children

We are lucky to be in a country composed of people from all over the world. The percentage of culturally and linguistically diverse children in the United States continues to increase. In 2012–2013, 9.2 percent, or about 4.4 million children, participated in an ELL program in public schools (Kena et al., 2015), and about 24 percent (almost 18 million) of U.S. children are Latino (Annie E. Casey Foundation, 2014). Collectively, our children provide rich diversity in cultural practices and languages, and this must be reflected in our mathematics classrooms. Teaching for access, equity and empowerment requires high expectations for all children and this means that in planning, teaching, and assessing, we are responsive to children's backgrounds, experiences, cultural perspectives, traditions, and knowledge (NCTM, 2014).

Funds of Knowledge

Children from different countries, regions, or experiences, including those who speak different languages, are often viewed as challenges to a teacher or school. Rather, children's varied languages and backgrounds should be seen as a resource in teaching (Gutiérrez, 2009). Valuing a person's cultural background is more than a belief statement; it is a set of intentional actions that communicate to the child, "I want to know about you, I want you to see mathematics as part of your life, and I expect that you can do high-level mathematics." In getting to know children, we access their funds of knowledge—the essential knowledge or information that they use to survive and thrive (Moll et al.,1992; Chao, Murray, & Gutiérrez, 2014). Unfortunately, too many teachers view non-Asian and non-European ELLs as behind academically and socially, and lacking the skills needed to succeed (Chval & Pinnow, 2010; Vollmer, 2000).

Instead of teaching children from a deficit model (i.e., focusing on their lack of knowledge and experience), we can connect children's experiences at home and with family to those of the mathematics classroom. Family and community activities, such as playing games, weaving, cooking, and story-telling, can serve as cultural and linguistic resources in learning mathematics.

Mathematics as a Language

Mathematics is commonly referred to as a "universal language," but this is not the case. Conceptual knowledge (e.g., what division is) is universal. Procedures (e.g., how you divide or factor) and symbols are culturally determined and are not universal. For example, the subtraction process varies from country to country in how it is notated and the language that is used to describe the process. Figure 5.1 illustrates three ways to subtract, along with the countries that teach that process (Perkins & Flores, 2002; Secada, 1983).

Figure 5.1

Subtraction algorithms from around the world.

Step in the Algorithm	Explanation or Think Aloud for the Step
Missing Addend Approach (used in France, Vietnam, Thailand, Laos, Mexico, Latin America, and other places)	
$\begin{array}{r} 5\ 2 \\ -1\ 7 \end{array}$	(Done mentally) Start with the ones place. Think 12 minus 7. Subtract.
$\begin{array}{r} 5\ 2 \\ -1^1\ 7 \\ \hline 5 \end{array}$	Because 10 is added to the 2 (ones), 10 is also added to the lower number, so mentally the lower number is now 27.
$\begin{array}{r} 5\ 2 \\ -1^1\ 7 \\ \hline 3\ 5 \end{array}$	What is 2 (tens) from 5 (tens)? 3 (tens). The answer: 35.
Equal Addition Subtraction (used in Latin America and the United States, less common)	
$\begin{array}{r} 5\ 2 \\ -1\ 7 \end{array}$	(Done mentally) I can't take 7 from 2, but I can add 3 to the 7 to get 0 (0 can be taken away from any number). If I add 3 to the bottom number, I must also add it to the top number.
$\begin{array}{r} 5\ 5\!\!\!/\,2 \\ -1\!\!\!/^2\ 7^0 \\ \hline 3\ 5 \end{array}$	Note: This is notated for the reader but is often done mentally in actual practice. 2 from 5 is 3 (tens). The answer is 35.

Figure 5.1   Subtraction algorithms from around the world. (continued)

Step in the Algorithm	Explanation or Think Aloud for the Step
Negative Numbers to Subtract (used in Eastern Europe, Russia, Latvia, Ukraine, and other places)	
$\begin{array}{r} 5\ 2 \\ -1\ 7 \\ \hline \end{array}$	7 from 2 is −5.
$\begin{array}{r} 5\ 2 \\ -1\ 7 \\ \hline -5 \\ \end{array}$	1 from 5 is 4.
$\begin{array}{r} 5\ \ 12 \\ -1\ \ \ 7 \\ \hline 4-5 \\ 3\ \ \ 5 \\ \end{array}$	40 minus 5 is 35.

Commas and periods are sometimes used in reverse, for example, 1,400 meaning 1.400 as written in the United States. Numerals are sometimes written differently. For example, in many countries the numeral 1 is written more like a 7 with a sharper angle (*1*), and the 7 has a horizontal line through it to distinguish it from the one (*7*) (Secada, 1983). Treating mathematics as a universal topic can lead to inequities in the classroom as children from other cultures may not recognize the symbols and processes being used in their class, even if they know the content, and therefore may not be able to participate and learn.

What we value and how we engage in "doing mathematics" is part of cultural practice. For example, mental mathematics is highly valued in other countries, whereas in the United States, recording every step is valued. Could you follow the first strategy in Figure 5.1? Each represents different, yet equally efficient and effective, strategies for solving subtraction problems. The critical equity question, though, is not just whether you can follow an alternative approach, but how will you respond when you encounter children using such an approach?

- Will you require children to show their steps (disregarding the way they learned it)?
- Will you ask children to elaborate on how they did it?
- Will you have these children show other children their way of thinking?

Teaching Tip

Instead of requiring children to write all their steps, ask them to think aloud as they solve a problem, or ask how they did it in their head.

The latter two responses communicate to the child that you are interested in his or her way of knowing mathematics, and that there are many ways in which different people and different cultures approach mathematics. Supporting a range of strategies for algorithms is an important way to show that you value children as individuals and is a good way to gain insights into possible culturally influenced strategies (Gutiérrez, 2015).

Culturally Responsive Mathematics Instruction

Culturally responsive mathematics instruction includes attention to mathematical thinking, language, and culture. And, it applies to all children, including children from different ethnic groups, different socioeconomic levels, and so on. It includes consideration for content, relationships, cultural knowledge, flexibility in approaches, use of accessible learning contexts (i.e., contexts familiar or interesting to children), a responsive learning community, and working in cross-cultural partnerships (Aguirre & del Rosario Zavala, 2013; Averill, Anderson, Easton, Te Maro, Smith, & Hynds, 2009). Culturally responsive mathematics instruction can improve the performance of all children, as well as narrow the academic performance gap (Boaler, 2008; Kisker, Lipka, Adams, Rickard, Andrew-Ihrke, Yanez, & Millard, 2012). Table 5.1 lists four **Aspects of culturally responsive mathematics instruction**, along with questions to guide planning, teaching, and assessing.

Table 5.1. Aspects of culturally responsive mathematics instruction.

Aspect of Culturally Responsive Instruction	Teacher Reflection Questions
Communicate high expectations.	Does teaching focus on understanding big ideas in mathematics? Are children expected to engage in problem solving and generate their own approaches to problems? Are connections made among mathematical representations? Are children justifying their strategies and answers, and are they presenting their work?
Make content relevant.	In what ways is the content related to familiar aspects of children's lives? In what ways is prior knowledge elicited/reviewed so that all children can participate in the lesson? To what extent are children asked to make connections between school mathematics and mathematics in their own lives? How are child interests (events, issues, literature, or pop culture) used to build interest and mathematical meaning?
Attend to children's mathematical identities.	In what ways are children invited to include their own experiences within a lesson? Are story problems generated from children and teachers? Do stories reflect the real experiences of children? Are individual's approaches presented and showcased so that each child sees his or her ideas as important to the teacher and peers? Are alternative algorithms shared as a point of excitement and pride (as appropriate)? Are multiple modes used to demonstrate knowledge (e.g., visuals, explanations, models) valued?
Ensure shared power.	Are children (rather than just the teacher) justifying the correctness of solutions? Are children invited (expected) to engage in whole-class discussions in which they share ideas and respond to one another's ideas? In what ways are roles assigned so that every child feels that he or she is contributing to and learning from other members of the class? Are children given a choice in how they solve a problem? In how they demonstrate knowledge of the concept?

Communicate High Expectations

Too often, our first attempt to help children, in particular ELLs, is to simplify the mathematics and/or remove the language from the lesson. Simplifying or removing language can take away opportunities to learn. Culturally responsive instruction stays focused on the big ideas of mathematics (i.e., is based on standards such as the *Common Core State Standards*) and helps children engage in and stay focused on those big ideas. In addition to focusing on the big ideas, using tasks worthy of groupwork, emphasizing multiple representations, incorporating student justifications and presentations are features of classrooms that support equitable opportunities to learn mathematics (Cabana, Shreve, & Woodbury, 2014; Dunleavy, 2015). For example, a critical area in grades 1 and 2 is addition, which includes moving between stories and equations. The stories can be carefully selected to use contexts

Teaching Tip

When looking at a textbook lesson, consider rearranging and prioritizing those tasks that (1) make connections between children's prior knowledge and experiences, (2) lend to children using their own strategies, and (3) encourage children to explain their thinking (Drake et al., 2015).

that are familiar to ELLs and that lend themselves to using visuals (such as cars). Rather than having a new context for every story, the stories can focus on the same theme (and connect to the English that children are learning in their ESL instruction, if possible). This provides a context for the mathematics without adding unnecessary linguistic demands. The teacher can incorporate opportunities for children to share their approaches to adding and illustrate (with the visuals) how they thought about it. In this way, ELLs are able to learn the important content and engage in classroom discourse.

Make Content Relevant

There are really two components to making content relevant. One is to think about the *mathematics*: Is the mathematics itself presented meaningfully, and is it connected to other content? The second is to select *contexts*: Is the mathematics presented so that it connects to relevant/authentic situations in children's lives?

Mathematical Connections

Helping children see that mathematical ideas are interrelated will fill in or deepen their understanding of and connections to previously taught content. Consider the following first-grade problem:

Edwin has some trains. He gives 2 to Marta. Edwin now has 6 trains. How many did Edwin have before he gave some away?

You may recognize that this task connects addition and subtraction, and that the initial value (how many trains Edwin had before he gave any away) is the unknown amount. Although the mathematics is already presented in a conceptual and meaningful manner, it is important to connect addition and subtraction, as well as to connect the symbols to the situation. For example, one child might use a think-addition approach: "I know that he had 6 and plus the 2 from Marta means he ended up with 8." Another child might think: "I thought 'what minus 2 is 6 and I know that is 8." The symbols for each child's thinking are $6 + 2 = ?$ and $? - 2 = 6$, respectively. Having children connect the symbols back to their thinking and to the story helps build strong mathematical connections and understanding of addition and subtraction.

Context Connections

Making content relevant is also about contexts. If the "trains" context is familiar, it can ground children's thinking so they can focus on reasoning about the mathematical relationships. Using problems that connect children to developmentally appropriate social or peer connections is one way to contextualize learning. Another is to make connections to historical or cultural contexts. Seeing mathematics from various cultures provides opportunities for children to "put faces" on mathematical contributions. For example, you can introduce the Mayan place-value system as a way to think about how we write numerals (grade K) and to think about our place-value (base-ten) system (grade 2).

You can also have children create freedom quilts, which tell stories about the Underground Railroad (Neumann, 2005), or other geometric art patterns can be used to develop standards content such as partitioning circles or rectangles into halves and fourths (grade 1) or into halves, fourths, and thirds (grade 2).

Analyze existing textbook lessons to see if the contexts used actually help children make sense of the mathematics—if they do not, then adapt the contexts so that they do (Drake et al., 2015). Additionally, sometimes data is provided in textbook tasks that can be replaced with data from your community, making it much more relevant and interesting to children, as well as potentially teaching children something important about their community (Simic-Muller, 2015). Using everyday situations can increase student participation, use of different problem strategies, and consequently help children develop a productive disposition (Tomaz & David, 2015).

Attend to Children's Mathematical Identities

A focus on children's mathematical identities overlaps with the previous category, but it merits its own discussion. A child's *mathematical identity* is their disposition toward mathematics and sense of competence as learner and a contributor in mathematics classrooms (Cobb, Gresalfi, & Hodge, 2009). Whether it is intentional or not, all teaching is identity work, as children are constantly adapting and redefining themselves based on their experiences in mathematics classrooms (Gutiérrez, 2015). Our goal is to develop productive dispositions in all children (i.e., the tendency to believe that steady effort in math learning pays off and to see oneself as an effective learner and doer of mathematics [NRC, 2001]). There are a number of ways that teachers can shape children's mathematical identities. One way to do this is "assigning competence" (Boaler & Staples, 2014, p. 27). As the teacher listens during small group work, they hear different contributions from children. During later discussion, the teacher can attribute ideas to individuals, saying something like, "That relates to the strategy Nicolas used." This strategy recognizes Nicolas as capable in mathematics, influencing how he perceives himself, as well as how other classmates might perceive him.

Additionally, telling stories about their own lives, or asking children to tell stories, makes mathematics relevant to children and can raise student achievement (Turner, Celedón-Pattichis, Marshall, & Tennison, 2009). Table 5.2 provides ideas for making mathematics relevant to a child's home and community.

Table 5.2. Where to find mathematics in children's homes and community.

Where to Look	What You Might Ask Children to Record and Share (and Mathematics That Can Be Explored)
Grocery store or market advertisements	• Cost of an item of which they bought more than one (repeated addition or multiplication) • Cost of an item that came with a quantity (e.g., dozen eggs) (number combinations, division) • Better buy of same item, different brands (subtraction) • Shapes of different containers (geometry) • Different types/brands of different foods they select, such as what kind of bread (data)
Photographs	• A person they admire (data) • A favorite scene (geometry, measurement) • 2-D and 3-D shapes in their home or neighborhood (geometry, measurement) • Flowers (counting, skip counting, or multiplication with number of petals)
Artifact (game or measuring device) from their culture or that is a favorite	• Mathematics used in the game (counting, operations, other) • Measuring devices (nonstandard and standard measures) for length and volume

Read the following teacher's story to see how she incorporated family history and culture into her class by reading *The Hundred Penny Box* (Mathis, 1986). In Mathis's story, a 100-year-old woman remembers an important event in every year of her life as she turns over each of her 100 pennies. Each penny is more than a coin; it is a "memory trigger" for her life.

> Taking a cue from the book, I asked all the children to collect one penny from each year they were alive, starting from the year of their birth and not missing a year. Children were encouraged to bring in additional pennies their classmates might need. Then, the children consulted with family members to create a penny time line of important events in their lives. Using information gathered at home, they started with the year they were born, listing their birthday and then recording first steps, vacations, pets, births of siblings, and so on.

Children in grades K–2 can increase their understanding of numbers and the number line by determining when between 0 (i.e., the day they were born) and their current age a memorable event happened. The number line is an important model to use in counting, adding, and subtracting, and this context helps children better understand the number line, which is abstract and more challenging than using set models (e.g., counters). For example, you can ask children "How many years between [these two events]?" and "How many years ago was [this event]?" These questions focus on subtraction as difference, rather than as take-away, an important and underemphasized subtraction situation.

Ensure Shared Power

When we think about creating a positive classroom environment, one in which all children feel as if they can participate and learn, we are addressing considerations related to power. The teacher plays a major role in establishing and distributing power, whether intentional or not. In many classrooms, the teacher has the power—telling children whether answers are right or wrong (rather than having children determine correctness through reasoning), dictating processes for how to solve problems (rather than giving choices for how children will engage in the problems), and determining who will solve which problems (rather than allowing flexibility and choice for children). Effective teachers encourage children to make mathematics contributions and validate reasoning, reaching a higher level of rigor (Gresalfi & Cobb, 2006). The way that you assign groups, seat children, and call on children sends clear messages about who has power in the classroom. The "assigning competence" strategy just described in student mathematical identities is a teacher move to distribute power (who knows the math in our class). When teachers position ELLs as contributing in meaningful ways to the group, other children begin to see ELLs in similar ways, eliciting and valuing their ideas (Yoon, 2008). And, when teachers delegate authority to marginalized children, they learn more (Dunleavy, 2015).

 **Teaching Tip**

In reflecting on teaching, focus on student participation. Which children struggled most? Were there multiple entry points? How might certain children have been encouraged to participate more?

Teaching Strategies That Support Culturally and Linguistically Diverse Children

Culture and language are interwoven and interrelated. Therefore, teaching strategies that support diverse learners often attend to a children's background, as well as their language. Creating effective learning opportunities for ELLs involves integrating the principles of bilingual education with those of standards-based mathematics instruction. When learning about mathematics, children may be learning content in English for which they do not know the words in their native language. For example, words such as *hexagons*, *cylinders*, and *prisms* may be entirely new terminology.

Stop and Reflect

Consider recent lessons you have taught, or look at four or five pages in a textbook. See how many words you can identify that are unique or take on a specialized meaning in mathematics.

Story problems may also be difficult for ELLs not just because of the language but also because the sentences in story problems are often structured differently from sentences in conversational English (Janzen, 2008). ELLs need to use both English and their native language to read, write, listen, and speak as they learn appropriate content—a position similarly addressed in NCTM standards documents and position statements. The strategies discussed in this section are the ones that appear most frequently in the literature as critical to increasing the academic achievement of ELLs in mathematics classrooms (e.g., Celedón-Pattichis & Ramirez, 2012; Echevarria, Vogt, & Short, 2008). Table 5.3 **Reflective questions for planning and teaching mathematics lessons for ELLs** offers an "at-a-glance" format of some reflective questions related to instructional planning and teaching to support ELLs.

Teaching Tip

Any one of the categories in Table 5.3 could be the focus of a lesson study, discussions with colleagues, or the basis for individual reflection. The importance lies not in the specific suggestions, but in the concept of having an eye on language development *and* mathematics content.

Table 5.3. Reflective questions for planning and teaching mathematics lessons for ELLs.

Process	Mathematics Content Considerations	Language Considerations
Reflective Questions for Planning		
1. Determine the mathematics.	• What mathematical concepts (aligned to grade-level standards) am I teaching? • What child-friendly learning objectives will I post? • How does this mathematics concept connect to other concepts children have learned?	• What language objectives might I add (e.g., reading, writing, speaking, and listening)? • What visuals or words will I use to communicate the content and language objectives?
2. Consider student needs.	• How can I connect the content to be taught to content that children have learned? Or, how will I fill in gaps if children don't have prerequisite content needed for the lesson?	• What context or models might I select that are a good match to children's social and cultural backgrounds and previously learned vocabulary?
3. Select, design, or adapt a task.	• What task can I use that addresses the content identified in No. 1 and the needs of my children identified in No. 2? • How might I adapt a task so that it has multiple entry and exit points (i.e., is challenging and accessible to a range of children)?	• What context might I use that is meaningful to the children's cultures and backgrounds? • What language pitfalls does the task have? Which of these will I eliminate, and which of these need explicit attention? • Which words or phrases, even if familiar to children, take on new meaning in a mathematics context (e.g., homonyms, homophones, and words such as sum, value, find)?

(continued)

Table 5.3. Reflective questions for planning and teaching mathematics lessons for ELLs. (*continued*)

Process	Mathematics Content Considerations	Language Considerations
Reflective Questions for Teaching		
1. Introduce the task (the *Before* phase).	• How will I introduce the task in a way that elicits prior mathematics knowledge needed for the task? • Is a similar task needed to build background related to the content (or would such a preview take away from the purpose or challenge of the task)?	• How can I connect the task to children's experiences and to familiar contexts? • What key vocabulary do I want to introduce so that the words will be used throughout the lesson? (Post key vocabulary in a prominent location.) • What visuals and real objects can I use that bring meaning to the selected task? • How can I present the task in visual, written, and oral formats? • How will I be sure that children understand what they are to do in the *During* phase?
2. Work on the task (the *During* phase).	• What hints or assists might I give as children work that help them focus without taking away their thinking? • What extensions or challenges will I offer for children who successfully solve the task? • What questions will I pose to push the mathematics identified in the learning goals?	• Have I grouped children for both academic and language support? • Have I encouraged children to draw pictures, make diagrams, and/or use manipulatives? • Have I used strategies to reduce the linguistic demands (e.g., graphic organizers, sentence starters such as, "I solved the problem by . . .," recording tables, and concept maps) without hindering the problem solving?
3. Debrief and discuss the task and the mathematics (the *After* phase).	• How will children report their findings? • How will I format the discussion of the task? • What questions will I pose to push the mathematics identified in the learning goals?	• In what ways can I maximize language use in nonthreatening ways (e.g., think–pair–share)? • How can I encourage and reinforce different formats (multiple exit points) for demonstrating understanding of the lesson content? • How might I provide advance notice, language support, or rehearsal to English language learners so that they will be comfortable speaking to their peers? • Am I using appropriate "wait time"?
Formative Assessment		
Throughout lesson and unit	• What questions will I ask during the lesson, or what will I look for in the children's work as evidence of learning the objectives (*During* and *After* phases)? • What follow-up might I provide to children who are not demonstrating understanding of the mathematics?	• What words will I use in my questions to be sure the questions are understood? How might I use a translator to assist in assessing? • If a child is not succeeding, how might I diagnose whether the problem is with language, content, or both? • What accommodations can I provide to be sure I am accessing what the children know?

Focus on Academic Vocabulary

ELLs enter the mathematics classroom from homes in which English is not the primary language of communication. Although a person may develop conversational English language skills in a few years, it takes as many as seven years to learn *academic language*, which is the language specific to a content area such as mathematics (Cummins, 1994).

Academic language is harder to learn because it is not used in a child's everyday world. In addition, there are unique features of the language of mathematics that make it difficult for many children, in particular those who are learning English. Teaching the academic language of mathematics evolves over time and requires thoughtful and reflective instructional planning.

Honor Use of Native Language

Valuing a child's native language is one of the ways you value his or her cultural heritage. In a mathematics classroom, children can communicate in their native languages while continuing their English language development (Haas & Gort, 2009; Moschkovich, 2009; Setati, 2005). For example, a good strategy for children working individually or in small groups is having them think about and discuss the problem in their preferred language. If a child knows enough English, then the presentation in the *After* phase of the lesson can be shared in English. If the child knows little or no English and does not have access to a peer who shares his or her native language, then a translator, the use of a Web-based dictionary, or a self-made mathematics-focused dictionary can be a strong support. Children within the small group can also be coached to use visual aids and pictures to communicate. Bilingual children will often code-switch, moving between two languages. Research indicates that the practice of code-switching supports mathematical reasoning because children select the language in which they can best express their ideas (Moschkovich, 2009).

Certain native languages can support learning mathematical words. Because English, Spanish, French, Portuguese, and Italian all have their roots in Latin, many math words are similar across languages (Celedón-Pattichis, 2009; Gómez, 2010). For example, *aequus* (Latin), *equal* (English), and *igual* (Spanish) are cognates. See if you can figure out the English mathematical terms for the following Spanish words: *número, diferencia, hexágano, ángulo, triángulo, quadra,* and *cubo.* Children may not make this connection if you do not point it out, so it is important to explicitly teach children to look for cognates.

Use Content and Language Objectives

If children know the purpose of a lesson, they are better able to make sense of the details when they are challenged by some of the oral or written explanations. When language expectations are explicitly included, children will know that they will be responsible for reaching certain language goals alongside mathematical goals and will be more likely to attempt to learn those skills or words. Here are two examples of dual objectives:

1. Children will determine the defining attributes of a triangle (mathematics).
2. Children will describe in writing and speaking characteristics that are true for any triangle (e.g., three angles) and that characteristics do not define a triangle (e.g., color, size) (language and mathematics).

Explicitly Teach Vocabulary

Intentional vocabulary instruction must be part of mathematics instruction for all children. There is strong evidence that teaching a set of academic vocabulary words intensively across several days using a variety of instructional activities supports ELLs (Baker et al., 2014). Vocabulary support can happen throughout a lesson, as well as reinforced before or after a lesson. These additional opportunities can reinforce understanding as they help children learn the terminology. Examples include these:

- Picture dictionaries linking concepts and terms with drawings or cut out pictures
- Foldables of key words for a topic (for example, see *Dinah Zike's Teaching Mathematics with Foldables* (Zike, n.d.), a free download)

- Games focused on vocabulary development (e.g., "Pictionary" or "Concentration")
- Interactive word walls, including visuals and translations
- Graphic organizers that look at multiple ways to help define a term (for example, **Vocabulary Reference Card Template**)

All children benefit from an increased focus on language; however, too much emphasis on vocabulary can diminish the focus on mathematics. Importantly, the language support should be *connected* to the mathematics and the selected task or activity (Bay-Williams & Livers, 2009).

As you analyze a lesson, you must identify terms related to the mathematics and to the context that may need explicit attention. Consider the following kindergarten question:

MacKenna and Sydney pick red and yellow apples from the apple orchard. Sydney picks five apples to take home. How many of each kind of apple might she take?

In order for children to engage in this task, the contextual terms *pick*, *apples*, and *orchard* must be understood. The phrase *how many of each* must be understood, as it may not be clear that this means to have some apples of each color so that the total is five apples. In first and second grades, children could be asked to list all the combinations in a table.

> **Stop and Reflect**
>
> *Table* is among hundreds of words whose meanings in mathematics are different from everyday usage. Other such terms include *difference*, *foot*, *multiple*, *partition*, *side*, and *angle*. Can you name five others?

Foster Student Participation during Instruction

Student participation is important to learning (Tomaz & David, 2015; Wager, 2014). Facilitating discourse that provides access to ELLs is critical. This includes (1) efforts to ensure that ELLs understand and have the background for engaging in the focus task(s), and (2) the need to put structures in place for student participation throughout the lesson.

Build Background Knowledge

Similar to building on prior knowledge, building background also takes into consideration native language and culture as well as content (Echevarria, Vogt, & Short, 2012). If possible, use a context and appropriate visuals to help children understand the task you want them to solve. This is a nonthreatening and engaging way to help children make connections between what they have learned and what they need to learn.

Some aspects of English and mathematics are particularly challenging to ELLs (Whiteford, 2009/2010). For example, teen numbers sound a lot like their decade number—if you say *sixteen* and *sixty* out loud, you can hear how similar they are. Emphasizing the *n* sound helps ELLs hear the difference. For example, in a lesson on the teen numbers and place value, a teacher may have children partner and have one say the place-value words and the partner say the actual teen name (emphasizing the *n*):

Partner A: Ten and four

Partner B: Fourteen

And the teacher can help children see the connection between *ten* and *teen*.

Remember, too, that the U.S. measurement system may be unfamiliar to ELLs. When encountering content that may be unfamiliar or difficult for ELLs, devote additional time to build background so that children can engage in the mathematical tasks without also having to navigate language and background knowledge.

Use Comprehensible Input

Comprehensible input means that the message you are communicating is understandable to children. Modifications include simplifying sentence structures and limiting the use of nonessential or confusing vocabulary (Echevarria, Vogt, & Short, 2012). Note that these modifications do not lower expectations for the lesson. Sometimes, teachers put many unnecessary words and phrases into questions, making them less clear to nonnative speakers. Compare the following two sets of teachers' instructions:

NOT MODIFIED:

You have a worksheet in front of you that I just gave out. For every story problem, I want you to draw a picture and write an equation. You will be working with your partner, but each of you needs to record your answers on your own paper. If you get stuck on a problem, raise your hand.

MODIFIED:

Please look at your paper. (Holds paper and points to the first story, which now has a picture next to it.) Let's read together. (Everyone reads.) What is this story about? (Waits) What words tell us what the story is about (points to story itself)? (Notes context-related words on board, as well as words that indicate the action in the problem, so they can be used for reference.) Talk to your partner about how to find the answer. (Points to mouth and then to a pair of children as she says this.) Write your answers. (Makes a writing motion over paper.)

Notice that four things have been done differently in the teacher talk: Sentences have been shortened, confusing words have been removed, attention is drawn to making meaning of the first example, and related gestures and motions have been added to the oral directives. Also notice the visuals that were added and the wait time the teacher gives. It is very important to provide extra time after posing a question or giving instructions to allow ELLs time to translate, make sense of the request, and then participate.

Another way to provide comprehensible input is to use a variety of tools to help children visualize and understand what is verbalized. In the preceding example, the teacher models the instructions. Effective tools include manipulatives, real objects, pictures, visuals, multimedia, demonstrations, and literature. When introducing a lesson, include pictures, real objects, and diagrams. Children should be expected to include various representations of their understandings, such as drawing and writing to explain what they have done. Doing so helps to develop children's understanding and language, and also gives the teacher a better idea of what they do and do not understand.

Engage Children in Discourse That Reflects Language Needs

Discourse, or the use of classroom discussion, is essential for *all* learning (Cirillo, Steele, Otten, Herbel-Eisenmann, McAneny, & Riser, 2014), but is particularly important for ELLs, who need to engage in productive language (writing and speaking), not just receptive language (listening and reading) (Baker et al., 2014). As noted in *Application of Common Core State Standards for English Learners*:

> ELLs are capable of participating in mathematical discussions as they learn English. Mathematics instruction for ELL children should draw on multiple resources and modes available in classrooms—such as objects, drawings, inscriptions, and gestures—as well as home languages and mathematical experiences outside of school. Mathematical instruction should address mathematical discourse and academic language (CCSSO, 2011, p. 2).

There are strategies you can use in classroom discourse that help ELLs understand and participate in discussions. Practicing an explanation first with a partner can increase participation. Revoicing, using gestures and visuals, inviting sharing and justification, and asking other children to respond to ELLs' ideas are all ways to support participation (Shein, 2012; Turner, Dominguez, Maldonado, & Empson, 2013). *Revoicing* is a research-based strategy that helps ELLs hear an idea more than once and hear it restated with the appropriate language applied to concepts. Children from other countries often solve or record problems differently, so inviting ELLs to share how they solved a problem can enhance the richness about a task. Importantly, ELLs cannot always explain their ideas fully, but rather than call on someone else; press for details. This pressing, or expansion move (Choppin, 2014), helps the teacher decide whether the idea makes sense *and* it helps other children make sense of the ideas (Maldonado, Turner, Dominguez, & Empson, 2009). Note that these teacher moves also attribute ideas to children, thereby enhancing their mathematical authority (power), as discussed earlier in this chapter.

Teaching Tip

> Making the strategies of ELLs public and connecting their strategies to others supports the learning of all children while building the confidence of the ELLs.

Plan Cooperative/Interdependent Groups to Support Language Development

The use of cooperative groups is a valuable way to support ELLs (Baker et al., 2014). For ELLs, groups provide the opportunity to use language, but only if the groups are carefully formed in a way that considers children's language skills. Placing an ELL with two English-speaking children may result in the ELL being left out. On the other hand, grouping all Spanish speakers together prevents these children from having the opportunity to hear and participate in mathematics in English. Consider placing a bilingual child in a group with a child who has limited English, or place children who have the same first language together with native speakers so that they can help one another understand and participate (Garrison, 1997; Khisty, 1997).

CLASSROOM VIGNETTE

The strategies just described are subtle moves in teaching. As you read the following vignette, look for strategies that the teacher applies to provide support for ELLs while keeping expectations high.

Ms. Cruz is teaching a second-grade lesson that involves the standard units for measuring length (in feet). The lesson begins with nonstandard units, and then moves to measuring in feet. Ms. Cruz has four English language learners in her class including a child from Korea, who knows very little English, and three children from Mexico, who speak English to varying degrees; all are recent arrivals in the United States. These children are not familiar with U.S. measurements and may or may not have had other experiences in measuring. Ms. Cruz knows she needs to build background to ensure they can participate in the lesson.

The lesson begins by asking children to count how many thumbs to get from one side of their desk to the other. Ms. Cruz motions using the length of her thumb as a unit on a child's desk as she asks the question. She asks children to write their number of thumbs on a Post-it note and then stick the note on the board (using motions to illustrate instructions). After the answers are posted, she brings children up to the carpet. She states, "You measured your desk with your thumbs. What does measure mean?" After hearing responses and examples, she says, "Look at the answers when you measured. Can they all be right?" As children suggest that the thumb length might matter, she calls up pairs of children and has them compare their thumbs. She has the class state in full sentences whose is "longer" and "shorter" (e.g., Annie's thumb is longer than Eun's thumb). Ms. Cruz says that the big idea today is to figure out how we can measure so we all agree on how long something (like our desk) is.

She then pulls out her book *How Big Is a Foot?* and begins to read, showing and pointing at pictures as she reads. When the bed turns out to be too small, she stops and asks, "What happened—any ideas?" She waits and then asks them to share with a partner before sharing with the group. One child explains that her foot is much smaller than Ms. Cruz's foot and gets up to show the difference.

Ms. Cruz finishes the book and asks, "How is the king's problem with the bed like our thumb measures?" She then suggests that we all agree on one thumb length to use and to re-measure our desks to see if we agree on how many thumbs it is. She hands out thumb cut-outs and asks children to use this second-grader's thumb to measure. She will see how they do in iterating the unit (not overlapping, end-to-end) and then bridge to measuring the carpet with a standard foot, being sure to talk about the meaning of the word *foot*.

Stop and Reflect

What specific strategies to support English language learners can you identify?

There are a number of strategies in the vignette that provide support for ELLs: recognizing the potential language support for *measure* and later for *foot*, as well as lack of familiarity with measuring, which was supported by having an opportunity to measure prior to hearing the story (building background). Ms. Cruz has children saying in full sentences whose thumb is longer and shorter. She employs the think-pair-share technique, concrete models (the thumb cut-out), the story, and the children's own measures to build meaning and scaffold to measuring with a foot. Most importantly, Ms. Cruz did not diminish the challenge of the task with these strategies. If she had altered the task, for example, not expecting the ELLs to explain why their measures turned out differently or what they predicted would happen in the story, they would not be learning what they needed to learn. Conversely, if she had simply asked children to begin measuring in feet, she might have kept her expectations high but failed to provide the support that would enable her children to succeed.

Assessment Considerations for ELLs

If a teacher wants to understand what a child knows about mathematics, then the child should be able to communicate that understanding in a way that is best for the child, even if the teacher may need a translation. Research shows that ELLs perform better when a test is given in their native language (Robinson, 2010). Several strategies can assist teachers in using formative assessments with ELLs, including tasks with multiple entry and exit points, diagnostic interviews, tasks that limit the linguistic load, accommodations, and self-assessment.

Select Tasks with Multiple Entry and Exit Points

An aspect of teaching mathematics through problem solving that is important, particularly for ELLs, is to select tasks carefully. If a problem can be solved in multiple ways, an ELL is more likely to be able to design a strategy that makes sense and then illustrate that strategy. Inviting children to show and/or explain their strategy provides options for ELLs to use words and pictures to communicate their thinking.

Use Diagnostic Interviews

When ELLs do not get a correct answer or cannot explain a response, it is easy to assume it is a lack of mathematical understanding rather than a language issue. Diagnostic interviews provide a chance to observe what content or language the child does or does not understand. Consider the following task that could be part of a diagnostic interview focused on place value (grade 2):

If you have 2 dimes and 3 pennies, how many cents do you have?

Stop and Reflect 500 250 3X 50 2.5

If a child missed this problem, what do you think might be the reason?

There are numerous reasons children might have struggled with this problem, including a lack of understanding the mathematical concept of place value or the values of the coins. Or it could be due to vocabulary, such as not knowing what the word *cents* means. It also could be because of the sentence structure. Diagnostic interviews have found that the word *if*, and the implied "If . . . then" sentence structure common to mathematics but not in other reading, can prevent children from comprehending what the sentence is asking (a challenge for native English speakers as well) (Fernandez, Anhalt, & Civil, 2009). The fact that there are many possible reasons why a child might not be able to solve a task, some related to language and others to mathematics, is a strong argument for using diagnostic interviews. If we misdiagnose the reason for a child's struggles, our interventions will be misguided.

Diagnostic interviews also can be used before instruction in order to assess the mathematical and language needs of children. Hearing an ELL's interpretation of a problem and seeing how he or she approaches the problem provide valuable insights. For example, a child might say "three *from* seventeen" rather than "seventeen *minus* three," which indicates the way the child talks about subtraction at home. Using and connecting both ways of talking about subtraction strengthen everyone's understanding.

Limit Linguistic Load

If you are trying to assess child understanding, look for language that can interfere with children' understanding the situation (e.g., unneeded elaboration in a story, difficult or unfamiliar vocabulary). Removing pronouns such as *they, this, that, his,* and *her* and using actual names can assist ELLs in understanding some problems. For example, a typical story problem follows:

Jacob had 9 comic books. For his birthday, his grandpa gives him some more for his collection. If he has 13 now, how many did he get for this birthday?

Rewritten, it might read:

Jacob had 9 comic books. <u>Jacob's</u> grandpa gave <u>Jacob</u> some more comic books. If Jacob has 13 <u>comic books</u> now, how many <u>comic books</u> did <u>Jacob</u> get from his grandpa?

Notice that it is not only reducing unnecessary language (e.g., birthday, collection), but also adding specific referents that make the meaning of the story more clear. Of course, this particular problem could be adapted further by using illustrations or actual comic books.

If there are more problems in a lesson or assessment, staying with the same scenario/context allows children to focus their thinking on the mathematics without getting bogged down in different contexts. For example, children need opportunities to interpret story problems in which different parts are missing (the starting part, the part being added, and the whole). In this example, the part being added is what was missing. A collection of stories can be created with different parts missing (and different values used). Using the comic book context but changing the problem type reduces the linguistic load while keeping the mathematical challenge high.

Teaching Tip

To reduce the linguistic load for children, pick one scenario/context, and stay with it for an entire lesson or series of lessons.

Provide Accommodations

For assessing, *providing accommodations* refers to strategies for making sure that the assessment itself is accessible to children. This might mean allowing children to hear the question (children often can understand spoken English better than written English), shortening the assessment, or extending the time (Kersaint, Thompson, & Petkova, 2009). In addition, you can refer to word walls and provide sentence starters so that the ELL knows what type of response you want. For example, "My **equation** fits the story because . . . " In general, the goal with assessment accommodations, like teaching accommodations, is to put structures in place so that ELLs can understand what you want them to learn and you can understand what they have learned.

Stop and Reflect

The goal of equity is to offer every child access to important mathematics. What might you have on a list of things to do (and things not to do) that support equity, access and empowerment?

6

Planning, Teaching, and Assessing Children with Exceptionalities

Instructional Principles for Diverse Learners

The NCTM position statement on Access and Equity in Mathematics Education states that we should hold the expectation that all children can reach mathematics proficiency and that high levels of performance must be attained regardless of race, ethnicity, gender, socioeconomic status, ability, or linguistic background including those in special education and gifted education (NCTM, 2014). Children need opportunities to advance their knowledge supported by teaching that gives attention to their individual learning needs. Children's backgrounds are not only an important part of who they are as people, but who they are as learners—and this background enriches the classroom.

Many *achievement* gaps are actually *instructional* gaps or *expectation* gaps. It is not helpful when teachers set low expectations for children, as when they say, "I just cannot put this class into groups to work; they are too unruly" or "My students with disabilities can't solve word problems—they don't have the reading skills." Operating under the belief that some children cannot do mathematics ensures that they don't have ample opportunities to prove otherwise. Instead, we suggest you consider Storeygard's (2010) mantra for teachers which proclaims—"My kids can!"

We know that teaching for equity is much more than providing children with an equal opportunity to learn mathematics, instead, it attempts to attain equal outcomes for all children by being sensitive to individual differences. How you will maintain equal outcomes and high expectations while providing for individual differences with strong support can be challenging. Equipping yourself with an ever-growing collection of instructional strategies for a variety of students is critical. A strategy that works for one child may be completely ineffective with another, even for a child with the same exceptionality. Addressing the needs of *all* means providing access and opportunity for:

- Children who are identified as struggling or having a disability.
- Children who are mathematically gifted.
- Children who are unmotivated or need to build resilience.

You may think, "I do not need to read the section in this chapter on mathematically gifted children because they will be pulled out for math enrichment." Children who are mathematically talented need to be challenged in the daily core instruction, not just when they are participating in a gifted program.

One of the basic tenets of education is individualizing the content taught and methods used for children who struggle, particularly those with special needs. Mathematics learning disabilities are best thought of as cognitive differences, not cognitive deficits (Lewis, 2014). Children with disabilities often have mandated individualized education programs (IEPs) that guarantee access to grade-level mathematics content—preferably in a general education classroom. This legislation also implies that educators consider individual learning needs not only in terms of *what* mathematics is taught but also *how* it is taught.

Essential in making decisions about how you can adapt instruction to meet individual learner's needs is the use of accommodations and modifications. An accommodation is a response to the needs of the environment or the learner; it does not alter the task. For example, you might write down directions for a child instead of just saying them orally. A modification changes the task, making it more accessible to the child. For example, if kindergartners are asked to try to use simple geometric shapes to form larger shapes, you might show the outlines of the two smaller shapes for the children to find and place directly on top of their exact outlines. Then give them the outline of the larger shape they will form. Then the next shape they will attempt without the modification. When modifications result in an easier or less demanding task, expectations are lowered. Modifications should be made in a way that leads back to the original task, providing scaffolding or support for learners who may need it. Complete an **Accommodation or Modification Needs** table to reflect on how you will plan for children in your classroom who have special needs. Record the evidence that you are adapting the learning situation.

In this chapter, we share research-based strategies that reflect these equity principles while providing appropriate accommodations and modifications for the wide range of children in your classroom.

Prevention Models

In many school systems, a systematic process for achieving higher levels performance for all children often includes a multitiered system of support (MTSS) frequently called response to intervention (RtI). This approach commonly emphasizes ways for struggling students to get immediate assistance and support rather than waiting for children to fail before they receive help or also for identifying children who are far exceeding standards and need additional challenges. Multitiered models are centered on the three interwoven elements: high-quality curriculum, instructional support (interventions), and formative assessments that capture children's strengths and weaknesses. Often this model is used to determine whether low achievement is due to a lack of high-quality mathematics (i.e., "teacher-disabled students") (Baroody, 2011; Ysseldyke,

Figure 6.1

Response to intervention—using effective prevention strategies for all children.

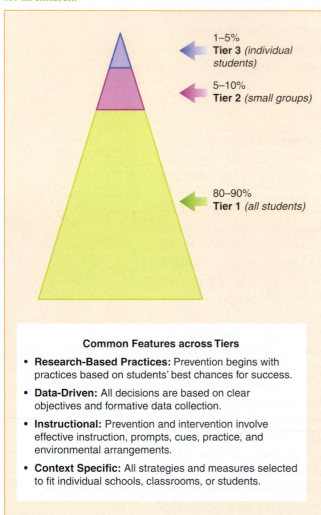

1–5%
Tier 3 *(individual students)*

5–10%
Tier 2 *(small groups)*

80–90%
Tier 1 *(all students)*

Common Features across Tiers

- **Research-Based Practices:** Prevention begins with practices based on students' best chances for success.
- **Data-Driven:** All decisions are based on clear objectives and formative data collection.
- **Instructional:** Prevention and intervention involve effective instruction, prompts, cues, practice, and environmental arrangements.
- **Context Specific:** All strategies and measures selected to fit individual schools, classrooms, or students.

Source: Based on Scott, Terence, and Lane, Holly. (2001). *Multi-Tiered Interventions in Academic and Social Contexts.* Unpublished manuscript, University of Florida, Gainesville.

2002) or due to an actual learning disability. This model can also help determine more intensive, instructional options for students who may need to have additional advanced mathematical challenges beyond what other children study.

Response to Intervention

RtI (**https://www.youtube.com/watch?v=nkK1bT8ls0M**) is a multitiered student support system often represented in a three-tier triangle format. As you might guess, there are a variety of RtI models developed by school systems as they structure their unique approaches to meeting children's needs. As you move up the tiers the number of children involved decreases, the teacher–student ratio decreases, and the level of intervention increases. Each tier in the triangle represents a level of intervention with corresponding monitoring of results and outcomes, as shown in Figure 6.1. The foundational and largest portion of the triangle (Tier 1) represents the core instruction for **all** children based on high-quality mathematics curriculum, highly engaging instructional practices (i.e., manipulatives, conceptual emphasis, etc.) and progress monitoring assessments. For example, if using a graphic organizer in Tier 1 core instruction the following high-quality practices would be expected in the three phases of the lesson—*Before, During,* and *After*:

Before. States purpose, introduces new vocabulary, clarifies concepts from needed prior knowledge in a visual organizer, and defines tasks of group members (if groups are being used).

During. Displays directions in a chart, poster, or list; provides a set of guiding questions in a chart with blank spaces for responses.

After. Facilitates a discussion to highlight or make more explicit the significant concepts or skills and then presents a summary and list of important concepts as they relate to one another.

Tier 2 represents children who did not reach the level of achievement expected during Tier 1 instruction. Children who move to Tier 2 should receive supplemental targeted instruction (interventions) using more explicit strategies with systematic teaching of critical skills and concepts, more intensive and frequent instructional opportunities, and more supportive and precise prompts (Torgesen, 2002). The National Council of Teachers of Mathematics' position statement on Interventions (2011) endorses the use of interventions that increase in intensity as children demonstrate continuing struggle with learning mathematics. Interventions may require "heroic action to preclude serious complications" (Fuchs & Fuchs, 2001, p. 86).

If further assessment reveals children have made favorable progress, the extra interventions are faded and discontinued. But, if difficulties and struggles still remain, the interventions can be adjusted in intensity, and in rare cases, children are referred to the next tier of support. Tier 3 is for children who need more intensive assistance, which may include comprehensive mathematics instruction or a referral for special education evaluation or special education services. Instructional strategies for the three tiers are outlined in Table 6.1.

Table 6.1. Interventions for teaching mathematics in a multitiered model.

Tiers	Interventions
Tier 1	**Highly qualified regular classroom teacher:** • Incorporates high-quality, engaging, and rigorous curriculum • Expects that all children will be challenged • Builds in CCSSO Standards for Mathematical Practice and NCTM process standards • Commits to teaching the curriculum as defined • Uses multiple representations such as manipulatives, visual models, and symbols • Monitors progress to identify struggling students and students who excel at high levels for possible interventions • Uses flexible student grouping • Fosters active student involvement • Communicates high expectations
Tier 2	**Highly qualified regular classroom teacher, with collaboration from other highly qualified educators (i.e., special education teacher):** • Works with children (often in small groups) in engaging, high-quality, and rigorous supplemental sessions outside of the core instruction • Conducts individual diagnostic interviews to target a student's strengths and weaknesses to facilitate next instructional steps • Slices back (Fuchs & Fuchs, 2001) to material from a previous grade to ramp back up to grade-level curriculum • Collaborates with special education, gifted, and/or ELL specialists • Creates lessons that emphasize the big ideas (focal points) or themes • Incorporates CSA (concrete, semi-concrete, abstract) approach • Shares thinking in a think-aloud to demonstrate how to make problem-solving decisions • Incorporates explicit systematic strategy instruction (summarizes key points and reviews key vocabulary or concepts prior to the lesson) • Models specific behaviors and strategies, such as how to handle measuring tools or geoboards • Uses mnemonics or steps written on cards or posters to help children follow, for example, the stages of problem solving • Uses peer-assisted learning, where another child can provide help to a child in need • Supplies families with additional instructional support materials to use at home • Encourages children's use of self-regulation and self-instructional strategies such as revising notes, writing summaries, and identifying main ideas • Teaches test-taking strategies and allows the children to use a highlighter on the test to emphasize important information
Tier 3	**Highly qualified special education teacher:** • Works one-on-one with children • Uses tailored instruction based on specific areas of strengths and weaknesses • Modifies instructional methods, motivates children, and adapts curricula • Uses explicit contextualization of skills-based instruction

Progress Monitoring

A key to guiding children's movement within the multitiered prevention model is the monitoring of their progress. One way that you can collect evidence of children's knowledge of concepts through the use of diagnostic interviews (examples are described in Chapter 3 and throughout the book in a feature called Formative Assessment Notes) (Hodges, Rose & Hicks, 2012). Another approach is to assess children's growth toward fluency in basic facts, an area that is well-documented as a barrier for children with learning disabilities (Mazzocco, Devlin, & McKenney, 2008). Combining instruction with short daily assessments proved to be a way to help children not only be better at remembering the facts but better at generalizing to other facts (Woodward, 2006). The collection of information gathered from these assessments will reveal whether children are making the progress expected or if more intensive instructional approaches need to be put into place.

Implementing Interventions

NCTM has shared a set of effective, research-based strategies (NCTM, 2007b) for teaching the subset of children for whom the initial core instruction was not effective (the children needing Tier 2 or Tier 3 interventions). These strategies include systematic and explicit instruction, think-alouds, concrete and visual representations of problems, peer-assisted learning activities, and formative assessment data provided to children and teachers. These interventions, proven to be effective for children with disabilities, may represent principles different from those used at Tier 1.

Explicit Strategy Instruction

Explicit instruction is characterized by highly structured, teacher-led instruction on a specific strategy. When engaging in this explicit instruction you do not merely model the strategy and have children practice it, instead you try to illuminate the decision-making along the way—a process that may be troublesome for these particular learners without support. In this instructional strategy, after you assess the children so that you know what to target, you use a tightly organized sequence from modeling the strategy to prompting children through the model, to practice. Your instruction uses these teacher-led explanations of concepts and strategies, including the critical connection building and meaning making that help learners relate new knowledge with concepts they know. Let's look at a classroom teacher using explicit instruction:

> As you enter Mr. Logan's classroom, you see a small group of young children seated at a table listening to the teacher's detailed explanation and watching his demonstration of addition concepts. The children are using manipulatives, as suggested by Mr. Logan, and moving through carefully selected tasks. He tells the students to take out three cubes and asks them to take out five more cubes. Mr. Logan asks the children, "Now how many do you have?" He asks, "Is **add** a word you know?" Then, to make sure they don't overcount, he asks them to talk about their reasoning process by asking the question, "What are some things you need to keep in mind as you put the two groups together?" Mr. Logan writes their responses on the adjacent board along with $3 + 5 = 8$ to connect the ideas that they share with the symbolic representation. During the lesson Mr. Logan frequently stops the group, interjects points of clarification, and directly highlights critical components of the task. For example, he asks, "Can you count from three by adding the five cubes on?" and "Would it be the same if you started with the five cubes and counted on the three cubes? Why?" The children take turns answering these questions aloud. Vocabulary words, such as **add**, **combine**, and **equals**, are written on the "math word wall" nearby and the definitions of these terms are reviewed and reinforced throughout the lesson. At the completion of the lesson, children are given several similar examples of the kind of combination discussed in the lesson as independent practice.

A number of aspects of explicit instruction can be seen in Mr. Logan's approach to teaching addition concepts. He employs a teacher-directed teaching format, carefully describes the use of manipulatives, and incorporates a model-prompt-practice sequence. This sequence starts with verbal instructions and demonstrations with concrete models, followed by prompting, questioning, and then independent practice. The children are deriving mathematical knowledge from Mr. Logan's oral, written, and visual clues.

As children with disabilities solve problems, explicit strategy instruction can help guide them in carrying out tasks. First ask them to read and restate the problem, draw a picture or make a model with materials, develop a plan by linking this problem to previous problems, write the problem in a mathematical sentence, break the problem into smaller pieces, carry out operations, and check answers using a calculator, hundreds chart or other appropriate tools. These self-instructive prompts, or self-questions, structure the entire learning process from beginning to end. Unlike more inquiry-based instruction, the teacher models these steps and explains components using terminology that is easily understood by children who struggle—children who did not discover them independently through initial Tier 1 or 2 activities. Yet, consistent with what we know about how all children learn, children are still doing problem solving (not just skill development).

Concrete models can support explicit strategy instruction. For example, a teacher demonstrating the properties of two-dimensional shapes, might say, "Watch me. Now make a rectangle with these four straws that looks just like mine." In contrast, a teacher with a more inquiry-oriented approach might say, "Using these different sized pieces of straws, how can you show me a rectangle?" Although initially more structured, the use of concrete models in this fashion will provide children with disabilities with greater access to abstract concepts.

There are a number of possible advantages to using explicit strategy instruction for children with disabilities. This approach helps you make more explicit for these children the covert thinking strategies that others use in mathematical problem solving. Although children with disabilities hear other children's thinking strategies in the *After* phase of each lesson, they frequently cannot keep up with the rapid pace of the sharing. Without extra time to reprocess the conversation, children with disabilities may not have access to these strategies. More explicit approaches are also less dependent on the child's ability to draw ideas from past experience or to operate in a self-directed manner.

There are some aspects of explicit strategy instruction that have distinct disadvantages for children with special needs, particularly the times children must rely on memory—often one of their weakest skills. There is also the concern that highly teacher-controlled approaches promote prolonged student dependency on teacher assistance. This is of particular concern for children with disabilities because many are described as passive learners.

Children learn what they have the opportunity to practice. Children who are never given opportunities to engage in self-directed learning (based on the assumption that this is not an area of strength) will be deprived of the opportunity to develop skills in this area. In fact, the best explicit instruction is scaffolded, meaning it moves from a highly structured, single-strategy approach to multiple models, including examples, and nonexamples. It also includes immediate error correction followed by the fading of prompts to help children move to independence. To be effective, explicit instruction must include making mathematical relationships explicit (so that children, rather than only learning how to do that day's mathematics, make connections to other mathematical ideas). Because making connections is a major component in how children learn, it must be central to learning strategies for children with disabilities.

Concrete, Semi-Concrete, Abstract (CSA)

The CSA (concrete, semi-concrete, abstract) intervention has been used in mathematics education for a variety of topics for years (Dobbins, Gagnon, & Ulrich, 2014; Griffin, Jossi, & van Garderen, 2012; Heddens, 1964; Hunter, Bush, & Karp, 2014). Based on Bruner and Kennedy's stages of representation (1965), this model reflects concrete representations such as manipulative materials that encourage learning through movement or action (enactive stage) to semi-concrete representations of drawings or pictures (iconic stage) and learning through abstract symbols (symbolic stage). Built into this approach is the return to visual models and concrete representations as children need or as children begin to explore new concepts or extensions of concepts learned previously. As children share reasoning that shows they are beginning to understand the mathematical concept, there can be a shift to semi-concrete representations. This is not to say that this is a rigid approach that only moves to abstraction after the other phases. Instead, it is essential that there is parallel modeling of number symbols throughout this approach to explicitly relate the concrete models and visual representations to the corresponding numerals and equations. CSA also includes modeling the mental conversations that go on in your mind as you help children articulate their own thinking. Used particularly in a combination with explicit strategy instruction, this approach has met with high levels of success for children with disabilities (Flores, Hinton, & Strozier, 2014; Mancl, Miller, & Kennedy, 2012, Miller & Kaffar, 2011).

Peer-Assisted Learning

Children with special needs also benefit from other children's modeling and support (McMaster & Fuchs, 2016). The basic notion is that children learn best when they are placed in the role of an apprentice working with a more skilled peer or "expert." Although the peer-assisted learning approach shares some of the characteristics of the explicit strategy instruction model, it is distinct because knowledge is presented on an "as-needed" basis as opposed to a predetermined sequence. The children can be paired with older children or peers who have more sophisticated understandings of a concept. At other times, tutors and tutees can reverse roles during the tasks. Having children with disabilities "teach" others is an important part of the learning process, so giving children with special needs a chance to explain their thinking to a peer or younger child is a valuable learning tool.

Think-Alouds

When you use a "think-aloud" as an instructional strategy you demonstrate the steps to accomplish a task while verbalizing the thinking process and reasoning that accompany the actions. Remember, don't start with where your thinking is; assess and start where the child's thinking is. Let's look at an example. Consider a problem in which first graders are given the task of determining which of two children is taller and by how much by having the students lying on the floor. Rather than merely demonstrating, for example, how to use connecting cubes to measure the length of the children, the think-aloud strategy would involve talking through the steps and identifying the reasons for each step while measuring each child and then comparing the difference between the children's heights. As you place a tick mark on the floor to indicate where the cubes should start, you might state, "I used this line to mark off where Rebecca's foot ends. How should I use this line as I measure Rebecca? I know I have to add on cubes, but how do I know when to stop adding cubes?" "How can I use both lengths of cubes to find out if Rebecca is taller than Emma and by how much?" "Do I need to count all the cubes?" All of this dialogue occurs prior to counting the difference in the amount of cubes.

Often teachers share alternatives about how else they could have carried out the task. When using this metacognitive strategy, try to talk about and model possible approaches (and the reasons behind these approaches) in an effort to make your invisible thinking processes visible to children.

Although you will choose any of these strategies as needed for interventions, your goal is always to work toward high student responsibility for learning. Movement to higher levels of understanding of content can be likened to moving up a hill. For some, formal stair steps with support along the way is necessary (explicit strategy instruction); for others, ramps with encouragement at the top of the hill will work (peer-assisted learning). Other children can find a path up the hill on their own with some guidance from visual representations (CSA approach). All people can relate to the need to have different support during different times of their lives or under different circumstances, and it is no different for children with special needs (see Table 6.2). Yet children with special needs must eventually learn to create a path to new learning on their own, as that is what will be required in the real world after formal education ends. Leaving children with only knowing how to climb steps with support and then later in life having them face hills without constant assistance and encouragement from others will not help them attain their life goals.

Teaching and Assessing Children with Learning Disabilities

Children with learning disabilities have very specific difficulties with perceptual or cognitive processing that may affect memory; general strategy use; attention; the ability to speak or express ideas in writing; the ability to perceive auditory, visual, or written information; or

Table 6.2. Common stumbling blocks for children with disabilities.

Stumbling Blocks for Children	What Will I Notice?	What Should I Do?
Trouble forming mental representations of mathematical concepts	• Has difficulty identifying a triangle when the top of the triangle points down • Can't interpret a number line	• Explicitly teach the representation—for example, demonstrate exactly how to draw a triangle while identifying the critical properties • Use larger versions of the representation so that children can move on (e.g., number line) or interact with the model
Difficulty accessing numerical meanings from symbols (issues with number sense)	• Has difficulty with basic facts; for example, doesn't recognize that 3 + 5 is equal to 5 + 3, or that 5 + 1 is the same as the next counting number after 5 • Does not understand the meaning of the equal sign • Can't interpret if an answer is reasonable	• Explicitly teach multiple ways of representing a number showing the variations at the same time • Use a number balance to support understanding of the equal sign • Use multiple representations for a single problem to show how it would be carried out in a variety of ways (base-ten blocks, illustrations, and numbers) rather than using multiple problems
Difficulty keeping numbers and information in working memory	• Loses track of counts of objects • Gets confused when multiple strategies are shared by other children during the *After* portion of the lesson • Forgets how to start the problem-solving process	• Use ten-frames or organizational mats to help the child organize counts • Explicitly model using counters or how to use skip counting to count • Record in writing the ideas of other children during discussions • Incorporate a chart that lists the main steps in problem solving as an independent guide or make bookmarks with questions the children can ask themselves as self-prompts
Lacks organizational skills and the ability to self regulate	• Misses steps in a process • Writes computations in a way that is random and hard to follow	• Use routines as often as possible or provide self-monitoring checklists to prompt steps along the way • Use graph paper to record problems or numbers • Create math word walls as a reference
Misapplies rules or overgeneralizes	• Applies rules such as "Always subtract the smaller from the larger" too literally, resulting in errors such as 25 − 9 = 24	• Always give examples as well as counter examples to show how and when "rules" should be used and when they should not. • Tie all rules into conceptual understanding, don't emphasize memorizing rote procedures or practices

the ability to integrate abstract ideas (Berch & Mazzocco, 2007). Although specific learning needs and strategies that work for one child may not work for another, there are some general ideas that can help as you plan instruction for children with special needs. The following questions should guide your planning:

1. What organizational, behavioral, and cognitive skills are necessary for the children with special needs to derive meaning from this activity?

2. Which children have significant weaknesses in any of these skills or concepts?

3. What are the children's strengths?

4. How can I provide additional support in these areas of weakness so that children with special needs can focus on the conceptual task in the activity? (Karp & Howell, 2004, p. 119)

Each phase of the lesson evokes specific planning considerations for children with disabilities. Some strategies apply throughout a lesson. The following discussion is based on Karp and Howell (2004) and although not exhaustive provides some specific suggestions for offering support throughout the lesson while maintaining the challenge.

1. *Structure the Environment*
   - *Centralize attention.* Move the child close to the board or teacher. Face children when you speak to them and use gestures. Remove competing stimuli.

   - *Avoid confusion.* Word directions carefully and ask the child to repeat them. Give one direction at a time. Use the same language for consistency. For example, talk about base-ten materials as ones, tens, and hundreds rather than interchanging those names with "flats," "rods," and other words about their shape rather than their value.

   - *Create smooth transitions.* Ensure that transitions between activities have clear directions and there are limited chances to get off task.

2. *Identify and Remove Potential Barriers*
   - *Help children remember.* Recognize that memory is often not a strong suit for children with disabilities and therefore develop mnemonics (memory aids) for familiar steps or write directions that can be referred to throughout the lesson. For example, **STAR** is a mnemonic for problem solving: **S**earch the word problem for important information; **T**ranslate the words into models, pictures, or symbols; **A**nswer the problem; **R**eview your solution for reasonableness (Gagnon & Maccini, 2001).

   - *Provide vocabulary and concept support.* Explicit attention to vocabulary and symbols is critical throughout the lesson. Preview essential terms and related prior knowledge/concepts, create a "math wall" of words and symbols to provide visual cues, and connect symbols to their precise meanings.

   - *Use "friendly" numbers.* Instead of using $6.13 use $6.00 to emphasize conceptual understanding rather than mixing computation and conceptual goals. Incorporate this technique when computation and operation skills are *not* the lesson objective.

   - *Vary the task size.* Assign children with special needs fewer problems to solve. Some children can become frustrated by the enormity of the task.

   - *Adjust the visual display.* Design assessments and tasks so that there is not too much on a single page. The density of words, illustrations, and numbers on a page can overload children. Find ways to put one problem on a page, increase font size, or reduce the visual display.

Teaching Tip

Note that searching the word problem for important information is different from identifying "key words" as the use of a "key word approach" is not effective.

3. *Provide Clarity*
   - *Repeat the timeframe.* Give children additional reminders about the time left for exploring materials, completing tasks, or finishing assessments. This helps children with time management.
   - *Ask children to share their thinking.* Use the think-aloud method or think-pair-share strategy.
   - *Emphasize connections.* Provide concrete representations, pictorial representations, and numerical representations. Have children connect them through carefully phrased questions. Also, connect visuals, meanings and words. For example, as you count a series of items, point out that you touch each item, say the number name in sequence, and write the last number stated as the total amount (cardinality).
   - *Adapt delivery modes.* Incorporate a variety of materials, images, examples, and models for visual learners. Some children may need to have the problem or assessment read to them or generated with voice creation software. Provide written instructions in addition to oral instructions.
   - *Emphasize the relevant points.* Some children with disabilities may inappropriately focus on the color of a cube instead of the quantity of cubes.
   - *Support the organization of written work.* Provide tools and templates so children can focus on the mathematics rather than the creation of a table or chart. Also use graphic organizers, picture-based models, and paper with columns or grids.
   - *Provide examples and nonexamples.* To define triangles, give examples of triangles as well as shapes that are not triangles. Help children focus on the characteristics that differentiate the examples from those that are not examples.

4. *Consider Alternative Assessments*
   - *Propose alternative products.* Provide options for how to demonstrate understanding (e.g., a verbal response that is written by someone else, voice recorded, or modeled with a manipulative). Use voice recognition software or word prediction software that can generate a whole menu of word choices when children type a few letters.
   - *Encourage self-monitoring and self-assessment.* Children with learning disabilities often need support in self-reflection. Asking them to review an assignment or assessment to explain what was difficult and what they think they got right, can help them be more independent and take greater rcsponsible for their learning.
   - *Consider feedback charts.* Help children monitor their growth by charting progress over time.

5. *Emphasize Practice and Summary*
   - *Consolidate ideas.* Create study guides that summarize the key mathematics concepts and allow for review. Have children develop their own study guides.
   - *Provide extra practice.* Use carefully selected problems (not a large number) and allow the use of familiar physical models.

Not all of these strategies will apply to every lesson or every child with special needs, but as you are thinking about a particular lesson and certain individuals in your class, you will find that many of these will allow your children to engage in the task and accomplish the learning goals of the lesson. Explore **Strategies for Making Math Accessible** for a handy collection of cards that you can use to think about particular children as you plan.

The Center for Applied Special Technology (CAST) website contains resources and tools to support the learning of all children, especially those with disabilities, through universal design for learning (UDL).

Adapting for Children with Moderate/Severe Disabilities

Children with moderate/severe disabilities (MSD) often need extensive modifications and individualized supports to learn mathematics. This population of children may include those with severe autism, sensory disorders, limitations affecting movement, cerebral palsy, processing disorders such as intellectual disabilities and combinations of multiple disabilities.

Originally, the curriculum for children with severe disabilities was called "functional," in that it often focused on life-related skills such as managing money, telling time, using a calculator, measuring, and matching numbers to complete such tasks as entering a telephone number or identifying a house number. Now directives and assessments have broadened the curriculum to address the grade-level expectations in the *Common Core State Standards* (CCSSO, 2010) or other curriculum policy documents.

When possible, the content should be connected to life skills and when appropriate features of jobs. To develop number sense, counting can be linked to daily counting tasks to be accomplished, and counting down can mark a period of cleanup after an activity or to complete self-care routines (washing hands). Children with moderate or severe disabilities should have opportunities to use measuring tools, compare graphs, explore place-value concepts (sometimes linked to money use), use the number line, and compare quantities. Shopping skills or activities in which food is prepared are both options for mathematical problem solving. At other times, link mathematical learning objectives to everyday events in a practical way. For example, when the operation of addition is studied, figuring out how many forks are needed for a birthday party that includes two classes would be appropriate. Children can also undertake a small project such as making a placemat for lunch as a way to explore shapes and measurements.

Do not believe that all basic facts must be mastered before children with moderate or severe disabilities can move forward in the curriculum; children can learn geometric or measuring concepts without having mastered all basic facts. Teaching geometry to children with moderate and severe disabilities should include more than merely identifying shapes. It is, in fact, critical for orienting children with moderate and severe disabilities into the real world. Concepts such as parallel and perpendicular lines and curves and straight sides become helpful for interpreting maps of the local area. Children who learn to count bus stops and judge time can be helped to successfully navigate their world. The handout **Math Activities for Children with Moderate or Severe Disabilities** offers ideas across the curriculum appropriate for teaching children with moderate to severe disabilities. Also, look at the **Additional Strategies for Supporting Children with Moderate/Severe Disabilities** handout for more ideas on how you can modify grade-level instruction.

Planning for Children Who Are Mathematically Gifted

Children who are mathematically gifted include those who have high ability or high interest. Some may be gifted with an intuitive knowledge of mathematical concepts, whereas others have a passion for the subject even though they may work hard to learn it. Many children's giftedness becomes apparent to parents and teachers when they grasp and articulate mathematics concepts at an age earlier than expected. They are often found to easily make connections between topics of study and frequently are unable to explain how they quickly got an answer (Rotigel & Fello, 2005).

Many teachers have a keen ability to spot talent when they note children who have strong number sense or visual/spatial sense (Gavin & Sheffield, 2010). Note that these teachers are not pointing to children who are fast and speedy with their basic facts, but those who have the ability to reason and make sense of mathematics.

Do not wait for children to demonstrate their mathematical talent; instead develop it through a challenging set of tasks and inquiry-based instruction (VanTassel-Baska & Brown 2007). Generally, as described in the RtI model, high-quality core instruction is able to respond to the varying needs of diverse learners, including the talented and gifted. Yet for some of your gifted children, the core instruction may prove not to be enough of a challenge.

Pre-assessing children by curriculum-based tests and also other measures such as concept maps prior to instruction allows the evaluation of what the child already knows and in some cases identifies how many grade levels ahead they might be (Rakow, 2012). Without this information the possibility of targeting the next steps and adaptations becomes guesswork.

There are four basic categories for adapting mathematics content for gifted mathematics students: *acceleration and pacing*, *depth*, *complexity*, and *creativity* (Johnsen, Ryser, & Assouline, 2014). In each category, your children should apply, rather than just acquire, information. The emphasis on applying, implementing, and extending ideas must overshadow the mental collection of facts and concepts.

Acceleration and Pacing

Acceleration recognizes that your children may already understand the mathematics content that you plan to teach. Some teachers use "curriculum compacting" (Reis & Renzulli, 2005) to give a short overview of the content and assess children's ability to respond to mathematics tasks that would demonstrate their proficiency. Allowing children to increase the pace of their own learning can give them access to curriculum different from their grade level while demanding more independent study. But, moving children to higher mathematics (by moving them up a grade, for example) will not succeed in engaging them as learners if the instruction is still at a slow pace. Research reveals that when gifted children are accelerated through the curriculum they are more likely to explore STEM (science, technology, engineering, and mathematics) fields (Sadler & Tai, 2007).

Depth

Enrichment activities go into depth beyond the topic of study to content that is not specifically a part of your grade-level curriculum but is an extension of the original mathematical tasks. For example, while studying place value to very large numbers, mathematically gifted children can stretch their knowledge to study other large numbers such as a google. This provides an extended view of how our base-ten numeration system fits within the broader systems of recording very large numbers. Other times the format of enrichment can involve studying the same topic as the rest of the class while differing on the means and outcomes of the work. Examples include group investigations, solving real problems in the community, writing data-based letters to outside audiences, or identifying applications of the mathematics learned.

Complexity

Another strategy is to increase the sophistication of a topic by raising the level of complexity or pursuing greater depth to content, possibly outside of the regular curriculum or by making interdisciplinary connections. For example, while studying a unit on place value, mathematically gifted children can deepen their knowledge to study other numeration systems such as Roman, Mayan, Egyptian, Babylonian, Chinese, and Zulu. This provides a multicultural view of how our numeration system fits within the historical number systems (Mack 2011). In the algebraic-thinking strand, when studying sequences or patterns of numbers, mathematically gifted children can learn about Fibonacci sequences and their appearances in the natural world in shells and plant life. See the **Mathematics Integration Plan**. Use this plan to integrate core content for a gifted child or, depending on the child's ability, use it to help children create independent explorations or research. When using this approach, children can think about a mathematics topic through another perspective or through an historic or even futuristic viewpoint.

Creativity

By presenting open-ended problems and investigations children can use divergent thinking to examine mathematical ideas—often in collaboration with others. These collaborative experiences could include children from a variety of grades and classes volunteering for special mathematics projects, with a classroom teacher, principal, or resource teacher taking the lead. Their creativity can be stimulated through the exploration of mathematical "tricks" using binary numbers to guess classmates' birthdays or design large-scale investigations of the amount of food thrown away at lunchtime (Karp, K. & Ronau, R., 1997). A group might find mathematics in art (Bush, Karp, & Nadler, 2015). Another aspect of creativity provides different options for children in culminating performances of their understanding, such as demonstrating their knowledge through inventions, experiments, simulations, dramatizations, visual displays, and oral presentations.

Noted researcher on the mathematically gifted, Benbow (Read, 2014), states that acceleration combined with depth through enrichment is best practice. Then learning is not only sped up but the learning is deeper and at more complex levels.

Strategies to Avoid

There are a number of ineffective approaches for gifted children, including the following:

1. *Assigning more of the same work.* This is the least appropriate way to respond to mathematically gifted children and the most likely to result in children hiding their ability.

2. *Giving free time to early finishers.* Although children find this rewarding, it does not maximize their intellectual growth and can lead to children hurrying to finish a task.

3. *Assigning gifted children to help struggling learners.* Routinely assigning gifted children to teach other children who are not meeting expectations does not stimulate their intellectual growth and can place them in socially uncomfortable or sometimes undesirable situations.

4. *Providing gifted pull-out opportunities.* Unfortunately, generalized gifted programs are often unrelated to the regular mathematics curriculum (Assouline & Lupkowski-Shoplik, 2011). Disconnected, add-on experiences are not enough to build more complex and sophisticated understanding of mathematics.

5. *Offering independent enrichment on the computer.* Although there are excellent enrichment opportunities to be found on the Internet and terrific apps, the practice of having gifted children use a computer program that focuses on skills does not engage them in a way that will enhance conceptual understanding, critical thinking, or support children's ability to justify their thinking.

Sheffield writes that gifted children should be introduced to the "joys and frustrations of thinking deeply about a wide range of original, open-ended, or complex problems that encourage them to respond creatively in ways that are original, fluent, flexible, and elegant" (1999, p. 46). Accommodations, modifications, and interventions for mathematically gifted children must strive for this goal.

Stop and Reflect

How is equity in the classroom different from teaching all children equitably?

7

Collaborating with Families and Other Stakeholders

Sharing the Message with Stakeholders

Teaching mathematics developmentally, addressing the increased content demands articulated in the *Common Core State Standards* initiative (CCSSO, 2010), and ensuring that children are mathematically proficient requires *everyone's* commitment. We often hear educators make statements such as "You must have the principal's support" and "You need to get parents on board," and we nod our heads in agreement. As educators it is not enough to know what the changes are; we must also understand *why* change in mathematics content and teaching strategies is needed and be able to share this message in jargon-free ways with families, administrators, politicians, and other stakeholders. And, involving stakeholders is not only about getting support for your mathematics program—it is about supporting student learning! Parental involvement at school results in higher levels of student academic achievement (Barnard, 2004; Lee & Bowen, 2006).

In this chapter, we discuss ideas for developing a collaborative community that understands and is able to support high-quality mathematics teaching and learning for every student. Also, we hope that this chapter (and the rest of this book) is helpful in presenting a strong case for why we need to teach developmentally-appropriate, student-centered mathematics.

Table 7.1. Questions related to change in mathematics teaching and learning.

Category	Types of Questions
Why Change?	• Why is mathematics teaching changing? • Is there evidence that this approach or curriculum is effective? • What are the *Common Core State Standards* and why do we have national standards? • Where can I learn more about the *Common Core State Standards*?
Pedagogy	• Why isn't the teacher teaching? (And what is the point of reinventing the wheel?) • Why is my child struggling more than in previous years? • Are children doing their own work when they are in groups? Is my child doing the work of other children? • Are calculators and other technology interfering with my child's fluency?
Content	• Is my child learning the basic skills? • Why is my child learning different algorithms/strategies (than I learned) for doing the operations? • Why are there less skills and more story problems?
Student Learning and Outcomes	• Will these standards prepare my child for middle school, high school, college, and beyond (e.g., ready for ACT, SAT, Algebra in eighth or ninth grade)? • Why is my child struggling more than in previous years? • How can I help my child with their homework; to be successful?

Changes to the mathematics curriculum—new textbooks, content topics, technologies, teaching philosophies, instructional strategies, and routines—warrant communication with parents, principals, and community leaders. Communicating with families is one of the most important components of successfully implementing a new mathematics curriculum (Bay, Reys, & Reys, 1999). Without such opportunities for communication, people may draw their own conclusions about the effectiveness of the mathematics curriculum, develop frustrations and negative opinions about what is happening in their child's classroom or school, and communicate this apprehension to other parents and community leaders. This has certainly been the case in states that initially adopted the *Common Core State Standards* (CCSS-M), and then had it voted out again. The reasons people opposed the standards (or support them) are sometimes not actually characteristics of the CCSS-M but, rather, characteristics that have been assigned to the CCSS-M.

Rather than hope that there will be support for changes in mathematics teaching and learning, it is important to anticipate possible questions and concerns and develop a plan to address them (Bay-Williams & Meyer, 2003). Table 7.1 highlights common questions parents and other stakeholders ask about mathematics programs.

Be proactive! Don't wait for concerns or questions to percolate. Providing a forum for parents, administrators, and community leaders around mathematics highlights the importance of the subject and gives stakeholders confidence that your school is a great place for preparing children for college and beyond. In the sections that follow, we share possible responses to the four areas of concerns in Table 7.1.

Why Change?

Change in many domains is considered a good thing. Why, then, is any change in mathematics teaching met with resistance? Additionally, the same people who claim to not be good at math or to not like math, are often the ones most concerned about changes in mathematics teaching and learning. Navigating through change in mathematics requires strong justification for why the change is occurring, and the justification must resonate with the particular stakeholders' concerns and experiences.

Changes in Content

Reflecting on how other professions—from doctors to mechanics to dentists to bankers to hair stylists have changed their practices over the past 25-plus years can make for an interesting comparison. Many fields have changed based on changes in society, different desired outcomes, available tools and technologies, research on what works, and new requirements within the job.

Another approach is to share research on the *ineffectiveness* of the traditional U.S. approach to teaching mathematics. The Trends in International Mathematics and Science Study (TIMSS), an international study conducted regularly that includes many countries, continues to find that U.S. students achieve at an average level in fourth grade, then below average in mathematics than international students in eighth grade and high school. Discuss the implications of unpreparedness for children who want to seek higher-paying jobs on what is now an international playing field.

Evidence for Change

Just as research and advancements have changed procedures doctors and mechanics use, research and advancements have informed alterations in procedures used in mathematics. In teaching mathematics, this can be what we have learned about teaching (e.g., to start with concrete tools or to make connections explicit) or what we have learned about specific content (e.g., that writing equations in nontraditional ways improves student understanding of equivalence [McNeil, Fyfe, Petersen, Dunwiddie, & Brletic-Shipley, 2011]). Also, in nearly all careers, certain mathematical proficiencies are essential: being able to select appropriate tools, determine and implement a strategy or algorithm, communicate and compare approaches, and reflect on the result of a procedure or solution. In other words, preparing children to be college and career ready means addressing the mathematical proficiencies described in the CCSS Mathematical Practices and NCTM Process Standards.

CCSS Mathematics

Chapter 1 addressed the CCSS. Here we focus on advocating with stakeholders related to the standards. If you are teaching in a "Common Core" state, then you may have encountered a number of questions about the CCSS and/or heard various incorrect facts communicated about the CCSS-Mathematics. CCSSI provides a list of myths and facts (see **http://www .corestandards.org/about-the-standards/myths-vs-facts/**). Here we summarize six common (and detrimental) myths related to mathematics (with facts in *italics* afterward):

Myth 1. CCSS are national standards. *Fact: CCSS was designed by Governors and State School Officers. They were adopted by states, and states can add to the core as they see fit. States are in charge of implementation and assessment of children.*

Myth 2. CCSS-Mathematics lowers existing state standards. *Fact: An analysis of state standards shows that the common core sets higher expectations than any individual state standards (and states can add more rigor if they choose).*

Myth 3. CCSS are not internationally benchmarked. *Fact: This was a significant purpose in creating the standards.*

Myth 4. CCSS do not prepare students for algebra in grade 8. *Fact: Those that complete CCSS-M through grade 7 can take algebra in grade 8.*

Myth 5. CCSS content is not in the right place. *Fact: Content was placed based on learning trajectories and research on student learning.*

Myth 6. CCSS dictates how teachers should teach. *Fact: The standards simply list what mathematics should be learned at what level. The Mathematical Practices describe what a mathematically proficient child can do. How to reach these outcomes for what a child should know and do are not addressed in the standards.*

Table 7.2. Statements and possible (unintended) interpretations of the statements.

Original Statement	What a Stakeholder Might Think	A Stronger, Carefully Composed Statement
"The [mathematics program] still addresses skills, but it also includes concepts."	"Why are they bringing skills up? They must be taking those away. My child/U.S. children have to know basics. How can I put a stop to this?"	"The skills in the [mathematics program] are expanding from what we once learned and now include . . ."
"It is important for children to learn from one another, so I will be more in the role of facilitator."	"The teacher is not teaching? My child does better when things are explained clearly. When I come to see you teach, what am I looking for if you are just letting the kids learn on their own?"	"In our classroom, we learn from one another. I give carefully selected tasks for children to discuss, and then we talk about them together so that everyone has a chance to learn the mathematics we are doing, and that approach gives me the chance to work one-on-one as needed."
"This year, we are doing a whole new mathematics program that the state has adopted."	"My worst nightmare—an experiment of something new during the years my child is in elementary school. This will cause problems for the rest of his life."	"We are doing some new things in order to make sure your child is well prepared for . . . [or that our program is the best available]. You might have noticed that last year we [added writing as a component to our math program]. This year, here are the big things we hope to accomplish . . ."

Stop and Reflect

Consider a statement you have heard or used with families. Ask yourself, "How might a parent (or other stakeholder) respond if he or she heard this statement?" "What might the parent misinterpret?" "How might my principal respond?" Then, read the responses in the table to see whether they represent stakeholders like those in your setting.

Whether your state is or is not using the CCSS-M, there are no doubt times when changes in mathematics teaching and learning need to be communicated to various stakeholders. These messages must be carefully composed! We sometimes say things that, although well intentioned, increase the concerns of stakeholders rather than reassure them. Table 7.2 provides three such examples.

Initially, these statements may not seem harmful, but they can set off alarms from the lens of a stakeholder. Consider these reactions, and then review the shifted language in the third column, which communicates a stronger (and less potentially disconcerting) message. It is very important to convey to stakeholders an excitement for and pride in your mathematics program. Being tentative, reserved, vague, or silent on the mathematics program can only raise concerns in the community. Help parents and administrators to understand that the mathematics program children are experiencing aligns with best practices in education, represents what children need to know in today's world, and prepares children for mathematics at the next level as well as the mathematics they need for life.

Pedagogy

When stakeholders ask questions that point to their belief that mathematics is best learned through direct instruction—just as they learned it—it is important to provide a rationale for why mathematics teaching and learning might be different now.

Teacher as Facilitator

Recall that two important findings about how children develop conceptual understanding is through (1) engaging in productive struggle and (2) making connections explicit (Hiebert & Grouws, 2007). Related to these two important research findings, compare the difference between being *shown* how to do something (e.g., "This is how you add; now practice this") and *developing* an understanding of something (e.g., "How many ways can you partition 6? How do you know if you have found all the ways?"). Ask, "In what ways are children learning about addition? About subtraction? How do the different ways support eventual mastery of the basic facts?" Point out that skills are still important, and children benefit by generating their own procedures. As children explore carefully selected tasks they engage in productive struggle and have the opportunity to make connections among mathematical ideas and strategies.

Address the role of the teacher as *organizer* (organizes a worthwhile mathematical task), *facilitator* (facilitates student interaction), and *questioner* (asks questions to help children make connections or to deepen their understanding). Remind parents that just because the teacher is not *telling* their child what to do does not mean that the teacher is not teaching. The teacher is orchestrating the class so that each child develops the appropriate connections, understands the mathematics, has the ability to solve problems and is developing a disposition that they can do mathematics.

Cooperative Groups

Parents and other stakeholders may also wonder about how frequently their child works in cooperative groups because this may differ from their own mathematics learning experiences. Help parents see the role of others in their learning as they solved the problems and as they heard solutions from those who were working at other tables. Connect that experience to the value of cooperative learning. You can do this in a variety of ways:

1. *Include a feature in your parent newsletter.* Early in the year, you can feature cooperative learning and address its importance across content areas. In mathematics, this can include the following benefits: hearing different strategies, building meaning, designing solution strategies, and justifying approaches—all of which are essential to building a strong understanding of mathematics and important life skills.

2. *Send home letters introducing math units.* If you are about to teach a unit on adding and subtracting two-digit numbers, a letter can help parents know the important aspects of the content. This is a great time to mention that children will work in groups so that they can see different ways to add or subtract two numbers.

3. *Do a cooperative learning mathematics activity at a family math night or back-to-school event.* Use a task that lends itself to assigning roles to different members of the group and won't take long to solve. Have parents work with two to three others to solve the task.

4. *Invite parents to assist in a mathematics group assignment.* Seeing firsthand the dialogue and thinking that happens in cooperative groups can go a long way in illustrating how valuable cooperative groups can be!

Parents may initially worry that children working in groups are simply copying from other children and not learning. Share strategies you use to build in individual accountability

Teaching Tip

Being proactive about communicating the *benefits* of cooperative learning, as well as how you build in *individual accountability* and *shared responsibility,* will go a long way toward converting parent concerns into parent support.

and shared responsibility. For example, teachers may ask each child to draw or write a solution in his or her notebook.

Use of Technology

Parents may be avid users of technology yet still have concerns about their child's use of calculators and computers in grades K–2, when children haven't yet mastered their basic facts for addition and subtraction. Even though research overwhelmingly finds that children using calculators achieve at least as well as those not using calculators, calculators are widely blamed for children's lack of reasoning and sense making. Reassure parents that children *will* learn the basic facts and procedures and the calculator can support that learning. Consider sharing or doing any of the following activities:

---

1. Type in 5 + 5 = . Continue to push the = key (most calculators continue to add 5 every time you push =). What patterns do you notice as you count by fives?
2. Broken Key. Suppose the following keys do not work on your calculator: 5 and 8. Figure out another way to add or subtract these numbers using the calculator:
   6 + 5   15 − 6   35 + 28

Debrief parents about the ways in which the calculator can be used as a learning tool. An important message to parents is that mastery of basic facts should *not* be a prerequisite to using a calculator. Instead, children and teachers should be making good decisions about whether a calculator supports or detracts from doing the problem at hand (and learning the intended mathematics).

> ### 🌿 Teaching Tip
>
> Families need to see specific ways to use the calculator to support learning of numbers and operations. Sharing or posting calculator activities is one way to help them understand the role calculators can play in young children's learning.

Content

Basic Facts and Standard Algorithms

A common concern of parents is that their children are not learning standard algorithms or the procedures they remember using when they were in elementary school. You must address (at least) two points related to this critical issue. First, the skills that parents are looking for (e.g., invert and multiply for dividing fractions) are still in the curriculum—they just may look different because they are presented in a way based on understanding, not just memorization. Standard algorithms are still taught but they are taught *along with* alternative (or invented) strategies that build on students' number sense and reasoning. Let parents experience that both invented and standard algorithms are important in being mathematically proficient by inviting them to solve the following problems:

$$1399 + 547 = \underline{\hspace{1.5cm}} \qquad 5009 - 998 = \underline{\hspace{1.5cm}}$$

$$487 + 345 = \underline{\hspace{1.5cm}} + 355$$

Ask for volunteers to share the ways that they thought about the problems. For the subtraction problem, for example, the following might be shared:

5000 take away 1000 is 4000, then add the 9 and 2 back on to get 4011.

998 up to 1000 is 2, up to 5000 is 4002, and up 9 more is 4011.

5009 to 5000 is 9, then down to 1000 is 4000 more (4009), and then down to 998 is 2 more (4011).

These invented strategies, over numerous problems, reinforce place-value concepts and the relationship between addition and subtraction. Noticing that these values are both near 1000 helps to select a strategy. The standard algorithm for this problem is very messy, and one that frequently results in computational errors. The best choice for solving this problem is one of the ways described above. The key to procedural fluency is to first assess the values in the problem and then decide how to solve it. This bird's-eye view of the problem is important in doing mathematics—rather than always doing the same thing regardless of the numbers. This is very evident in the third example, which can be solved with no computation if the relationships among the numbers are first noticed.

Second, what is "basic" in the 21st century is much more than computation. Many topics in early elementary school were not a part of the curriculum a generation ago (e.g., connecting numbers and algebra). Looking together through the essential concepts in the *Common Core State Standards* or the NCTM *Curriculum Focal Points* helps parents see that the curriculum is not just an idea generated at their child's school but the national consensus on what children need to learn.

Practice and Problem Solving

Parents may also wonder why there are fewer skill/practice problems and more story problems in the curriculum. Effective mathematics learning environments are rich in language. Real mathematics involves more "word" problems and far fewer "naked number" skill problems. In contrast to when the parents went to school, skills are now less needed in the workplace because of available technology, but the importance of number sense, reasoning, and being able to solve real problems has increased. Because some children struggle with reading and/or writing, share strategies you use to help them understand and solve story problems (Figure 7.1).

Figure 7.1

Share with parents how you support reading and problem solving.

Reading Strategies for Mathematics Problems

- Read math story problem aloud (whole class)

- Read a math story problem with a friend

- Say or write the question in the problem

- Draw a picture of the problem

- Act out the problem

- Use a graphic organizer (recording page with problem-solving prompts)

- Discuss math vocabulary

- Play math vocabulary games

Student Learning and Outcomes

At the heart of parents' interest in school mathematics is wanting their child to be successful, not only in the current classroom but also at the next level of school.

Preparation for College and Career

If your state has implemented the *Common Core State Standards*, you can share that the standards are for K–12 and designed to prepare students for college and future careers. The *Common Core State Standards* website has an increasing number of resources for parents (http://corestandards.org) to help them ensure that their child is college- and career-ready. Because the standards are at least as rigorous as prior state standards, and have an increased focus on student reasoning and sense making, they better prepare children for high-stakes assessments such as the ACT or SAT, which over the years have adapted to reflect changes in content expectations in high school curriculum, such as the increased focus on statistics (Jaschik, 2014; Peterson's, 2015). As noted in the CCSS myths and facts, these standards are more rigorous, and therefore better prepare children for high-stakes assessments, and still prepare children to take algebra in eighth or ninth grade.

Parents may be more interested in how your specific school is doing in preparing children for the future. Share evidence from your school of mathematics success, including stories about an individual child (no name given) or the success of a particular classroom, like the following one received by a principal:

> I was worried at the start of the year because my son didn't have a lot of confidence in math and he was coming home with problems that he was supposed to figure out his own way to solve. I wondered why the teacher hadn't shown him how to add or subtract. But now I can really see his number sense—he has all kinds of ways he adds numbers and can do it in his head. And he is really good at solving and writing his own story problems! As an aside, I am also learning a lot—I didn't learn this way, but I am finding the homework problems are really interesting as we figure them out. I am just curious if this is something he will get to do again in second grade, or if this is just the way first-grade teachers introduce the ideas.

Such communications help parents see that there is a transition period and that in the end a standards-based approach helps engage children and build their understanding over time.

Productive Struggle

Parents may worry when they see their child struggle with a single mathematics problem because they may believe that fast means successful. But faster isn't smarter. The book *Faster isn't Smarter* (Seeley, 2009) is a great read on this topic written for families, educators, and policy makers. Seeley offers 41 brief messages, many of which can address parent questions about mathematics (e.g., "A Math Message to Families: Helping Students Prepare for the Future," "Putting Calculators in their Place: The Role of Calculators and Computation in the Classroom," and "Do It in Your Head: The Power of Mental Math"). As noted above, engaging children in productive struggle is one of the two most effective ways teachers can help children develop conceptual understanding (the other is making connections among mathematical ideas) (Bay-Williams, 2010; Hiebert & Grouws, 2007). Rather than presenting a series of simpler problems for children to practice, standards-based curricula characteristically focus on fewer tasks, each of which provides children with an opportunity for higher-level thinking, multiple strategy solutions, and more time focused on math learning.

Share the first Standard for Mathematical Practice (Figure 7.2), and ask the parents what they notice. Focus on the importance of *perseverance*. This is true in mathematics and in life.

Figure 7.2

Standard 1 from the Standards for Mathematical Practice.

---

1. **Make sense of problems and persevere in solving them.**

Mathematically proficient children start by explaining to themselves the meaning of a problem and looking for entry points to its solution. They analyze givens, constraints, relationships, and goals. They make conjectures about the form and meaning of the solution and plan a solution pathway rather than simply jumping into a solution attempt. They consider analogous problems, and try special cases and simpler forms of the original problem in order to gain insight into its solution. They monitor and evaluate their progress and change course if necessary. Older children might, depending on the context of the problem, transform algebraic expressions or change the viewing window on their graphing calculator to get the information they need. Mathematically proficient children can explain correspondences between equations, verbal descriptions, tables, and graphs or draw diagrams of important features and relationships, graph data, and search for regularity or trends. Younger children might rely on using concrete objects or pictures to help conceptualize and solve a problem. Mathematically proficient children check their answers to problems using a different method, and they continually ask themselves, "Does this make sense?" They can understand the approaches of others to solving complex problems and identify correspondences between different approaches.

Common Core State Standards was developed by the Council of Chief State School Officers. Copies may be downloaded from the Council's website at http://www.ccsso.org/.

Reassure parents that some tasks take longer because of the nature of the tasks, not because their child lacks understanding. Mathematics is not nearly as much about speed and memorization as it is about being able to grapple with a novel problem, try various approaches from a variety of options, and finally reach an accurate answer.

Administrator Engagement and Support

Teachers cite a supportive principal as one of the most essential components in successfully implementing a standards-based curriculum (Bay, Reys, & Reys, 1999). Principals play pivotal roles in establishing a shared vision for a problem-based mathematics program. Principals, however, often cannot take the time to attend the professional development workshops that are designed for teachers who will be teaching the mathematics program. And what they need to know is qualitatively different from what a classroom teacher needs to know.

Since the launch of the *Common Core State Standards*, school administrators, parents, and community members are more aware than ever about mathematics standards. If your state has not adopted the *Common Core State Standards*, there are still state-level standards that are the focus of mathematics goals and assessments. Even though principals are hearing more about mathematics standards, higher standards, and the need to ensure that all children are successful, it does not mean they understand what standards-based mathematics curriculum *is* in terms of the content or the related CCSS Standards for Mathematical Practice or NCTM Process Standards.

Administrators are likely to get bombarded with broad or specific questions from parents: "Is 'New Math' back?," "Why isn't the teacher teaching the procedures for multiplying and dividing?," "What are the Standards for Mathematical Practice?," or any of the other questions offered earlier in this chapter. When a principal is asked these questions, he or she needs to give a convincing response that is accurate and that also addresses the heart of the parents' concerns—that their child is going to get a sound math experience that will prepare him or her for college and career.

Meyer and Arbaugh (2008) suggest professional development specifically for principals. Although their focus is on the adoption of standards-based textbooks, the plan they outline applies to all principals who are seeking to be knowledgeable and effective advocates for implementing new standards or mathematics curricula. The following ideas are adapted from their suggested professional development to focus on one-on-one conversations.

1. *Contrast old and new curriculum.* As a first step, it is important to know what is new and different in the mathematics program. One way to start is to provide a set of materials that represent typical *Common Core State Standards*–aligned tasks alongside the previous curriculum. Point out the noticeable similarities and differences or the key features of the curriculum. (Note: It is important to focus on *both* similarities *and* differences—not *everything* is being replaced, and this is an important message.)

2. *Discuss how parents and children will respond.* Anticipate what will be noticed by parents (or their children): Which changes might be welcomed? Which changes might be worrisome? How will the welcome aspects be promoted and the worrisome aspects be explained?

3. *Experience the curriculum.* Invite the principal to visit your classroom or other classrooms where the Standards for Mathematical Practice or the NCTM Process Standards are being infused. Ask the principal to join a group of children and listen to their discussion of how they are solving a problem. Or organize a lesson when, in the *After* phase, the children actually present their solutions to the principal. For example, in a kindergarten class, ask children to take pictures (or draw pictures) representing the two-dimensional shapes in the school. If possible, ask the principal to solve one of the problems the children are doing and share his or her strategy with the class. This firsthand experience can provide the principal with a wonderful story to share with parents and with insights that won't be gained from reviewing standards documents.

4. *Discuss emerging issues.* Plan a regular time to meet with the principal to discuss what he or she has heard from families about the mathematics program. Discuss what you might do to respond to questions (some of the anticipated issues may already have been described in the preceding section on parents' concerns). If there is a question about a problem-based approach, Chapter 2 should be a great read for a principal, and contains talking points to share with others.

Finally, keep your principal apprised of successes and breakthroughs. These stories provide the principal with stories and evidence to share when pressed by parents or community members. Principals are very often your strongest advocates and are in a position to serve as buffers between school mathematics and the community.

Stop and Reflect

What do you think the parents of your children would most value about "teaching mathematics *through* problem solving," and how will you use your response to this question to build strong family support and engagement? (Repeat the question for other stakeholders, such as your principal.)

Family Engagement

Parents know the importance of mathematics for their child's future. They participate in their child's learning by supporting homework, attending back-to-school nights or PTA meetings, and by meeting with teachers, even if they may recall unpleasant experiences or difficulties with school mathematics from their own schooling. Understanding that memories of mathematics classes are not always pleasant for parents and appreciating parental support prepare us to suitably identify for parents the mathematics goals that children should be experiencing in the 21st century.

Communication with families is key to encouraging their support and involves using one-way, two-way, and three-way communication strategies (Figure 7.3).

Figure 7.3

Ways to communicate with families.

One-way communication strategies	Letters sharing the goals of a unit	Websites where resources and curriculum information are posted	Newsletters
Two-way communication strategies	Log of child's work (signed or commented on by parent)	PTA meetings/open houses	One-on-one meetings, class or home visits
Three (or more)– way communication strategies	Family math nights	Conferences (with parent and child)	Log/journal of child's learning with input from child, parent, and teacher

Numerous studies have found a positive relationship between the level of parental involvement and their child's achievement in school (e.g., Aspiazu, Bauer, & Spillett, 1998; Henderson et al., 2002). Parents need frequent opportunities to get information directly from the school leaders and teachers about their child's mathematics program, including the kind of instruction that might differ from what they experienced in their own schooling. Even if your school has been engaged in implementing a mathematics program for a decade that reflects the NCTM *Principles and Standards for School Mathematics* and now the *Common Core State Standards*, the program will still be new to the parents of your children.

Family Math Nights

There are many ways to conduct a family or community mathematics event, such as including a math component in a back-to-school night, discussing it in a PTA meeting, or hosting a showcase for a new mathematics program. One idea is to host a Math Orientation Workshop (Ernst & Ryan, 2014). The purpose of this even is to develop consistency between the way math is taught in school and the way parents help at home. Beyond a focus on the content, parents can learn about *dispositions* of effective problem solvers, including the importance of asking questions; developing persistence; using multiple ways to solve problems; learning from mistakes; and reflecting on whether solutions make sense (see Ernst and Ryan [2014] for more details on designing and implementing this event). Providing opportunities to parents to learn about specific mathematics topics prior to their children learning the topics can lead to increased relationships with parents and increased student achievement (Knapp, Jefferson, & Landers, 2013).

Critical to any plan is providing opportunities for parents to be learners of mathematics so that they can experience what it means to *do mathematics* (just like their children). When choosing mathematical tasks to use with parents, be sure the tasks focus on content that really mat-

Teaching Tip

Welcome back or family math nights are a great time to have parent–child teams experience doing math tasks together.

ters to them and relates to what they already know is a part of the elementary curriculum (e.g., addition and subtraction, including basic facts, as well as place value are good ideas in grades K–2). There are tasks throughout this text that are ideal for a math night. Figure 7.4 contrasts two examples of first-grade problems for learning about combinations (sums) that make 6—one is straightforward and lends to a single procedure (solve the problems as modeled by the teacher using counters) and one that is designed for a teaching-through-problem-solving experience (explore and find different combinations).

Stop and Reflect

What distinctions do you notice between the two tasks? What is valued as "doing mathematics" in both of the problems?

Figure 7.4

Problems to explore at a parent or community night.

Problem 1: Find the answers to these equations. Use counters or draw pictures to show your work.

$$1 + 5 = \underline{\hspace{1cm}} \qquad 0 + 6 = \underline{\hspace{1cm}}$$
$$3 + 3 = \underline{\hspace{1cm}} \qquad 2 + 4 = \underline{\hspace{1cm}}$$

Problem 2: The parking lot has only blue and red cars. There are 6 cars parked. How many blue and how many red cars might be in the parking lot? Use counters to find as many ways as you can. Draw a picture and write an equation for each answer.

Extensions: Can you find all of the ways to have 6 red and blue cars in the parking lot? How many ways can you find to have a total of 5 cars? How many ways can you find to have a total of 7 cars? Do you see a pattern?

The contrasting addition problems are perfect for discussing with parents what it means to do mathematics because they (1) address critical areas in the *Common Core State Standards* and focal points in the *Curriculum Focal Points*, (2) involve using manipulatives (color tiles or counters), (3) connect the mathematical ideas of partitioning and addition, and (4) (in the latter example) have multiple solution strategies.

The potential each of these problems has to support and challenge children in making sense of mathematics should be made explicit during a discussion with parents. After giving parents time to do both tasks and discuss solution strategies (as you would with children), connect the learning experience to their questions and concerns. Ask participants to consider the learning opportunities in the two contrasting tasks. Ask questions such as the following:

- What skills are being developed in each problem?
- Which problem gives more opportunity to make connections between mathematics and the real world?
- Which task would your child be more motivated to solve? Why?

Help parents identify the depth of the mathematics in the teaching-through-problem-solving task. Remind them that in grades K through 2, children are building important foundations of number and operations through algebraic reasoning—looking for patterns, reasoning, and generalizing. Help parents see these aspects in the car combination problem. Share the *Common Core State Standards* and the NCTM standards (in parent-friendly language), and focus on the goal of having children becoming mathematically proficient as described in those standards. Ask parents, "Where do you see these proficiencies being supported in the two tasks we did?"

Another good choice for family math nights is basic fact strategies, as addition and subtraction facts are a central part of the curriculum in grades K–2, and developing *reasoning strategies* is essential to learning the facts well. (Parents may only know flash cards or other memorization activities.) See Chapter 10 for the three phases of fact mastery, as well as games and activities for developing reasoning strategies.

Address any or all of the questions in Table 7.1 that apply to your setting. One way to do this is to have parents write their questions on note cards and collect them so you can identify common questions and decide the order in which to discuss each one.

Teaching Tip

Provide copies of the appropriate *Common Core State Standards* Introduction and Overview pages (the first two pages for each grade), and allow parents time to think about each "Critical Area."

Classroom Visits

Invite parents to engage in your mathematics lessons, observing or interacting with students. An invitation to come to a mathematics lesson or a math event (e.g., family math night) gives parents the chance to witness firsthand such things as how you ask questions, how problems can be solved in many ways, and how calculators can be used to support reasoning. They may notice that you encourage children to select their own strategy and explain how they know it works. Parents will also pick up on the language that you are using and will be able to reinforce that language at home. You can even provide a note-taking template that includes categories such as the following:

- What is the big idea of the lesson?
- What illustrations or tools are being used to help students (your child) understand?
- What are some questions the teacher is asking that I could also ask?
- What does the teacher do when a student (my child) is stuck or needs challenged?

Involving ALL Families

Some families are at all school events and conferences; others rarely participate. However, all families want their children to be successful in school. Parents who do not come to school events may have anxiety related to their own school experiences, or they may feel completely confident that the school and its teachers are doing well by their child and that they do not need to participate. In some cultures, questioning a teacher may be perceived as disrespectful. Rodríguez-Brown (2010, p. 352), a researcher on Hispanic families, writes, "It is not that Latino parents do not want to support their children's learning. . . . [They] believe that it is disrespectful to usurp the teacher's role."

Try to find ways to build a strong rapport with all families. Some strategies to consider include the following:

1. *Honor different strategies for doing mathematics.* Although this is a recommendation in standards documents, it is particularly important for children from other countries because they may have learned different ways to do the operations (Civil & Planas, 2010).

2. *Communicate with positive notes and phone calls.* Be sure to find a way to compliment each child's mathematical thinking (not just a good score on quiz) at some point early in the school year.

3. *Host informal gatherings to discuss mathematics teaching and learning.* Having regular opportunities to meet with the parents allows the development of rapport and trust. Consider hosting events in out-of-school facilities. Schools in communities with a high level of poverty have found that having parent events at a community center or religious institution brings in families that are reluctant to come into a school.

4. *Incorporate homework that involves the family.* When a child brings in homework that tells about his or her family and you provide positive feedback or a personal comment, then you are establishing a two-way communication with the family via homework.

5. *Translate letters that are sent home.* If you are doing a class newsletter (for families) or a letter describing the next mathematics unit, make an effort to translate the letter into the native language of the families represented in your class. If you cannot do this, consider having the first class session include a component in which children write to their families about what they are about to do. Ask them to write in their parents' first language and to include visuals to support their writing. Ask parents to respond (in their language of choice). This is a great practice for helping children know what they need to learn, and it communicates to families that they are an important part of that learning.

6. *Post homework on your webpage.* For parents who are not native speakers of English, posting problems on your site makes it easier to take advantage of online translations. While these translations may not be perfectly accurate, they can help parents and children understand the language in the problems.

For more suggestions on ensuring that your mathematics tasks and homework are meeting the needs of culturally and linguistically diverse children, see Chapter 5 and read "NCTM Research Brief: Involving Latino and Latina Parents in Their Children's Mathematics Education" (Civil & Menéndez, 2010). For suggestions on students with special needs, see Chapter 6.

Homework Practices and Parent Coaching

You may have heard parents say, "I am not good at math" or "I don't like solving math problems." While parents may feel this way, such messages to their child can impede their success in mathematics. In fact, a parent's emotions are connected to the student's emotions, and these positive emotions are connected to better performance (Else-Quest, Hyde, & Hejmadi, 2008). It is our responsibility as educators to figure out ways to redirect parents to portray mathematics in a positive light.

Tips for Helping Parents Help Their Child

Explicitly teaching parents *how to* help their children has also been found to make a difference in supporting student achievement and student attitudes (Cooper, 2007; Else-Quest et al., 2008; Patall, Cooper, & Robinson, 2008). Take the following recommendations into consideration when thinking about the homework that you will assign to your children.

1. *Mimic the three-phase lesson model.* Table 2.5 describes the three-phase lesson model. Homework can reflect these general phases. Complete a brief version of the *Before* phase of a lesson to be sure the homework is understood before children go home. At home, children complete the *During* phase. When they return with the work completed, apply the sharing techniques of the *After* phase of the homework.

Children can even practice the *After* phase with their family if you encourage this through parent or guardian communications. Some form of written work must be required so that children are held responsible for the task and are prepared for the class discussion.

2. *Use a distributed-content approach.* Homework can address content that has been taught earlier in the year as practice, that day's content as reinforcement, or upcoming content as groundwork. Interestingly, research has found that distributed homework (homework that combines all three components) is more effective in supporting student learning (Cooper, 2007). The exception is students with learning disabilities, who perform better when homework focuses on reinforcement of skills and current class lessons.

3. *Promote an "ask-before-tell" approach with parents.* Parents may not know how best to support their child when he or she is stuck or has gotten a wrong answer. One important thing you can do is to ask parents to implement an "ask-before-tell" approach (Kliman, 1999). This means that before parents explain something, they should ask their child to explain how he or she did it. The child may self-correct (a life skill), and if not, at least the parents can use what they heard from their child to provide targeted assistance. Teach successful homework strategies to children, and share these strategies with parents. For example, the following ideas, suggested by Wieman and Arbaugh (2014), can be posted in your classroom and sent home:

   • Look for examples in our notes or daily work. Try those problems again.

   • If you are stuck, take a break, then come back and try again.

   • If you are confused, write a statement or question describing what is confusing.

   • Ask for help using specific questions (from parents, peers, or online support sites)

4. *Provide good questioning prompts for parents.* Providing guiding questions for parents or guardians supports a problem-based approach to instruction as they help their children. Figure 7.5 provides guiding questions that can be included in the children's notebooks and shared with families. Translating questions for parents who are not native speakers of English is important. Often, a child can help you with this task.

5. *Use Games and Interactives.* Find opportunities to assign games or interactives for homework. The intent is that the child plays with family members (e.g., parent, sibling). The game can be played as part of a lesson and then sent home to play two to three times, with a written summary of what happened as they played due the next day. Games can be assigned to develop fluency with such concepts as reinforcing basic facts, operations, number recognition, counting, and so on. Fixed-Addend War (adapted from Britt, 2015), is one such engaging activity that can be offered as a homework option at various times throughout the year.

Several features of this game make it a great choice for homework: It only requires a deck of cards. Children can choose the fixed addend, or the parent can pick one for which they think their child needs practice. Finally, it sets up opportunities for mathematical discussion. For example, asking "How did you solve it?" and "What reasoning strategy might you use?" help the student to develop and practice strategies and parents to hear those strategies.

Many interactives and applets are available across content strands (some of which are shared throughout Part 2 of this book). Asking children to explore, play, or solve on an

🌱 *Teaching Tip*

Providing specific guidance to families makes a big difference in what to do (and *not* do) to help their children learn mathematics and be confident in doing mathematics.

Figure 7.5

Questions for families to help their children with homework.

These guiding questions are designed to help your child think through his or her math homework problems. When your child gets stuck, ask the following:

- What do you need to figure out? What is the problem about?
- What words are confusing? What words are familiar?
- Do you have similar problems to look at?
- What words or pictures do you use in class?
- Where do you think you should begin?
- What have you tried so far? What else can you try?
- Can you describe where you are stuck or what is confusing?
- Can you draw a picture to help you think about the problem?
- Does your answer make sense?
- Is there more than one answer?

GAME: FIXED ADDEND WAR

Use a deck of cards, removing face cards. Identify an addend (e.g., 9) and place one of those values in the middle. Deal the rest of the cards to the two players, face down. Each player turns up a card, says the sum, followed by the addition sentence, taking turns with who goes first. The player with the larger sum gets the cards.

Example: Fixed Addend is 9. Player one turns up a 2 and says "Eleven—Nine plus two equals eleven (or two plus nine is eleven)." Player 2 two turns up a 6 and says, "15—Nine plus six equals fifteen." If there is a tie—it is a 'war' and they repeat the process, but the winner of the next round wins both sets of cards.

applet can be another way to engage families with doing mathematics. A favorite is *Deep Sea Duel*, which can be found in Classroom Resources on the NCTM website. This is a fun strategy game that helps children practice sums and differences, as they are trying to reach a target and win the game.

Homework of this nature communicates to families the problem-based or sense-making nature of your classroom and might help them see the value in this approach. A final note: A little bit goes a long way—if children are to spend time solving meaningful problems, then just a few engaging problems a night can accomplish more than a long set of practice problems.

Resources for Families

Parents will be better able to help their child if they know where to find resources. The Internet can either provide a wealth of information or be an overwhelming distraction. Help parents locate the good places to find math support. First, check whether your textbook provides websites with online resources for homework, including tutorials, video tutoring, videos, connections to careers and real-world applications, multilingual glossaries, audio podcasts, and more. Second, post websites that are good general resources. Here are some examples:

- *Math Forum@NCTM.* This popular and useful site includes many features for teachers and families. Parents may want to read or participate in math discussion groups, read about key issues for the mathematics community, or download some of the very interesting problems posted here.

- *National Library of Virtual Manipulatives* (NLVM) This site has many applets and virtual tools for learning about many mathematics topics, appropriate for the classroom and the home.

There are also great websites for specific content. For example, Thinking Blocks has excellent applets for exploring addition and subtraction. Finally, print books can be important resources for teachers. Here are a couple that we recommend:

- *It's Elementary: A Parent's Guide to K-5 Mathematics* (Whitenack, Cavey, & Henney, 2015). This book explains current teaching practices and fundamental math concepts, with many examples and student work.
- *What's Math Got to Do with It? How Parents and Teachers Can Help Children Learn to Love Their Least Favorite Subject* (Boaler, 2009). Jo Boaler describes how math can be understandable and fun, how children can excel in math, and how parents and schools can help.

Seeing and Doing Mathematics at Home

In the same way that families support literacy by reading and talking about books with their children, families can and should support numeracy. Because this has not been the practice in many homes, it means you, as the teacher, have the responsibility to help parents see the connection between numeracy and everyday life. Consider asking families to make the *Math Promise* (Legnard & Austin, 2014). Family members make this promise to one another, which means they explicitly agree they will do math together—get to know each other's mathematical reasoning, play math games, and notice mathematics in their daily lives. In her article "Beyond Helping with Homework: Parents and Children Doing Mathematics at Home," Kliman (1999) offers some excellent suggestions, which include asking parents to share anecdotes, find mathematics in the books they read, and create opportunities during household chores. Figure 7.6 provides a sample letter home that suggests these ideas to parents.

Trips in the car can include informal and fun mathematics explorations. For example, license plates can be noted and family members can try to use the numbers on the plate to create a true mathematics equation or someone can select a target number, and the values from the plate are used to try to reach that target number (Hildebrandt, Biglan, & Budd, 2013). Today's Date (Mistretta, 2013) is another activity that can be a part of informal family discussions. Today's Date involves taking the date (e.g., 18) and thinking of different expressions, ways to write it, and connections to personal interests (e.g., a favorite athletes number or the age of a cousin). These tasks have many possible solutions and can be used repeatedly at any time of the year.

Figure 7.6

Sample letter to parents regarding ways to infuse mathematics into their interactions with their child.

 # Making Math Moments Matter (M⁴)

Dear Families:

As a second grader, your child is increasingly aware of what is going on in the world. In that world is a lot of math! In our class this year we are working on **place value**, as well as learning about **standard units of measurement**, **describing and analyzing shapes**, and **addition and subtraction of three-digit numbers**. It will really help your child to <u>understand</u> and <u>see the importance</u> of math if you find ways to talk about "math moments" (on any math topic, but especially these four critical areas). We call it Making Math Moments Matter (M⁴ for short). Here are some ways to have fun with M⁴ at home.

Share stories. Share a math moment at dinner (or in the car). When have you used math today (shopping, laundry, budgets, etc.)? Think of the many things you might have estimated—how long it will take to get to work, or to run a series of errands. Take turns sharing stories. We will share family math moments in class!

 Connecting to reading. As they tell you about the book they are reading, ask quantity-type questions: How many shapes do you see in that picture? How many more pages do we have to finish the book? How long (in inches or centimeters) do you think that animal is?

Chores. Yes, chores! If it takes 45 minutes to do a load of laundry, how long will 3 loads take? If you walk the dog for 10 minutes twice each day, how many hours is the dog walked in 10 days? 100 days? If you earn $5 an hour walking dogs, what might you earn in a week?

Scavenger hunts. Riding in the car can be more interesting if there are things to look for. Consider challenging your child to look for numbers on signs and to say them correctly. Search for as many shapes as you can (e.g., a train car is a rectangular solid, a trash can is a cylinder, etc.).

8

Developing Early Number Concepts and Number Sense

BIG IDEAS

1 Counting tells how many things are in a set. When counting a set of objects, the last word in the counting sequence names the quantity for that set. (*cardinality*)

2 Numbers are related to each other through a variety of number relationships. The number 7, for example, is three more than 4, two less than 9, composed of 3 and 4 as well as 2 and 5, is three away from 10, and can be quickly recognized in several patterned arrangements of dots. These ideas further extend to an understanding of 17, 57, and 370.

3 Number concepts are intimately tied to the world around us. Application of number relationships to problem solving marks the beginning of making sense of the world in a mathematical manner.

4 *Number sense* means that you can think about and use numbers and their relationships in multiple ways to estimate and solve problems.

Research indicates that early number sense predicts school success more than other measures of cognition, such as verbal, spatial, or memory skills or reading ability (Jordan, Kaplan, Locuniak, & Ramineni, 2007; Locuniak & Jordan, 2008; Mazzocco & Thompson, 2005; Watts, Greg, Duncan, Siegler, & Davis-Kean, 2014). So the importance of young children developing strong number sense cannot be overstated. To many adults, number may seem like a simple idea. But number is actually a complex and multifaceted concept. A rich and flexible understanding of number involves many different ideas, relationships, and skills. Young children enter school with many ideas about number and these ideas should be built upon to develop new relationships over time. With time and a variety of experiences, children can develop a thorough understanding of number that will in turn support the development of more advanced mathematical concepts.

The emphasis that number and number sense receive in the National Council of Teachers of Mathematics' *Curriculum Focal Points* (NCTM, 2006) and the *Common Core State Standards* (CCSSO, 2010) speaks to their importance in the early childhood curriculum. *Curriculum Focal Points* emphasize that children in prekindergarten should work on concepts of one-to-one correspondence, counting, cardinality, and comparing small amounts using language such as "more than" and "less than." According to the CCSS-M expectations, in kindergarten, children learn the counting sequence from 1 to 100, continue to connect counting to cardinality, and compare numbers from 1 to 10. First graders extend the counting sequence to 120 and begin to explore two-digit numbers as tens and ones. Second graders extend counting to 1000, explore three-digit numbers, and learn to skip count by 5s, 10s, and 100s.

In 2009, the Committee on Early Childhood Mathematics, established by the National Research Council (NRC), identified three foundational areas in mathematics content for early learners: the number core, the relations core, and the operations core. This chapter focuses on the first two core areas while Chapter 9 addresses the third core by examining the meaning of operations. Note that as you help children develop their initial abilities with counting, conversations about number relationships begin. Therefore, the activities and concepts in this chapter are not sequential but coexist in a rich mathematical environment where children make connections between numbers.

In particular, this chapter looks at the development of number ideas for 0 up through 20. These foundational ideas can be extended to content that enhances the development of number (e.g., measurement, data, operations) and content directly affected by how well early number concepts have been developed (e.g., larger numbers, basic facts, place value, and computation). It all begins, though, with the critical ideas of counting and comparing quantities to build young children's rich understanding of number concepts and robust number sense.

The Number Core: Early Counting and Number Concepts

Families help children as young as two or three years of age count their fingers, toys, people at the table, and other small sets of objects. Questions such as "Who has more?" or "Are there enough?" are part of many children's daily lives. Evidence indicates that when children have such experiences, they begin to develop understanding of the concepts of number and counting (Baroody, Li, & Lai, 2008; Clements & Sarama, 2014; National Research Council, 2009). In addition, findings from recent brain research suggest that children who are most proficient with number are those who flexibly use different brain pathways—one associated with numbers and symbols and the other associated with spatial reasoning (Park & Brannon, 2013). We therefore include an abundance of activities in this chapter to support the different experiences children need to gain a thorough understanding of number concepts.

Early Counting

No matter what prior experiences children have had before coming to school, we need to strive to help all children develop the following four interrelated aspects of early numerical knowledge (Clements & Sarama, 2014):

1. *Number sequence.* The names and the ordered list of number words

2. *One-to-one correspondence.* Counting objects by saying number words in a one-to-one correspondence with the objects

3. *Cardinality.* Understanding that the last number word said when counting tells how many objects have been counted

4. *Subitizing.* Quickly recognizing and naming how many objects are in a small group without counting. Young children can recognize and name quantities of objects that are less than four without counting.

Children must construct these ideas through a variety of experiences and activities. They cannot be forced. As children work on each of these aspects of early counting, their understanding about counting is continually refined. For example, children will learn *how* to count (matching counting words with objects) before they understand that the last count word indicates the *amount* of the set or the *cardinality* of the set. A teacher can at the same time use subitizing to emphasize the notion of cardinality and to help emphasize the notion that counting tells "how many."

Research-based learning trajectories (also called *learning progressions*) can help you use information about your children's current knowledge to design and sequence instructional tasks to move children to more advanced ways of reasoning. One such learning trajectory for counting identifies increasingly sophisticated levels of reasoning that range from having no counting skills (i.e., precounter) to being able to count using complex strategies that move beyond counting by ones (Clements & Sarama, 2014). Table 8.1, based on this research, provides a selection of levels and sublevels identified as benchmarks in the trajectory (pp. 36–46). Teachers who are aware of this learning trajectory for counting are better able to design instructional tasks that are purposefully targeted at moving children along the trajectory from one level to the next.

Table 8.1. Learning trajectory for counting.

Levels of Thinking	Characteristics
Precounter	Here the child has no verbal counting ability. A young child looking at three balls will answer "ball" when asked how many. The child does not associate a number word with a quantity.
Reciter	This child verbally counts using number words, but not always in the right order. Sometimes they say more numbers than they have objects to count, skip objects, or repeat the same number.
Corresponder	A child at this level can make a one-to-one correspondence with numbers and objects, stating one number per object. If asked "How many?" at the end of the count, they may have to recount to answer.
Counter	This student can accurately count objects in an organized display (in a line, for example) and can answer "How many?" accurately by giving the last number counted (this is called *cardinality*). They may be able to write the matching numeral and may be able to say the number just after or before a number by counting up from 1.
Producer	A student at this level can count out objects to a certain number. If asked to give you five blocks, they can show you that amount.
Counter and Producer	A child who combines the two previous levels can count out objects, tell how many are in a group, remember which objects are counted and which are not, and respond to random arrangements. They begin to separate tens and ones, like 23 is 20 and 3 more.
Counter Backwards	A child at this level can count backward by removing objects one by one or just verbally as in a "countdown."
Counter from Any Number	This child can count up starting from numbers other than one. They are also able to immediately state the number before and after a given number.
Skip Counter	Here the child can skip-count with understanding by a group of a given number—tens, fives, twos, etc.

Source: Based on Clements, D., & Samara, J. (2014). *Learning and teaching early math: The learning trajectories approach (2nd ed.).* New York, NY: Routledge.

Learning Number Sequences

One of the first necessary skills for verbal counting is to be able to produce the standard list of counting words in order: "One, two, three, four . . ." Although learning the forward and backward number sequence may be considered a rote procedure, effort should be made to help children build the number sequence in a meaningful way, especially numbers in the teens. One recommendation is to play off number words in other languages where the structure of the numbers is more explicit. For example, in Japanese the number 11 is *ju ichi*, which translates to "ten and one," the number 12 is *ju ni*, which translates to "ten and two," and so on. You can also use a vertical number line to help children visualize how numbers change as they begin writing two-digit numbers (see Figure 8.1). A vertical number line is more intuitive than the typical horizontal number line because as numbers become larger they are higher on the number line as opposed to further to the right.

Although the forward number sequence is relatively familiar to most young children, mastering the backward number sequence, counting back, and counting on from a particular number are often difficult for young children. Eventually, first graders should be able to start from any number less than 120 and count on from there (CCSSO, 2010). Provide children frequent opportunities to practice the number-word sequence in both forward and reverse order and begin counts with numbers other than 1 through short and engaging activities such as the following.

Standards for Mathematical Practice

7 **Look for and make use of structure.**

Activity 8.1

CCSS-M: K.CC.A.1; K.CC.A.2

Counting Up and Back

Counting up to and back from a target number in a rhythmic fashion is an important counting exercise. Line up five children and five chairs in front of the class. As the whole class counts from 1 to 5, the children sit down one at a time. When the target number, 5, is reached, it is repeated; the child who sat on 5 now stands, and the count goes back to 1. As the count goes back, the children stand up one at a time, and so on, "1, 2, 3, 4, 5, 5, 4, 3, 2, 1, 1, 2, ..." Any rhythmic movement (clapping, turning around, doing jumping jacks) can be used as the count goes up and back. Vary the activity by starting at numbers other than one. For example, use 15 to 20 if the class is working on the teen numbers and use something like 55 to 65 if the class is ready to move to larger numbers (both of these ranges fit with kindergarten expectations in CCSS). Children find exercises such as this both engaging and challenging. To modify this activity for English language learners, give each child who is in front of the class one card from a set of cards with the target numerals (e.g., 1 to 5, 15 to 20, or 55 to 65) and the corresponding number word. These cards will provide a visual to help children connect the written numeral and number word to the number being said.

An extension for the previous activity involves having children stand in a circle and count around the circle to a target number. One child starts the count at number 1; the next child says the next number in the sequence, and so on, until a child says the target number. That child sits down and the next child starts the count again at number 1. The activity continues until one child is left standing. Challenge children by asking them to predict who will sit down next or who will say a particular number. You can vary the activity by using shorter or longer sequences, by starting the count at a number other than 1, or by having the children count backward.

Teaching Tip

When learning the number sequence, some children do not realize that each number word represents a separate number, so they may touch two objects as they say two-syllable counting words such as "se-ven" or "thir-teen."

Figure 8.1

A vertical number line can help children visualize patterns in our written numbers.

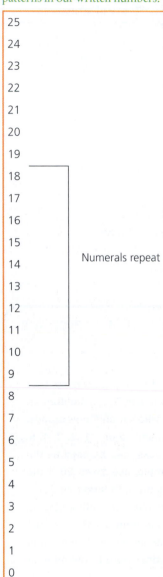

| 25 |
| 24 |
| 23 |
| 22 |
| 21 |
| 20 |
| 19 |
| 18 |
| 17 |
| 16 |
| 15 |
| 14 | Numerals repeat |
| 13 |
| 12 |
| 11 |
| 10 |
| 9 |
| 8 |
| 7 |
| 6 |
| 5 |
| 4 |
| 3 |
| 2 |
| 1 |
| 0 |

Activity 8.2 merges the idea of a number line with number sequences.

Activity 8.2

CCSS-M: K.CC.A.1; K.CC.A.2; K.CC.A.3

Line Them Up!

To prepare for this activity, stretch a clothesline across a bulletin board or off to the side of your classroom at a level where children can reach it. Use the **Numeral Cards** to prepare a set of cards (one numeral per card) that represents a sequence of numbers you want the children to work with, say, 0 through 20 for kindergarten. Mix the cards and then place them face down in a pile. Ask a child to take the top card and use a clothespin to place the card on the clothesline. Have a second child take the next card and place that card on the clothesline in the appropriate position relative to the first card. Before children place their numeral cards, ask the class questions such as "Is this number before or after . . ." and "Does this number go on the left or the right of . . .?" Continue until all the cards are placed on the clothesline in a sequence. Then have the children read the sequence forward as well as backward and discuss the need for equal spacing. If any number is out of sequence or is too closely spaced, see if the children can determine how to correct the order and placement of the cards. You can modify this activity by using shorter or longer sequences and by using number sequences that start at different numbers. Once children are familiar with this activity, use the **Line Them Up!** Activity Page to have children order any ten numbers that you insert at the top of the Activity Page.

You can use children's literature as a lead-in to counting objects and counting backward. For example, *Pete the Cat and his Four Groovy Buttons* (Litwin, 2012) is a story about a cat who starts with four groovy buttons on his shirt. But one by one they pop off and he ends up with zero—or does he? As he counts down, the numeral is shown, along with the written word. (Note there is also a related subtraction equation shown.) *Ten in the Bed* (Dale, 2007) is another book that offers practice opportunities to count backward from ten to one using the classic song chorus, "roll over, roll over."

Numeral recognition and writing are part of learning to count. Kindergartners are expected to write numbers from 0 to 20 in the *Common Core State Standards* (2010). Helping children read and write the 10 single-digit numerals is similar to teaching them to read and write letters of the alphabet. Neither has anything to do with number concepts. However, numeral writing can be engaging. For example, ask children to trace over numerals in shaving cream on their desks, make numerals from clay, press the numeral on a calculator, write them on the interactive whiteboard or on a partner's back, and so on. In the following activity, children work on number recognition as a class.

Activity 8.3

CCSS-M: K.CC.A.3

Number Necklaces

Use the **numeral cards** to prepare number necklaces (cards with a yarn string) that have a numeral on each card. Initially, show numbers on cards and ask children who are wearing that number to step forward. Now is a good time to show numbers written backwards to highlight how that is not a match to anyone in the room. Alternatively children can find a peer with the same numeral. This activity can progress to including cards that show the corresponding amount instead of the numeral. A further extension involves calling out a number, and then two children who add to that number pair up.

Developing One-to-One Correspondence

After learning the number sequence a child must be able to connect this sequence in a one-to-one correspondence with the objects in the set being counted. Each object must get one and only one count. Regular classroom activities, such as matching the number of napkins or snacks needed at snack time and the number of materials needed for an activity to the children in the class, or even simply taking attendance where each child posts a smiley face sticker, are opportunities for children to engage in purposeful counting that emphasizes one-to-one correspondence. Make sure during these activities that children have sets of blocks or counters to move as they count and that the activity is more than the children simply following the teacher's count. The following activities provide specific opportunities focused on one-to-one correspondence.

Activity 8.4

CCSS-M: K.CC.B.4.A

Counting Moose Tracks

Before this activity, read *Moose Tracks!* by Karma Wilson (2006). This book is a delightful story about a moose that thinks someone has been in his house because of all the footprints he keeps finding. In the end, it is revealed that he is the one creating all the footprints! Give pairs of children a **Moose Tracks Game Board**, one die, and two game pieces, such as different colored centimeter cubes. Children take turns rolling the die and moving their game piece along the game board. Play is collaborative with players helping each other. Play continues until both children have traveled the length of their tracks. Because the board has separate spaces for each "moose track," children work on one-to-one correspondence as they move their game piece along the board. Alternatively, rather than moving one game piece along the board, have children place the number of same colored centimeter cubes along their track that corresponds to the number on the die. For example, if the child rolls a 4, he places 4 red cubes along his track in 4 separate spaces. For his next turn, he uses a different color of cube, say 3 blue cubes for a 3 on the die. By using several of the same colored cubes, as opposed to moving just one cube along the board, the child has a visual record of the one-to-one correspondence. This representation also provides a more explicit visual of cardinality—the number of cubes in a group.

Simple board games such as the Moose Tracks game in Activity 8.4, in which children count one space for each number in the sequence, helps to emphasize the one-to-one correspondence between objects and numbers in the count sequence. Egg cartons, as used in the next activity, also provide a similar structure to support children as they work on one-to-one correspondence.

Standards for Mathematical Practice

◄ **7** **Look for and make use of structure.**

Activity 8.5

CCSS-M: K.CC.B.4.A

Egg Carton Counting

In pairs, children roll one die. For each dot on the die, they place one counter into each compartment of an egg carton (you can also use a plastic ice cube tray). Ask the children, "How do you know you have the right number of counters?," "How many counters do you now have in the carton?," and "How many more do you need to fill the carton?" They continue to take turns rolling the die and placing counters into the egg carton until the carton is full. Require that they roll the exact amount needed to fill the carton. For example, if there are two empty compartments, someone must roll a two to fill the carton. This requirement reinforces the idea of one-to-one correspondence.

Activity 8.6

CCSS-M: K.CC.B.4.A

Seashell Counts

Children roll one or two dice, depending on the numbers they are ready to work with. For each dot on the die/dice, they place a seashell into a box of sand. Ask the children, "How do you know you have the right number of shells?" and "How many shells do you now have in the sand?" Alternatively, they can plant artificial flowers into a ball of playdough or place buttons on a picture of a shirt (see **Button Counts**).

Figure 8.2

The child has learned cardinality if, after counting five objects, he or she can answer the question "How many do you have in all?" with "Five."

Figure 8.3

In counting, each number is one more than the previous number.

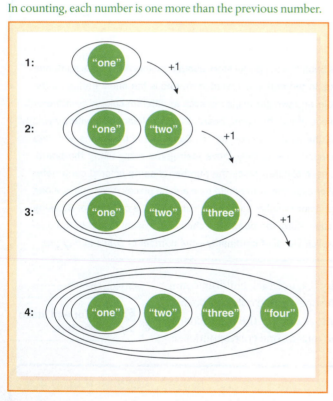

Source: National Research Council. (2009). *Mathematics learning in early childhood: Paths toward excellence and equity*, p. 27. Reprinted with permission from the National Academy of Sciences, courtesy of the National Academies Press, Washington, DC.

In counting activities, for many children, especially children with disabilities, it is important to have a plan for counting. The children should count objects from left to right, move the objects as they count, or touch them as they say each number word aloud.

Developing Cardinality

Fosnot and Dolk (2001) state that an understanding of cardinality and its connection to counting is not a simple task for four-year-olds. Children will learn how to count (matching counting words with objects) before they understand that the last number stated in a count indicates the amount of the set (how many you have in all) or the set's cardinality as shown in Figure 8.2. Children who make this connection are said to have the cardinality principle, which is a refinement of their early ideas about quantity and is required for kindergartners (CCSSO, 2010). Most, but certainly not all, children by age $4\frac{1}{2}$ make this connection (Fosnot & Dolk, 2001).

Related to cardinality, children should also recognize that each counting number identifies a quantity that is one more than the previous number and that the new quantity is embedded in the previous quantity (see Figure 8.3). This knowledge will be helpful later in breaking numbers apart.

To develop their understanding of counting, engage children in almost any game or activity in which they have to purposefully count objects, make comparisons between counts, and consistently answer the question "How many do you have in all?" at the end of each count, as in Activity 8.7, Fill the Tower.

 Activity 8.7

CCSS-M: K.CC.B.5

Fill the Tower

 Children take turns rolling a die and collecting the indicated number of counters. They then place these counters on one of the towers on their **Fill the Tower Game Board.** The object is to fill all of the towers with counters. As an option, require that the towers be filled exactly so that a roll of 5 cannot be used to fill four empty spaces. To modify this activity for a child with disabilities or for any child who is struggling with counting, use a die with only 2 or 3 dots or numerals on the sides. Using a larger-sized die also makes it easier for the child to count the dots. You can increase the number choices on the die when you have evidence that the child is counting accurately. A modification for gifted children is to have them use a die with higher numbers and a game board with larger towers.

Playing Fill the Tower provides opportunities for you to talk with children about number and assess their thinking. Observe how they count the dots on the die. Ask the children, "How do you know you have the right number of counters?," "How many counters did you put in the tower?," and "How many more do you need to fill the tower?"

Look for ways to make counting situations into real problems. Chapter 2 includes an example of how to turn a routine snack time into an opportunity for children to learn more about number and counting (see section on multiple entry and exit points). You can also count groups of children, as in the video "Mingle and Count," which can be found on the Teaching Channel website.

The following counting activity incorporates estimation to increase the level of difficulty.

Activity 8.8

CCSS-M: K.CC.B.4; K.CC.B.5; K.CC.A.3

Number Tubs

Give each child four to six closed margarine tubs, each containing a different number of pennies or counters. The child is asked to find a tub with a particular number of counters. Challenge them to first estimate the number by either shaking the tub or by quickly glancing at the amount inside. Then have the child count the coins to find the correct tub. Ask the child to label the tubs with sticky notes to show the amount inside. At first, the child may make four dots to represent four counters, but eventually, with encouragement, the numeral will be written. Make sure to discuss how this demonstrates the value of writing the numbers in a form that all can understand and that doesn't require recounting.

 Formative Assessment Note

Children who successfully count orally may not have attached meaning to their counts. To determine whether a young child understands cardinality, listen to how the child responds when you discuss counting tasks with him or her. For example, show the child a card with five to nine large dots in a row so that they are easy to count. Ask the child to count the dots. If the count is accurate, ask, "How many dots are on the card?" Early on, the child may need to recount again, but a child who is beginning to grasp the meaning of counting will not have to recount. If the child points to the last object counted as representing the number of dots on the card, this can be an indication that the child has not constructed the idea of cardinality of a set. If the child correctly responds with and refers to the total counters, now say, "Please give me the same number of counters as there are dots on the card." Here is a sequence of indicators to look for, listed in order from a child who does not attach meaning to the count to a child who is using counting as a tool:

Does the child not count but instead take out counters and make a similar pattern?

Does the child recount?

Does the child point to the last object counted to represent the total?

Does the child place the counters in a one-to-one correspondence with the dots?

Does the child just count the dots and retrieve the correct number of counters?

Can the child show that there are the same number of counters as dots?

As the child shows competence with patterned sets of dots, move to using random dot patterns to raise the level of difficulty.

The following activity introduces the idea of counting different kinds of objects within the same set.

Activity 8.9

CCSS-M: K.CC.B.4; K.CC.B.5

The Find!

Place index cards numbered 1 to 10 in a box. Depending on your children's readiness, you may need to include a dot representation of the number on the card. In pairs, children pull out a card and then collect that number of objects from a designated area in the classroom. The objects could be books, pencils, cubes, crayons, counting bears, and so on. They place their numbered card and the collected objects in a container. In pairs they check the other children's collections to make sure they have collected the correct number of objects. Vary the difficulty of this activity by using smaller numbers (2–5) or larger numbers (15–20). Initially you want children to collect the same kind of object, but eventually have them collect a mix of objects to introduce the idea that you can count different kinds of objects in a collection. For example, they can collect two crayons, one marker, and one pencil for the number 4—four things to write with! Children can use **The Find!** Activity Page to represent their number.

Use a computerized version of the game Concentration at NCTM's Illuminations website to help children relate numerals to number words and quantities. If needed, you can reduce the level of difficulty by selecting the option to have all the numerals, numbers, and quantities visible so that the child can focus on moving back and forth between the representations without having the added difficulty of remembering the locations of specific cards.

Subitizing

Children explore quantity before they can count. For example, they can identify which cup is bigger or which plate of blueberries has more berries. Eventually they need to attach an amount to the quantities to explore them in greater depth. When you look at an amount of objects, sometimes you are able to just "see" how many are there, particularly for a small group. For example, when you roll a die and know that it is five without counting the dots, that ability to "just see it" is called *subitizing*. There are times when you are able to do this for even larger amounts, say when you break apart a group of eight dots shown in a pattern by seeing five dots and then three dots. "Subitizing is a fundamental skill in the development of children's understanding of number" (Baroody, 1987, p. 115) and can be developed and practiced through experiences with patterned sets such as those that can be found on dice and dominoes.

Many children easily recognize patterned sets of dots on dice due to the many games they have played. Similar instant recognition (*subitizing*) can be developed for other patterns (see Figure 8.4). Naming these amounts

Figure 8.4

Recognizing a patterned set.

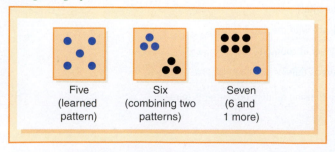

| Five (learned pattern) | Six (combining two patterns) | Seven (6 and 1 more) |

immediately without counting facilitates *counting on* (from a known patterned set) or learning combinations of numbers (seeing a patterned set of two known smaller patterns). To support young children with subitizing begin with three or four objects arranged in symmetric patterns before moving to larger numbers such as five or more challenging arrangements.

Children can play Okta's Rescue at NCTM's Illuminations website to work on subitizing with a variety of sets. The activity is timed to provide that additional push to move children beyond counting by ones.

Activity 8.10

CCSS-M: K.CC.B.4

Learning Patterns

 Provide each child with about 10 counters and a piece of paper or a paper plate as a mat. Hold up a dot plate for about five seconds and say, "Make the pattern you saw on my plate using the counters on your plate. How many dots did you see? What did the pattern look like?" Spend some time discussing the configuration of the pattern and the number of dots. Then show the plate so they can self-check. Do this with a few new patterns each day. To modify this activity for a child with disabilities, begin by giving the child a small selection of premade dot plates. Then instead of the child creating a given pattern with counters, the child finds the matching dot plate.

Standards for Mathematical Practice

◀ **7 Look for and make use of structure.**

Good materials to use in pattern recognition activities include a set of dot plates made with paper plates or large index cards and the sticky dots commonly available in office supply stores (see Figure 8.5). Note that some patterns are combinations of two smaller patterns or a pattern with one or two additional dots. These should be made in two colors to distinguish each of the smaller patterns. Keep the patterns compact and organized. If the dots are too spread out, the patterns are hard to identify.

The next activity displays images quickly so that children do not have time to count the dots one by one. Consequently, they are challenged to find another way to determine how many. Dot plates

Teaching Tip

Use quick images to encourage children to move beyond counting by ones.

Activity 8.11

CCSS-M: K.CC.B.4a; K.CC.B.4b

Dot Plate Flash

Hold up a dot plate for three seconds and say, "How many dots do you see? What did the pattern look like?" Include easy patterns first and then add more dots as children's confidence and skill build. When needed, show a plate a second time so that children can get another look. Children like to see how quickly they can recognize the pattern and say how many dots. Children can also flash dot plates to each other as a workstation activity.

Figure 8.5

A collection of dot patterns for "dot plates."

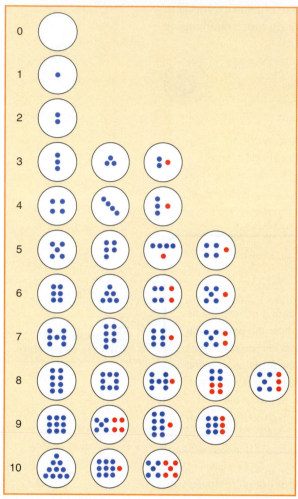

that have three to five dots are useful to start work on subitizing. Dot plates that have more than five dots are useful in helping children work on advanced subitizing or decomposition where they quickly see and use small groups within the larger amount to quickly determine how many.

Instant recognition activities with the plates or index cards are exciting and can be done in 5 minutes at any time of day or between lessons. There is value in using them at any primary grade level and at any time of year. On the Teaching Channel website, you can watch a kindergarten teacher using quick images to help her children use subitizing to think about the number 8 (search for "Quick Images" on the website).

t e c h n o l o g y ⏻
note

Explore the web-based activities called "Speedy Pictures 1" and "Speedy Pictures 2" (on the MathLanding website) where children can practice subitizing and basic addition using flashed images of fingers, dice, beads on a frame, or eggs in a carton holding ten. There are also a variety of apps available for phones and tablets, such as the Little Monkey Apps, that provide a variety of quick images to help young children practice their subitizing skills.

Thinking about Zero

We find that because early counting often involves touching an object, zero is sometimes not included in discussions about numbers and counting. Children need to explore the number zero because it is one of the most important digits in the base-ten system, and purposeful conversations about it and its position on the number line are essential—and it is a required standard for kindergartners (CCSSO, 2010). Surprisingly, zero is not a concept that is easily grasped without intentionally building understanding. In fact, it took quite a long time for zero to be accepted as a number in many cultures because its nature is so different from other numbers (Kaplan, 2000). But three- and four-year-olds can begin to meaningfully use the word zero and the numeral 0 to communicate that there are no objects in the set (Clements & Sarama, 2014). With the dot plates discussed previously (see Figure 8.5), use the zero plate to discuss what it means when there is no dot on the plate. Relate zero to meaningful contexts to which your children are familiar. In particular, Activities 8.10, 8.11, and 8.15 are useful in exploring the number zero.

Counting On

Initially, when asked to combine two sets, children will have to count from one, even if they have already counted one of the sets. For example, if after counting five bears a child is given three more and asked how many there are in all, the child may need to recount the five bears, starting the count from one. Eventually, children will be able to start counting a quantity from a given number other than one. This is called "counting on." Using the previous example, a child who can count on will usually say, "Five (referring to the group of five bears), six, seven, eight. I have eight bears." The child may keep track of the count by holding up a finger with each number (six, seven, eight). Fosnot and Dolk (2001) describe counting on as a *landmark* on a child's path to number sense.

Let's consider two activities that are designed to help children move from counting from one to counting on. In both activities the counted objects are hidden to encourage the child to create a mental image of the quantities—which helps children move away from relying on counting the objects from one.

 ## Activity 8.12

CCSS-M: K.CC.A.2; K.CC.B.5

Counting On with Counters

Give each child a collection of 10 or 12 counters that the children line up left to right on their desks. Tell them to count four counters and push them under their left hands or place them out of sight in a cup (see Figure 8.6). Then, pointing to the hidden counters in the child's hand or cup, ask, "How many are there?" (Four.) "So let's count like this: f-o-u-r (pronouncing the number slowing and pointing to their hand), five, six, ..." Repeat with other numbers of counters under the hand or in a cup.

 ## Activity 8.13

CCSS-M: K.OA.A.1; 1.OA.B.5

Real Counting On

 This game for two children requires a deck of cards (numbers 1 to 7), a die, a paper cup, and counters. The first player turns over the top number card and places the indicated number of counters in the cup. The card is placed next to the cup as a reminder of how many are inside. The second player rolls the die and places that many counters next to the cup. (See Figure 8.7.) Together they decide how many counters in all. Give children the **Real Counting on Recording Sheet** with columns for "In the Cup," "On the Side," and "In All" to support their organization. Increase the highest number in the card deck when children have mastered the smaller numbers. For children with disabilities, keep the number of counters in the cup constant (such as five) and have them count on from that number until they are fluent. Then move to the full game.

Observe how children determine the total amounts in Activity 8.13. Children who are not yet counting on may want to empty the counters from the cup or will count up from one using their fingers to keep track of the count. As children continue to play "Real Counting On," they will eventually use counting on as that strategy becomes meaningful and useful.

Figure 8.6

Counting on: "Hide four. Count, starting from the number of counters hidden."

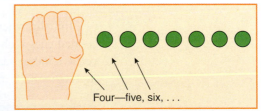

Four—five, six, . . .

The Relations Core: More Than, Less Than, and Equal To

The concepts of "more," "less," and "same" are basic relationships contributing to children's overall understanding of number. Almost any child entering kindergarten can choose the set that is *more* if presented with two sets that are quite obviously different in number. In fact, Baroody (1987) states, "A child unable to use 'more' in this intuitive manner is at considerable education risk" (p. 29). Classroom activities should help children build on and refine this basic notion.

Figure 8.7

How many in all? How do children count to tell the total?

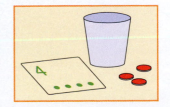

Although the concept of *less* is logically related to the concept of *more* (selecting the set with more is the same as *not* selecting the set with less), the concept of *less* proves to be more difficult for children than *more*. A possible explanation is that children have many opportunities to use the word *more* but have limited exposure to the word *less*. To help children with the concept, frequently pair the idea of *less* with *more* and make a conscious effort to ask "Which is less?" questions as well as "Which is more?" questions. In this way, the concept of *less* is connected with the better-known idea of *more* and children become familiar with the term.

For all three concepts (more/greater than, less/less than, and same/equal to), children should construct sets using counters as well as make comparisons or choices between two given sets. Conduct the following activities in a spirit of inquiry with requests for children's explanations: "Can you show me how you know this group has less?"

Figure 8.8

Making sets that are more, less, and the same.

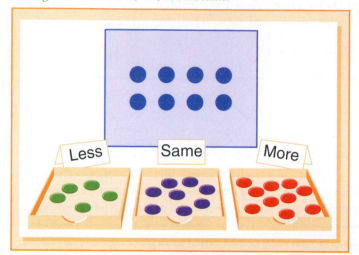

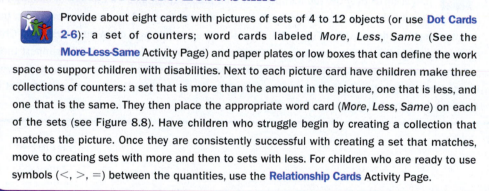

Activity 8.14

CCSS-M: K.CC.C.6

Make Sets of More/Less/Same

Provide about eight cards with pictures of sets of 4 to 12 objects (or use **Dot Cards 2-6**); a set of counters; word cards labeled *More, Less, Same* (See the **More-Less-Same** Activity Page) and paper plates or low boxes that can define the work space to support children with disabilities. Next to each picture card have children make three collections of counters: a set that is more than the amount in the picture, one that is less, and one that is the same. They then place the appropriate word card (*More, Less, Same*) on each of the sets (see Figure 8.8). Have children who struggle begin by creating a collection that matches the picture. Once they are consistently successful with creating a set that matches, move to creating sets with more and then to sets with less. For children who are ready to use symbols ($<$, $>$, $=$) between the quantities, use the **Relationship Cards** Activity Page.

Initially, when young children begin comparing sets, they may be easily confused by perceptual cues such as the length of the row of counters or the spacing of counters in one set versus another set. If needed, encourage children to use matching to compare sets. For example, in Activity 8.14, suggest that they stack counters on top of the images to match the sets.

Activity 8.15

CCSS-M: K.CC.A.3; K.CC.C.6

Find the Same Amount

Give children a collection of cards with pictures of sets on them, such as **Dot Cards 1-6**. Have the children pick up any card in the collection and then find another card with the same amount to form a pair. Continue finding other pairs. This activity can be altered to have children find dot cards that are "less" or "more." Some children with disabilities may need a set of counters with a blank ten-frame to help them "make" a pair instead of finding a pair.

Formative Assessment Note

Observe children as they do these activities. Children whose number ideas are completely tied to counting and nothing more will select cards at random and count each dot. Others will begin by estimating and selecting a card that appears to have about the same number of dots. This demonstrates a significantly higher level of understanding. Also, observe how the dots are counted. Are the counts made accurately? Is each counted only once? Does the child touch the dot? A significant milestone for children occurs when they recognize small patterned sets without counting (subitizing).

Activity 8.16

CCSS-M: K.CC.A.3; K.CC.C.6; K.O.A.A.1

More, Less, or the Same

This activity is for partners or a small group. Make four to five sets of cards from the **More-or-Less Cards** and two sets of the **Number Cards 0-10** (Blackline Master 1). Put these cards face down into two separate decks. To play, one child draws a number card, places it face up, and puts that number of counters into a cup. Next, another child draws one of the more-or-less cards and places it next to the number card (see Figure 8.9). For the More cards, the designated number of counters are added to the cup; for the Less cards, counters are removed; and, for Zero cards, no change is made. Children then predict how many counters are in the cup. The counters are emptied and counted and then the game is repeated by drawing new cards. Eventually, the words *more* and *less* can be paired or substituted with *add* and *subtract* to connect these ideas with the arithmetic operations.

Developing Number Sense by Building Number Relationships

Howden (1989) described *number sense* as a "good intuition about numbers and their relationships. It develops gradually as a result of exploring numbers, visualizing them in a variety of contexts, and relating them in ways that are not limited by traditional algorithms" (p. 11). *Principles and Standards for School Mathematics* (NCTM, 2000) identifies the ability to think flexibly about numbers, including various ways to represent and use numbers, as an indication of having number sense.

In the remainder of this chapter, we look at the kinds of relationships and connections children should be making about smaller numbers up to about 20 to aid in their development of number sense. But "good intuition about numbers" does not end with these smaller whole numbers. Children continue to develop number sense as they

Figure 8.9

Materials to play "More, Less, or the Same."

use numbers in operations, build an understanding of place value, devise flexible methods of computing, and make estimates involving large numbers. Flexible, intuitive reasoning with numbers—number sense—should continue to be developed throughout the school years as fractions, decimals, and percentages are added to children's repertoire of number ideas.

Relationships between Numbers 1 through 10

Once children have acquired the concept of cardinality and can meaningfully use their counting skills, they need to expand their collection of ideas about number sense to develop the knowledge needed to meaningfully work with operations. But too often teachers move directly from the beginning ideas of counting to addition and subtraction, leaving children with a very limited collection of ideas about number to bring to these new topics. We want children, as they solve problems, to move away from counting by ones and to develop strategies for mastering basic facts by emphasizing the development of number relationships such as those in Figure 8.10 and as follows:

Figure 8.10

Three relationships to be developed involving small numbers.

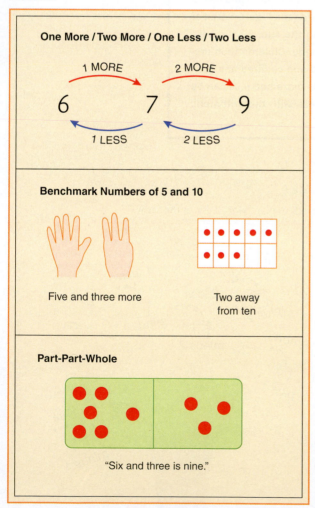

- *One and two more, one and two less.* The two-more-than and two-less-than relationships involve more than just the ability to count on two more or count back by two. Children should know that 7, for example, is 1 more than 6 and also 2 less than 9.

- *Benchmark numbers of 5 and 10.* Because the number 10 plays such a large role in our numeration system and because two fives equal 10, it is very useful to develop relationships between the numbers 1 to 10 and the benchmark numbers of 5 and 10.

- *Part–part–whole relationships.* The most important relationship that can be developed about numbers is to conceptualize a number as being composed of two or more parts. For example, 7 can be thought of as a set of 3 and a set of 4 or a set of 2 and a set of 5.

The principal tool that young children will use as they construct these relationships is the one number tool they possess: counting. Initially, you will notice a lot of counting by ones, and you may wonder if you are making progress. Have patience! As children construct new relationships and begin to use more powerful ideas, counting by ones will become less and less necessary.

One and Two More, One and Two Less

When children count, they don't automatically think about how one number is related to another. Their goal is only to match number words with objects until they reach the end of the count. To learn that six and eight are related by the corresponding relationships of "two more than" and "two less than" requires reflection on these ideas. Counting on (or back) one or two counts is a useful tool in constructing these ideas.

Activity 8.17

CCSS-M: K.OA.A.2;
K.CC.A.3; K.CC.B.4c; 1.OA.C.5

One/Two Less and More Dominoes

Use the dot-pattern dominoes (**Dot Cards 1-6**) or a standard set of dominoes. Lay out one domino. To play the "one-less-than" version, children place a new domino that is one less than the end domino on the board. A similar game can be played for two less, one more, or two more.

Activity 8.18

CCSS-M: K.OA.A.2; 1.OA.C.5

Make a Two-More-Than Set

Provide children with about six cards from **Dot Cards 1-6**. For each card, children should display a set of counters that is two more than the set shown on the card. Similarly, spread out eight to ten dot cards and, for each card, find a card that is two less than it. (Omit the 1 and 2 cards for two less than, and so on.)

In activities in which children find a set or make a set, they can also select the matching **Number Cards 0-10** (Blackline Master 1) that identify the quantity in the set. Children can be encouraged to take turns reading the associated number sentence to their partner. If, for example, a set has been made that is two more than a set of four, the child can say, "Two more than four equals six" or "Six is the same as two more than four." The next activity moves to a purely symbolic representation of the relationships.

Activity 8.19

CCSS-M: 1.OA.C.5

A Two-More-Than Machine

To teach children how to make a two-more-than machine, ask them to press 0 + 2 = on their calculators. Now have them press any number—for example, 5. Children should hold their finger over the = key and predict the number that is two more than 5. Then they press = to confirm. If they do not press any of the operation keys (+, −, ×, ÷), the "machine" will continue to perform in this way.

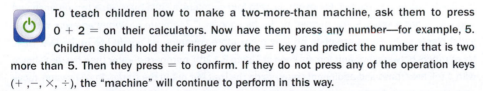

Formative Assessment Note

To assess children's grasp of relationships involving one and two more or less than, simply write a few numbers on a sheet of paper. Point to a number and have the child tell you the number that is "*two less than* this number," varying the specific request with different numbers. It is not necessary to check every possibility.

Using Benchmark Numbers 5 and 10

Here again, we want to help children relate a given number to other numbers, specifically 5 and 10, to support thinking about various number relationships.

Stop and Reflect	500 ⌇ ²⁵⁰ 3X ▱ 5° 0 ⟋ 2.5

Consider the role that 5 and 10 play in helping to think about the following:
5 + 3, 8 + 7, 8 − 2, 8 − 3, 8 − 4, 13 − 8.

Figure 8.11

Ten-frames.

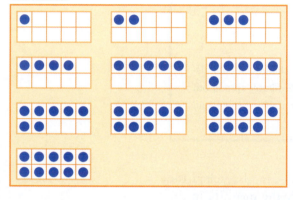

The knowledge of 8 as "5 and 3 more" and as "2 away from 10" can play a role in how a child thinks about these examples. For example, 8 + 7 may be thought of as 8 + 2 + 5 ("Making 10" strategy). Later, similar relationships can be used in the development of mental computation skills on larger numbers such as 68 + 7.

The most common models for exploring benchmark numbers 5 and 10 are **Five-Frames** (Blackline Master 12) and **Ten-Frames** (Blackline Master 13). The five-frame is a 1 × 5 array and the ten-frame is a 2 × 5 array, both positioned horizontally, in which counters or dots are placed to illustrate quantities (see Figure 8.11). Each child should have their own frame when working on the activities.

For prekindergarten or kindergarten children who have not yet explored a ten-frame, it is a good idea to begin with a five-frame. Provide about 10 counters that will fit in the five-frame sections and try the following activity.

Activity 8.20

CCSS-M: K.CC.C.7; K.OA.A.5

Five-Frame Tell-About

Explain that only one counter is permitted in each section of the **Five-Frame** (Blackline Master 12). Have the children show three on their five-frame (see Figure 8.12(a) for an example of how three can be displayed). Ask, "What can you tell us about three from looking at your mat?" After hearing from several children, try other numbers from 0 to 5. Children may initially place their counters on the five-frame in any manner. For example, with four counters, a child may place two on each end and say, "It has a space in the middle" or "It's two and two." There are no wrong answers with the initial placements. Focus attention on how many more counters are needed to make five. Next, try numbers between five and ten. As seen in Figure 8.12(b), numbers greater than five are shown with a full five-frame and additional counters on the mat but not in the frame. In discussion, focus attention on these larger numbers as five and some more: "Seven is five and two more."

Standards for Mathematical Practice

3 Construct viable arguments and critique the reasoning of others.

Standards for Mathematical Practice

7 Look for and make use of structure.

Notice that the five-frame focuses on the relationship to five as a benchmark but does not help children relate numbers to ten. After five-frames have been used for a week or so, consider introducing ten-frames. Play a ten-frame version of a "Five-Frame Tell-About" but soon introduce the following convention for showing numbers on the ten-frame: *Always fill the top row first, starting on the left, the same way you read. When the top row is full, place counters in the bottom row, also from the left.* This approach will provide structure for seeing a full row in the ten-frame as five without the need to count, as can be seen in Figure 8.11. At first, children may continue to count every counter by ones. So look for opportunities to draw children's attention to this characteristic of the ten-frame. Make sure to spend time asking questions such as "What are you looking at in the ten-frame to help you find how many?" and "How does knowing you have a full row help you find how many?"

You can find virtual activities with five- and ten-frames on NCTM's Illuminations website. These versions allow children to build target numbers and include an option that asks children to determine how many counters are displayed as well as how many empty spaces are in a given frame. These activities can be used with individual learners as there is a voice-over option that will ask children questions about the tasks.

The next activity, "Number Medley," is much more of a problem-solving situation than it first appears because children have to decide how to change their ten-frame to make the new number.

Activity 8.21

CCSS-M: K.CC.C.6; K.CC.C.7

Number Medley

 First, have all children make the same number on their **Ten-Frame** (Blackline Master 13). Then call out or hold up random numbers between 0 and 10. After each number, the children change their ten-frames to show the new number. Ask, "How do you decide how to change your ten-frame?" If working with English language learners (ELLs), consider saying the number in their native language or writing the number. Children can do this activity independently by using a prepared list of about 15 random numbers. One child plays "teacher" while the rest use the ten-frames.

How children use the ten-frame provides insight into their current number concept development. Consequently, activities like this one can be used as a diagnostic interview. For example, when making a new number, some children will remove all the counters from the ten-frame and begin from a blank frame. Others will have learned what each number looks like and will soon learn to adjust numbers by adding on or taking off only what is required, often capitalizing on a row of five without counting. Do not pressure children to use one approach or another but have children share their strategies for how and why they make changes to the ten-frame.

In the previous activity, encourage children to think about how their current number relates to the new number by having them tell, before changing their ten-frames,

Figure 8.12

A five-frame focuses on 5 as the benchmark.

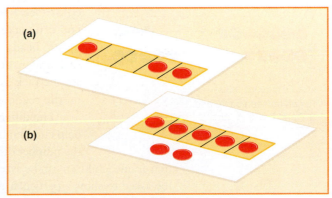

how many more counters need to be added ("plus") or removed ("minus"). They then call out plus or minus whatever amount is appropriate. If, for example, the frames showed six, and the teacher called out "Four," the children would respond "Minus two!" and then change their ten-frames accordingly. A discussion of how they know what to do is valuable. With continued experiences, all children can make new numbers on the ten-frame more efficiently.

Small ten-frame cards are an important variation of ten-frames and can be made from cardstock using the **Little Ten-Frames** Activity Page. Each set consists of 20 cards: a 0 card, a 10 card, and two each of the numbers 1 to 9. The cards allow for simple practice activities to reinforce the 5 and 10 as benchmarks, as in Activity 8.22.

◣ **Activity 8.22**   **CCSS-M: K.CC.B.5**

Ten-Frame Flash

Flash **Little Ten-Frames** Activity Page to the class or small group and see how quickly the children can tell how many dots are shown. This fast-paced activity takes only a few minutes, can be done at any time, and is highly engaging. For ELLs, producing the English word for the number may take more time, so either pair children with similar language skills, or encourage children to use their preferred language.

Important variations of "Ten-Frame Flash" include

- Saying the number of empty spaces on the card instead of the number of dots
- Saying one more than the number of dots (or two more, one less, or two less)
- Saying the "ten fact"—for example, for six dots in the frame, saying, "Six and four equals ten"
- Saying the sum by adding the flashed card to a card children have at their desk

Ten-frame tasks are surprisingly challenging for children because there is a lot to keep in their working memory. Children must reflect on the two rows of five, the spaces remaining, and how a particular number is more or less than five and how far away it is from ten. How well children can respond to "Ten-Frame Flash" is a quick diagnostic assessment of their current number concept level. Consider interviews that include the variations of the activity listed earlier.

Figure 8.13

An arithmetic rack provides a visual model of the benchmarks of 5 and 10.

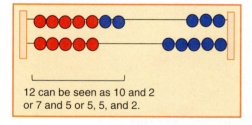

12 can be seen as 10 and 2 or 7 and 5 or 5, 5, and 2.

Another model for benchmarks of five and ten is an arithmetic rack, also called a number rack. An arithmetic rack can have one or more rows of ten beads. Each row has five beads of one color and five beads of another color (see Figure 8.13). Arithmetic racks are available commercially or you can make an arithmetic rack with cardstock, pipe cleaners, and small plastic beads. You can also find a free electronic version of an arithmetic rack under the Math Learning Center's free apps. In this e-version you can set the rack as a single row of 10 or create up to 10 rows of 10, depending on the readiness of your children.

The different colors and embedded five structure of the arithmetic rack help children build mental images of numbers. Children can be asked to name the number displayed on an arithmetic rack—and if flashed quickly as with the ten-frame, children can be asked how they know how many beads are displayed. They can also be asked to show a particular number using the arithmetic rack. The class can then share the different ways that the same number was displayed.

Stop and Reflect

Before reading on, gather eight counters. Count out the set in front of you as if you were a four- or five-year old.

Part–Part–Whole Relationships

Any child who has learned how to count meaningfully can count out eight objects as you just did. What is significant about the experience is what it did *not* cause you to think about. Nothing in counting a set of eight objects will cause a child to focus on the fact that it could be made of two parts. For example, separate the counters you just set out into two piles and reflect on the combination. It might be 2 and 6 or 7 and 1 or 4 and 4. Make a change in your two piles of counters and say the new combination to yourself. Focusing on a quantity in terms of its parts (*decomposing numbers)* has important implications for developing number sense. Of the three number relationships show in Figure 8.10, part-part-whole ideas are easily the most important. In fact, the ability to think about a number in terms of a *part-part-whole* relationship is a major milestone in the development of number sense.

Most part–part–whole activities focus on a single number for the entire activity. For example, children might work on breaking apart or building the number 7 throughout an activity. They can either build (*compose*) the designated quantity in two or more parts (also known as a "both addends unknown" situation), or they start with the full amount and partition it into two or more parts (*decompose*). Kindergarteners usually begin these activities working on the number 4 or 5. As concepts develop, the children extend to numbers 6 to 12.

When children do part–part–whole activities, have them say or "read" the parts aloud and then write them down on some form of recording sheet. Reading and writing the combinations encourages reflective thought focused on the part–part–whole relationship. Writing can be in the form of drawings, numbers written in blanks (a group of _____ cubes and a group of _____ cubes), or addition equations ($3 + 5 = 8$ or $8 = 2 + 6$). There is a clear connection between part–part–whole concepts and addition and subtraction ideas.

The following activity and its variations may be considered the "basic" part–part–whole task.

▶ Activity 8.23

CCSS-M: K.OA.A.3; 1.OA.C.6

Build It in Parts

 The task is to see, for a given number, how many different combinations children can make using two parts. (If you wish, you can allow for more than two parts.)

Provide one type of material in different colors, such as connecting cubes or squares of colored paper. Use a context either from children's daily lives that will be familiar to most or from a piece of children's literature. For example, ask how many different combinations of six hats the peddler in the children's book *Caps for Sale* (Slobodkina, 1938) can wear, limiting the color choices to two and keeping the colors together (i.e., three red and three blue caps, four red and two blue, etc.). (Note that the book is also available in Spanish for some ELLs and may be found as a YouTube video.) Each different combination can be displayed on a small mat. Have children say or read, and eventually write, a number sentence that matches their partner's representation. Here are just a few ideas of materials you can use, each of which is illustrated in Figure 8.14.

- Use two-color counters, such as lima beans spray-painted on one side (also commercially available in plastic).

(continued)

- Make bars of connecting cubes of two different colors. Keep the colors together on the bar.
- Make combinations using two dot strips—strips of cardstock about 1 inch wide with stick-on dots.
- Make combinations of "two-column strips" from cardstock using the **Two-Column Cards** Activity Page. All pieces except the single squares are cut from two columns of the cardstock.
- Color rows of squares on 1-inch grid paper.
- Use arithmetic racks that have 10 beads in two rows.

Standards for Mathematical Practice

8 **Look for and express regularity in repeated reasoning.**

As you observe children working on the "Build It in Parts" activity, encourage them to reflect on the combinations they have found. Two or three children working together may have quite a large number of combinations, including repeats. Encourage them to look for patterns. Ask, "Do you have all of the possible combinations? How do you know?"

In the "Build It in Parts" activity, the children are focusing on the combinations. To add some interest, vary the activity by adding a design component. Rather than creating a two-part illustration for a number, children create an interesting design with an assigned number of elements. For each design, they are then challenged to see and read the design in two parts. Here are some ideas.

- Make arrangements of wooden cubes.
- Make designs with pattern blocks. It is a good idea to use only one or two shapes at a time.
- Make designs with flat toothpicks. These can be dipped in white glue and placed on small squares of cardstock to create a permanent record.
- Make designs with touching squares or triangles. Cut a large supply of small squares or triangles out of cardstock. These can also be glued down.

Challenge children to describe their designs in different ways to produce different number combinations. For example, Figure 8.15 shows different number combinations for the same designs.

You can also use children's literature to provide contexts for part-part-whole activities. For example, *10 Little Hot Dogs* (Himmelman, 2010), a predictable-progression counting book, features 10 dachshund puppies climbing on and off a chair. Using a mat illustrated with a **Chair** and counters representing the puppies, children can show different ways to put, say, six puppies on and off the chair. Two children can compare the numbers of puppies on their chairs. Who has more puppies on their chair? How many more?

Activity 8.24 is a quick part–part–whole activity that can be done anywhere because children use their fingers to show the two parts.

Figure 8.14

Assorted materials for building parts of six.

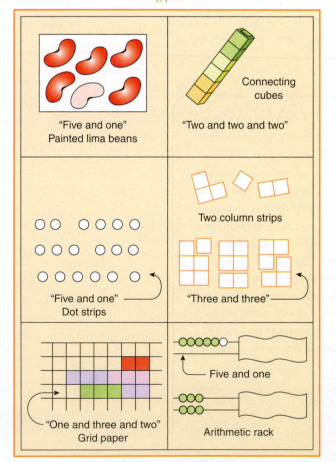

"Five and one" Painted lima beans

Connecting cubes
"Two and two and two"

"Five and one" Dot strips

Two column strips

"Three and three"

"One and three and two" Grid paper

Five and one

Arithmetic rack

Activity 8.24

CCSS-M: K.OA.A.3; 1.OA.C.6

Show Me the Parts!

Tell children their task is to hold up a given number of fingers when you state the number. For example, ask them to hold up five fingers. Initially, children may just show five fingers on one hand. Encourage them to think of different ways they can hold up five fingers (e.g., two on one hand, three on the other; four on one hand, one on the other). Ask children questions to encourage them to think about the commutative property. For example, "Kane is showing two on his right hand and three on his left hand. Rina is showing three on her right hand and two on her left hand. How are those different? How are they the same?"

Figure 8.15

Representations for six.

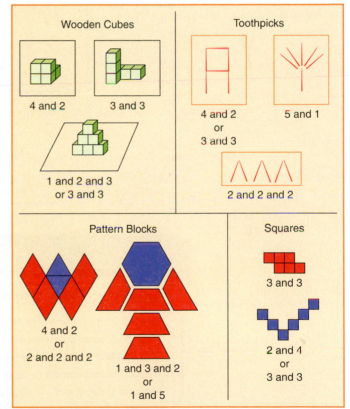

An important variation of part–part–whole activities is referred to as *missing-part* activities. In a missing-part activity, children are given the whole amount and part of the whole. They then use their already developed knowledge of the parts of that whole to try to tell what the covered or hidden part is. If they are unsure, they simply uncover the unknown part and say the full combination. Missing-part activities can be challenging for children not only because the missing part increases the difficulty level but also because they encourage children to continue to reflect on the combinations for a number. They also serve as the forerunner to subtraction. With a whole of eight but with only three showing, the child can later learn to write "8 − 3 = 5."

The next four activities illustrate variations of this important idea of a missing part. For any of these activities you can use a context from familiar classroom events or from a children's book, such as the animals hiding in the barn in *Hide and Seek* (Stoeke, 1999).

Activity 8.25

CCSS-M: K.OA.A.2

Covered Parts

A set of counters equal to the target amount is counted out, and the rest are put aside. One child places the counters under a margarine tub or piece of cardstock and then pulls some out into view. (This amount could be none, all, or any amount in between.) For example, if six is the whole and four are showing, the other child says, "Four and *two* is six." If there is hesitation or if the hidden part is unknown, the hidden part is shown (see Figure 8.16).

Figure 8.16

Missing-part activities.

Activity 8.26

CCSS-M: K.OA.A4

Missing-Part Cards

For each number from 4 to 10, make missing-part cards using the **Missing-Part Cards** Activity Page. Each card has a numeral for the whole and two dot sets with one set that needs to be covered by a flap. For the number 8, you will create nine cards with the visible part ranging from 0 to 8 dots. Children use the cards as in "Covered Parts," saying, "Four and two is six" for a card with four dots showing and two dots hiding under the flap (see Figure 8.16).

Activity 8.27

CCSS-M: K.OA.A.1; K.OA.A.2; K.OA.A.3

I Wish I Had

Hold out a bar of connecting cubes, a dot strip, a two-column strip (use the **Two Column Cards**), or a dot plate showing six or less and say, "I wish I had six." The children respond with the part that is needed to make six. Counting on can be used to check. The game can focus on the same "I wish I had" number (a good starting point for children with disabilities), or the number can change each time (see Figure 8.16). Consider adding a familiar context, such as "I wish I had six books to read." See the corresponding **Expanded Lesson: I Wish I Had** for a detailed version of this activity.

Activity 8.28

Number Sandwiches

Select a number between 5 and 12. Have children find combinations of two **Dot Cards 1-6** totaling that number. Children make a "sandwich" with the two cards by placing them back-to-back with the dot sides out. When they have found at least 10 pairs, the next challenge is for the partner to name the number on the other side. The cards are turned over to confirm. The same sandwiches can then be used again to name the other hidden part.

You can also incorporate digital formats for any of the preceding part–part–whole activities. All you need is a program that permits children to create sets of objects on the screen. Look at Scott Foresman's eTools and choose "Counters." Under "work-spaces" on the bottom left, select the bucket icon and then pick the bathtub and add boat, duck, or goldfish counters. As shown in Figure 8.17(a), children can stamp different bathtub toys either in the bathtub (unseen) or outside the tub. The numeral on the bathtub shows how many are in the tub, or it can show a question mark (?) for missing-part thinking. The total is shown at the bottom. By clicking on the light bulb, the contents of the bathtub can be seen, as shown in Figure 8.17(b). This program offers a great opportunity to develop both part–part–whole and missing-part concepts.

Figure 8.17

Scott Foresman's eTools software is useful for exploring part–part–whole and missing-part ideas.

Formative Assessment Note

To assess part–part–whole relationships, use a missing-part diagnostic interview (similar to Activity 8.25 "Covered Parts"). Begin with a number you believe the child has "mastered," such as 5. Have the child count out that many counters into your open hand. Close your hand around the counters and confirm that child knows how many are hidden there. Then remove some and show them in the open palm of your other hand. (See Figure 8.18.) Ask the child, "How many are hidden?" Repeat with different amounts removed, checking three or four missing parts for each number. If the child responds quickly and correctly and is clearly not counting in any way, call that a "mastered number" and check it off the child's assessment record. Repeat the process with the next higher number. Continue until the child begins to struggle. In early kindergarten you will find a range of mastered numbers from four to eight. By the end of kindergarten, children should have mastered numbers up to 10 (CCSSO, 2010).

Figure 8.18

A missing-part number assessment. Eight in all. "How many are hidden?"

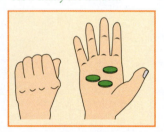

Teaching Tip

Children do not have to have formal place-value instruction before working with numbers beyond 10.

Relationships for Numbers 10 to 20

Although preK, kindergartners, and first-graders experience numbers up to 20 and beyond daily, it should not be assumed that they will automatically extend the set of relationships they developed with smaller numbers to numbers beyond 10. And yet these numbers play a big part in many counting activities, in basic facts, and in much of what we do with mental computation. In fact, several researchers suggest number instruction should move beyond 10 and even beyond 20 as soon as possible—even before formal place-value instruction (Fosnot & Dolk, 2001; Wright, Stranger, Stafford, & Martland, 2006). Although children may count by ones to count sets beyond 10, the experiences of counting and grouping help children build important initial place-value knowledge. The emphasis should be on helping children learn the number words and numerals beyond 10 rather than the traditional notions of place value (e.g., names of places). That will come in time as children develop strategies to add and subtract two-digit numbers.

Pre–Place-Value Concepts of Ten

Stop and Reflect

Say to yourself, "One ten." Now think about that from the perspective of a child just learning to count to 20! What could one ten possibly mean when ten tells me how many fingers I have and is the number that comes after nine? How can it be one?

Wright and his colleagues (2006) outlined a three-level progression of children's understanding of ten:

1. *An initial concept of ten.* The child understands ten as ten ones and does not see ten as a unit. When children at this level work on a task involving tens, they will count by ones.

2. *An intermediate concept of ten.* The child understands ten as a unit composed of ten ones but relies on materials or representations to help complete tasks involving tens.

3. *A facile concept of ten.* The child can solve tasks involving tens and ones without using materials or representations. At this level children can mentally think about two-digit numbers as groups of tens and ones.

The *Common Core State Standards* suggests that first-graders should know that "10 can be thought of as a bundle of ten ones—called a 'ten:'" (CCSSO, 2010, p. 15). The difficulty of children understanding "one ten and six ones" (what's a one?) does not mean that a set of ten should not figure prominently in the discussion of the teen numbers. To help children move their understanding of "ten" forward, consider providing lots of purposeful opportunities for them to count and group objects. For example, Fosnot and Dolk (2001) describe a K–1 teacher who used the context of making necklaces using five beads of one color, then five beads of another color, and then repeating these groups of five. Children could count by ones if they needed to, but the teacher built in the constraint of creating necklaces with a five structure to encourage the children to begin to count by fives. Eventually she introduced the idea of selling the necklaces as a school fundraiser and suggested charging a penny per bead. Because the beads were in groups of five, the children worked with nickels and dimes, further encouraging the children to begin to see five and ten as units.

Initially, children do not see a numeric pattern in the numbers between 10 and 20. Rather, these number names are simply ten additional words in the number sequence. Building from the idea mentioned earlier, mapping the teens number names to a ten and one structure is an important idea (i.e., matching thirteen to "ten and three"). The activity that follows provides a way to help children visualize and reinforce the meaning of "teen" numbers.

Standards for Mathematical Practice

7 Look for and make use of structure.

Activity 8.29

CCSS-M: K.NBT.A.1

Ten and Some More

Use a simple two-part mat and a story that links to whatever counters you are using. Then have children count out ten counters (e.g., bears, beans, coffee stirrers, etc.) onto the left side of the mat. Next have them put five counters on the other side. Together, count all of the counters by ones. Chorus the combination: "Ten and five equals fifteen." Turn the mat around: "Five and ten equals fifteen." Repeat with other numbers in a random order but always start with the ten on the left side of the mat. After children have had some experience with this activity, bundle the counters (with a rubber band or plastic baggie) into groups of ten.

"Ten and Some More" is designed to teach the numbers in the "teens" and, thus, requires some explicit teaching. Watch this **video (https://www.youtube.com/watch?v=2ZV4Oq7Xaew)** of a kindergarten teacher who is working with her children in a more explicit manner to decompose teen numbers into ten and some leftovers.

Following the Activity "Ten and Some More," explore numbers through 20 in a more open-ended manner. Provide each child with a **Double Ten-Frame** mat (Blackline Master 15). In random order, have children show numbers to 20 on their frames. Have children discuss how the counters can be arranged on the Double Ten-Frame mat so that it is easy to see how many are there. At first, not every child will create a full set of 10, but as this idea becomes more popular, they will develop the notion that teens are 10 and some more. Eventually challenge children to show larger amounts, such as 26 counters or even more. In this video called **Beyond Fingers (https://www.youtube.com/watch?v=3fTCAicmUWY)** you will see how a teacher works with a group of kindergartners to explore combinations of ten and some more to make the numbers from 11 to 19.

The following activity moves to a symbolic representation of multidigit numbers that explicitly shows how a multidigit number is composed ten and some more.

Activity 8.30

CCSS-M: K.NBT.A.1; 1.NBT.B.2; 2.NBT.A.1

Build the Number with Cards

Using the **Build the Number Cards** Activity Pages, create a set of cards from cardstock. The tens card is twice as long as the ones card and the hundreds card is three times as long as the ones card (see Figure 8.19). To start, children use the cards to create "teen" numbers and then move on to other two-digit numbers. For example, write a two-digit number, say, 16, where children can see it. Children are to find the two cards that can be used to make 16 (a 10 and a 6). Select children to demonstrate to the class how to make the given number. Point out that you can still see the 10 hiding under the overlay of the 6. Repeat the activity with different two-digit numbers. When children are ready, extend the activity to three-digit numbers. You can also have children represent the numbers with concrete materials, such as base-ten materials or ten-frames.

Standards for Mathematical Practice

8 **Look for and express regularity in repeated reasoning.**

Extending More-Than and Less-Than Relationships

The relationships of one more than, two more than, one less than, and two less than are important for all numbers and are built from children's knowledge of the same concepts for numbers less than 10. The fact that 17 is one less than 18 is connected to the idea that 7 is one less than 8. Children may need explicit support in making this connection.

Activity 8.31

CCSS-M: K.CC.C.6; K.NBT.A.1

More and Less Extended

Project an image of seven counters and ask what is two more, or one less, and so on. Now add a filled ten-frame to the display (or 10 in any pattern) and repeat the questions. Pair up questions by covering and uncovering the ten-frame as illustrated in Figure 8.20.

Figure 8.19

Building numbers with cards that show place value explicitly.

Figure 8.20

Extending relationships to the teens.

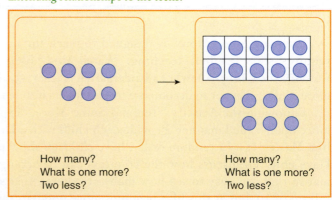

Numbers to 100: Early Introductions

According to the *Common Core State Standards* (CCSSO, 2010), kindergartners are expected to be able to count to 100 by the end of the school year. Therefore, early exposure to numbers to 100 is important. Although it is unlikely that children in kindergarten or first grade will initially have a facile understanding of tens and ones related to place value, they should learn much about the sequence of numbers and counting patterns to 100, if not beyond.

The **Hundreds Chart** (Figure 8.21) is an essential tool for every K–2 classroom (see Blackline Master 3). Children can orally count to 100 as you or a child points to each number on the chart. Whenever collections of things are counted, it is a good idea to pause long enough to find the number on the chart. This can help put numbers for large quantities in perspective. Point out, for example, that 87 is a big number that is close to 100. The number 35 is also big but is closer to 20 than 100 and is far away from 87.

An extremely useful version of the chart is made of transparent pockets into which each of the 100 numeral cards can be inserted. You can hide a number by inserting a blank card in front of a number in the pocket. You can insert colored pieces of paper in the slots to highlight various number patterns. And you can remove some or all of the number cards and have children replace them in their correct slots.

A hundreds chart displayed using a projection device is almost as flexible as the pocket chart version. Numbers can be hidden by placing opaque counters on them. Patterns can be marked with a pen or with transparent counters. A blank 10 × 10 grid serves as an empty hundreds chart on which you can write numbers (See **Blackline Master 2**). A computerized version can be found at the NCTM Illuminations website under "Learning about Number Relationships." This eChart uses a calculator and hundreds chart together so that children can visually see the patterns generated by the calculator.

There are many different patterns on the hundreds chart that children can explore, which is the focus of Activity 8.32.

Figure 8.21

A hundreds chart.

1	2	3	4	5	6	7	8	9	10
11	12	13	14	15	16	17	18	19	20
21	22	23	24	25	26	27	28	29	30
31	32	33	34	35	36	37	38	39	40
41	42	43	44	45	46	47	48	49	50
51	52	53	54	55	56	57	58	59	60
61	62	63	64	65	66	67	68	69	70
71	72	73	74	75	76	77	78	79	80
81	82	83	84	85	86	87	88	89	90
91	92	93	94	95	96	97	98	99	100

Activity 8.32

CCSS-M: K.CC.A.1; K.CC.A.2; 1.NBT.A.1; 1.NBT.C.5; 2.NBT.A.2

Patterns on a Hundreds Chart

Have children work in pairs to find patterns on the hundreds chart. Solicit ideas orally from the class. Have children explain patterns found by others to be sure that all understand the ideas that are being suggested.

In a discussion, different children will describe the same pattern in several ways. Accept all ideas. Here are some of the patterns they may point out:

- The numbers in a column all end with the same number, which is the number at the top.
- In a row, one number "counts" (the ones digit goes 1, 2, 3, . . ., 9, 0); the "first" number (tens digit) stays the same but the "second" number (ones digit) goes up by ones.
- In a column, the first number (tens digit) "counts" or goes up by ones.
- You can count by tens going down the right-hand column.
- If you count by fives, you get two columns: the 5 column and the last column.
- The number right above a given number is 10 less; the number right below a given number is 10 more.

For children, these patterns are not at all obvious or trivial. For example, one child may notice the pattern in the column under the 4—every number ends in a 4. Two minutes later another child will "discover" the parallel pattern in the column headed by 7. That there is a pattern like this in every column may not be completely obvious.

Knowing the number sequence up to 100 by 10s is a kindergarten expectation in the Common Core and skip-counting by 5s, 10s, and 100s is a second grade expectation. Keep in mind that children commonly learn number sequences before they consider the value of the number words. Watch a video of **Nicole**, a second grader who skip counts by 10s up to 100. It is not until she is asked, "What comes after 100" and she responds, "200" that you realize that she may not be considering the meaning of the 10-count and the value of the number words. The hundreds chart is a useful tool to help children explore skip-count patterns. However, they will need additional work to ensure they are also considering the value of the numbers in the skip count sequence.

The next activity challenges children to use the patterns they have noticed and discussed in Activity 8.32 to find missing numbers in the hundreds chart.

Activity 8.33

CCSS-M: K.CC.A.1; K.CC.A.2; 1.NBT.A.1; 1.NBT.C.5; 2.NBT.A.2

Missing Numbers

Provide children with a hundreds chart on which some of the number cards have been removed. (One option is to use a classroom pocket chart. Another option is to fill in parts of an empty hundreds chart **Blackline Master 2**). The children's task is to replace the missing numbers in the chart. Beginning versions of this activity have only a random selection of individual numbers removed. Later, remove sequences of several numbers from three or four different rows. Finally, remove all but one or two rows or columns. Eventually, challenge children to replace all of the numbers in a blank chart. If you use a classroom hundreds chart, provide children with disabilities their own copy using an empty hundreds chart. Having their own copy allows them to write possible numbers in the missing spots on the chart so they do not have to keep the numbers in short term memory. This allows them to focus on the more cognitively demanding task of reasoning about the numbers and their relationships.

 Formative Assessment Note

Replacing the number cards or tiles from a blank chart is a good learning center activity for two children to work on together. By listening to how children go about finding the correct locations for numbers, you can learn a lot about how well they have constructed an understanding of the 1-to-100 sequence.

Number Sense and the Real World

Here we examine ways to broaden early knowledge of numbers. Relationships of numbers to real-world quantities and measures and the use of numbers in simple estimations can help children develop flexible, intuitive ideas about numbers.

Calendar Activities

Although 90 percent of the classrooms surveyed in a study reported using calendar-related activities (Hamre, Downer, Kilday, & McGuire, 2008), calendar activities are not the kind of mathematics instruction that will support young learners in developing mathematical literacy. The calendar may be helpful in developing a sense of time, however, the National Research Council Committee (2009) has stated that "using the calendar does not emphasize foundational mathematics" (p. 241)—in particular, the calendar does not align with the need to develop key mathematical relationships related to the number 10 because the calendar is based on groups of seven. The committee concludes, "Doing the calendar is not a substitute for teaching foundational mathematics" (p. 241). Ethridge and King (2005) suggest that during calendar activities children learn to parrot the response for the predictable questions and they don't always understand some of the concepts presented. Clements, Baroody, and Sarama (2013) recommend avoiding the inappropriate use of the calendar, as it engages only a few children. The key message is that doing calendar mathematics should be thought of as an "add on" and should not take time away from developing essential pre K–2 mathematics concepts.

Estimation and Measurement

One of the best ways for children to think of real quantities is to associate numbers with measures of things. In the early grades, measures of length, weight, and time are good places to begin. Just measuring and recording results will not be very effective unless there is a meaningful reason for children to be interested in or to think about the result. To help children think about the numbers in a context and what they mean (e.g., how long the desk is, how heavy the book is), ask them to first write down or tell you an estimate. To produce an estimate is, however, a very difficult task for young children. They do not easily grasp the concept of "estimate" or "about." So children need lots of opportunities to explore what is meant by "estimate" and "about." As an example, suppose that you have cut out an ample supply of very large footprints, each about 18-inches long. You would ask the class, "About how many of the giant's footprints will it take to measure across the rug in our reading corner?" The key word here is *about*, and it is one that you will need to spend a lot of time helping your children understand. To this end, the request for an estimate can be made in ways that help develop the concept of *about*. For example, rather than asking children for a specific number, begin by asking whether the amount will be more or less than a target number. The following questions can be used with most early estimation activities:

Standards for Mathematical Practice

◀ **2** Reasoning abstractly and quantitatively.

- *More or less than* _____? Will the rug be more or less than 10 footprints long? Will the apple weigh more or less than 20 blocks? Are there more or less than 15 connecting cubes in this long bar?

- *Closer to* _____ *or to* _____? Will the rug be closer to 5 footprints or closer to 20 footprints long? Will the apple weigh closer to 10 blocks or closer to 30 blocks? Does this bar have closer to 10 cubes or closer to 50 cubes?

- *About* _____? About how many footprints long is the rug? About how many blocks will the apple weigh? About how many cubes are in this bar? (You can suggest possible numbers as options.)

Asking for estimates using these formats helps children learn what you mean by *about*. Every child can make an estimate with some supportive questions and examples. However, rewarding children for the closest estimate in a competitive fashion will often result in their trying to seek precision and not actually estimate. Instead, discuss all answers that fall into a reasonable range. One of the best approaches is to give children ranges as their possible answers: "Does your estimate fall between 10 and 30? Between 50 and 70? Or 100 and 130?" Of course, you can make the choices more divergent until they grasp the idea.

To help with numbers and measures, estimate several things in succession using the same unit. For example, suppose that you are estimating and measuring "around things" using a string. The string is wrapped around the object and then measured in some unit such as popsicle sticks. After measuring the distance around Demetria's head, estimate the distance around the wastebasket or around the globe or around George's wrist. Each successive measure helps children with the new estimates. See Chapter 15 for a complete discussion of measurement.

Here are some activities that can help children connect numbers to real situations.

Activity 8.34
CCSS-M: K.MD.A.1; 1.MD.B.3; 2.MD.A.3

Add a Unit to Your Number

 Write a number on the board. Now suggest some units to go with it, and ask the children what comes to mind when they hear the number and unit. For example, suppose the number is 9. "What do you think of when I say 9 *dollars*? 9 *hours*? 9 *cars*? 9 *kids*? 9 *meters*? 9 *o'clock*? 9 *hand spans*? 9 *gallons*?" Spend some time discussing and exploring each unit. Let children suggest other appropriate units. Children from different cultures may be able to share different units used in their culture.

Activity 8.35
CCSS-M: K.MD.A.1; 1.MD.A.2; 2.MD.A.3

Is It Reasonable?

Standards for Mathematical Practice

> **3 Construct viable arguments and critique the reasoning of others.**

Select a number and a unit—for example, 15 feet. Could the teacher be 15 feet tall? Could a house be 15 feet wide? Can a man jump 15 feet high? Could three children stretch their arms 15 feet? Pick any number, large or small, and a unit with which children are familiar. Then make up a series of these questions. Also ask, "How can we find out if it is reasonable or not? Who has an idea about what we can do?" When children are familiar with this activity, have them select the number and unit and create the questions to ask.

These activities are problem based in the truest sense. Not only are there no clear answers, but children can easily begin to pose their own questions and explore the numbers and units most interesting to them. You can also use the Toy Shop activities at the NCTM Illuminations website as a setting that focuses on finding numbers in the real world.

Data Collection and Analysis

Graphing activities are good ways to connect children's worlds with number and relationships. (Chapter 17 discusses ways to make graphs with children in grades pre K–2.) Graphs can be quickly made from any data gathered with children: favorites (ice cream flavor, color, sports team, type of pet); number of sisters, brothers, pets; transportation modes to school;

types of shoes children are wearing (sneakers, sandals, etc.); and so on. Graphs can be connected to content in other subjects, such as an investigation of objects that float or sink. Or a unit on sea life might lead to a graph of favorite sea animals. Here are some other options for graphs that are linked to children's literature:

- *Chrysanthemum* (Henkes, 2008): Create a graph of the length of children's first names (i.e., use categories 3, 4, 5 letters and so on).

- *This is the Way We Go to School* (Baer, 1990): Make a graph of the way children come to school.

- *We're Going on a Leaf Hunt* (Metzger, 2008): Have children collect a leaf from around their home or around the school, create a graph of different types of leaves.

- *3 Little Firefighters* (Murphy, 2003): Use children's career aspirations to make a graph (i.e., sort jobs into public service, entertainment, education, and so on).

In the early stages of number development, the use of graphs is primarily for developing number relationships and for connecting numbers to real quantities in the children's environment. The graphs focus attention on counts of realistic things. Once a graph is made, it is very important to take the time to ask questions (e.g., "What do you notice about the ice cream choices our class made?" "How many more children ride the bus to school than come in cars?"). Equally important, graphs can elicit comparisons between numbers that are rarely made when only one number or quantity is considered at a time. See Figure 8.22 for an example of a graph and corresponding questions. At first, children may find it challenging to respond to questions involving differences, but these comparison concepts add considerably to children's understanding of number and are a focus of 1.MD.C.4 in the Common Core State Standards (CCSSO, 2010).

Figure 8.22

Relationships and number sense in a bar graph.

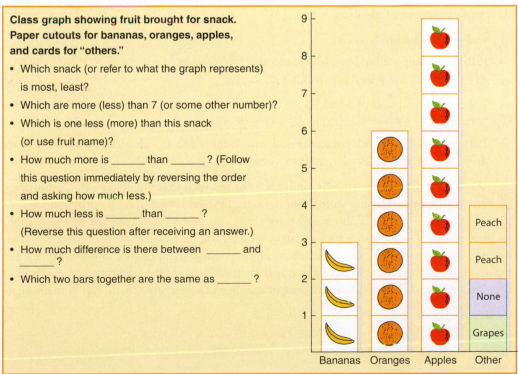

Revisiting the Big Ideas for Number Concepts

As a recap of the big ideas from this chapter, here is a list of the kinds of things that children should learn about the number 8 (or any number up to about 20) while they are in pre K and kindergarten:

- Count to 8 (know the number words and their order)
- Count 8 objects and know that the last number word tells how many
- Recognize, read, and write the numeral 8 and pair it with an amount of objects
- State more and less by 1 and 2—8 is one more than 7, one less than 9, two more than 6, and two less than 10
- Recognize patterned sets for 8 such as:

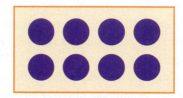

- Relate to the benchmark numbers of 5 and 10: 8 is 3 more than 5 and 2 away from 10
- State part–part–whole relationships: 8 is the same as 5 and 3, 2 and 6, 7 and 1, and so on (this includes knowing the missing part of 8 when some are hidden)
- Identify doubles: double 4 equals 8
- State relationships to the real world: my brother is 8 years old; my reading book is 8 inches wide

First and second graders extend these ideas to numbers beyond ten and further refine their understanding of number:

- One ten is equal to ten ones
- Fifteen is composed of ten and five more
- 632 is composed of 600 and 30 and 2 more
- Benchmark numbers of 5 and 10 can be used for mental computation with larger numbers: think of $68 + 7$ as equal to $68 + 2 + 5$, which is the same as $70 + 5 = 75$.
- Larger numbers are related to the real world: there are 457 children in my school; we drove almost 900 miles over summer vacation

We started the chapter sharing findings from research that underscore the importance of young children developing strong number sense. We end the chapter by providing a summary of common misconceptions and errors children make when they are learning about number concepts along with ways you can help (see Table 8.2). Being aware of these common misconceptions will allow you to anticipate and recognize them in your children so you can purposefully address the misconceptions with instruction and ultimately support children to develop a rich and flexible understanding of number that will serve them well in mathematics and in life.

Table 8.2. Common errors and misconceptions in number concepts and how to help.

Misconception/Error	What It Looks Like	How to Help
1. Child makes mistakes with the counting sequence	Child may be able to orally count to a certain point (e.g., from 1 to 10) but then either skips number words or uses student-generated number words (e.g., ten, one-teen, two-teen, three-teen, . . .).	• Practice counting together out loud (forward and backward number sequences). • Read counting books and make them available to children. • Prepare cards with numerals and have children place them in order on a number line (see Activity 8.2). • Match the written numeral with the written number word.
2. Child does not use one-to-one correspondence	Child does not attach one number word to each object. He either double counts, saying two number words for one object or touches more than one object as he says one number word. For example, he may touch two objects as he says two-syllable counting words such as "se-ven" or "thir-teen."	• As the child counts objects, have him place one object in each space of an egg carton or ice cube tray. • Slow down the count by having the child put counters into a bag or by picking up object with salad tongs as it is counted. • Make a plan for counting: arrange objects in a row, count objects from left to right, touch one object and say each number word out loud, move each object as it is counted across a line on a work mat or place into a bag or box. • If a child splits the count across two-syllable counting words, have the child work on matching the written numeral with the written number word.
3. Child is confused by perceptual cues (i.e., spacing or length of row of counters)	 Child thinks the top row has more circles because the row is longer.	• Use matching to compare sets. For example, stack counters on top of images to match the sets.
4. Child does not have cardinality principle	When asked "How many?" recounts or points to the last object counted.	• Play board games that have a linear path and instead of moving one marker along the path, leave one counter in each space. For example, if the child rolls a 4 on the die, she places 4 counters, one in each space on the board. Ask, "How many spaces did you travel?" • Provide lots of counting opportunities, followed by asking "How many?" • When counting collections together, say, "1, 2, 3, 4, 5. We have 5 pencils." • Have children get into groups of called out numbers (e.g., get into groups of 2, groups of 5, groups of 4). See "Mingle and Count" video on the Teaching Channel website.
5. Child does not count on	Child counts out one set and then when given more objects, recounts the first set, starting back at one.	• After child counts out one set and states how many, cover the collection with a sheet of paper or put the collection in a cup. The idea is to remove the objects from sight, forcing the child to create a mental image of the objects. Child may still want to peek at the collection. Encourage child to think about how many before peeking. • Use quick images to work on child's subitizing skills.

9

Developing Meanings for the Operations

BIG IDEAS

1 Addition can be thought of as physically or conceptually placing two or more quantities together.

2 Subtraction can be thought of as taking an amount away from a given quantity, comparing two quantities, or finding a missing part given the whole and the other part.

3 Multiplication in grades preK–2 involves counting groups of equal size and determining how many are in all.

4 Division in grades preK–2 can be thought of as sharing equal amounts among a given number of groups or as repeatedly measuring out the same amount from a given total.

5 The four operations are related to each other. Addition names the whole in terms of the parts, and subtraction names a missing part. Multiplication can be thought of as repeated addition. Division names a missing factor in terms of the known factor and the product. Division can also be thought of as repeated subtraction.

6 Models can be used to solve contextual problems for all operations and to figure out what operation is involved in a problem. Models also can be used to give meaning to number sentences.

This chapter is about helping children connect different meanings, interpretations, and relationships to the four operations of addition, subtraction, multiplication, and division so that they can accurately and fluently apply these operations in real-world settings. This is all part of the Operations Core (National Research Council [NRC], 2009), in which children learn to see mathematical situations in their daily lives or in story problems and begin to make models of these situations using a variety of representations such as words, diagrams, manipulatives, and/or numbers (e.g., equations). The Operations Core builds and expands on the NRC's Number Core and Relations Core discussed in Chapter 8 and will be extended in the discussion of place value in Chapter 11. As children learn to connect the big ideas listed above, they can and should simultaneously be developing more sophisticated ideas about number, recognizing ways to think about basic fact combinations, and accurately and fluently applying these operations in real-world situation. All of this develops *operation sense*.

In the *Common Core State Standards* (CCSSO, 2010), children in K-2 are expected to be able to think about addition and subtraction situations that involve adding to, taking from, putting together, and taking apart using increasingly sophisticated strategies. In kindergarten, children model the situations using fingers, manipulatives, drawings, and mental images. In first grade, children expand their modeling to the use of equations and in second grade, children use primarily diagrams, equations, and mental strategies to model and reason through situations. Solving comparison situations is added to the expectations in first and second grades. Second graders also begin to explore multiplication as equal groups, using rectangular arrays to model problems.

Teaching Operations through Contextual Problems

Contextual problems are the primary teaching tool to use to help children construct a rich understanding of the operations. These contexts are what elicit problem-solving strategies (Schwartz, 2013) and help children make sense of the operations. What might a good lesson that is built around contextual problems look like? The answer comes more easily if you think about children not just solving the problems but also using words, pictures, and numbers to explain how they reasoned about solving the problem and why they think they are correct. Children should solve problems using whatever physical materials or drawings they feel will help them. They explain either verbally or in writing what they did and why it makes sense within the context of the situation—with enough detail (e.g., a written explanation, a drawing they used to help them solve the problem, modeling with manipulatives) to allow someone else to track on their reasoning and understand their solution. With the emphasis on children explaining their ideas and reasoning, lessons should focus on two or three problems and the related in-depth discussions rather than a lot of problems with little elaboration.

Standards for
Mathematical Practice

◄ **3 Construct viable arguments and critique the reasoning of others.**

Children's Conceptions of Addition and Subtraction

From an adult's perspective the ideas of addition and subtraction seem quite simple. For example, think about how you would solve the following problem.

Aidan had 7 beads. After she bought some more beads, she had 15 beads. How many beads did Aidan buy?

Most adults and older students solve this problem by subtracting 15 – 7. But young children do not initially view this as a subtraction situation because 15 – 7 is the "opposite" operation or action implied in the problem. Instead, they will mimic the implied action in the problem and solve it by adding on or counting up from 7 until they reach 15. Their approach may seem less efficient than simply subtracting, but it makes sense to young children because it mirrors the situation in the problem. Watch **Arriel** solve a similar problem by adding on or counting up. Eventually, after having much experience making sense of story problems, working with different combinations of numbers, and examining the results of using addition and subtraction in these situations (possibly at their teacher's request), they will begin to generalize that they get the same result by subtracting and will join older students and adults in using subtraction for these kinds of problems. This example illustrates how children's initial conceptions are different from those of adults—even with something we consider so basic as addition and subtraction.

Children's conceptions are the best foundation on which to build future learning. Therefore, the perspective on addition and subtraction taken in this chapter is based on what has been learned from numerous research studies about children's understanding of operations (Gutstein & Romberg, 1995; Carpenter, Fennema, Franke, Levi, & Empson, 2014; NRC, 2009; Verschaffel, Greer, & De Corte, 2007; Clements & Sarama, 2014). Through this research, we are aware that children can solve contextual or story problems involving age-appropriate numbers by reasoning through the relationships in the problems. We also know that different problems have different structures that can affect the difficulty level of the problem. When teachers are familiar with these structures, they are better able to plan and differentiate instruction.

Addition and Subtraction Problem Structures

Addition and subtraction situations have been studied extensively and categorized in multiple ways (Gutstein & Romberg, 1995; Carpenter, Fennema, Franke, Levi, & Empson, 2014; Verschaffel, Greer, & De Corte, 2007; Clements & Sarama, 2009; NRC, 2009; CCSSO, 2010). Table 9.1 illustrates one categorization scheme that identifies four types of problems based on the relationships involved. These problem types include *change* problems (*join* and *separate*), *part–part–whole* problems, and *compare* problems (Carpenter, Fennema, Franke, Levi, & Empson, 2014). Each structure has three numbers. For example, the *Join* problem type has a start number, a change number, and a result number. The *Part–part–whole* problem type has two part numbers and one whole. Any one or more of the three numbers can be unknown in a story problem.

In Table 9.1, each of the problem types and structures are illustrated with a story problem that uses the number family 4, 8, 12. Depending on which of the three quantities is unknown, a different problem structure results. Note that the problems are described in terms of their type and structure and not as addition or subtraction problems. Contrary to what you may have thought, a joining action does not always mean addition, nor does separate or remove always mean subtraction, as can be seen in the number sentences in Table 9.1.

Change Problems
Join/Add To Problems

Join problems describe situations in which quantities are physically being brought together. These problems are also known as *add to* problems because the action or change occurring in the problem is a result of adding or joining quantities. For joining problems,

---

Standards for Mathematical Practice

1 Make sense of problems and persevere in solving them. ▶

Standards for Mathematical Practice

7 Look for and make use of structure. ▶

Table 9.1. Basic types and structures for addition and subtraction story problems.

Problem Type and Structure with Physical Action Involved: Change Problems			
	Result Unknown	**Change Unknown**	**Start Unknown**
(a) Join (Add To)	Sandra had 8 pennies. George gave her 4 more. How many pennies does Sandra have altogether? $8 + 4 = \square$	Sandra had 8 pennies. George gave her some more. Now Sandra has 12 pennies. How many did George give her? $8 + \square = 12$ or $12 - 8 = \square$	Sandra had some pennies. George gave her 4 more. Now Sandra has 12 pennies. How many pennies did Sandra have to begin with? $\square + 4 = 12$ $12 - 4 = \square$
(b) Separate (Take From)	Sandra had 12 pennies. She gave 4 pennies to George. How many pennies does Sandra have now? $12 - 4 = \square$	Sandra had 12 pennies. She gave some to George. Now she has 8 pennies. How many did she give to George? $12 - \square = 8$ $8 + \square = 12$ $12 - 8 = \square$	Sandra had some pennies. She gave 4 to George. Now Sandra has 8 pennies left. How many pennies did Sandra have to begin with? $\square - 4 = 8$ $8 + 4 = \square$

Problem Type and Structure with No Physical Action Involved: Part–Part–Whole and Compare Problems			
	Whole Unknown	**One Part Unknown**	**Both Parts Unknown**
(c) Part–Part–Whole	George has 4 pennies and 8 nickels. How many coins does he have? $4 + 8 = \square$	George has 12 coins. Eight of his coins are pennies, and the rest are nickels. How many nickels does George have? $12 = 8 + \square$ or $12 - 8 = \square$	George has 12 coins. Some are pennies and some are nickels. How many of each could he have? $12 = \square + \square$
	Difference Unknown	**Larger Quantity Unknown**	**Smaller Quantity Unknown**
(d) Compare	Situations of "How many *more*?" George has 12 pennies and Sandra has 8 pennies. How many more pennies does George have than Sandra? $8 + \square = 12$ $12 - 8 = \square$	Sandra has 8 pennies. George has 4 more pennies than Sandra. How many pennies does George have? $8 + 4 = \square$ $8 = \square - 4$	George has 12 pennies. George has 4 more pennies than Sandra. How many pennies does Sandra have? $\square + 4 = 12$ $12 - 4 = \square$
	Situations of "How many *fewer*?" George has 12 pennies. Sandra has 8 pennies. How many fewer pennies does Sandra have than George? $12 - 8 = \square$ $12 = 8 + \square$	Sandra has 4 fewer pennies than George. Sandra has 8 pennies. How many pennies does George have? $\square - 4 = 8$ $8 + 4 = \square$	Sandra has 4 fewer pennies than George. George has 12 pennies. How many pennies does Sandra have? $12 - 4 = \square$ $12 = \square + 4$

there are three quantities involved: an initial or *start amount*, a *change amount* (the part being added or joined), and the *resulting amount* (the total amount after the change takes place). In Table 9.1(a), this is illustrated by the change being "added" to the start amount. Provide children the **Join Story** Activity Page where they can work with counters and model the problem on the story situation graphic organizer. Watch this video of **Jocelyn** solving a change unknown addition problem. You will see how she reasons to get the answer using doubles facts she already knows.

Separate/Take From Problems

Separate problems are commonly known as *take away* or *take from* problems in which part of a quantity is physically being removed or taken away. Notice that in the *separate* problems, the start amount is the whole or the largest amount, whereas in the *join* problems, the result is the largest amount (the whole). Children can use the **Separate Story** Activity Page as a graphic organizer.

Part–Part–Whole Problems

Part–part–whole problems, also known as *put together* and *take apart* problems in the *Common Core State Standards* (CCSSO, 2010), involve two parts that are conceptually or mentally combined into one collection or whole, as in Table 9.1(c). These problems are different from *change* problems in that there is no action of physically joining or separating the quantities. In these situations, either the missing whole (total unknown), one of the missing parts (one addend unknown), or both parts (two addends unknown) must be found. There is no meaningful distinction between the two parts in a part–part–whole situation, so there is no need to have a different problem for each part as the unknown. The third situation in which the whole or total is known and the two parts are unknown creates opportunities to think about all the possible decompositions of the whole. This structure links directly to the idea that numbers are embedded in other numbers (part of the Number Core). For example, children can break apart 7 into 5 and 2, where each of the addends (or parts) is embedded in the 7 (whole). These kinds of problems can conceptually combine different kinds of objects, such as 5 red balls and 6 blue balls or 3 cars and 4 trucks, into one collection. Combining different kinds of objects into one set can be challenging for young children to understand because they have to generalize what the different objects have in common. See the **Part–part–whole Story** Activity Page for the corresponding graphic organizer.

Compare Problems

Compare problems involve the comparison of two quantities. The third amount in these problems does not actually exist but is the *difference* between the two quantities (see Table 9.1(d)). Like part–part–whole problems, comparison situations do not typically involve a physical action. The corresponding **Compare Story** Activity Page can help children model the situation. The unknown quantity in compare problems can be one of three quantities: the smaller amount, the larger amount, or the difference. For each of these situations, two examples are provided: one problem in which the difference is stated in terms of "how many more?" and the other in terms of "how many less?" Note that the language of "more" and "less" can present a challenge to many children as they attempt to interpret the relationships between the quantities using these ideas.

You can find more examples of compare problems as well as the other problem types in the *Common Core State Standards* (see Table 1 in the CCSSI Math Standards Glossary; CCSSO, 2010, p. 88).

Stop and Reflect

500　250　3x　5°　2.5

Go back through the example story problems in Table 9.1 and match the numbers in the problems with the components of the structures. For example, which numbers in the Join Problems match to start, change, and result and which are unknown? For each problem, if possible, first print off the corresponding graphic organizer Activity Page, and second, use a set of counters or coins to model (solve) the problem as you think children in the primary grades might do. Write either an addition or subtraction equation that you think best represents the problem as you did it with counters and then compare your equation to the ones in Table 9.1. If you did not use a listed equation, try to recreate the reasoning that could result in that equation.

As you look back at the equations for each of the problems in Table 9.1, you may have written some equations where the unknown quantity is not isolated on one side of the equal sign. For example, a likely equation for the join problem with start unknown is $\square + 4 = 12$. This is referred to as the *semantic* equation for the problem because the numbers are listed in the order that follows the sequence of the story problem. When the semantic form does not isolate the unknown on one side of the equation, an equivalent equation can be written for the same problem. In this case, for $\square + 4 = 12$, we can write the equivalent equation $12 - 4 = \square$ (see Figure 9.1). This is referred to as the *computational* form of the equation; it isolates the unknown and is typically how most older students and adults think about the problem. This may be an efficient way to solve the problem, but children typically begin to think about and model the situation based on the sequence played out in the problem, which is modeled more appropriately by the semantic equation—and this way of reasoning should be valued. When the semantic form is not also the computational form, help children see how these equations are equivalent and that there are several equivalent equations to represent a given situation. The structure of the equations also may cause difficulty for English language learners (ELLs), who may not initially have the flexibility in creating equivalent equations due to reading comprehension issues with the story situation.

The categories in Table 9.1 help children develop a schema to identify important information and to structure their thinking. In particular, researchers suggest that children (particularly those with disabilities) should be explicitly taught these underlying structures so that they can identify important characteristics of the situations and determine when to add or subtract (Fagnant & Vlassis, 2013; Fuchs, Fuchs, Prentice, Hamlett, Finelli, & Courey, 2004; Xin, Jitendra, & Deatline-Buchman, 2005). When children are exposed to new problems, the familiar characteristics will assist them in generalizing from similar problems on which they have practiced. Furthermore, teachers who are not aware of the variety of situations

Standards for Mathematical Practice

◀ **4 Model with mathematics.**

Figure 9.1

The semantic and computational equations for each of the six join and separate problems in Table 9.1(a) and (b). Notice that for the result-unknown problems, the semantic form is the same as the computational form.

Quantity Unknown	Join Problems	Separate Problems
Result Unknown	$8 + 4 = \square$	$12 - 4 = \square$
Change Unknown	$8 + \square = 12$ (semantic) $12 - 8 = \square$ (computational)	$12 - \square = 8$ (semantic) $12 - 8 = \square$ (computational)
Start Unknown	$\square + 4 = 12$ (semantic) $12 - 4 = \square$ (computational)	$\square - 4 = 8$ (semantic) $8 + 4 = \square$ (computational)

and corresponding structures may randomly offer problems to children without the proper sequencing to support their full grasp of the meaning of the operations. By knowing the logical structure of these problems, you will be able to help children interpret a variety of real-world contexts. More importantly, you will need to pose a variety of problem types with different structures (i.e., unknowns) as well as recognize which types and structures produce the greatest challenge for children—the topic of the next section.

Problem Difficulty

The structure of some problem types is more difficult than others. Problems in which a physical action is taking place, as in join and separate problems, are easier because children can model or act out the situation. However, even within these types of problems, some problems are more difficult than others. Consider each of the following three problems.

Maggie had 7 bracelets. She bought 8 more bracelets. How many bracelets does Maggie now have?

Maggie had 7 bracelets. She bought some more bracelets. She now has 15 bracelets. How many did Maggie buy?

Maggie had some bracelets. She bought 8 more bracelets. She now has 15 bracelets. How many bracelets did Maggie start with?

Stop and Reflect

Use a set of counters to model (solve) these problems as you think children in the primary grades might do. Rank order the problems in terms of which ones you think would be more difficult for children. Why do you think one problem might be more difficult than another?

The Join and Separate problems in which the start is unknown (e.g., Maggie had some bracelets) are often most difficult, probably because children attempting to model the problems directly do not know how many counters to put down to begin. Instead, they often use a trial-and-error approach to determine the unknown start amount (Carpenter, Fennema, Franke, Levi, & Empson, 2014). Problems in which the change amounts are unknown, like the second problem above, can also be difficult.

Part–part–whole problems can be difficult for children for two reasons: (1) There is no action to model because the situation describes a conceptual bringing together of quantities, which is difficult to directly model, and (2) it is a challenge for children to grasp that a quantity can represent two things at once. For example, if the problem describes 3 cars and 4 trucks in a parking lot and asks how many vehicles are in the lot, children have to understand that the cars and trucks are also part of the larger category of vehicles.

Compare problems are often challenging because the language used to compare the two quantities can be complex for children. Fewer, less than, more, bigger, and greater than are the terms typically used to describe the relationships in comparison problems. Children often have more experiences with the

Teaching Tip

Many children have difficulty with problems in which the start is unknown because they try to model the problem in chronological order and they cannot make the set that represents the beginning of the problem. Suggest that children use an index card with a question mark written on it to represent the unknown start amount.

relationships of more and greater than, so you need to ensure they have opportunities to think about relationships described using fewer and less than. Even so, some children misinterpret the language of "how many more" as meaning "to add" instead of "find the difference." Note that when the larger amount is unknown, stating the problem using the term *more* is easier for children because the relationships between the quantities and the operation more readily correspond to each other. In the smaller unknown situation, stating the problem using the term *fewer* is easier for children for the same reason. Similar to the part–part–whole problems, the lack of a physical action in these situations makes it difficult for children to model or act out these kinds of problems. In fact, many children will solve compare problems as part–part–whole problems without making separate sets of counters for the two amounts. The whole is used as the large amount, one part for the small amount and the second part for the difference.

Teaching Tip

If children struggle to make sense of the relationship between the quantities in a comparison problem, suggest they cover up the number that comes before the word more/fewer (e.g., George has ■ more pennies than Sandra; Sandra has ■ fewer pennies than George). This strategy temporarily removes the number which can be a distractor so they can determine which quantity is larger or smaller.

In most curricula in the United States, the overwhelming emphasis is on the easier join and separate problems with the result unknown. Consequently these become the de facto definitions of addition and subtraction: Addition is "put together" and subtraction is "take away." But these are not the only situations in which we use addition and subtraction, as you can see from Table 9.1. When children develop these limited put-together and take-away definitions for addition and subtraction, they often have difficulty later when addition or subtraction is called for but the structure of the problem is something other than put together or take away. It is important that children experience all the problem types and structures to ensure they are developing a broader understanding of addition and subtraction.

Take a look at this **video clip** of a diagnostic interview of a second-grader named Richard. Note that Richard struggles with both the addition and subtraction problems he is given. What surprised you in Richard's interview? How might this child struggle to solve problems in a whole class setting? What might be some next steps in Richard's instruction? Now let's look at ideas for supporting the teaching of addition and subtraction.

Teaching Addition and Subtraction

Combining the use of the story problem structures and models (counters, drawings, number lines, bar diagrams) is important in helping children construct a deep understanding of addition and subtraction. Building the understanding of these operations now will support children's understanding of these operations with larger numbers, fractions, and decimals later on. As you read this next section, note that addition and subtraction are taught at the same time.

Contextual Problems

There is more to think about than simply giving children problems to solve. In contrast with the rather straightforward and brief contextual problems in the previous section, consider the following problem, which a child has solved in Figure 9.2.

Yesterday we were measuring how tall we were. You remember that we used the connecting cubes to make a big train that was as long as we were when we were lying down. Dion and Rosa were wondering how many cubes long they would be together if they lie down head to foot. Dion had measured Rosa, and she was $49\frac{1}{2}$ cubes long. Rosa measured Dion, and he was 59 cubes long. Can we figure out how long they will be end to end?

Fosnot and Dolk (2001) point out that in story problems, children tend to focus on getting the answer. "Context problems, by contrast, are connected as closely as possible to children's

Figure 9.2

Student work shows a child's thinking as she calculates the total measurement of Rosa's and Dion's heights.

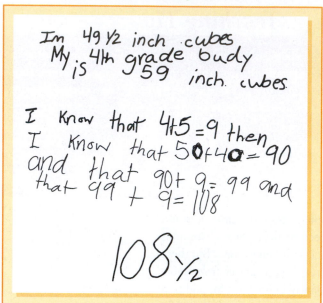

lives, rather than to 'school mathematics.' They are designed to anticipate and to develop children's mathematical modeling of the real world" (p. 24). Contextual problems might derive from recent experiences in the classroom; a field trip; a discussion in art, science, or social studies; or from children's literature. Because contextual problems connect to life experiences, they are important for ELLs, too, even though it may seem that the language presents a challenge to them. Some strategies to support comprehension of contextual problems include using a noun-verb word order, replacing terms such as "his/her" and "it" with a name, and removing unnecessary words. A visual aid, or having actual children model this story, would also be effective strategies for ELLs and children with disabilities. As an example, the preceding problem could be rewritten as:

Yesterday, we measured how long you were using cubes. Dion and Rosa asked how many cubes long they are when they lie down head to foot. Rosa was $49\frac{1}{2}$ cubes long, and Dion was 59 cubes long. How long are Rosa and Dion when lying head to foot?

Bedtime Math (Overdeck, 2013) is a series of books (with an accompanying website) that is the author's attempt to get parents to incorporate math problems into the nighttime (or daytime) routine. There are three levels of difficulty, starting with problems for "wee ones" (preK), "little kids" (K–2), and "big kids" (grade 2 and up). Each set of problems revolves around a high-interest topic such as roller coasters, foods, and animals. Teachers can use these problems in class for engaging children in interesting contextual problems.

Wording of Problems

Contextual and story problems that are worded so that the actions and quantities flow in a chronological or natural story order are generally easier than those in which the order is inverted. For example, in the following pair of story problems, the natural order of events in the second problem is easier for children to follow:

Mike's grandpa gave him some money for his birthday. Mike already had 6 dollars. Now Mike has 9 dollars. How much money did Mike's grandpa give him?

Mike had 6 dollars. His grandpa gave him some money for his birthday. Now he has 9 dollars. How much money did Mike's grandpa give him?

Join problems with the change unknown can be thought of in terms of "how much more is needed" or "how much was added." Some children find story problems with actions that happened in the past more difficult to process and so would find the first of the following two problems easier:

Joyce has 3 eggs in her basket. How many more eggs does she need to find to have 8 eggs?

Joyce has 3 eggs in her basket. She found some more eggs in the chicken coop. Now she has 8 eggs. How many more eggs did Joyce find in the chicken coop?

When you suspect that wording is the cause of children's difficulty, pose problems with *similar structure* but with wording in which the actions and quantities follow a chronological or natural story order. Children can gain confidence with the easier wording, but eventually they need to be challenged to make sense of the more difficult wording. Here are some strategies to help support children when they are challenged with more difficult wording:

- Ask children to talk about what is happening in the problem. (See the suggestions in the later section, "Analyzing Contextual Problems.")
- Have children use counters to act out the problem, explaining what the counters stand for and what is happening in the problem.
- Have children draw pictures that represent each of the quantities in the problem. Then have them describe the relationships between these quantities.

Choosing Numbers for Problems

The structure of the problem will change the challenge of the task, but you can also vary the challenge by the numbers you choose to use. If a child struggles with a problem, use smaller numbers to see if it is the size of the numbers causing the difficulty. You can also intensify the challenge by increasing the size of the numbers. In general, the numbers in the problems should be in accord with the children's number development. According to the *Common Core State Standards* (CCSSO, 2010), by the end of their respective school years, kindergartners should be able to count as many as 20 objects to answer "how many?" and solve addition and subtraction word problems to 10; first graders should add and subtract up to 20 and demonstrate fluency up to 10; and second graders should be able to add and subtract fluently up to 20 using mental strategies. Kindergartners are also expected to decompose numbers between 11 and 19 into tens and ones; first graders are learning about decomposing two-digit numbers up to 100; and second graders are learning about decomposing three-digit numbers up to 1000.

We can see that children in grades K–2 are learning about multidigit numbers and are beginning to understand how our base-ten system works. Rather than wait until children develop techniques for computing numbers, use word problems as an opportunity for them to learn about number and computation simultaneously. For example, a problem involving the combination of 30 and 42 has the potential to help first and second graders focus on sets of 10. As they decompose 42 into 40 and 2, it is not at all unreasonable to think that they will add 30 and 40 and then add 2 more. The structure of a word problem can strongly influence the type of strategy a child uses to solve a multidigit problem. This is especially true for children who have not been taught the standard algorithms for addition and subtraction. For example, consider the following problem.

A school of 28 fish was swimming together in the ocean. Another school of fish decided to join them, making a larger school of fish. The new larger school has 64 fish. How many fish were in the second school of fish that joined the first group of fish?

Because the preceding problem has a join action, this increases the probability that children will use a counting-on or an add-on approach to solve the problem. Using an open number line to support a more efficient strategy than simply counting on by ones, a child might reason as follows: Add 2 to 28 to reach 30, add 30 more to get to 60, add 4 more to reach 64. Then add 2 + 30 + 4 (the amounts added to 28 to reach 64). Another child might add 40 to 28 which equals 68 and then take off the 4 extra—4 back from 40 is 36. You can learn more about *invented strategies* for addition and subtraction in Chapter 12.

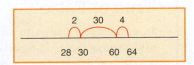

Introducing Symbolism

Preschool children initially have no need for the symbols $+$, $-$, and $=$ as they listen and respond orally to addition and subtraction situations. However, by kindergarten and first grade these symbolic conventions are required. To build up to this requirement, whenever young children are engaged in solving story problems, introduce symbols as a way to record what they did as they share their thinking during the discussion portion of a lesson. Say, "You had the number 12 in your problem and the number 8 was one of the parts of 12. You found out that the unknown part was 4 by removing 8. Here is a way we write that: $12 - 8 = 4$." Some children may describe a counting-up strategy to find the solution of 4, so it is important to also introduce the equivalent equation $8 + 4 = 12$. The minus sign should be read as "minus" or "subtract" but *not* as "take away" because not all subtraction situations are take away situations. The plus sign is easier because it is typically a substitute for "and."

◢ Activity 9.1

CCSS-M: 1.OA.A.1; 2.OA.A.1

Build It in Parts Equations

Recall Activity 8.23, called "Build It in Parts," and its variations in which children build sets or make designs to represent combinations for a particular number (e.g., 3 green hats and 2 blue hats equals 5 hats). In Activity 8.23, children are challenged to find different combinations for the same number. When children are ready for written symbolism, simply show them how to write an addition number sentence (equation) for each set or design. Initially with "Build It in Parts" children said a combination, such as "Four and five is the same as nine." Now they have a new symbolic way to represent and record what they say.

Some care should be taken with the equal sign. The equal sign is a relational symbol meaning "is the same as" and is not an operation symbol (such as $+$ and $-$). However, many children think of the equal sign as a symbol that signals that the "answer is coming up" or "it is time to do a computation." In fact, children often interpret the equal sign in much the same way as the $=$ key on a calculator: the key you press to get the answer. **This video (https://www.youtube.com/watch?v=eO3OQI9Jwts)** illustrates these misconceptions.

 Teaching Tip

When reading equations, avoid using phrases such as 2 + 2 "makes" 4 because the word "makes" sounds like an action or operation. Instead use the phrase "is the same as" in place of or together with "equals."

An equation such as $4 + 8 = 3 + 9$ has no "answer" and is still true because both sides represent the same quantity. As you record and read the equal sign in equations, use the phrase "is the same as" in place of or in conjunction with "equals." Use a variety of equations, such as $9 = 5 + 4$, $6 = 6$, and $3 + 5 = 4 + 4$, to help children understand the meaning of the equal sign. For example, if a child has described how she broke or decomposed 8 into 3 and 5, record that idea as $8 = 3 + 5$. The next activity helps to emphasize the meaning of the equal sign.

◢ Activity 9.2

CCSS-M: 1.OA.D.7

True or False?

To encourage children to examine their understanding of the equal sign, show a list of number sentences and ask whether each number sentence is true or false and how they know. The following are some examples: $7 = 3 + 4$; $3 + 6 = 6 + 3$; $2 + 6 = 4 + 4$; $3 = 10 - 7$; and $5 = 5$. Make sure to include some false number sentences such as $9 = 6 + 4$; $8 - 2 = 5$; $5 + 6 = 11 + 3$. Also pose problems such as $3 + 4 = \square + 5$ in which the task is for children to make a true number sentence. Encourage children to explain their reasoning.

Another approach is to think of the equal sign as a balance; whatever is on one side of the equation "balances" or equals the other side. This concept of the equal sign will support algebraic thinking in future grades if developed early (Knuth, Stephens, McNeil, & Alibali, 2006). (See Chapter 13 for a detailed look at ways to teach the equal sign as a balance and as "is the same as".)

Formative Assessment Note

Observing how children solve story problems will provide information about their understanding of number, strategies they are using to answer basic facts, and methods they are using for multidigit computation. Look beyond the answers they get on a worksheet. For example, a child who uses counters and counts each addend and then recounts the entire set for a join-result-unknown problem (this is called *count all*) needs to develop more sophisticated strategies. With more practice, they will count on from the first set. This strategy will be modified to count on from the larger set; that is, for 4 + 7, the child will begin with 7 and count on, even though 4 is the start amount in the problem. Eventually, children use facts retrieved from memory, and their use of counters fades completely when working with numbers within their comfort zone. Observations of children solving problems can inform what numbers to use in subsequent problems and what questions to ask that will focus children's attention on more efficient strategies.

Model-Based Problems for Addition and Subtraction

Many children will use models such as counters, diagrams, or number lines to solve story problems. These models are thinking tools that help them understand what is happening in the problem and help them keep track of the numbers and steps in solving the problem. Problems can also be posed using models when there is no context involved.

Standards for Mathematical Practice

5 **Use appropriate tools strategically.**

Addition

When the parts of a set are known, addition is used to name the whole in terms of the parts. This simple definition of addition serves both *action situations* (join and separate) and static or *no-action situations* (part–part–whole).

Each part–part–whole model shown in Figure 9.3 represents 5 + 3 = 8. Some of these are the result of a definite put together (i.e., add to) or joining action, and some are not. Notice that in every example, both of the parts are distinct, even after the parts are combined. For children to see a relationship between the two parts and the whole, the image of the 5 and 3 must be kept as two separate sets. In other words, the two parts should be in separate piles, on separate sections of a mat, or should be two different colors. This helps children reflect on the action after it has occurred: "These red chips are the ones I started with. Then I added these three blue chips, and now I have eight chips altogether."

The use of *bar diagrams* (also called *strip* or *tape diagrams*) as semiconcrete visual representations is a central fixture of both Japanese curriculum and what is known as *Singapore mathematics* and can be found in increasingly more classrooms

Figure 9.3

Part–part–whole models for 5 + 3 = 8 and 8 − 3 = 5.

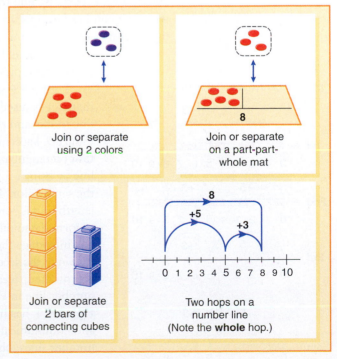

in the United States. As with other tools, these diagrams support children's mathematical thinking by generating "meaning-making space" (Murata, 2008, p. 399) and are a precursor to the use of number lines. Murata states, "Tape diagrams are designed to bring forward the relational meanings of the quantities in a problem by showing the connections in context" (p. 396).

Technology Note. You can find online bar diagram tools called *Thinking Blocks* at Math Playground's website and as a free app in the iTunes Store. *Thinking Blocks* can be used to help children model and solve contextual problems involving operations with whole numbers and fractions.

Activity 9.3

CCSS-M: K.OA.A.3; 1.OA.A.1; 1.OA.B.4

Guinea Pigs in Cages

Appropriate for the preK–1 child, use the book *Guinea Pigs Add Up* (Cuyler, 2010) to think about a growing and changing population of class pets—guinea pigs! There are many options for using this story, such as starting with two unknown addends: "How many ways can you place 10 guinea pigs in two cages?" Children can use the **Both Addends Unknown** Activity Page to record their ideas. Another idea is to use the book context for thinking of missing-part as subtraction. Use the **Guinea Pig Problem** Activity Page to pose questions to the children about the numbers of pigs in the cage, numbers adopted, and how many are left. Children can use the **Cage Mat** and the little **Guinea Pig Counters** Activity Pages to model the problem. Encourage children to pose their own questions and record the appropriate number sentences.

A *number line* is an essential model, but it can initially present conceptual difficulties for children below second grade and children with disabilities (National Research Council, 2009). This is partially due to children's difficulty in seeing the unit, which is a challenge when the number line appears as a continuous line. A number line is also a shift from counting a number of objects in a collection to counting length units. There are, however, ways to introduce and model number lines that support young learners as they learn to use this representation (see Figure 9.4).

Figure 9.4 shows an instructional sequence of four number line models that can be used to introduce children to the more commonly used number line model and then to the open number line model. The first number line in Figure 9.4 accentuates the spaces (or the units) between the numerals by using thin rectangular strips in alternating colors. Children can also build a number line by using a given length, such as a set of Cuisenaire rods or linking cubes of the same color. The rectangular strips, rods, and linking cubes show that each length unit is "one unit," and that same unit is repeated over and over (iterated) to form the number line (Dougherty, Flores, Louis, & Sophian, 2010). Eventually introduce the tick marks in between the accentuated spaces or intervals as shown in the second number line. Over time remove the rectangular strips that accentuate spaces and move to the more commonly seen number line, the third number line in Figure 9.4. The open number line, the fourth model shown in Figure 9.4, has been found to be an effective way for children to keep track of and communicate their reasoning (Fosnot & Dolk, 2001). Before using open number lines, children need to demonstrate the understanding that they are counting spaces as opposed to numbers or tick marks.

Figure 9.4

Instructional sequence of number lines.

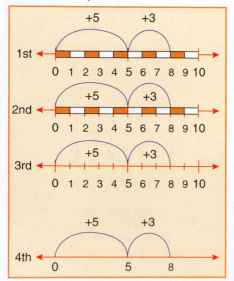

A number line measures distances from zero the same way a ruler does. If you don't emphasize the unit (length) when teaching how to use the number line, children may focus on the tick marks or numerals instead of the spaces (a misunderstanding that becomes apparent when their answers are consistently off by one). In each version of the number line model, use arrows (hops) for each number in an expression to illustrate the length concept more clearly (see Figure 9.4). To model the part–part–whole concept of 5 + 3 on any version of the number line, start by drawing an arc from 0 to 5, indicating, "This much is five." Do **not** point to the tick mark for 5 and say, "This is five." Then show the three hops, counting, "six seven, eight" (not "one, two, three") to demonstrate the counting-on model and reinforce the mental process.

The next activity provides opportunities for children to make sense of a number line.

Activity 9.4

CCSS-M: K.OA.A.2;
1.OA.A.1; 1.OA.A.2; 2.OA.A.1

Up and Down the Number Line

Create a large number line on the floor of your classroom, or display one in the front of the room. Make sure your line starts with a zero and has arrows at each end of the line. Use a stuffed animal, like a frog or rabbit, for hopping along the number line, or if using a large floor model of the number line, ask a child to walk on the number line. Pose a variety of problem situations and talk about the movement required for each. Start with a context that requires moving a distance, such as a frog hopping away from a lily pad or a baby rabbit hopping towards its mother, to emphasize the spaces (units of length) on the number line. This activity can help children create a mental image for thinking about the meaning of addition and subtraction.

Standards for Mathematical Practice

2 **Reason abstractly and quantitatively.**

Figure 9.5

Models for 9 − 4 as a missing-part problem.

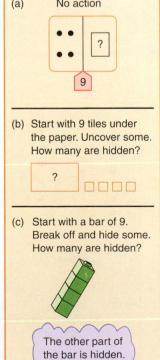

(a)   No action

(b) Start with 9 tiles under the paper. Uncover some. How many are hidden?

(c) Start with a bar of 9. Break off and hide some. How many are hidden?

The other part of the bar is hidden.

technology note

You can find a free interactive number line on the Houghton Mifflin eManipulatives website that emphasizes the length unit with animals (a frog, a rabbit, or a kangaroo) that hop along the number line. Each hop is marked with an arc and a length and you can change the length of the hops from one to ten. You can also change the direction of the hop so that the animal hops forward (addition) or backward (subtraction). The Math Learning Center website also offers an interactive number line that helps children model strategies for addition and subtraction.

Subtraction

In a part–part–whole model, when the whole and one of the parts are known, subtraction can be used to name the missing part (see Figure 9.5). If you start with a whole set of 8 and from that remove a set of 3, the two sets that you know are the sets of 8 and 3. The expression 8 − 3, read "eight minus three," names the set of five remaining. (Note that we did not say "take away.") Notice that the models in Figure 9.3 are models for subtraction as well as addition (except for the action). Helping children see that they are using the same models or pictures connects the two operations through their inverse relationship.

Activity 9.5

Missing-Part Subtraction

 Use a context or story about something that is hiding to introduce this activity. For example, the book *Five Little Monkeys Play Hide-and-Seek* (Christelow, 2004) and the "lift the flap" book *What's Hiding in There?* (Drescher, 2008) offer scenarios where various animals are hiding. Explain to the children that they will model the animals using a fixed number of tiles placed on a mat. One child separates the tiles into two parts while another covers his or her eyes. The first child covers one of the two parts with a sheet of paper or a large index card, revealing only the other part (see Figure 9.5(b)). The second child says the subtraction sentence. For example, "Nine minus four [the visible part] is five [the hidden part]." The hidden part can be revealed for the child to self-check. Have children record both the subtraction equation and the addition equation. ELLs may need sentence prompts such as "_____ minus _____ equals _____."

Subtraction as Think-Addition

Note that in Activities 9.3 and 9.5, the situations end with two distinct parts, even when there is a remove action. The removed part remains on the mat as a model for an addition equation to be written after writing the subtraction equation. A discussion of how these two equations can be written for the same situation is an important opportunity to connect the operations of addition and subtraction. This is more cognitively engaging than the traditional worksheet activity of "fact families" in which children are given a family of numbers, such as 3, 5, and 8, and are asked to write two addition equations and two subtraction equations. This often becomes a meaningless process of dropping the numbers into slots without much thought.

Thinking about subtraction as "think-addition" rather than "take-away" is significant for mastering subtraction facts. Because the tiles for the remaining or unknown part are left hidden under the cover in Activity 9.5, when children do such activities they are encouraged to think: "What goes with the part I see to make the whole?" For example, if the total or whole number of tiles is nine, and six tiles can be seen, the child is likely to think in terms of "6 and what amount add to 9?" or "What goes with 6 to equal 9?" The mental activity is "think-addition" instead of "count what's left." Later, when working on subtraction facts, a subtraction fact such as $9 - 6 = \square$ should trigger the same thought pattern: "6 and what equals 9?" Watch **Andrew** solve a missing-part problem by thinking "8 plus what equals 14?"

Comparison Models

Comparison situations involve two distinct sets or quantities and the difference between them. Several ways of modeling the difference relationship are shown in Figure 9.6. The same model can be used whether the difference or one of the two quantities is unknown.

Note that typically it is not immediately clear to children how to associate either the addition or subtraction operations with a comparison situation. From an adult vantage point, you can see that if you match part of the larger amount with the smaller amount, the large set can be thought of as the whole in a part–part–whole model that can help you solve the problem.

Figure 9.6

Models for the difference between 8 and 5.

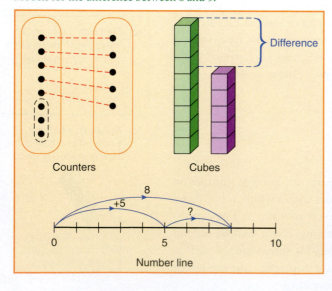

Counters

Cubes

Difference

Number line

In fact, children may model compare problems in just this manner. But it is a challenge for children to track on this idea if they do not construct the idea themselves.

The more obvious strategy is to have pairs of children show two amounts, perhaps with two bars of connecting cubes, of say, how many pencils are in each of their backpacks. Discuss the difference between the two bars to generate the third number. For example, if the children make a bar of 10 and a bar of 6, ask, "How many more do we need to match the bar of 10?" The unmatched cubes in the longer bar represent the difference of 4. Ask, "What equations can we make with these three numbers?" You can also have children make up story problems that involve the two amounts of 10 and 6. Discuss which equations go with the problems that are created.

Standards for Mathematical Practice

2 **Reason abstractly and quantitatively.**

Properties of Addition and Subtraction

Although the properties we discuss in this section are algebraic in nature (because they are generalized rules), they are discussed here because the meanings of the properties are essential to understanding how numbers can be added and subtracted. Explicit attention to these concepts, with the goal of building the terminology over time, will help children become more flexible and efficient in how they combine numbers.

The Commutative Property for Addition

The *commutative property* (sometimes known as the *order property*) for addition means that you can change the order of the addends and it does not change the answer. Although the commutative property may seem obvious to us (simply reverse the two piles of counters on the part–part–whole mat), it may not be obvious to children. Because this property is essential in problem solving (e.g., counting on from the larger number), mastering basic facts (if you know 3 + 9 you also know 9 + 3), and mental mathematics, there is value in spending time helping children construct the relationship (Baroody, Wilkins, & Tiilikainen, 2003). First graders do not need to be able to name the property as much as they need to understand and visualize it, know why it applies to addition and not subtraction, and apply it (CCSS 1.OA.B.3). But, as a caution, you should always name the property accurately and avoid using a "nickname" that will confuse the child (and subsequent teachers), such as calling it the "ring around the Rosie" property. Such arbitrary names are confusing as children progress. Use the precise terminology.

Standards for Mathematical Practice

6 **Attend to precision.**

Schifter (2001) describes children who discovered the commutative property while examining sums to ten. When the children were asked whether they thought it would always work many were unsure if it worked all of the time and were especially unsure about it working with large numbers. The point is that children may see and accept the commutative property for sums they've experienced but not be able to explain or even believe that this important property works for all addition combinations. Asking children to think about when properties do (and don't) apply is at the heart of mathematics, addressing numeration, reasoning, generalizing, and algebraic thinking.

To help children focus on the commutative property, pair problems that have the same addends but in different orders. Using different contexts for each problem can help children focus on the similarity in the problems (i.e., the same addends). For example:

Tania is on page 8 in her book. Tomorrow she hopes to read 6 more pages. What page will she be on if she reads that many pages?

The recycling bin in the cafeteria had 6 bottles in it. During lunch 8 more bottles were put in the bin. How many bottles were in the bin after lunch?

Ask if anyone can describe how these problems are alike. When done as a pair of problems, some children (not all) will see that having solved one they have essentially solved the other. Pose multiple problem pairs across time to help children learn from experience that the two addends can be added in either order without changing the answer. Note that some children will overgeneralize the commutative property to subtraction. Use contextual situations and story problems to help them confront this misconception.

The Associative Property for Addition

Standards for Mathematical Practice

8 **Look for and express regularity in repeated reasoning.** ▶

The *associative property* for addition states that when adding three or more numbers, it does not matter whether the first pair is added first or if you start with any other pair of addends. This knowledge is expected of first graders in the CCSS in Standard 1.OA.B.2 (CCSSO, 2010). This property allows a lot of flexibility so children can change how they group numbers to work with combinations they know. For example, knowing this property can help children identify "combinations of ten" from the numbers they are adding by mentally grouping numbers differently than just reading the expression from left to right.

    The following activity provides opportunities to explore the associative property for addition.

◢ Activity 9.6

CCSS-M: 1.OA.B.2

More Than Two Addends

 Give children six sums to find involving three or four addends. Prepare these on one page divided into six sections with space to write beneath each sum. Within each problem, include at least one pair of addends with a sum of 10 or perhaps a double: $4 + 7 + 6$, $5 + 9 + 9$, or $3 + 4 + 3 + 7$. Children should show how they added the numbers. For children with disabilities, you may need to initially support their decision making, suggesting that they look for a 10 or a double and have them underline or circle those numbers as a starting point.

Figure 9.7

Children show how they added.

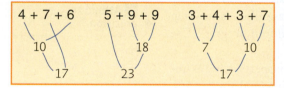

Figure 9.7 illustrates how children might show what they did. As they share their solutions, there will be some who added numbers together using different pairs and in a different order but got the same result. They used both the associative and the commutative properties here, but it is more important to highlight the commutative property because of its usefulness to mental strategies, mastering basic facts, and problem solving. This is also an excellent number sense activity because many children will find combinations of 10 in these sums or will use doubles. Learning to adjust strategies to fit the numbers is the beginning of the road to computational fluency.

The Zero Property for Addition

Story problems involving zero and using zeros in three-addend sums (e.g., $4 + 0 + 2$) are also good opportunities to help children understand zero as the identity element in addition or subtraction (see Table 3 in the CCSS Mathematics Glossary, p. 90). Occasionally children believe that $6 + 0$ must be more than 6 because "addition makes numbers bigger" or that $12 - 0$ must be 11 because "subtraction makes numbers smaller." Instead of making meaningless rules about adding and subtracting zero, create opportunities for discussing adding and subtracting zero using contextual situations.

Children's Strategies for Solving Addition and Subtraction Problems

PreK–1 grade children have little or no means of efficiently computing, so when faced with solving word problems, they often use counters or other models to help them figure out the solution based on the meaning in the story. Research in mathematics education describes three levels through which children progress as they make sense of and solve addition and subtraction situations. The levels are direct modeling, counting strategies, and derived facts (Carpenter, Fennema, Franke, Levi, & Empson, 2014; Clements & Sarama, 2007; NRC, 2009). Over time, after having multiple experiences with different addition and subtraction situations, children eventually become fluent with individual sums and differences and these become known facts to the children.

Let's consider how children might solve the following story problem depending on the level at which they are functioning.

Standards for Mathematical Practice

2 Reason abstractly and quantitatively.

Jacob has 5 cards. His brother gives him 8 more cards. How many cards does Jacob have now?

Children who use *direct modeling* to find a solution model every number and action described in the situation using actual objects, fingers, or drawings. So a child who is working at the direct modeling level would count out 5 blocks, then count out 8 more blocks, and then count them all to find 13—this is called a *count all* strategy. You can watch videos of two first graders using direct modeling: **Arlene (5 + 3)** and **Cheyenne (14 − 5)**.

A child who is using more efficient *counting strategies* does not need to model every number in the situation: the child will start at 8 and count up 5, holding up one finger for each number word from 9 up to 13—this is called a *counting on* strategy. You can watch **Andrew**, a first grader, use a counting on strategy to solve 5 + 3.

A child functioning at the *derived facts* level often looks for ways to decompose the numbers in a given situation to make an easier problem. This child may reason that because 8 is 2 away from 10, he can decompose 5 into 2 and 3, add the 2 to the 8 which equals 10, and then add 3 more which is 13—this is called *a Making 10* or an *Up Over 10* strategy. A child who is using derived facts may reason so quickly that it appears that the fact is a known fact. In this case, the distinction between derived and known facts is arbitrary. In these videos, **Cheyenne** and **Edgar** explain how they used derived facts.

 # Formative Assessment Note

The strategies that children use to solve problems provide you with important information concerning their number development, how they are reasoning to answer basic facts, and methods that they are using for multidigit computation. Therefore, it is essential that you look at more than the answers children get. These observations can give you insight into what numbers to use in problems for the next day, including any special number or computation development work needed for individual children.

For example, a child who counts out counters for each of two addends and then counts all of the counters again might be encouraged to count on by posing a problem involving adding a large number and a small one, such as 14 + 3. If you have been working on the meaning of the teens or other ideas about tens, you should pose problems that offer opportunities for children to use these ideas. For example, pose problems for 14 − 10 or 10 + 10 + 10 + 6. Then you can observe children's use of the ideas you have been working on. You can also pose problems involving number concepts or computations that you have not yet explored with your children. How they approach the problems will give you insight as to where that portion of your number instruction can best begin.

The point is to use story problems to assess more than problem solving. Number and computation skills are often much more clearly visible in children's work with story problems than on exercises devoid of a context.

Laying the Foundation for Multiplication and Division

The *Common Core State Standards* recommends that second graders work with equal groups of objects to build a foundation for the formal study of multiplication (CCSSO, 2010). Multiplication and division are often taught separately, with multiplication preceding division. It is important, however, to combine multiplication and division soon after multiplication has been introduced to help children see how these operations have an inverse relationship. In most curricula, these topics are first presented in grade 2 and then become a major focus of the third grade and beyond. When approached with a problem-solving perspective, kindergarten through second-grade children can be quite successful at solving contextual and story problems involving multiplication and division, even division with remainders, prior to being taught formal computational methods and the symbols used for multiplication and division (Carpenter, Fennema, Franke, Levi, & Empson, 2014; Schifter, Bastable, & Russell, 1999; Roberts, 2003). Young children engage in situations such as counting equal groups (multiplication) and fairly sharing or measuring out (division) in their daily lives. Capitalizing on these kinds of informal experiences can help lay a good foundation for more formal study of these operations in later grades. Multiplication and division problems also provide children with opportunities to work with the idea of groups, which helps with the development of place value and grouping in tens.

Multiplication and Division Problem Structures

Although there are structures for multiplication other than *equal groups* (also known as repeated addition) and *arrays* (CCSS includes arrays with area), we will focus on these particular structures because they relate well to the addition work in which children in grades preK–2 have been involved and are typically how multiplication and division are explored in the earlier grades.

Examples of the problem types for multiplication and division are shown in Table 9.2. Problems matching these structures can be modeled with sets of counters, number lines, or arrays. (The term multiplicative is used here to describe all problems that involve multiplication and division.) You can find more examples of these problem types in the *Common Core State Standards* (see Table 2 in the CCSSI Math Standards Glossary; CCSSO, 2010, p. 89).

Standards for Mathematical Practice

▸ **7** **Look for and make use of structure.**

Equal-Group Problems

Equal-group problems involve three quantities: the number of groups, the size of each group, and the total. These quantities are illustrated in the following problem:

Jill has 4 bags of crayons. There are 3 crayons in each bag. All together she has 12 crayons.

In a given problem, any of these three quantities can be unknown (see Table 9.2(a)). When the number and size of groups are known (total is unknown), the problem is a *multiplication* situation. When either the group size is unknown (How many in each group?) or the number of groups is unknown (How many groups?), the problem is a *division* situation. But note that these division situations are not alike. When the size of the groups is unknown but the number of groups is known, the problems are called *fair-sharing* or *partition* problems. The whole is shared or distributed among the known number of groups to determine the group size. When the number of groups is unknown but the size of the equal groups is known, the problems are called *measurement division* or sometimes

Table 9.2. Multiplication and division problem types.

Problem Type and Structure: Equal-Groups Problems	Whole Unknown (Multiplication)	Group Size Unknown (Partition Division)	Number of Groups Unknown (Measurement Division)
(a) Equal groups	Mark has 4 bags of apples. There are 6 apples in each bag. How many apples does Mark have altogether? $4 \times 6 = \square$	Mark has 24 apples. He wants to share them equally among his 4 friends. How many apples will each friend receive? $24 \div 4 = \square$	Mark has 24 apples. He put them into bags containing 6 apples each. How many bags did Mark use? $24 \div 6 = \square$
	If apples cost 7 cents each, how much did Jill have to pay for 5 apples? $5 \times 7 = \square$	Jill paid 35 cents for 5 apples. What was the cost of 1 apple? $35 \div 5 = \square$	Jill bought apples at 7 cents apiece. The total cost of her apples was 35 cents. How many apples did Jill buy? $35 \div 7 = \square$

Problem Type and Structure: Array Problems			
	Product Unknown	**Group Size Unknown**	**Number of Groups Unknown**
(b) Array	A carton has 3 rows of soup cans with 5 cans in each row. How many soup cans are there? $3 \times 5 = \square$	There are 15 soup cans placed in a carton in 3 equal rows. How many soup cans are in each row? $15 \div 3 = \square$	There are 15 soup cans placed in a carton in equal rows of 5 cans. How many rows are there? $15 \div 5 = \square$

repeated subtraction problems. The whole is "measured off" or repeatedly subtracted in groups of the given size. Watch this **video clip** where you will see a child demonstrating measurement division as he uses the known total and group size to find the number of groups (unknown).

For K–2 children, equal-group problems can be related to *repeated addition* problems: 4 equal groups of 3 or $3 + 3 + 3 + 3$. This is an important initial connection for young learners to make, as multiplication and repeated addition produce the same results for positive whole numbers.

There is also a subtle difference between problems that might be termed equal-group problems (e.g., If 3 children have 4 apples each, how many apples are there?) and those that might be termed *rate* problems (e.g., If there are 4 apples per child, how many apples would 3 children have?). Note that rate problems can be more difficult for younger children because they involve working with a composed unit (a rate, such as number of apples per child) rather than a number of countable objects. When the rate is something children can concretely model (number of apples per child as opposed to miles per hour), rate problems can be thought of in much the same way as the equal-group problems. You should consider posing such problems.

Array Problems

Arrays are initially considered in second grade in the CCSS as addition situations with equal groups. The array is a model for an equal-group situation (Table 9.2(b)). It is shown as a rectangular grouping, with one factor representing the number of rows and the other representing the number found in each row. CCSS groups arrays with area rather than with the equal-group problems because arrays can be thought of as a logical lead-in to the row-and-column structure of an area problem. Note that area problems are not introduced until third grade in the CCSS.

Teaching Multiplication and Division

A major conceptual hurdle in working with multiplicative structures is understanding that while a group contains multiple items these groups can also be seen as single entities (Blote, Lieffering, & Ouewhand, 2006). Children can solve the problem, "How many apples are in 4 baskets with 8 apples each?" without thinking multiplicatively simply by counting out four sets of eight counters and then counting all. To think multiplicatively about this problem requires children to conceptualize each group of eight as a single item to be counted four times. Experiences with making and counting equal groups, especially in contextual situations, are extremely useful in preparing children to develop multiplicative thinking.

Contextual Problems

As with addition and subtraction, there is more to think about than simply giving children word problems to solve. Use contexts based on children's experiences and ones that all children can access. For children who are beginning to talk about fractions, include partition problems in which items can be subdivided into fractional parts (brownies, pies, cups of milk, etc.). When a familiar context is used, children are more likely to demonstrate a spontaneous and meaningful approach to solve the problem because they are comfortable with it.

The tendency in the United States is to have children solve many problems in a single class period with a focus on getting the answers. But if you change the focus to sense making, solving only a few problems, strategically using tools such as physical materials, drawings, as well as equations, can be a better approach. Whatever children write on paper, they should explain it in enough detail for someone else to follow their thinking. Leave enough space on an activity sheet to encourage multiple strategies and explanations—leaving only a small space will prompt just an answer and nothing more.

Snack time is a familiar context that provides lots of opportunities for children to explore the notion of fair sharing or partition division as the next activity illustrates.

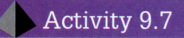

Activity 9.7

CCSS-M: K.CC.B.4; K.CC.B.5; K.CC.C.6; 1.OA.A.1; 2.OA.C.4

Snack Time Sharing

Read *Snack Attack* (Ruschak & Carter, 1990) as a lead-in to this activity. In pairs or small groups, children work with a bag of snacks, such as crackers or cookies, to determine how many each child in the group will get. Because the children will be handling the snacks, you can either use pictures of the snacks that have been cut out or have additional snacks on hand for children to eat after the activity. To differentiate, prepare baggies of different amounts of the snack and place children in different-sized groups. For example, give a bag of 12 cookies to a group of 3 children; a bag of 10 cookies to 3 children; a bag of 16 cookies to 4 children; or a bag of 15 cookies to 4 children. The scenarios depend on whether your children are ready for the challenge of dealing with leftovers. As children are engaged in this sharing activity, circulate and ask children to explain their reasoning. In particular, look for ways that children deal with leftovers as well as whether children distribute the snacks in amounts other than by ones. Capture their ideas on a note pad or an iPad to help them share their ideas in a discussion later.

Roberts (2003) described a teacher who used the children's book *Snack Attack* and a similar sharing activity with her kindergartners. The article describes the various strategies children used to fairly share their snack and how the teacher supported the children as they shared their strategies during discussion time. You can refer to the article for more ideas. *One Hundred Hungry Ants* (Pinczes, 1999) and *Remainder of One* (Pinczes, 2002) are two additional children's books that provide engaging contexts for children to explore multiplication and division.

Symbolism for Multiplication and Division

When children solve simple multiplication story problems before learning about multiplication symbolism, they will most likely begin by writing addition equations to represent what they did. In fact, the *Common Core State Standards* recommends that second graders begin to write equations to express the total as a sum of equal addends (CCSSO, 2010). If you feel your children are ready, introduce the multiplication sign and explain what the two factors mean. You can also write one sentence that expresses both concepts at once, for example, $9 + 9 + 9 + 9 = 4 \times 9$.

Standards for Mathematical Practice

6 Attend to precision.

In the United States, the usual convention is that 4×8 refers to four sets of eight, not eight sets of four. (In other countries such as Japan and Korea, the convention is that 4×8 refers to four taken eight times or eight sets of four.) In vertical form, usually the bottom factor indicates the number of sets or groups. These conventions allow us to communicate with each other more clearly about the problem and help build toward the commutative property of multiplication. However, with younger children, the more important idea is the informal explorations with multiplication and division situations and not the introduction of symbolism.

Related to communication about these operations is the use of the unfortunate phrase "goes into," as in "6 goes into 24," when referring to division. This phrase carries little meaning about division, especially in connection with a fair-sharing or partitioning context. The "goes into" terminology is simply ingrained in adults' speech; it has not been in textbooks for years. Instead of this phrase, use appropriate terminology with children, such as "How many groups of 6 are in 24?"

Choosing Numbers for Problems

An understanding of the idea of products or quotients is not affected by the size of the numbers involved as long as the numbers are within your children's grasp. Although a CCSS expectation for second graders is to work with arrays with up to 5 rows and up to 5 columns, a contextual problem involving 6 equal groups of 8 stickers or 24 grapes fairly shared with 3 people is not out of reach for second graders. When given the challenge of making sense of these contextual situations, children will invent computational strategies (e.g., two 8s or 16 three times) or they will model the problem with manipulatives (e.g., sharing 24 tiles among three friends).

More often than not, in real world situations, division does not result in a whole number. So even in the early grades, pose division story problems with remainders. Discuss the different ways that children think about dealing with remainders in a given context. Remainders can be handled in these ways:

1. The remainder is identified as simply left over.
2. The remainder is partitioned into fractional parts.
3. The remainder is discarded, leaving a smaller whole-number answer.
4. The remainder can "force" the answer to the next highest whole number.
5. The answer is rounded to the nearest whole number for an approximate result.

The following story problems illustrate all five possibilities for handling remainders. As can be seen in these examples, *partition division* story problems lend themselves more readily to fraction remainders (as opposed to *measurement division* story problems).

1. *Left over.* You have 10 pieces of candy to share fairly with 3 children. How many pieces of candy will each child receive? *Answer:* 3 pieces of candy and 1 left over.

2. *Partitioned as a fraction.* You have 9 brownies and you want to fairly share with 4 children. How many brownies will each child receive? *Answer:* 2 and one-fourth brownies.

3. *Discarded.* A rope is 15 feet long. How many 7-foot jump ropes can be made? *Answer:* 2 jump ropes.

4. *Forced to next whole number.* If 4 children can ride in each car, how many cars are needed to take to 23 children to the museum? *Answer:* 6 cars.

5. *Rounded, approximate result.* If 6 children are planning to share a bag of 50 pieces of bubble gum, about how many pieces will each child get? *Answer:* About 8 pieces for each child.

In making sense of their answers, children need to pay attention to the context. For example, in problem 4 above, answering *5 and three-fourths* cars does not make any sense. Addressing what to do with remainders, given the context, should be central to teaching about division.

Model-Based Problems for Multiplication and Division

In the beginning, children will be able to use the same models—sets, bar diagrams, and number lines—for all four operations. A model not often used for addition but extremely important and widely used for multiplication and division is the array. An *array* is any arrangement of objects in rows and columns, such as a rectangle of square tiles or blocks (see Blackline Master 16 called the **10 × 10 Multiplication Array** for an example of an array). Figure 9.8 shows a variety of models that are useful for multiplication and division. Note in Figure 9.8 that an addition sentence is written with the corresponding multiplication sentence to clearly connect the two operations.

Figure 9.8

Models for equal-group multiplication.

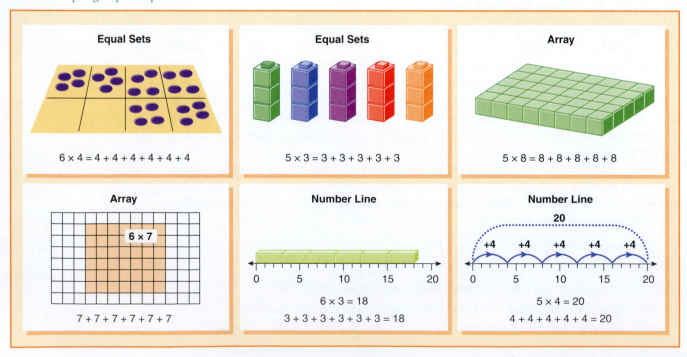

The *Common Core State Standards* recommend that second graders work with the array model with no more than five rows and five columns to lay the foundation for multiplication (CCSSO, 2010). However, even younger children can use the array model to begin to help them organize quantities and skip-count. Because you want to move children beyond counting by ones and encourage children's use of rows and columns as units, use small quantities arranged in arrays to play off their ability to *subitize* (quickly recognize the amount without counting).

Standards for Mathematical Practice

7 **Look for and make use of structure.**

Stop and Reflect

Compare the arrays in Figure 9.9. Children who need to count by ones can do so with any of the arrays, but which array subtly suggests skip counting?

Figure 9.9

Use arrays to help children construct multiplicative strategies. Which array subtly suggests skip counting?

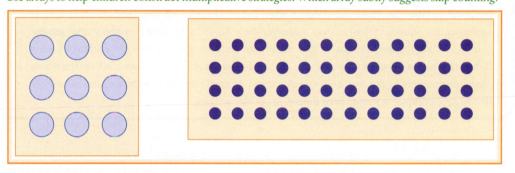

The following activity uses contexts and the idea of using small numbers of rows and columns to help children make sense of the array model as well as move beyond counting by ones.

Activity 9.8

CCSS-M: K.CC.B.5; 1.OA.C.5; 2.NBT.A.2; 2.OA.C.4

Quick! How Many Are There?

Find places where you live that organize items into arrays, such as a bakery or a grocery store. Take pictures of these items—for example, a tray of doughnuts or muffins, a box of oranges or apples. You can also find pictures online for this purpose. (Check out the website for the Harry & David stores as one possibility.) Show these pictures to your children and set up the task by telling them that the baker, grocer, or person making an online order needs their help to determine how many items are on the tray or in the box. Allow children to use a strategy that makes sense to them, which initially may be counting by ones. Look for children who use skip counting and have them share their strategy so that this idea is introduced to other children (make sure to emphasize the structure of the rows/columns). You can repeat this activity several times with different contexts and different pictures.

Even when using arrays that are arranged in quantities more likely to be subitized, some children may not be ready to move beyond counting by ones. Allow them to count by ones but continue to provide them opportunities to work with these kinds of arrays and to hear how other children are paying attention to the structure of the rows/columns and using small amounts to efficiently skip-count. Given time, these children will also begin to track on the structure of arrays and use equal groups to count more efficiently.

 **Teaching Tip**

The idea of organizing quantities into rows and columns might seem a bit arbitrary to children. So it is important to use contexts in which this arrangement seems natural (e.g., a muffin pan, doughnuts on a tray, fruit displayed at a grocery store, a checkers board, a parade formation).

Activity 9.9 has a good problem-solving spirit to help children explore the different meanings of division.

 Activity 9.9

CCSS-M: 2.OA.C.4

Divide and Conquer!

Using the context of a story about sharing, such as *Bean Thirteen* (McElligott, 2007), provide children with a supply of counters (beans) and a way to place them into small groups (small paper cups). Have children count out a number of counters to be the whole or total amount (e.g., start with 16) and record this number. Next specify either the number of equal groups to be made or the size of the groups: "Separate your counters into four equal-sized groups," or "Make as many groups of four as possible." Next, if ready for symbolism, have the children write the corresponding repeated addition and/or multiplication equation for what their materials show. For ELLs, be sure they know what *groups*, *equal-sized groups,* and *groups of four* mean. For children with disabilities, consider having them start with a partition approach (i.e., separate your counters into 2 groups), in which they share the counters by placing them one at a time into each cup. Explore the **Expanded Lesson: Divide and Conquer** for additional details about this activity.

In Activity 9.9, "Divide and Conquer," be sure to include both types of situations: number of equal groups unknown and size of groups unknown. Discuss with the class how these two situations are different, how each is related to multiplication, and how each can be written as repeated addition and multiplication equations. Do Activity 9.9 several times. Start with whole quantities that are multiples of the divisor (no remainders) but soon include situations with remainders. Note that it is technically incorrect to write the answer to a division problem, like 18 cookies shared equally with 4 people, as 4 R 2 because this is not a number (the answer should be a number). As written, the 2 is not well defined because it is really two-fourths. If your children have experience working with the resulting fractional parts, have them write or say the fractional part (e.g., two-fourths). Otherwise, in the beginning, the form 4 R 2 may be appropriate until children have experience with the given fractional parts.

"Divide and Conquer" can be varied by changing the model. Have children build arrays using square tiles or have them draw arrays on square grid paper. Present the exercises by specifying how many squares are to be in the array. Then specify the number of rows that should be made (partition) or the length of each row (measurement). How could children model remainders using drawings of arrays on grid paper? Explore the applet "Rectangle Division" on the National Library of Virtual Manipulatives website for an interactive illustration of division with remainders.

 ## Formative Assessment Note

A good way to check on children's understanding of the operations is to pose several story problems with different operations. Have them work on two or three problems a day over the course of a week. If your objective is to find out about their understanding of the operations, rather than having them actually do the computations, have them indicate what operation(s) they would use and with what numbers. To avoid guessing, you can have children draw a picture to explain why they chose the operation that they did. Alternatively, you can have the children come up with story problems to go with given models or equations.

Laying the Foundation for Multiplication Properties in Earlier Grades

As with addition and subtraction, there are some multiplicative properties that are useful and, although they will be highlighted in third grade and beyond, are still worthy of attention in the earlier grades. The emphasis should be on the ideas and not on the terminology, symbols, or definitions.

The Commutative Property of Multiplication

It is not intuitively obvious that 3×8 is the same as 8×3 or that, in general, the order of the numbers does not change the answer (*commutative property*). A picture of 3 groups of 8 objects cannot immediately be seen as 8 groups of 3 objects. Likewise, eight hops of 3 land at 24, but it is not clear that 3 hops of 8 will land at the same point.

The array, by contrast, is quite powerful in illustrating the order property, as shown in Figure 9.10. Children can draw or build arrays and use them to demonstrate why each array represents two equivalent totals (products).

The Role of Zero and One in Multiplication

Factors of zero and, to a lesser extent, 1 can be conceptually challenging for children. Make up story problems to help children reason about situations such as 0×5 or 3×0. Note that on a number line, 5 hops of 0 land at 0 (5×0). What would 0 hops of 5 be? Another fun activity is to try to model 6×0 or 0×8 with an array. (Try it!) Arrays for factors of one are also worth investigating with story problems or real-life situations providing a context. Avoid telling children rules. Instead, challenge children to articulate general statements about the role of zero and one in multiplication based on their experiences thinking about different contexts.

Children's Strategies for Solving Multiplication and Division Problems

As with addition and subtraction situations, children progress through different levels of strategies as they solve multiplication and division situations. Initially, they solve these kinds of problems by directly modeling the relationships and action described in the problems. In time children move from directly modeling to using counting strategies and then to using derived facts.

Let's consider how children who are using different levels of strategies might solve the following situation that involves repeated addition or multiplication:

There are 3 golf balls in a box. How many balls are in 6 boxes?

Figure 9.10

Two models to illustrate the commutative property for multiplication.

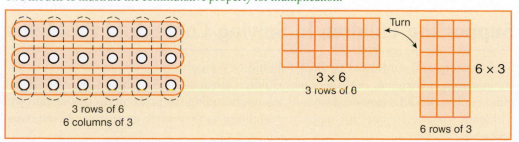

3 rows of 6
6 columns of 3

3 × 6
3 rows of 6

Turn

6 × 3

6 rows of 3

A child who is directly modeling would make 6 groups with 3 counters in each group and would count all the counters to find the answer. A child who has moved to using counting strategies might hold up a finger one at a time as she counts by three 6 times: 3, 6, 9, 12, 15, 18. Another child who is not as proficient at skip counting by threes may start skip counting and then revert to counting by ones: 3, 6, 9, 12, . . . 13, 14, 15, . . . 16, 17, 18. This child is still using a counting strategy. When a child is using derived facts, she uses known facts to find unknown facts. For this problem, a child might reason that because 3×5 equals 15, 3 more is 18.

For partition division, let's look at the following situation:

Arielle has 12 lollipops. She wants to share them equally among 4 of her friends. How many will each friend get?

When direct modeling, a child will count out 12 counters and then separate them into 4 groups, probably placing one counter in each of the 4 groups until all 12 counters are distributed. He would then count the counters in one of the groups to find the answer (how many will each friend get). You can watch a video of **Rosa**, a first grader, who uses a drawing to directly model a fair sharing or partition division problem. For a child who is using a counting strategy to solve this kind of division problem, the child will typically use trial and error to determine how many might be in each group because she is trying to mimic the action in the problem. So the child might first skip-count by twos, keeping track of the number of twos on her fingers: 2, 4, 6, 8. Because 4 twos is not enough, she tries another number, say, 3: 3, 6, 9, 12. When she reaches 12 with 4 fingers raised, she realizes each friend would get 3 lollipops. A child who uses derived facts may know 5×3 is 5 groups of 3 or 15, so 4 groups of 3 would be three less or 12.

For measurement division, consider this situation:

Parker has 24 cupcakes. He wants to store 6 cupcakes in each box. How many boxes will he need?

A child who is directly modeling will count out 24 counters and then repeatedly measure out groups of 6 counters until no more groups of 6 are possible. He will then count the number of groups to find the answer. For a child who is using a counting strategy, he will count by sixes, keeping track of each count, say, by extending a finger: 6, 12, 18, 24. Looking at 4 extended fingers, he knows Parker will need 4 boxes. Here is a video of **Connor**, a first grader, who attempts to use skip counting by fours to solve a measurement division problem. If a child is using derived facts, he may think 5×6 equals 30, but one less 6 would be 24—so, 4 boxes.

Supporting Children in Solving Contextual Problems

Solving story and contextual problems should be a significant part of your number and computation curriculum. But sometimes children are at a loss for what to do. Also, struggling readers or ELLs may need support in understanding the problem. In this section you will learn some techniques for supporting children as they work on story and contextual problems.

Standards for Mathematical Practice

1 Make sense of problems and persevere in solving them.

Analyzing Contextual Problems

Regardless of what grade you are teaching, it is important to always have children spend time thinking about a problem before they get started. For example, let's consider the following problem:

Luke is saving money to buy a new model boat that costs $33. Each week his dad agrees to put $6 in a savings account if Luke does chores around the house. Luke works about 2 hours each week on his chores. How many weeks will Luke have to work before he has enough money to buy the model boat?

At least two strategies can be taught that are very helpful in preparing to solve a problem: (1) think about the answer before solving the problem, and (2) work a simpler problem first.

Think about the Answer before Solving the Problem

Instead of rushing in to model the numbers or do calculations, children should spend some time thinking and talking about what the answer might look like. A great strategy for differentiation is to pose the problem with the numbers missing or covered up. This eliminates the rush to a solution. For our sample problem above, here are some questions that you might have the children think about and discuss:

- *What is happening in this problem?* Luke is working to save money to buy a boat.
- *Is there any extra information we don't need?* We don't need to know how many hours Luke works doing his chores each week.
- *What will the answer tell us?* The answer will tell us how many weeks Luke will have to work in order to have enough money. The answer will be some number of weeks.
- *Will the answer be a big number or a small number?* Well, each week he gets $6. If he works 10 weeks, he would have $60. He only needs $33. So it must be less than 10 weeks.
- *About how many weeks do you think he will have to work?* If he works 10 weeks, he would have $60. He only needs $33. So it is about half of that or 5 weeks.

With this type of discussion, three things are happening. First, children are focusing on the problem and the meaning of the answer instead of solely on numbers. The specific numbers are not important in thinking about the structure of the problem. Second, with the focus on the structure of the problem, children are able to identify the numbers that are important and those that are not. Third, the thinking leads to a rough estimate of the answer. Reflecting about the meaning of the answer and about how large it might be is a useful starting point and will help in judging the reasonableness of the answer when the problem is solved.

Work a Simpler Problem

When the numbers in a problem overwhelm a child, the general problem-solving strategy of "try a simpler problem" can help the child think about the solution process without dealing with the cognitive overload of larger numbers or complex relationships between the numbers. A simpler problem strategy has the following steps:

1. Substitute small whole numbers for all relevant numbers in the problem.
2. Model the problem (with counters, drawings, number lines, bar diagrams, or arrays) using the new numbers.
3. Describe in words how to use the model to solve the problem. (If appropriate for your children, write an equation that solves the simpler version of the problem.)

4. Using the description from #3, substitute the original numbers. (If using equations, write the corresponding equation, substituting the original numbers.)

5. Use the description and model (or equation) to find the answer.

6. Write the answer in a complete sentence, and decide whether it makes sense.

With younger children, initially it will be you who is identifying how to create a simpler problem (e.g., which smaller numbers or model to use). For example, you could suggest to a struggling child to substitute $10 for the cost of the boat and $2 for the amount Luke earns per week. With these new numbers, the answer will be a whole number. When the child can describe a correct strategy and solution with these numbers, have the child solve the problem using the numbers $11 and $2 per week. These new numbers are close to the ones in the problem just successfully solved by the child but introduce the fractional idea that is present in the original problem. Through this process, children are introduced to the strategies and tools they can use to analyze and approach a problem when they are struck. Again, the focus remains on using reasoning and sense making.

Caution: Avoid Relying on the Key Words Strategy!

It is often suggested that children should be taught to use "key words" in story problems to decide whether to add, subtract, multiply, or divide. For example, with the key words approach "altogether" and "in all" mean you should add and "left" and "fewer" indicate you should subtract. To some extent, the overly simple and formulaic story problems sometimes found in textbooks reinforce this approach (Sulentic-Dowell, Beal, & Capraro, 2006). When problems are written in this way, it may appear that the key word strategy is effective.

In contrast with this belief, researchers and mathematics educators have long cautioned against the strategy of key words (e.g., Clement & Bernhard, 2005; Sowder, 1988). Here are four arguments against relying on the key word approach.

Standards for Mathematical Practice

1 **Make sense of problems and persevere in solving them.**

1. The key word strategy sends a terribly wrong message about doing mathematics. The most important approach to solving any contextual problem is to analyze it and make sense of it using all the words. The key word approach encourages children to ignore the meaning and structure of the problem and look for an easy way out. Mathematics is about reasoning and making sense of situations. Sense-making strategies *always* work!

2. Key words are often misleading. Many times the key word or phrase in a problem suggests an operation that is incorrect. For example, consider this story problem:

Maxine gave 28 stickers she no longer wanted to Zandra. Now Maxine has 73 stickers *left*. How many stickers did Maxine have to begin with?

A child using the word "left" as a suggestion to subtract 73 − 28 will generate the incorrect answer of 45. Instead of making sense of the situation, the key word approach is used as a shortcut in making a decision about which operation to select.

3. Many problems have no key words. Especially when you get away from the overly simple problems found in primary textbooks, you will find that a large percentage of problems have no key words. A child who has been taught to rely on key words is then left with no strategy. In both the addition and the multiplication problems in

this chapter, you will find numerous examples of problems with no key words. Here's an example:

Aidan has 28 goldfish. Twelve are orange and the rest are yellow. How many goldfish are yellow?

---

4. Key words don't work with two-step problems or more advanced problems, so using key words for simpler problems sets children up for failure because they are not learning how to read for meaning.

Require Explanations

In the early years, solving story problems provides an excellent place to develop children's habit of providing explanations. For children in grades preK–2, explanations can range from verbal statements to drawings to written words. You may find that children who know their basic facts or have learned traditional methods of computing will write little more than the computations they used. It is important to make clear that you want explanations that use words, numbers, and drawings so that someone else can follow their reasoning and understand their solution.

The solutions shown in Figure 9.11 are from children aged 4 to 7. Laura, a beginning second grader, used separate equations to represent the amounts. Emma, who was just beginning first grade, chose to use a weekly calendar format to help her think about the problem and keep track of the amounts. Abby, a prekindergarten child, after hearing the story problem read twice, drew her circles using spacing to help organize her ideas. When asked how many eggs were found, she counted and got 15. She wrote the numeral 15 with help.

As children continue be asked to show their reasoning, they will improve both from practice and from seeing the methods used by others. In the examples in Figure 9.11, the children are showing how they solved the problem. To extend their explanations, you might ask questions such as, "Why do you think your answer is correct?" or "Why did you decide that addition (or whatever operation was used) was the right thing to do in this problem?"

Teaching Tip

Sometimes children can become so involved in drawing detailed realistic pictures of objects mentioned in problems that they lose sight of the mathematics (Crespo & Kyriakides, 2007). Engage in a discussion about what makes a good drawing in mathematics versus a good drawing for other purposes. In mathematics, drawings should be simple and only include information relevant to solving the problem.

Multistep Problems

Two-step word problems appear for the first time in the *Common Core State Standards* (CCSSO, 2010) when second-graders are expected to solve two-step addition and subtraction word problems (2.OA.A.1). You can watch **Connor** solve a multistep story problem using the computation $6 \times 2 - 5$. First, be sure children can analyze the structure of one-step problems in the way that we have discussed. The following ideas, adapted from Huinker (1994), are designed to help children see how two problems can be linked together to help think about multistep problems.

1. Give children a one-step problem and have them solve it. Before discussing the answer, have the children use the answer to the first problem to create a second problem. The

Figure 9.11

Three preK–2 children solve a complex problem using different types of drawings and explanations for their work.

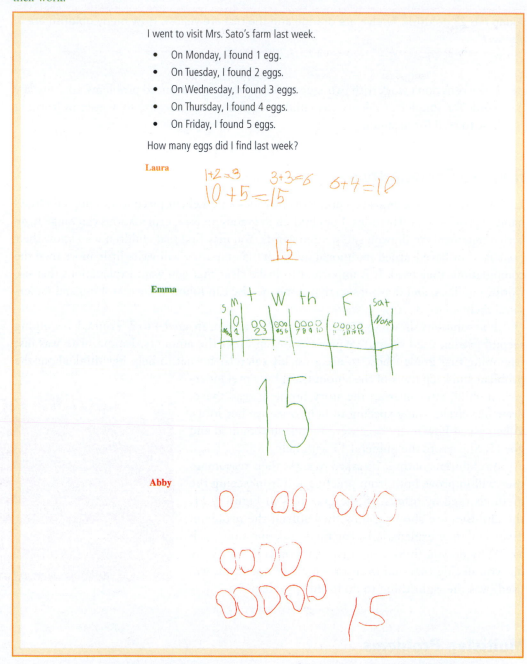

I went to visit Mrs. Sato's farm last week.

- On Monday, I found 1 egg.
- On Tuesday, I found 2 eggs.
- On Wednesday, I found 3 eggs.
- On Thursday, I found 4 eggs.
- On Friday, I found 5 eggs.

How many eggs did I find last week?

rest of the class can then be asked to solve one of these created problems, as in the following example:

Given problem: Ryan has 14 crayons and Nathan gives Ryan 11 crayons. Now how many crayons does Ryan have?

Second Problem: Some of Ryan's crayons are broken. If 20 of his crayons are not broken, how many crayons are broken?

2. Make a "hidden question." Repeat the approach above by giving groups different one-step problems. Have them solve the first problem and write a second problem. Then

they should write a single combined problem that leaves out the question from the first problem. The question in the given problem is the "hidden question," as in this example:

Given problem: Toby brought 24 cupcakes to school. Bree brought 18 cookies. How many sweets did they bring to school?

Second Problem: How many more sweets do they need to reach 50 sweets?

Hidden Question Problem: Toby brought 24 cupcakes to school. Bree brought 18 cookies. How many more sweets do they need to reach 50 sweets?

Have other groups identify the hidden question. Because all children are working on a similar task (be sure to mix the operations), they will be more likely to understand what is meant by a *hidden question*.

3. Pose standard two-step problems, and have the children identify and answer the hidden question. Consider this problem:

Rebekah hits a tennis ball against a wall 28 feet away. It hits the wall and bounces back 13 feet and then rolls another 6 feet towards her. How far from Rebekah does the ball stop?

Begin by considering the questions that were suggested earlier: "What's happening in this problem?" "What will the answer tell us?" These questions will get you started. If children are stuck, you can ask, "Is there a hidden question in this problem?" Although the examples given here provide a range of contexts, using the same (and familiar) context across this three-step process would reduce the linguistic demands for ELLs and therefore make the stories more comprehensible—and the mathematics more accessible.

 ## Formative Assessment Note

One of the best ways to assess knowledge of the meaning of the operations is to have children generate story problems for a given equation or result (Drake & Barlow, 2007; Whitin & Whitin, 2008). Use a diagnostic interview to see whether your children can flexibly think about an operation. Fold a sheet of paper into quarters or use the Translation Task based on the work of Shield and Swinson (1996). Give children an expression such as $15 - 7$; ask that they record and answer it in the upper-left-hand quarter, write a story problem representing the expression in the upper right quarter, draw a picture (or model) in the lower left section, and describe how they would tell a younger child how to solve this problem in the last section. (For a child with disabilities, the child could dictate the story problem and the description of the solving process while the teacher transcribes.) Children who can ably match scenarios, models, and explanations to the computation will demonstrate their understanding, whereas children who struggle will reveal areas of weakness. Adapt the assessment by giving children the result (e.g., "24 cents") and asking them to write an addition problem (or any other appropriate type of problem) that will generate the given answer, along with models and word problems written in the remaining quarters. Another option is to use the context from a piece of children's literature to create a word problem that emphasizes the meaning of one of the four operations; each child then has to complete the other three sections.

Final Thoughts: Outcomes Related to Teaching and Learning Operations

In a chapter about developing the meanings of operations, we have spent quite a bit of space emphasizing the use of story problems and contextual problems to achieve this goal. It is primarily through analyzing, making sense of, and solving story problems and contextual problems that children will gain a full understanding of which operation to use in any given situation. As children are engaged in this work they are also developing number skills and concepts that eventually will provide the foundations for mastery of basic facts. They also are developing computational fluency as they develop and master many different methods for computing. Place-value ideas will be enhanced and utilized as children find new and better ways to break numbers apart and combine them.

The hope is that we have made clear that there is much more to story problems than simply having children get answers. We want them to develop number skills and computational techniques as well as to have a rich understanding of the operations. To attend to these goals requires that we think carefully about the problems we pose. What operation structures do children need to work on? What numbers will challenge children but not overwhelm them? In other words, think of story problems and contextual situations as a means to an end rather than an end in themselves.

In helping children develop an understanding of operations, we also need to be aware of and look for common misconceptions that children develop along the way so that we can purposefully address these in a timely manner. Table 9.3 provides a list of common misconceptions related to operations and ways we can help children move beyond them.

Table 9.3. Common errors and misconceptions in operations and how to help.

Misconception/Error	What it Looks Like	How to Help
1. Child thinks that addition only means "join" or "put together" and subtraction only means "separate" or "take away"	Struggles to solve part–part–whole and compare problems. For example, the child consistently adds the two given numbers without regard to the numbers' relationship within the situation. When asked to write a story problem for $9 - 5 = \square$ can only write "separate"/"take away" problems. When reading a subtraction number sentence, such as $9 - 5 = \square$, reads it as "9 take away 5." Struggles with understanding how another child uses $12 - 8 = \square$ to solve the following part–part–whole problem: • George has 12 coins. Eight of his coins are pennies, and the rest are nickels. How many nickels does George have?	• Make sure to pose story problems and contextual problems that include all four problem types (join, separate, part–part–whole, compare) with the unknown quantity in different locations so children gain experience thinking about and solving a variety of situations. • Have available and encourage the use of physical materials for children to model story/contextual problems. Discuss what they have done to determine the answer. When children are ready for symbols, symbolically record what they have done. • Explicitly discuss and highlight situations where children used subtraction/addition but the situation was not "take away"/"put together." • Read the "−" sign as "minus" not "take away" and the "+" sign as "plus." • When children use equivalent equations to solve the same story problem ($\square + 4 = 12$ and $12 - 4 = \square$), ask children to discuss why this is possible.
2. Child treats the equal sign as an operator and as a signal to do a computation	For $5 + 4 = \underline{} + 3$, says the __ should be 9 because $5 + 4 = 9$. When asked if $6 = 6$, says no, because there is no computation to do. When asked if $7 = 3 + 4$, says no, because "you can't write it that way because there is no computation to do with 7."	• Use a balance to illustrate the relational meaning of the equal sign (see Chapter 13 for details) • Read the equal sign as "is the same as" and "equals" • Avoid saying $5 + 3$ "makes" 8 because the word "makes" sounds like an operation or that you have to do something. • Pose true/false number sentences like in Activity 9.2.

Table 9.3. Common errors and misconceptions in operations and how to help.

Misconception/Error	What it Looks Like	How to Help

3. Child overgeneralizes the commutative property of addition to subtraction	In solving 54 − 17, subtracts 4 − 7 as 7 − 4.
	
	When asked to think about what 3 − 8 could mean, child responds it is 5 because 8 − 3 equals 5.
		• Pose story problems, such as "separate" or "take away" situations that switch the two numbers. Have children model the problems with counters and compare the results. Examples:
		  • Katie has 7 cookies and gives 4 of them to her brother.
		  • Katie has 4 cookies and wants to give 7 cookies to her brother.

4. Child thinks that adding zero makes a number bigger and subtracting zero makes a number smaller	6 + 0 = 7 (because addition makes bigger) 12 − 0 = 11 (because subtraction makes smaller)	• Use story problems that introduce the idea of adding and subtracting zero in a meaningful context that children can act out. • Avoid offering meaningless rules or rhymes for children to memorize.
5. Child counts tick marks or numbers on the number line instead of the intervals between the numbers	When the child counts using a number line, the count is consistently off by 1. Points to the tick marks or numbers as they count.	• Use the sequence of number line models in Figure 9.4 to emphasize what is counted on a number line. • When using a number line in a class discussion, use physical hops and arrows to emphasize what is being counted. • Use e-manipulatives (like those described in the chapter) that use animals that hop along the number line to emphasize it is the space or interval that is counted. • Pose story problems that involve the action of hopping, such as hopping frogs or jumping bunnies.
6. Child treats factors of 0 and 1 as if the operation is addition/subtraction	Child responds as follows: 5 × 0 = 5 5 × 1 = 6	• Use story problems that introduce the idea of equal groups or number of groups of zero/one in a meaningful context that children can act out. • Avoid offering meaningless rules or rhymes for children to memorize.

7. Child interprets particular words to always mean specific operations (e.g., left means subtract; more means add)	Child solves story problems by using key words to decide which operation to use. For example, sees the word "more" in the following problem and adds the numbers given (8 + 13 = 21):
	
	  Josie has 13 puppies. Randy has 8 puppies. How many more puppies does Josie have?
	
	Child is stumped when faced with story problems that have no key words, such as:
	
	  Josie has 13 puppies. 8 of them are brown. The others are white. How many are white?
		• Do not teach key words to solve word problems.
		• Make sure to pose story problems and contextual problems that include all four problem types (join, separate, part–part–whole, compare) with the unknown quantity in different locations so children gain experience thinking about and solving a variety of situations.
		• Have available and encourage the use of physical materials for children to model story/contextual problems. Discuss what they have done to determine the answer. When children are ready for symbols, symbolically record what they have done.
		• Use the suggestions for analyzing contextual problems shared in the chapter to help those children who struggle with where to begin (e.g., think about the answer before solving the problem; solve a simpler problem).

10

Helping Children Develop Fluency with Basic Facts

BIG IDEAS

1 Children move through three phases in developing fluency with basic facts: counting, reasoning strategies, and mastery (Baroody, 2006). Instruction and assessment must help children move through these phases without rushing them.

2 Number relationships provide the foundation for strategies that help children to remember basic facts or figure out unknown facts from those already known. For example, knowing how numbers are related to 5 and 10 helps children master facts such as 3 + 5 (think of a ten-frame) and 8 + 6 (since 8 is 2 away from 10, take 2 from 6 to make 10 + 4 = 14).

3 When children are not fluent with the basic facts, they often need to drop back to earlier phases and revisit foundational ideas, such as number relationships. More drill is not the answer.

4 Helping children build a foundation for multiplication involves connecting their experiences with addition doubles and skip counting to the foundational multiplication facts of 2s and 5s.

Basic facts for addition are the number combinations in which both addends are less than 10. Subtraction facts correspond to the addition facts. Thus, 15 − 8 = 7 is a subtraction fact because both the corresponding addition parts are less than 10. The goal with basic facts is to develop fluency, which the *Common Core State Standards* (CCSSO, 2010) describe as being able to flexibly, accurately, efficiently, and appropriately solve problems. Plan your instruction and assessment for learning basic facts around these ideas.

According to the CCSS-M, second graders should be able to use mental strategies to fluently add and subtract within twenty, with the goal that by the end of second grade, they know their basic facts up to 20 from memory. It is critical that children know their basic facts well, but developing fluency does not start in second grade. If you teach in grades preK–1, this chapter is also for you because you have a very important role in helping children become fluent with their basic facts—aspects of number sense that are critical to developing fluency begin in prekindergarten and continue throughout the primary grades. The *Curriculum Focal Points*, (NCTM, 2006) recommend that children in preK should be able to compare quantities and use language such as "more than" and "less than." The *Common Core State Standards* (CCSSO, 2010) indicate that by the end of kindergarten children should be able to fluently add and subtract within five. First graders should be able to add and subtract within 20 using a variety of methods, but should be fluent within 10. When we consider these standards, clearly fluency with basic facts occurs over a long period of time.

K	1	2
Fluently add and subtract *within 5*	Fluently add and subtract *within 10*	Fluently add and subtract *within 20*

The Developmental Nature of Learning Basic Facts

Developing fluency with basic facts is an incremental process. It may surprise you to hear that flash cards and timed tests are not the best way to help children develop fluency. Instead, the key to teaching basic facts effectively is to focus on number sense and the development of reasoning strategies (Baroody, 2003; Fuson, 1992; Henry & Brown, 2008; Verschaffel, Greer, & De Corte, 2007).

Baroody (2006) describes three phases in the process of learning basic facts:

1. *Phase 1: Counting strategies.* Counts physical objects (e.g., manipulatives, fingers, tallies) or uses oral counting to find an answer. (Example: For 4 + 7, the child starts with 7 and counts on saying, "8, 9, 10, 11".)

2. *Phase 2: Reasoning strategies.* Uses basic facts and number relationships that they know to figure out an unknown fact. (Example: For 4 + 7, the child knows that 3 + 7 is 10, so 4 + 7 is one more or 11.)

3. *Phase 3: Mastery.* Generates an answer quickly and accurately. (Example: For 4 + 7, the child quickly responds, "11; I just know it.")

In any one classroom there will be children at all three phases. In fact, a child can be at different phases for different groups of facts. Table 10.1 outlines the ways children solve basic addition and subtraction problems as they move from counting to reasoning to mastery. You will see some ideas, such as the different counting strategies (phase 1), were discussed in Chapters 8 and 9. In this chapter, we will focus on reasoning strategies (phase 2) and moving children to mastery (phase 3).

Table 10.1. The developmental process for basic fact mastery for addition and subtraction.

	Addition	Subtraction
Counting	Direct modeling (counting objects and fingers) • Counting all • Counting on from first • Counting on from larger	Counting objects • Separating from • Separating to • Adding on
	Counting abstractly • Counting all • Counting on from first • Counting on from larger	Counting fingers • Counting down • Counting up
		Counting abstractly • Counting down • Counting up
Reasoning	Properties • $a + 0 = a$ • $a + 1 =$ next whole number • Commutative property	Properties • $a - 0 = a$ • $a - 1 =$ previous whole number
	Known-fact derivations (e.g., $5 + 6 = 5 + 5 + 1$; $7 + 6 = 7 + 7 - 1$)	Inverse/complement of known addition facts (e.g., $12 - 5$ is known because $5 + 7 = 12$)
	Redistributed derived facts (e.g., $7 + 5 = 7 + (3 + 2) = (7 + 3) + 2 = 10 + 2 = 12$)	Redistributed derived facts (e.g., $12 - 5 = (7 + 5) - 5 = 7 + (5 - 5) = 7$)
Retrieval	Retrieval from long-term memory	Retrieval from long term memory

Source: From *First-Grade Basic Facts: An investigation into teaching and learning of an accelerated, high-demand memorization standard* by Valerie J Henry and Richard S Brown. Published by National Council of Teachers of Mathematics, © 2008.

 Formative Assessment Note

How will you know when your children are ready to work on reasoning strategies? When they are able to (1) use counting-on strategies (start with the larger number and count up) and (2) decompose numbers (e.g., 6 as 5 + 1). Pose one-digit addition problems to children in a one-on-one setting and ask how they solved it. For example, for 3 + 8, do they count on from the larger? Do they see 5 + 6 as 5 + 5 + 1?

Different Approaches to Teaching Basic Facts

Three somewhat different approaches to teaching basic facts have been used in the United States. We briefly describe the pros and cons of each approach in this section.

Memorization

This approach moves from presenting concepts of addition and subtraction straight to memorization of facts, devoting no time to develop reasoning strategies (Baroody, Bajwa, & Eiland, 2009). With this approach, children have 100 separate addition facts for the various combinations of 0 through 9 to memorize. They may even have to memorize subtraction separately, bringing the total to over 200! There is strong evidence that this method simply does not work. Too many fourth and fifth graders have not developed fluency with their addition and subtraction facts and continue to count on their fingers. You may be tempted to say that you learned your facts in this manner, as did many other children. However, studies as long ago as

1935 found that many children independently develop a variety of strategies for learning basic facts despite the amount of isolated drill they may experience (Brownell & Chazal, 1935). You may have even independently found your own strategies for difficult basic facts.

Memorization does not encourage children to develop strategies that could help them master their basic facts. Baroody (2006) points out three limitations to learning basic facts this way.

- *Inefficiency*. There are too many facts to memorize in a rote fashion.
- *Inappropriate applications*. Children misapply the facts and don't check their work.
- *Inflexibility*. Children don't learn flexible strategies for finding sums and, therefore, continue to count by ones.

Notice how a memorization approach works against the development of *fluency* (i.e., being able to flexibly, accurately, efficiently, and appropriately solve problems).

When taught basic facts via memorization, many struggling learners and children with learning disabilities continue to use counting strategies because they have not had explicit instruction on reasoning strategies (e.g., Mazzocco, Devlin, & McKenney, 2008). In addition, drill can cause unnecessary anxiety and undermine children's interest and confidence in mathematics (Boaler, 2016).

Explicit Strategy Instruction

This approach to basic fact instruction involves explicitly teaching strategies that are applicable to a collection of facts. Children learn a strategy (e.g., combinations of 10) and then explore and practice the strategy (e.g., using a ten-frame to see which facts equal 10). There is strong evidence to indicate that such methods can be effective (e.g., Baroody, 1985; Bley & Thornton, 1995; Fuson, 1984, 1992). Many of the ideas developed and tested by these researchers are discussed in this chapter.

Explicit strategy instruction is intended to *support* children's thinking rather than to give them something new to memorize. Emphasizing memorization of a strategy and which facts work with that strategy is ineffective. This emphasis on memorization does not work for the same reasons that memorizing isolated facts does not work. In fact, children who memorize basic fact strategies wind up with less number sense in the long run (Henry & Brown, 2008). The key is to introduce strategies to children and then let them *choose* one that helps them find the answer without counting.

Guided Invention

Guided invention also emphasizes strategies but children generate the strategies based on their knowledge of number relationships (Gravemeijer & van Galen, 2003). For example, some children may think of 6 + 7 as "double 6 is 12 and one more is 13." Others in the same class may recognize that 7 is 3 away from 10, so they take 3 from 6 to add to 7 to equal 10, and then add the remaining 3 which equals 13. Still other children may take 5 from each addend to make 10 and then add the remaining 1 and 2 to equal 13. The crucial point is that children are using number combinations and relationships that make sense to them.

Gravemeijer and van Galen (2003) called this approach *guided invention* because not all children will independently develop many of the strategies that are efficient without some guidance. That is, you need to purposefully design tasks and problems that help children notice number relationships. For example, to elicit the Make 10 strategy using the 6 + 7 task, you might have children place counters in two ten-frames and then have them think of different ways to mentally move the counters to find the total.

Standards for Mathematical Practice

> **7** Look for and make use of structure.

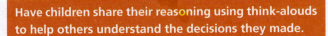

Teaching Tip

Have children share their reasoning using think-alouds to help others understand the decisions they made.

Teaching Basic Facts Effectively

Boaler (2015a) describes an important research study in which researchers found a striking difference between low and high achieving children: when given computational problems, the high achieving children used number sense and strategies to change the numbers into easier numbers to work with; low achieving children did not. Instead, the low achieving children used inefficient counting strategies (Gray & Tall, 1994). Boaler (2015b, 2016) describes similar findings from data collected through the Programme for International Student Assessment (PISA)—high achievers focused on reasoning and making connections between big ideas in math while low achievers focused on memorization.

To ensure that all children move away from inefficient counting strategies and become fluent with their basic facts, we need to commit to making reasoning strategies a central part of basic fact instruction. As you plan learning experiences to help children learn their basic facts, use the three phases described earlier to help guide your instruction. In particular, when discussing children's strategies, focus their attention on the methods that will help them move from one phase to the next. For example, when solving 7 + 4 some children will have used counting on (phase 1). Others will use the Making 10 strategy (7 + 3 is 10 and 1 more equals 11). Help children who are counting on to see the connections to Making 10. To move from phase 2 to recall, continue to provide engaging and diverse experiences where children are using and talking about their strategies. Through these varied experiences and discussions all children will become quicker and eventually will "just know" more and more facts.

Because the approaches of guided invention and teaching strategies explicitly emphasize reasoning and making connections, we focus on these two effective approaches for helping children move from counting to strategies to recall. For a guided invention approach we recommend using purposefully designed story problems to elicit particular strategies. To add to children's existing strategies, use the second approach, explicitly teach reasoning strategies. You will find a combination of these two approaches will serve your children well.

Use Purposefully Designed Story Problems

Research has found that when a strong emphasis is placed on solving problems, children not only become better problem solvers but also master more basic facts than children in a drill-oriented program (National Research Council, 2001). In fact, posing a story problem each day, followed by a brief discussion of the strategies that children used, can improve children's accuracy and efficiency with basic facts (Rathmell, Leutzinger, & Gabriele, 2000). Story problems provide context that can help children make sense of the situation and provide opportunities for children to explore a variety of strategies for doing computation.

A guided invention approach to teaching basic facts means that you purposefully design tasks and problems that help children notice number relationships. Story problems lend themselves well to this purpose because they can be structured to increase the likelihood that children will develop the target strategy. For example, if you want to try to elicit the Make 10 strategy from your children, you could pose the following story problem:

Standards for Mathematical Practice

> **1** Make sense of problems and persevere in solving them. ▶

Rachel sold 9 boxes of Girl Scout cookies on Friday and 6 boxes on Saturday. How many boxes did she sell?

How does this problem increase the likelihood that children will develop the Make 10 strategy?

The numbers and situation in this story lend themselves to thinking of $9 + 6$ as $10 + 5$ (one box of cookies could be moved from Saturday to Friday). By having children place 9 counters in one ten-frame and 6 counters in another ten-frame, the structure of the ten-frame may also help elicit the Make 10 strategy. Even if children do not use the strategy you were intending, have them explain the strategies they did use. You can always share the Make 10 strategy as one you have seen other children use and ask your children to try it with another story problem.

Some teachers are hesitant to use story problems with ELLs or children with disabilities because of the additional language or reading required. However, using story problems with all children is important because language supports understanding. Nonetheless, it is crucial that the contexts you use are relevant and understood by all the children.

Standards for Mathematical Practice

> **3** Construct viable arguments and critique the reasoning of others.

Explicitly Teach Reasoning Strategies

Explicitly teaching reasoning strategies helps children expand their own collection of strategies and will help them move away from counting to more efficient ways of recalling facts quickly and accurately. The key idea is for children to make use of *known relationships* and *known facts* to *derive* unknown facts. For example, children might use one of their Combinations of 10 strategies, like $7 + 3$, to solve an unknown fact, like $7 + 5$, noticing that $7 + 5 = 7 + 3 + 2$. Keep this key idea in mind as you review each of the reasoning strategies described in this chapter. Watch how **Connor**, **Myrna**, and **Miguel** use known facts to solve $6 + \underline{\quad} = 13$.

You can design a lesson to help children examine a specific collection of facts for which a particular type of strategy is appropriate. Discuss as a class how these facts are alike, or you might suggest a strategy and see if children are able to use it with similar facts.

Do not expect to introduce a strategy and have children understand and use the strategy after just one lesson or activity. Children need lots of opportunities to make the strategy their own. Make games and interactive activities part of daily work at school and home. Godfrey and Stone (2013) offer helpful tips on how to productively use game binders that children can take home. One of the most valuable points they make is the need to communicate with families about the importance of developing fact fluency through the development of strategies. Encourage families to play the games together and discuss the strategies they use.

> ♪ *Teaching Tip*
>
> Display reasoning strategies for children to reference. Give the strategies names that make sense so that children know when to apply them (e.g., Make 10, Doubles).

Encourage children to use particular strategies, but do not require them to do so—this is the opposite of what you are trying to accomplish as it takes the reasoning right out of strategy development. Instead, emphasize making good choices and justifying those choices.

Assessing Basic Facts Effectively

Chapter 3 illustrated many formative assessment strategies—observations, interviews, performance tasks, and writing—ways to help you figure out what children know and what they do not know so that we can design instruction accordingly. Yet assessment of basic facts is often limited to timed tests. We must do better if we are going to ensure that all children learn their basic facts.

What Is Wrong with Timed Tests?

First, timed tests do not assess the four elements of fluency (e.g., being able to flexibly, accurately, efficiently, and appropriately solve problems). Timed tests provide no insights into which strategies children are using, nor if they are flexible in using those strategies. From timed tests, you have a little insight into how efficient children might be overall, but you don't really know whether children have used very inefficient strategies for some facts while going quickly through others. So, at best, you can see which facts they are getting correct (accuracy). Second, timed tests negatively affect children's number sense and recall of facts (Boaler, 2012, 2014; Henry & Brown, 2008; Ramirez, Gunderson, Levine, & Beilock, 2013). Third, timed tests are not needed for children to master their facts (Kling, 2011), so they take up time that could be used for meaningful and more appealing learning experiences.

How Might I Assess Basic Fact Fluency?

One way to assess fact fluency is to use a hiding assessment with individual children to assess their knowledge of various number combinations (Godfrey & Stone, 2013; Richardson, 2002). In this assessment, the teacher has the child count out five cubes and then explains that she will hide some of the cubes. The child is to say how many she's hiding by looking at how many are left on the table. If the child can respond quickly and accurately (without counting), then the teacher increases the number of cubes, up to ten. When the child is no longer able to respond quickly with a noncounting strategy, this identifies the child's baseline or working number to focus on during instructional activities and games. Watch this video to see the **hiding assessment in action (https://www.youtube.com/watch?v=x_NsgRcjB88)**.

Thinking about each of the aspects of fluency is also a useful approach to assess. Ask yourself, "How can I determine if each of my children is able to do that particular aspect for this set of facts?" Table 10.2 offers a few ideas for each component of fluency (based on Kling & Bay-Williams, 2014). As you assess, keep in mind that there is no one "best" strategy for

Table 10.2. Effective strategies for assessing basic fact fluency.

Aspects of Fluency	Observation	Interview Probes	Writing (Journals or Tests)
Appropriate strategy selection	As they play a game, are they picking a strategy that makes sense for that fact? For example, for 9 + 2 they might count on, but not for 9 + 6.	Nicolas solved 6 + 8 by changing it in his mind to 4 + 10. What did he do? Is this a good strategy? Tell why or why not.	Review the addition facts table and write which facts are your "toughies." Next to each one, tell a strategy that you want to remember to use.
Flexibility	As for strategy selection, do they pick Making 10 for 9 + 6? Do they notice that 8 + 3 is also 3 + 8?	Solve 6 + 7 using one strategy. Now try solving it using a different strategy.	Explain how you think about these two problems: 13 − 3 = 12 − 9 =
Efficiency	How long does it take to select a strategy? Are they quick to use doubles? Does efficiency vary with certain facts, like facts over 10 (add)?	Go through this stack of cards and sort by the ones you just now and the ones you use a strategy.	Solve these [basic fact] problems (provide a set of 10). If you just knew the answer, circle it. If you used a strategy, write the strategy's name (e.g., Near-Doubles).
Accuracy	Which facts are they consistently getting correct?	What is the answer to 7 + 8? How do you know it is correct (how might you check it)?	Review your [3s facts] with your partner. Make a stack of the ones when you were correct and not correct. Record which facts you have "down pat" and which you are still learning.

any fact. For example, 7 + 8 could be solved using Making 10 or Near-Doubles. The more you emphasize choice, the more children will be able to find strategies that work for them, and that will lead to their own fact fluency.

Activity 10.1 is a good way to assess children's ability to select appropriate strategies for a fact and their flexibility in strategy use.

Activity 10.1

CCSS-M: 1.OA.C.6; 2.OA.B.2

If You Didn't Know

Pose the following task: If you did not know the answer to 8 + 5 (or any fact that you want children to think about), how could you figure it out without counting? Encourage children to come up with more than one way. To strengthen children's communication skills and increase confidence, especially that of ELLs and children with disabilities, have children share their ideas with a partner before sharing with the class.

The more children are engaged in activities and games, the more opportunities you have to observe and interview them to monitor which strategies and facts they know and don't know (games are discussed in the *Reinforcing Basic Fact Mastery* section of this chapter). As you gather this information, you can adapt the games and instruction to address their needs.

Reasoning Strategies for Addition Facts

Recall that basic fact mastery depends on progressing through three phases. The second phase, reasoning strategies, warrants significant attention; too often children are asked to go from counting (phase 1) to memorization (phase 3). Therefore, a significant part of this chapter is devoted to the reasoning strategies that are important to teach including how to teach them well. The reasoning strategies children can and will develop are directly related to one or more number relationships that were discussed in Chapter 8. In that chapter, numerous activities were suggested to help children develop these relationships. Now the teaching task is to help children connect these number relationships to the basic facts. In kindergarten and first grade, significant time should be devoted to decomposing and composing numbers and exploring number combinations (e.g., combinations that equal 5 and combinations that equal 10, respectively). In grade 2, children continue to develop reasoning strategies until they know their addition facts from memory. It takes many experiences over many months for children to move from using strategies to just knowing their facts. Note that no memorization is needed—just many activities like the ones shared here! The first four strategies described are foundational to the later strategies and so should be developed first.

One More Than and Two More Than

Each of the 36 facts highlighted in the accompanying chart has at least one addend of 1 or 2. These facts are a direct application of the one-more-than and two-more-than relationships described in Chapter 8. Consequently, children need to be able to count on before they are able to successfully use this strategy (Baroody et al., 2009).

Story problems in which one of the addends is a 1 or a 2 are easy to create. For example:

Six children were waiting in line for ice cream. Two more children got in line. How many children are waiting in line?

+	0	1	2	3	4	5	6	7	8	9
0		1	2							
1	1	2	3	4	5	6	7	8	9	10
2	2	3	4	5	6	7	8	9	10	11
3		4	5							
4		5	6							
5		6	7							
6		7	8							
7		8	9							
8		9	10							
9		10	11							

Ask different children to explain how they got 8 as the answer. Some will count on from 6. Some may still need to count 6 and 2 and then count all. Others will say they knew that 2 more than 6 is 8. To help children move from counting strategies to reasoning strategies, draw their attention to the connection between counting on and adding two using a number line, ten-frame, or arithmetic rack.

◀ Activity 10.2　CCSS-M: 1.OA.A.1; 1.OA.C.6; 2.OA.B.2

How Many Feet in the Bed?

 Read *How Many Feet in the Bed?* by Diane Johnston Hamm. On the second time through the book, when a new person gets in the bed, ask children how many *more* feet are in the bed. Have children record the equation (e.g., $4 + 2$) and tell how many feet in all. As family members get out of the bed, two less can be explored.

Find opportunities to make the connection between counting on and adding two using a number line, ten-frame, or arithmetic rack. For ELLs, clarify the meaning of *foot* (it is used here as a body part, not as a unit of measure) and be sure they know what the phrases "two more" and "two less" mean. You can further support ELLs and children with disabilities by acting out the story with children in the classroom.

The different responses you hear will provide you with a lot of information about children's number sense. As children are ready to use the two-more-than idea without counting all, they can begin to practice with activities such as the following.

Figure 10.1

One more and two more activities.

◀ Activity 10.3　CCSS-M: 1.OA.C.5; 1.OA.C.6; 2.OA.B.2

One More Than and Two More Than with Dice and Spinners

Label one die with +1, +2, +1, +2, "one more," and "two more." Label another die with the values 3, 4, 5, 6, 7, and 8 (or whatever values children need to practice). After each roll of the dice, children should say the complete fact: "Four and two is six." Alternatively, in place of the first die, use a spinner with "1 more" on one half and "2 more" on the other half (see Figure 10.1). For children with disabilities, you may want to start with a die that just has +1 and "one more" and then move to a +2 and "two more" die on another day. This will help emphasize and practice one approach. See the **Expanded Lesson: One-Two More/One-Two Less Than** where children use dot cards to connect the idea of more and less to adding and subtracting.

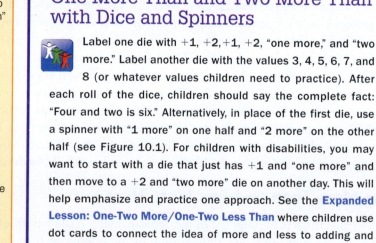

Adding Zero

Nineteen facts have zero as one of the addends (see chart). Although adding zero is generally easy, some children overgeneralize the idea that answers to addition problems are bigger than the addends. They also may find it more difficult when zero comes first (e.g.,

$0 + 6$). Use story problems involving zero and drawings that show two parts with one part empty.

The following activity provides children opportunities to generalize from a set of problems, which reinforces reasoning and gives you a chance to address any overgeneralizations.

+	0	1	2	3	4	5	6	7	8	9
0	0	1	2	3	4	5	6	7	8	9
1	1									
2	2									
3	3									
4	4									
5	5									
6	6									
7	7									
8	8									
9	9									

Activity 10.4

CCSS-M: 1.OA.C.5;
1.OA.B.3; 1.OA.C.6; 2.OA.B.2

What's Alike? Zero Facts

Write about 10 zero facts on the board, some with the zero first and some with the zero second. Discuss how the equations are alike. Ask children to create their own stories and to illustrate the problems. Alternatively, children can use counters and a part–part–whole mat to model the situations.

Standards for Mathematical Practice

◄ **8** Look for and express regularity in repeated reasoning.

Doubles

There are ten doubles facts from $0 + 0$ to $9 + 9$, as shown in the chart here. These facts can be anchors for other facts.

Many children find doubles easier to grasp than other facts. However, all children, and especially children with disabilities, can benefit from using and creating picture cards for each of the doubles as shown in Figure 10.2. Story problems can focus on pairs of like addends:

+	0	1	2	3	4	5	6	7	8	9
0	0									
1		2								
2			4							
3				6						
4					8					
5						10				
6							12			
7								14		
8									16	
9										18

Alex and Zack each found 7 seashells at the beach. How many seashells did they find together?

Figure 10.2

Double facts.

Activity 10.5

CCSS-M: 1.OA.C.5; 1.OA.C.6; 2.OA.B.2

Double Magic

Read *Two of Everything* (Hong, 1993), a Chinese folktale in which a couple (the Haktaks) find a magic pot that doubles everything that goes into it. Use the story as a context to create your own double machine using a plastic cauldron (easily purchased around Halloween) or any container for the magic pot. Make a set of cards with an "input number" on the front side and the double of the number on the reverse. The card is flipped front to back as it comes out of the pot. You can do this activity as a whole class, having children write the double on a personal whiteboard. Or have children work as partners taking turns with one showing the "input number" and the other stating the fact. Use the **Double Magic** Activity Page as a recording page for children. A double machine is a fun concept for children and provides good practice for thinking about doubles as well as algebraic thinking.

Activity 10.6

CCSS-M: 1.OA.C.6; 2.OA.B.2

Calculator Doubles

For this activity, children work in pairs with a calculator. The children enter the "double maker" (2 × _____) into the calculator. Then one child says a double—for example, "Seven plus seven." The other child presses 7 on the calculator, says what the double is, and then presses = to see the correct double (14) on the display. The children then switch roles. Remind them to reset the calculator before each turn by entering 2 × .
For ELLs who are just learning English, invite them to say the double in their native language or in both their native language and English. (Note that the calculator is also a good way to practice +1 and +2 facts.)

Combinations of 10

Perhaps the most important strategy for children to know is the combinations that equal 10. Combinations of 10 are foundational facts from which children can derive many facts. In fact, when children master two types of facts—the Doubles and the Combinations of 10—they can then use those to derive most of the other challenging basic facts (Kling, 2011).

Use story problems such as the following to provide children opportunities to develop the Combinations of 10 strategy.

Standards for Mathematical Practice

> **4 Model with mathematics.** ▶

There are ten boys and girls on the playground. How many girls and how many boys might be on the playground?

The ten-frame and the arithmetic rack are useful tools for creating visual images of the number relationships. The next activity, which incorporates the ten-frame, is a good way to introduce the Combinations of 10 strategy.

Activity 10.7

CCSS-M: 1.OA.B.4; 1.OA.C.6; 2.OA.B.2

How Many More to Equal 10?

Place counters on a ten-frame and ask, "How many more to equal 10?" (See Figure 10.3.) This activity can be repeated using different starting numbers. Eventually, show an empty ten-frame and say a number less than 10. Children start with that number and complete the "10 fact." If you say, "four," they say, "four plus six is ten." This activity can be completed as a whole class or in pairs. Children who are still in phase 1 of learning the facts (using counting strategies) or children with disabilities may need one-on-one support to help them focus their attention on how the structure of the ten-frame (e.g., groups of 5, empty places within the 5) can help them move away from counting by ones.

Standards for Mathematical Practice

7 Look for and make use of structure.

There are several children's books whose storylines lend themselves to finding the combinations that make ten. *Anno's Counting House* (Anno, 1982), an older book for which used copies can be found online, tells the story of ten children who move one by one from their old house to a new house. The context suggests a systematic way to think about the changing combinations, which can help children verify that they have found all the possible combinations of ten. *There Were Ten in the Bed* (Kubler, 2001) is another book that can be used to spur children to think about the Combinations of 10. The book is based on the nursery song with the chorus, "roll over, roll over." Ten children start in the bed and as one child says "roll over, roll over," they all roll over and one of the children falls out of the bed. This pattern continues until only one child is left in the bed. All the combinations of 10, except 0 + 10 and 10 + 0, can be systematically found by following the storyline.

Figure 10.3

Combinations of 10 on a ten-frame.

6 and 4 is 10.

Making 10

All of the basic facts with sums greater than 10 can be solved using the Making 10 strategy (about a third of the facts). With this strategy, children use their known facts that equal 10 and then add the rest of the number onto 10. For example, to solve 6 + 8, children may recognize that 8 is 2 from 10; so they take 2 from the 6 and add the 2 to 8 to equal 10 and then add on the remaining 4 to equal 14. When trying to encourage children to come up with this strategy on their own, pose problems that have at least one addend of 8 or 9. Making 10 is also called Break Apart to Make Ten, or BAMT (Sarama & Clements, 2009) and Up Over Ten.

This reasoning strategy is greatly emphasized in high-performing countries (e.g., Korea, China, Taiwan, and Japan) where children learn facts sooner and more accurately than children in the United States (Henry & Brown, 2008). A study of California first graders found that this strategy contributed more to developing fluency than using doubles (even though using doubles had been emphasized by teachers and textbooks in the study) (Henry & Brown, 2008).

The Making 10 strategy can also be applied to adding larger numbers. For example, when adding 28 + 7, a child can take 2 from 7 and add it to 28 to equal 30 and then add 5 more, which is 35. This strategy can even be extended to make 100. Thus, this reasoning strategy deserves significant time and attention when teaching basic addition (and subtraction) facts.

Activity 10.8

CCSS-M: 1.OA.B.3; 1.OA.C.6; 2.OA.B.2

Move It, Move It

This activity is designed to elicit the Making 10 strategy. Give children a mat with a **Double Ten-Frame** (Blackline Master 15). Flash cards are placed next to the ten-frames, or a fact can be given orally. Children place counters in each frame to represent the problem (e.g., for 9 + 6, children would cover nine places on one frame and six on the other). Then children are to decide how to "move it"— how to move the counters so that they can find the total without counting. Ask children to explain what they did and connect their ideas to the new equation. For example, 9 + 6 may become 10 + 5 by moving one counter to the first ten-frame. Highlight strategies that are working for children (e.g., 5 as an Anchor, Combinations of 10, Making 10). Provide children the Activity Page for **Move It, Move It** as a way to record their ideas.

Activity 10.9

CCSS-M:1.OA.B.3; 1.OA.C.6; 2.OA.B.2

Frames and Facts

Make **Little Ten-Frame** cards and display an 8 (or 9) card on a projector. Place other cards beneath it one at a time and ask children to respond with the total. Have children explain what they are doing. For 8 + 4, they might say, "Take 2 from the 4 and put it with 8 to equal 10. Then 10 and 2 left over is 12." Move to more difficult cards, like 7 + 6. Have children record each equation as shown in Figure 10.4. Look for opportunities to highlight that filling in the little ten-frame starting with the larger number is a faster approach. As a counterexample, show and discuss how it is more challenging to start with the smaller number. The activity can also be done independently with the little ten-frame cards.

Figure 10.4

Frames and facts activity.

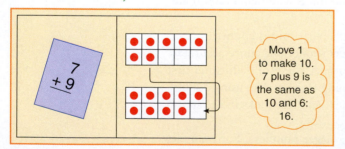

Note that children may have many other ways of using 10 to add with 8 or 9. For example, with the fact 9 + 5, some will add 10 + 5 and then subtract 1. This is a perfectly good strategy that uses 10.

Using 5 as an Anchor

Using an anchor (5 or 10) is a reasoning strategy that builds on children's knowledge of number relationships and so is a great way to reinforce number sense and learn the basic facts. Using 5 as an anchor means looking for fives in the numbers in the problem and building from those to determine the sum. For example, in 7 + 6, a child may think of 7 as 5 + 2 and 6 as 5 + 1. The child would add 5 + 5 and then the extra 2 from the 7 and the extra 1 from 6, adding up to 13.

The five- and ten-frames and the arithmetic rack discussed in Chapter 8 can help children visualize numbers as 5 and some more. The following activity extends the use of these visual models to support children's reasoning strategies for addition.

Activity 10.10

CCSS-M:1.OA.B.3;
1.OA.C.5; 1.OA.C.6; 2.OA.B.2

Flash

Project a **Double Ten-Frame** (Blackline Master 15) on the board. Without letting children see, place counters on each ten-frame so that the top row is full (five counters) and the extras are in the bottom row. Flash (uncover) the Double Ten-frame for about 3 to 5 seconds and then recover. Ask children how many counters they saw. Accept all answers. Again quickly uncover and then cover the ten-frames and ask if anyone wants to change their answer. Finally, uncover the ten-frames and have children explain how they saw the counters. Alternatively, you can use two of the **Little Ten-Frames** or two arithmetic racks. You can also have children do this activity with partners.

Near-Doubles

Near-doubles are also called the "doubles-plus-one" or "double-minus-one" facts and include all combinations in which one addend is one more or one less than the other. This strategy uses a known fact to derive an unknown fact. The strategy is to double the smaller number and add 1 or double the larger number and subtract 1. Therefore, children must know their doubles before they can work on this strategy.

To introduce Near-Doubles, write a doubles fact and a near-doubles fact right under it, as illustrated here.

$$5 + 5$$
$$5 + 6$$

Ask children how the first fact might help them find the second fact. Activity 10.11 elaborates this idea.

 Activity 10.11   CCSS-M: 1.OA.B.3; 1.OA.C.6; 2.OA.B.2

On the Double!

Create a display (on a board or on paper) that shows doubles and prepare cards with near-doubles (e.g., 4 + 5) (see Figure 10.5). Ask children to find the doubles fact that could help them solve the fact on the card and place the card on that spot. Ask children if there are other doubles that could help as well.

Figure 10.5

Near-double facts activity.

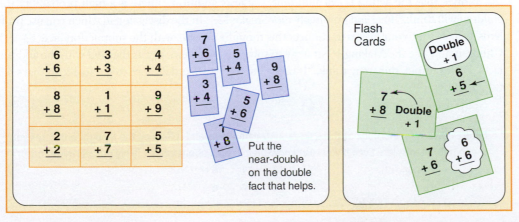

Near-doubles are more difficult for children to recognize and, therefore, may not be a strategy that all children find useful. In that case, do not force it.

Reasoning Strategies for Subtraction Facts

Subtraction facts prove to be more difficult than addition. This is especially true when children have been taught subtraction through a "count-count-count" approach; for $13 - 5$, *count* 13, *count* off 5, *count* what's left. Remember that counting is the first phase in reaching basic fact mastery. The goal is to move children beyond counting strategies to ensure they master their basic facts.

Table 10.1 at the beginning of this chapter lists the ways children might subtract as they move from counting to reasoning to mastery. Without opportunities to learn and use reasoning strategies, children continue to rely on counting strategies for subtraction facts, which can be slow and too often result in inaccurate answers. Spending sufficient time on the following reasoning strategies can help children move to phase 2 and eventually on to mastery (phase 3). You can also help children build stronger connections between addition and subtraction by posing more join and separate story problems with start and change unknowns as well as more part-part-whole and comparison story problems (see Chapter 9).

Think-Addition

As the label implies, in this strategy children use known addition facts to produce the unknown quantity or part (see Figure 10.6). If this important relationship between parts and wholes—between addition and subtraction—can be made, subtraction facts will be much easier for children to learn. As with addition facts, it is helpful to begin with facts that have totals of 10 or less (e.g., $8 - 3$, $9 - 7$) before working on facts that have a total higher than 10 (e.g., $13 - 4$).

The value of think-addition cannot be overstated. However, if children are to effectively use the think-addition strategy, they first must master the basic addition facts. Evidence suggests that children learn very few, if any, subtraction facts without first mastering the corresponding addition facts. So, for example, mastery of $3 + 5$ is prerequisite knowledge for learning the facts $8 - 3$ and $8 - 5$.

Story problems that promote think-addition are those that sound like addition but have a missing addend: *join, start unknown; join, change unknown;* and *part–part–whole, part unknown* (see Chapter 9). Consider this problem:

Janice had 5 fish in her aquarium. Grandma gave her some more fish. Then she had 12 fish. How many fish did Grandma give Janice?

Notice that the action is *join* and, thus, suggests addition. There is a high probability that children will think, "Five and how many more make 12?" In the discussion in which you use problems such as this, your task is to connect this thought process with the subtraction fact, $12 - 5$. Children may use the Making 10 strategy to solve this problem, just as they did with the addition facts. For example, they may think, "It takes 5 to get to 10 and 2 more to get to 12, so that's 7."

Figure 10.6

Using a think-addition model for subtraction facts.

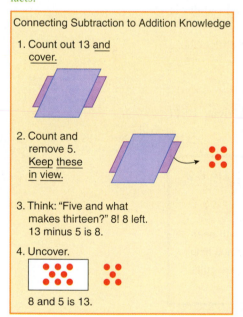

Connecting Subtraction to Addition Knowledge

1. Count out 13 <u>and</u> cover.

2. Count and remove 5. Keep <u>these</u> in <u>view</u>.

3. Think: "Five and what makes thirteen?" 8! 8 left. 13 minus 5 is 8.

4. Uncover.

8 and 5 is 13.

Stop and Reflect

Before reading further, look at these three subtraction facts and reflect on the thought processes you use to get the answers. Even if you "just know them" think about what a likely process might be.

$$14 \qquad 13 \qquad 15$$
$$\underline{-9} \qquad \underline{-7} \qquad \underline{-6}$$

Down Under 10

There are two ways to think about Down Under 10. The first is to think about it as a "separate" situation. For 14 − 8, first take away 4 from 14 to equal 10, then take away 4 more, which is 6. Another way to think about this is as a "comparison" or "finding the difference or distance" between the two numbers. In other words, how far apart are 14 and 8? From 14, jump down 4 to the 10 and 2 more to the 8—they are 6 apart. These two interpretations are illustrated in Figure 10.7.

Down Under 10 is a derived fact strategy because children use what they know (that 14 minus 10 is 4) to derive a related fact (14 − 8). Like the Combinations of 10 and Making 10 strategies discussed previously, this strategy is emphasized in high-performing countries but not emphasized enough in the United States (Fuson & Kwon, 1992).

One way to develop the Down Under 10 strategy is to give children pairs of facts in which the difference for the first fact is 10 and the second fact is either 8 or 9 (e.g., 16 − 6 and 16 − 7; 14 − 4 and 14 − 6). Have children solve each pair of problems and discuss their strategies. If children do not naturally

Figure 10.7

Down Under 10 illustrated on the number line for 14 − 8.

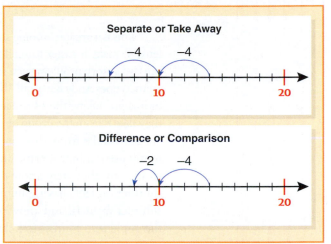

Bekah had 15 bracelets. She gave 6 to a friend. How many does Bekah have left? (Separate)

Bekah rode her bike for 15 minutes. Fabi rode her bike for 9 minutes. How many more minutes did Bekah ride than Fabi? (Comparison)

Activity 10.12

CCSS-M:1.OA.B.4; 1.OA.C.6; 2.OA.B.2

Apples in a Tree

 Display a **Double Ten-Frame** (Blackline Master 15) with chips covering the first ten-frame and some of the second (e.g., for 16, cover 10 in the first frame and 6 on the second frame). Tell children these chips represent apples that were in a tree but that some apples have fallen to the ground—you will tell them how many have fallen and they will tell you how many are still in the tree. Ask children to explain their thinking. Repeat this activity multiple times with different amounts of apples. For ELLs or culturally diverse children, you can change to a context that is familiar.

see the relationship, ask them to think about how the first fact can help them solve the second. Use a number line to illustrate the reasoning used. You can also pose story problems such as the following to elicit the Down Under 10 strategy:

You can also use children's literature to offer contexts to work on reasoning strategies. For example, *One Less Fish* (Toft & Sheather, 1998) is a beautiful book with an important environmental message that starts with 12 fish and counts back to zero fish. On a page with 8 fish, ask, "How many fish are gone?" and "How did you figure it out?" Encourage children to use the Down Under 10 strategy. Any counting-up or counting-back book can be used in this way!

Take from 10

This strategy capitalizes on children's knowledge of the combinations that make 10 and decomposing the initial value into 10 and ones. For example, consider the problem 16 − 7. Children would pull apart the 16 into 10 + 6, and then subtract 10 − 7 (because they know this fact). They would then add the resulting 3 to the remaining 6 to get 9. Try this strategy on these examples:

$$15 - 8 = \qquad 17 - 9 = \qquad 13 - 8 =$$

This is a great reasoning strategy, although it may seem uncomfortable at first. Use story problems to make it easier for children to keep track of the quantities. For example, for $14 - 8$, you can use a story problem such as "Andy had 14 toy animals. He gave 8 to a friend. How many toy animals does Andy have left?" To reason through the strategy, children can either use manipulatives or imagine taking the 14 toy animals and splitting them into a group of 10 and a group of 4. Then they take 8 from the group of 10 to get 2. They add the 2 to the 4 to see they have 6 left.

The Take from 10 strategy, although not as well known in the United States, is consistently used in high-performing countries. If you have children from other countries in your classroom, they may know this strategy and can share it with others. It can be used for all subtraction facts having minuends greater than 10 (the "toughies") by just knowing how to subtract from 10 and knowing addition facts with sums less than 10. The next activity uses the apple tree context to help children work through the Take from 10 strategy.

Activity 10.13

CCSS-M: 1.OA.B.3;
1.OA.B.4; 1.OA.C.6; 2.OA.B.2

Apples in Two Trees

Adapting Activity 10.12, explain that each ten-frame is a different tree and that you will tell them how many apples fall out of the "full" tree. The children's task is to tell how many total apples are left on the trees. Ask children to explain their thinking.

Reinforcing Reasoning Strategies

It is important to note that while the strategies explained so far may appear as if they are best used for particular basic facts, the reality is there is no one "best" strategy for any fact. For example, $6 + 8$ could be solved using Making 10, Using 5 as an Anchor, or even Doubles (i.e., move one from 8 to the 6 to get $7 + 7$). The more you emphasize choice, the more children will be able to flexibly, accurately, efficiently, and appropriately solve problems, which will lead to fact fluency.

Stop and Reflect

Most addition facts lend themselves to a variety of different reasoning strategies. What are three strategies children could use to get the answer to $8 + 5$?

📋 Formative Assessment Note

Using diagnostic interviews with children learning their basic facts is critical. Many children will be stuck on counting strategies (phase 1) and can be so adept at counting that you may be unaware that they are counting. Quick counting is not a substitute for fact mastery. Use a short diagnostic interview that includes a variety of facts that lend themselves to different strategies. After the child records or states the answer, ask the child to explain how his or her thinking led to the answer.

Building a Foundation for Multiplication Facts

To lay a foundation for multiplication, the CCSSO (2010) recommends that children in second grade begin working with equal groups of objects arranged in rectangular arrays (up to five rows and up to five columns). Although it is appropriate for second graders to use skip counting at this stage, emphasizing reasoning strategies is just as important for moving toward mastery of multiplication facts as it is with addition facts (Baroody, 2006; Wallace & Gurganus, 2005).

When opportunities arise, draw children's attention to the commutative property of multiplication. As discussed in Chapter 9, this property can be best visualized by using arrays as opposed to equal groups of objects. For example, a 2×8 array can be described as 2 rows of 8. When rotated 90 degrees, it is an 8×2 array and described as 8 rows of 2. In both cases, the total is 16. It will take time for children to understand and feel confident with this significant idea but understanding it will cut in half the number of multiplication basic facts to be learned.

Teaching Tip

As with addition and subtraction facts, start with story problems to develop reasoning strategies for multiplication facts.

Standards for Mathematical Practice

7 Look for and make use of structure.

technology

note

The applet on the Illuminations website called "Factorize" allows children to visually explore multiplication by creating rectangular arrays.

A good place to start work on multiplication is with 2s and 5s because these facts build on children's strengths and prior knowledge. In particular, these facts connect to children's experiences with addition doubles and skip counting (Heege, 1985; Kamii & Anderson, 2003; Watanabe, 2006). Next, work can begin on 0s and 1s but be sure these are understood, not just memorized. Experiences with these foundational multiplication facts can begin toward the end of second grade.

×	0	1	2	3	4	5	6	7	8	9
0			0							
1			2							
2	0	2	4	6	8	10	12	14	16	18
3			6							
4			8							
5			10							
6			12							
7			14							
8			16							
9			18							

Twos

Facts that have 2 as a factor are equivalent to addition doubles and should already be known by children by the time you begin introducing them to multiplication. The goal is to help children realize that 2×7 is the same as double 7 or $7 + 7$. Start with story problems in which 2 is the number of groups, as in 2×7. Later, use problems in which 2 is the size of each group, as in 7×2, to help children develop an understanding of the commutative property of multiplication. Here are two corresponding examples:

Our field trip is in 2 weeks. How many days will we need to wait? [two groups of 7]

A kindergarten class is making clay animals. If there are 7 rabbits made, how many rabbit ears are there? [seven groups of 2]

Standards for Mathematical Practice

2 Reason abstractly and quantitatively.

Fives

Facts with 5 as the second factor can be related to skip counting by fives. Practice counting by fives and keep track of how many fives have been counted (e.g., 5, 10, 15 is 3 groups of five or 3×5). Use a number line to keep track of the jumps of five: If we jump by 5s four

×	0	1	2	3	4	5	6	7	8	9
0						0				
1						5				
2						10				
3						15				
4						20				
5	0	5	10	15	20	25	30	35	40	45
6						30				
7						35				
8						40				
9						45				

×	0	1	2	3	4	5	6	7	8	9
0	0	0	0	0	0	0	0	0	0	0
1	0	1	2	3	4	5	6	7	8	9
2	0	2								
3	0	3								
4	0	4								
5	0	5								
6	0	6								
7	0	7								
8	0	8								
9	0	9								

Figure 10.8

Fives facts.

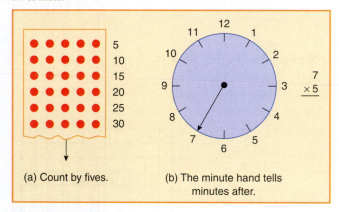

(a) Count by fives. (b) The minute hand tells minutes after.

Standards for Mathematical Practice

8 Look for and express regularity in repeated reasoning.

times, where will we land? Connect counting by fives with arrays that have 5 dots in each rows (see Figure 10.8(a)). Point out that such an array with four rows of five is a model for 4 × 5, six rows of five is 6 × 5, and so on. As illustrated in the following activity, you can also connect fives facts to telling time on an analog clock to the nearest five minutes, an expectation for second graders in the *Common Core State Standards*.

▶ Activity 10.14

CCSS-M: 2.NBT.A.2

Clock Facts

Focus on the minute hand of the clock. When it points to a number, how many minutes after the hour is it? Point to numbers 1 to 9 on a large clock face in random order. Children respond with the minutes after. (See Figure 10.8(b)). Connect this idea to the multiplication facts with 5. For example, when the minute hand is pointing at the "6," that is 6 groups of 5 or 6 × 5 = 30. In this way, the fives facts become the "clock facts."

Zeros and Ones

Thirty-six facts have at least one factor that is either 0 or 1. These facts, though apparently easy on a procedural level, tend to get confused with "rules" that some children learned for addition – for example, the fact 6 + 0 stays the same, but 6 × 0 is always 0; and the $n + 1$ fact is the next counting number, but $n \times 1$ stays the same. To prevent this confusion, use story problems to develop the concepts underlying these facts and avoid rules that are not conceptually based, such as "Any number multiplied by zero is zero." You can start by having children describe stories to match a problem. For example:

---

6 × 0: six rows of chairs with no people in each

0 × 6: zero spiders with six legs each

For the 1s facts, use stories like the ones described above for zero. In addition, use arrays to illustrate commutativity ($8 \times 1 = 1 \times 8$). With the use of stories and arrays, help children generalize what it means to have $n \times 0$, $0 \times n$, $1 \times n$ and $n \times 1$ without just memorizing these properties.

Reinforcing Basic Fact Mastery

When children "just know" a fact or can apply a reasoning strategy so quickly that they almost don't realize they have done it, they have reached phase 3: mastery. CCSS-M refers to this as "know from memory" (CCSSO, 2010, p. 19) and the expectation is that children by the end of second grade will know from memory their basic facts for addition and subtraction. Repeated experiences with reasoning strategies are effective for committing facts to memory; memorizing is not. Therefore, games and activities that focus on reasoning strategies are more effective than drilling with flash cards—and are more appealing to children.

When children do not become fluent with their basic facts, they will certainly struggle with multi-digit computation. Furthermore, children who do not know their facts often struggle to understand more complex mathematical concepts because their cognitive energy must be spent on computation rather than on the more sophisticated concepts being developed (Forbringer & Fahsl, 2010). Commit to using the effective strategies described in this chapter to ensure all children become fluent with their basic facts. When children are not developing fluency, do not resort to drill. Instead drop back to work on foundational ideas, such as number relationships.

Supporting Basic Fact Fluency through Games

Games are an excellent way to provide repeated and engaging experiences for children to learn their basic facts. Playing games that infuse reasoning strategies support children to be able to flexibly choose strategies, decide which strategy is the most appropriate for a given problem, and become more efficient and accurate in finding the answer. These are the four tenants of fluency described earlier in the chapter and are what it takes to become fluent with the basic facts. Also, games increase children's involvement, encourage student-to-student interaction, and improve communication—all of which are related to improved academic achievement (Bay-Williams & Kling, 2014; Forbringer & Fahsl, 2010; Kami & Anderson, 2003; Lewis, 2005).

As you use games, focus on related clusters of facts and on what individual children need to practice. When appropriate, encourage children to self-monitor by creating their own game board or fact cards that include the facts they are working on (their personal "toughies").

Activity 10.15   CCSS-M: 1.OA.B.4; 1.OA.C.6; 2.OA.B.2

Salute!

Place children in groups of three and give each group a deck of cards (omit face cards and use aces as ones). Two children draw a card without looking at it and place it on their forehead facing outward so the others can see it. The child with no cards tells the sum of the two cards. The first of the other two children to correctly say the number on their forehead "wins" the card set. For ELLs, children with disabilities, or reluctant learners, speed can increase anxiety and inhibit participation. You can remove the issue of speed by having children write down the card they think they have (within 5 seconds) and getting a point if they are correct. This activity can be differentiated by including only certain cards (e.g., addition facts using only the numbers 1 through 5).

Activity 10.16   CCSS-M:1.OA.B.4; 1.OA.C.6; 2.OA.B.2

What's under My Thumb?

Create a set of missing-number cards with fact families for each pair of children in your class (see Figure 10.9(a)). Begin this activity as a whole class and then move to partners. Show children one of the cards and ask why they think the numbers go together and why one number is circled. When this number family idea is understood, draw a different card and cover one of the numbers with your thumb, asking, "What is under my thumb?" Ask children to name the missing number and explain their thinking. After you have modeled this process, children can do this activity with partners. Have children create their own cards based on the facts they need to practice. They can also work alone with cards like the ones in Figure 10.9(b) where the answer is written on the back. Alternatively, you can use strips for the missing-number cards instead of circles, such as those in Figure 10.9(c).

Figure 10.9

Introducing missing-number cards.

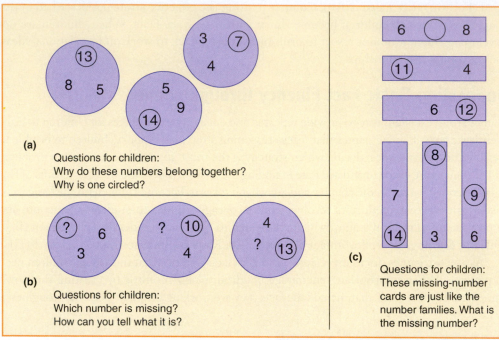

(a)

Questions for children:
Why do these numbers belong together?
Why is one circled?

(b)

Questions for children:
Which number is missing?
How can you tell what it is?

(c)

Questions for children:
These missing-number
cards are just like the
number families. What is
the missing number?

As a follow-up to Activity 10.16, children can complete "cards" on a **Missing-Number Worksheet**. On the worksheet, fill in two of the three numbers for a set of facts. You can create differentiated worksheets for children using clusters of facts that each child is ready to work on. An example is shown in Figure 10.10 where Make 10 facts are in one column, Near-Doubles facts make up the middle column, and in the third column are combinations from two fact families. Have children write an equation for each missing-number card. This helps children connect the missing addend problems to subtraction.

Standards for Mathematical Practice

7 **Look for and make use of structure.** ▶

📋 Formative Assessment Note

As children are engaged in games and activities, interview them to determine whether they are using counting strategies, reasoning strategies, or quick recall. Ask them to tell you what strategy they just used. If you observe counting, ask the child to try a particular reasoning strategy. If children are counting, more experiences to develop number relationships, such as activities with ten-frames and arithmetic racks, are needed.

Table 10.3 offers ideas for how to adapt some classic games to focus on basic fact mastery (reflects ideas from Forbinger & Fahsl, 2010 and Kamii & Anderson, 2003). Suggestions for differentiation are also included.

When all facts are learned, continued reinforcement through occasional games and activities is important. The next activity engages children in flexibly applying addition and subtraction.

Activity 10.17

CCSS-M:2.OA.B.2

Bowl-a-Fact

For this activity (modified from Shoecraft, 1982), create a game board by drawing circles placed in triangular fashion to look like bowling pins, with the front circle labeled 1 and the others labeled consecutively through 10. Give children the **Bowl-A-Fact** Activity Page so they can record their equations. For culturally diverse classrooms, be sure that children are familiar with bowling. (If they are not, consider showing a YouTube clip or photographs.)

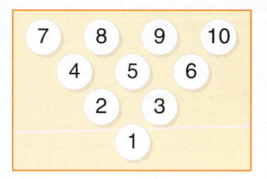

Take three dice and roll them. Children use addition and/or subtraction with at least two of the numbers on the three dice to come up with equations that result in answers that are on the pins. For example, if you roll 4, 2, and 3 they can "knock down" the 3 pin with $4 + 2 - 3$. They can also knock down the 7 pin with $4 + 3$. If they can produce equations to knock down all 10 pins, they get a strike. If not, roll again and see whether they can knock the rest down for a spare. After doing this with the whole class, children can work in small groups. To decrease the challenge, roll four dice at a time.

Figure 10.10

Examples of missing-number worksheets. The blank version can be used to fill in any sets of facts you wish to emphasize. The column headings shown are not included on student pages.

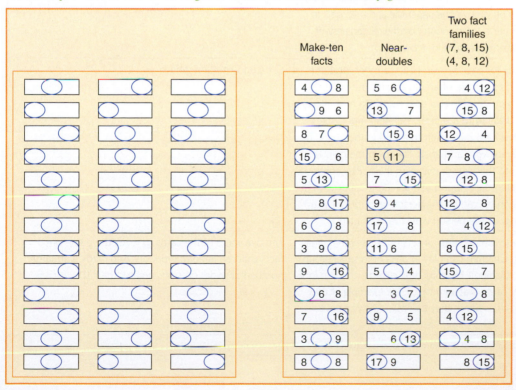

Table 10.3. Classic games adapted to basic fact mastery.

Classic Game	How to Use it with Basic Fact Mastery	Suggestions for Differentiation
Bingo	Each bingo card has a fact problem (e.g., 2 + 3 in each box. The same fact will be on multiple bingo cards but in different locations on each card. You will call out an answer (e.g., 6), and the children will find a matching problem (or more than one problem) on their card.	Create bingo boards that focus on different clusters of facts (e.g., doubles or doubles +1 on some boards, and Making 10 on other boards). Be sure that the answers you call out are an even mix of the clusters so that everyone has the same chance to win.
Concentration	Create cards that have a fact problem (e.g., 6 + 7) on one half and the answers (e.g., 13) on the other half. Shuffle the cards and turn them face-down in a 6 × 4 grid. (If you like, you can make the grid larger to use more cards.)	Select cards that focus on a particular cluster of facts (e.g., +1 and doubles) for each round of the game. Multiple groups can play the game simultaneously—each group will use the parts of the deck that contain the facts they are working on. Also, consider making cards that show the ten-frames below the numbers to help provide a visual for children.
Dominoes	Create (or find online) dominoes that have a fact on one side and an answer (not to that fact) on the other. Each gets the same number or dominoes (around eight). On his or her turn, they can play one of the dominoes in their hand only if they have an answer or a fact that can connect to a domino on the board.	As with other games, select the dominoes that focus on a particular clusters of facts.
Four in a Row	Create a 6 × 6 square game board with a sum written on each square. Below, list the numbers 0 through 9. Each of the two players has counters of a different color to use as their game pieces. On the first turn, Player I places a marker (paper clip) on two addends and then gets to place his or her colored counter on the related answer. (If you have repeated the same answer on different squares of the board, the player only gets to cover one of them.) Player 2 can only move one paper clip and then gets to place his or her colored counter on the related answer, The first player to get four in a row wins.	Rather than list all the values below the chart, just list the related addends. For example, use 1, 2, 6, 7, 8, 9 if you want to work on +1 and +2.
Old Maid (retitled as Old Dog)	Create cards for each fact and each answer. Add one card that has a picture of an old dog (or use your school mascot). Shuffle and deal cards. On each player's turn, they draw from the person on their right, see whether that card is a match to a card in their hand (a fact and its answer), and, if so, lay down the pair. Then the person to their left draws from them. Play continues until all matches are found and someone is left with the Old Dog. Winner can be the person with (or not with) the Old Dog, or the person with the most pairs.	See Concentration (above).
Go Fish for 10	Create a set with 44 cards: 4 sets of cards with a digit 0–10 on it. Children can play in pairs or in small groups. Instead of "fishing" for pairs of like cards, children look for pairs of cards that sum to 10. For example, if they have a 6 in their hand, they can ask, "Do you have a 4?"	Remove some of the cards to focus the game on facts children need to work on. Add cards with larger numbers to work on sums greater than 10.

Source: Based on ideas from Forbringer & Fahsl, 2010, and Kamii & Anderson, 2003.

Effective Drill

Drill—repetitive nonproblem-based activity—in the absence of reasoning has repeatedly been shown to be ineffective. Nonetheless, drill can strengthen memory and retrieval capabilities (Ashcraft & Christy, 1995) but it should be low-stress and engaging. Drill is only appropriate after children know strategies and have moved from phase 2 to phase 3. The games and activities from this chapter can be played even after children know the facts from memory and will serve as a low-stress and engaging way to strengthen memory and retrieval.

Too often drill includes too many facts too quickly, causing children to become frustrated and overwhelmed. Also, children will progress at different rates—gifted children tend to be good at memorizing; whereas, children with intellectual disabilities have difficulty memorizing (Forbringer & Fahsl, 2010). Rather than work on all facts, identify a group of related facts (e.g., near-doubles) and look at patterns within that set. By organizing the work around related facts, if a child needs any further discussion and illustrations, the focus will be beneficial. Children can create their own cards with each fact written both ways (e.g., 3 + 5 and 5 + 3), with addends represented in ten-frames, and the answer on the back. They can work with these at home or with a partner, and keep track of the ones they "just know" and the ones for which they use a strategy.

There are several websites and software programs that provide children opportunities to drill basic facts (see Table 10.4). None of these currently support strategy development, but these programs can be a great support for children who are near mastery or who are maintaining mastery. One disadvantage of most of these sites is that they focus on all the facts at one time. Two exceptions—*Fun 4 the Brain* and *Math Fact Café*—allow you to target groups of related facts.

Table 10.4. Online resources for mastery of basic math facts.

Name	Description
Fun 4 the Brain: *Math Games*	This site offers over a dozen games for addition facts. Pick a game (e.g., Snowy's Friend) and then pick the fact families you would like to explore.
Math Fact Café	Here you will find a lot of downloadable practice: premade fact sheets, flashcards, and practice pages, or create your own practice pages, selecting the number of practice problems, the level of difficulty, and which fact families.
NCTM Illuminations *Deep Sea Duel*	Play this applet: The first person to choose a set of digit cards with a specified sum wins. You can choose how many cards, what types of numbers, and the level of strategy.
NCTM Illuminations *Let's Learn Those Facts*	Six complete lessons for addition facts are provided, including links to resources and student recording sheets.
BBC *Cross the Swamp*	This British applet asks children to supply a missing operation (+/ −) and a number to complete an equation (e.g., 4__ __ = 12). There are five questions in a set, each with three levels of difficulty.
NLVM *Diffy*	Diffy is a classic mathematics puzzle that involves finding the differences of given numbers. Here it is presented as an applet.
IXL Learning	IXL contains interactive practice tools to monitor children's progress toward basic fact mastery. Connections with the Common Core State Standards, Department of Defense Education Activity standards, and existing state standards are provided.

Do's and Don'ts for Teaching Basic Facts

We close this chapter with some important reminders for effectively teaching basic facts. This is such an important life skill for all learners that it is important that we, as teachers, use what research suggests are the most effective practices.

What to Do

The following recommendations can support the development of quick recall.

1. *Ask children to self-monitor.* As with all learning, having a sense of what you know, what you don't know, and what you need to learn is important. This certainly holds true with learning basic facts. Have children identify which basic facts are their personal "toughies" and continue to work with reasoning strategies to help them derive those facts.

2. *Focus on self-improvement.* Emphasize a growth mindset, as described in Chapter 2, by helping children notice that they are getting quicker or learning new facts or strategies. For example, children can keep track of how long it took them to go through their "fact stack" and then two days later, work through the same stack and check to see whether they were quicker (or more accurate or used a new strategy) compared to the last time.

3. *Limit practice to short time segments.* Long periods (10 minutes or more) for basic fact practice are not effective. Instead use the first 5 to 10 minutes of the day, or extra time before lunch, to provide continued support on fact development and retention without using mathematics instructional time that is better devoted to other topics. You can project numerous examples of double ten-frames in relatively little time. Or you can pose a story problem each day and take 5 minutes to share strategies. You can also have children pair up and go through each of their individualized sets of flash cards in 2 minutes.

4. *Work on facts over time.* Rather than do a unit on fact memorization, work on facts throughout the year, working on one reasoning strategy or set of facts until it is learned, then move on. Focus on foundational facts first and be sure those are mastered before teaching derived fact strategies.

5. *Involve families.* Share your plan for how children will work on learning facts over the year, including that you will first emphasize reasoning strategies. Ask family members to help children by using reasoning strategies when they don't know a fact.

6. *Make fact practice enjoyable.* There are many games and activities, including those in this chapter, that are designed to reinforce facts without competition and without inducing anxiety.

7. *Use technology.* Technology offers children immediate feedback and reinforcement, helping them to self-monitor.

8. *Emphasize the importance of knowing their facts.* Without trying to create pressure or anxiety, emphasize to children that they must learn their basic facts and learn them well because they will be using them all the time in real life and throughout the rest mathematics.

What Not to Do

The following list describes strategies that may have been designed with good intentions but hinder children's recall of basic facts.

1. *Don't use timed tests.* As we have mentioned, little insight is gained from timed tests and they can negatively affect children by creating unneeded anxiety. Turn those timers off!

2. *Don't use public comparisons of mastery.* You may have experienced as a student or even used as a teacher a bulletin board display that identifies which children are on which step of a staircase to mastering their basic facts. Imagine how the child who is on step 3 feels when most others are on step 6. Similarly, avoid public competition with flash cards. It is great to celebrate children's successes, but avoid comparisons between children to prevent the development of anxiety as they learn mathematics.

3. *Don't proceed through the facts in order from 0 to 9.* Begin work on the foundational facts first. Be sure children really know these facts before moving on. Then move on to the tougher facts.

4. *Don't work on all the facts all at once in a given activity or game.* Because some children will learn some facts more quickly than other children, you will need to differentiate. Using observations and diagnostic interviews, help children identify which facts they need more experience with and have them focus on that target set of facts during an activity or game.

5. *Don't expect quick recall too soon.* Quick recall or mastery can be attained only after significant time has been spent on reasoning strategies.

6. *Don't use facts as a barrier to good mathematics.* Mathematics is not solely about computation. Mathematics is about problem solving, reasoning, using patterns, and making sense of things. There is no reason that a child who has not yet mastered all basic facts should be excluded from any mathematical experiences. When working on more complex tasks, allow calculators so that children don't get bogged down on computation.

7. *Don't use fact mastery as a prerequisite for calculator use.* Insisting that children master the basic facts before allowing them to use a calculator denies them important learning opportunities. Calculator use should be based on the instructional goals of the day. For example, if the learning goal for a lesson is for children to explore even and odd numbers, then they might build different array representations of numbers, recording the amounts of different parts while they look for patterns. Using a calculator can quicken computation in this lesson and keep the focus on reasoning about even and odd numbers.

11

Developing Whole-Number Place-Value Concepts

BIG IDEAS

1 Sets of ten (and tens of ten) can be perceived as single entities or units. For example, "three sets of ten and two singles" is base-ten language to describe 32 single objects.

2 The positions of digits in numbers determine which size group they count. This is the major organizing principle of place-value numeration and is central to developing number sense.

3 There are patterns to the way that numbers are formed. For example, each decade has a symbolic pattern reflective of the 0-to-9 sequence (e.g., 20, 21, 22, . . . 29).

4 The groupings of ones, tens, and hundreds can be taken apart in different but equivalent ways. For example, beyond the typical way to decompose 256 into 2 hundreds, 5 tens, and 6 ones, 256 can be represented as 1 hundred, 14 tens, and 16 ones, or 25 tens and 6 ones. Decomposing and composing multidigit numbers in flexible ways is a necessary foundation for computational estimation and exact computation.

5 Children progress through three levels of understanding the concept of "ten." First, one ten means ten ones. Children then progress to seeing ten as a unit (i.e., as one thing) but rely on physical or mental models to work with units of ten. Finally, they are able to easily work with units of ten as numbers and are no longer dependent on physical or mental base-ten models.

> **6** Children can develop place-value understanding as a *result* of finding their own methods of adding and subtracting two- and three-digit numbers. Relying on their own methods requires that they focus on the value of the numbers involved, reinforcing the development of place value concepts.
>
> **7** "Really big" numbers are difficult to conceptualize and are best understood in terms of familiar real-world referents. The number of people who can fill the seats in the local high school auditorium is, for example, a meaningful referent for the number 1,000 for children who have visited that venue.

Number sense is linked to a complete understanding of place value and our base-ten number system. In kindergarten and first grade, children count up to 100 and 120, respectively, and consider patterns in these numbers. But, most importantly, they begin to be able to think about groups of ten objects as one thing or as a unit. This understanding takes time for children to develop and is a critical milestone for young children (Wright, Martland, & Stafford, 2008). But in the meantime, they can and should explore larger numbers as they enrich their understanding of "ten-ness." The *Common Core State Standards* (CCSSO, 2010) recommend that kindergartners work with numbers between 11 and 19 by putting them together (composing) and taking them apart (decomposing) into tens and ones using physical materials and drawings. By second grade, these initial ideas are extended to three-digit numbers. A firm understanding of place value with whole numbers lays the foundation for work with decimals as well as larger numbers in upper elementary and middle school.

A significant part of the development of place value understanding includes children putting numbers together (composing) and taking them apart (decomposing) in a wide variety of ways as they solve addition and subtraction problems with two- and three-digit numbers. In other words, computation instruction should be interwoven with place-value instruction. Children's efforts in simultaneously making sense of place value and computation enhance their ability to invent their own computation strategies and strengthen their place value understanding.

Pre–Place-Value Understandings

Children know a lot about numbers with two digits (10 to 99) as early as kindergarten. After all, kindergartners learn to count to 100 and count out sets of items with as many as 20 or more objects (CCSSO, 2010). They count children in the room, turn to specific page numbers in their books, and so on. However, initially their understanding is quite different from yours. It is based on a count-by-ones approach to determine quantity and so the number 18 to them means 18 ones. They are not yet able to separate the quantity into place-value groups. For example, after counting 18 teddy bears, a young child might tell you that the 1 in the number stands for 1 teddy bear and the 8 stands for 8 teddy bears. Such children have not had enough experiences to move beyond this initial understanding of two-digit numbers.

Researchers have identified three levels of understanding about the concept of "ten" through which children progress (Wright, Martland, Stafford, & Stanger, 2008).

- *Level 1:* Initial Concept of Ten. Children understand ten not as a unit but only as ten ones. When solving addition or subtraction problems involving tens, they count only by ones.
- *Level 2:* Intermediate Concept of Ten. Children see ten as a unit, as one thing that consists of ten ones, but they must rely on physical or mental models to help them work with units of ten.
- *Level 3:* Facile Concept of Ten. Children are able to easily work with units of ten without the use of physical or mental base-ten models.

Consider the suggestions in the following Formative Assessment Note as ways to assess where children are in this trajectory.

Formative Assessment Note

In a diagnostic interview, ask first- or second-graders to count out 35 tiles. Watch closely to determine whether they count out the tiles one at a time and push them aside without any type of grouping or if they group them into tens. Have the children write the number that tells how many tiles they just counted. Some may write "53" instead of "35," a simple reversal. You will likely find that early on children count the tiles one by one and are not yet thinking of ten as a unit (level 1), and are therefore in a pre–place-value stage.

The children just described know that there are 35 tiles "because I counted them." Writing the number and saying the number are usually done correctly, but their understanding of 35 derives from and is connected to the count-by-ones approach. Without your help, children do not easily or quickly develop a meaningful use of groups of ten to represent quantities.

Even if children can tell you that in the numeral 35 the 3 "is in the tens place" or that there are "5 ones," they might just know the name of the positions without understanding that the "tens place" represents how many groups of ten. Similarly, if children use base-ten blocks, they may name a rod of ten as a "ten" and a small cube as a "one" but may not be able to tell how many ones are required to make a ten. In other words, children may attach words to both materials and groups without realizing what the materials or symbols represent.

Children may know that 35 is "a lot" and that it's more than 27 (because you count past 27 to get to 35). But initially they think of the "35" as a single numeral. At this stage, they do not know that the 3 represents three groups of ten things and the 5 represents five single things (Fuson, 2006). Fuson and her colleagues refer to children's pre–place-value understanding of number as *unitary*. That is, there are no groupings of ten, even though a two-digit number is associated with the quantity. They initially rely on unitary counts to understand quantities.

Teaching Tip

Children may attach words to both materials and groups without realizing what the materials or symbols represent. Look for evidence or counter-evidence of this level of understanding as children work on tasks.

Developing Foundational Ideas in Whole-Number Place Value

Place-value understanding requires an *integration* of new and sometimes difficult-to-construct concepts of grouping by tens (the base-ten concept) with procedural knowledge of how groups are recorded in our place-value system and how numbers are written and spoken. Note that learners must understand the word *grouping* in the context of place value, especially English language learners (ELLs) who may become confused because the root word *group* is often used to instruct children to work together.

Integrating Base-Ten Groupings with Counting by Ones

Each of the sets in Figure 11.1 has 35 tiles, but each set is organized differently. Before base-ten ideas develop, counting by ones is the only approach by which children can be convinced that all three sets are the same amount. Once children can count out a set of 35 by ones, help them see that making groupings of tens and leftovers is a way of counting that same quantity. Figure 11.1 shows three distinct stages of understanding related to base-ten groupings that children move through as they reason about grouping quantities.

Figure 11.1

Three stages of reasoning about 35 objects.

Grouping Stage	Visual Representation	Counting Approach	Children Can:
Unitary Count by ones	Set A	1, 2, 3, 4, 5, 6, 7, 8, 9, 10, 11, 12, and so on	• Name a quantity or "tell how many" by counting each piece. • Are not yet able to think of 10 as a single unit. • Use counting by ones as the only way they are convinced that different sets have the same amount.
Base Ten Count by groups of tens and ones	Set B	1, 2, 3 groups of 10 and 1, 2, 3, 4, 5 ones (singles) or 10, 20, 30, 31, 32, 33, 34, 35	• Count a group of 10 objects as a single unit (unitizing). • Coordinate the base-ten approach with a count by ones as a means of telling "how many."
Equivalent Can count by groups of tens and ones in a non-standard base-ten format	Set C	Before counting, children would group the singles into groups of ten, and then count 10, 20, 30, 31, 32, 33, 34, 35	• Recognize that amounts do not have to be in the standard base-ten format (i.e., ten ones are always in a group of ten) to be equivalent. • Use these alternate groupings to relate to computation by being able to regroup numbers in a variety of ways.

There is a subtle, yet profound, difference between children at these stages: Some know that set B in Figure 11.1 is 35 because they understand the idea that 3 groups of ten and 5 more is the same amount as 35 counted by ones; others simply say, "It's 35," because they have been told that when things are grouped this way, it's called 35. The children who understand place value will see no need to count set B by ones. They understand the "thirty-fiveness" of sets A and B to be the same. The children in the pre–place-value stage may not be sure how many they will get if they count the tiles in set B by ones or if the groups were "ungrouped" how many there would then be.

Your foremost objective should be helping children integrate what they already know about numbers from counting by ones with the grouping-by-tens concept. If they only count by ones, ask them, "What will happen if we count these by groups and singles (or by tens and ones)?" If a set has been grouped into tens and singles and counted, then ask, "How can we be really certain that there are 35 things here?" or "How many do you think we will get if we count by ones?" You cannot just tell children that these counts will all be the same and hope that will make sense to them—it is a relationship they must construct themselves.

Standards for Mathematical Practice

7 **Look for and make use of structure.**

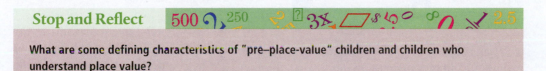

Stop and Reflect

What are some defining characteristics of "pre–place-value" children and children who understand place value?

Teaching Tip

Children's ability to label place values with base-ten names (e.g., ones, tens, hundreds) does not guarantee that they understand that 1 ten is the same as 10 ones or that 1 hundred is the same as 10 tens.

Groupings with fewer than the maximum number of tens are referred to as *equivalent groupings* or *equivalent representations*. Understanding the equivalence of sets B and C indicates a realization that grouping by tens is not just a rule that is followed, but that any grouping by tens, along with the singles, can help tell how many. Many computational techniques (e.g., regrouping in addition and subtraction) are based on equivalent representations of numbers.

Integrating Base-Ten Groupings with Words

The way we say a number such as "thirty-five" must also be connected with the grouping- by-tens concept. In particular, counting by tens and ones results in saying the number of groups and singles separately: "three tens and five." Saying the number of tens and singles separately in this fashion is called base-ten language. Children can associate base-ten language with standard language: "three tens and five is the same as thirty-five."

There are several variations of base-ten language for 35: "3 tens and 5," "3 tens and 5 ones," "3 groups of 10 and 5 ones;" "3 tens and 5 singles," and so on. Each may be used interchangeably with the standard name "thirty-five." If you have ELLs, it is best to select one variation (e.g., 3 tens and 5 ones) and consistently connect it to the standard language. Other languages often use the base-ten format (e.g., 17 in Spanish is *diecisiete*, 17 in Japanese is *juushichi*—both of which literally mean "ten and seven"), so this can be a good cultural connection for children.

It is important to be precise in your language. Whenever you refer to a number in the tens, hundreds, or thousands (or beyond), make sure you do not just say "six," but instead refer to it with its place value location, such as 6 tens (or 60). Children are often confused when numbers are discussed as digits rather that describing their actual value.

Standards for Mathematical Practice

6 Attend to precision. ▶

Integrating Base-Ten Groupings with Place-Value Notation

The symbolic scheme that we use for writing numbers (ones on the right, tens to the left of ones, and so on) must be coordinated with the grouping scheme. Activities can be designed so that children physically associate groupings of tens and ones with the correct recording of the individual digits, as Figure 11.2 illustrates.

Figure 11.2

Groupings by 10 are matched with numerals, which are recorded in labeled places and eventually written in standard form.

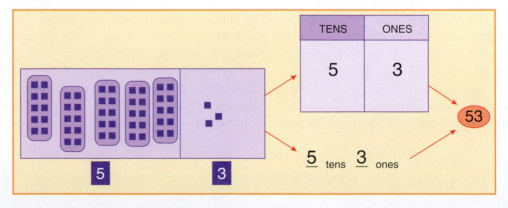

Language again plays a key role in making these connections. The explicit count by groups and singles matches the individual digits as the number is written in the usual left-to-right manner. A similar coordination is necessary for hundreds and other place values.

Keep in mind that children will find it initially challenging to see "ten" as both 10 ones and 1 ten.

Figure 11.3 summarizes the ideas of integrated place-value understanding that have been discussed so far. Note that all three methods of counting (from Figure 11.1) are coordinated as the principal method of integrating the base-ten concepts, the written names, and the oral names.

Base-Ten Models for Place Value

Note that when children are working on base-ten concepts, they combine multiplicative understanding (each piece is ten times the value of the place to the right) with a positional system (each place has a value)—something hard to do prior to multiplication being taught! Physical models for base-ten concepts support the development of place value and base-ten understanding. Physical models also play a key role in helping children develop the idea of "a ten" as both a single entity and as a set of 10 units. Remember, though, that the physical models do not "show" the concept to the children. The children must mentally construct the "ten makes one" relationship and impose it on the model.

An effective, base-ten model for ones, tens, and hundreds is one that is *proportional*. That is, a model for ten is physically ten times larger than the model for a one, and a model for one hundred is ten times larger than the ten model. Proportional models allow children to verify that ten of any given piece is equivalent to one piece in the column to the left (e.g., 10 tens equals 1 hundred). Base-ten proportional models can be categorized as *groupable* or *pregrouped*.

Groupable Models

Models that most clearly reflect the relationships of ones, tens, and hundreds are those for which children can build a place-value piece from other place-value pieces and verify it's value—for example, the ten can actually be made or grouped from the single pieces. When children put 10 beans in a cup, the cup of 10 beans literally *is the same as* the 10 single beans. Bundles of wooden craft sticks or coffee stirrers can be grouped with rubber bands. Plastic linking cubes can be built into bars of ten and also provide a good transition to pregrouped rods because they form a similar shape. Examples of these groupable models are shown in Figure 11.4(a).

When children become more familiar with these models, collections of tens can be made in advance by the children and kept as ready-made tens (e.g., craft sticks can be left bundled, linking cubes can be left connected). This is a good transition to the pregrouped models described in the next section.

Figure 11.3

Relational understanding of place value integrates three components: base-ten concepts, oral names for numbers, and written names for numbers.

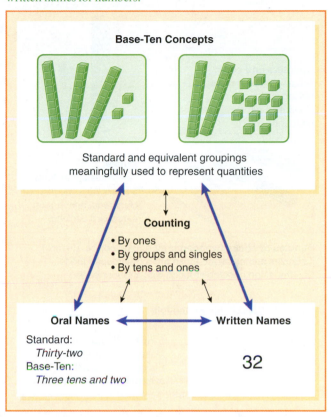

Base-Ten Concepts

Standard and equivalent groupings meaningfully used to represent quantities

Counting
- By ones
- By groups and singles
- By tens and ones

Oral Names

Standard:
Thirty-two
Base-Ten:
Three tens and two

Written Names

32

Teaching Tip

As children begin to make groupings of ten, start introducing the language of "tens" by matching the objects being used, such as "cups of ten and ones" or "bundles of ten and singles." Then move to a general phrase, such as "groups of ten and ones." Eventually you can abbreviate "groups of tens" as "tens" such as "four tens and seven."

Figure 11.4

Groupable and pregrouped base-ten models.

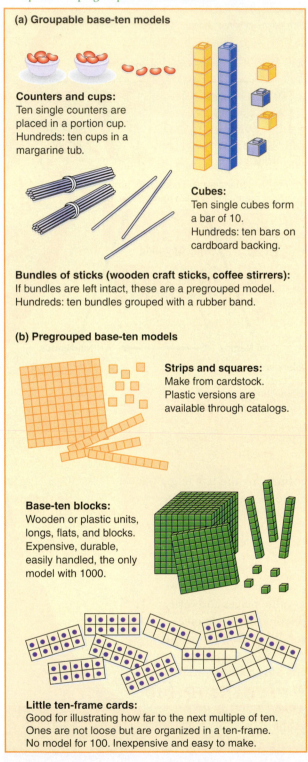

(a) Groupable base-ten models

Counters and cups:
Ten single counters are placed in a portion cup. Hundreds: ten cups in a margarine tub.

Cubes:
Ten single cubes form a bar of 10. Hundreds: ten bars on cardboard backing.

Bundles of sticks (wooden craft sticks, coffee stirrers):
If bundles are left intact, these are a pregrouped model. Hundreds: ten bundles grouped with a rubber band.

(b) Pregrouped base-ten models

Strips and squares:
Make from cardstock. Plastic versions are available through catalogs.

Base-ten blocks:
Wooden or plastic units, longs, flats, and blocks. Expensive, durable, easily handled, the only model with 1000.

Little ten-frame cards:
Good for illustrating how far to the next multiple of ten. Ones are not loose but are organized in a ten-frame. No model for 100. Inexpensive and easy to make.

Standards for Mathematical Practice

7 Look for and make use of structure.

Pregrouped Models

Models that are pregrouped are commonly shown in textbooks and are often used in instructional activities. Pregrouped models, such as those in Figure 11.4(b) and the **Base-Ten Materials** (see Blackline Master 32), cannot be taken apart or put together. When 10 single pieces are accumulated, they must be exchanged or traded for a ten, and likewise, tens must be traded for hundreds. The chief advantage of these physical models is their ease of use and the efficient way they model large numbers.

With pregrouped models, make an extra effort to make sure that children understand that a ten piece really is the same as 10 ones. Although there is a pregrouped cube to represent 1000, have children attach 10 hundred pieces together as a cube to show how the cube is formed. Otherwise, some children may count only the square units they see on the surface of the six faces and think the cube represents 600.

Games, such as Race to 100, offer a motivating format in which children can actively engage in making equal trades, reinforcing the use of pregrouped base-ten models. Here is a **video** of a child playing Race to 100 with a teacher. You may wish to provide children with a **Place Value Mat** that includes a ten-frame in the ones column to help keep track of the count (see Blackline Master 17).

The **Little Ten-Frames** effectively link to the familiar ten-frames children have been using to think about numbers as discussed in Chapters 8 and 10, and as such, may initially be more meaningful than base-ten materials made from paper strips and squares (like Blackline Master 32). The little ten-frames model has the distinct advantage of always showing the distance to the next decade. For example, when 47 is shown with 4 ten cards and a seven card, a child can see that three more will make five full cards, or 50.

A significant challenge with using the pregrouped physical models occurs when children have not had adequate experience working with groupable models. Then there is the potential for children to use them without reflecting on the ten-to-one relationships. For example, if children are *told* to trade 10 ones for a ten, it is quite possible for them to make this exchange without attending to the "ten-ness" of the piece they call a ten. Similarly, children can "make the number 42" by simply picking up 4 tens and 2 ones without understanding that if all the pieces were broken apart there would be 42 ones. Before moving to pregrouped models, pay attention to children's explanations for when and why they group pieces and then once you have moved to pregrouped models, continue to ask children to justify when and why they make trades. The ten-to-one relationship should play a prominent role in their explanations and justifications.

technology *note*

Using electronic versions of base-ten manipulatives, children (including those with disabilities) can place ones, tens, hundreds, or thousands on the screen with simple mouse clicks. In the *Base Blocks* applets at the National Library of Virtual Manipulatives, children place the base-ten models on a place-value mat. When children lasso 10 pieces of one type with a rectangle, the pieces snap together into a larger base-ten piece. When a piece is dragged one column to the right, the piece breaks apart into 10 of that unit. As pieces are moved onto the place-value mat, a numeral is displayed that corresponds to the current quantity of base-ten materials. You can also adjust the columns to display two, three, or four place values. Scott Foresman's *eTools* has a similar place-value tool with a few additional features. Place-value columns can be turned on and off, and the "odometer" option can show the number 523 as 5 *hundreds* + 2 *tens* + 3 *ones*, as 500 + 20 + 3, or as *five hundred twenty-three*. A hammer icon will break a piece into 10 smaller pieces, and a glue bottle icon is used to group 10 pieces together.

Compared to physical base-ten blocks, these virtual manipulatives are free, easily grouped and ungrouped, available in "endless" supply, and can be manipulated by children and displayed by projector or smart board. Even with all these advantages, virtual models are no more conceptual than physical models and as such are only a representation for children who understand the relationships involved.

Nonproportional Models

Nonproportional models or models where the ten is not physically ten times larger than the one, are *not* used for introducing place-value concepts. They are used once children have a conceptual understanding of the numeration system and need additional reinforcement. Examples of nonproportional models include an abacus that has the same-sized beads on wires in different columns; money using pennies, dimes, and dollars to represent the ones, tens, and hundreds; and chips that are assigned different place values by color.

Developing Base-Ten Concepts

Now that you have a sense of the important place-value concepts, we turn to activities that assist children in developing these concepts. This section focuses on base-ten concepts or grouping by tens (see the top of Figure 11.3). Connecting this important idea with the oral and written names for numbers (the rest of Figure 11.3) is discussed separately to help you focus on how to do each. However, in the classroom, the oral and written names for numbers can and should be developed in concert with conceptual ideas.

Grouping Activities

Reflect for a moment on how strange it must sound to say "seven ones." Certainly, children have never said they were "seven ones" years old. The use of the word *ten* as a singular group name is even more mysterious. Consider the phrase "Ten ones makes one ten." The first *ten* carries the usual meaning of 10 things, the amount that is 1 more than 9 things. But the other *ten* is a singular noun, one thing. How can something the child has known for years as the name for a lot of things suddenly become one thing? And if you think this is confusing for native speakers, imagine the potential difficulty for ELLs.

Because children start their development of base-ten concepts with a count-by-ones idea of number, you must begin there. You cannot arbitrarily impose grouping by ten on children.

Children need to experiment with gathering objects into groups of like size and perhaps come to an agreement that ten is a very useful size to use. The following activity could be done in kindergarten or first grade as an example of a first effort at developing grouping concepts.

Standards for Mathematical Practice

1 Make sense of problems and persevere in solving them.

Activity 11.1

CCSS-M: K.NBT.A.1; 1.NBT.B.2a

Counting in Groups

Find a collection of items between 25 and 100 that children might be interested in counting—perhaps the number of shoes in the classroom, a tub of cubes, the number of crayons in the classroom crayon box, or the number of books in the classroom library. Suppose the children decide to count the number of shoes. Then pose the question, "How could we count our shoes in some way that would be easier than counting by ones?"

Whatever suggestions children pose, try them. After testing several methods, you can have a discussion about what worked well and what did not. If no one suggests counting by tens, you might casually suggest that as an idea to try.

One teacher challenged her children to find a good way to count all the linking cubes being held by the class after each child had been given a cube for each of their pockets. The first suggestion was to count by sevens. That was tried but did not work very well because none of the children could count by sevens. In search of a more efficient way, the next suggestion was to count by twos. This did not seem to be much better than counting by ones. Finally, they settled on counting by tens and realized that this was a good and relatively "fast" way of counting.

This and similar activities provide you with the opportunity to suggest to children to arrange materials into groups of tens before they start the "fast" way of counting. Remember that children may count "ten, twenty, thirty, thirty-one, thirty-two" but not fully realize the "thirty-two-ness" of the quantity. To connect the count-by-tens method with their understood method of counting by ones, the children need to count both ways and discuss why they get the same result.

The idea in the next activity is for children to make groups of ten and record or say the amounts. Number words are used so that children will not mechanically match tens and ones with individual digits.

Activity 11.2

CCSS-M: K.NBT.A.1; 1.NBT.B.2a; 1.NBT.B.2b; 1.NBT.B.2c

Groups of Ten

Prepare bags of different types of objects such as toothpicks, buttons, beans, plastic chips, linking cubes, craft sticks, or other items. Children should use the **Bag of Tens** Activity Page, a recording sheet similar to the top example in Figure 11.5. The bags can be placed at stations around the room or given to pairs of children. Children empty the bags and count the contents. The amount is recorded as a number word. Then the objects are grouped in as many tens as possible. The groups are recorded on the form. After returning the objects to the bags, bags are traded or children move to another station. Note that children with disabilities may initially need to use a ten-frame to support their counting. Then the use of the ten-frame should eventually fade.

Variations of the "Groups of Ten" activity are suggested by the other recording sheets in Figure 11.5. On the **Get This Many** Activity Page, children count the dots and then count out the corresponding number of objects. Provide small cups to put the groups of ten in. Notice that the activity requires children to first count the set in a way they understand (e.g., count by ones), record the amount in words, and then make the groupings. The **Fill the Tens** and **Loop This Many** Activity Pages begin with a verbal name (number word), and children must count the indicated amount and then make groups.

Figure 11.5

Activities involving number words and making groups of ten.

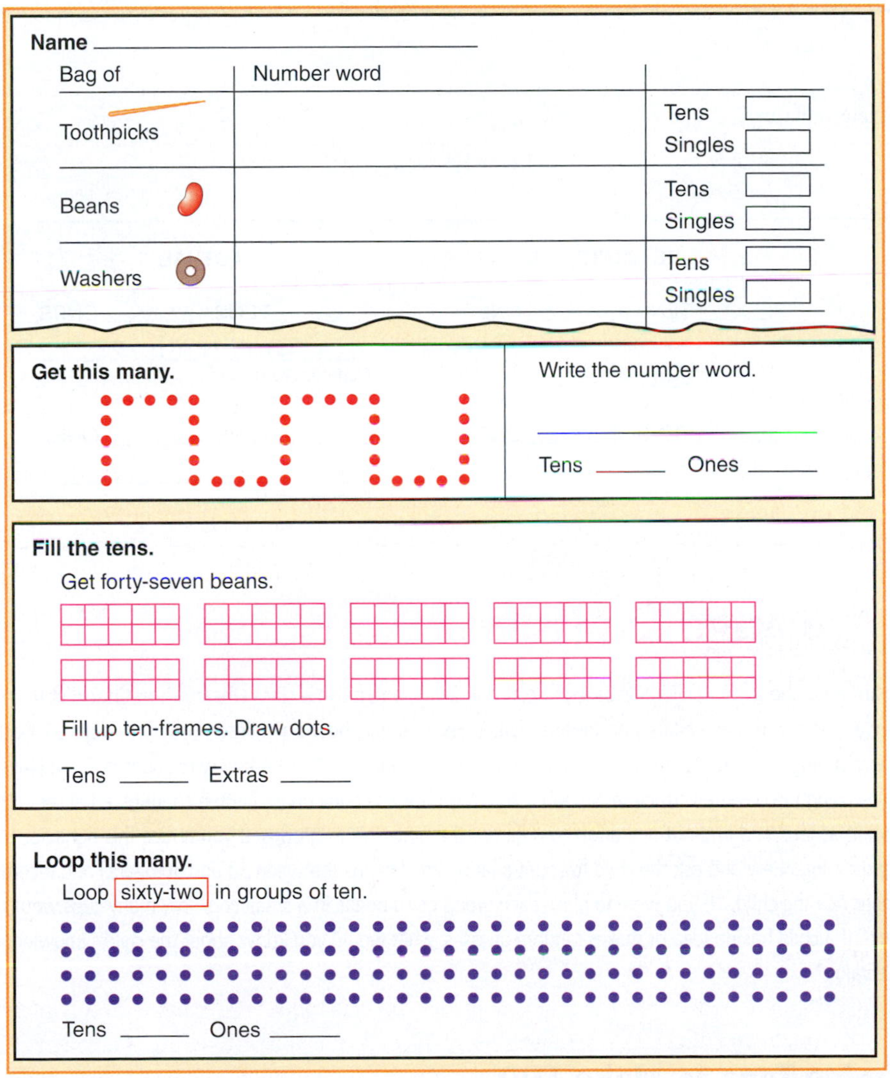

The following activity is another variant of the grouping activities but includes an estimation component that adds interest, makes the activity more problem based, and contributes to number sense. Listening to children's estimates is a useful assessment opportunity that tells you a lot about children's concept of numbers.

Activity 11.3

Estimating Groups of Tens and Ones

Give children a length that they are going to measure—for example, the length of a child lying down or the distance around the edge of a sheet of newspaper. At one end of the length, line up 10 units (e.g., 10 linking cubes, toothpicks, rods, or blocks). On a recording sheet (see Figure 11.6 and the **How Long?** Activity Page), children record an estimate of how many groups of 10 and ones they think will match the length. Next they find the actual measure, placing units along the full length. These are counted by ones and also grouped in tens. Both results are recorded. Estimating the groups of ten requires children to pay attention to the ten as a group or unit. Notice that all three place-value components from Figure 11.3 are included. Children work in pairs to measure several lengths around the room. **Click here** for an Expanded Lesson for this activity.

Figure 11.6

Recording sheet for estimating groups of tens and ones.

NAME *Jessica*

ITEM	ESTIMATE	ACTUAL
Straws	*5* TENS *6* ONES	*3* TENS *2* ONES
		Thirty-two
		Number Word
_____	_____ TENS _____ ONES	_____ TENS _____ ONES
		_____
		Number Word

Formative Assessment Note

To learn a lot about your children's base-ten concept development use a class **Observation Checklist** to record observations about how children do these activities. For example, how do children count the objects? Do they make groupings of ten? Do they count to 10 and then start again at 1? Children who count in these ways are already using the base-ten structure. But what you may likely see early on is children counting a full set without stopping at tens and without any effort to organize the materials in groups. If you notice this behavior, use a diagnostic interview and ask the child to count a jar of small beans (between 30 and 50 beans) and record the number. Ask the child, "If you were to place each group of 10 beans in a small cup, how many cups would you need?" If a child has no idea or makes random guesses, what would you know about the child's knowledge of place value?

Grouping Tens to Make 100

In second grade, numbers up to 1000 become important (CCSSO, 2010). Here the issue is not one of connecting a count-by-ones approach to a group of 100 but rather seeing the number in multiple ways, including as 100 single objects, as 10 tens, and as a singular unit. In textbooks these relationships are often presented on one page showing how 10 rods of ten can be put together to make 1 hundred piece. This quick demonstration may be lost on many children. Additionally, the word *hundred* is equally strange and can get even less attention. These word names are not as simple as they seem!

The 100th Day of School from the Black Lagoon (Thaler, 2014) and *100th Day Worries* (Cuyler, 2005) are two children's books that focus on the 100th day of school, which is one way to explore the benchmark number of 100. Through a variety of ways to think about 100 (such as collections of 100 items), children can use these stories to think about the relative size of 100 or ways to make 100 using a variety of combinations.

To reinforce the idea that a hundred is a group of 10 tens and also 100 singles, consider the estimation activity "Too Many Tens."

 Activity 11.4　　　　　　　　　　　　　　　　　CCSS-M: 2.NBT.A.1

Too Many Tens

Show children any quantity with 150 to 1000 items. For example, you might use a jar of lima beans, a clear bag of plastic beads, a long chain of connecting links or paper clips, a box of Styrofoam packing peanuts, or a grocery bag full of straws. First, have children make and record estimates of how many beads, for example, are in the bag. Discuss how children determined their estimates. Then distribute portions of the beads to pairs or triads of children to put into cups of 10 beads. Collect leftover beads and put these into groups of ten as well. Now ask, "How can we use these groups of ten to tell how many beads we have? Can we make new groups from the groups of ten? What is 10 groups of ten called?" Be prepared with some larger containers or baggies into which 10 cups (or other collections of 10 tens) can be placed. When all groups are made, count the hundreds, the tens, and the ones separately. Record the totals on the board as "4 hundreds + 7 tens + 8 ones."

In this activity, it is important to use a groupable model so that children can see how the 10 groups of ten are the same as 100 individual items. At first, you may think this activity will take too much time. But this activity helps cement the connection that is often lost in the rather simple display of a hundreds flat or a paper hundreds square in the pregrouped base-ten models.

Equivalent Representations

An important variation of the grouping activities is aimed at the equivalent representations of numbers. For example, pose the following task to children who have just completed the "Groups of Ten" activity (Activity 11.2).

What is another way you can show 42 besides 4 groups of ten and 2 singles? Let's see how many ways you can find.

Interestingly, most children will go next to 42 singles. The following activities focus on creating additional equivalent representations.

 Activity 11.5　　　　　CCSS-M: 1.NBT.B.2; 1.NBT.C.5

Standards for Mathematical Practice

◀ **8** Look for and express regularity in repeated reasoning.

Can You Make the Link?

Show a collection of materials that is only partly grouped in sets of ten. For example, you may have 5 chains of 10 links and 17 additional unconnected links. Be sure the children understand that each chain has 10 links. Have children count the number of chains and the number of singles in any way they wish to count. Ask, "How many in all?" Record all responses and discuss how they got their answers. Next, before their very eyes, change the groupings (make a ten from the singles or break apart one of the tens) and repeat the questions and discussion. Do not change the total number from one time to the next. Once children begin to understand that the total does not change, ask in what other ways the items could be grouped if you use tens and ones.

If you are teaching second grade, equivalent representations for hundreds as groups of tens can help children with the concept of a hundred as 10 tens. The next activity is similar to "Can You Make the Link?," but it is done using pregrouped materials and includes hundreds.

Activity 11.6

CCSS-M: 2.NBT.A.1; 2.NBT.A.3; K.CC.B.5

Three Other Ways

Children work in groups or pairs. First, they show 463 on their desks with base-ten materials in the standard representation (i.e., 4 hundreds pieces, 6 sticks of ten, and 3 ones). Next, they find and record at least three other ways of representing this quantity. As a variation, challenge children to find a way to show an amount with a specific number of pieces. For example, "Can you show 463 with 31 pieces?" (There is more than one way to do this.)

Although Burris (2013) identified benefits of using both virtual and physical base-ten manipulatives, he found virtual base-ten blocks more readily supported children as they explored nonstandard representations of numbers for a couple of reasons. (He used the virtual place value blocks from Scott Foresman's *eTools*.) First, children were able to compose and decompose numbers more quickly with the virtual blocks than with the physical blocks and so were able to generate many more different representations. And second, the virtual site included a place value mat that displayed the number represented by the base-ten blocks. As the base-ten blocks changed, the number remained the same, reinforcing the idea that the representations were indeed equivalent.

When children have had sufficient experiences with pregrouped materials, a semi-concrete "square-line-dot" notation can be used for recording hundreds, tens, and ones (see Figure 11.7 and the **Square Line Dot** Activity Page). Use the drawings to reinforce the notion of unitizing (i.e., *one* ten, *one* hundred) and also as a suggestion for how children can record their reasoning and results.

The next activity begins to incorporate oral language with equivalent representation ideas.

Activity 11.7

CCSS-M: 1.NBT.A.1; 2.NBT.A.1; 2.NBT.A.3

Base-Ten Riddles

Base-ten riddles can be presented orally or in written form (see **Base-Ten Riddle Cards**). In either case, children should use base-ten materials to help solve the riddles. The examples here illustrate different levels of difficulty. After children solve these riddles, have them write new ones:

- I have 23 ones and 4 tens. Who am I?

- I have 4 hundreds, 12 tens, and 6 ones. Who am I?

- I have 30 ones and 3 hundreds. Who am I?

- I am 45. I have 25 ones. How many tens do I have?

- I am 341. I have 22 tens. How many hundreds do I have?

- I have 13 tens, 2 hundreds, and 21 ones. Who am I?

- If you put 3 more tens with me, I would be 115. Who am I?

- I have 17 ones. I am between 40 and 50. Who am I? How many tens do I have?

Oral and Written Names for Numbers

In this section, we focus on helping children connect oral and written names for numbers (see bottom of Figure 11.3) with their emerging base-ten concepts of using groups of 10 or 100 as efficient methods of counting. Note that the ways we say and write numbers are conventions, not concepts. Children must learn these by being told rather than through problem-based activities.

🎵 Teaching Tip

It is important to note that for ELLs, the convention or pattern in our English number words is likely not the same as it is in their native language, especially for the numbers 11 to 19.

Figure 11.7

Equivalent representation exercises using square-line-dot pictures.

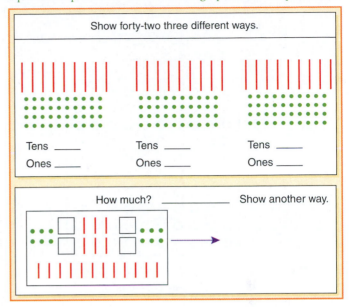

Two-Digit Number Names

In kindergarten and first grade, children need to connect the base-ten concepts with the oral number names they have repeatedly used. They know the words but may have not thought of them in terms of tens and ones. In fact, early on they may want to write twenty-one as 201.

When teaching oral names, you will almost always want to use base-ten models. Initially, rather than use standard number words, use the more explicit base-ten language (e.g., "4 tens and 7 ones" instead of "forty-seven"). Base-ten language is rarely misunderstood. When it seems appropriate, begin to pair base-ten language with standard language. Emphasize the teens as exceptions. Acknowledge that they are formed "backward" and do not fit the patterns. The next activity helps introduce oral names for numbers.

▲ Activity 11.8

CCSS-M: 1.NBT.B.2c

Counting Rows of Ten

Project the **10 × 10 Multiplication Array** of dots (Blackline Master 16). Cover up all but two rows, as shown in Figure 11.8(a). "How many tens? [2] Two tens is called twenty." Have the class repeat. Show another row. "Three tens is called thirty. Four tens is forty. Five tens could have been fivety but is just fifty. How many tens does sixty have?" The names *sixty, seventy, eighty,* and *ninety* all fit the pattern. Slide the cover up and down the array, asking how many tens and the name for that many. ELLs may not hear the difference between *fifty* and *fifteen, sixty* and *sixteen,* and so on, so explicitly compare these words and clearly enunciate and even overemphasize the word endings.

Use the same 10 × 10 multiplication array to work on names for tens and ones. Show, for example, four full lines, "forty." Next expose one dot in the fifth row. "Four tens and one. Forty-one." Add more dots one at a time. "Four tens and two. Forty-two." "Four tens and three. Forty-three." This is shown in Figure 11.8(b). When that pattern is established, repeat with other decades from 20 through 90. Eventually use a hundreds chart (See **Blackline Master 2**) in conjunction with the 10 × 10 multiplication array to connect the oral name with the written numeral. For example, children can locate "43" as down four rows of ten and over 3 ones.

The next activities show how this basic approach might be done with other base-ten models.

Figure 11.8

10×10 dot arrays are used to model sets of tens and ones (Blackline Master 16).

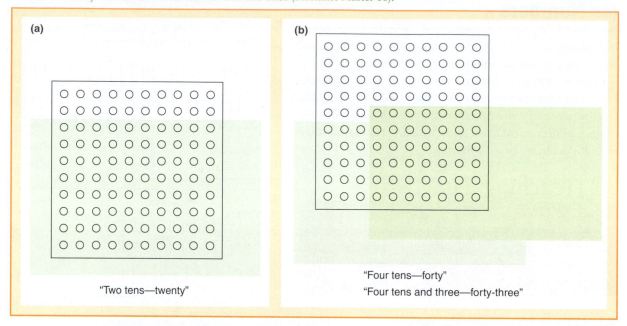

(a)

"Two tens—twenty"

(b)

"Four tens—forty"
"Four tens and three—forty-three"

 Activity 11.9

CCSS-M: 1.NBT.B.2; 1.NBT.C.5

Counting with Base-Ten Models

Show some tens (using base-ten pieces) on the projector or just place them on the carpet in a mixed arrangement. Ask how many tens. Add or remove a ten and repeat the question. Next add some ones. Always have children give the base-ten name and the standard name. (Refer children to examples of the base-ten name and the corresponding standard name that you have posted on the math word wall. These examples will be helpful for any ELLs and children with disabilities in your class.) Continue to make changes in the materials displayed by adding or removing 1 or 2 tens and by adding and removing ones. Avoid the standard left-to-right order for tens and ones so the emphasis is on the names of the materials, not the order they are in.

Reverse the activity by having children use base-ten blocks at their desks. For example, say, "Make 63." The children make the number with the models and then give the base-ten name (6 tens and 3 ones) and standard name (63).

 Activity 11.10

CCSS-M: 1.NBT.B.2a; 1.NBT.B.2b; 1.NBT.B.2c

Standards for Mathematical Practice

▸ **2** Reason abstractly and quantitatively.

Tens and Ones with Fingers

Ask your class, "Can you show 6 fingers (or any amount less than 10)?" Then ask, "How can you show 37 fingers?" Some children will figure out that at least four children are required. Line up four children, and have three hold up 10 fingers while the fourth child holds up 7 fingers. Have the class count the fingers by tens and ones. Ask other children to show different numbers. Emphasize the number of sets of 10 fingers and the single fingers (base-ten language) and pair this with standard language.

Activities 11.8, 11.9, and 11.10 will be enhanced by having children explain their thinking. If you don't require children to reflect on their responses, they soon learn how to give the response you want, matching number words to models without actually thinking about the total quantities. Also, consider occasionally counting an entire representation by ones. Remember that counting by ones is the young child's principal linkage with the concept of quantity. For example, suppose you have just had children use linking cubes to make 36. Try asking, "Do you think there really are 36 blocks there?" Many children may not be convinced, so the count by ones is very significant.

Teaching Tip

Post examples of base-ten names and the corresponding standard names on the math word wall. This is particularly helpful for ELLs and children with disabilities and will be helpful for other children as well.

Three-Digit Number Names

The approach to three-digit number names is essentially the same as for two-digit names. Show mixed arrangements of base-ten materials and have children give the base-ten name (4 hundreds, 3 tens, and 8 ones) and the standard name (438). Vary the arrangement from one example to the next by changing only one type of piece; that is, add or remove only ones or only tens or only hundreds. It is important for children with disabilities to see counterexamples, so purposefully point out that some (anonymous!) children wrote 200803 for two hundred eighty-three, and ask them whether that is correct and to explain their reasoning. The connection between oral and written numbers is not straightforward, with some researchers suggesting that an early milestone on the route to full understanding is this early (incorrect) expanded form of writing numbers (Byrge, Smith, & Mix, 2013). These discussions allow children to explore their initial ideas and clear up any misunderstandings.

Standards for
Mathematical Practice

3 Construct viable arguments and critique the reasoning of others.

The major challenge with three-digit numbers is with numbers involving no tens, such as 502. As noted earlier, the use of base-ten language is quite helpful here. The difficulty with zero tens (or more generally the internal zero) is more pronounced when writing numerals. For example, children frequently incorrectly write 7002 for seven hundred two. Emphasizing the meaning in the oral base-ten language will be a significant help. At first children do not see the importance of zero in place value and do not understand that zero helps us distinguish between such numbers as 203, 23, and 230 (Dougherty, Flores, Louis, & Sophian, 2010). Carefully avoid calling zero a "placeholder" because it is a number with a value. Pose tasks similar to the following to emphasize the importance of zero in place value. ELLs may need additional time to think about how to say and write the numerals, because they are translating all the terms involved with the number.

Use the standard names to say the following numbers: 203, 23, and 230. As you say a number, have children write the number and then model the number with base-ten materials. Then repeat the numbers orally using base-ten language and have children check their models and written numerals.

Written Symbols

Place-value mats are simple mats divided into two or three sections to hold ones and tens or ones, tens, and hundreds pieces as shown in Figure 11.9. You can suggest to children that the mats are a good way to organize their materials when working with

Figure 11.9

Place-value mats with two ten-frames in the ones place promote the concept of groups of ten.

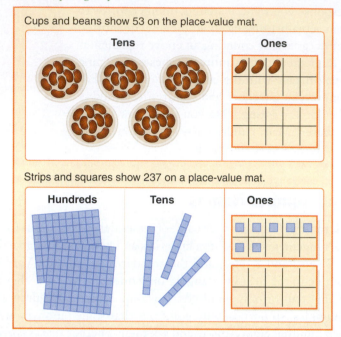

Cups and beans show 53 on the place-value mat.

Strips and squares show 237 on a place-value mat.

base-ten blocks. Explain that the standard way to use a place-value mat is with the space for the ones on the right and tens and hundreds places to the left.

Although it is not commonly seen in textbooks, it is strongly recommended that two ten-frames be drawn in the ones place as shown on the **Place-Value Mat**, Blackline Master 17. That way, the amount of ones on the ten-frames is always clearly evident, eliminating the need for repeatedly counting the ones. The ten-frame also makes it very clear how many additional ones are needed to make the next set of ten. If children are modeling two numbers at the same time, one ten-frame can be used for each number.

Be aware of how easy it is for a child to show a number on a mat using base-ten blocks and learn to write the number without any understanding of what the number represents. First- and second-grade textbooks often show a picture of base-ten materials and have children record numbers in this manner:

<u>7</u> tens and <u>3</u> ones is <u>7 3</u> in all.

Figure 11.10

Building numbers with a set of place-value cards.

It is all too easy to copy down the number of rods and single blocks and rewrite these digits as a single number 73 and not confront what these symbols stand for. Consider the following approach to address this issue.

As children use their place-value mats, they can be shown how the left-to-right order of the pieces is also the way that numbers are written. To show how the numbers are "built," have a set of 27 **Place Value Cards**—one for each of the hundreds (100–900), one for each of the tens (10–90), and cards for 1 through 9 (see Figure 11.10). Notice that the cards are made so that the tens card is twice as long as the ones card and the hundreds card is three times as long as the ones card.

As children place the materials for a number (e.g., 457) on the place-value mat, have them also place the matching cards (e.g., 400, 50, and 7) below the materials. Then starting with the hundreds card, layer the others on top, right aligned. This approach will show how the number is built while allowing children to see the individual components of the number. This is especially helpful when there are zero tens. The place-value mat and the matching cards demonstrate the important link between the base-ten models and the written form of the numbers.

The next two activities are designed to help children make connections between models, oral language (base ten and standard), and written forms. The activities can be done with two- or three-digit numbers depending on children's needs.

Teaching Tip

To support children struggling with reading a number with an internal zero (i.e., zero tens), show or say, for example, 7 hundreds and 4 ones. Then the class says, "Seven hundreds, zero tens, and four ones, which is—seven hundred (slight pause) four." The pause and the base-ten language suggest the correct reading of the three-digit number.

Activity 11.11

CCSS-M: 2.NBT.A.1a; 2.NBT.A.1b; 2.NBT.A.3

Say It/Display It

Display models of ones and tens (and hundreds, if appropriate) in a mixed arrangement. Use a projector, virtual manipulatives, or simply draw on the board using the square-line-dot method. Children say the amount shown in base-ten language ("four hundreds, one ten, and five ones") and then in standard language ("four hundred fifteen"); next they enter it on their calculators or write it on a small whiteboard or on paper. Have someone share his or her display and defend it. Make a change in the materials and repeat. You can also do this activity by saying the standard name for a number and then having children use base-ten materials to show that number and then enter it on their calculators (or write it). Again, pay special attention to numbers in the teens (e.g., 13 and 419) and to the case of zero tens (e.g., 305). ELLs may need additional time to think of the words that go with the numbers, especially as the numbers get larger.

The next activity is a wonderful challenge for children in early stages of place-value development. It can also be used as an assessment to see whether children really understand the value of digits in two- and three-digit numbers.

Activity 11.12

CCSS-M: 1.NBT.B.2; 1.NBT.C.5; 1.NBT.C.6; 2.NBT.A.1; 2.NBT.A.3; 2.NBT.B.5; 2.NBT.B.8

Digit Change

Have children enter a specific two- or three-digit number on the calculator. The task is to change one of the digits in the number without simply entering the new number. For example, change 48 to 78. Change 315 to 305 or to 295. Changes can be made by adding or subtracting an appropriate amount. Children should write or discuss explanations for their solutions. Children with disabilities may need the visual support of having cards that say "add ten" or "add one" first to explore how the number changes. They may also need to use base-ten materials to be able to conceptualize the number and then move to more abstract work using only the calculator.

Formative Assessment Note

Children are often able to disguise their lack of place value understanding by following directions, using the tens and ones pieces in prescribed ways, and using the language of place value.

The diagnostic tasks presented here are designed to help you look more closely at children's understanding of the integration of the three components of place value. Designed as diagnostic interviews rather than whole-class activities, these tasks have been used by several researchers and are adapted primarily from Kami (1985), Labinowicz (1985), and Ross (1986).

The first interview task is referred to as the Digit Correspondence Task. Take out 36 blocks. Ask the child to count the blocks, and then have the child write the number that tells how many there are. Circle the 6 in 36 and ask, "Does this part of your 36 have anything to do with how many blocks there are?" Then circle the 3 and repeat the question. As with all diagnostic interviews, do not give clues. Based on responses to similar tasks, Ross (1989, 2002) has identified five distinct levels of understanding of place value:

1. *Single numeral.* The child writes 36 but views it as a single numeral. The individual digits 3 and 6 have no meaning by themselves.

2. *Position names.* The child correctly identifies the tens and ones positions but still makes no connections between the individual digits and the blocks.

3. *Face value.* The child matches 6 blocks with the 6 and 3 blocks with the 3.

4. *Transition to place value.* The 6 is matched with 6 blocks and the 3 with the remaining 30 blocks but not as 3 groups of 10.

5. *Full understanding.* The 3 is correlated with 3 groups of 10 blocks and the 6 with 6 single blocks.

For the second interview, write the number 342. Have the child read the number. Then have the child write the number that is 1 more. Next, ask for the number that is 10 more. You may wish to explore further with models. One less and 10 less can be checked the same way. Observe whether the child is counting on or counting back or whether the child immediately knows that 10 more is 352. This interview can also be done with a two-digit number.

A third interview can also provide interesting evidence of depth of understanding. Ask the child to write the number that represents 5 tens, 2 ones, and 3 hundreds. Note that the task does not give the places in order. What do you think will be the common misunderstanding? If the child does not write 352, then ask the child to show you the number with base-ten materials and to say what number they have with the materials. Compare to what they wrote previously, if different. What information can you obtain from the results of this interview?

Watch this video clip and consider what this child knows about place value based on her responses to the interviewer's questions.

Table 11.1 provides a summary of the most common errors and misconceptions children will demonstrate in the early stages of learning about place value, along with suggestions about how to help them work through these issues.

Table 11.1. Common errors and misconceptions in place value and how to help.

Misconception/Error	What it Looks Like	How to Help
1. The child incorrectly writes numbers in an expanded form that mirrors the place value words.	When asked to write "two hundred eighty three" the child writes 200803.	• Have the child build numbers with a set of place-value cards as shown in Figure 11.10.
2. The child reverses the digits when writing two-digit numbers.	Writes "53" when should write "35."	• Have the child use virtual base-ten blocks that display the corresponding number. • Have the child use base-ten blocks to represent both two-digit numbers (such as 53 and 35) and then write the numbers using place-value columns. Now ask the child to describe how the numbers are similar and different. • Ask the child to read the number using base-ten language (e.g., 53 is 5 tens and 3 ones) and then match it with place-value cards (Figure 11.10).
3. The child represents the number with base-ten blocks using the face value of the digits.	When asked to represent "13" with base-ten materials, the child uses one piece for the "1" and three pieces for the "3" as in: 1 3 □ □ □ □	• Have the child use virtual base-ten blocks that display the corresponding number. • Have the child build the number with a set of place-value cards as shown in Figure 11.10 and then use base-ten blocks to represent the corresponding amounts.
4. When given an arrangement of base-ten blocks to count, the child ignores the 10-1 relationship between the pieces and uses the same count for different pieces.	When given the following arrangement of base-ten blocks the child either counts by ones and responds "5" or counts by tens and responds "50."	• Ask the child to count the given arrangement by ones. You will likely need to point out the "ones" in the rods of ten and the tens in the flat of a hundred. • Have the child use groupable base-ten blocks or ten-frames to build the number and then count the amount by ones to check.
5. The child is easily confused about the meaning of the digits in a multi-digit number.	When asked to identify which of the following shows 35, the child may say both or may select one and justify the response by saying that there are 3 pieces to match to the 3 and 5 pieces to match to the 5 (without connecting the meaning of the place value to the digit).	• Have the child represent numbers whose digits are reverses (e.g., 35 and 53) using physical base-ten blocks. Count the amounts by ones. Ask what is similar and what is different. • Have the child represent numbers whose digits are reverses using virtual base-ten blocks and compare the corresponding displayed numbers. • Have the child build the number with a set of place-value cards (see Figure 11.10).

Figure 11.11

A hundreds chart (Blackline Master 3).

1	2	3	4	5	6	7	8	9	10
11	12	13	14	15	16	17	18	19	20
21	22	23	24	25	26	27	28	29	30
31	32	33	34	35	36	37	38	39	40
41	42	43	44	45	46	47	48	49	50
51	52	53	54	55	56	57	58	59	60
61	62	63	64	65	66	67	68	69	70
71	72	73	74	75	76	77	78	79	80
81	82	83	84	85	86	87	88	89	90
91	92	93	94	95	96	97	98	99	100

Patterns and Relationships with Multidigit Numbers

In this section, we focus on developing the relationships of numbers to special numbers called *benchmark numbers* and in ten-structured thinking—that is, flexibility in using the structure of tens in our number system. These ideas begin to provide a basis for computation as children simultaneously strengthen their understanding of number relationships and place value.

The Hundreds Chart

The hundreds chart (Figure 11.11 and **Blackline Master 3**) is such an important tool in the development of place-value concepts that it deserves special attention. K–2 classrooms should have a hundreds chart displayed prominently and used often.

A useful version of a hundreds chart can be made of transparent pockets into which each of the 100 numeral cards can be inserted. You can hide a number in the chart by inserting a blank card in front of the number in the pocket. You can also insert colored pieces of paper in the slots to highlight various number patterns such as skip counting by 2 (even number), 5, and 10 (2.NBT.A.2). You can also remove some or all the number cards and have children return them to their correct positions. A blank 10 x 10 grid (see **Blackline Master 2**) serves as an empty hundreds chart on which you can write numbers. Discuss the pattern shown on the chart as well as the patterns in the numbers.

In kindergarten and first grade, children can count and recognize two-digit numbers with the hundreds chart. In first and second grades, children can use the hundreds chart to develop base-ten understanding, noticing that jumps up or down are jumps of ten (1.NBT.C.4), while jumps to the right or left are jumps of one.

There are lots of patterns on the hundreds chart. During discussions, different children may describe the same pattern in several ways. Accept all ideas and encourage children to consider how these descriptions are similar and different. Here are some of the important place-value related patterns children may point out:

- The numbers in a column all end with the same number, which is the same as the number at the top of the chart.
- In a row, the first number (tens digit) stays the same and the "second" number (ones digit) counts 1, 2, 3, . . . 9, 0) changes as you move across.
- In a column, the first number (tens digit) "counts" or goes up by ones as you move down.
- You can count by tens going down the far right-hand column.
- Starting at 11 and moving down on the diagonal, you can find numbers with the same digit in the tens and ones (e.g., 11, 22, 33, 44, and so on).

For children, these patterns are not obvious or trivial. For example, one child may notice the pattern in the column under the 4—every number ends in a 4. Two minutes later, another child will "discover" the parallel pattern in the column headed by 7. That there is a pattern like this in every column may not be completely obvious.

Once you've discussed some of the patterns on the chart, try Activity 8.33, "Missing Numbers" in Chapter 8.

Formative Assessment Note

Replacing the number cards from a blank chart is a good station activity for two children to try. By listening to how children determine the correct places for numbers, you can assess how well they have constructed an understanding of the 1-to-100 sequence and whether they recognize and purposefully use patterns in our number system to recreate the hundreds chart.

 ## Activity 11.13   CCSS-M: K.CC.A.1; K.NBT.A.1; 1.NBT.A.1; 1.NBT.B.2; 1.NBT.C.5

Finding Neighbors on the Hundreds Chart

Begin with a blank or nearly **Blank Hundreds Chart** (see Blackline Master 2), projecting it on a screen or giving copies to individual children. Then, circle a particular missing number. Children are to fill in the designated number and its "neighbors"—the numbers to the left, to the right, above, and below. After children become comfortable naming the neighbors of a number, ask what they notice about the neighboring numbers. The numbers to the left and right are one more and one less than the given number. Those above and below are ten less and ten more, respectively. What about those numbers on the diagonal? By discussing these relationships on the chart, children begin to see how the sequence of numbers is related to the numerical relationships.

Notice that children will first use the hundreds chart to learn about the patterns in the sequence of numbers. In the following activity, number relationships are made more explicit by including the use of base-ten materials in conjunction with the hundreds chart.

Standards for Mathematical Practice

◀ **2 Reason abstractly and quantitatively.**

 ## Activity 11.14   CCSS-M: K.CC.A.1; K.NBT.A.1; 1.NBT.A.1; 1.NBT.B.2; 1.NBT.C.5

The Hundreds Chart with Models

Use any base-ten model for two-digit numbers with which the children are familiar. Either the **Base-Ten Materials** (see Blackline Master 32) or the **Little Ten-Frame Cards** is recommended. Give children one or more numbers to first make with the models and then find on the hundreds chart. Use groups of two or three numbers either in the same row or the same column. Ask children, "How are the numbers in the row (or column) alike? How are they different?"

Then indicate a number on the hundreds chart. Ask children, "What would you have to change to make it into each of its neighbors (the numbers to the left, to the right, above, and below)?"

As a first step in moving to larger numbers, continue the hundreds chart to 200 and ask similar questions about these larger numbers. You can eventually extend the chart beyond 200.

Several web-based resources include hundreds charts that allow children to explore patterns. "Learning about Number Relationships" is an example (from NCTM's Illuminations website) that has a calculator and hundreds chart and allows for a variety of explorations. Children can skip-count by any number and also begin their counts at any number. ABCya's Interactive Number Chart (0-99 or 1-100) allows children to find and document patterns by coloring the squares that contain the numbers.

Activity 11.15

CCSS-M: 2.NBT.A.1; 2.NBT.A.2; 2.NBT.A.3; 2.NBT.B.8

The Thousands Chart

Provide children with several sheets of the **Blank Hundreds Chart** (see Blackline Master 2). Assign groups of three or four children the task of creating a 1-to-1000 chart. The chart is made by taping 10 blank hundreds charts together in a long strip. Children should decide how they will divide up the task of filling in the chart, with different children working on different parts of the chart. The thousands chart should be discussed as a class to examine how numbers change as you count from one hundred to the next, what the patterns are within and across each hundred, and so on. Note that all of the earlier hundreds chart activities can be extended to thousands charts.

Relationships with Benchmark Numbers

One of the most valuable features of both the hundreds chart and the little ten-frame cards is how clearly they illustrate the distance to the next multiple of 10—the number of spaces to the end of the row on the chart or the number of blank spaces on the ten-frame card. Multiples of 10, 100, and occasionally other special numbers, such as multiples of 25, are referred to as *benchmark numbers*. Children learn to use this term as they work with informal methods of computation. For example, when finding the difference between 74 and 112, a child might say, "First I added 6 onto 74 and that equals 80, which is a benchmark number. Then I added 2 tens onto 80 to get to 100 because that's another benchmark number." Whatever terminology is used, understanding how numbers are related to these special numbers is an important step in children's development of number sense and place-value understanding.

In addition to the hundreds chart, the number line is an excellent way to explore these relationships. The next two activities are suggestions for using number lines. Provide the **Number Lines** Activity Page as a recording sheet for children.

Activity 11.16

CCSS-M: 1.NBT.A.1; 1.NBT.B.2; 1.NBT.B.3; 2.NBT.A.1; 2.NBT.A.2; 2.NBT.A.4

Who Am I?

Sketch a long line (or use cash register tape) and label 0 and 100 at opposite ends. Mark a point with a "?" that corresponds to your secret number. (Estimate the position the best you can.) Children use estimation to try to identify your secret number. For each estimate, place and label a mark at that number on the line until your secret number is discovered. Have children explain how they are making their estimates. Highlight any use of benchmark numbers in their estimations. As a variation, the endpoints can be different from 0 and 100. For example, try 0 and 1000, 200 and 300, or 500 and 800.

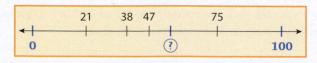

Activity 11.17

CCSS-M: 1.NBT.A.1; 1.NBT.B.2; 1.NBT.B.3; 2.NBT.A.1; 2.NBT.A.2; 2.NBT.A.4

Who Could They Be?

Label two points on a number line (not necessarily the ends) with benchmark numbers. Show children different points labeled with letters and ask what numbers they might be and why the children think that. In the example shown here, B and C are less than 100 but probably more than 60. E could be about 180. You can also ask where 75 might be or where 400 is located. About how far apart are A and D? Why do you think D is more than 100? For ELLs and children with disabilities, say as well as write the numbers on a note card, or ask children to both write and say the numbers.

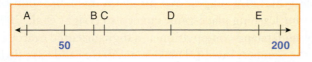

In the next activity children apply some of the same ideas about benchmark numbers that we have been exploring.

Activity 11.18

CCSS-M: 1.NBT.A.1; 1.NBT.B.2; 1.NBT.B.3; 2.NBT.A.1; 2.NBT.A.2; 2.NBT.A.4

Close, Far, and in Between

Put any three numbers on the board. Use two-digit numbers if those are more appropriate for the children.

With these three numbers as referents, ask questions such as the following, encouraging discussion of all responses:

- Which two numbers are closest? How do you know?
- Which number is closest to 300? To 250?
- Name a number between 457 and 364.
- Name a multiple of 10 between 219 and 364.
- Name a number that is greater than all of these numbers.
- Name an even number that is greater than all these numbers.
- About how far apart are 219 and 500? 219 and 1000?
- If these are "big numbers," what are some small numbers? What are some numbers that are about the same? What are some numbers that make these seem small?

For ELLs, modify this activity by using prompts that are similar to each other (rather than changing the prompts each time, which increases the linguistic demand). ELLs and children with disabilities will also benefit from using a visual, such as a number line, and from writing the numbers rather than just hearing them or saying them.

Connecting Place Value to Addition and Subtraction

As you can see, there is much more to learning about place value than having children state how many ones, tens, or hundreds are in a number. Children need ample time and opportunity to fully understand place value because it is a complex concept—so complex that it took humans centuries to develop. Recognizing this complexity, an effective shift has been to blend instruction on computation and place value. The NCTM *Principles and Standards for School Mathematics* suggest, "It is not necessary to wait for students to fully develop place-value understandings before giving them opportunities to solve problems with two- and three-digit numbers. When such problems arise in interesting contexts, students can often invent ways to solve them that incorporate and deepen their understanding of place value, especially when students have the opportunities to discuss and explain their invented strategies and approaches" (National Council of Teachers of Mathematics, 2000, p. 82*). Researchers also suggest that problems involving addition and subtraction are a good context for learning place-value concepts (Wright et al., 2008). We know that children who only understand computation as a digit-oriented exercise and not with full understanding of the numbers involved make many errors and have little judgment of the reasonableness of their answers. Chapter 12 focuses on helping children build flexible computational strategies using place-value knowledge. Here, in this section, we lay the groundwork for developing both conceptual and procedural knowledge as we connect place value to addition and subtraction.

Stop and Reflect

As you consider the activities in this section, you will find that although you are adding and subtracting multidigit numbers, the activities are structured so that you will not be regrouping or trading. If you find yourself using a standard procedure, do the activity again using decomposition (taking apart numbers) and composition (putting together numbers) rather than regrouping.

The key purpose of the following activities is to provide opportunities for children to apply their emerging understanding of place value to computation using benchmark numbers.

Activity 11.19

CCSS-M: 1.NBT.B.4

50 and Some More

Say or write a number between 50 and 100. Children respond with "50 and _____." For 63, the response is "50 and 13." Any benchmark number can be used instead of 50. For example, you could use any number that ends in 50 for the first part (e.g., 450 and some more). Or you could use numbers such as 70 or 230 as starting points.

The benchmark numbers we discussed in our discussions of place value are also used in computational strategies to make the calculations easier. The next activity is aimed at what may be one of the most important benchmark numbers: 100.

---

* From *Principles and Standards for School Mathematics*, Vol. 1. Published by National Council of Teachers of Mathematics. © 2000.

Activity 11.20

The Other Part of 100

Two children work together with a set of **Little Ten-Frame Cards**. One child makes a two-digit number using the ten-frame cards. Then both children work mentally to determine what goes with the ten-frame amount to make 100. They write their solutions on paper and then check by making the other part with the cards to see if the total is 100. Children take turns making the original number. Figure 11.12 shows three different thought processes that children might use. Provide children with **The Other Part of 100** Activity Page as a recording sheet.

   Have children take a look at **Maurice's Chart**. Ask them to decide whether Maurice is right or wrong and, if needed, describe how to correct the mistake.

If your children are adept at finding parts of 100, you can change the whole from 100 to other multiples of 10, such as 70 or 80, or extend the whole to any number less than 100.

Stop and Reflect

Suppose that the whole is 83. Sketch four little ten-frame cards showing 36. Looking at your "cards," what goes with 36 to make 83? How did you think about it?

What you might have done in finding the other part of 83 was added up from 36 to 83. Or you might have subtracted 33 from 83, which equals 50 and then subtracted 3 more. Either way, notice that you did not regroup. Most likely you did it in your head, possibly using benchmark numbers and place value. With more practice you (and children as early as the second grade) can do this without the aid of the cards.

   Compatible numbers for addition and subtraction are numbers that easily combine to make benchmark numbers. Numbers that make tens or hundreds are the most common examples. Compatible sums also include numbers that end in 5, 25, 50, or 75, because these numbers are easy to work with as well. Your task is to get children accustomed to looking for combinations that work together and then looking for these combinations in computational situations.

Figure 11.12

Thinking about the "other part of 100."

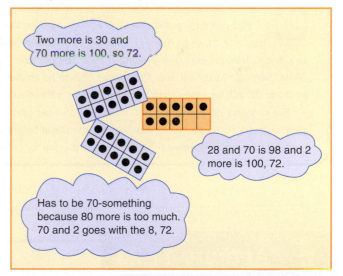

Activity 11.21

Compatible Pairs

Searching for compatible pairs can be done as an activity with the full class. One at a time, project the five suggested compatible pair searches shown in Figure 11.13. The possible searches vary in difficulty. Children name or connect the compatible pairs as they see them.

The next activity takes the next step to making addition more explicit while working on place value understanding. This bridging activity involves counting with a constant using the calculator. By adjusting the numbers, it can be made appropriate for almost any ability level.

Figure 11.13

Compatible pair searches.

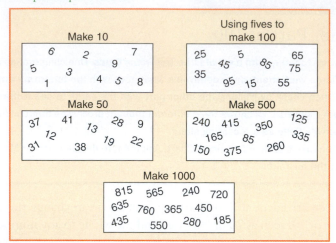

Activity 11.22

Calculator Challenge Counting

Children press any number on the calculator (e.g., 17), then + 10. They say the sum before they press =. Then they continue to add 10 mentally, challenging themselves to say the number before they press =. Challenge them to see how far they can go without making a mistake.

You can differentiate this activity by adjusting the numbers. You may want to begin with a starting number that is less than 10 (e.g., 6) for children with disabilities or with a larger number, such as 98 or 327, for children who need a challenge. Also, the constant addend (+10 in the preceding example) can be changed to any number with one, two, or three digits. Some children will even find jumps of 5 to be challenging if the starting number is not a multiple of 5. Skip counting by 20 or 25 will be easier than counting by 7 or 12 and will help develop important patterns and relationships.

You can also go in reverse. That is, enter a number such as 53 (or 123) in the calculator and press −10 (or for more of a challenge, try − 6). As before, children say the result before pressing =. Each successive press will subtract 10 or whatever constant was entered. Have children share strategies for determining the sum or difference and discuss patterns that appear.

You can also use a calculator, as in the following activity, to challenge children to determine how much to add to or subtract from a given number to reach a target amount.

Activity 11.23

Wipe Out!

Ask children to enter a given number, such as 384, into their calculators. Then their task is to determine a number to subtract from 384 or to add to 384 to wipe out or make the middle digit "0." Have them write down the number and operation they think will work. For example, they could subtract 80 from 384 to equal 304 (they would write − 80). Or they could add 20 to 384 to equal 404 (they would write + 20). Once they have written down their plan, they enter it into their calculator to check to see if the target digit is wiped out. If their plan does not work, they try again. This activity may at first seem too easy for your children, but it will surprise you to see how many think they need to subtract 8 (instead of 80) or add 2 (instead of 20). Once children catch on, you can challenge them with larger numbers and more digits to "wipe out." For example, to increase the challenge, have children start with 5,689 and their goal is to "wipe out" the "6" and the "8".

This next activity combines base-ten representations with symbolism.

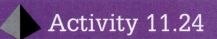

Activity 11.24

CCSS-M: 2.NBT.B.7

Numbers, Squares, Lines, and Dots

Use the **Square, Line, Dot** Activity Page to introduce children to the use of small squares (hundreds), lines (tens), and dots (ones) as a quick way to represent base-ten pieces with simple drawings. Then, as illustrated in Figure 11.14, display addition (or subtraction) problems using a number along with a quantity represented using squares, lines, and dots. Children are to mentally compute the totals (or differences).

Figure 11.15 is a take-away version of the same activity. Note that the subtraction problems with the removed amount represented by the numeral will be easiest to start with.

Figure 11.14

Flexible counting on or addition using both models and numerals.

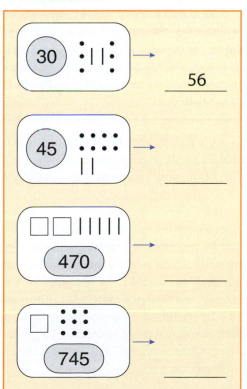

Figure 11.15

Take away or take from subtraction using both models and numerals.

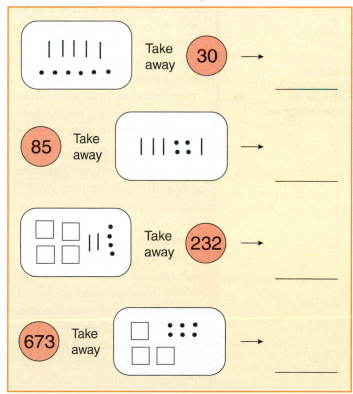

If this activity is done as a whole class, discuss each task before going on to the next. You can also have children write about how they solved each problem, but it is still important to have a discussion with the class. Children can also use the square, line, dot representations as a way to calculate or check answers on other tasks, as shown in the work of a second grader in Figure 11.16.

Figure 11.16

A second grader shows subtraction using a line and dot model.

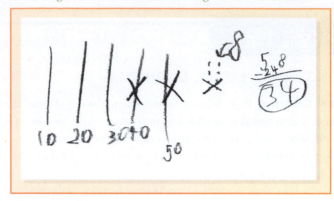

The next activity extends the use of the hundreds chart by using it for addition.

Standards for Mathematical Practice

> **3** Construct viable arguments and critique the reasoning of others.

▶

◢ Activity 11.25

CCSS-M: 2.NBT.B.5

Hundreds Chart Addition

Display a hundreds chart (or thousands chart) for all children to see or, alternatively, give children their own individual charts using the **Four Small Hundreds Charts** (see Blackline Master 4). Children use the hundreds chart to add two numbers (e.g., **38** and **24**). There are many ways that children can use the hundreds chart for addition, so the value is in the class discussions. Have children work on one sum at a time and then have a discussion to compare the different methods children used. Watch **this video** (**https://www.youtube.com/watch?v=cNLP8JylBvY**) that shows one way to add two numbers using a hundreds chart.

The hundreds chart can be thought of as a stacked number line—one that highlights the distance from any number to the next multiple of 10. A jump down a row is the same as adding 10, and a jump up a row is 10 less. To begin, pose problems with relatively small second numbers such as the following:

$$17 + 14 \quad 23 + 12 \quad 35 + 13 \quad 78 + 15$$

Many children will initially count on by ones from the first number, which is an indication that they may not understand how to count by tens from any starting value (an important place-value concept). A child who is using ten as a unit might explain for the problem $17 + 14$ that she started at 17 on the hundreds chart and added 10 by jumping down a row to 27, and then added 3 more by counting over to 30, and then one more to 31. Alternatively, a child might add $17 + 14$ by adding $10 + 10$ by starting at 10 and jumping down a row to 20, then moving over 7 spaces to 27, and then counting 4 more spaces to 31.

The following activity is similar to "Hundreds Chart Addition" but explores the idea of adding up or "think addition" as a method of subtraction.

◢ Activity 11.26

CCSS-M: 2.NBT.B.5

How Much Between?

Provide children with a **Blank Hundreds Chart** (see Blackline Master 2). Give them two numbers. Their task is to determine how much from one number to the next.

In "How Much Between?" the choice of the two numbers has an impact on the strategies children will use. The easiest pairs are ones in the same column on the hundreds chart (e.g., 26 and 76), which is a good place to begin. When the larger number is in a different column from the smaller number (e.g., 24 and 76), children can add on tens to get to the target number's row and then add or subtract ones. Of course, this is also a reasonable strategy for any two numbers. But consider 26 and 72, where the column of 72 is to the left of the column that 26 is in. A child might count by tens from 26 and go down 4 rows (+ 40) to get to 66 (the row before 72) and then count by ones to get to 72. Or a child might count by tens from 26 and go down 5 rows (+ 50) to get to 76 and then count back by ones to get to 72. There are also other possible approaches, which make the discussion of strategies again so important.

You may be so accustomed to thinking about addition and subtraction computation as involving "regrouping"—the trading of 10 ones for a ten or vice versa—that you tend to believe that regrouping is an integral part of computation. In fact, as you will see in Chapter 12, virtually all invented or alternative strategies for computation as well as mental strategies involve no regrouping at all. Rather, what happens in most cases might be called "bridging a ten." The row structure of the hundreds chart is especially useful in developing this understanding of bridging across ten. Children should have ample opportunities to develop their ideas in activities like the ones in this section. Many children are likely still developing their ideas about numbers and distances between them. These ideas are as much about place-value understanding as about addition and subtraction.

 Formative Assessment Note

Children who exhibit difficulty with any of these activities may be challenged with invented computation strategies. Therefore, conduct a diagnostic interview to determine how they are reasoning in activities, such as Activity 11.24, "Numbers, Squares, Lines, and Dots." That activity requires that children have sufficient understanding of base-ten concepts to use them in meaningful counts. If children are counting by ones, then more practice with activities like "Numbers, Squares, Lines, and Dots" may be ineffective. Rather, consider additional counting activities in which children have opportunities to see the value of grouping by ten. Using the little ten-frames can help highlight grouping in tens.

Connections to Real-World Ideas

As children study place-value concepts, encourage them to notice numbers in the world around them. Children in the first grade should be thinking about numbers up to 100 and second graders should be thinking about numbers up to 1000 (CCSSO, 2010). Where are numbers like this in your school? You might use the number of children in a particular grade, the number of children who ride to school on buses, the number of minutes devoted to mathematics each day or week, or the number of days since school has started. There are measurements and numbers discovered on field trips, in other subject areas, and so on. And then there are places outside of school to notice numbers: In grocery stores, sporting complexes, and newspapers to name just a few. Children's literature can also provide a springboard for connecting place value to real-world activities. For example, *Earth Day, Hooray!* (Murphy, 2004) combines place value and recycling as children at an elementary school struggle to keep track of the aluminum cans they collect to recycle.

Look for ways to help your children make sense of the size of the numbers they are learning about. For example, did you know that a horse, a polar bear, and a grand piano each weigh about 1,000 pounds? That the Eiffel Tower is about 1,000 feet tall? Or that a typical ear of corn has about 800 kernels? Check out other ideas to build familiarity with benchmark numbers and units in the chapter on measurement (Chapter 15).

You do not need a prescribed activity to bring real numbers into the classroom. You can turn them into interesting graphs, write stories using them, and make up problems. For example, children can investigate how many cartons of chocolate and plain milk are served in the cafeteria each month? Can they estimate how many cartons will be sold in a school year? Collecting such data and then grouping into tens and hundreds will help reinforce the value of grouping in situations when you need to count and compare quantities.

The particular way you bring numbers and the real world together in your class is up to you. But do not underestimate the value of connecting the real world to the classroom.

12

Building Strategies for Whole-Number Computation

BIG IDEAS

1 Flexible methods of addition and subtraction involve taking apart (decomposing) and combining (composing) numbers in a wide variety of ways. Much of decomposition of numbers is based on place value or compatible numbers—number pairs that work easily together, such as 25 and 75.

2 Invented strategies are flexible methods of computing that vary with the numbers and the situation. These strategies are generated by the person using them through reasoning about the numbers and situations.

3 Flexible methods for computation require a robust understanding of the operations and properties of the operations (commutative and the associative property) as well as how addition and subtraction are related as inverse operations.

4 The standard algorithms are elegant strategies for computing that are based on performing the operation on one place value at a time with transitions to an adjacent position (trading or regrouping). Standard algorithms tend to cause children to think in terms of digits rather than the composite number that the digits make up, resulting in children losing track of the actual value of the digits.

5 Multidigit numbers can be built up or taken apart in a variety of ways to make the numbers easier to work with. These parts can be used to create estimates in calculations rather than using the exact numbers involved. For example, 36 can be thought of as 30 and 6, 4 less than 40, and as 25 plus 10 plus 1. Likewise, 483 can be thought of as 500−20+3 and as 450 and 33 more.

6 Computational estimates involve parts of numbers that are easier to handle or substitute difficult-to-handle numbers with close compatible numbers so that the resulting computations can be done mentally.

Much of the public sees computational skill as the hallmark of what it means to know mathematics at the elementary school level. Although this is far from the whole story, learning computational skills with whole numbers is, in fact, a very important part of the elementary curriculum. Expectations for competency in today's workforce as well as in daily life mean that changes are warranted in how computation is taught. Rather than presenting a single method of adding or subtracting, children should learn that methods can and should change flexibly as the numbers and the context change. In the spirit of the *Common Core State Standards* (CCSSO, 2010) and the *Principles and Standards for School Mathematics* (National Council of Teachers of Mathematics, 2000), the goal is no longer just a matter of "knows how to subtract three-digit numbers;" rather, it is the development over time of an assortment of flexible skills that will best serve children as they prepare for college and careers. *Adding It Up* (National Research Council, 2001) describes it this way:

> More than just a means to produce answers, computation is increasingly seen as a window on the deep structure of the number system. Fortunately, research is demonstrating that both skilled performance and conceptual understanding are generated by the same kinds of activities. (p. 182)

According to the *Common Core State Standards*, children should solve addition and subtraction problems with numbers appropriate for their grade level (within 10 for kindergartners; within 100 for first graders; and within 1000 for second graders). First graders are expected to add two-digit numbers to one-digit numbers or to a multiple of 10. Second graders are expected to add two-digit and three-digit numbers. The solution methods range from using concrete models or drawings to strategies based on place value, meanings of operations, and number sense. To support the development of flexible addition and subtraction strategies, the *Common Core State Standards* also expect children to be able to compose and decompose numbers (numbers less than 20 for kindergartners; numbers less than 100 for first graders; and numbers less than 1000 for second graders).

A Move to Computational Fluency

Addition and subtraction strategies that build on decomposing and composing numbers in flexible ways contribute to children's overall number sense. In most everyday instances, these alternative strategies for computing are easier and faster than the standard algorithms (procedures for computing) and can often be done mentally. Therefore, it is advantageous to help children learn a variety of methods that they can select from as needed. In fact, more and more elementary classrooms are engaging in what has become commonly known as "number talks" (Humphreys & Parker, 2015) where children have opportunities to engage in solving and discussing alternative strategies to solve computation problems.

Consider the following problem.

Mary has 114 spaces in her photo album. So far she has 89 photos in the album. How many more photos can she put in before the album is full?

Stop and Reflect

Try solving the photo album problem using a method other than the standard algorithms you were taught in school. If you are tempted to start with the 9 and the 4, try a different approach. Can you solve it mentally using number sense? Can you solve it in more than one way? Work on this before reading further.

Here are just five of many methods that have been used by children in the primary grades to solve the computation in the photo album problem:

- $89+11$ is 100. $11+14$ is 25.
- $90+10$ is 100 and 14 more is 24. I need to add 1 more because we should have started at 89, not 90, so that is 25 total that I added on.
- From 114 subtract 14 to get 100, then subtract 10 more to get 90, and then 1 more to get to 89, which is subtracting 25 in all.
- 89, 99, 109 (that's 20). 110, 111, 112, 113, 114 (keeping track on fingers) is 25.
- $89+11$ is 100. Adding the same amount (11) to 114 is 125. Then the difference between 125 and 100 is 25.

Strategies such as these can be done mentally, are generally faster than the standard algorithms, and make sense to the person using them. Every day, too many children and adults resort to standard algorithms that they don't fully understand and so, are often error-prone when other, more meaningful methods, like these alternative strategies, would be faster and more accurate.

For a closer look at several alternative algorithms that explicitly emphasize place value and number sense, go to the University of Chicago's Everyday Mathematics website and search "Algorithms." This site provides video examples of these alternative computational algorithms as well as the research basis for why we should help children develop these alternative algorithms. In particular, as children learn these alternative algorithms they learn how quantities can be pulled apart and put back together in different ways (i.e., decomposition and composition of numbers), laying a foundation for understanding the properties of operations (e.g., NCTM, 2014). To get a better sense of the relationship between developing conceptual understanding and computational fluency, watch this **video (https://www.youtube.com/watch?v=ZFUAV00bTwA)** about how the Common Core Standards takes a balanced approach.

Flexibility with a variety of computational strategies is an important tool for a mathematically literate citizen to be successful in daily life. It is time to broaden our perspective of what it means to compute. If you haven't developed these strategies on your own, you will learn them as you read and work through the problems in this chapter and as you teach your children to use them!

Connecting Addition and Subtraction to Place Value

One important shift has been to blend instruction on numeration and place value with computation with two- and three-digit numbers (and beyond). Research suggests that problems involving addition and subtraction are a good context for learning place-value concepts (Carpenter, Franke, Jacobs, Fennema, & Empson, 1998; Cobb & Merkel, 1989; Kamii, 1985; Madell, 1985; Kamii & Joseph, 1988; Wright, Martland, Stafford, & Stanger, 2008). If children only understand computation as a digit-by-digit exercise and not based on the value of the numbers involved, they make many errors and are often unable to judge the reasonableness of their answers. In Chapter 11 in the section called "Connecting Place Value to Addition and Subtraction," we emphasized the connection between place value, addition, and subtraction. The key purpose of the activities in that section is to offer children opportunities to apply their emerging understanding of place value to computation using benchmark numbers. Remember, place value is not only a basis for computation; children also develop place-value understanding as a result of finding their own methods for adding and subtracting multidigit numbers.

Consider Jerrika, in January of the first grade, who solves a story problem for 10+13+22 using connecting cubes. Her written work (Figure 12.1) shows she is still at a pre–place-value stage (see Chapter 11). We can observe that she is beginning to use the idea of "1 ten" but most likely counted on the remaining 35 cubes by ones. Her classmate, Monica, solved the same problem but has clearly utilized more base-ten ideas (Figure 12.1). Ideas such as these continue to grow with further problem solving and sharing of ideas during class discussions.

Figure 12.1

The work of two first graders in January of the school year. They both solved the problem 10 + 13 + 22.

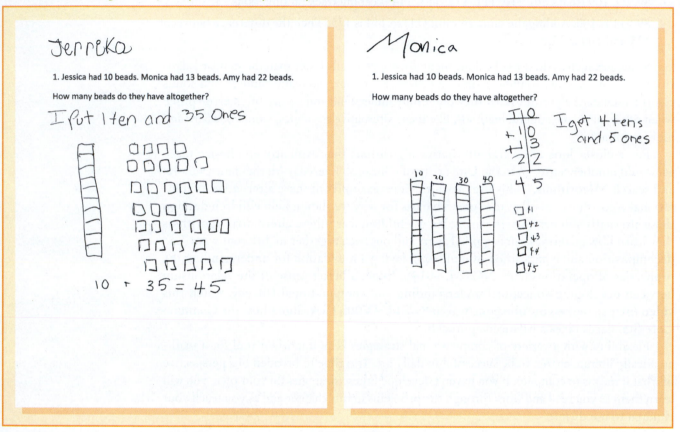

Chapter 11 contains several activities that are designed to further children's understanding of place value concepts while engaging them in addition and subtraction. The next activity continues with this goal by using little ten-frame cards instead of the hundreds chart you see in many of the activities in Chapter 11.

Activity 12.1

CCSS-M: 2.NBT.B.5

Little Ten-Frame Sums

Provide pairs of children with two sets of **Little Ten-Frames**. Each child chooses a number and represents it with the little ten-frames. An example (47+36) is shown in Figure 12.2. Partners work to find the total number of dots, recording the pair of numbers and the sum. The activity can also be done by showing the two sets of ten-frames on the projector for 10–15 seconds and asking the children to give the total. Show them a second time if children request another look.

Figure 12.2

Using little ten-frame cards to add.

Three Types of Computational Strategies

Figure 12.3 lists a general instructional sequence that includes three types of computational strategies. The direct modeling methods can, with guidance, develop into an assortment of more flexible and useful invented strategies, many of which can be carried out mentally. The standard algorithms remain an important part of what children need to learn; however, reinforce that, like the other strategies, the standard algorithms are more useful in some instances than in others. Make sure to discuss which methods seem best in which situations.

Direct Modeling

The developmental step that usually precedes invented strategies for addition and subtraction is called *direct modeling*. This involves the use of manipulatives, drawings, or fingers along with counting to directly represent the numbers involved and the meaning of an operation or story problem. Figure 12.4 shows an example of direct modeling in which a child has modeled the numbers in the problem using counters and then counted by ones to find the answer.

Children who consistently count by ones in additive situations most likely have not developed base-ten grouping concepts. That does not mean that you should avoid giving them problems involving two-digit numbers. Rather, as you work with children who are still struggling to see ten as a unit, suggest that they use a tool to help them think, such as placing counters into ten-frames or making bars of 10 from connecting cubes as they count. Some children will initially use the base-ten rod of 10 as a counting device to keep track of counts of 10, even though they are counting each 10 rod by ones. As children complete each intermediate count, have children write down the corresponding numbers for memory support.

When children have constructed the idea of ten as a unit, they begin to use this idea to move from direct modeling to invented strategies built from number sense and the properties of operations. But it is important to note that direct modeling is a necessary phase for children to work through. Do not push children to

Figure 12.3

A general instructional sequence for three types of computational strategies.

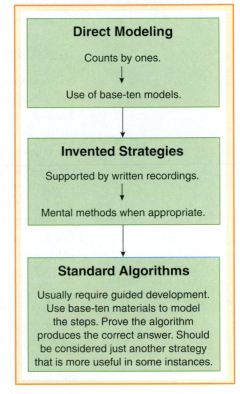

Figure 12.4

A possible direct modeling solution for a story problem.

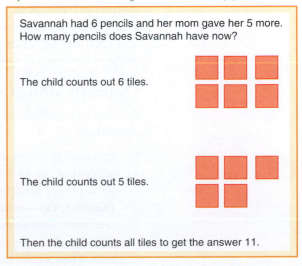

prematurely abandon concrete approaches using materials—including their fingers! However, some children may need encouragement to move away from direct modeling. Here are some ideas to promote the fading of direct modeling:

- Record children's verbal explanations on the board in ways that they and others can follow.

- Ask children who have just solved a problem with concrete materials if they can do a similar problem mentally.

- Ask children to make a written numeric record of how they solved the problem with concrete materials. Then have them try the same written method on a new problem.

Invented Strategies

An *invented strategy* is any strategy, other than the standard algorithm, that does not involve the use of physical materials or counting by ones (Carpenter, Franke, Jacobs, Fennema, & Empson, 1998). For first and second graders, the *Common Core State Standards* (CCSSO, 2010) describe these as "strategies based on place value, properties of operations, and/or the relationship between addition and subtraction" (pp. 16, 19). More specifically, children are expected to "develop, discuss, and use efficient, accurate, and generalizable methods to compute sums and differences of whole numbers in base-ten notation, using their understanding of place value and the properties of operations" (p. 17). At times, invented strategies become mental methods after ideas have been explored, used, discussed, and understood. For example, after some experience, children may be able to do 75+19 mentally (75+20 is 95, less 1 is 94). For 648+257, children may need to write down intermediate steps (i.e., add 2 to 648) to support their memory as they work through the problem. (Try that one yourself.) In the classroom, written records of thinking are often encouraged as strategies develop because they are more easily shared and help children focus on the reasoning used. Distinctions among written, partially written, and mental computation are not important, especially in the development period.

A number of research studies have focused attention on how children handle computational situations when they have been given options for multiple strategies (see, for example, Keiser, 2010; Lynch & Star, 2014; Rittle-Johnson, Star, & Durkin, 2010; Verschaffel, Greer, & De Corte, 2007). "There is mounting evidence that children both in and out of school can construct methods for adding and subtracting multi-digit numbers without explicit instruction" (Carpenter et al., 1998, p. 4). One of the best ways for children to grow their repertoire is to listen to the strategies invented by classmates as they are shared, explored, and tried out by others. However, children should not be permitted to use any strategy without understanding it.

Contrasts with Standard Algorithms

Consider the following significant differences between invented strategies and standard algorithms.

1. *Invented strategies are number oriented rather than digit oriented.* Using the standard algorithm for 45+32, children think of 4+3 instead of 40 and 30. Kamii, longtime advocate for invented strategies, claims that standard algorithms "unteach" place value (Kamii & Dominick, 1998). By contrast, an invented strategy works with the complete numbers. For example, an invented strategy for 618−254 might begin with 600−200 is 400. Another approach might begin with 254, and add 46 which is 300. Then 300 more to 600 and so on. In either case, the computation is number-oriented.

2. *Invented strategies tend to be left-handed rather than right-handed.* Invented strategies often begin with the largest parts of numbers (leftmost digits) because they focus on the entire number. For 86+17, many invented strategies will begin with 80+10 or 86+10 or even 86+20, providing some sense of the size of the eventual answer in just one step. In contrast, the standard algorithm begins with 6+7 is 13. By beginning on the right with a digit orientation, the result is hidden until the end. The standard long division algorithm is the exception.

3. *Invented strategies provide a range of flexible options rather than "one right way."* Invented strategies depend on the numbers involved. Children change the numbers in ways to make the computation easier. Try each of these mentally: 465+230 and 526+98. Did you use the same method? The standard algorithm suggests using the same approach on all problems. The standard algorithm for 7000−25 typically leads to student errors, yet a mental strategy is relatively simple.

Benefits of Invented Strategies

The development and use of invented strategies generate procedural proficiency and more. The positive benefits are difficult to ignore.

- *Children make fewer errors.* Research reveals that when children use their own computational strategies they tend to make fewer errors because they understand their own methods (Gravemeijer & van Galen, 2003). Even when well explained and illustrated with base-ten blocks, many children do not understand the underlying concepts of standard algorithms. Not only do these children make more errors, but the errors are often systemic and difficult to remediate. Errors with invented strategies are less frequent and rarely systemic.

- *Less reteaching is required.* Often teachers are concerned when children's early efforts with invented strategies are slow and time consuming. But the productive struggle in these early stages builds a meaningful and well-integrated network of ideas that is robust and long lasting and significantly decreases the time required for reteaching.

- *Children develop number sense.* Children's development and use of number-oriented, flexible algorithms help them cultivate a rich understanding of the number system, especially place-value concepts. In contrast, children who frequently use standard algorithms are unable to explain why they work and do not demonstrate robust number sense.

- *Invented strategies are the basis for mental computation and estimation.* When invented strategies are the norm for computation, there is no need to talk about mental computation and estimation as if they were separate skills. The number-oriented (as opposed to digit-oriented) perspective and the use of benchmark numbers in invented strategies helps children develop a sense of the magnitude of the answer (estimation). Also, as children become more and more proficient with these flexible methods, they find they are able to use them mentally without having to write down even intermediate steps.

- *Flexible methods are often faster than the standard algorithms.* Consider 300−98. A simple invented strategy might use 300−100 = 200. Adding 2 back (because we subtracted 2 too many), we get 202. This is easily done mentally, or even with some recording, in much less time than the steps to the standard algorithm. Those who become adept with invented strategies will consistently perform addition and subtraction computations more quickly than those using a standard algorithm.

- *Strategy invention is itself a significantly important process of "doing mathematics."* Children who invent a computational strategy or who adopt a meaningful strategy shared by a classmate are involved in the process of sense making and building confidence. This development of procedures is a process that is often hidden from children when the emphasis is only on standard algorithms. By engaging in this aspect of mathematics, a significantly different and valuable view of "doing mathematics" is revealed to learners.

- *Invented strategies serve children well on standardized tests.* Evidence suggests that children using invented strategies do as well or better than children using standard algorithms for computation on standardized tests (Fleischman, Hopstock, Pelczar, & Shelley, 2010; Fuson, 2003).

Mental Computation

A mental computation strategy is simply any invented strategy that is done mentally without recording steps. What may be a mental strategy for one child may require written support by another child. Initially, children may not be ready to do computations mentally, as they may still be at the direct modeling stage or need to notate parts of the problem as they think it through. As your children become more adept, they can and should be challenged to do appropriate computations mentally. You may be quite amazed at the ability of children (and at your own ability) to do mental mathematics. Watch **Connor** use two different invented strategies to mentally solve 39+25.

Try this example using mental mathematics:
342+153+481

Stop and Reflect

For this addition task, try this method: Begin by adding the hundreds, saying the totals as you go—3 *hundred*, 4 *hundred*, 8 *hundred*. Then add on to this amount the tens in successive manner and finally the ones. What mental strategy did (or could) you use as you add on the tens?

Standard Algorithms

More than a century of tradition combined with pressures from families who were taught only the standard algorithm may result in thinking that there is only one best approach and one "right" algorithm. Arguments for a single algorithm generally revolve around efficiency and the need for methods that work with all numbers. For addition and subtraction, however, well-understood and practiced invented strategies are more than adequate, sometimes more efficient, and often more accurate. And, as already mentioned, they have the added bonus of building place-value understanding and number sense.

The main focus in teaching the standard algorithm should be making sense of the procedure as a process and not learning a memorized series of steps. The *Common Core State Standards* (CCSSO, 2010) require that children eventually have knowledge of the standard algorithms (addition and subtraction with multidigit whole numbers in grade 4, multiplication with multidigit whole numbers in grade 5, and division of multidigit whole numbers in grade 6). Notice that the grades in which this knowledge of standard algorithms is required is long after the time where the topic is introduced. This timeline points to the need for full conceptual development to take place first. Importantly, the *Common Core State Standards* recognize that teaching only the standard algorithm doesn't allow children to explore other useful approaches. Understanding how standard algorithms work and when they are the best choice (over an invented approach) is central to development of procedural proficiency.

Standard Algorithms Must Be Understood

Children may pick up the standard algorithms from older siblings and family members while you are still trying to teach a variety of invented strategies. Some children who already know the standard algorithm may resist learning more flexible strategies, thinking they already know the "right" approach. What do you do then?

First and foremost, apply the same rule to standard algorithms as to all strategies: *If you use it, you must understand why it works and be able to explain it.* In an atmosphere that says, "Let's figure out why this works," children can profit from making sense of standard algorithms just as they can with invented strategies. But the responsibility for the explanations should be theirs, not yours. Remember, "Never say anything a kid can say!" (Reinhart, 2000).

Delay Teaching Standard Algorithms

Children are unlikely to invent the standard algorithms because methods that begin with the smaller numbers (the ones) are not as intuitive. Therefore, you will need to introduce and explain each algorithm and help children understand how and why they work. No matter how carefully you introduce these algorithms as simply another alternative, children may sense that "this is the real way" or the "one right way" to compute. So spend a significant amount of time with invented strategies—months, not weeks. Do not feel that you must rush to the standard algorithms. Delay! Again, note that the *Common Core State Standards* (CCSSO, 2010) require that children learn a variety of strategies based on place value and properties of the operations one to two years before the standard algorithms are expected to be mastered. The understandings children gain from working with invented strategies will make it much easier for you to teach the standard algorithms when the time comes. If you think you are wasting precious time by delaying, just be reminded of how many years you and others teach the same standard algorithms over and over to children who still make errors with them and are still unable to explain them. Here is a video of **Gretchen** who uses the standard algorithm incorrectly but still thinks that answer is correct—even when other approaches lead to a different answer.

Continue to Value All Methods

The standard algorithm (once it is understood) is one more strategy children can put in their "toolbox of methods." Reinforce the idea that just like the other strategies, it may be more useful in some instances than in others. Pose problems in which an invented or mental strategy is more useful, such as 504−498 or 61+19. Discuss whether an invented or mental strategy or the standard algorithm seems best. Point out that for a problem such as 568+347, the standard algorithm has advantages. Watch this video clip of **Estephania** who compares the use of a mental strategy with the standard subtraction algorithm.

> **Standards for Mathematical Practice**
>
> ◀ **1** Make sense of problems and persevere in solving them.

Cultural Differences in Algorithms

Some people falsely assume that mathematics is easier than other subjects for children who are not native English speakers. However, the reality is that there are many international differences in notation, conventions, and algorithms. Knowing more about the diverse algorithms children might bring to the classroom and their ways of recording symbols for "doing mathematics" will assist you in supporting these children and responding to their families. It is important to realize that an algorithm we call "standard" may not be customary in other countries. So encouraging a variety of algorithms is important in valuing the experiences of all children.

For example, equal additions is a subtraction algorithm used in many Latin and European countries. It is based on the knowledge that adding (or subtracting) the same amount to both the minuend and the subtrahend will not change the difference (answer). Therefore, if the problem to solve is $25-15$, there is no change to the answer (or the difference) if you subtract 10 from the minuend and subtrahend and solve $15-5$. There is still a difference of 10. Consider the problem $62-27$. Using the algorithm you may think of as "standard," you would likely regroup by crossing out the 6 tens, adding the 10 with a small "1" to the 2 in the ones column (making 12 ones), and then subtract 7 from the 12, and so forth. In the "equal additions" approach (see Figure 12.5(a)), you add 10 to the ones place (2) in 62 to get 12 ones. You would then counteract that addition of 10 to the minuend by adding 10 to the 27 (subtrahend), making 37. Now you subtract the 37. Alternatively, a child, using a strategy based on equal additions (also called "same difference") (Humphreys & Parker, 2015) might add 3 to both 62 and 27, which results in $65-30$, a much easier problem to solve (Figure 12.5(b)). Both of these may sound confusing to you, but try them. Especially when there are zeros in the minuend (e.g., $302-178$), you may find this a productive option over our "standard" algorithm. More important, your possible confusion can give you a sense of how your children (and their families) may react to a completely different procedure from the one they know and find successful. This **video (https://www.youtube.com/watch?v=lIY8rQQqgpw)** demonstrates the equal additions algorithm.

Figure 12.5(a)

The "equal additions" algorithm.

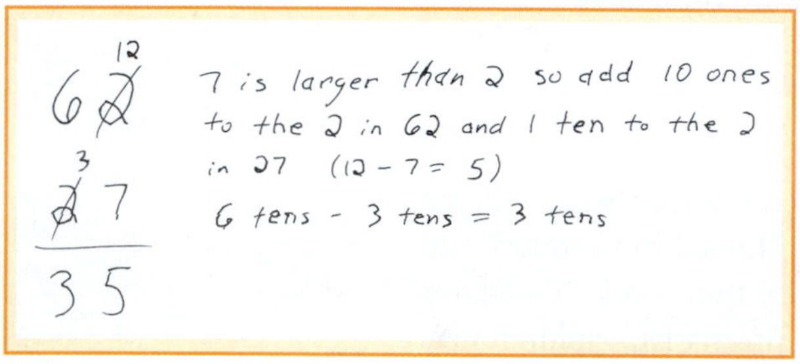

Figure 12.5(b)

A strategy using "equal additions" or "same difference."

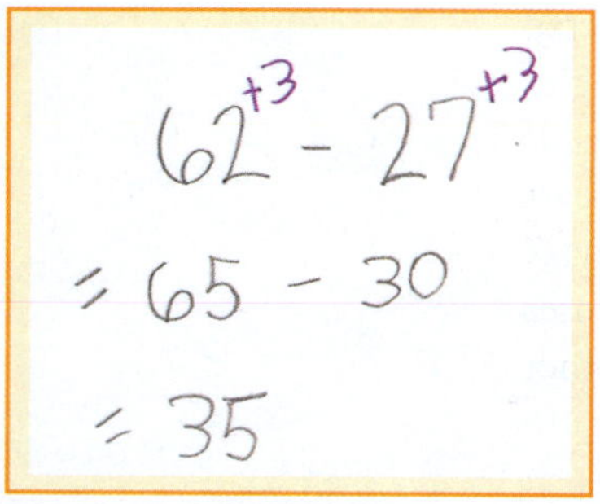

Why does the equal additions method result in the same answer? Using an open number line, mark the two numbers in the original subtraction problem, such as 302 and 178 in $302-178$. Note the difference or the distance between the two numbers (124). Now, using equal additions, change the numbers to create an easier problem to subtract. Note the difference or distance between the two numbers in this new problem is the same as in the original problem. Adding (or subtracting) the same amount from the minuend and the subtrahend just shifts the numbers the same distance along the number line but maintains the difference or distance *between* the two numbers.

Another key component to understanding cultural differences in algorithms is the emphasis on mental mathematics in other countries (Perkins & Flores, 2002). In fact, some children pride themselves on their ability to do math mentally. Don't be surprised if children from other countries can produce answers without written work.

Development of Invented Strategies

You won't be surprised to read that children do not spontaneously invent wonderful computational methods while you sit back and watch. Children tend to develop or gravitate toward different strategies they are exposed to, suggesting that teachers and programs do have an effect on the methods children develop (Verschaffel et al., 2007). The following sections discuss general pedagogical methods that support children's development of invented strategies for multidigit addition and subtraction.

Creating a Supportive Environment

Invented strategies are developed from a strong understanding of numbers. The development of place-value concepts begins to prepare children for the challenges of inventing computational strategies. For example, the CCSSO (2010) suggests that second graders should be able to use mental computation to find a number that is 10 or 100 more (or less) than a given number between 100 and 900. This standard calls for young learners to publicly share emerging ideas. Therefore, children need a classroom environment where they can act like mathematicians and explore ideas without fear. When children in your classroom attempt to investigate new ideas such as invented strategy use, they should find your classroom a safe and nurturing place for expressing naïve or rudimentary thoughts.

Some of the characteristics described previously regarding the development of a problem-solving environment need to be reiterated here to establish the climate for taking risks, testing conjectures, and trying new approaches. Children also need to know that they must persevere and be ready for productive struggle; as that is when learning takes place. Hiebert and Grouws (2007) stated, "We use the word *struggle* to mean that students expend effort to make sense of mathematics, to figure something out that is not immediately apparent. . . . We do not mean the feelings of despair that some students can experience when little of the material makes sense" (p. 387). We need to encourage children to persist with material that is challenging but within their grasp and understandable.

Here are some factors to keep in mind:

Standards for Mathematical Practice

3 Construct viable arguments and critique the reasoning of others.

- Avoid immediately identifying the right answer when a child states it. Give other children a chance to consider whether they think the answer and approach are correct.

- Expect and encourage student-to-student interactions, questions, discussions, and conjectures. Allow plenty of time for discussions.

- Encourage children to clarify previous knowledge and make explicit how they are relating this previous knowledge to new ideas.

- Promote curiosity and openness to new ideas and trying new things.

- Talk about both right and wrong ideas in a nonevaluative and nonthreatening way and emphasize both as places to learn.

- Move less sophisticated ideas to more sophisticated thinking through coaching and strategic questioning.

- Use familiar contexts and story problems to build background and connect to children's experiences. Avoid using "naked numbers" as a starting point, as they do not encourage strategy development.

- Show samples of anonymous children's work and allow children to critique the reasoning of others. *The Great Math Tattle Battle* (Bowen, 2006) is an entertaining book largely about correcting errors in double-digit addition calculations. You can share a "student worksheet" that contains lots of mistakes and see whether your class can find and correct the errors.

Models to Support Invented Strategies

There are three common types of invented strategies to solve addition and subtraction situations that can be extended to larger numbers: **split strategy (https://www.youtube .com/watch?v=XjRiQpMMI-k)** (also called *decomposition*), **jump strategy (https:// www.youtube.com/watch?v=w9haFFL-AMs)** (similar to counting on or counting back), and **shortcut strategy (https://www.youtube.com/watch?v=_v9Kb-qFVxY)** (sometimes known as *compensation*) (Torbeyns, De Smedt, Ghesquiere, & Verschaffel, 2009). The notion of "splitting" a number into parts (often by place value) is a useful strategy for all operations. Both the word *split* and the use of a visual diagram help children develop strategies (Verschaffel et al., 2007). When recording children's ideas, try using arrows or lines to explicitly indicate how two computations are joined together, as shown in Figure 12.6(a).

Figure 12.6

Two methods of recording children's thought processes on the board so that the class can follow the strategy.

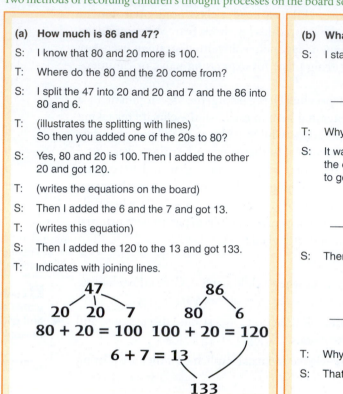

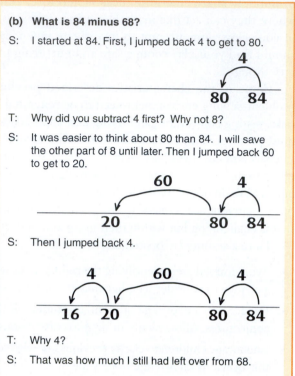

The *empty number line* (also known as the *open number line*) shown in Figure 12.6(b) is a number line with no prewritten numbers or tick marks. Children can use it to support their use of a sequential *jump strategy* that is very effective for thinking about addition and subtraction situations (Caldwell, Kobett, & Karp, 2014; Gravemeijer & van Galen, 2003; Verschaffel et al., 2007). The empty number line is much more flexible than the usual number line because it works with any numbers, eliminates the confusion with tick marks and the spaces between them, and it can be jotted down anywhere. Also, children are less prone to making computational errors when using it (Gravemeijer & van Galen, 2003; Klein, Beishuizen, & Treffers, 2002; Verschaffel et al., 2007).

You can introduce the empty number line by using it to model a child's thinking for the class. Make sure to emphasize that the number line, like a ruler, is a length marked off into particular units—and in the case with the open number line, children create their own units with jumps. Children have to determine the range of numbers to use on the empty number line based on the problems they are solving. They often use "friendly numbers" for the jumps or jump to benchmark numbers on the number line and then calculate the total of the jumps (Barker, 2009). The jumps on the number line can be recorded as children share or explain each step of their solution, counting up or down from an initial number. With time and practice, children find the empty number line to be an effective tool to support and explain their reasoning.

Bar diagrams can also be used to support children's thinking and help them explain their ideas to others. Bar diagrams work particularly well for contexts that fit a comparison situation and a part-part-whole model. See Figure 12.7 for a sample of each.

Standards for Mathematica Practice

5 **Use appropriate tools strategically.**

Figure 12.7

Using bar diagrams to think about quantities and their relationship to each other.

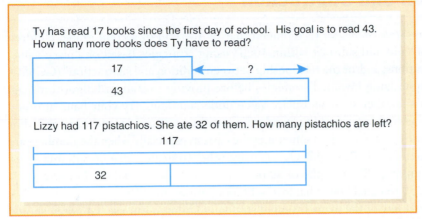

Ty has read 17 books since the first day of school. His goal is to read 43. How many more books does Ty have to read?

17	← ? →
43	

Lizzy had 117 pistachios. She ate 32 of them. How many pistachios are left?

117	
32	

note

You will find a few interactive number lines on the internet where children can practice using a jump strategy to find the distance between two numbers. One of these can be found by searching for "ICT games number line jump." With this version you can change where the number line starts (-100 to 200), the number of spaces on the number line (26 spaces versus 66 spaces), and the size of the jumps. Another version can be found by searching for "dreambox number line jumps" and is limited to jumps of size ten.

The *shortcut strategy* involves the flexible adjustment of numbers. Just as children used 10 as a benchmark number in learning their basic facts, they can move from numbers such as 38 or 69 to the nearest 10 (in this case 40 or 70) and then later take the 2 or 1 off to compensate. For example, if we are adding $38+69$, we can adjust these numbers to $40+70$—which equals 110—and then take off the three extras to get 107. As another example, $51-37$ can be thought of as $51+6$ to get 57 and $57-37 = 20$; then subtract 6 (because you added 6 to the start amount to make the problem easier) to get 14. So $51-37 = 14$. Alternatively, you can adjust the 37 to 41 and subtract $51-41$, which equals 10. Because you subtracted 4 more than you needed to (by changing 37 to 41), you need to add 4 back: $10+4$ is 14.

As these examples suggest, the numbers involved in a problem as well as the type of problem will influence the strategies children use. Therefore, it is important to think carefully about the type of story problem you pose as well as the numbers you use!

◢ Activity 12.2

CCSS-M: 2.OA.A1

Exploring Subtraction Strategies

 Use the set of problems on the **Looking at Collections** Activity Page. Ask children to use bar diagrams or open number lines to show how they are solving these problems and to be ready to explain their strategies.

 For children with disabilities, cut the recording sheet into three pieces to reduce the visual display or put one problem on a page. If children are struggling with where to start, suggest the use of a particular strategy (such as the empty number line). If ELLs have limited English, you can modify this activity by using the same subject in all the stories. If proficiency is stronger, ensure that the contexts are understood.

See the **Expanded Lesson: Exploring Subtraction Strategies** for more details on how to implement this activity.

Development of Invented Strategies for Addition and Subtraction

The *Common Core State Standards* recommend that by the end of second grade, children should be able to "add and subtract within 1000" using strategies based on "place value, properties of operations, and/or the relationship between addition and subtraction" (CCSSO, 2010, p. 19). Emphasizing invented strategies before moving to standard algorithms can enhance children's number sense and place value understanding. Try your hand at doing these computations without using the standard algorithms: 487+235 and 623−587. For subtraction, a counting-up strategy is sometimes the easiest, especially when the numbers are relatively close together as in 623−587. Occasionally, other strategies are more advantageous. For example, "chunking off" multiples of 50 or 25 is often a useful method. For 462+257, pull out 450 and 250 to equal 700. That leaves 12 and 7 more, for 719.

These are just a few of the many invented strategies children can use. Children should use strategies for addition and subtraction that they understand and can use efficiently. Your goal might be that each of your children has at least one or two methods that are reasonably efficient, mathematically correct, and useful with lots of different numbers. Expect different children to settle on different strategies that play to their strengths. In other words, all children do not have to use the same strategy for the same problem. The following sections suggest a variety of invented strategies that children often use.

Adding and Subtracting Single-Digit Numbers

When adding or subtracting small amounts or finding the difference between two reasonably close numbers, many children will use counting to solve the problem. One goal should be to extend children's knowledge of basic facts and the ten-structure of the number system so that counting is not required. When the calculation crosses a ten (e.g., 58+6), using the decade number (60) and thinking 58+2+4, for example, extends children's use of the Make 10 strategy (e.g., add on to equal to 10 and then add the rest). Similarly, for subtraction, children can extend the Down Under 10 strategy. For instance, for 53−7, take off 3 to equal 50, then 4 more is 46.

The next activity helps children think explicitly about making these extensions.

 Teaching Tip

Using the empty number line to support and make explicit children's initial reasoning with jumps can help children develop mental models that will allow them to solve problems in their head.

▶ Activity 12.3

CCSS-M: 1.NBT.C.4; 2.OA.A.2

Crossing a Decade

Quickly review the Make 10 and Down Under 10 strategies from basic facts (see Chapter 10) using little ten-frames. Then have available for children's use **Little Ten-Frames** as well as **Base-Ten Materials** (Blackline Master 32), a **Place-Value Mat** (with ten-frames Blackline Master 17), or a **Hundreds Chart** (Blackline Master 3). Pose an addition or subtraction story problem that crosses a decade number and involves a change or difference of less than 10. The following problems are examples.

- Tommy was on page 47 of his book. Then he read 9 more pages. What page did he end on?

- How far is it from 68 to 75?

- Meghan had 42 cents. She bought a small toy for 8 cents. How much money does she have left?

Two children can work together to determine how to quickly find the total.

Listen for children who are counting on or counting back by ones without paying attention to the ten. For these children, suggest that they use either a hundreds chart or the little ten-frames, shown in Figure 12.8, to support their thinking. Also find out how they solve fact combinations such as $8+6$ and $13-5$. The use of tens for these facts is essentially the same as for the higher-decade problems. Have children who are using the strategy share their ideas with others. They might say, for $47+6$, "I added 3 from the 6 to the 47 to equal 50. Then I added the remaining 3 and that is 53."

As you transition children from single-digit to two-digit numbers, adding and subtracting tens and hundreds is an important intermediate step. Sums and differences involving multiples of 10 or 100 are easily computed mentally. Write a problem such as the following on the board:

$$300+500+20$$

Challenge children to solve it mentally. Ask them to share how they did it. Listen for the use of place-value words: "3 *hundred* and 5 *hundred* is 8 *hundred*, and *20* is *820*." Start with problems that do not require regrouping and then move to more difficult problems such as $70+80$. Continue to encourage children to use base-ten models to help them think in terms of units of tens and hundreds.

Standards for Mathematical Practice

7 Look for and make use of structure.

Figure 12.8

Children extend the Make 10 idea to larger numbers.

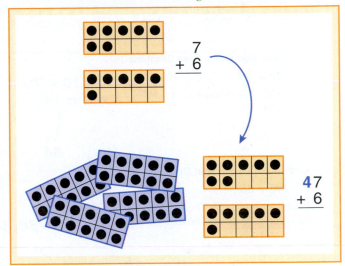

▲ **Activity 12.4**

CCSS-M: 1.NBT.C.4; 1.NBT.C.5; 1.NBT.C.6

I Am . . . , Who is . . . ?

Have children practice their mental calculations and prepare for multidigit computation by adding or subtracting multiples of tens (or other familiar combinations) with two-digit numbers. Use the **I Am/Who Is? Game Cards** for a class up to 30 children. If you have fewer than 30 children, give children who need a challenge two cards. There are also some easier combinations (e.g., Who is 20 + 10? Who is 37 + 10?), so give those cards initially to children with disabilities to ensure they understand the game and are tracking on and using units of ten. Start the game by calling out any number you see on a card, such as "Who is 22?" The child should respond with "I am 22, who is . . ." and then read the rest of the card. The game will loop all the way around through the thirty problems.

Adding Two-Digit Numbers

In the CCSS-M the development of fluency with multidigit addition and subtraction begins in grade 1 with the addition of multiples of ten (1.NBT.C.5) and continues through grade 4, when children are expected to "Fluently add and subtract multidigit whole numbers using the standard algorithm" (4.NBT.B.4) (CCSSO, 2010). This fluency must be built through years of explorations using concrete models or drawings and strategies based the inverse relationship between addition and subtraction, place value, and the properties of operations. Problems involving the sum of 2 two-digit numbers will usually elicit a wide variety of invented strategies from children. Some strategies will involve starting with one or the other number and working from that point, either by adding on to get to the next ten or by adding tens to get from one number to the other. These strategies build the foundation for adding three-digit numbers (and beyond).

Let's start by looking at the following story problem:

Standards for Mathematical Practice

2 Reason abstractly and quantitatively.

Two Scout troops went on a field trip. There were 46 Girl Scouts and 38 Boy Scouts. How many Scouts went on the trip?

Figure 12.9 illustrates four different invented strategies for this story problem, which involves the addition of 2 two-digit numbers. The ways that the solutions are recorded are suggestions but note the frequent use of the empty number line.

Figure 12.9

Four different invented strategies for addition with two-digit numbers.

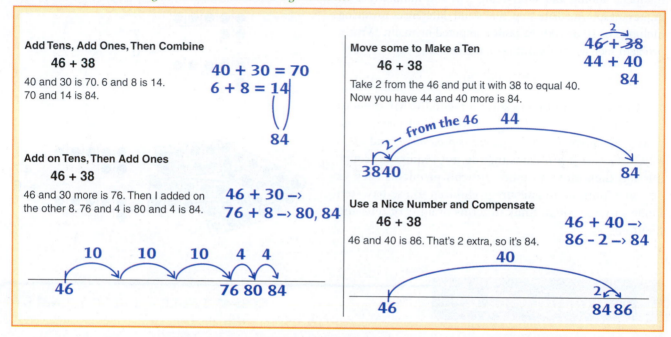

Try adding 367 + 155 in as many different ways as you can. How many of your ways are like those in Figure 12.9?

The shortcut and compensation strategies that focus on making ten are useful when one of the numbers ends in 8 or 9. To promote these strategies, present problems with addends like 39 or 58. Note that it is only necessary to adjust one of the two numbers.

The following activity supports children's thinking about adjusting numbers by using 10 as an anchor.

Activity 12.5

CCSS-M: 1.NBT.C.4; 2.NBT.B.5; 2.NBT.B.9

Just Adjust It

Create a series of problems using numbers that will increase the likelihood that children will gravitate toward the idea of using 10, but do not require children to do so. The point is to help children become more aware of different ways to adjust numbers. Consider using this series of problems:

50 + 30   48 + 30   50 + 32   51 + 28   53 + 29   20 + 60   18 + 58

Project one problem at a time and give children time to solve it before you ask first for answers and then for explanations of their approaches. Record children's strategies so that you can refer back to them when appropriate. If no child suggests the idea of using 50 + 30 or 20 + 60 to help solve the subsequent related problems, you may want to challenge them to determine how they could use that problem to help them solve the others. By listening to classmates and seeing their ideas recorded on the board or projector, other children, particularly those with disabilities, can become more aware of different ways to adjust numbers.

Note that there are multiple ways to add the numbers from the preceding activity by using 10 as an anchor. For example, for 51+28, a child may change 51 to 50 and 28 to 30, add 50+30 to get 80, and then subtract 2 to adjust for adding 30 (instead of 28) and add 1 for adding 50 (instead of 51) to get 79. Other children may think that 51 is really close to 50 and they move 1 to the 28 and add 50+29 to get 79. Still other children may add the tens (50+20) and then the ones (1+8) to get 79. Although this last strategy does not use 50+30, remember your goal is to help children develop strategies that are efficient and that make sense to them. By listening to how their classmates reasoned to find the sums, children will be exposed to a variety of strategies.

 ## Formative Assessment Note

Periodically you will want to focus on a particular child to determine his or her strategy use. Pose the following problem to the child in a diagnostic interview: 46 + 35. See if the child begins by splitting the numbers. That is, for 46 + 35, the child may add on 4 to the 46 to get to 50 and then add the remaining 31. Or the child may add 30 to 46 to get to 76, then add 4 more to get to 80, and then add the remaining 1. In either case, be mindful of how flexibly the child uses ten as a unit or how the child uses a shortcut strategy. Some children may use an open number line and count up with jumps of ten, saying "46, 56, 66, 76" as they draw a corresponding arc and numbers such as +10 and so on. Another approach the child may use involves splitting the numbers into parts and adding the easier parts separately. The split usually involves tens and ones, or the child may use other parts of numbers such as 50 and 25 as easier *compatible numbers* to work with.

Some children may use a counting-by-tens-and-ones technique where they start counting by tens and then revert to counting by ones. That is, instead of quickly saying, "46 + 30 is 76" or even "46, 56, 66, 76," they may say "46, 56, 57, 58, 59, 60, ...75, 76," attempting to keep track of the count-by-ones using their fingers. If child is not consistently using ten as a unit, he or she likely needs more work with place-value ideas.

This last activity in this section provides children with experience in determining whether a sum of two numbers is odd or even.

 ## Activity 12.6

CCSS-M: 2.OA.C.3

Odd or Even?

Start the class off with a two-digit addition problem that uses two consecutive numbers such as 44 + 45. Have them write the problem on the top line of the **Odd or Even** Activity Page. Ask, "Is the sum odd or even? How do you know?" Try other two- or three-digit consecutive addends. Ask, "Are these sums odd or even?" Challenge children to generalize their reasoning by asking, "Do you think the sum of two 'side-by-side' numbers will always be that way? Why or why not?"

Standards for Mathematical Practice

◀ **1** Make sense of problems and persevere in solving them.

Subtraction as "Think Addition"

Children who know the *think-addition* strategy for their basic facts can also use this strategy to solve problems with multidigit numbers. This is an amazingly powerful way to subtract and is particularly successful with children with disabilities (Peltenburg, van den Heuvel-Panhuizen,

& Robitzsch, 2012). For example, for 45 − 29, the idea is to think, "How much do I add to 29 to get to 45?" Notice that this strategy is not as efficient for 45 − 6 because of the distance between the two numbers, 45 and 6. Using *join with change unknown* problems or *missing-part* problems (discussed in Chapter 9) will encourage the use of the think-addition strategy. Here is an example of each.

Sam had 46 baseball cards. He bought some more cards for his collection. Now he has 73 cards. How many cards did Sam buy? (*join with change unknown*)

Juanita has 73 crayons in all. Some are broken and some are not. 46 crayons are not broken. How many are broken? (*missing-part*)

Standards for Mathematical Practice

2 Reason abstractly and quantitatively.

Figure 12.10 shows invented strategies that use addition to solve "subtraction" story problems. As you can see, using tens is also an important part of these strategies. Simply asking for the difference between two numbers may also prompt these strategies.

Figure 12.10

Three different invented strategies for subtraction by "think addition".

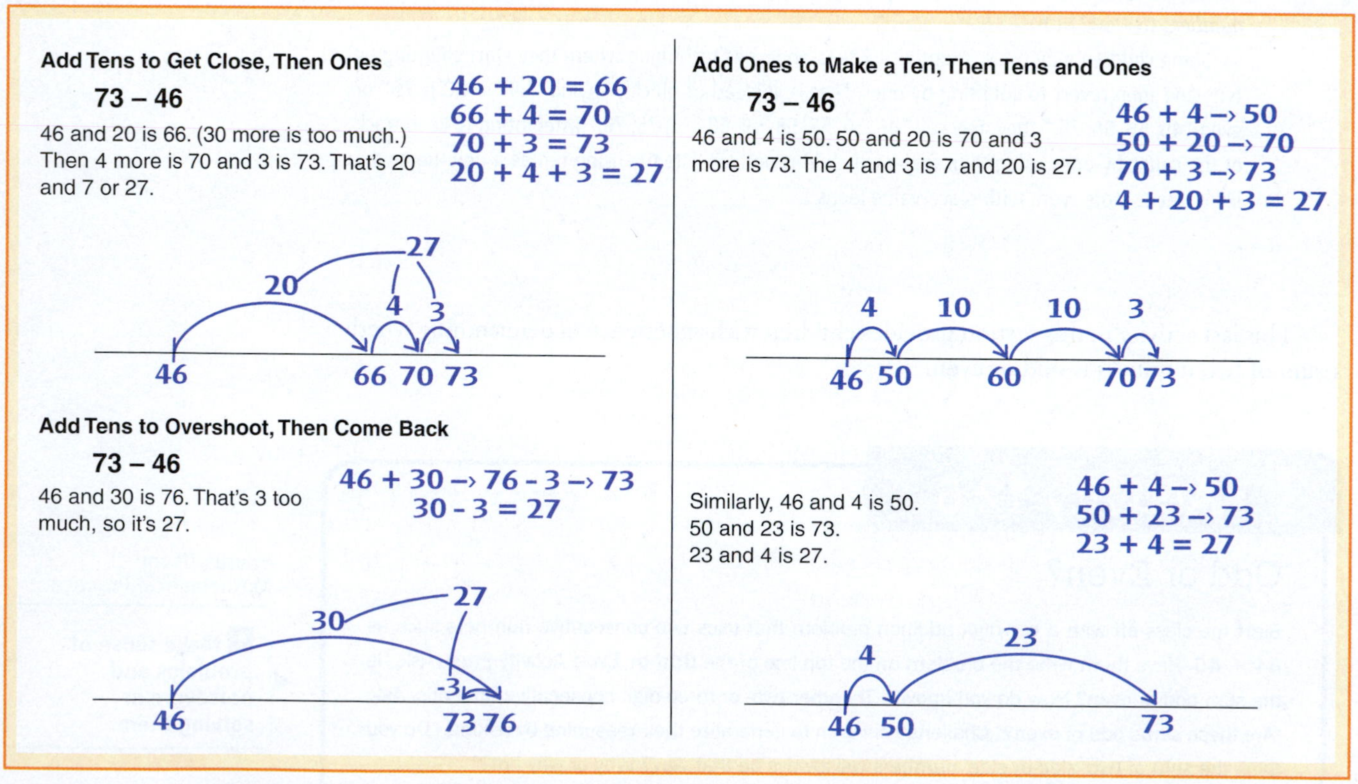
Add Tens to Get Close, Then Ones
73 – 46
46 and 20 is 66. (30 more is too much.) Then 4 more is 70 and 3 is 73. That's 20 and 7 or 27.
46 + 20 = 66
66 + 4 = 70
70 + 3 = 73
20 + 4 + 3 = 27
27
20
4
3
46
66 70 73
Add Tens to Overshoot, Then Come Back
73 – 46
46 and 30 is 76. That's 3 too much, so it's 27.
46 + 30 -> 76 - 3 -> 73
30 - 3 = 27
27
30
-3
46
73 76
Add Ones to Make a Ten, Then Tens and Ones
73 – 46
46 and 4 is 50. 50 and 20 is 70 and 3 more is 73. The 4 and 3 is 7 and 20 is 27.
46 + 4 -> 50
50 + 20 -> 70
70 + 3 -> 73
4 + 20 + 3 = 27
4
10
10
3
46 50
60
70 73
Similarly, 46 and 4 is 50. 50 and 23 is 73. 23 and 4 is 27.
46 + 4 -> 50
50 + 23 -> 73
23 + 4 = 27
4
23
46 50
73

Activity 12.7

CCSS-M: 2.NBT.B.5; 2.NBT.B.9

How Far to My Number?

Children work in pairs with a single set of **Little Ten-Frame.** One child uses the cards to make a number less than 50 while the other child writes a number greater than 50 on a piece of paper, as shown in Figure 12.11). For children with disabilities or children who need a challenge, you may choose to suggest the size of the second number (e.g., less than 100; less than 500). The children work together to find out how much more must be added to the number shown with the ten-frame to get to the larger number written on paper and to write a corresponding equation. Once an answer is determined, they should demonstrate how their answer combined with the smaller number matches the larger number. Over time, you can fade the use of the little-ten frames.

You can repeat "How Far to My Number?" with three-digit numbers with or without the use of models. As always, it is important to have children share their strategies during a discussion.

Take-Away Subtraction

Take-away subtraction is considerably more difficult to do mentally. However, take-away strategies are common, probably because many textbooks emphasize take-away as the meaning of subtraction (even though there are other meanings). Four different strategies are shown in Figure 12.12 for the following story problem.

Figure 12.11

Use think-addition to solve "How Far?" problems.

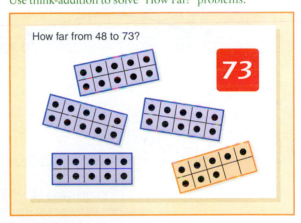

How far from 48 to 73?

73

There were 73 children on the playground. The 46 second-graders came inside first. How many children were still on the playground?

The methods that begin by taking tens from tens are reflective of what most children do with base-ten pieces. The other methods leave one of the numbers intact to do the subtraction. When the subtracted number is a multiple of 10 or close to a multiple of 10, take-away subtraction can be an easy method to do mentally. Try 83−29 in your head by first taking away 30 and adding 1 back. Some children will become confused when they hear a classmate describe this strategy for 83−29. In particular, they do not understand why you add 1 back. They think because you added 1 to 29 to make it 30, then you should subtract 1 from the answer. Use a story problem with the numbers and let them act it out with **Base-Ten Materials** (Blackline Master 32) so that they can see that when they take away 30, they took 1 too many away and that is why they need to add 1 back.

Figure 12.12

Four different invented strategies for take-away subtraction.

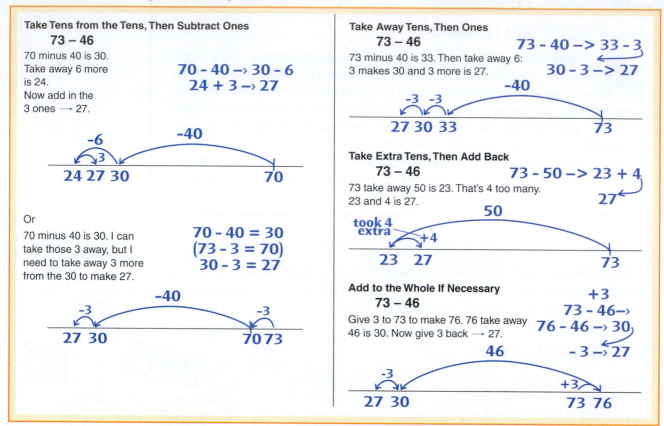

Try computing 82 − 57. Use both take-away and "think addition" methods. Can you use all of the strategies in Figures 12.10 and 12.12?

Remember the "equal additions" or "same difference" strategy (Humphreys & Parker, 2015) that was described earlier in this chapter? There are some children who use this strategy as an invented strategy with take-away subtraction. For example, for 32−17, children might think that 17 is 3 away from 20, so if they add 3 to 17 to equal 20, they need to add 3 to 32 to get 35 (to maintain the difference between the two numbers). Now the problem is 35−20 or 15. Encourage children to use an empty number line to see why 32−17 and 35−20 have equivalent answers.

Keep in mind that for many subtraction problems, especially those with three digits, a "think addition" approach is significantly easier than a take-away approach. For children who could benefit from a "think addition" approach but are not using it, you may want to revisit some simple missing-part activities to encourage that type of thinking.

Extensions and Challenges

Each of the examples in the preceding sections involved sums less than 100 and all involved *crossing a ten*; that is, if done with a standard algorithm, they required regrouping or trading. As you choose problems when planning instruction, you should consider whether the problems require crossing a ten (hundred, or thousand), the size of the numbers in the problems, and the potential for doing the problems mentally.

Crossing a Ten (or More)

For most of the strategies, it is easier to add or subtract when crossing a ten is not required. Try each strategy with 34+52 or 68−24 to see what we mean. Easier problems have their purpose, one of which is to build confidence. They also permit you to challenge children by asking, "Would you like a harder one?" Crossing 100 or 1000 is also more difficult as you can see by trying 58+67 with different strategies. Crossing across hundreds when subtracting can also present a challenge. For example, problems such as 128−50 or 128−45 are more difficult than ones that do not cross a hundred as in 298-187.

Larger Numbers

The *Common Core State Standards* recommend that second graders add and subtract three-digit numbers using a variety of strategies. How would *you* do these problems without using the standard algorithms: 487+235 and 623−247. Again, for subtraction, a "think-addition" strategy is usually the easiest. But occasionally, children will use other strategies with larger numbers. For example, "chunking off" multiples of 50 or 25 is a useful method. For 462+257, pull out 450 and 250 to equal 700. That leaves 12 and 7 more, which is 719. As with smaller numbers, continue to expect children to explain the strategies they use.

Standard Algorithms for Addition and Subtraction

As noted earlier, children are not likely to invent the standard algorithms because they are less intuitive, so your instruction when teaching these algorithms will need to be more directed. Given that, it is critical that you teach the algorithms in a conceptual manner, helping children understand the units of hundreds, tens, and ones as they work.

The standard algorithms require an understanding of *regrouping*, exchanging 10 in one place-value position for 1 in the position to the left—or the reverse, exchanging 1 for 10 in the position to the right. The corresponding terms *borrowing* and *carrying* are obsolete and conceptually misleading. The word *regroup* may have little meaning for young children, so start with the term *trade*: Ten ones are *traded* for a ten. A hundred is *traded* for 10 tens. Notice that none of the invented strategies involves regrouping.

Remember to emphasize that standard algorithms are a good choice in some situations, just as invented strategies are good choices in some situations. The numbers involved are the determining factor. As mentioned earlier, take time to discuss when it is more appropriate to use standard algorithms versus invented strategies.

Teaching Tip

Even after you have taught the standard algorithms, it is important to continue to encourage and promote the use of invented strategies. Children must learn to choose the method that best fits the numbers in the problem.

Standard Algorithm for Addition

When teaching any procedure (algorithm), you need to begin with the concrete. Then make explicit connections between the concept (regrouping) and the procedure. Teaching how to record the steps to the procedure comes after much work and discussion with concrete materials.

Begin with Models Only

In the beginning, focus on regrouping without recording the numerical process. Provide children with **Place-Value Mats** and **Base-Ten Models** (Blackline Masters 17 and 32).

Figure 12.13

Working from right to left with the standard addition algorithm.

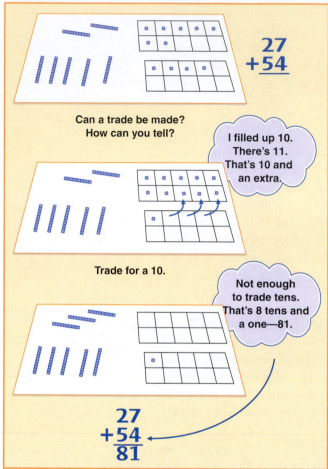

Have children use the base-ten materials to make one number at the top of the mat and a second beneath it as shown in Figure 12.13. If children are still developing base-ten concepts, a groupable model such as counting chips in cups or connecting cubes is helpful. Point out this one rule: *Begin in the ones column*. Then let children solve the problem on their own. Allow plenty of time and then have children explain what they did and why. Let children display their work on a projector or use interactive white boards to help with their explanations. One or two problems in a lesson with lots of discussion are much more productive than a lot of problems based on rules children don't understand.

Develop the Written Record

Use the **Addition and Subtraction Recording Sheets** similar to those in Figure 12.14 to help children record numerals in columns as they model each step of the procedure with the base-ten materials. The first few times you do this, guide each step carefully through questioning, as shown in Figure 12.15. A similar approach would be used for three-digit problems. Have children work in pairs with one responsible for the base-ten materials and the other recording the steps. They should reverse roles with each problem.

A common error children make is to record their answers in this way:

$$
\begin{array}{r}
57 \\
+\ 69 \\
\hline
1116
\end{array}
$$

Figure 12.14

Blank recording charts are helpful for children to record their work.

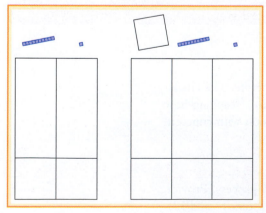

As you can see, this child has lost her connection to the place value and is treating the ones and tens as two separate problems. The child should try to use another way to check her answer—in this case, suggest having her estimate a reasonable answer and then use manipulatives, such as base-ten blocks, to help her model the problem. Cover up her initial answer and ask, "Do you think your answer will be between 100 and 200 or 200 and 300?" to help the child see that an answer in the thousands is not logical. Take a look at **Talecia** as she, too, loses her connection to the real value of the numbers she is recording when she adds 638+476.

Figure 12.16 shows a variation of the traditional recording scheme that is very effective because it highlights the actual value of the numbers and is relatively efficient, at least for up to three digits. This is known as the partial sums approach and avoids the "carried ones." If children start adding on the left as they are inclined to do, partial sums would just be a vertical recording scheme for the invented strategy "add tens, add ones, then combine" (see Figure 12.9). This adaptation is particularly effective for children with disabilities.

Figure 12.15

Help children record on paper each step they do on their place-value mats.

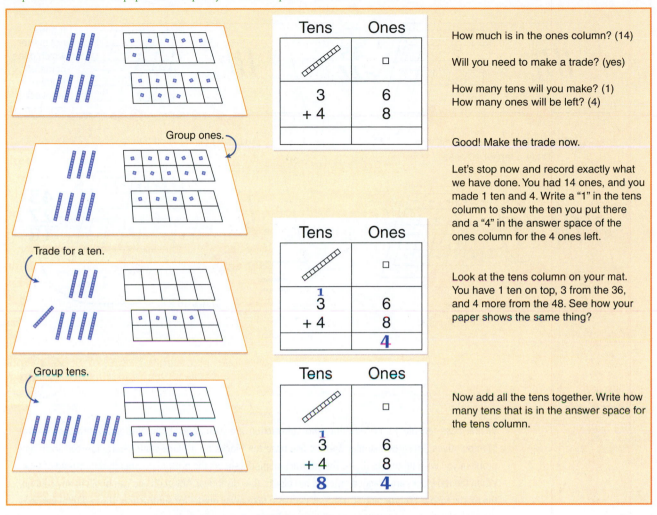

How much is in the ones column? (14)

Will you need to make a trade? (yes)

How many tens will you make? (1)
How many ones will be left? (4)

Good! Make the trade now.

Let's stop now and record exactly what we have done. You had 14 ones, and you made 1 ten and 4. Write a "1" in the tens column to show the ten you put there and a "4" in the answer space of the ones column for the 4 ones left.

Look at the tens column on your mat. You have 1 ten on top, 3 from the 36, and 4 more from the 48. See how your paper shows the same thing?

Now add all the tens together. Write how many tens that is in the answer space for the tens column.

Standard Algorithm for Subtraction

The general approach to developing the subtraction algorithm is the same as for addition. When the procedure is completely understood with models, a do-and-record approach connects it with a written form.

Begin with Models Only

Start by having children treat the subtraction problem as a "take-away" situation. With this meaning of subtraction, they model only the first (top) number in a subtraction problem (minuend) on the top half of their place-value mats. For the amount to be subtracted, have children write each digit on a small piece of paper and place these pieces near the bottom of their mats in the respective columns, as in Figure 12.17. To avoid errors, suggest making all necessary trades first. That way, the full amount on the paper slip can be taken off at once. Also explain to children that they are to begin working with the ones column first, as they did with addition.

Figure 12.16

The partial sums approach can be used from left to right as well as from right to left.

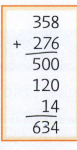

```
   358
+  276
   500
   120
    14
   634
```

Figure 12.17

Two-digit subtraction with the standard algorithm and models.

Not enough ones to take off 7.
Trade a ten for 10 ones.

$$\begin{array}{r} 45 \\ -27 \\ \hline \end{array}$$

And now I can take off 2 tens.

It does not matter which ones come off. Put the leftovers together.

Now there are 15 ones.
I can take 7 off easily.

$$\begin{array}{r} 45 \\ -27 \\ \hline 18 \end{array}$$

That's 18 left.

Anticipate Difficulties with Zeros

Problems that include numbers in which zeros are involved tend to cause special difficulties. The common errors that emerge when "regrouping across zero" are best addressed at the modeling stage. For example, in $403 - 138$, children must make a double trade: trading a hundreds piece for 10 tens and then a tens piece for 10 ones. After children have experience with making trades using base-ten materials, use the following activity before giving children any hints about how they might deal with regrouping across a zero.

Activity 12.8

CCSS-M: 2.NBT.B.7; 2.NBT.B.9

Tricky Trading

Pose a problem to the class that requires regrouping across zero, such as $103 - 78$. Children work in pairs using **Base-Ten Materials** (Blackline Master 32) and **Place-Value Mats** (Blackline Master 17). Once they have identified an answer, they now check their answer using an invented strategy. If they did not get the same answer with the base-ten materials and their invented strategy, encourage them to try to determine why. Follow up with a discussion that starts with children sharing their ideas.

Develop the Written Record

The process of recording each step as it is done is the same as was suggested for addition using the **Addition and Subtraction Recording Sheets** (Blackline Master 20). When children can explain the use of the symbols involved in the recording process, fade the use of physical materials and move to the complete use of symbols. Again, be attentive to problems with zeros.

If children are permitted to follow their natural instincts and begin with the biggest pieces (from the left instead of the right), recording schemes similar to that shown in Figure 12.18 are possible. The trades are made from the pieces remaining *after* the subtraction in the column to the left has been done. The "regroup across zero" difficulty will still occur in problems like 462−168 when working left to right. Try it.

Figure 12.18

A left-hand recording scheme for subtraction.

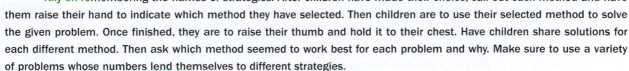

Stop and Reflect

Contrast teaching children to regroup in subtraction, especially regrouping across zero, with think-addition. For example, try solving this: 428 and how much equals 703? Now think about teaching children to regroup across zero to solve 703 − 428. Which is easier? Why?

Once children understand the standard algorithms for addition and subtraction of multidigit numbers, it is important to provide them opportunities to determine which strategy from a variety of strategies might be more useful, given the specific numbers involved. The following activity provides this experience.

Activity 12.9

CCSS-M: 1.NBT.C.4; 2.NBT.B.5; 2.NBT.B.6; 2.NBT.B.7; 2.NBT.B.9

Pick Your Strategy

Tell children you are going to show them a problem, but they are NOT to solve it—they are simply to decide which method from their invented strategies and standard algorithms they would choose to solve the problem and be ready to explain why. Projecting a list of strategies for addition (or subtraction) problems will support children with disabilities and English Language Learners by allowing them to focus on the task at hand without requiring them to rely on remembering the names of strategies. After children have made their choice, call out each method and have them raise their hand to indicate which method they have selected. Then children are to use their selected method to solve the given problem. Once finished, they are to raise their thumb and hold it to their chest. Have children share solutions for each different method. Then ask which method seemed to work best for each problem and why. Make sure to use a variety of problems whose numbers lend themselves to different strategies.

Helping children develop flexible methods of adding and subtracting strengthens their understanding of place value, number relationships, and operations. Comparing methods used, including the standard algorithms, supports children in better understanding these methods, which results in their making fewer computational errors. An assortment of computational strategies will serve children well on assessments, in later grades, and in life.

Introducing Computational Estimation

As mentioned earlier, when invented strategies are the norm for computation, there is no need to talk about mental computation and estimation as separate topics because they are an integral part of invented strategies. As children become more and more proficient with these flexible methods, they find they are able to use them mentally without having to write down even intermediate steps.

Even so, computational estimation is a higher level thinking skill that involves many decisions that children need opportunities to think about and discuss. Whenever we are faced with a computation in real life, we have a variety of choices to make concerning how we will find a reasonable answer. A first decision is: "Do we need an exact answer, or will an approximation be okay?" If an approximation is deemed appropriate, we need to decide the level of precision called for and which estimation strategy is most suitable for that purpose. We can choose to use an invented strategy, a standard algorithm, or even a calculator. How close an estimate must be to the actual computation is a matter of context, as was the original decision to use an estimate. Even if we do need an exact answer, children can "detect possible errors by strategically using estimation and other mathematical knowledge," as highlighted in the *Common Core State Standard* Mathematical Practice 5 (CCSSO, 2010, p. 7). Good estimators tend to employ a variety of computational strategies they have developed over time.

Standards for Mathematical Practice

6 **Attend to precision.** ▶

Understanding Computational Estimation

The goal of computational estimation is to be able to flexibly and quickly produce a reasonable estimate that is a suitable approximation for an exact number given the particular context. In the K–8 mathematics curriculum, estimation refers to three quite different ideas:

Measurement estimation: Determining an approximate measure without making an exact measurement. For example, we can estimate the length of a room or the weight of a watermelon.

Quantity estimation: Approximating the number of items in a collection. For example, we might estimate the number of children in the auditorium or jelly beans in the "estimation jar."

Computational estimation: Determining a number that is an approximation of a computation that we cannot or do not need to determine precisely. For example, we might want to know the approximate amount we are spending at a store and need to add the cost of several items to see whether $20.00 will cover the amount.

As early as grade 2, we teach strategies to help children develop an understanding of what it means to estimate computations and length measurements (2.MD.A.3) as well as time to the nearest five minutes (2.MD.C.7).

Children are not as good at computational estimation as they are at producing exact answers and sometimes find computational estimation uncomfortable (Siegler & Booth, 2005). In particular, many children confuse the idea of estimation with guessing. None of the three types of estimation involves guessing. Each involves reasoning and sense making. Computational estimation, for example, actually involves computing. Therefore, it's important to (1) avoid using the words *guess* and *guessing* when working on estimation activities and (2) explicitly help children see the difference between a guess and a reasonable estimate.

Computational estimation may be underemphasized in situations where the focus is on the standard algorithm. But, when approaching mathematics as a sense-making endeavor, once children have found a solution, they should look back at the end of a computation and be able to see whether the answer is in the ballpark—to "detect possible errors by strategically using estimation and other mathematical knowledge" (CCSSO, 2010, p. 7). Take 403 − 138, mentioned previously. At a glance, this answer has to be less than 300, so an incorrect answer of 375 (a common error) would be recognized as impossible.

Suggestions for Teaching Computational Estimation

Here are some general principles that are worth keeping in mind as you help your children develop computational estimation skills.

Use Real Examples

Discuss real-life situations in which computational estimations are used. Some common examples include adding up the cost of several items in a store to make sure you have enough money; determining approximate weekly totals (milk cartons purchased in the school cafeteria, school supplies used in class, time playing games on a tablet or smartphone); and determining the lengths of several objects together (tables in cafeteria, desks in classroom, class pets, children's shoes). Look at newspaper headlines to find where numbers are the result of estimation and where they are the result of precision (e.g., "Hundreds of Students Leave School Ill" versus "Fourteen Local Students Place in Regional Destination Imagination Competition"). Children are more motivated by real examples—for example, asking children, "About how many hours do you spend watching TV in one week? One month? How can you figure it out?"

Use Estimation Language

Words and phrases such as *about*, *close*, *just about*, *a little more* (or *less*) *than*, and *between* are part of the language of estimation. Children should understand that they are trying to get as close as possible using efficient methods, but there is no "one correct" or "winning" estimate. Language can help convey that idea.

Use a Context

Situations play a role in estimation. For example, is it a reasonable expectation for the cost of a game to be $9 or $90. Could attendance at the school musical be 30 or 300 or 3000? A simple computation can provide the important digits, with knowledge of the context providing the rest.

Accept a Range of Estimates, Offer a Range As an Option

Because estimates are based on computation, how can there be different answers? The answer, of course, is that any particular estimate depends on the strategy used and the kinds of adjustments made in the numbers. Estimates also vary with the level of precision needed. Estimating how much time it will take someone to drive to the store is quite different from trying to decide whether your last $5 will cover three items you need at Fast Mart. What estimate would you give for 270+325? If you use 200+300, you might say 500. Or you might use 250 for the 270 and 350 for the 325, which is 600. You could also use 300 for 270 and add 325, equaling 625. Is only one of these "right"? By sharing children's estimates and letting them discuss how and why different estimates emerged, they can begin to see that estimates generally fall in a range around the exact answer.

Important teacher note: Do not reward or overemphasize the estimate that is the closest. It is already very difficult for children to handle "approximate" answers; worrying about accuracy and pushing for "the one" closest answer exacerbates this problem. Instead, focus on whether the answers given are *reasonable* for the situation or problem at hand. Especially when introducing estimation, it is a good idea to offer ranges for the estimates. Ask whether the answer will be between 300 and 400, 450 and 550, or 600 and 700.

Focus on Flexible Methods, Not Answers

Remember that having children reflect on the strategies used by classmates will lead to additional strategy development. Class discussions about estimation are just as important as they were for the development of invented strategies for computation. For any given situation, there are often several very good but different methods of estimation.

Here is an activity in which a specific number is not required to answer the questions that involve addition and subtraction. The amounts used can represent lengths, time, or simply numbers without a context.

Activity 12.10

CCSS-M: 2.NBT.B.5; 2.MD.A.3; 2.MD.C.7

Is It Over or Under?

 Here are some addition/subtraction examples that do not use a context. The children are to use estimation to determine whether the answer would be over or under a target amount.

37 + 75 (over/under 100)

712 − 458 (over/under 300)

You can add an interesting context to make this activity accessible to more learners, but remember that using multiple contexts can be difficult for ELLs, who must learn each new context. Consider playing "Is It Over or Under?" several times using one context (e.g., the length of classroom objects) and then varying the values each time. Project the lengths of various objects on a document projector, such as the following. The children are to determine whether the total of the lengths are over or under the target amount of 30 feet. (Note that the target amount need not be the same for each problem.)

Over/Under 30 feet:

Bulletin Board: 6 feet

Table: 3 feet

Shelf: 10 feet

Teacher's Desk: 5 feet

You can also use time as a context, having children estimate using the nearest five minutes (**2.MD.C.7**). For example, if the target time is 1 hour, children use time to the nearest five minutes to determine how these amounts relate to 1 hour:

23, 11, 18 minutes, (over/under 1 hour)

5 time slots, 13 minutes each (over/under 1 hour)

Computational Estimation Strategies

There are numerous strategies that are helpful in computing estimates in addition and subtraction. Here are a few to present to children.

Front-End Methods

A front-end approach is reasonable for addition or subtraction when all or most of the numbers have the same number of digits. Figure 12.19 illustrates this idea. Notice that when a number has fewer digits than the rest, that number may be ignored initially. Also note that only the front (leftmost) number is used and the computation is then done as if there were zeros in the other positions.

After adding or subtracting the front digits, an adjustment is made to correct for the digits or numbers that were ignored. Making an adjustment is actually a separate skill. Initially, practice just using the front digits. Make sure that children pay close attention

Figure 12.19

Front-end estimation in addition.

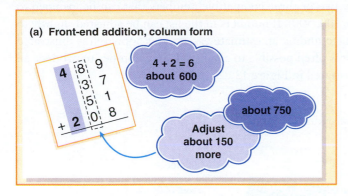

(a) Front-end addition, column form

4 + 2 = 6
about 600

Adjust
about 150
more

about 750

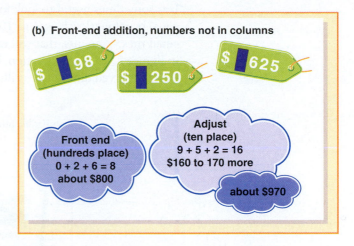

(b) Front-end addition, numbers not in columns

$ 98 $ 250 $ 625

Front end
(hundreds place)
0 + 2 + 6 = 8
about $800

Adjust
(ten place)
9 + 5 + 2 = 16
$160 to 170 more

about $970

to place value and only consider digits in the largest place, especially when the numbers vary in the number of digits. The front-end strategy can be easy to use because it does not require rounding or changing numbers.

Rounding Methods

Children are not required to use rounding in the *Common Core State Standards* until third grade, but rounding can help children build number sense and use invented strategies efficiently to find exact sums and differences. If your children are ready, you can use the following activity to introduce them to the concept of rounding. When several numbers are to be added, it is usually a good idea to round them to the same place value. Keep a running sum as you round each number. Figure 12.20 shows an example of rounding.

Figure 12.20   Rounding using place value.

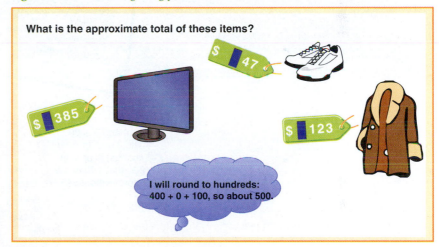

What is the approximate total of these items?

$ 47

$ 385

$ 123

I will round to hundreds:
400 + 0 + 100, so about 500.

Activity 12.11

CCSS-M: 2.NBT.B.5

Round Up?

Create a number line on the floor with painter's tape, a rope, or cash register tape. Use sticky notes or pieces of paper to label the benchmark numbers of tens (10, 20, 30, . . .), hundreds (100, 200, 300, . . .) or whatever range of numbers you are considering as a class. Have the numbers far apart so that 3 to 4 children can stand facing forward between each number. Then distribute numbers for children to round. For example, give a child the number 53. The child stands on the line where 53 should be, then rounds to the nearest ten (50). Talk about the case of a 5 in the ones position (or in other halfway positions for larger numbers) as a convention—we all agree that we round up when we are midway between numbers.

For addition and subtraction problems involving only two numbers, one strategy is to round only one of the two numbers. For example, you can round only the subtracted number such as 624−83 becomes 624−100, resulting in 524. You can stop here, or you can adjust. Adjusting might go like this: Because you subtracted a bigger number, the result must be too small—by about 20, the difference between 100 and 80. Adjust to about 540.

Compatible Numbers

It is sometimes useful to look for two or three compatible numbers that can be grouped to equal benchmark values (e.g., 10, 100, 500). If numbers in the list can be adjusted slightly to equal these amounts, that will make finding an estimate easier. This approach is illustrated in Figure 12.21. In subtraction, it is often possible to adjust only one number to produce an easily observed difference, as illustrated in Figure 12.22.

Figure 12.21

Compatible numbers used in addition.

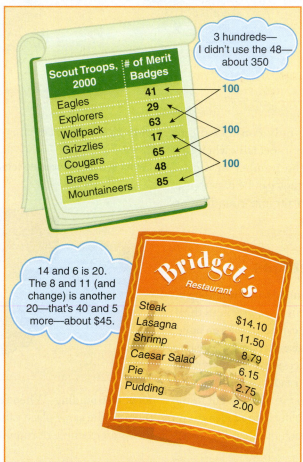

Figure 12.22

Compatible numbers are useful in finding the difference.

The following activity (adapted from Coates & Thompson, 2003) is a blend of mental computation and estimation. Figuring out where the numbers go to create the exact solution involves estimation.

 Activity 12.12

CCSS-M: 2.NBT.B.5

Box Math

 Using the **Number Cards**, give children three digits to use (e.g., 3, 5, 7) and two operations (+ and −), cut out from card stock so they can manipulate them easily. Then show children a set of equations with answers only and ask them to use their number cards (in the squares) and operations (in the circle) so that the computation results in the answers shown.

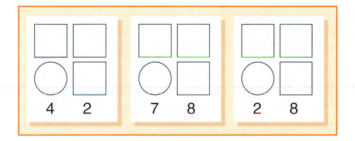

For children who have disabilities, you may want to have the operation signs already displayed with answers (such as an addition or a subtraction sign for the answer 42). These fixed problems will reduce the amount of decision making needed and allow children to focus on the numbers.

📋 Formative Assessment Notes

To get a sense of a child's estimation skills and understanding, in a diagnostic interview, ask the child to solve the following: "Charlie wants to estimate how much he needs to save to buy two video games. One game is $99 and the other is $118. How much should he save to purchase the two games?" Ask the child how he came up with his estimate. If the child is trying to mentally carry out the standard algorithm in the air or on the table with a finger, he likely has a limited ability with estimation strategies. Because $99 is so close to $100, it would be important for the child to use that idea in combining the two prices. If the child is unclear whether to change 99 to 100 or to 98 (as it is equally as close), that would pinpoint a lack of understanding of the purpose of estimation. Estimation cannot be easily assessed with paper-and-pencil tasks, so interviews that require explanations give more substantial evidence of a child's understanding.

Common Misconceptions with Whole-Number Computation

Table 12.1 provides a summary of the most common errors and misconceptions children will demonstrate with whole-number computation, along with suggestions about how to help them work through these issues. Notice that many of the misconceptions are related to children's use of the standard algorithms, not invented strategies. The reason for this is primarily because a child's invented strategies are ones that the child generates using ideas about place value, properties, and operations that make sense to him or her.

Table 12.1. Common errors and misconceptions in whole number computation and how to help.

Misconception/Error	What It Looks Like	How to Help
1. Child loses track of the value of the digits when adding or subtracting.	65 +43 The child uses the incorrect place value names such as reading the above problem as "six hundred plus 4 hundred is ten hundred" and writes: 65 +43 110 + 8 118 The child may read the answer as "one thousand eighteen."	• Ask the child to use estimation to check for reasonableness of answer. • Have the child use base-ten materials and a place-value mat to represent the quantities and the operation. • Have the child use another strategy to check answer.
2. When adding 2 multidigit numbers, child records entire sum of digits in each column.	87 +69 1416	• Ask the child use estimation to check for reasonableness of answer. • Have the child use base-ten materials and a place-value mat to represent the quantities and the operation. • Have the child use partial sums to record and find total. Then ask child to compare the numbers found in each of the methods. • Have the child use another strategy to check answer.
3. When subtracting 2 multidigit numbers, child always subtracts the lesser digit from the greater digit.	76 −39 43	• Ask the child to use estimation to check for reasonableness of answer. For example, keep 76 the same and round 39 to 40. 76-40 is 36. Ask child if his/her answer is reasonable given this estimate. • Have the child use base-ten materials and a place-value mat to represent the quantities and the operation. • Have the child use another strategy to check answer.
4. Child relies solely on key words to determine operation to use.	When solving a word problem like the following, the child scans the problem for the numbers and a key word to help determine which operation to use. *Sarah ate 34 marshmallows. Sarah ate 6 more marshmallows than Rich. How many marshmallows did Rich eat?* The child solves the problem by adding 34 and 6 because s/he interprets the word "more" to mean "add." The child is stumped when faced with story problems that have no key words, such as: *Laurie has 83 pennies. 16 of them are shiny. The others are dull. How many are dull?*	• Covering up the number "6" in the word problem, ask the child to read the problem. Then ask the child who ate more marshmallows. • Have the child use bar diagrams to represent the amounts for Sarah and the amounts for Rich to help make more explicit the relationship between the quantities. • Do not teach key words to solve word problems. • Make sure to pose story problems and contextual problems that include all four problem types (join, separate, part-part-whole, compare) with the unknown quantity in different locations so children gain experience thinking about and solving a variety of situations. • Have available and encourage the use of physical materials for children to model story/contextual problems. Discuss what they have done to determine the answer. • Suggest to the struggling child some of the recommendations for analyzing contextual problems (in Chapter 9) (e.g., think about the answer before solving the problem; solve a simpler problem).

Table 12.1. Common errors and misconceptions in whole number computation and how to help.

Misconception/Error	What It Looks Like	How to Help
5. Child overgeneralizes the "equal additions" or the "same difference" strategy to addition situations.	 For problems like 38+75, the child reasons that because 38 is 2 away from 40, s/he will add 2 to 38 (which is 40) and then thinks s/he needs to add 2 to 75 (which is 77) because s/he does not understand the "equal additions" strategy and why it is only applicable to subtraction situations.	• Have the child use concrete materials to represent the quantities and solve the original addition problem and the problem s/he created. Then ask the child to compare. • Have the child use a number line to represent and solve the original addition problem and the problem s/he created. Ask the child to try to determine why the answers are different. • Have the child solve a subtraction problem using "equal additions." Then show the original and the modified subtraction problems on a number line. Challenge the child to determine why the "equal additions" strategy results in equivalent answers by considering the number line representation of the problems.
6. Child makes mistakes when regrouping across zeroes in a subtraction problem.		• Have the child use estimation to check for reasonableness of answer. • Have the child use base-ten materials and a place-value mat to represent the quantities and the operation. • Ask the child to use another strategy to check answer.
7. Child thinks that s/he has to find an exact answer after finding an estimation.	When asked to estimate say, 624−83, the child changes 83 to 100 to find 624−100 or 524. But then immediately works to find the exact answer.	• Avoid having children check their estimates by finding the exact answer every time they find estimates. • Use real situations as examples for when estimations (and not exact answers) are useful. • Discuss why an exact answer is unnecessary when finding estimates.

13

Promoting Algebraic Reasoning

BIG IDEAS

1 Algebra is a useful tool for generalizing arithmetic and representing patterns in our world. Explaining regularities and consistencies across many problems gives children the chance to generalize. (Mathematical Practice 8)

2 The methods we use to compute and the structures in our number system can and should be generalized. For example, the generalization that $a + b = b + a$ tells us that $38 + 72 = 72 + 38$ without having to compute the sums on each side of the equal sign. (Mathematical Practice 7)

3 Symbols, especially those involving equality and variables, must be well understood conceptually for children to be successful in mathematics. (Mathematical Practice 6)

Algebraic reasoning (also called algebraic thinking) in grades preK−2 involves forming generalizations from experiences with number and computation and formalizing these ideas with the use of meaningful representations and symbols. Looking for and finding relationships and building a structure with those relationships are the core ideas involved in forming these generalizations. Algebraic thinking is used across all areas of mathematics and is central to mathematical reasoning in general, as can be seen from the strong connections to the Standards for Mathematical Practice.

According to the *Curriculum Focal Points* (National Council of Teachers of Mathematics, 2006), preK children should engage in algebraic thinking through recognizing and generating simple patterns—in other words, looking for and finding relationships. In kindergarten, young children engage in algebraic thinking as they "represent addition and subtraction with objects, fingers, mental images, drawings, sounds (e.g., claps), acting out situations, verbal explanations, expressions, or equations" (CCSSO, 2010, p. 11). Similar connections between arithmetic and algebra are noted in every grade from kindergarten through second grade, where number and algebra are combined in the discussions of clusters and standards under the domain of Operations and Algebraic Thinking. CCSS-M introduces function as a domain in grade 8, but functional thinking begins in the early grades as children consider situations that covary, such as the relationship between the number of pencils purchased and the cost of those pencils.

Strands of Algebraic Reasoning

In *Young Mathematicians at Work: Constructing Algebra*, Fosnot and Jacob (2010) write, "It is human to seek and build relations" (p. 12). Algebraic thinking is used to generalize arithmetic, to notice patterns that hold true in algorithms and with properties, and to reason quantitatively about such things as whether expressions are equivalent or not. Algebra must be approached in a way that children, as they seek and build relations, see it is a useful tool for making sense of all areas of mathematics and real-world situations.

Researchers suggest three strands of algebraic reasoning, all integrating the central notions of generalizations and symbolism (Blanton, 2008; Carraher & Schliemann, 2007; Kaput, 2008).

1. Study of structures in the number system, including those arising in arithmetic (algebra as generalized arithmetic).
2. Study of patterns, relations, and functions.
3. Process of mathematical modeling, including the meaningful use of symbols.

🌱 *Teaching Tip*

> Your success in helping children see relationships and think algebraically is driven by your questions. Record the questions suggested throughout this chapter on note cards and keep them handy for lesson planning and classroom discussions.

Although algebra is often considered a separate strand of the mathematics curriculum, algebra can and should be approached as an integral part of all areas of mathematics. This chapter is organized around these three strands. In each section we share how these ideas develop across grades preK–2.

Structure in the Number System: Connecting Number and Algebra

Algebra is often referred to as generalized algebra. For children to generalize say, an operation, they must consider several examples and identify commonalities that can be used to describe any of the examples—in other words, they have to go beyond individual examples to make claims about the operation for an entire type of number (e.g., whole numbers, natural numbers, fractions). These generalizations help children gain insights into the structure of the number system. The process of generating generalizations from number and arithmetic begins as early as prekindergarten and continues as children learn about all aspects of number and computation, including basic facts and meanings of the operations. Here we share three ways to connect arithmetic to algebra.

Generalization with Number Combinations

Looking for generalizations in sets of problems can begin in the early grades as young children decompose and compose numbers and use a variety of strategies to add and subtract. Consider the following problem that provides children a chance to think about decomposing numbers while building a sense of what the operation of addition involves:

> There are 5 frogs in a pond. Some jump onto a lily pad and some jump onto a rock. How many frogs might be on the lily pad and how many might be on the rock?

This problem provides children with the opportunity to notice generalizable characteristics, such as increasing the number on the lily pad by one means reducing the number on the rock by one. To facilitate the generalization, children can be challenged to find all the ways the frogs might be on the lily pad and the rock. The significant algebraic question is how to decide when all the solutions have been found. Give children a recording sheet, such as the **Frogs on a Pond** recording sheet, so it will be easier for they to record their solutions and look for patterns. To begin with, children might reply they cannot think of any different ways to place the frogs. Ask questions to focus children's attention on the relationship between adjacent solutions (e.g., 1+4 and 2+3) (e.g., "How are the first numbers, 1 and 2, related; how are the second numbers, 4 and 3, related?"). As children recognize these relationships, they will begin to strategically use each number from 0 to 5 for the lily pad and the corresponding number for the rock.

Teaching Tip

> In these kinds of problems, children often do not consider the combinations with zero. If this happens, simply ask, "Could the lily pad or the rock be empty?"

As shown on the **Frogs on a Pond** recording sheet, continue to work toward generalization by looking at other quantities of frogs (e.g., how many ways for 7 frogs? for 10 frogs?). Ask children what patterns or consistencies do they notice across these cases. Once they have found all the solutions for each case, ask, "What do you notice about the number of solutions and the number of frogs?" When a child is able to explain that for each number 0 to 5 there is one solution, he or she no longer has to partition 5 into parts to find solutions but is making a generalization about how to determine the number of solutions without having to list them. For example, the child might explain, "There is always one more way than the number of frogs."

Standards for Mathematical Practice

> **8** Look for and express regularity in repeated reasoning.

This reasoning can be applied to other numbers and in other contexts, which is an important step in generalization. The children's book *The Sleepover* (Fosnot, 2007) describes a context with eight children rearranging themselves on a pair of bunk beds. This situation offers another opportunity for children to grapple with the idea of finding all the possible combinations for a given number. And yet another children's book, *The Double-Decker Bus* (Liu & Fosnot, 2007), uses a double-decker bus to provide opportunities to think about possible number combinations.

The following activity purposefully focuses children's attention on the adjacent combinations in an effort to help them generalize and reason more strategically.

▲ Activity 13.1

CCSS-M: K.OA.A.3; 1.OA.D.7; 1.OA.C.6; 2.OA.B.2

One Up and One Down with Addition

Have children select a number, such as 7, and add it to itself. The task is to find out what happens to the sum if you add 1 to one of the sevens and subtract 1 from the other seven (e.g., 8+6). You can refer to this action as "one up" and "one down" but be sure English Language Learners know the words "up" and "down" and how those relate to the action taking place. You can model moving *up one space* and *down one space* on a number line.

A mathematics balance (a plastic "number line" on a fulcrum) can be useful, especially for children with disabilities, to physically model the movement of one hanging weight and the effect it has on the balance of the equation. If you do not have such a balance, use a two-sided mat with an equal sign in the middle to demonstrate making equations that show that what is on the left side of the mat is the same as (or equal to) what is on the right side of the mat. You can also find an interactive version by searching for "Number Balance" on the University of Cambridge's NRICH website.

To facilitate generalization, ask children, "Does this "one up" and "one down" action work with other numbers? Does it only work if you start with a number plus itself? Can you explain why it works? What else can you find out?" See the corresponding **Expanded Lesson: One Up and One Down**.

Some children may wonder if "One Up and One Down" works for "really big numbers." Suggest they test their ideas with a calculator. It is also useful to explore the idea of two up and two down, and so on. Note that the results are the same as long as the same amount is added and subtracted. This exploration can be useful when learning basic facts ($6+8$ is the same as $7+7$ or double 7).

Children may want to know if the one-up/one-down idea works for subtraction. (It does not.) But there is an important pattern to discover: If both numbers change in the same direction, up or down, the result is the same. (This is called "equal additions" or "same difference" [Humphreys & Parker, 2015] and is described in Chapters 5 and 12.) Recognizing this allows us to change $12-8$ to $10-6$, or $83-48$ to $85-50$, changing potentially difficult problems to easier ones. Pose a story problem like the following example to help children build a sense of what the operation of subtraction involves. Change the problem type to offer opportunities to consider other meanings of subtraction (e.g., comparison, missing part).

Standards for Mathematical Practice

2 Reasoning abstractly and quantitatively.

Ben had 16 pretzels. If he ate one pretzel, he'd have 15 left. What other numbers of pretzels could Ben start with and how many would he have to eat to always have 15 left?

Have children generate several subtraction expressions that equal 15. Arrange them in a sequence to increase the likelihood that children will notice that both numbers increase by 1:

$$16-1$$

$$17-2$$

$$18-3$$

$$19-4$$

$$20-5$$

Encourage them to describe what is happening across the examples. Children may say something like, "When the number is smaller, you don't have to subtract as much to get 15. But with bigger numbers, you have to subtract more because there are more." Or "As it gets bigger, he has to take away more to equal 15." You will need to help children refine their language and explanations as they learn to describe generalizations to ensure they are being explicit. For example, require children to be clear about what they mean by "it" and "this"—as seen in the second child's explanation—and look for opportunities to refine language and introduce vocabulary when appropriate (Russell, Schifter, & Bastable, 2011). The generalization that the difference is maintained when both numbers are increased (or decreased) by the same amount supports the development of the "equal additions" strategy.

Standards for Mathematical Practice

6 Attend to precision.

Generalization with Place Value

Fundamental to mental mathematics is generalizing place-value concepts. For example, consider how you would do the sum 49+18 in your head. Many people, because of their past experiences with similar sums, will move one over from 18 to make a ten and think 50+17. Alternatively, they could move two over from 49 to make a ten and think 47+20. Either way, the idea of changing the numbers so that you are working with a multiple of ten is a powerful strategy based on place-value that is generalized from experiences with previous examples. Many of these strategies and examples have been addressed in the previous four chapters.

Standards for Mathematical Practice

7 **Look for and make use of structure.** ▶

The hundreds chart is a useful tool to help children generalize the relationship between tens and ones. Ask children, "What did we add to get from 72 to 82? From 5 to 15? From 34 to 44?" Children notice across these examples (and more like them) that they are adding 10 and, on the hundreds chart, moving down exactly one row. Moves on the hundreds chart can be represented with arrows (for example, $\rightarrow$ means move right one column or plus 1, and $\uparrow$ means move up one row or subtract 10). Consider asking children to complete these problems:

$$14 \rightarrow \; \rightarrow \; \leftarrow \; \leftarrow \quad\quad 63 \uparrow\uparrow\downarrow\downarrow \quad\quad 45 \rightarrow \uparrow \leftarrow \downarrow$$

Some children may count up or back using a count-by-ones approach. Others may know to jump 10 or 1 (up or down). Still others may recognize that a downward arrow "undoes" an upward arrow—an indication that these children are moving toward generalizations (Blanton, 2008). In other words, they recognize that +10 and −10 results in zero change.

 ## Formative Assessment Note

As children work on tasks like the one just described, you can observe while using a checklist to note which children solve tasks by counting by ones, by jumping, or by noticing the "doing" and "undoing." What you observe can help you identify which children's approaches to highlight during the subsequent discussion. For example, you can start the discussion by having children who used the more basic strategies (e.g., a count-by-ones approach or a jumping strategy) share and then have children who have generalized the situation share how they think about it.

The next activity provides an engaging context for children to explore patterns involving place value and addition.

◢ Activity 13.2

CCSS-M: 1.NBT.C.4; 2.NBT.B.9

Diagonal Sums

   Provide children with a copy of a **Hundreds Chart** (Blackline Master 3) or you can use an interactive virtual hundreds chart (several are available online). Children select any four numbers in the hundreds chart that form a square. They are to add the two numbers on each diagonal as in the example shown here. For younger children or children who struggle, allow them to use calculators so that they can explore the pattern without getting bogged down in computations.

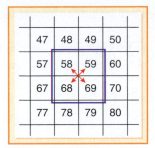

Have children share their diagonal sums and compare what happened. Then invite children to explore other diagonal sums on the chart. Ask them to describe why this pattern works. Extend their exploration to diagonals of any rectangle. For example, the numbers 15, 19, 75, and 79 form four corners of a rectangle children can explore.

Stop and Reflect 500 ♫ 250 ... 3x ▱ ... ∞ ⌐ 2.5

Before reading further, stop and explore why the diagonal sums described in the previous activities are the same. What questions might you ask children to ensure they are noticing the relationship between tens and ones?

Here are some additional tasks you might explore on a hundreds chart. With each task, notice how the first part is about number. The latter part asks questions that focus on generalizations (algebraic thinking).

- Pick a number. Move down two and over one. What is the relationship between the original number and the new number?
- Skip count by different values (e.g., 2, 3, 5). Which numbers make diagonal patterns? Which numbers make column patterns? What is true about all the numbers that make a column pattern?
- Find a two skip-count pattern in which one number lands "on top of" the other (that is, all of the shaded values for one pattern are part of the shaded values for the other)? How are these two skip-count numbers related? Is this true for any pair of numbers that have this relationship?

Asking questions such as "When will this be true?" and "Why does this work?" requires children to generalize and consequently, strengthen their understanding of the number concepts they are learning.

Generalization with Algorithms

When studying operations, children are often asked to explain how they solved a problem. As you listen to children's explanations, listen for strategies that can be generalized. In fact, you can purposefully select numbers that are likely to elicit particular strategies. For example, the problem 504−198 will likely elicit the strategy of using a close benchmark number to make a problem easier. You might record a child's mental strategy such as 504−200+2 on the board for the class to consider. You can ask, "Why did you use 200?" to help children track on this strategy. Follow up with a series of related computation problems for which children can use and discuss this strategy. By considering several examples and their commonalities, children will be able to generalize and recognize when particular strategies can be useful.

Sets of problems are good ways for children to look for and describe patterns across the problems, patterns that build an understanding for the operation and related algorithms:

$$2+8 \quad 5+8 \quad 8+9 \quad 8+7 \quad 6+8$$

Once children have solved sets of related problems, you can start with general questions: What do you notice? How are the problems alike? Different? But you may need to focus their attention on what you want them to generalize by asking more specific questions: How can using 10 help you solve each problem? Why? In this set of problems, such a discussion can help children appreciate how the relationship between 8 and 10 can make the problems easier to solve. Children can also develop a better understanding of addition situations—for example, how if you add an amount to one addend (to make 10) you must subtract that same amount from the other addend. This strategy of Making 10 can be applied to any of the basic addition facts for 8 (and 7 and 9 for that matter), helping children with what is often some of the more challenging facts to learn.

Meaningful Use of Symbols

Algebraic notation in the form of equations and variables are powerful tools for representing mathematical ideas and the primary grades are not too early to begin using them. Note that algebraic notation needs to be built from a firmly established understanding of the arithmetic symbols $+, -, \times, \div,$ and $=$. Many misconceptions often develop in these early years that unfortunately stay with children into later years. So before we talk further about algebraic thinking and generalization, in particular, we first emphasize how preK–2 teachers can help children develop a strong understanding of the equal sign and variables through meaningful instruction.

The Meaning of the Equal Sign

The equal sign is one of the most important symbols in mathematics, especially in elementary arithmetic and in early algebra. The *Common Core State Standards* explicitly address developing an understanding of the equal sign as early as the first grade. Sometimes children begin to write equations using the equal sign as early as kindergarten, and they continue to work with equations in every subsequent grade. Unfortunately, research dating from 1975 to the present indicates that children have a very poor understanding of the equal sign (Kieran, 2007; McNeil, 2014; RAND Mathematics Study Panel, 2003). In addition, the equal sign is rarely represented in U.S. textbooks in ways that facilitate children's understanding of the equivalence relationship (Powell, 2012)—an understanding that is critical to understanding algebra (Knuth, Alibali, McNeil, Weinberg, & Stephens, 2011; McNeil et al., 2006).

Stop and Reflect

In the following equation, what number do you think belongs in the box?

$$8 + 4 = \square + 5$$

How do you think children in the early grades or even in middle school typically answer this question?

In one study, no more than 10 percent of children in grades 1 to 6 put the correct number (7) in the box. The common responses were 12 and 17. (How did children get these answers?) None of the sixth graders (out of 145) put a 7 in the box (Falkner, Levi, & Carpenter, 1999).

Where do such misconceptions come from? A large majority of equations that children encounter in elementary school look like this: $5+7 =$ ___ or $4 \times 3 =$ ___. As a consequence, children come to see $=$ as signifying "and the answer is" rather than as a symbol that indicates equivalence (Carpenter, Franke, & Levi, 2003; McNeil & Alibali, 2005; McNeil, 2014; Molina & Ambrose, 2006).

Subtle shifts in how you approach teaching computation can alleviate this significant misconception. For example, a simple change such as writing basic facts as $7 = 2+5$ can cause children to stop and question why this is the same as $2+5 = 7$. Also, rather than always asking children to solve a problem like $19+23$, ask them to find an equivalent expression and use both to write an equation (Blanton, 2008). For $19+23$, children might write $19+23 = 20+22$. Activity 13.3 is a way to work on equivalent expressions while supporting the development of the Making 10 strategy for learning basic facts.

◀ Activity 13.3

CCSS-M: 1.OA.C.6; 1.OA.D.7; 2.OA.B.2

Ten and Then Some

In this activity (based on **Fosnot & Jacobs, 2010**), each pair of children will need eight note cards labeled with the equations $10+1$ to $10+8$ (see the **Equation Cards**). They lay the cards out on their desks face up.

Each pair will also need a deck of playing cards with all the face cards, aces, and tens removed. Each child draws one playing card from the deck. Together the partners decide which note card is equivalent to the sum of their playing cards and they place the playing cards behind the identified note card (i.e., if they drew 8 and 5, they place these cards behind the $10+3$ note card). If the sum of the playing cards is less than 10, they slide the cards back in the deck in random places. Have children write the two expressions as an equation (e.g., $5+8 = 10+3$) to reinforce the idea that these quantities are equal. Children can also play this game independently.

As an alternative to using note cards, you can prepare a game board whose spaces are all the expressions $10+1$ to $10+8$. The children then place their two playing cards below the appropriate space on the board.

For struggling learners, have ten-frames or arithmetic racks available so they can model the sums. Initially have them move counters to make **10** to reinforce the Making 10 strategy. Eventually have them only describe how they would move the counters to make **10** and then fade the use of manipulatives altogether.

Initially, children will struggle to understand how amounts that look different can actually be equivalent. In other words, they wonder why the numbers do not have to be identical. Consequently, at first children will need to add the numbers on each side to verify for themselves that they are the same quantity. As they come to understand compensation (e.g., how part of one number can be moved to another number), they begin to understand how equivalent quantities do not have to be identical. Once you know children can use compensation, challenge them to find the equivalent expression without computing first.

Standards for Mathematical Practice

◀ **7** **Look for and make use of structure.**

The next activity continues to challenge children to work on equivalent expressions.

Activity 13.4

CCSS-M: 1.OA.C.6; 1.OA.D.7; 2.OA.B.2

Different but the Same

Challenge children to find different ways to express a particular number, say, 6. Encourage children to create both addition and subtraction expressions. Give a few examples, such as 3+3 or 12−6. Ask questions such as, "How many ways can you make 6 using at least one number greater than 10?" "What patterns do you notice?" Have children write equations using their expressions (e.g., 12−6 = 0+6; 15−9 = 2+4). For equations that use the same operation, challenge the children to explain why the quantities on each side are equivalent without doing the computation. Adding a context (e.g., Legos, trading cards) can support children's reasoning.

Why is it so important that children in grades preK−2 correctly understand the equal sign? First, it is important for children to understand and symbolize relationships in our number system and the equal sign is a principal method of representing these relationships. For example, $8+5 = 8+2+3$ shows the basic fact strategy of Making 10. Understanding the equal sign as equivalence supports children as they explore the behavior of operations because they can focus on the relationship between the numbers and not on doing the computation. A second reason, although removed from the preK−2 classroom, is that when older students have a poor understanding of the equal sign, they typically have difficulty working with algebraic expressions (Knuth, Alibali, McNeil, Weinberg, & Stephens, 2011; Knuth, Stephens, McNeil, & Alibali, 2006). For example, the equation $5x+24 = 54$ requires students to see both sides as equivalent. When students interpret the equal sign as "do a computation," they think it is impossible to "do" the left-hand side of the equation. However, if both sides are understood to be equivalent expressions, students can reason that $5x$ must be 24 less than 54 or $5x = 30$. Therefore, x must equal 6. Helping preK−2 children develop a solid understanding of the equal sign can in turn help them avoid such difficulties in later grades.

Conceptualizing the Equal Sign as a Balance

Children's understanding of the idea of equivalence can and must be developed through meaningful contexts and concrete methods. Children's literature offers some ways to introduce equivalence in terms of a balance. For example, *Equal Shmequel* (Kroll, 2005) is a story about a mouse and her friends who want to play tug-of-war. To do so, they must determine how to make both sides equal so that the game is fair. In the end, they use a teeter-totter to balance the weight of the friends. This focus on equal sides and balance make this a great book for focusing on the meaning of the equal sign as a balance.

The next two activities use kinesthetic approaches, tactile objects, and visualizations to reinforce the "balancing" notion of the equal sign (ideas based on Mann, 2004).

Activity 13.5

CCSS-M: 1.OA.D.7; 2.NBT.A.4

Seesaw Comparisons

Ask children to raise their arms to look like a seesaw. Explain that you have softballs, all weighing the same, and tennis balls, all weighing the same, but the softballs are heavier than the tennis balls. (Have some softballs and tennis balls available in case children, especially ELLs, are not familiar with these items.) Ask children to imagine that you have placed a softball in each of their left hands. Ask them what would happen to their seesaw (children should bend to the left side). Ask children to imagine that you place another softball in their right hands (children should level off). Next, with the softballs still there, ask them to imagine a tennis ball added to the left. Finally, say you are adding another tennis ball in the left hand again. Then ask them to imagine a tennis ball moving over to the right hand. This is a particularly important activity for children with disabilities who may be challenged with the abstract idea of balancing values of expressions.

After acting out several seesaw examples, ask children to share their observations. For example, one child may share, "If you have a balanced seesaw and add something to one side, it will tilt to that side." Another child may explain, "If you take away the same object from both sides of the seesaw, the seesaw will still be balanced."

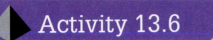

Activity 13.6   CCSS-M: K.MD.A.2; 1.OA.D.7; 2.NBT.A.4

What Do You Know about the Shapes?

Show children a balance scale with objects on both sides. Here is an example:

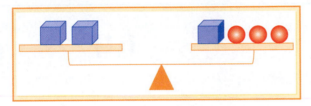

Tell children that the cubes weigh the same and the balls weigh the same. Then ask the children, "What do you know about how the weights of the balls and the cubes compare?" Have children explain their thinking first with a partner and then with the class.

Figure 13.1 shows a series of other examples for the pan balance. Two or more balances for a single problem provide different information about the shapes or variables. Problems of this type can be adjusted in difficulty for children in grades K−2. When no numbers are given, as in the top three examples in Figure 13.1, children look for combinations of numbers for the shapes that make the pans balance. The different shapes represent different amounts (variables) and so would have different values. There are often different paths to finding a solution so discussion of solution strategies is a must. To create your own pan balance problems, start by assigning values to two or three shapes. Place shapes in groups and add the values. Be sure your problems can be solved!

Standards for Mathematical Practice

◄ **2 Reason abstractly and quantitatively.**

Stop and Reflect

How would you solve the last problem in Figure 13.1? Can you solve it in two ways?

t e c h n o l o g y ⏻
note

There are several excellent online pan balance explorations to continue work on equivalence:

- NCTM's Illuminations "Pan Balance—Shapes" and "Pan Balance—Numbers," where children enter what they believe to be equivalent expressions.
- PBS Cyberchase Poddle Weigh-In, where shapes are balanced with numbers between 1 and 4.
- Agame Monkey Math Balance, where children select numbers for each side of a balance to make the two sides balance. The level of difficulty can be adapted.

Figure 13.1

Examples of problems using pan balances.

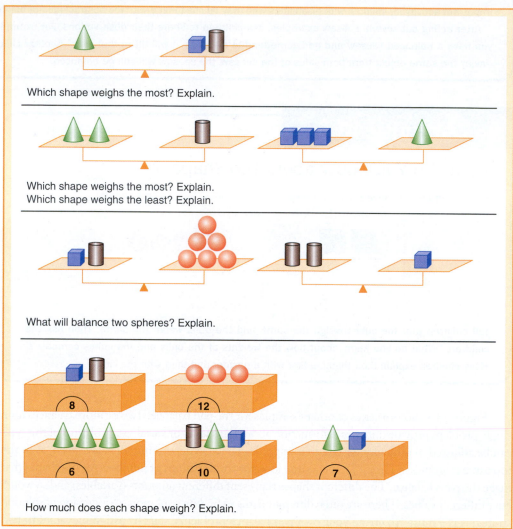

After children have experienced pan balance tasks involving shapes, they can explore pan balances using numbers and then variables.

Activity 13.7

Tilt or Balance?

Draw or project a simple two-pan balance. In each pan, write a numeric expression and ask which pan will go down or whether the two will balance (see Figure 13.2(a)). Select expressions that are appropriate for the grade level of children (e.g., sums within 100 for grade 1 and within 1000 grade 2). Challenge children to write expressions for each side of the scale to make it balance and then to write the corresponding equation to illustrate the meaning of =. Note that when the scale tilts, either a "greater-than" or "less-than" symbol ($>$ or $<$) is used, and if it is balanced, an equal sign ($=$) is used. Include examples such as the third and fourth balances for which children are asked to analyze the relationships on both sides (as opposed to doing the computation) to determine whether the pan tilts or balances. For children with disabilities, rather than have them write expressions for each side of the scale, share a small collection of cards with expressions and have them identify the ones that will make the scale balance.

Figure 13.2

Using expressions and variables in equations and inequalities. The two-pan balance helps develop the meaning of $=$, $<$, and $>$.

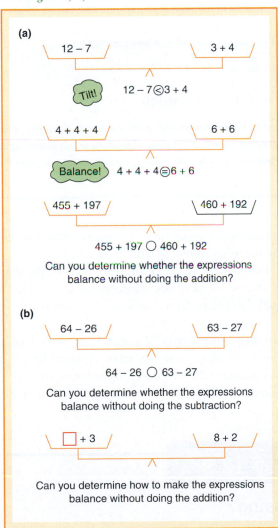

(a)

| 12 − 7 | 3 + 4 |

Tilt!   12 − 7 ⧀ 3 + 4

| 4 + 4 + 4 | 6 + 6 |

Balance!   4 + 4 + 4 ⊜ 6 + 6

| 455 + 197 | 460 + 192 |

455 + 197 ◯ 460 + 192

Can you determine whether the expressions balance without doing the addition?

(b)

| 64 − 26 | 63 − 27 |

64 − 26 ◯ 63 − 27

Can you determine whether the expressions balance without doing the subtraction?

| ☐ + 3 | 8 + 2 |

Can you determine how to make the expressions balance without doing the addition?

True/False and Open Sentences

Carpenter and colleagues (2003) suggest that a good starting point for helping children make sense of the equal sign is to explore equations as being either true or false. Clarifying the meaning of the equal sign is just one of the outcomes of this type of exploration, as seen in the next activity.

Activity 13.8

CCSS-M: 1.OA.B.3; 1.OA.D.7; 1.NBT.B.4; 2.NBT.B.5

True or False Equations

Introduce true/false sentences or equations with simple examples to explain what is meant by a true equation and a false equation (e.g., $2+3 = 5$ is a true equation; $4+3 = 2$ is a false equation). Then put several simple equations on the board, some true and some false. Here are some examples:

$$5+2 = 7 \qquad 4+1 = 6$$

$$8 = 10-1 \qquad 7 = 12-5$$

To begin with, keep the computations simple. Ask children to talk with their partners and decide which of the equations are true (and why) and which are false (and why).

After this initial exploration, have children explore equations that are in a less familiar form:

$$3+7 = 7+3 \qquad 10-3 = 11-4 \qquad 9+6 = 0+14$$

$$8 = 8 \qquad 15+7+3 = 16+10$$

Listen to the types of reasons children use to justify their answers and plan additional equations accordingly. ELLs and children with disabilities will benefit from first explaining (or showing) their reasoning to a partner as a low-risk speaking opportunity and then sharing with the whole group. Children can use "Pan Balance—Numbers" on NCTM's Illuminations website to explore and/or verify equivalence.

Children will typically agree about equations when there is an expression on one side and a single number on the other, although initially equations such as $7 = 12-5$ may generate discussion. For equations with no operation (e.g., $8 = 8$), the discussion may be lively. Children often believe there must be an operation on one side and an "answer" on the other. Reinforce that the equal sign means "is the same as" by using that language as you read the symbol.

After children have experienced true/false sentences, introduce open sentences—that is, equations with a box or blank (or variable) to be replaced by a number. To develop an understanding of open sentences (also called missing-value equations), encourage children to look at the number sentence holistically and describe in words what the equation represents.

Activity 13.9

CCSS-M: 1.OA.D.7; 1.OA.D.8; 2.OA.A.1

What's Missing?

Write several open sentences on the board. Ask children to figure out what number is missing and how they know. Notice that most of the equations are set up so that children do not have to do the computation to figure out what is missing. Encourage them to first try to figure out the missing number without doing the computation. Challenge children to find more than one way to figure out the missing number. Here are some examples:

$$5+2 = \square \qquad 4+\square = 6 \qquad 4+5 = \square-1$$

$$6-\underline{} = 7-4 \qquad \underline{}+5 = 5+8 \qquad 15+27 = \underline{}+28$$

Relational Thinking

Children usually think about the equal sign in one of three ways (Stephens et al., 2013). First, as noted previously, they may have an *operational view*, meaning that the equal sign means "do something." Second, children may hold a *relational–computational view* in which the equal sign symbolizes a relation between answers to two calculations, but they see computation as the only way to determine if the two sides are equal or not. Finally, children can develop a *relational–structural view* of the equal sign (we will refer to this as relational). With the relational conception of the equal sign, a child uses numeric relationships between the two sides of the equal sign rather than actually computing the amounts.

Standards for Mathematical Practice

◀ **2** **Reason abstractly and quantitatively.**

Consider two distinctly different explanations for placing an 8 in the box for the open sentence $7 + \square = 6 + 9$.

> Explanation 1: Because 6+9 is 15, I need to figure out 7 plus what equals 15. It is 8, so the box is 8.

> Explanation 2: Seven is one more than the 6 on the other side. That means that the box should be one less than 9, so it must be 8.

The first child computes the sum on one side of the equation and then uses the sum to determine the missing part on the other side (relational–*computational* view). The second child uses a relationship between the expressions on either side of the equal sign. This child does not need to compute the values on each side (relational–*structural* view). When numbers are large, a relational-structural view is much more efficient and useful.

Stop and Reflect

If the children used the same reasoning they used to solve $7 + \square = 6 + 9$, how would they each solve the following open sentence?

$$534 + 175 = 174 + \square$$

The first child would likely do the computation and might have difficulty finding the correct addend because of the size of the numbers. The second child would reason that 174 is one less than 175, so the number in the box must be one more than 534.

📎 Teaching Tip

Children sharing their reasoning promotes relational thinking and can help other children improve their noticing skills and analysis of relationships in problems.

📋 Formative Assessment Note

As children work on these types of tasks, you can interview them one on one (though you may not get to everyone). Listen for whether they use relational–structural thinking. If they do not, ask, "Can you find the answer without actually doing any computation?" This questioning helps nudge children toward relational thinking and helps you decide the next instructional steps.

Children need many and ongoing opportunities to explore problems that encourage relational thinking (Stephens et al., 2013). Explore increasingly complex true/false and open sentences with your class, perhaps as daily problems, warm-ups, or at centers/stations. Posing problems with larger numbers that make computation difficult (not impossible) can prompt children to try a relational–structural approach. Here are some examples to consider.

TRUE/FALSE:

674−369 = 664−379   37+54 = 38+53   376−329 = 76−29

OPEN SENTENCES:

73+56 = 71+□   126−37 = □−40   68+58 = 57+69+___

Stop and Reflect

Before reading on, try using relational–structural thinking to reason about these true-false and open sentences.

Using such equations can prompt children to look at equations in their entirety rather than just jumping right into a series of computations, an important aspect of algebraic thinking (Blanton, Levi, Crites, & Dougherty, 2011). Molina and Ambrose (2006) found that asking children to write their own open sentences was particularly effective in helping them solidify their understanding of the equal sign. This is the focus on the next activity.

Activity 13.10

CCSS-M: 1.OA.D.7; 1.OA.D.8; 2.OA.A.1

Make a Statement!

Ask children to make up their own true/false and open sentences that they can use to challenge their classmates. To support student thinking, provide dice with numerals on them. They can turn the dice to different faces to try different possibilities.

Each child should write three equations with at least one true and at least one false sentence. For children who need additional structure, in particular children with disabilities, provide the **Make a Statement** Recording Sheet. Children can trade their equations with other children to find each other's false statements. Interesting equations can be the focus of a follow-up, whole-class discussion.

When children write their own true/false sentences, they often are intrigued with the idea of using large numbers and lots of numbers in their sentences. Support their efforts, as these kinds of problems tend to help move children toward relational–structural thinking.

The Meaning of Variables

Variables are first mentioned in the CCSS-M standards in grade 6, but researchers suggest starting much earlier so that students are more adept at using variables when they encounter more complex mathematical situations in middle school (Blanton et al., 2011). Variables can be interpreted in many ways. They can be used to represent unique but unknown quantities or quantities that vary. Unfortunately, children often think of all variables as placeholders for specific numbers (unique, unknown quantities) and not representations for multiple or even infinite values (quantities that vary). Children need experiences that build meaning for both.

Variables Used as Unknown Values

Standards for Mathematical Practice

◀ **2** Reason abstractly and quantitatively.

In the open sentence explorations, the $\square$ and the ____ are precursors of a variable used to represent a unique, unknown value. You can also use a letter, such as an n, instead of a box or a blank in your open sentences, to stand for the missing number.

Consider the following open sentence:

$$\square + \square + 7 = \square + 17$$

This equation could have also been written as $n + n + 7 = n + 17$. When the same symbol or letter is used in multiple places in an expression or equation, the convention is that it stands for the same number every place it occurs. (Point this out to children.) In this example, the $\square$ or n must be 10.

Many story problems describe a situation involving a specific unknown. Here is an example where the change is unknown:

Rebekah had 5 apples in her basket. She picked some more after lunch. Then she had 13. How many apples did she pick after lunch?

Although children can solve this problem without using algebra, they can represent the equation as $5 + \_\_\_ = 13$ or even as $5 + a = 13$ as a way to begin to learn about variables.

When writing equations for story problems, different equations may occur. For example, consider this story problem:

If Gabbie has 12 cards and Karl has 5 cards, write an equation for how many more cards Gabbie has than Karl.

Standards for Mathematical Practice

◀ **4** Model with mathematics.

Notice the instructions did not ask children to solve the problem but rather to write an equation. Some children might write $12 - 5 = \square$ whereas others may write $5 + \square = 12$. The latter equation can be interpreted as "Karl's 5 cards plus some more cards are the same as Gabbie's 12 cards." Facilitate a discussion with children to help them understand that both equations show the same relationships and both are correct. Children should be able to write and justify *both* equations by connecting the equations to the story.

With a context, children can even explore three variables, each one standing for an unknown value as in the following activity (adapted from Maida, 2004).

Activity 13.11

CCSS-M: 1.OA.A.1; 1.OA.C.6; 2.OA.A.1

Toys, Toys, Toys

Children are challenged to figure out the cost of three toys, given the following three facts:

Ask children to look at each fact and make observations that can help them figure out the cost of each toy. For example, they may notice that the soccer ball costs $1 more than the teddy bear (i.e., compare the first two equations). Help children write this observation in the same format as the other statements. Continue until these discoveries lead to finding the cost of each toy. Encourage children to use manipulatives to represent and explore the problem.

Stop and Reflect   500 ⌕ 250   ⁇ 3x ▱ ∫⌂5○ ∞ ∩ ✗ 2.5

Work on the problem in Activity 13.11 before reading further. Using the observation that the soccer ball cost $1 more than the bear, that means that the third fact can be thought of as a bear+$1+bear = $5. So, how much is a teddy bear? Notice the work done in building the concept of the equal sign is now applied to understanding and solving for variables.

Variables Used as Quantities That Vary

The shift from the variable representing a specific quantity to a variable representing multiple possibilities can be difficult for children and is not as explicit in the curriculum as it should be. Children need experiences with variables that vary early in the elementary curriculum. For example, second graders can begin to describe patterns using variables, as when describing how much many legs for any number of dogs: $L = D \times 4$ (the number of legs is the number of dogs times four).

Make sure to emphasize that the variable stands for *the number of* because children can confuse the variable with a label (Blanton et al., 2011; Russell, Schifter, & Bastable, 2011). For example, in solving the problem, *There are 13 dogs and cats at the kennel. How many dogs and how many cats are at the kennel?*, you may find a variety of solutions that use the following notation:

$$6D+7C \qquad 5D+8C \qquad 10D+3C$$

Here children are using letters as labels, not variables. D does not represent a *number*, but rather it is shorthand for *dog*. When introducing the concept of variable, you need to be aware of this tendency to use letters as labels.

Slight shifts in how arithmetic problems are presented can also open up opportunities to help children develop this second meaning of variables (Blanton, 2008). As an example, let's revisit the previous story problem, but remove the result:

Rebekah had 5 apples in her basket. She picked some more after lunch. How might you describe the total number of apples Rebekah had in her basket after lunch?

With the total removed, the goal becomes writing the expression: $5+a$. This can also be illustrated on a number line:

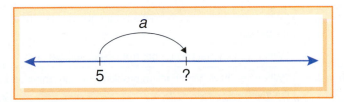

As another example, consider the following tasks. Think about how the second task is modified from the first:

NUMBER TASK:

Sandra has 10 pennies. George has 4 more pennies than Sandra. How many pennies does George have?

ALGEBRA TASK:

Sandra has some pennies. George has 4 more pennies than Sandra. How many pennies does George have?

Notice in the modified version there is no way to do a computation because you are not given specific values. Children can list possible ways in a table (see Figure 13.3) and eventually represent the answer as $George = Sandra+4$, or more briefly, $G = S+4$.

Another opportunity to use variables as quantities that vary is when children make conjectures about the number system (e.g., when you add zero to any number, you get that number back). These statements are the properties of our number system and are true for all numbers, making them appropriate places to use variables that vary. The next section looks at ways to help children recognize, understand, and describe these important generalizations about our number system.

Figure 13.3

Possible ways variables can vary in value.

Number of Pennies for Sandra	Number of Pennies for George
2	6
3	7
4	8
10	14
23	27

Structure in the Number System: Properties

The importance of properties cannot be overstated. Table 13.1 provides a list of the ones that children in the primary grades must know and be able to use, and includes how children might describe the property. Importantly, in the CCSS-M, the emphasis is on *using* and *applying* the properties (not identifying them); for example, in grade 2, one standard states, "Explain why addition and subtraction strategies work, using place value and the properties of operations" (CCSSO, 2010, p. 19).

Table 13.1. Properties of the Operations for PreK–2.

Name of Property	Symbolic Representation	How Children Might Describe the Pattern or Structure
Commutative	$a+b = b+a$	"When you add two numbers in any order, you'll get the same answer."
Associative	$(a+b)+c = a+(b+c)$	"When you add three numbers, you can add the first two and then add the third or add the last two numbers and then add the first number. Either way, you will get the same answer."
Additive Identity	$a+0 = 0+a = a$	"When you add zero to any number, you get the same number you started with."
	$a-0 = a$	"When you subtract zero from any number, you get the number you started with."
Additive Inverse	$a-a = 0*$	"When you subtract a number from itself, you get zero."
Inverse Relationship of Addition and Subtraction	If $a+b = c$ then $c-b = a$ and $c-a = b$	"When you have a subtraction problem you can 'think addition' by using the inverse."

* The additive inverse property is usually written as $a + (-a) = 0$, but the symbolic representation $a-a = 0$ will make more sense to children in the primary grades.

Correctly using and applying the properties is essential to computation (Blanton et al., 2011). Traditionally, instruction on the properties has involved matching equations to which property they illustrate. That is not sufficient and should not be the focus of your instruction on the properties. Instead, focus on helping children recognize and understand these important generalizations—and use them to generate equivalent expressions in order to solve problems efficiently and flexibly (for example, understanding the commutative property for both addition and multiplication substantially reduces the number of facts to be memorized). The properties of the operations have been discussed in several chapters in this book, in particular Chapter 9 and Chapter 10. In this chapter, the focus is on exploring the properties as generalizations of number.

Making Sense of Properties

Standards for Mathematical Practice

8 Look for and express regularity in repeated reasoning.

Children begin to notice equivalent expressions as they engage in their work with numbers. Contexts like the frogs on a pond used earlier in the chapter can provide opportunities to focus on the properties. For example, some children might consider pairs of solutions such as $2+7$ and $7+2$ as different solutions because of the contextual situation; that is, $2+7$ could represent 2 frogs on the lily pad and 7 frogs on the rock and then $7+2$ would represent 7 frogs on the lily pad and 2 frogs on the rock. Others may argue that they are the "same," meaning that although $2+7$ and $7+2$ are modeling different situations, they still result in 9 frogs. It is important to allow children to work through and process this idea of commutativity so look for multiple places to revisit the idea. Consider the suggestion in the next paragraph.

Again, making slight changes in how arithmetic problems are presented can open up more opportunities to examine the mathematical ideas at hand (Blanton, 2008)—in this case, properties. For example, instead of a series of unrelated addition problems, consider the following list of related problems:

$$4+7 \quad 7+4 \quad 23+15 \quad 15+23$$

Once children have solved these problems, focus their attention on the addends, asking questions such as, "What do you notice?" Some children may say that these equal the same amount, but it is important to discuss why this is true. A child might explain that the numbers could be the number of grapes on two plates and that no matter if the plates trade places, the total will be the same amount.

The pivotal question for generalization, however, asks, "Is it true for any numbers?" Some children will agree that although it seems to be true all of the time, maybe there are two numbers they haven't tried yet for which it does not work. Other children might explain that the numbers can be added in any order and it does not matter what the numbers are. Challenge children to try a lot of different examples. When they want to check larger numbers, give them a calculator so they can focus on checking the sums and not on doing the calculation. To be clear, it is important to recognize that even if children show some understanding of commutativity of single-digit addends, you may need to help them recognize the *generalizability* of the property with larger numbers. Using and applying this property means that in an equation such as $394+176 = \square+394$, a child recognizes the commutative property and uses it to efficiently solve the problem. She may say that the $\square$ must be 176 because $394+176$ is the same as $176+394$.

A next step toward generalization is to have children express these properties in general terms without reference to specific numbers—first in their own language and then using symbols. For instance, after examining several examples of adding zero, a child might observe, "When you add zero to any number, you get that number back." If the verbal generalization is not clear or entirely correct, have children discuss and modify the wording until all agree with and understand the wording. Write this verbal statement of the property on the board.

Articulating this property (and any other properties of our number system) in a general way, in either words or symbols (e.g., $a+0 = a$ or $\square+0 = 0+\square$), noting that it is true for all numbers, makes the structure of our number system and the connection between arithmetic and algebra explicit. (Note that using letters to describe the properties can be used as early as first grade as long as it is done meaningfully [Blanton et al., 2011; Carpenter, Franke, & Levi, 2003].) When these structures are made explicit and are understood, they not only add to children's tools for computation, but they also enrich their understanding of the number system, providing a base for even higher levels of reasoning (Carpenter, Franke, & Levi, 2003).

Activity 13.12 provides a creative way for children to develop experience with the identity property for addition, as well as other properties.

> **Standards for Mathematical Practice**
>
> **3** Construct viable arguments and critique the reasoning of others.

Activity 13.12

CCSS-M: 1.OA.B.3; 1.OA.C.6; 1.OA.D.7; 2.OA.B.2

Five Ways to Zero

Give each pair of children a number (you can use a deck of cards to do so). If they get a 7, they are to write 5 different ways to get to 0 using number sentences that start with 7. For example, they could write 7 5 2 = 0 or it could be 7 + 3−10 = 0. Be sure children are using correct notation and grouping so that their statements are true. There will be opportunities to also discuss the associative property for addition and whether it also works for subtraction because of the placement of children's numbers. All children might benefit from using counters or a number line in exploring the possibilities. After they find five ways, ask children what was true about all of the problems they wrote.

Discussing problem sets such as these and others helps children make sense of the properties. In the following first grade vignette, the teacher is using true/false sentences to help children reason about the commutative property of addition.

Teacher: [*Pointing at* $5+3 = 3+5$ *on the board*] Is it true or false?

Carmen: True, because $5+3$ is 8 and $3+5$ is 8.

Andy: There is a 5 on both sides and a 3 on both sides and nothing else.

Teacher: [*Writing* $6+9 = 9+6$ *on the board*] True or false?

Children:	True. It's the same!
Teacher:	[*Writing* 25+48 = 48+25 *on the board*] True or false?
Children:	True!
Teacher:	Who can describe what is going on with these examples?
Rene:	If you have the same numbers on each side, you get the same thing.
Teacher:	Does it matter what numbers I use?
Children:	No.
Teacher:	[*Writing a+7 = 7+ a on the board*] What is *a*?
Michael:	It can be any number because it's on both sides.
Teacher:	[*Writing a+ b = b+ a on the board*] What are *a* and *b*?
Children:	Any number!

Notice how the teacher is developing the aspects of the commutative property in a conceptual manner—focusing on exemplars to guide children to generalize rather than asking them to memorize or identify the properties, which can be a meaningless, rote activity.

Making and Justifying Conjectures

Noticing generalizable properties and attempting to prove that they are true is a significant form of algebraic reasoning and is at the heart of what it means to do mathematics (Ball & Bass, 2003; Carpenter, Franke, & Levi, 2003; Schifter, 1999; Schifter, Monk, Russell, & Bastable, 2007). Children can make conjectures about properties as early as first and second grade, and this must be encouraged by the teacher. For example, as first graders are exploring addition, a child might observe that the order you add two numbers does not matter (1+6 = 6+1). This idea can be presented to the group. Children can test the idea with other numbers and eventually try to explain why this is true. They can write it in symbols: a+b = b+a (yes, first graders can understand and benefit from using variables). It is important to ask, how can this help us do math problems? For first graders, recognizing that when they see 1+6 that they can start with 6 and add on 1 is an important step toward learning how to add efficiently (as well as learn the basic facts).

Standards for Mathematical Practice

> **7 Look for and make use of structure.** ▶

The most common form of justification for young children is the use of examples (Russell, Schifter, & Bastable, 2011). Some children will be satisfied to try one or two examples. Others will try several examples but will not vary those examples in terms of size or other characteristics, such as using even and odd numbers. Still others will try very large numbers as substitutes for "any" number. Encourage children to use a wide variety of examples. After trying their examples, they may respond, "See? It works for any number you try." Proof by example will hopefully lead to someone asking, "How do we know there still aren't some numbers that it doesn't work for?"

Children can use physical materials or representations to justify the reasoning behind the conjecture (see Figure 13.4). What moves this beyond "proof by example" is that the argument does not depend on particular numbers and emerges from the structure of the representation (Schifter, Russell, & Bastable, 2011). Children might explain the generalization using statements such as "These could be any numbers and would work this way no matter what the numbers are."

Figure 13.4

Using manipulatives to generalize the commutative property.

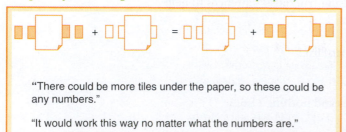

"There could be more tiles under the paper, so these could be any numbers."

"It would work this way no matter what the numbers are."

Odd or even numbers provide an excellent context for exploring structure in our number system. All too often children are simply told that the even numbers are those that end in 0, 2, 4, 6, or 8 and odd numbers are those that end in 1, 3, 5, 7, or 9. Although this is true, it is only an attribute of even and odd numbers rather than a definition that explains what *even* or *not even* (i.e., *odd*) really means. The next three activities help children develop conceptual ideas of even and odd numbers without forcing definitions. In fact, after these activities children should be able to describe in their own words what we mean by odd and even numbers.

 Activity 13.13   CCSS-M: 1.OA.B.3; 2.OA.C.3; 2.NBT.B.5

Fair Shares for Two

Tell a story about two twin sisters (or brothers). The twins always share whatever they have equally. If they find some pretty seashells, they will count them out and share them so that each has the same number of shells. When their Mom gives them cookies for lunch, they are always sure that each get the same number of cookies. Sometimes they are not able to share things fairly because there is something left over. For example, this happened when Dad gave them five marbles. (Discuss why they could not share five marbles equally.) Whenever there is a leftover, the twins put the extra item in a special box of "leftovers" for their baby brother.

Now assign three or four numbers from 6 to 40 to pairs of children, depending on readiness. Their task is to decide which of their numbers could be shared fairly and which would have a leftover. Provide linking cubes to use for their investigations. Display a list of numbers that can be shared and a list of those that will have a leftover. Examine the lists as a class and ask for observations. Select numbers not in the list and ask if children can tell which list they belong in and how they know.

The critical portion of "Fair Shares for Two" is the discussion about children's investigations and findings. Notice how children use the linking cubes in their investigations. Some children will count out the number of cubes and then distribute the cubes one by one to each twin. They either keep track of the fair sharing (e.g., one for this twin, one for that twin; two for this twin, two for that twin, and so on) or they have to count at the end to determine if each twin received the same amount. Others might organize their cubes by pairing them together to make sure that each twin receives the same amount (see Figure 13.5). Have children share how they used their linking cubes and ask how can they quickly see whether the twins received the same amount. Challenge the children to use their own words to describe the numbers that can be fairly shared (evens) and those that cannot (odds). Based on this activity, *an even number is an amount that can be shared fairly or split into two equal parts with no leftovers. An odd number is one that cannot be split into two equal parts.* The number endings (e.g., 0, 2, 4, 6, and 8) are only an interesting and useful pattern or observation and should not be used in their definition (of an even number).

In the next activity, children start with visual representations of even and odd numbers.

Figure 13.5

Sharing cubes fairly with two people.

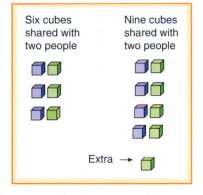

 Activity 13.14   CCSS-M: 1.OA.B.3; 2.OA.C.3; 2.NBT.B.5

Bumps or No Bumps

Create sets of **Two-Column Cards** on card stock (see Figure 13.6) for pairs of children. Children are to work together to describe as many things as they can about the pieces. (For example: There are cards for each number 1 to 10. Some are like rectangles. Some have a part sticking out.) For those who need help to get started, suggest that they put the cards in order from one to ten. After having some time to explore and share ideas they have noticed, ask children to find a way to sort their cards into two sets. If no pair sorts the cards like in

(continued)

Figure 13.6, do so on a projector and ask what rule you are using to sort the cards. Use children's language to describe the pieces representing the odd numbers. For example, someone may describe the seven card as having a "bump."

Next, assign the pairs of children three or four numbers between 11 and 50 and have them decide whether two-column cards for these numbers would have bumps or no bumps (or whatever language children used). Provide linking cubes for their investigations. Ask them to use words and pictures to explain their conclusions.

To extend "Bumps or No Bumps," ask children what kind of card they will get when two cards in the set are added together to create a new two-column card.

Figure 13.6

Two-column cards are separated into groups with "bumps" and "no bumps."
Note that these are also odd and even numbers. Why?

Stop and Reflect

Think for a moment how you might prove that the sum of two odd numbers is always even. How might the two-column cards used in the activity "Bumps or No Bumps" be useful?

As in "Fair Shares for Two," challenge the children to use their own words to describe the numbers. In "Bumps or No Bumps," *an even number is an amount that can be formed into pairs (i.e., the columns) with no leftovers. An odd number is an amount that, after forming pairs, will always has one not paired.* After refining children's definitions of these numbers, you can introduce the terms *even* and *odd*. Children will notice see that numbers with "bumps" end in 1, 3, 5, 7, or 9 and even numbers end in 0, 2, 4, 6, or 8. Again, these characteristics should not be included in the definitions.

After experiences with "Fair Shares for Two" and "Bumps or No Bumps," the next activity moves children's thinking about evens and odds to a more abstract level.

Activity 13.15

CCSS- M: 1.OA.B.3; 2.OA.C.3; 2.NBT.B.5

Broken Calculator: Can You Fix It?

 Distribute calculators to every child. In partners, have children select one of the following two problems to explore.

1. If you cannot use any of the even keys on the calculator (0, 2, 4, 6, 8), can you create an even number in the calculator display? If so, how?

2. If you cannot use any of the odd keys on the calculator (1, 3, 5, 7, 9), can you create an odd number in the calculator display? If so, how?

They must decide if it is possible and if so, share an example of how to do it. Finally they are to prepare a justification or illustration to describe why it does or doesn't work (in general).

For children with disabilities, provide linking cubes so they can concretely model numbers to support their thinking. Invite early finishers to take on the other problem or to write their justifications using variables. In the follow-up discussion, ask children for other patterns or generalizations they notice about odd and even numbers.

Making, testing, and proving conjectures should become a routine activity in your classroom (Russell, Schifter, & Bastable, 2011). This next activity suggests one way to make this happen.

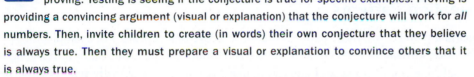

Activity 13.16   CCSS- M: 1.OA.B.3; 2.NBT.B.9

Convince Me Conjectures

  To begin, offer children a conjecture to test (see **Conjecture Cards for K-2** for ideas). For example, "If you add one to one addend and take one away from the other addend, the answer will be the same." Ask children to (1) test the conjecture and (2) prove it is true for any number. Point out the difference between testing and proving. Testing is seeing if the conjecture is true for specific examples. Proving is providing a convincing argument (visual or explanation) that the conjecture will work for *all* numbers. Then, invite children to create (in words) their own conjecture that they believe is always true. Then they must prepare a visual or explanation to convince others that it is always true.

All children, particularly **ELLs**, may struggle with correct and precise terms. When needed, "revoice" their ideas using appropriate phrases to help them learn to communicate mathematically, but be careful to not make this the focus—the focus should be on the ideas presented. Children with disabilities will benefit from the presentation and discussion of counterexamples.

Using and *applying* the properties is central to mathematical proficiency—it is not only emphasized in the CCSS-M content, but also in the Mathematical Practices (CCSSO, 2010). An explicit focus on seeking generalizations and looking for structure is also important in supporting the range of learners in the classroom from those who struggle to those who excel (Schifter, Russell, & Bastable, 2009). Doing so requires planning—deciding what problems to pose and what questions to ask to help children think about generalized ideas—across the mathematical strands, not just during the "algebra" unit.

Patterns and Functions

Patterns are found in all areas of mathematics. Learning to look for, describe, and extend patterns are important processes in thinking algebraically. Two of the eight mathematical practices (CCSSO, 2010) actually begin with the phrase "look for," implying that children who are mathematically proficient pay attention to patterns as they do mathematics. Functional thinking begins in preK–2 when children make observations like, "Each person we add to the group means we add 2 more feet" (Blanton et al., 2011).

Standards for
Mathematical Practice

7 **Look for and make**
use of structure.

8 **Look for and**
express regularity
in reasoning.

In grades preK−2, repeating and then growing patterns have often been a primary focus, but they are not explicitly mentioned in the *Common Core State Standards*. This does not mean that patterns are not useful. In fact, patterns provide opportunities for children to look for structure and express regularity in situations. The point is that the goal is not to have children do patterns just to do patterns; rather, children should be engaged in looking for, describing, and extending patterns to help them develop the skills to look for structure and express regularity in all mathematical situations.

When possible, patterning activities should involve some form of physical materials. Many kindergarten and first-grade textbooks have pages where children are shown a picture of a pattern such as a string of colored beads. The task is to color the last few beads in the string according to the pattern. There are a few differences between this and the same activity done with physical materials. First, by coloring on the page without an initial investigation with physical materials, the activity takes on a sense of right versus wrong rather than a sense-making activity. If a mistake is made, correction on the page is difficult and can cause frustration. Physical materials, on the other hand, allow a trial-and-error approach that can allow for learning from mistakes or missteps. Second, pattern activities on worksheets prevent children from extending patterns beyond the few spaces provided on the page. By using materials such as colored blocks, buttons, and connecting cubes, children gain more experience thinking about patterns because the patterns can be extended well beyond those few spaces. Plus, by using a variety of materials to create patterns, children can begin to generalize patterns across the different materials.

Repeating Patterns

Repeating patterns are those patterns that have a core that repeats. For example, if red-blue is the core, a string of beds could be used to continue to repeat this pattern: red-blue-red-blue-red-blue . . . . Notice in Figure 13.7 that the core is always fully repeated and never only partially shown.

An important goal when working with repeating patterns is to help children identify the *core* of the pattern (Warren & Cooper, 2008). One possible way to emphasize the core is to place shape patterns under a document camera, state aloud what is there and ask what comes next. After adding on a few shapes, ask children to describe the pattern. To help children, especially those with disabilities, track on the core of the pattern, highlight the core by drawing a circle around the shapes that form the core, repeating the circle each time the core is repeated. You can also highlight the core by labeling the pattern with letters as shown in Figure 13.7. For example, the first pattern in Figure 13.7 shows an AB pattern because the core has two different elements, A and B. The red-blue pattern described earlier is also an AB pattern. An ABBB pattern (the last pattern shown in Figure 13.7) uses 2 different elements but because B is repeated 3 times, the core has 4 elements.

Teaching Tip

When first starting to work with patterns, ask children to describe three things they notice. Once they share their ideas, then point out the pattern if no one else does, and ask them, "What comes next?"

Repeating patterns are everywhere! The seasons, days of the week, and months of the year are just a beginning. Challenge children to find real-life AB patterns—for example, "day, night," "open a door, close the door," "to school, home from school," or "set the table before eating, clear table after eating." Children's books often have patterns in repeating rhymes, words, or phrases. *Pattern Fish* (Harris, 2000) and *My Mom and Dad Make Me Laugh* (Sharratt, 1996) are two great choices. A very long repeating pattern can be found in *If You Give a Mouse a Cookie* (Numeroff, 1985) (or any books in this series), in which each event eventually leads back to giving a mouse a cookie, with the implication that the sequence would be repeated. In addition, you can recite oral patterns. For example, "do, mi, mi, do, mi, mi, . . ." is a simple singing pattern. Also, body movements such as moving the arm up, sideways, and then down can be used to make patterns: up, side, down, up, side, down (ABC).

Figure 13.7

Examples of repeating patterns using manipulatives.

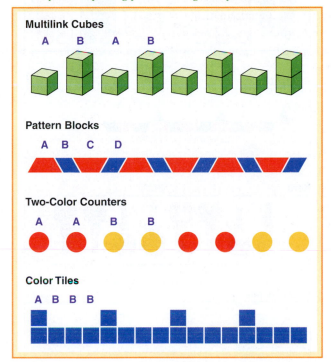

There are numerous websites that offer children opportunities to explore repeating patterns. For example, PBS Kids offers several interactive pattern activities for young children (search for PBS Kids patterns). An Activity called "Patch Tool" on NCTM's Illuminations website allows children to flip and rotate shapes to create various patterns, which informally introduces them to geometric transformations while they explore patterns. The National Library of Virtual Manipulatives also has several applets that support the exploration of repeated (and growing) patterns, including Attribute Trains, Color Patterns, and Pattern Blocks.

The following activity helps children work on identifying the core of a pattern.

Activity 13.17

CCSS-M: K.MD.B.3; K.G.A.1; K.G.B.4; 1.G.A.2

Can You Match It?

Show six or seven patterns with different materials or pictures (see Figure 13.8 for examples). In pairs, one child closes his eyes while the other child uses the A, B, C method to read a pattern that you point to. After hearing the pattern, the child who had his eyes closed examines the patterns and identifies which pattern was read. If two of the patterns in the list have the same structure, the discussion can be very interesting.

Figure 13.8

Examples of pattern cards on card stock. Each pattern completely repeats its core at least twice.

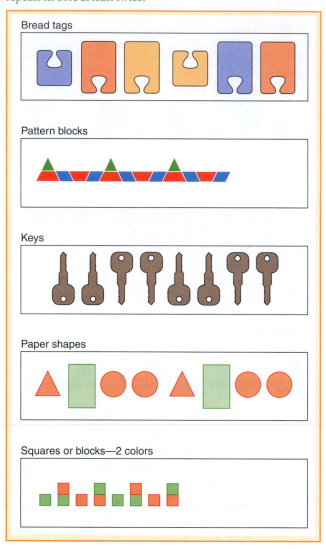

A significant step forward mathematically is to see that two patterns constructed with different materials are actually the same pattern. For example, the second pattern in Figure 13.7 and the second pattern in Figure 13.8 can both be "read" A-B-C-D-A-B-C-D, and the third pattern in both figures is A-A-B-B-A-A-B-B. Translating two or more patterns with the same structure into some form of symbolism (in this case, the alphabet) moves beyond doing patterns for the sake of doing patterns and helps children gain experience with generalization.

Standards for Mathematical Practice

 Look for and make use of structure.

Activity 13.18

CCSS-M: K.MD.B.3; K.G.A.1; K.G.B.4; 1.G.A.2

Same Pattern, Different Stuff

Give each child a pattern strip like those shown in Figure 13.8 and a set of materials that is different from that on the pattern strip. Have children make a pattern with the set of materials that has the same structure as the pattern on the strip. You can also mix up the pattern strips and have children find strips that have the same pattern structure. To test if two patterns are the same, children can translate each of the strips into a third set of materials or they can write down the A, B, C pattern for each.

After children have experiences identifying, building, and extending repeating patterns, you can step up the challenge by introducing a functional aspect to their work by asking them to predict which element will be in a particular position, as done in the next activity.

Activity 13.19

CCSS-M: K.MD.B.3; K.G.A.1; K.G.B.4; 1.G.A.2; 2.OA.C.3

Predict Down the Line

Provide children with a pattern to extend (e.g., ABC pattern made with colored links). Before children begin to extend the pattern, have them predict exactly what elements (colored links) will be in, say, the twelfth position. (Notice that in an ABC pattern the third, sixth, ninth, and twelfth terms are the C element because they are multiples of 3.) After children predict, have them complete the pattern to check. Ask them how they knew. You can differentiate this lesson by starting with a more basic AB pattern or by having different groups of children work on different types of patterns based on their readiness. Children should be required to provide a reason for their prediction in writing supported with visuals. After the discussion, extend the challenge by asking children to predict what element will be in a position further down the line, such as the 20th or 24th position. Again, children should be required to provide a reason for their prediction.

In "Predict Down the Line, "some children will check their prediction by continuing to build onto the patterns they had already constructed. Others may combine their 12-cube pattern with a partner's and use the new 24-cube pattern to check their prediction. Still others may use skip counting by 3s to help them check their prediction.

Growing Patterns

Growing patterns, which involve a progression from step to step, are precursors to functional relationships and should be explored in the primary grades. In technical terms, these patterns are called *sequences;* we will simply call them *growing patterns*. With these patterns, children identify the core, but they also look for a generalization or a relationship that will tell them how the core is changing—and, ultimately, in later grades, what the pattern will be at any point along the way (e.g., the *n*th term).

Children's experiences with growing patterns should start with fairly straightforward patterns using visuals, such as those in Figure 13.9. Geometric patterns made with physical materials (e.g., tiles, counters, cubes) are good exemplars because the pattern is easier to see (than with numbers) and because children can manipulate the objects.

Figure 13.9(d) is a growing pattern in which a square made of 4 cubes is added to the middle as you go from one step to the next. Describing how a growing pattern changes from step to step is known as *recursive* thinking (Bezuszka & Kenny, 2008; Blanton, 2008) and is how most younger children will be able to reason about these kinds of patterns. Therefore, when discussing a growing pattern, encourage children to consider how each step in the pattern differs from the preceding step. When a child observes that each new step can be built by adding on to or changing the previous step, the discussion should include a demonstration of how this can be done. Circling or color coding the part that is the same in adjacent terms can help identify what is changing.

🌱 *Teaching Tip*

Two important questions help children analyze growing patterns in order to determine the general relationship: What is staying the same? What is changing?

Figure 13.9
Geometric growing patterns using manipulatives.

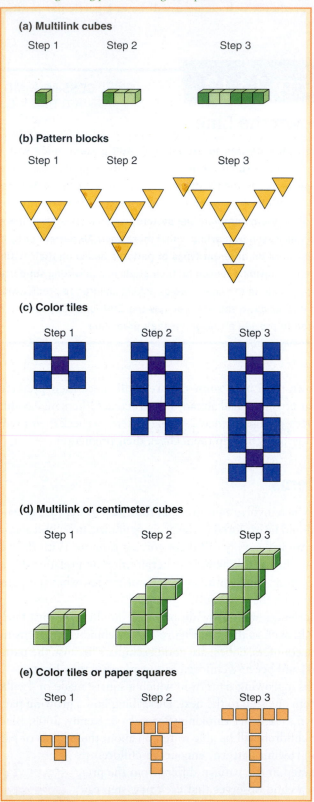

(a) **Multilink cubes**

Step 1   Step 2   Step 3

(b) **Pattern blocks**

Step 1   Step 2   Step 3

(c) **Color tiles**

Step 1   Step 2   Step 3

(d) **Multilink or centimeter cubes**

Step 1   Step 2   Step 3

(e) **Color tiles or paper squares**

Step 1   Step 2   Step 3

Stop and Reflect 500 250 3 2.5

Before reading further, what is the relationship between the steps in the each of the patterns shown in Figure 13.9? What changes from the first step to the second step? From the second step to the third step?

Each triangle design in Figure 13.9(b) can be made by adding three triangles to the corners of the preceding design. Circle the three triangles in the center of each design to highlight what is staying the same. The pattern in Figure 13.9(e) involves adding three tiles to each new figure, two to the vertical part and one to the horizontal part of the figure. You can use color coding to highlight what is changing from one figure to the next.

Functional Thinking

Although young children initially use recursive thinking when making sense of growing patterns, they can be encouraged to explore more sophisticated functional thinking using input–output activities. The children's book *Two of Everything* (Hong, 1993) works well for this purpose because it describes putting things "in a magic pot" and then taking things "out of the pot." The book tells the story of a magic pot in which anything that falls into it is doubled, but that rule can be changed to explore other relationships. (See McNamara [2010] for ideas for using this book with second graders.)

The next activity builds on a similar idea by creating a function machine. Shoeboxes or large refrigerator boxes can be turned into input–output boxes. Decorate the box to look like a machine and add buttons labeled "easy," "medium," and "hard," and design functions that are appropriate for your children (Fisher, Roy, & Reeves, 2013).

Activity 13.20

CCSS-M: 1.OA.C.6; 2.OA.B.2; 2.OA.C.4

What Is My Rule?

"What Is My Rule" can be played with the whole class, or children can play in small groups, perhaps as a station activity. Provide a collection of rules on cards, such as "double the input number and add 1." Include at least three examples so that the function machine operator is sure to understand the rule (e.g., 3 → 7; 6 → 13; 10 → 21).

Children suggest input numbers and the "operator" indicates the output. A list of in–out pairs is kept on the board, as shown in Figure 13.10, for children to refer to as they reason to determine the rule. Children who think they have determined the rule can hold their thumbs up to their chest. As more numbers are put into the machine, those children tell what comes out. Continue until most children have determined the rule.

Eventually children can make up their own rules to try to stump their classmates.

Figure 13.**10**

A function machine is used to play "What Is My Rule?" Children suggest input numbers and the machine operator indicates the output value.

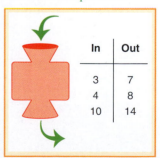

In	Out
3	7
4	8
10	14

Number Patterns

Our number system is also full of wonderful patterns that can be useful to children for counting and making sense of number relationships and place value ideas. The simplest form of a number pattern is a string of numbers that follows some rule for determining how the string continues. The following activity includes some repeating patterns and some growing patterns as well as a few other types of relationships.

Activity 13.21

CCSS-M: 1.OA.C.6; 1.NBT.C.4; 2.OA.B.2; 2.NBT.A.2; 2.NBT.B.5

What's Next and Why?

This activity can be done as a whole class or in pairs at a station. Provide children five or six numbers from a number pattern. Children are to extend the pattern for several more numbers and explain the rule for generating the pattern. The difficulty of the task depends on the number pattern and how familiar the children are with searching for patterns. Here are some recommended patterns to try.

1, 2, 1, 2, 1, 2, . . .	a simple alternating pattern
1, 2, 2, 3, 3, 3, . . .	each digit repeats according to its value
2, 4, 6, 8, 10, . . .	even numbers—skip counting by 2
1, 2, 4, 8, 16, . . .	double the previous number
2, 5, 11, 23, . . .	double the previous number and add 1
1, 2, 4, 7, 11, 16, . . .	successively increase the skip count
2, 2, 4, 6, 10, 16, . . .	add the preceding two numbers

Have children make up their own number pattern rules to challenge their classmates.

You can use a calculator to skip-count by any amount beginning anywhere. For example, to count by fives, enter 0+5 = . (The 0 isn't necessary but is a good idea with young children.) Successive presses of the = key will count on from 5 by fives. To skip count by fives from a different number, say, 16, simply press 16+5 and continue pressing the = key. The calculator "remembers" the last operation, in this case "+5," and adds that to whatever is currently in the window whenever the = key is pressed. The = will continue to have this effect until an operation key is pressed. The next activity uses the calculator as a tool to explore patterns.

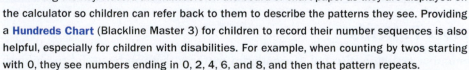

Activity 13.22

CCSS-M: 1.NBT.C.5; 2.NBT.A.2

Calculator Skip Counting

Teach children how to make their calculators skip count by different numbers. As they work in pairs, challenge them to say the next number before pressing the = key. Have them hold their finger over the = button and say the next skip count, press the = to confirm or correct, and then continue, always trying to say the next count before pressing the key. Record the numbers on the board or chart paper as they are displayed on the calculator so children can refer back to them to describe the patterns they see. Providing a **Hundreds Chart** (Blackline Master 3) for children to record their number sequences is also helpful, especially for children with disabilities. For example, when counting by twos starting with 0, they see numbers ending in 0, 2, 4, 6, and 8, and then that pattern repeats.

When children are comfortable starting their skip counting from zero, teach them how to use the calculator to start at a different number, and note any patterns. For example, what do they notice about the number sequence when they begin with any even number, such as 34, and skip count by twos? What happens if they count by twos and begin with 1?

When children have become comfortable skip counting by small numbers, suggest that they try skip counting by a "big" number such as 20 or 50. Children will be surprised to see familiar patterns in the tens and hundreds places. Continue as appropriate with challenges to count by other numbers such as 15, 25, or 30.

Focusing on patterns in skip counting will support children's use of invented strategies for addition as well as multiplication. In fact, a key reason for exploring number patterns in the elementary curriculum is to strengthen children's understanding of number relationships and properties. The more often you ask children, "Did you notice a pattern?," and then expect them to explain the pattern, the more often they are making sense of the mathematics they are doing.

Standards for Mathematical Practice

1 **Make sense of problems and persevere in solving them.**

Common Misconceptions with Algebraic Reasoning

Table 13.2 provides a summary of the most common errors and misconceptions children will demonstrate with algebraic reasoning, along with suggestions about how to help them work through these issues. Although all of these misconceptions are ones that you should help children clear up, the misconceptions related to children's understanding of equality are critical to address. Children who hold misconceptions of the equal sign will struggle when solving more sophisticated problems in the elementary curriculum. Moreover, a robust understanding of equality is crucial to understanding and doing well in algebra (Knuth, Alibali, McNeil, Weinberg, & Stephens, 2011; McNeil et al., 2006).

Table 13.2. Common errors and misconceptions in algebraic reasoning and how to help.

Misconception/Error	What It Looks Like	How to Help
1. Child thinks of the equal sign as a signal to "do something."	Child identifies 12 as the missing number for problems like: $5+7 = \underline{\quad} + 8.$ Child resists writing equations in the form: $8 = 5+3$ because he or she thinks the answer should always be written on the right side after *doing* the computation. Equations such as $6 = 6$ does not make sense to the child because no computation is involved.	• Read and emphasize the equal sign as "is," "is the same as," or "is equal to." For example, read $4+5 = 9$ as "four plus five *is the same as* 9." • Restate children's remarks that imply the equal sign "makes" another number or signals an action to emphasize $=$ means "is" or "is the same as." • Relate the concept of equality to a balance (see Section called "Conceptualizing the Equal Sign as a Balance"). • Use true/false and open sentences to emphasize equality. • Record children's equivalent expressions when they solve problems in different ways (e.g., $8+7 = 8+2+5 = 5+3+7 = 10+5 = 5+10 = 15$).
2. When checking to see "does this always work?" child only checks a few examples.	Child explains that two numbers can be added in any order because $3+5 = 5+3$ and $1+3 = 3+1$. Child is satisfied with one or two examples.	• Although the child may not be ready to generalize using variables, you can encourage them to check a wider range of numbers (e.g., two really large numbers, one small number and one really large number, two even numbers, two odd numbers, one even and one odd number, and so on). • Ask the child to describe in general terms what is happening, without referring to specific numbers. • Encourage them to try to use physical materials or representations in a general way to justify their claim (see Figure 13.4 as an example).

(continued)

Table 13.2. Common errors and misconceptions in algebraic reasoning and how to help. (continued)

Misconception/Error	What It Looks Like	How to Help
3. Child overgeneralizes +1/−1 in addition to subtraction.	Child explains that 5+6 = 6+5 because for 5+6, they can subtract one from the 6 and add it to the 5 to get 6+5. So because 5+6 = 6+5, using the same reasoning, the child argues that 7−4 = 8−3.	• Have child model the numbers and the operation using physical materials to check his or her claim. • Ask child to model the subtraction situations on number line to check to see if they are equivalent. • Put the situations (addition and subtraction) into story problem contexts so children can act out the situation to check their claim.
4. Child overgeneralizes that all patterns repeat.	For a growing pattern, such as 2, 4, 6, . . . the child identifies 2, 4, 6 as the core of a repeating pattern and extends the pattern as: 2, 4, 6, 2, 4, 6, . . .	• Present growing patterns in the following format and ask the child to fill in the blanks: 2, 4, 6, __, __, __, 14, 16, 18 • Show growing patterns that appear in nature and in children's environment. • When posing geometric growing patterns, use color coding to highlight what is staying the same in each term so that the child can better see what is changing.
5. Child confuses labels as variables and vice versa.	In solving a problem, like *There are 8 birds in the yard. Some are in the tree and some are in the bird bath. How many birds might be in the tree and how many might be in the bird bath?*, the child might write expressions such as: 3T+5B 2T+6B 0T+8B where T is shorthand for "tree" and B is shorthand for "birdbath." Then when asked to solve problems like *n+3 = 8* or *9−n = 4*, the child is confused because he thinks the *n* stands for an object, not a number.	• If children use labels with their numbers, have them write out the word instead of just using a letter. • Use boxes, blanks, and letters interchangeably in equations, emphasizing that each of these represent numbers.

14

Exploring Early Fraction Concepts

BIG IDEAS

1 Fractions are numbers. They describe a quantity and can be compared with other quantities.

2 Equal sharing is a way to build on whole-number knowledge to introduce fractional amounts as equal shares or equal-sized portions of a whole.

3 Partitioning and iterating are two ways children can reason about fractions. Partitioning can be thought of as cutting or splitting an amount equally. Iterating can be thought of as physically or mentally making copies of a piece, such as a unit fraction, and counting those pieces.

4 Three categories of models can be used when working with fractions—area (e.g., *one-fourth* of a garden), length (e.g., *three-quarters* of an inch), and set (e.g., *one-half* of the class).

Fractions are one of the most important topics students need to understand to be successful in algebra and beyond, yet it is an area that presents a considerable challenge for students. NAEP results have consistently shown that students have a weak understanding of fraction concepts (Sowder & Wearne, 2006; Wearne & Kouba, 2000). This lack of understanding is then translated into difficulties with fraction computation, decimal and percent concepts, and the use of fractions in other areas of mathematics, such as algebra (Bailey, Hoard, Nugent, & Geary, 2012; Brown & Quinn, 2007; National Mathematics Advisory Panel, 2008).

You can help children in the primary grades begin to construct a solid foundation for fraction concepts that will prepare them for the more complex concepts and skills that come later in the elementary and middle school curricula.

The *Common Core State Standards* (CCSSO, 2010) recommend that formal instruction on fraction concepts begin in third grade. However, you can develop informal knowledge and understanding about fractions before third grade by building on children's everyday experiences of fair sharing. In fact, the *Common Core State Standards* include at both the first and second grade levels partitioning geometric shapes into equal shares. In first grade, children are introduced to fractions through the partitioning of circles and rectangles into two and four equal-sized shares (Standard 1.G.A.3). First graders are also expected to know the vocabulary *halves*, *fourths*, and *quarters* and to tell time to the nearest half hour. Second graders extend this work to partitioning circles and rectangles into *thirds* or three equal-sized shares (Standard 2.G.A.3). Although neither the *Curriculum Focal Points* (National Council of Teachers of Mathematics, 2006) nor the *Common Core State Standards* (CCSSO, 2010) identify informal fractional ideas for the preK and kindergarten levels, even young children experience plenty of everyday opportunities that involve fair sharing that can prepare them for making sense of fractions.

Meanings of Fractions for PreK–2 Children

Understanding fractions involves much more than recognizing that $\frac{3}{4}$ is three shaded parts of a shape partitioned into four sections. Fractions have numerous meanings and can be represented as areas, sets, or lengths. The different meanings include part–whole, division, measurement, ratio, and operator. To help children develop a comprehensive understanding of fractions, researchers recommend that children have experiences with all the meanings of fractions (Clarke, Roche, & Mitchell, 2008; Lamon, 2012; Siegler et al., 2010). For grades preK–2, we emphasize part–whole, division as equal sharing, and measurement.

Part–Whole

One of the most commonly used meanings of fractions is the part–whole relationship. In early childhood classrooms, part–whole fractions are typically represented by shading part of a whole that has been partitioned into equal parts—for example, three-fourths of a rug is thought of as three parts *out of* four. Part–whole situations can also be described as part of a group of children (one-third of the class brought their lunch) or as part of a length (we walked one and one-half miles). The first example (shading part of a whole to indicate area) and the third example (walked $1\frac{1}{2}$ miles) involve continuous quantities, that is, quantities that are measured and that can be cut into as many equal parts as we wish. The second example (one-third of the class) involves discrete quantities, that is, quantities that are counted and cannot be divided further (e.g., people, chairs, cars).

Using the part–whole meaning of fractions can be an effective starting point for building meaning of fractions (Cramer & Whitney, 2010). However, too often instruction is based only on the part–whole relationship, which limits children's ability to reason about fractions as numbers (Mack 2001; Olive & Vomvoridi 2006; Streefland 1991). In particular, when children are able to only think of fractions as part–whole, they tend to struggle with making sense of fractions greater than one (Hackenberg, 2007; Thompson & Saldanha 2003; Tzur 1999). For example, when $\frac{3}{4}$ only makes sense as three parts *out of* four, children find it difficult to make sense of $\frac{5}{3}$ as five parts *out of* three. Part–whole reasoning also does not necessarily result in children thinking about the relative size of the part to the size of the whole (e.g., Steffe & Olive, 2010).

Equal Sharing

Equal sharing, a form of division, is an idea that young children understand intuitively because of their experiences sharing things with brothers, sisters, friends, and so on. Consider the idea of four children fairly sharing two sticks of clay so they can make clay animals. Fractions emerge naturally from this scenario. Note that this is not a part–whole scenario, although it still results in each child getting two-fourths or one-half of a stick of clay. Because of the meaningful connections that can be made, early fraction instruction should build from young children's experiences of sharing and partitioning (Empson & Levi, 2011; Lamon, 2012; Siegler et al., 2010).

Standards for Mathematical Practice

◀ **2** **Reason abstractly and quantitatively.**

Equal sharing situations can involve continuous or discrete quantities. The example with two sticks of clay is an example of a continuous quantity because theoretically we could cut the stick into as many equal pieces as we want. With young children, when using discrete quantities for equal sharing situations, it is best to use story problems that have whole-number solutions with no remainders. (These story problems with discrete quantities are the same as the partition division problems discussed in Chapter 9.) Consider these story problems:

- There are 12 chairs and 4 tables in a classroom. If we want the same number of chairs around each table, how many chairs will be placed around a table?
- There are 14 chairs and 4 tables in a classroom. If we want the same number of chairs around each table, how many chairs will be placed around a table?

The solution for both problems (how many chairs will be placed around a table) is a whole number (3). But in the second problem there are two chairs that cannot be placed and, because chairs are discrete objects, they cannot be split or cut into smaller parts that can be shared. If your goal is to have children think about fractional parts, you want them to be able to share fairly all the objects in the situation. So it is important to use continuous quantities when there are remainders so those can be cut into as many equal parts as needed.

Measurement

Although the *Common Core State Standards* recommend limiting linear measurement in grades K–2 to whole units (e.g., inches, feet, centimeters, meters), fractions often emerge naturally in many measurement situations. Linear measurement involves identifying a length and then using that length as a measurement piece to determine the length of an object. For example, using the length of an inch, a child could use multiple copies of an inch to determine that a pencil is 5 inches long. Similarly, for fractions, a child can use a fraction strip that represents the unit fraction $\frac{1}{3}$ and then count or measure to show that it takes four of those to reach $\frac{4}{3}$.

Measurement also includes time. The most obvious place to relate fractions and time is when telling time to the half hour and quarter hour. This would involve explicitly identifying the unit of time as an hour. Using an analog clock, you can emphasize how the minute hand sweeps a full turn around the clock face to measure an hour. Halfway around the face measures half that time or half of an hour. Half of that measures a quarter of the time by splitting the hour into four equal quantities of time. When second graders progress to telling time in smaller increments of 5-minute intervals, the connection between time and fractions becomes less obvious.

Measurement situations by their very nature consist of measuring a quantity that we could cut into as many equal-sized pieces as we need and so involve continuous quantities. As we will see, the measurement meaning of fractions connects well with the number line model.

Introducing Fraction Language

Fraction symbolism represents a fairly complex convention that can be misleading to children. That is why it is important in grades preK–2 to use fraction words and postpone introducing fraction symbolism (e.g., Empson & Levi, 2011). Allow children to first focus on making sense of fractions without the complication of also trying to make sense of the symbolism.

In the *Common Core State Standard for Mathematics*, children are expected to learn the fraction vocabulary of *halves*, *fourths*, and *quarters* in first grade and then *thirds* in second grade. A good time to introduce the vocabulary of fractional parts is *during* the discussions of children's solutions to story problems and not before. When a brownie or other whole has been partitioned into equal shares, simply say, "We call these *fourths*. The whole is cut into four equal-sized parts—fourths."

Initially, children need to be aware of two aspects of fractional parts: (1) the number of parts and (2) the equality of the parts (in size, not necessarily in shape). Emphasize that the number of equal parts or fair shares (i.e., unit fractions) that make up a whole determines the name of the fractional parts or shares. For example, it takes *four* one-fourths to create the whole. Children will likely be familiar with halves but should quickly learn to describe thirds and fourths. In time, children should begin to consider the relationship between the size of the part and the whole.

 Formative Assessment Note

Some children think that all fractional parts are called halves. Once a child has completed a partitioning story problem, ask the child to tell you how much each person gets. The word the child uses to describe the fractional amount will tell you if the child is overgeneralizing the word *half*.

Notice that in the *CCSM-M*, halves and fourths are developed in first grade prior to thirds in second grade. This is done because successive halving of parts is a natural process for young children. Once children have been successful dealing with and explaining halves and fourths, pose sharing tasks that involve eighths. They will likely rely on their halving strategy to find a solution. Likewise, once children have demonstrated an understanding of thirds, pose sharing tasks that involve sixths. Using this progression from parts that can be found through halving to parts that require a different strategy is a great way to differentiate as some children will require more time than others to demonstrate understanding of partitioning into different amounts.

In addition to helping children use the words *halves*, *thirds*, *fourths*, and *quarters*, be sure to make regular comparisons of fractional parts to the whole. Make it a point to use the term *whole*, *one whole*, or simply *one* so that children have a language that they can use regardless of the model involved.

Standards for Mathematical Practice

6 Attend to precision. ▶

Models for Fractions

Substantial evidence suggests that the effective use of visuals in fraction tasks is important in building children's understanding of fractions (Cramer & Henry, 2002; Empson & Levi, 2011; Petit, Laird, Marsden, & Ebby, 2016; Siebert & Gaskin, 2006). Unfortunately, when textbooks incorporate visuals or manipulatives, they tend to use only area models (Hodges, Cady, & Collins, 2008; Watanabe, 2007). Using a variety of physical tools that represent both continuous and discrete quantities is critical for children to make sense of fractions as they explore fractions in a variety of situations (Siegler et al., 2010; Zhang, Clements, & Ellerton, 2015).

Table 14.1 provides a quick overview of three types of models—area, length, and set—defining the wholes and their related parts for each model. Using different models for fractions can enhance children's understanding as the models offer different opportunities or ways to think about fraction ideas. For example, an area model can be helpful in visualizing parts of a whole as well as the relationship between the size of the part to the whole while a linear model can reinforce the notion of a fraction as a measure. When appropriate, doing the same activity with two different representations and asking children to make comparisons between them can help clarify ideas.

Table 14.1. Models for fraction concepts and related visuals and contexts.

Model Type	Description	Sample Contexts	Sample Manipulatives and Visuals
Area	Fractions are determined based on how a part of a region or area relates to the whole area or region.	Quesadillas (circular food) Pan of Brownies Garden Plot or Playground	Fraction Circles/ Rectangles Pattern Blocks Tangrams Geoboards Grid paper regions
Length	Fractions are represented as a subdivision of a length of a paper strip (representing a whole), or as a length/distance between 0 and a point on a number line, subdivided in relation to a given whole unit.	Walking/Distance travelled String lengths Music measures Measuring with inches, fractions of miles, etc.	Cuisenaire Rods Paper strips Number lines
Set	Fractions are determined based on how many discrete items are in the whole set, and how many items are in the part.	Children in the class, school, stadium Type of item in a bag of items	Objects (e.g., pencils, toys) Counters (e.g., two color counters, colored cubes, teddy bear, sea shells)

It is important for children to experience fractions through contexts that are meaningful to them (Cramer & Whitney, 2010). These contexts may align well with one representation and not as well with another. For example, if children are being asked who walked the farthest, a linear model will be better than an area model in supporting their thinking.

Area Models

Circular fraction pieces are by far the most commonly used area model. One advantage of the circular model is that it emphasizes the part–whole concept of fractions and so are good for introductory activities but they also can be used to emphasize the relative size of a part to the whole (Cramer, Wyberg, & Leavitt, 2008). What is being compared is the area of the part to the area of the whole. Because we can cut area into as many equal-sized pieces as we want and because area is measured, it falls into the category of a continuous quantity. Notice that when drawing circles, children (and adults) can find it difficult to partition the circle into reasonably equal-sized parts. Regions, such as rectangles, can be drawn on blank or grid paper and are easier to partition. There are many other area models including pattern blocks, geoboards, color tiles, and fraction bars. The physical models in Figure 14.1 demonstrate how different shapes can represent the whole.

Figure 14.1

Area models for fractions.

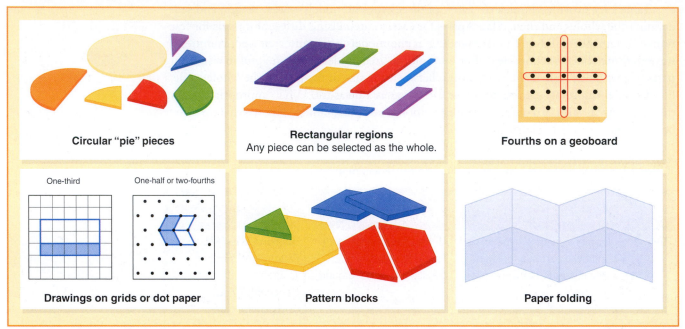

Circular "pie" pieces

Rectangular regions
Any piece can be selected as the whole.

Fourths on a geoboard

One-third

One-half or two-fourths

Drawings on grids or dot paper

Pattern blocks

Paper folding

Too often we only provide area models for children that are already partitioned into equal-sized parts so they do not have to attend to this critical feature of fractional parts (Watanabe, 2007). It is important to provide children opportunities to explicitly confront this issue of equal-sized parts. Activities like Activity 14.1 provide such opportunities.

Activity 14.1

CCSS-M: 1.G.A.3; 2.G.A.3

Halves or Not Halves?

Use the **Halves or Not Halves** Activity Page showing examples and nonexamples of halves. (Note that examples and nonexamples are very important to use with children with disabilities.) Have children identify the wholes that are correctly divided into halves (equal shares) and those that are not. For each response, have children explain their reasoning.

Repeat with other fractional parts, such as fourths (see Figure 14.2) or thirds. (See **Fourths or Not Fourths** Activity Page and **Thirds or Not Thirds** Activity Page.)

Figure 14.2

Children need to recognize when shares are not equal.

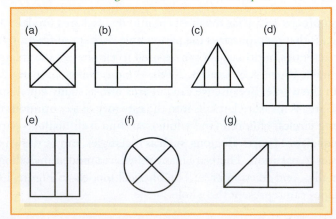

In the "Halves or Not Halves" activity, the wholes are already partitioned either correctly or incorrectly; the children are not involved in the partitioning. So the most important part of this activity is the discussion. Use the discussion to reinforce the idea that all the pieces need to be shared and shared equally. Tell children to pretend they are sharing a food that they all like and when there are unequal parts, pose questions such as "Which piece would you like and why?" and "Will everyone think they have a fair share?"

The *Common Core State Standards* set as an expectation for second graders that they will recognize that "equal-sized parts" does not necessarily mean the same shape when using an area model. So with second graders, make sure to include examples that illustrate this concept. The next two activities address this idea.

Standards for Mathematical Practice

▶ **3** Construct viable arguments and critique the reasoning of others.

Activity 14.2

CCSS-M: 2.G.A.3

Size and Shape Check

 Challenge children by asking them to draw shapes that fit each of the four categories listed below for any grade appropriate fractional parts. (Notice that creating fourths and eighths tends to be easier than creating thirds and sixths because children can use a halving strategy to create fourths and eighths.)

1. Same shape, same size (equivalent)
2. Different shape, same size (equivalent)
3. Different shape, different size (not equivalent)
4. Same shape, different size (not equivalent)

Provide children with recording sheets such as the **Eighths or Not Eighths** Activity Page and the **Sixths or Not Sixths** Activity Page. Many children, in particular children with disabilities, will need to cut and move pieces around to check to make sure that parts that are different shapes are indeed equal in size.

Activity 14.3

CCSS-M: 1.G.A.3; 2.G.A.3

Different Shapes for Fair Shares

 Give children **Dot Paper** (Blackline Master 8) and ask them to enclose a region that lends itself to partitioning with a particular fractional part (e.g., halves, fourths, thirds). For example, you might ask them to enclose a 4-by-2 rectangle if they are going to partition into halves or fourths, or a 3-by-6 rectangle if they are going to partition into thirds. (Make sure to point out that they are counting the space in between the dots, not the dots, to create the rectangles.) If using, say, the 4-by-2 rectangle, ask children to find a way to partition their rectangle into halves. Then have them draw another rectangle that is the same size (4-by-2) and partition it a different way to show halves. Encourage children to find a way to show halves where the halves are different shapes. See how many ways they can

(continued)

find. Note that the areas do not need to be adjacent. See Figure 14.3 for some possibilities. Emphasize "ths" as you say the fractional parts, particularly for ELLs who may not hear the difference between fractional parts and wholes (e.g., *fourths* sounds like "fours"). Explicitly discuss the difference between *four* areas and a *fourth of* an area. Also discuss the meaning of the words *whole* and *hole*.

Formative Assessment

The previous three activities offer good diagnostic interviews to assess whether children understand that it is the *size* that matters, not the shape. When working with fourths as shown in Figure 14.2, if children get all correct except (e) and (g), they hold the misconception that parts should be the same shape. Future tasks are needed that focus on equivalence.

Figure 14.3

Given a whole, find fractional parts that are different shapes but the same size.

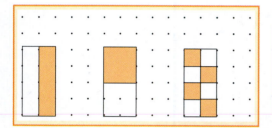

Cyberchase, a popular PBS television series, offers fraction activities on their website such as "Thirteen Ways of Looking at a Half." In this activity, children are challenged to find all the ways they can shade half of a geometric shape that is cut into eighths.

Length Models

With length models, lengths or linear measurements are compared instead of areas. In this model, a unit of length is compared to the whole length. We can cut a length into as many equal-sized pieces (units) as we want; therefore, length models represent continuous quantities. Length models appropriate for preK–2 include fraction strips, paper strips (e.g., adding-machine tape), Cuisenaire rods, and line segments (see Figure 14.4). All of these models provide flexibility because any length can represent the whole.

Virtual Cuisenaire rods and accompanying activities can be found online at various websites including the University of Cambridge's NRICH website.

Researchers have identified number line models as useful in fraction instruction because they help children understand that a fraction is a quantity or a number (Petit, Laird, & Marsden, 2010; Siegler et al., 2010; Watanabe, 2007). Locating fractions on a number line also highlights their relationship to other numbers, including other fractions. The number line has been shown as extremely effective with young children when working with whole numbers (e.g., Booth & Siegler, 2008; Fosnot & Dolk, 2001; Siegler & Ramani, 2009). Using

Figure 14.4

Length or measurement models for fractions.

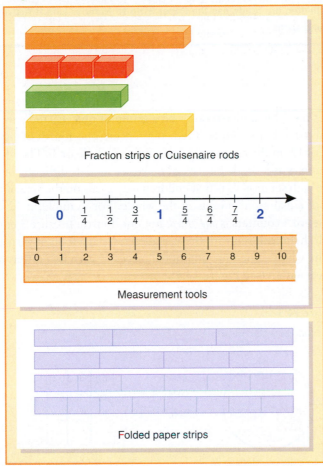

Fraction strips or Cuisenaire rods

Measurement tools

Folded paper strips

this model with whole numbers can help prepare these children to be ready to use this model with fractions in later grades. Using line segments, a modified version of a number line, for fraction instruction in grades preK–2 is ideal. Children can develop an understanding of the number line by folding paper strips as described in Activity 14.4 (adapted from Zhang, Clements, & Ellerton, 2015).

Activity 14.4

CCSS-M: 1.G.A.3; 2.G.A.3

Paper Strip to Number Line

The **Paper Strip to Number Line I** Activity Page, which focuses on halves, fourths, and eighths, can be used for this activity. On this activity page, you will see several line segments that are all the same length. Give pairs of children three different colored strips of paper (e.g., blue, green, red) that are each the same length as one of the line segments on the Activity Page. Their task is to fold, say, the blue strip into two equal parts, the green strip into four equal parts, and the red strip into eight equal parts. Then they use their unfolded strips to locate various fractions (e.g., one-half, two-halves, one-fourth, two-fourths, and so on) on the number lines on the Activity Page. To reinforce the notion that three-fourths, for example, is 3 *one-fourths*, have

(continued)

children cut each strip into its respective unit fraction parts. They can use the unit fractions to count the fractional amounts.

When your children are ready, use the **Paper Strip to Number Line II** Activity Page, which involves thirds and sixths.

Set Models

The whole in a set model is understood to be a group of objects, and subsets of the whole make up fractional parts. For example, 3 red counters are one-fourth of a group or set of 12 counters. The set of 12, in this example, represents the whole or 1. The idea of referring to a collection of counters as a single entity can make set models difficult for young children. Another challenge with set models is that children may focus on the size of the subset rather than the number of equal-sized subsets in the whole. For example, if 12 counters make a whole, then a subset of 4 counters is *one-third*, not one-fourth, because 3 equal-sized subsets make the whole. To help children with these challenges, put a loop of yarn around the set to help them "see" the whole. Then use additional pieces of yarn in a different color or sticks to group the subsets within (see Figure 14.5).

Figure 14.5

Set models for fractions.

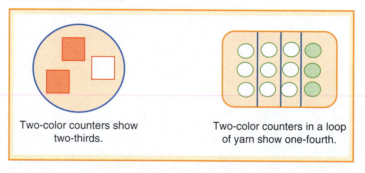

Two-color counters show two-thirds.

Two-color counters in a loop of yarn show one-fourth.

Discrete objects, like two-color counters, are effective for set models. They can easily be flipped to change their color to model various fractional parts of a whole set. Any countable objects, such as a box of crayons or a tin of muffins, can work as a set model (one box or tin could be the unit or whole). The next activity engages children in fairly sharing with a set model.

 Activity 14.5

CCSS-M: 1.G.A.3; 2.G.A.3

Sets in Equal Shares

Give pairs of children 16 crayons in a box or clear plastic bag. Explain to the children that although there are 16 individual crayons, the "whole" consists of all 16 crayons in the box (or bag). Their task is to determine and be ready to explain how the 16 crayons can be equally shared with two, four, and then eight friends. They can use the **Sets in Equal Shares** Activity Page to record their ideas. When children demonstrate confidence and accuracy with halves, fourths, and eighths, they can be challenged to share, say, 12 crayons with three and then six friends.

Virtual manipulatives are available for all three models of fractions. When paired with using actual manipulatives, virtual manipulatives have been found to improve student achievement (Moyer-Packenham, Ulmer, & Anderson, 2012). Your children can explore length, area, and set models of fractions using the applet called "Fractions Model" at the NCTM Illuminations website.

 Formative Assessment Note

Children should have opportunities to explore fractions across the three models for fractions. A good way to assess children's knowledge of a fractional amount is to give them the **Meaning of a Fraction** Activity Page along with a fractional value (e.g., *three-fourths*). Their task is to think of the fractional amount in terms of *area, length,* and *set* and for each model (1) draw a picture and (2) write a sentence describing a context or example for the selected fraction.

Building Fractional Parts through Partitioning and Iterating

The first goal in the development of fractions is to help children construct the idea of *fractional parts of the whole*—the parts that result when the whole or unit has been partitioned into *equal-sized portions or fair shares*. Recall that Table 14.1 describes the meanings of parts and wholes for each type of fraction model. We can build on children's experiences of fair sharing to begin to establish this idea of fractional parts.

One of the most significant ideas for children to develop about fractions is the sense that fractions are numbers—quantities that have values. You may not be familiar with the terms *partitioning* (splitting equally) and *iterating* (counting a repeated amount) but, as you will see, they connect to whole-number concepts you will recognize. Researchers have acknowledged for some time how important these two actions are to meaningfully working with fractions (e.g., Olive, 2002; Pothier & Sawada, 1990). These actions, in particular, emphasize the numerical nature of fractions. Look to create and use tasks embedded in contexts that explicitly require children to engage in these actions. When children explain how they thought about fractional situations, listen for these ideas.

Partitioning

Partitioning can be thought of as splitting or cutting a quantity equally. Young children are engaged in the act of partitioning from an early age when they split a group of 6 into 3 and 3 or when they share items among family and friends. Given children's experiences with fairly sharing items among family and friends, sharing tasks are a good place to begin the development of fractions (Siegler et al., 2010). Sharing tasks allow children to develop concepts of fractions from an activity that makes sense to them, rather than having the structure imposed on them. In this approach children do not begin with traditional part–whole tasks of identifying halves, thirds, fourths, and so on. These fractional parts and children's understanding of part–whole fractions emerge as a result of their fair sharing in meaningful contexts. See **Expanded Lesson: Equal Sharing Stories for Early Fractions** for a lesson designed for grades 1 or 2.

Sharing tasks are generally posed in the form of a story problem involving a given number of objects that are to be shared equally among a given number of people: *Four friends share two cookies. How many cookies will each friend get?* The problems become more difficult by increasing the numbers of objects to be shared or increasing the number of sharers, for example: *Suppose there are four cookies to be shared fairly with three children. How much will each child get?* You can see how **Eduardo** reasons about this sharing situation. Like Eduardo, often children initially solve sharing tasks by distributing items one at a time. When this process leaves leftover pieces, they must figure out how to subdivide so that every person (or group) gets a fair share. When children answer questions such as "how much will each child get?" the idea that fractions are numbers will be reinforced.

Considerable research has been done with children from first through eighth grades to determine how they go about the process of forming fair shares and how the tasks posed to children influence their responses (e.g., Empson & Levi, 2011; Lamon, 2012; Mack, 2001; Pothier & Sawada, 1990; Siegler et al., 2010). Researchers recommend following a progression of sharing tasks that builds on children's understanding of whole-number quantities and informal partitioning strategies (e.g., Empson & Levi, 2011; Siegler et al., 2010). Table 14.2 provides an overview of the following progression and examples of corresponding story problems.

Table 14.2. Progression for teaching with equal shares story problems.

Progression	Example Problems
1. Problems whose solutions are whole numbers.	Three children want to fairly share 15 grapes. How many grapes will each child get?
2. Problems with 2, 4, or 8 sharers and whose solutions are mixed numbers (greater than 1).	Two children want to share 5 quesadillas so that everyone gets the same amount. How much will each child get?
3. Problems with 2, 4, or 8 sharers and whose solutions are less than 1.	Four children want to share 3 cookies so that everyone gets the same amount. How much will each child get?
4. Problems with 3 sharers and whose solutions are mixed numbers (greater than 1).	Three children want to share 10 sticks of clay to make clay animals. If everyone gets the same amount, how much does each child get?
5. Problems with 3 sharers and whose solutions are less than 1.	Three children want to equally share 2 pizzas. How much does each child get?

1. *Begin with equal sharing problems whose solutions are whole numbers.* To begin with, it is easier for young children to share fairly a number of discrete objects (e.g., 14 apples with 7 people) than for them to share fairly one object (e.g., 1 pancake with 4 children). So begin with equal sharing situations in which the quantities to be shared are discrete objects with whole number solutions. (Again, these situations are the same as the partition or fair-sharing (i.e., division) problems discussed in Chapter 9.) In the *before* and the *after* portions of the lessons, emphasize that all of the objects must be shared and shared equally. This is an important idea to stress because once the scenarios require partitioning quantities into smaller pieces, some children will either not share all of the objects or not share them equally.

2. *Use equal sharing problems with 2, 4, or 8 sharers and whose solutions are mixed numbers.* Because children's initial strategies for sharing single objects involve halving, begin with 2, 4, and then 8 sharers. Using problems that have solutions that are larger than 1 enable children to relate their understanding of whole numbers to fractions and they actually find them easier to solve than problems whose solutions are less than 1.

3. *Use equal sharing problems with 2, 4, or 8 sharers and whose solutions are less than 1.* Again, problems with 2, 4, or 8 sharers capitalize on children's halving strategies. Problems with solutions less than 1 tend to be more difficult for young children because they have to anticipate how to partition.

4. *Next, use equal sharing problems with 3 sharers and whose solutions are mixed numbers.* For 3 sharers, children have to anticipate how to slice or cut the objects. Many children will attempt to use a repeated halving strategy or trial and error. Moving to 3 (and then 6 sharers) will force children to confront their tendencies to use halving strategies.

5. *Use equal sharing problems with 3 sharers and whose solutions are less than 1.* Again, children have to anticipate how to partition the objects.

As discussed in other chapters, when using story problems to help children construct mathematical ideas, having children share their solutions and explain their reasoning to each other is key. Make sure to look for significant ideas in children's work while they are solving the story problems that you can then highlight in the discussion (*after*) portion of the lesson.

Sharing brownies is a classic activity that focuses on partitioning to create equal shares (see for example, Empson, 2002, and Russell & Economopoulos, 2008). Using concrete tools that can be partitioned, such as play dough, squares of cheese, or paper rectangles, can make sharing activities accessible even for prekindergartners (Cwikla, 2014).

 Activity 14.6　　　　CCSS-M: 1.G.A.3; 2.G.A.3

Cut Me a Fair Share!

 Give each child some play dough and a plastic knife. Explain that they are going to be finding a way to share a number of brownies fairly with a group of children. Start with an example that is not too difficult. For example:

> Four friends want to share six brownies so that each friend gets the same amount of brownies. How much will each friend get?

To ensure "brownies" of about the same size, have children use square cookie cutters to create their "brownies" from the play dough. (You can make square cookie cutters by repeatedly folding a sheet of aluminum foil until you have a long, sturdy strip of foil; cut into an appropriate length, fold into a square shape, and tape the ends together.) Show how to share the brownies fairly with four friends, using a plastic knife if necessary. Encourage children to share their ways of thinking about this problem. It will be helpful for many children, especially those with disabilities, to give them the **Cut Me a Fair Share!** Activity Page that provides a visual for the number of brownies and the number of friends. A strategy many children will use for this problem is to deal out one brownie to each child and then halve each of the remaining brownies to fairly share all the brownies (see Figure 14.6). Then, pose a selection of other sharing tasks with different numbers of brownies and different number of sharers (see additional examples below).

You can differentiate these tasks by changing the numbers involved. Consider these variations in numbers:

- 5 brownies shared with 2 children
- 2 brownies shared with 4 children
- 5 brownies shared with 4 children
- 4 brownies shared with 8 children
- 4 brownies shared with 10 children
- 3 brownies shared with 4 children

Standards for Mathematical Practice

1 Make sense of problems and persevere in solving them.

Figure 14.6

Six brownies shared with four children. Each child gets one and one-half brownies.

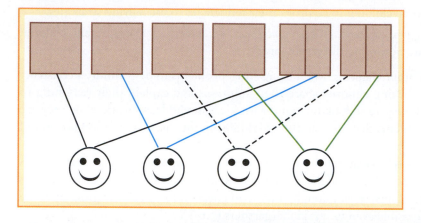

Stop and Reflect

Try drawing pictures for each of the preceding sharing tasks. Which do you think is most difficult? Which of these represents essentially the same degree of difficulty? What other tasks involving two, four, or eight sharers would you consider as similar, easier, or more difficult than these tasks?

When the numbers allow for some items to be distributed whole (five shared with two), some children will first share whole items and then cut up the leftovers. Others will slice every piece in half and then distribute the halves. When there are more sharers than items, some partitioning must happen at the beginning of the solution process. When children who are still using a halving strategy try to share five things among four children, they will eventually get down to two halves to give to four children. For some, the solution is to cut each half in half; that is, "each child gets a whole (or two halves) and a half of a half." Some children will partition each item into an equal number of sharers and then will distribute the pieces to each child. **Felisha** uses this strategy to find the fractional amount each of five children get when sharing two cookies, but loses track of what the whole is in determining each person's share.

The last example, three brownies shared with four children, is more challenging because there are more sharers than items, and it involves more than just finding halves. One strategy is to partition each brownie into four parts and give each child one-fourth from each brownie for a total of three-fourths. Children (even adults) are surprised at the relationship between the problem and the answer.

Partitioning into three or six equal parts is challenging for children because they naturally want to use a halving strategy that does not work in these cases. Here are some examples:

- 4 pizzas shared with 6 children
- 4 pizzas shared with 3 children
- 5 pizzas shared with 3 children

Stop and Reflect

Try solving these problems using drawings. Can you solve them in different ways?

Figure 14.7 shows some different sharing solutions that might be observed when children are partitioning into 3 or 6 equal parts.

Figure 14.7

Three different sharing processes for thirds and sixths.

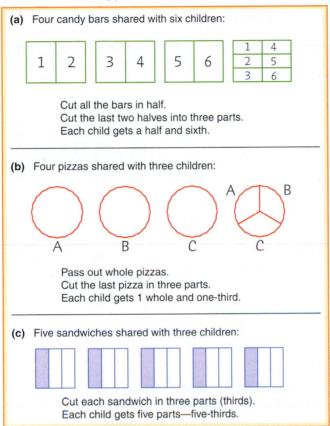

(a) Four candy bars shared with six children:

Cut all the bars in half.
Cut the last two halves into three parts.
Each child gets a half and sixth.

(b) Four pizzas shared with three children:

Pass out whole pizzas.
Cut the last pizza in three parts.
Each child gets 1 whole and one-third.

(c) Five sandwiches shared with three children:

Cut each sandwich in three parts (thirds).
Each child gets five parts—five-thirds.

Figure 14.8 shows how a child partitioned to solve "5 pizzas shared with 3 children." This took a lot of guess and check, at which point the teacher asked, "Can you see a pattern in how you have divided the pizza and how many people are sharing?" At this point, the child noticed a pattern: If there are three people, the remaining pizzas need to be partitioned into thirds.

The varied difficulty levels of these sharing tasks lend themselves to creating a tiered lesson. In a tiered lesson, the goal (sharing) is the same, but the specific tasks vary in their challenge. Figure 14.9 shows how one teacher offers three tiers for a lesson on sharing brownies (Williams, 2008).

These kinds of story problems include the following features:

- The objects in the story are easy to draw and partition (e.g., apples, carrots, bagels, granola bars, cookies, brownies, quesadillas, pancakes, sticks of gum, sandwiches, pizzas, crackers, cake, candy bars, sticks of modeling clay, pretzel sticks, and so on).

- The story problem does not contain fractions. The fractions emerge as a result of the relationship between the number of objects to be shared and the number of people sharing. This allows children to make connections between their whole-number knowledge and their developing fraction knowledge.

Standards for Mathematical Practice

◄ **2 Reason abstractly and quantitatively.**

Figure 14.8

A child explains a pattern for finding equal shares of a pizza.

Figure 14.9

Example of a tiered lesson for the brownie-sharing problem.

Tier 1 task: For students who still need experience with halving	Tier 2 task: For students comfortable with halving and ready to try other strategies	Tier 3 task: For students ready to solve tasks in which students combine halving with new strategies
How can 2 people share 3 brownies?	How can 4 people share 3 brownies?	How can 3 people share 5 brownies?
How can 2 people share 5 brownies?	How can 3 people share 4 brownies?	How can 3 people share 2 brownies?
How can 4 people share 3 brownies?	How can 3 people share 5 brownies?	How can 6 people share 4 brownies?
How can 3 people share 4 brownies?	How can 6 people share 4 brownies?	How can 5 people share 4 brownies?

Standards for Mathematical Practice

> **1 Make sense of problems and persevere in solving them.**

- Children can solve these kinds of problems without formal instruction and without knowing anything about fraction symbols. They can represent how much one person gets by shading in one share or showing one share with manipulatives.

technology note

"Kids and Cookies" is an applet on the Mathlanding website where children can work on partitioning strategies in the context of fairly sharing cookies with friends. You can change the number of friends (up to 6), the shape of the cookie (round or rectangular), the number of cookies to share (up to 12), and the number of equal pieces you can cut a cookie into (halves, thirds, fourths, fifths, and sixths). The applet is also available in Spanish.

To reinforce the idea of equal shares, you may want to start with activities where children create designated equal shares using physical models before asking children to draw and partition their own representations. Patterns blocks are a good tool to use to help emphasize equal shares because the different pattern blocks are *not* equal shares (i.e., equal area). Creating shapes with pattern blocks and asking about equal shares helps children focus on the important idea of fair (equal) shares. For example, ask children to create a "cookie" using the six different pattern block shapes and ask, "Can this cookie be shared fairly with 6 people?" (Ellington & Whitenack, 2010). The answer is "no." Then, ask children to build a cookie that can be shared fairly.

 ## Teaching Tip

Children do not necessarily have to consciously think of equal-sized pieces when using fraction manipulatives because the manipulatives automatically create the equal-sized parts. Emphasize the need for equal-sized pieces whether manipulatives or student-generated representations are used.

 ## Formative Assessment Note

Young children can have difficulty drawing equal parts because they do not initially anticipate how to slice the object into equal parts (Empson & Levi, 2011; Siegler et al., 2010). Observe children as they draw pictures and begin to partition the objects. Note if they automatically begin halving for every scenario, even those for which halving will not work (e.g., 5 children equally sharing 3 bananas). This could be an indication that they are not anticipating how to partition objects. Especially when partitioning into 3 and 6 equal groups, children have to pay attention to the relationship between the number of objects and the number of sharers.

Initially, some children do not partition amounts into equal-sized groups and, in particular, some children do not distinguish between the number of objects shared and the quantity shared—in other words, they may find an equal number of pieces without considering the size of the pieces. To develop a more comprehensive understanding of fractions, children need experiences partitioning regions or shapes (area models) as well as lengths and sets of objects. Activity 14.7 uses examples of line segments (length model) in which the partitioning is not completely illustrated. This can help children strengthen their understanding of the importance of equal parts as opposed to simply the number of parts.

Teaching Tip

For children who have difficulty drawing equal parts, give them wooden coffee stirrers or thick uncooked spaghetti noodles to show the partitioning. This allows children to think about anticipating how to partition objects and to easily move the partitions as needed.

Teaching Tip

Using the same physical model, designate different wholes. That way, a given fractional part does not get identified with a special shape or color but instead with the relationship of the part to the designated whole.

Activity 14.7

CCSS-M: 1.G.A.3; 2.G.A.3

How Much Did She Share?

Give children line segments partitioned such that only some of the partitions are showing. Use a context such as someone sharing licorice strings. For each line segment, ask "How much did Holly share? How do you know?"

Children can justify their reasoning by measuring the size of the sections that have been partitioned using paper strips or Cuisenaire rods.

(continued)

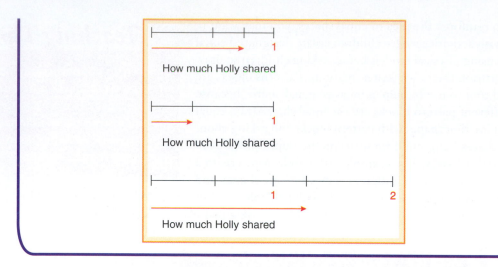

In the story problems you pose, make sure to include a variety of situations that can be represented with these different models. For example, the following story problems fit a length model, a set model, and an area model, respectively:

- Marley, Zack, Rita, and Hannah want to share 5 pretzel sticks equally. How much will each of them get? (length)
- Marley and Zack want to share 11 grapes equally. How much will each of them get? (set)
- Marley, Zack, and Mia want to share 7 pieces of construction paper equally. How much will each of them get? (area)

✿ Teaching Tip

Make sure to use fractions greater than 1 (*ten-fourths*) and mixed numbers (*two and two-fourths*) along with fractions between 0 and 1. This helps children see that fractions can be any size and that they often fall between whole-number values.

The objects to be shared can be drawn on paper as rectangles, circles, or line segments along with a statement of the problem. Some children may need to cut and physically distribute the pieces, so another possibility is to cut out construction paper circles or rectangles to represent the objects to be shared. You could use thin rectangles to represent objects of length. Children can use connecting cubes to make bars that they can separate into pieces. Or they can use more traditional fraction models such as circular "pie" pieces (area), Cuisenaire rods (length), or counters of different colors (sets).

Iterating

In whole-number learning, counting precedes learning to add and subtract. This is also true of fractions. Children should come to think of counting fractional parts in much the same way they might count apples or any other objects. Counting fractional parts to see how multiple parts compare to the whole helps children to understand the relationship between the parts and the whole. Children should be able to answer the question, "How many fourths are in one whole?" just as they know how many ones are in ten. Counting a repeated amount (e.g., unit fraction) is called *iterating*. Understanding that *three-fourths* can be thought of as a count of three parts called *fourths* is an important idea for children to develop (Post, Wachsmuth, Lesh, & Behr, 1985; Siebert & Gaskin, 2006; Tzur, 1999).

Children should engage in counting by fractional amounts to reinforce that fractions are numbers. With young children, iterating or counting should be done with length or area models. (Set models are too difficult for young children to use for iteration.) For example, display some circular fractional pieces in groups as shown in Figure 14.10. For each collection, tell children what type of piece is being shown and simply count them together: "*One*-fourth, *two*-fourths, *three*-fourths, *four*-fourths, *five*-fourths." To reinforce the iteration or count even more, you can slightly alter your language to say, "*One* one-fourth, *two* one-fourths, *three* one-fourths," and so on.

Figure 14.10

Iterating fractional parts in an area model.

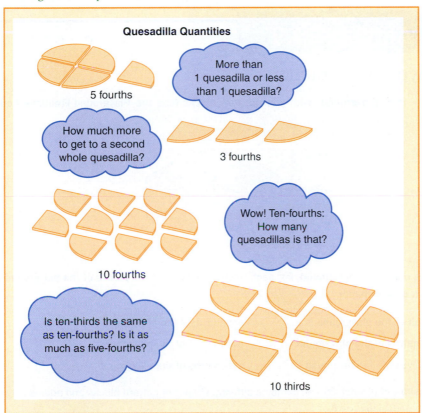

With this introduction, children are ready for the following activity.

◀ **Activity 14.8**

CCSS-M: 1.G.A.3; 2.G.A.3

More, Less, or Equal to One Whole

Give children a collection of fractional parts (all the same size pieces) and indicate the kind of fractional part they have. (Use either area or length models. Avoid using set models for iteration with young children.) Parts can be drawn on a worksheet or physical models can be placed in plastic bags with an identifying card. For example, if done with Cuisenaire rods or fraction strips, the collection might have seven light green rods/strips with a caption or note indicating "each piece is an eighth." The task is to decide whether the collection is less than one whole, equal to one whole, or more than one whole. Ask children to draw pictures and/ or use fraction words to explain their answer. Adding a context, such as people sharing candy bars, pizzas, or sticks of clay, can help children understand and reason through the problem.

As children count collections of parts, discuss the relationship to one whole. Make informal comparisons between different collections. "Why does it take more fourths to make a whole than thirds?" "Why did we get two wholes with four halves but just a little more than one whole with four thirds?" Take this opportunity to connect this language to mixed numbers. "What is another way we could say ten-fourths?" (Possible responses are two wholes and two-fourths, or two wholes and one-half, or one whole and six-fourths.)

Activity 14.9 (adapted from Roddick & Silvas-Centano, 2007) uses pattern blocks to help children work on the concepts of partitioning and iterating.

 Activity 14.9　　　　　　CCSS-M: 1.G.A.3; 2.G.A.3

Playground Fractions

Create this "playground" with your pattern blocks (see the **Playground Fractions** Activity Page).

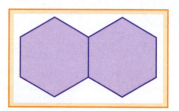

This is one whole playground. For each fraction below, find the pieces of the playground and draw it on your paper.

one-half of the playground	one-fourth of the playground
three-halves of the playground	two-fourths of the playground
five-halves of the playground	five-fourths of the playground

Extensions of this activity can combine different shapes of pattern blocks and address eighths, thirds, and sixths.

The next activity also uses patterns blocks to help children focus on the size of the parts as opposed to the number of pieces or partitions (Champion & Wheeler, 2014; Ellington & Whitenack, 2010). It also provides them opportunities to continue to count fractional parts.

 Activity 14.10　　　　　　CCSS-M: 1.G.A.3; 2.G.A.3

Pattern Block Creatures

Ask children to build a Pattern Block Creature that fits with a set of rules (a creature represents one whole). These rules can begin with just stating a fractional quantity for a color, such as "The red trapezoid is one-fourth of the creature." More constraints can be added to the rules. For example:

The yellow hexagon is one-half of the creature. Use two colors to build your creature.

The blue parallelogram is one-sixth of the creature. Use at least two colors to build your creature.

After children build their creature based on your rules, have them count the fractional amounts to make sure they have an exact whole (i.e., *one*-fourth, *two*-fourths, *three*-fourths, *four*-fourths).

Then have them create fraction rules for their own Pattern Block Creature and sketch the outline of the creature on paper. Have them write their rule, such as "The red trapezoid is _____ of my creature." They then trade creatures and rules with other children to see if they can figure out the fractional amount for each other's creatures.

Partitioning and iterating tasks are challenging but very effective in helping children understand the meaning of fractions. As you create story problems and tasks for the children, remember the big ideas you are trying to help them construct: (1) Fractions are numbers that we can use to count and (2) fractional parts are equal shares or equal-sized portions of a whole or unit.

Fraction Size Is Relative

Another foundational idea pertaining to fractions is that a fraction by itself does not describe the size of the whole or the size of the parts. A fraction tells us only about the *relationship between* the part and the whole. To illustrate, consider the following situation:

Pizza Fallacy: Mark is offered the choice of a third of a pizza or a half of a pizza. Because he is hungry and likes pizza, he chooses the half. His friend Jane gets a third of a pizza but ends up with more than Mark. How can that be?

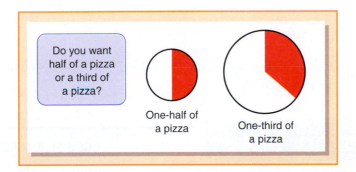

The visual illustrates how Mark was mistaken in his choice. The point of the "pizza fallacy" is that whenever two or more fractions are discussed in the same context, one cannot assume (as Mark did) that the fractions are all parts of the same size whole. Teachers can help children become aware of the crucial idea that a fraction is necessarily related to its whole by regularly asking, "What is the whole?" or "What is the unit?"

Fraction Equivalence and Comparison

Look for opportunities when children are solving equal-sharing story problems in which they have what appear to be different answers but which are actually equivalent amounts. For example, for the problem *4 children equally share 6 pancakes*, one child may distribute one whole pancake to each person and then halve the remaining two and say that each person gets *one and one-half* pancakes. A second child may also distribute one whole pancake to each person but partition the remaining two pancakes into fourths and say that each person gets *one and two-fourths*. A third child may partition each of the 6 pancakes into 4 equal parts (fourths) and say that each person gets *six-fourths*. (See Figure 14.11.) Use the children's solutions to help them see that the same quantity is shared in each case.

Figure 14.11

Solutions for an equal sharing story problem.

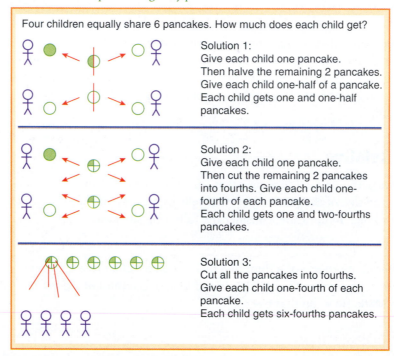

Four children equally share 6 pancakes. How much does each child get?

Solution 1:
Give each child one pancake.
Then halve the remaining 2 pancakes.
Give each child one-half of a pancake.
Each child gets one and one-half pancakes.

Solution 2:
Give each child one pancake.
Then cut the remaining 2 pancakes into fourths. Give each child one-fourth of each pancake.
Each child gets one and two-fourths pancakes.

Solution 3:
Cut all the pancakes into fourths.
Give each child one-fourth of each pancake.
Each child gets six-fourths pancakes.

Like Activity 14.3, the following activity has children purposefully looking for different ways to partition the same quantity.

Activity 14.11

CCSS-M: 1.G.A.3; 2.G.A.3

Cut Them Up Again!

Pose a sharing story problem for which children could partition the objects in multiple ways. For example, "*4 children share 10 brownies so that each one will get the same amount. How much will each child get?*" Tell children that their task is to find at least two different ways to share the objects. Some children will use trial and error while others will be more systematic in finding different ways to partition the objects. Have children share the different ways they have found to partition the objects. Then challenge them to determine if the different ways result in each child getting a different or equal amount of brownie. Have children explain their reasoning.

The next activity uses the idea of a missing value to challenge children to find equivalent fractional amounts. This activity provides a genuine problem for second graders.

Activity 14.12

CCSS-M: 1.G.A.3; 2.G.A.3

Keeping It Fair

Pose a problem such as the following: *"Suppose 6 children shared 8 cookies equally. If 3 more children arrive, how many cookies would you need if you want to give them the same amount as the first 6 children?"* Some children will share 8 cookies equally among the 6 children to determine how much each person will get in that situation and then use that information to determine how much is needed for the additional 3 children. Others may reason that because 3 is half of 6, they can halve the 8 cookies to see that 4 cookies are needed for the additional 3 children. Make sure to have children share their reasoning for keeping it fair!

Once children are successful with equal sharing problems over an extended period of time (months, not days), you can pose situations where children compare fractional amounts. Fair-sharing situations offer productive opportunities for children to compare fractional amounts. For example, children can compare the amounts people would get if 2, 3, 4, and 6 people shared a brownie. *The Doorbell Rang* (Hutchins, 1986) is a great children's book that builds on the idea that as the number of sharers involved increases, the smaller the shares become. Encourage children to use the formal fraction names in their comparisons; for example, one-third of a brownie is less than one-half of a brownie.

Using a length model helps to emphasize that a fraction is a quantity and it also allows children to compare fractions in terms of relative size. The following activity (adapted from Bay-Williams & Martinie, 2003) is a fun way to use a real-world context to engage children in thinking about comparing fractions through a linear model.

Activity 14.13

CCSS-M: 1.G.A.3; 2.G.A.3

Who Is Winning?

Explain to the children that friends are playing the game "Red Light–Green Light." The fractions tell how much of the distance each child has already moved. Who is winning? Challenge children to place the friends on a line to show where they are between the start and finish.

Mary: three-fourths	Harry: one-half	Larry: two-fourths
Hans: two-thirds	Angela: five-eighths	Greta: four-sixths

The game "Red Light–Green Light" may not be familiar to all children, especially ELLs. Modeling the game with children in the class is a good way to build background knowledge and also support children with disabilities.

From Fraction Words to Symbols

Notice that throughout this chapter we have used words to name fractional amounts. In the CCSS-M, understanding fraction symbols is an expectation in grade 3. The earliest that we recommend introducing fraction symbolism is toward the end of second grade. If you

🎵 Teaching Tip

The phrase "improper fraction" is a misleading phrase that implies something is wrong or unacceptable about the fraction, when it is simply an equivalent representation. Instead use the phrase "fraction greater than 1."

Standards for Mathematical Practice

2 **Reason abstractly and quantitatively.** ▶

choose to do so, you will need to spend time helping children develop a strong understanding of what the numerator and denominator of a fraction tell us.

The way that we write fractions symbolically is a convention—an arbitrary agreement for how to represent fractions. (By the way, always write fractions with a horizontal bar, not a slanted one: $\frac{3}{4}$, not $^3/_4$. It is easier for children to tell which is the numerator and which is the denominator.) Understanding of the convention can be developed through attention to how we use the numerator and denominator, in particular, in iterating activities.

Pose iterating tasks to children that include a range of fractions less than 1, equal to 1 (e.g., $\frac{4}{4}$), and greater than 1 (e.g., $\frac{4}{3}$). After the children have counted the fractional parts in the iterating task, write the corresponding fraction symbol. Then pose questions to help children make sense of the symbols, such as:

What does the numerator in a fraction tell us?

What does the denominator in a fraction tell us?

How do you know if a fraction is greater than or less than 1? Greater than or less than 2?

Stop and Reflect

Before reading further, answer these three questions in terms of what we have been talking about—namely, counting, or iterating, fractional parts.

Here are some reasonable explanations for the numerator and denominator.

- *Numerator.* This is the counting number. It tells how many equal shares or parts we have. It is the number of repetitions of the unit fraction.
- *Denominator.* This tells what size piece, or fractional part, is being counted. It is the number of repetitions of the unit fraction needed to create the whole. For example, it takes *four* one-fourths to create the whole.

Making sense of symbols requires making connections to visuals. Illustrating what $\frac{5}{4}$ looks like in terms of the amount of pizza (area), the distance on a number line (length), or the number of objects in a bag (set) will help children make sense of this value. One of the best things that we can do for children is to emphasize equivalence and different ways to write fractional amounts.

Teaching Considerations for Fraction Concepts

Because the teaching of fractions is so important, and because fractions are often not well understood even by adults, we revisit some of the more significant ideas offered in this chapter here. Hopefully you have recognized that one reason fractions are not well understood is that there is a lot to know about them, from part–whole relationships to division (fair sharing), and understanding includes being able to represent fractions across area, length, and set models and includes contexts that fit these models. Many of these ideas may not have been part of your own learning experience, but they must be part of your teaching experience so that your children can fully understand fractions and in the future be successful with fraction computation, algebra, and mathematics beyond.

The following research based recommendations for instruction provide an effective recap of the big ideas in this chapter (e.g., Clarke, Roche, & Mitchell, 2008; Cramer & Whitney, 2010; Siegler et al., 2010; Steffe & Olive, 2010).

1. Give a greater emphasis to the variety of meanings of fractions, moving children's understanding of fractions beyond part–whole.
2. Incorporate a variety of models and contexts to represent fractions.
3. Emphasize that fractions are numbers, making use of measurement contexts and number lines in representing fractions.
4. Spend whatever time is needed for children to understand equivalences (concretely), including flexible naming of fractions.
5. Iterating and partitioning must be a significant aspect of fraction instruction.

Finally, in closing this very important chapter, we share Table 14.3, which provides a summary of common misconceptions and errors children make when they are learning about fraction concepts along with ways you can help them work through these issues.

Table 14.3. Common errors and misconceptions in fraction concepts and how to help.

Misconception/Error	What It Looks Like	How to Help
1. Child does not share all parts.	Child has an extra piece and chooses to ignore it.	• Revisit fair-sharing tasks that have whole number solutions, emphasizing that all parts must be distributed and fairly shared. • Continue to emphasize that the child must find a way to distribute all parts and to do so fairly.
2. Child does not understand that parts need to be equal in size.	Child thinks the following shape is one-fourth red and three-fourths green.	• Use a context with something the child really likes. Then ask, "Which piece would you want and why?" and "What if I gave you this piece?" (indicating a smaller piece). • Revisit fair-sharing tasks that have whole number solutions, emphasizing that all parts must be equal in size. • Have children create and compare their own representations of a given fraction using representations they have drawn on paper. Have them also use different manipulatives to create the given fraction and compare across representations. • Pose tasks such as the one illustrated in which all the partitions are not already made to draw attention to the issue of equal-sized parts. • Have children use uncooked spaghetti noodles or popsicle sticks to decide how to partition.
3. Child confuses equal *number* of shares with equal *amount* shared.	Child thinks the clay pieces have been shared fairly because each child has four pieces.	• Color code the different sized pieces to distinguish between them. Ask child, "Would you get the same amount as your friend if you got the 4 small blue pieces and your friend got the 4 large green pieces?" • Exaggerate the different sizes to help the child notice that one child will receive more than another.

(continued)

Table 14.3. Common errors and misconceptions in fraction concepts and how to help. (continued)

Misconception/Error	What It Looks Like	How to Help
4. Child loses sight of the whole.	Child thinks the trapezoid is one-half when it represents one-fourth of the following area: 	• Using same model, change the whole so that children do not get used to thinking the whole is always say, one hexagon. • Have children explicitly identify the whole before identifying the fractional amount. Use yarn to loop around one whole.
5. Child tries to use repeated halving for all sharing problems.	When solving a problem like *5 children sharing 3 pretzel sticks*, child tries to use a halving strategy: The child is not anticipating how to partition objects based on the numbers in the problem but is overgeneralizing the use of a halving strategy. The child is unsure what to do with the leftover part or how to partition the pretzels so he can fairly share them.	• Give tasks that require partitioning into equal groups of 3 (and 6) to provide opportunities to confront an overgeneralizing of the halving strategy. • Use a context with something the child really likes. Then ask, "Which piece would you want and why?" and "What if I gave you this piece?" (indicating a smaller piece). • Have children use uncooked spaghetti noodles or popsicle sticks to represent their cuts/partitions to help with anticipating how to partition.
6. Child thinks same-sized parts have to be the same shape.	Child thinks the following parts are not equal in size because they are different shapes: Child thinks the following parts are not the same size because they are arranged differently: 	• Use tasks that ask the child to partition the whole to find the same fractional amount in a different way and have them verify parts are the same size (e.g., cutting parts out and laying on top of each other to check size, moving manipulatives to check size). • See Activities 14.1, 14.2, and 14.3.

Table 14.3. Common errors and misconceptions in fraction concepts and how to help.

Misconception/Error	What It Looks Like	How to Help
7. Child counts tick marks on linear models rather than the spaces between.	The child says the number line below is portioned into thirds rather than halves. 	• Emphasize that what is being counted are the segments *between* the ticks. Use narrow strips of paper to represent the equal-sized segments and to emphasize what is being counted.
8. With set models child focuses on the size of the subset rather than the number of equal-sized subsets in the whole.	With 12 counters as the whole, child thinks the equal-sized parts of 3 create thirds, not fourths. 	• Use one color of yarn to loop around the whole and another color of yarn or popsicle sticks to partition into equal-sized groups. Have the child count the fractional parts to see if she gets less than a whole, more than a whole, or exactly a whole. • Use a smaller set of counters and start by having the child find halves and then fourths. For example, using 8 counters, ask the child to find a half. Then ask the child to find one-fourth. Ask the child to compare these amounts. • Have the child do the same problem with an area or linear model and compare their solutions. For the given example, the area or linear model would use a whole partitioned into twelfths, with those grouped into groups of 3 or grouped into fourths.

15

Building Measurement Concepts

BIG IDEAS

1 Measurement involves a comparison of an attribute of an item or situation with a unit that has the same attribute. Lengths are compared to units of length, areas to units of area, time to units of time, and so on.

2 Before anything can be measured meaningfully, it is necessary to understand the attribute to be measured.

3 Estimation of measures and the development of benchmarks for frequently used units of measure help children increase their familiarity with units, preventing errors and aiding in the meaningful use of measurement.

4 Measurement instruments (e.g., rulers) are tools that group multiple units so that you do not have to iterate a single unit multiple times.

Measurement can be thought of as the "assignment of a numerical value to an attribute or characteristic of an object" (National Council of Teachers of Mathematics, 2003, p. 1). It is one of the most useful mathematics content strands because it is an important component in everything from occupational tasks to life skills for the mathematically literate citizen. From gigabytes that measure amounts of information, font size on computers, recipes for a meal, to deciding whether you need the 6-foot or 12-foot power cord, we are surrounded with measurement concepts that apply to many real-world contexts and applications.

However, measurement is not an easy topic for children to understand. Data from international studies consistently indicate that children in the United States are weaker in the area of measurement than any other topic in the mathematics curriculum (Provasnik et al., 2010; Thompson & Preston, 2004).

In grades preK–2, the primary emphasis of measurement instruction is developing a conceptual understanding of the measurement process as well as the units and tools for measuring length and time. Kindergartners should learn to describe the length and weight of objects, directly comparing two objects using words such as *taller, shorter, heavier, lighter, more,* and *less* (CCSSO, 2010). By first grade, children should compare objects indirectly using a third object and understand how to use multiple copies of a unit to measure the length of an object. Second graders move to using standard measuring tools, such as rulers, yardsticks, and meter sticks, and to using number lines to represent whole numbers as lengths from zero. They also begin to explore the inverse relationship between the size of the measuring unit and the measure (i.e., number of units used). First graders begin to tell and write time in hours and half-hours and second graders extend that to 5-minute intervals and use a.m. and p.m. Money is also included under the study of measurement but does not occur until second grade.

The Meaning and Process of Measuring

Suppose that you asked your children to measure an empty bucket (see Figure 15.1). The first thing they would need to know is *what* about the bucket is to be measured. They might measure the height, depth, diameter (distance across), or circumference (distance around). All of these are length measures. They could determine the surface area of the side as well as the volume (or capacity) and weight of the bucket. Each aspect that can be measured is an *attribute* of the bucket.

Once children determine the attribute to be measured, they then choose a unit that has the attribute being measured. Length is measured with units that have length, area with units that have area, volume with units that have volume, weight with units that have weight, and so on.

Figure 15.1

Measuring different attributes of a bucket.

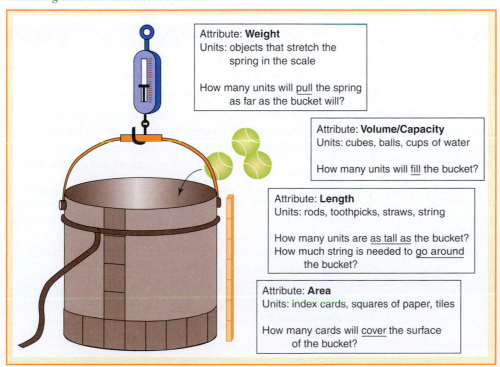

Attribute: **Weight**
Units: objects that stretch the
spring in the scale

How many units will <u>pull</u> the spring
as far as the bucket will?

Attribute: **Volume/Capacity**
Units: cubes, balls, cups of water

How many units will <u>fill</u> the bucket?

Attribute: **Length**
Units: rods, toothpicks, straws, string

How many units are <u>as tall as</u> the bucket?
How much string is needed to <u>go around</u>
the bucket?

Attribute: **Area**
Units: index cards, squares of paper, tiles

How many cards will <u>cover</u> the surface
of the bucket?

Technically, a *measurement* is a number that indicates a comparison between the attribute of the object (or situation, or event) being measured and the same attribute of a given unit of measure. We commonly use small units of measure to determine a numeric relationship (the measurement) between what is measured and the unit. For example, to measure a length, the comparison can be done by lining up copies of the unit directly against the length being measured. For most attributes measured in schools, we can say that *to measure* means that the attribute being measured is "filled," "covered," or "matched" with a unit of measure having the same attribute (as illustrated in Figure 15.1).

In summary, to measure something, one must perform three steps:

1. Decide on the attribute to be measured.
2. Select a unit that has that attribute.
3. Compare the units—by filling, covering, matching, or using some other method—with the attribute of the object being measured. The number of units required to match the object is the measure.

Measuring instruments such as rulers, meter sticks, scales, and clocks are devices that make the filling, covering, or matching process easier. A ruler lines up the units of length and numbers them. A clock lines up units of time and marks them off.

Measurement Concepts and Skills

If a typical group of first graders attempts to measure the length of their classroom by laying strips 1 meter long end to end, the strips sometimes overlap, and the line can weave in a snake-like fashion. Do they understand the concept of length as an attribute of the classroom? Do they understand that each 1-meter strip has this attribute of length? They most likely understand that they are counting a line of strips stretching from wall to wall. But they may not be explicitly aware that, when measuring, they are comparing the same attribute of the measuring unit (the 1-meter strip) and the object being measured (the classroom). The skill of measuring with a unit must be explicitly linked to the concept of measuring as a process of comparing attributes. Table 15.1 describes an instructional sequence that can help explicitly link measurement concepts

Table 15.1. Measurement instruction: A sequence of experiences.

Step	Goal	Type of Activity	Notes
1—Making Comparisons	Children will understand the attribute to be measured.	Make comparisons based on the attribute, for example, longer/shorter, heavier/lighter. Use direct comparisons whenever possible.	When it is clear that the attribute is understood, there is no further need for comparison activities.
2—Using Models of Measuring Units	Children will understand how filling, covering, matching, or making other comparisons of an attribute with measuring units produces a number called a *measure*.	Use physical models of measuring units to fill, cover, match, or make the desired comparison of the attribute with the unit.	Begin with nonstandard units. Progress to the direct use of standard units when appropriate and certainly before using measuring tools.
3—Using Measuring Instruments	Children will use common measuring tools with understanding and flexibility.	Make measuring instruments (grouped units) and compare them with the individual unit models to see how the measurement tool performs the same function. Make direct comparisons between the student-made tools and the standard tools. Standard measuring instruments, such as rulers and scales, make the filling, covering, or matching process easier.	Without a careful comparison of the nonstandard (or informal) tools with the standard tools, much of the value in making the tools can be lost.

and skills. As the first step in the instructional sequence highlights, before anything can be measured meaningfully, it is necessary to understand the attribute to be measured (Battista, 2012).

Making Comparisons

With a measure, such as length, you can sometimes make a direct comparison by lining up one object against another. But often an indirect method using a third object must be used. For example, if children compare the height of a wastebasket to the distance around, they must devise an indirect way to compare, such as using a string to make that comparison. The string is the intermediary, as it is impossible to directly compare these two lengths.

> ## 🌿 *Teaching Tip*
>
> Use and encourage precise language when helping children make comparisons. Avoid using the ambiguous phrases "bigger than" and "smaller than"; instead use more specific language such as "longer than" or "is heavier than."

Using Physical Models of Measuring Units

For most attributes measured in elementary schools, it is possible to have physical models of units of measure. Time and temperature are exceptions. Units models can represent both nonstandard (sometimes referred to as *informal*) units and standard units. For length, for example, drinking straws (nonstandard) and 1-foot-long paper strips (standard) might be used.

Standards for Mathematical Practice

◀ **6** Attend to precision.

To help make the notion of units explicit, use as many copies of the unit as are needed to fill or match the attribute measured (this is called *tiling* and involves equal partitioning). The length of the room could be measured with giant footprints (nonstandard) by placing multiple copies of the footprint end to end, completely "covering" the length of the room. Somewhat more difficult is using a single copy of the unit to complete the measurement (this is called *iteration*. You may recall that counting same-size fractional parts is also called *iteration*). That means measuring a given length (say, with a single footprint) by repeatedly moving it from position to position and keeping track of where the last unit ended. Not only is this more difficult for younger children, but it also obscures the meaning of the measurement—to see how many units will fill the length.

It is useful to measure the same object with units of different size to help children understand that the size of the unit used is important. (This is an expectation for second graders in the *Common Core State Standards*.) For each different-sized unit, estimate the measure in advance and discuss the estimate afterward. Children should start to observe that smaller units produce larger numeric measures, and vice versa. This is a difficult concept for young children to understand but they can make sense of it (e.g., National Research Council, 2009). Children mentally construct this inverse relationship by estimating, then experimenting, and finally reflecting on the measurements.

Building and Using Measuring Instruments

On the 2003 NAEP exam (Blume, Galindo, & Walcott, 2007), only 20 percent of fourth graders could give the correct measure of an object not aligned with the end of a ruler, as in Figure 15.2. Even at the middle school level, only 56 percent of eighth graders answered the same situation accurately (Kloosterman, Rutledge, & Kenney, 2009). Students on the same exam also experienced difficulty when the increments on a measuring tool were not one unit. These results point to the difference between using a measuring tool and understanding how it works.

Only after children understand and can use single units of measurement should they move to working with common measuring tools. When children build simple measuring instruments using unit models with which they are familiar, it is more likely

Figure 15.2

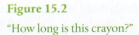
"How long is this crayon?"

📙 *Teaching Tip*

If your children have been using individual paper clips as units of measurement, have them create a chain of paper clips to use as a ruler for an initial transition from single units to instruments.

that they will understand how an instrument measures. A ruler is a good example. If children line up individual physical units, such as 1-inch-long paper clips or 1-inch-long tiles, along a strip of card stock and mark them off, they can see that it is the *spaces* on rulers and not the tick marks or numbers that are important. It is essential that children discuss how measurement with iterating individual units compares with measurement using an instrument. Without this comparison and discussion, children may not understand that these two methods are essentially the same. Then they are ready to compare their "ruler" with standard rulers and can compare their use.

Introducing Nonstandard Units

A common approach in primary grades is to begin measurement of any attribute with nonstandard units. Although the primary emphasis at the preK-2 level is on the development of linear measurements, establishing a conceptual foundation for measuring other attributes, such as area, volume, capacity, and weight, is common. The use of nonstandard units for beginning measurement activities is beneficial for the following reasons:

- Nonstandard units can emphasize the attribute being measured. For example, when discussing how to measure the length of a bulletin board, units such as toothpicks, straws, or paper clips may be suggested. Each of these units covers length—and actually accentuates length because each unit is thin and long. With the visual support of such nonstandard units, the discussion can focus on what it means to measure length.

- The use of nonstandard units avoids conflicting objectives in introductory lessons. Is your lesson about what it means to measure length or about understanding inches?

- By carefully selecting nonstandard units, the size of the numbers in early measurements can be kept reasonable. Length measures for first graders can be kept at fewer than 20 units even when measuring long distances simply by using longer units.

- Nonstandard units provide a good rationale for standard units. The need for a standard unit has more meaning when your children measure the same objects with their own collection of nonstandard units and arrive at different answers.

Although nonstandard units offer these benefits, based on several research studies, Clements and Sarama (2009) caution that early measuring experiences with several different units can confuse children. While children are grappling with the concept of measurement, it is important to use a few nonstandard units that clearly demonstrate the attribute being measured (e.g., for length, toothpicks as opposed to square tiles or linking cubes). Early on, children need to first understand the attribute being measured, and then the notion of matching and the use of units of equal size. Once they demonstrate understanding of these concepts, you can introduce nonstandard units of different sizes to provide the rationale for standard units. The move to standard units should be guided by how well your children understand measurement of the target attribute.

How Big Is a Foot? (Myller, 1991) tells the story of a king who measures the queen using his feet and orders a bed to be made that is 6 king's feet long and 3 king's feet wide. The carpenter's apprentice, who is very small, makes the bed according to his own feet, demonstrating the need for standard units. Another tale about nonstandard units that children enjoy is *Twelve Snails to One Lizard* (Hightower, 1997).

Introducing Standard Units

Perhaps the biggest error in measurement instruction is the failure to recognize and separate two types of objectives: (1) understanding the meaning and technique of measuring a particular attribute and (2) learning about the standard units commonly used to measure that attribute.

Teaching standard units of measure can be organized around three broad goals:

Teaching Tip

As you teach standard units, make sure children, especially ELLs, understand the terms (e.g., feet, yard) and abbreviations (e.g., in, ft, cm). Include these on your math word wall.

1. *Familiarity with the unit.* Children should have a basic idea of the size of commonly used units and what they measure. Being able to estimate a shelf as 5 feet long is as important as being able to measure the length of the shelf accurately.

2. *Ability to select an appropriate unit.* Children should know both what is a reasonable unit of measure in a given situation and the precision that is required. (Would you measure your lawn to purchase grass seed with the same precision you would use to measure a window to buy a pane of glass?) Children need practice in selecting appropriate standard units and judging the level of precision.

3. *Knowledge of relationships between units.* Children should know the relationships that are commonly used, such as those between inches, feet, and yards or minutes and hours.

Children who exhibit measurement sense are familiar with the standard measurement units, are able to make estimates in terms of these units, and meaningfully interpret measures depicted with standard units.

Developing Unit Familiarity

Two types of activities can develop familiarity with standard units: (1) comparisons that focus on a single unit and (2) activities that develop personal referents or benchmarks for single units or easy multiples of units.

Activity 15.1

CCSS-M: 1.MD.A.2; 2.MD.A.1; 2.MD.A.3

About One Unit

Give children a physical model of a standard unit and have them search for objects that have about the same measure as that one unit. For example, to develop familiarity with the meter, give children a piece of rope 1 meter long and challenge them find objects in the classroom, outside on the playground, around the school building, or at home that are about 1 meter in length (see **About a Meter** Activity Page). Have them make separate lists of things that are about 1 meter long, things that are a little shorter (or a little longer), or things that are twice as long (or half as long). Be sure to include curved or circular lengths. Later, children can try to predict whether a given object is longer, shorter, or close to 1 meter. (Notice the use of terms such as *longer* rather than *more than*. Remember to use precise language!)

"About One Unit" can be done with other unit lengths. Enlist families to help children find familiar distances that are about 1 mile or 1 kilometer. Suggest in a take-home letter that families check the distances around the neighborhood, to the school or grocery store, or along other frequently traveled paths. If possible, send home (or use in class) a 1-meter or 1-yard trundle wheel to measure distances. Watch this **video (http://www.youtube.com/watch?v=6iK5b2uA2Ac)** of a class estimating while using a trundle wheel to measure the length of the school hallway.

For other interesting locations to measure, go online to Google Earth and use their Measuring Tools. Children can measure distances in centimeters, inches, feet, yards, kilometers, and miles. If needed, watch a **tutorial** beforehand on how to measure distances on Google Earth (**https://www.youtube.com/watch?v=TYBoI7hZKss**).

ℒ **Teaching Tip**

Meter trundle wheels measure off one meter with every rotation. Children may not understand that the circumference of the wheel is the same length as the flat meter stick. Help children make the connection by having them match a rope or strip of paper that is 1 meter in length to a meter stick and then to the wheel. You can also lay a meter stick down and roll the trundle wheel along the length of the stick.

For the standard weights of gram, kilogram, ounce, and pound, children can compare objects on a two-pan balance with single copies of these units in one pan and objects in the other. Note that one slice of store-bought sandwich bread usually weighs about 1 ounce, so many objects will weigh much more than 1 ounce. Children can be encouraged to bring in familiar objects from home to compare on the classroom scale.

To develop unit familiarity, you can also begin with familiar items and use their measures as references or benchmarks. For example, a doorway is a bit more than 2 meters high. A bag of flour is a good reference for 5 pounds. A paper clip weighs about a gram and is about 1 centimeter wide. A gallon of milk weighs a little less than 4 kilograms. The next activity engages children in measuring familiar items in a variety of ways.

▲ Activity 15.2

CCSS-M: 1.MD.A.2; 2.MD.A.1

Familiar References

Read *Measuring Penny* (Leedy, 2000) to introduce children to the variety of ways familiar items can be measured. In this book, the author bridges between nonstandard units (e.g., dog biscuits, swabs, etc.) and standard units (inches, centimeters, etc.) to measure her pet dog Penny. Using the idea of measuring Penny for inspiration, have children find something at home (or in class) to measure in as many ways as they can think of using standard units. The measures should be rounded to the nearest whole numbers. Discuss in class the familiar items chosen and their measures so that different ideas and benchmarks are shared. Many of the units used in *Measuring Penny* are common in the United States but not in other countries. Still, the book can be used to relate to how children from other countries measure length and volume.

There are other children's books that can also engage children in developing familiarity with various lengths. For example, the children's book *Actual Size* (Jenkins, 2011a) portrays several different animals and insects (or a part of their body) in their actual size. From the head of a 23-foot-long crocodile to the hand of a gorilla to the 2.5-inch-tall mouse lemur, children can compare themselves and their classmates to these fascinating creatures while learning about linear measurement.

It can be interesting for children to find length benchmarks on their bodies. Have children compare their benchmarks with those of their parents or an older sibling to see how they differ in size. Point out that children will likely need to adjust their benchmarks over time as they grow.

◢ Activity 15.3

CCSS-M: 2.MD.A.1

Personal Benchmarks

Measure various parts of your body. About how long is your foot, your stride, your hand span (stretched or with fingers together), the width of your index finger or pinky finger, your arm span (finger to finger and finger to nose), and the distance around your wrist and around your waist? What is the height to your waist, shoulder, and head? Some of these measures may prove to be useful benchmarks for single or multiples of standard units. (The average child's fingernail is about **1** cm wide and most people can find a **10-cm** length somewhere on their hands.)

Choosing Appropriate Units

Should the room be measured in feet or inches? Should concrete blocks be weighed in grams or kilograms? The answers to questions such as these involve more than simply knowing how big the units are, although that is certainly required. Another consideration involves the need for precision. If you were measuring your wall in order to cut a piece of molding to fit, you would need to measure it very precisely. The smallest unit would be an inch or a centimeter, and you would also use small fractional parts. But if you were determining how many 8-foot molding strips to buy, the nearest foot would probably be sufficient.

Standards for Mathematical Practice

◄ **6** Attend to precision.

◢ Activity 15.4

CCSS-M: 2.MD.A.3

Guess the Unit

Find examples of measurements of all types in newspapers, in stores, on signs, online, or in other everyday situations. For example, you may consider various distances or lengths at your school (e.g., desks, hallway, playground, gym, cafeteria). You can also use the ideas on **Measurement Cards**. Present the context and measures but without units. The task is to predict what units of measure were used. Have children discuss their choices. For children with disabilities you may want to provide the possible units (e.g., inches, feet, yards, miles) so they can sort the real-world measures into these groups.

Important Standard Units and Relationships

Although a conceptual foundation for measuring many attributes is developed during grades preK–2, the primary emphasis with standard units is on linear measurements, both customary and metric. The National Council of Teachers of Mathematics (2011b) takes a strong position on the metric system, because it is a globally used system and if U.S. students are going to be prepared for the global workplace, they must be knowledgeable about and comfortable with metric units. NCTM's position statement goes on to say that because we are still using customary measures in day-to-day life children must work in that system as well. The *Common Core State Standards* specifically state that, by the end of second grade, children should be familiar with centimeters and meters as well as inches and feet.

The relationships between units within either the metric or customary systems are conventions. As such, children must simply be told what the relationships are (e.g., 3 feet or 36 inches in a yard; 100 cm in a meter), and instructional experiences must be devised to reinforce them. Knowing basic relationships between units in a given measurement system becomes important in the intermediate grades as they work on conversions between units. At the primary level, being able to pace off 3 meters—unit familiarity—is more important than knowing how many cups in a quart or inches in a yard. However, by gaining familiarity with various units, some children may begin to automatically use these relationships in their work.

The Role of Estimation and Approximation

Measurement estimation is the process of using mental and visual information to measure or make comparisons without using measuring instruments. People use this practical skill almost every day. Do I have enough sugar to make cookies? Can you throw the ball 15 meters? Is this suitcase over the weight or size limit? Will my car fit into that parking space? Here are several reasons for including estimation in measurement activities:

- Estimation helps children focus on the attribute being measured and the measuring process. Think how you would estimate the area of the cover of this book using playing cards as the unit. To do so, you have to think about what area is and how the units might be placed on the book cover.

- Estimation provides an intrinsic motivation for measurement activities. It is interesting to see how close you can come in your estimate to the actual measure.

- When standard units are used, estimation helps develop familiarity with the unit. If you estimate the height of the door in meters before measuring, you must think about the size of a meter.

- The use of a benchmark to make an estimate lays the foundation for multiplicative reasoning. For example, someone might reason that the width of a picture is about twice the length of a ruler, or 2 groups of 12 inches or 24 inches or 2 feet.

In all measuring activities, emphasize the use of approximate language. The desk is *about* 15 orange rods long. The chair is a *little less than* 4 straws high. Approximate language is very useful for young children because many measurements do not result in whole numbers. As children get older, they will begin to use fractional units or smaller units to measure with more precision. When this happens, acknowledge that the smaller unit or subdivision produces a greater degree of *precision*. This is also an opportunity to develop the idea that all measurements include some error. For example, a length that has been measured accurately can never be more than one-half unit in error. And because there is no "smallest unit," there is always some error involved. In other words, all measurements are approximations.

Standards for Mathematical Practice

6 Attend to precision. ▶

Stop and Reflect

Why is it the case that a length that has been measured accurately can never be more than one-half unit in error? Use a specific context and measure to help you think about this situation.

Suppose that you are measuring a length of ribbon with a ruler that only shows quarter inches—so our unit is a quarter of an inch. If the length of ribbon falls between $3\frac{3}{4}$ and 4 inches, we would usually round to whichever number is closer to the length of ribbon. If the length of ribbon is more than halfway towards the 4-inch mark, we say it's 4 inches long. However, if the length of ribbon is less than halfway from $3\frac{3}{4}$ we say it is closer to $3\frac{3}{4}$ inches long. In either case, we are within $\frac{1}{8}$ of an inch or one-half of the unit and are essentially ignoring the difference—and this constitutes our "error." If we need more precision in our measurement, we use smaller units to ensure that our measurement rounding or error is within an acceptable range.

Strategies for Estimating Measurements

Always begin a measurement activity with children making an estimate—whether they are using nonstandard or standard units. Just as for computational estimation, specific strategies exist for estimating measures. Here are four specific strategies:

1. *Develop and use benchmarks or referents.* Research suggests that children who acquire mental benchmarks or reference points for measurements *and* practice using them in class activities are much better estimators than children who have not learned to use benchmarks (Joram, 2003). Children must pay attention to the size of the unit to estimate well (Towers & Hunter, 2010). Referents should be things that are easily envisioned by the child. One example is the height of an average child (see Figure 15.3). Children should have a good referent for single units and also useful multiples of standard units.

Standards for Mathematical Practice

◄ **7 Look for and make use of structure.**

Figure 15.3

Estimating measures using benchmarks and chunking.

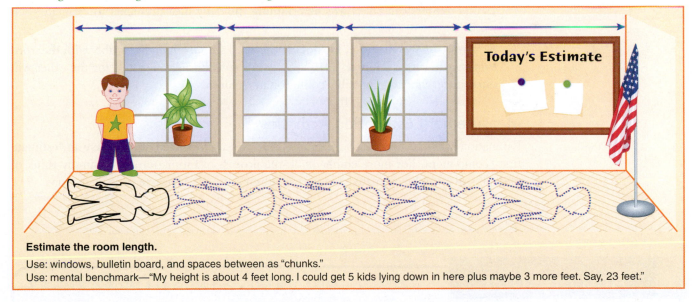

Estimate the room length.

Use: windows, bulletin board, and spaces between as "chunks."

Use: mental benchmark—"My height is about 4 feet long. I could get 5 kids lying down in here plus maybe 3 more feet. Say, 23 feet."

2. *Use "chunking" or subdivisions.* The weight of a stack of books is easier to estimate if some referent is given to the weight of an "average" book. If a wall length to be estimated has useful chunks that can be used, it is usually easier to estimate the shorter chunks along the wall than to estimate the whole length. Figure 15.3 shows an example using windows, bulletin boards, and spaces between as chunks. Alternatively, if the wall length to be estimated has no useful chunks, it can be mentally divided in half and then in fourths or even eighths by repeatedly subdividing it until a more manageable length is found. Length, volume, and area measurements all lend themselves to chunking or subdividing.

3. *Iterate units.* For length, area, and volume, it is sometimes easy to mark off single units mentally or physically. You might use your hands or make marks or folds to keep track as you go. If a child knows, for example, that her stride is about one-half of a meter long, she can walk off a length and then add to get an estimate. Hand and finger widths are useful for shorter measures.

Each strategy just listed should be explicitly taught and discussed with children. Suggested benchmarks for useful measures can be developed and recorded on a class chart. Include items found at home. But the best approach to improving estimation skills is to have children do a lot of estimating. Keep these teaching tips in mind:

1. *Help children learn strategies by having them first try a specified approach.* Later activities should permit them to choose whatever techniques they wish.

2. *Discuss how different children made their estimates.* This will confirm that there is no single right way to estimate while reminding children of other useful approaches.

3. *Accept a range of estimates.* Think in relative terms about what is a good estimate. Within 10 percent for length is quite good. Even 30 percent "off" may be reasonable for weights or volumes.

4. *Do not promote a "winning" estimate.* This discourages estimation and promotes only seeking the exact answer.

5. *Encourage children to give a range of estimates that they believe includes the actual measure.* For example, the door is between 7 and 8 feet tall. This not only is a practical approach in real life but also helps focus on the approximate nature of estimation.

6. *Make measurement estimation an ongoing activity.* Post a daily measurement to be estimated. Children can record their estimates and discuss them in a 5-minute period. Teams of second graders can take turns determining the daily measurements to estimate each week.

7. *Be precise with your language.* Do not use the word *measure* interchangeably with the word *estimate* (Towers & Hunter, 2010). Randomly substituting one word for the other will cause uncertainty and possibly confusion in children.

Measurement Estimation Activities

Estimation activities need not be elaborate. Any measurement activity can have an "estimate first" component. For more emphasis on the process of estimation itself, simply think of measures that can be estimated and have children estimate. Here are two suggestions.

 **Activity 15.5**   CCSS-M: K.MD.A.1; K.MD.A.2; 1.MD.A.1; 1.MD.A.2; 2.MD.A.3

Estimation Quickie

 Select a single object such as a box, a jar, a pumpkin, a painting on the wall of the school, or even the principal! Each day, select a different attribute or dimension to estimate. For the pumpkin, for example, children can estimate its height, circumference, weight, and volume. Remember you can use nonstandard units to give children practice measuring various attributes until they are ready for standard units. If you have ELLs, be sure to include metric measures when you have moved to standard units. You can also help children compare the centimeter to the inch. Watch this short **video** (**http://www .youtube.com/watch?v=ygeIbA4TJNk**) about a kindergarten class exploring various measures of a pumpkin.

Activity 15.6

CCSS-M: 1.MD.A.2; 2.MD.A.1; 2.MD.A.3

Estimation Scavenger Hunt

Conduct estimation scavenger hunts. Give teams a list of either familiar nonstandard or familiar standard measurements and have them find things that are close to having those measurements. Do not allow children to use measuring instruments at first. Look at the **Estimation Scavenger Hunt** Activity Page for some possible ideas.

Let children suggest how to judge results in terms of accuracy.

Formative Assessment Note

Estimation tasks are a good way to assess children's understanding of both measurement and units. Use an **Observation Checklist** (Blackline Master 33) to take notes about children's estimates and measures of a variety of real objects and distances. Prompt children to explain how they arrived at their estimates to get a more complete picture of their measurement knowledge. Asking only for a numeric estimate and no explanation can mask a lack of understanding and will not give you the information you need to inform next instructional steps.

Length

Length is usually the first attribute children learn to measure. Length of an object is found by locating two endpoints and examining how far it is between those points. We measure lengths by selecting a unit (that has length) and repeatedly matching that unit to the object.

Be aware, however, that length measurement is not immediately understood by young children. Here are some of the more common misconceptions and difficulties children have when measuring length (Clements & Sarama, 2009; Curry, Mitchelmore, & Outhred, 2006):

- Leaving gaps between units or overlapping units
- Using units that are not of equal size (e.g., measuring with paper clips of different sizes)
- Combining units of different sizes as if they were the same unit (e.g., combining 2 feet and 4 inches as "6 long")
- Measuring from the wrong end of the ruler or beginning at "1" rather than "0"
- Counting the tick marks on a ruler or the "points" between heel-to-toe steps rather than the spaces (units)
- Not aligning two objects when comparing them

Keep these misconceptions and difficulties in mind as you plan lessons and observe your children during measurement activities.

Comparison Activities

At the preK and kindergarten level, children should begin with direct comparisons of two or more lengths and then move to indirect comparisons by the first grade (CCSSO, 2010;

NCTM, 2006). Throughout the school day, look for opportunities for children to compare lengths directly. For example, which block tower is taller, which clay snake is shorter, which chair is wider, and so on. The next two activities offer direct comparison experiences.

Activity 15.7

CCSS-M: K.MD.A.2; 1.MD.A.1; 2.MD.A.3

Longer, Shorter, Same

Create learning stations where children can explore which objects in a group are longer, shorter, or about the same in length as a specified "target" object. Change the target object and children may find that the shorter object is now longer than the target. A similar task can involve putting a set of objects in order from shortest to longest.

Activity 15.8

CCSS-M: K.MD.A.2; 1.MD.A.1; 1.MD.A.2; 2.MD.A.3

Length (or Unit) Hunt

Give pairs of children a strip of card stock, a stick, a length of rope, or some other object with an obvious length dimension that will serve as a "target" unit. The task is for children to find five things in the room that are shorter than, longer than, or about the same length as their target unit. They can record what they find in pictures or words.

By making the target length a standard unit (e.g., a meter stick or a 1-meter length of rope), the activity can be repeated to provide familiarity with important standard units.

Indirect comparison, which means using another object to help make the measure, is the focus of the next activity. Children who can use a third object to compare the lengths of two other objects must have a transitive understanding of measurement. For example, if the length of a green pencil is shorter than the length of a blue pencil, and the length of the blue pencil is shorter than the length of a red pencil, then the length of the green pencil must be shorter than the length of the red pencil. Not all children in grades K–1 will be able to follow this argument (Curry, Mitchelmore, & Outhred, 2006); however, through indirect comparison activities, they can begin to build this understanding.

Activity 15.9

CCSS-M: 1.MD.A.1; 2.MD.A.3; 2.MD.A.4

Will It Fit?

Challenge children to determine whether an object in the classroom or outside the classroom (maybe in the library or cafeteria or on the playground) would fit through the doorway of the classroom. For example, ask, "Is the classroom doorway wide enough for one of the tables in the cafeteria to go through?" or "Will one of the shelves in the library fit through the doorway?" or "What about the monkey bars on the playground? Will those fit through the school's front door?" Have pairs of children brainstorm ways they can check and then discuss and try some of their suggestions.

Children should also compare lengths that are not in straight lines. One way to do this is by using indirect comparisons.

Activity 15.10

Crooked Paths

 Make some crooked or curvy paths on the floor (or outside) with masking tape or chalk. Ask children to determine which path is longest, next longest, and so on. (Some children may focus on the straight-line distance from the beginning of the curved path to its end [Battista, 2012]. So make sure to emphasize that the length you want them to consider is along the curved path.) Children should suggest ways to measure the crooked paths so that they can be compared easily. If you wish to offer a hint, provide pairs of children with a long piece of string (at first make it longer than the path). Have children explain how they solved the problem. For children with disabilities, you may need to tape the end of the string to the beginning of the path and help them mark the final measurement on the string with a marker. Use another string in the same way for the other path. Then compare the string lengths.

Some children may argue that the path that "looks longer" (i.e., is more spread out) is the longer path, when the crooked and more compact path may actually be longer. For these children, show them an example of two paths on the floor (one really crooked, compact path and one straight path that "looks longer" than the crooked path) and have children walk each path to see which takes longer to walk. See the **Expanded Lesson: Crooked Paths** for an enhanced version of this activity.

Using Physical Models of Length Units

There are four important principles of iterating units of length, whether they are nonstandard or standard (Dietiker, Gonulates, Figueras, & Smith, 2010, p. 2). You will notice that these principles are related to some of the common difficulties children have with linear measurement that were identified earlier.

- Units must have equal length; otherwise you cannot iterate them to obtain a count.
- Units must be aligned with the length being measured; otherwise a different quantity is being measured.
- Units must be placed without gaps, or a part of the length is not being measured.
- Units must be placed without overlaps, or the length has portions that are measured more than once.

Children can begin to measure length using a variety of nonstandard units, including the following:

- *Giant footprints.* Cut out about 20 copies of a large footprint about $1\frac{1}{2}$ to 2 feet long on poster board.
- *Measuring ropes.* Cut rope into lengths of 1 meter. These ropes can measure the perimeter and the circumference of objects such as the teacher's desk, a tree trunk, or the class pumpkin.
- *Drinking straws.* Straws are useful in that they are easily cut into smaller units. They can also be linked together with a long string or slid onto a length of pipe cleaner, creating an excellent bridge to a ruler or measuring tape.
- *Shorter units.* Flat toothpicks, linking cubes and paper clips are useful nonstandard units for measuring shorter lengths. Cuisenaire rods are also useful because they are easily

placed end to end and are also metric (centimeters). Paper clips can also be made into chains, again making an excellent bridge to a ruler. Note that individual linking cubes do not explicitly exhibit the attribute of length as well as Cuisenaire rods, toothpicks, paper clips, and straws.

Keep in mind that using a few well-chosen nonstandard units can avoid confusing children with too many kinds of units. Once children demonstrate, in particular, that all the units used to measure a given length must be the same length, then you may want to increase the variety of nonstandard units available.

The following activity encourages children to develop their own approach to measuring lengths.

◢ Activity 15.11

CCSS-M: 1.MD.A.2; 2.MD.A.1; 2.MD.A.2; 2.MD.A.3

How Long Is the Teacher?

Explain that you have just received an important request from the principal. She needs to know exactly how tall each teacher in the building is. The children are to decide how to measure the teachers and write a note to the principal explaining how tall their teacher is and detailing the process that they used. If you wish to give a hint, ask, "Would it help if I lie down?" Have children make marks at your feet and head and draw a straight line between these marks.

Explain that the principal says they can use any nonstandard or standard unit to measure with (provide choices). For each choice of unit, supply enough units to more than cover your length. Put children in pairs and allow them to select one unit with which to measure. Ask children to estimate first and then use their unit to measure. For those ready for a challenge, have them do the measurement twice, with two different units.

Follow up with questions such as "What did you do to get your measurement?" "Did children who measured with the same unit get the same answers? If not, why not?" "How could the principal make a line that was as long as the teacher?" Focus on the value of carefully lining up units end to end. Discuss what happens if you overlap units, have gaps in the units, or don't follow a straight line.

You can repeat the basic task of "How Long Is the Teacher?" by measuring a variety of items. It is helpful when several pairs of children use the same unit to measure the target lengths (e.g., heights, distances around) so that possible errors can be discussed and the measuring process refined.

The following measurement activity adds an explicit estimation component.

◢ Activity 15.12

CCSS-M: 1.MD.A.2; 2.MD.A.1; 2.MD.A.3

Estimate and Measure

Make lists of things in the room to measure (see Figure 15.4) or use the **Estimating and Measuring with Nonstandard Units Recording Sheet**. Run a piece of masking tape along the dimension of the objects to be measured. Include curves or other distances that are not straight lines. Have children make estimates before they measure. Young children and children with disabilities may find it difficult to come up with a reasonable estimate, so provide possible strategies. For example, make a row or chain of exactly 10 of the units to help them visualize their estimates. They first lay 10 units against the object and then make their estimate. You can also do this activity using standard units.

Figure 15.4

Example of a recording sheet for measuring with nonstandard length units.

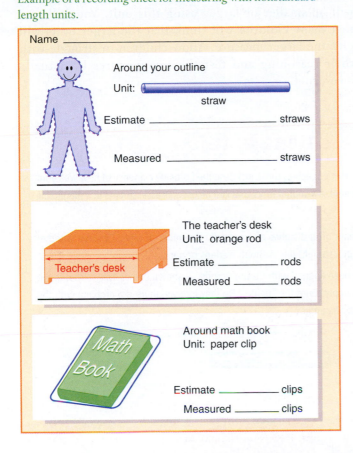

Laying the Foundation for Conversions

The *Common Core State Standards* recommend that second graders consider the relationship between the size of a unit and the resulting measure. Children can find it a challenge to understand that larger units will create a smaller measure and vice versa. Engage children in activities in which this issue is emphasized.

Activity 15.13

CCSS-M: 2.MD.A.2; 2.MD.A.3

Changing Units

Have children measure a length with a specified unit. Then provide them with a different unit that is either twice as long or half as long as the original unit. Their task is to predict the measure of the same length using the new unit. Children should write down their predictions and discuss how they made their estimations. Provide the **Changing Units Recording Sheet**. Cuisenaire rods are excellent for this activity. Challenge ready children with units that are more difficult multiples of the original unit.

Standards for Mathematical Practice

◀ **2** Reason abstractly and quantitatively.

Teaching Tip

> Start with simpler multiples (e.g., halving and doubling) so children will more easily be able to unpack the inverse relationship of size of unit to the numeric measure.

When first doing the "Changing Units" activity, show the second unit and discuss only if the measure will be smaller or larger using this unit. You will find that many children will think that the larger units will give the larger measure. Allow children to struggle with their reasoning and test their conjectures by actually measuring.

📋 Formative Assessment Note

Observation and discussion during activities such as those just described provide evidence of how well your children understand length measurement. Additional tasks that can be used as assessments in a diagnostic interview format are:

- Ask children to draw a line or mark off a distance of a prescribed number of units. Observe whether children know to align the units in a straight line without overlaps or gaps.

- Show children objects that have been aligned with Cuisnaire rods, as shown below. Ask, "What is the length of each object?" Do they simply count the "units"? Do they indicate there is a problem with the different length units in the second example?

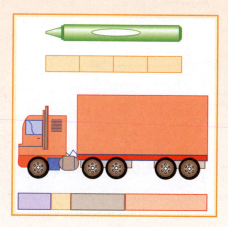

Standards for Mathematical Practice

3 Construct viable arguments and critique the reasoning of others. ▶

- Alternatively, provide a box with assorted units of different sizes, such as Cuisenaire rods. Have children use the materials in the box to measure a given length. Observe whether the child understands that all units must be of similar size. If different lengths of units are used, ask the child to describe his or her measurement.

- Demonstrate to the class how a fictitious child used a ruler to measure the length of an object. Make many errors such as showing gaps, overlaps, and a wavy line of alignment in the placement of the ruler. The children's task is to explain why these measurements may be inaccurate.

- Have children measure two different objects. Then ask how much longer the longer object is. Observe whether children can use the two measurements they have to answer or whether they need to make a third measurement to find the difference.

- Have children measure a length with small paper clips and then again with large paper clips. Can they identify and describe the inverse relationship between the measures they find and the size of the units?

If your assessment indicates that there is some confusion about how length is measured, use the class discussion of these results to help your children self-assess and refine their understanding.

Making and Using Rulers

The jump from measuring with actual units to using standard rulers is challenging. One method to help children understand rulers is to have them make their own rulers.

▲ Activity 15.14   CCSS-M: 1.MD.A.2; 2.MD.A.1; 2.MD.A.3

Make Your Own Ruler

Use two colors of precut narrow strips of construction paper for the units. Each unit should have a length that is at least twice as long as the width so that the notion of length is emphasized. For example, if you use inches as the unit, your narrow strips could be 1 inch long and $\frac{1}{2}$ inch wide (or tall). Or you could use a nonstandard unit of 5 cm long and about $2\frac{1}{2}$ cm wide. Discuss how the units could be used to measure a length by laying them end to end. Provide long strips of card stock at least twice the width of your unit. Have children make their own ruler by gluing the units in alternating colors onto the card stock, as shown at the top of Figure 15.5.

Have children use their new rulers to measure items on a list you provide. Include items that are longer than their rulers. Discuss the results, including how they measured the longer items. There might be discrepancies due to rulers that were not made properly or because a child does not understand how a ruler works.

Also, consider using larger nonstandard units such as multiple tracings of a child's footprint glued onto strips of cash register tape (without gaps or overlaps). These rulers can be used to measure longer lengths or distances.

Challenge children to find more than one way to measure a length with a ruler. Do you have to start at the end? What if you start at another unit in the center? Does that matter? Children can eventually put numbers on their handmade rulers, as shown in Figure 15.5. To begin with, numbers can be written in the center of each unit as a way to precount the units. When numbers are written in the standard way, at the ends of the units, the ruler becomes a number line. This format is more sophisticated and should be carefully discussed with children—in particular, why the numbers are at the end of the unit. (See the discussion in Chapter 9 about meaningfully developing a number line representation with children. Look for opportunities to help children relate the number-line representation to length measurement.)

Be explicit in making the connection between the handmade rulers and standard rulers. Give children a standard ruler and have them identify and discuss how the rulers they have made and standard rulers are alike and how they are different. Ask questions such as "What are the units?" "What do the numbers mean?" "What are the other marks for?" "Where do the units begin?" "Could you make a ruler with the same units as the standard ruler?"

Figure 15.5

Give meaning to numbers on rulers.

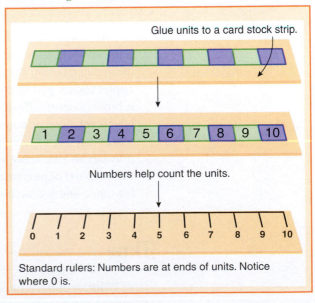

Glue units to a card stock strip.

Numbers help count the units.

| 1 | 2 | 3 | 4 | 5 | 6 | 7 | 8 | 9 | 10 |

Standard rulers: Numbers are at ends of units. Notice where 0 is.

Formative Assessment Note

Research indicates that when children see standard rulers with the numbers on the tick marks, they often incorrectly believe that the numbers are counting the marks rather than indicating the units or spaces between the marks. This is a misconception about rulers that can lead to wrong answers. As a performance assessment, provide children with a ruler, as shown in Figure 15.6, with tick marks but no numbers. Have children use the ruler to measure an item that is shorter than the ruler. Use an **Observation Checklist** (Blackline Master 33) to record whether children count spaces between the tick marks or count the tick marks.

Another good performance assessment of ruler understanding is to have children measure with a "broken" ruler, one with the first two units broken off. Use your **Observation Checklist** to note whether children say that it is impossible to measure with such a ruler because there is no starting point. Also note on your checklist those who match and count the units meaningfully in their measures, indicating understanding.

Observing how children use a ruler to measure an object that is longer than the ruler is also informative. If a child simply reads the last mark on the ruler, this is an indication that he or she does not understand how a ruler is a representation of a continuous row of units.

Figure 15.6

Use an unmarked ruler and ask children to measure an object. In the example shown, the correct length is 8 units. A child counting tick marks would respond with 9 units.

GeoGebra offers a couple of interactive applets in which children are asked to measure given objects using a broken ruler (search for "GeoGebra broken rulers"). The interactive applet allows you to change the ruler from a standard ruler to a standard ruler that is broken along different intervals. There are nine objects children can measure, all of which are close enough in length to approximate to whole units. The rulers on this worksheet are all divided into fourths. Maine's Education Development Center also provides an interactive applet that uses a ruler that is divided into sixteenths to measure various parts of pets (search for "Maine EDC broken rulers"). If children click on the hint button, a line is drawn along the path that should be measured.

Time

Time is different from most other attributes that are commonly measured in school because it cannot be seen or felt. This difference makes it more difficult for children to comprehend units of time and how those units are matched against a given time period or duration.

Comparison Activities

Time can be thought of as the duration of an event from its beginning to its end. As with other attributes, for children to adequately understand the attribute of time, they should make comparisons of events that have different durations. If two events begin at the same time, the shorter duration will end first and the other last longer—for example, which wind-up toy lasts longer? However, this form of comparison focuses on the ending of the duration rather than the duration itself. In order to think of time as something that can be measured, we need to focus on the duration itself. This requires that some form of measurement of time be used.

As children learn about seconds, minutes, and hours, they should develop some concept of how long these measurement units are. Have children time familiar events in their daily lives, such as brushing teeth, eating dinner, riding to school, and doing homework. Point out to children the duration of short and long events during the school day. Timing short events of $\frac{1}{2}$ minute to 2 minutes can be fun and helpful to children as they become familiar with measuring the duration of an activity. Children can work in pairs and use a timer, such as a stopwatch, to time engaging tasks that address duration. Here are some suggestions:

- Stacking 10 blocks one at a time and then removing them one at a time
- Saying your full name
- Walking along a designated path from beginning to end
- Watering a plant
- Reading a page in a book

For other examples, check out *Just a Second* where author Steve Jenkins (2011b) shares some interesting events that occur in just 1 second, 1 minute, and 1 hour. For example, a hummingbird beats its wings 50 times in one second; a hamster's heart beats about 450 times in one minute; and an adult takes about 900 breaths in one hour. As children compare the duration of various events to the units of seconds, minutes, and hours, they become more comfortable with the idea of measuring time.

Reading Clocks

The common instrument for measuring time is the clock. However, learning to tell time has little to do with time measurement and more to do with the skills of learning to read an instrument. Clock reading can be a difficult skill to teach. Starting in first grade, children are usually taught to read clocks to the hour and then to the half hour. In second grade, they learn to read to 5-minute intervals (CCSSO, 2010). In the early stages of this sequence, children are shown clocks set exactly to the hour or half hour. Thus, many children who can read a clock at 7:00 or 2:30 are initially challenged by 6:58 or 2:33.

Digital clocks permit children to read times easily but do not relate times very well to benchmark times. To know that a digital reading of 7:58 is nearly 8:00, the child must know that there are 60 minutes in an hour, that 58 is close to 60, and that 2 minutes is not a very long time. The analog clock shows "close to" times visually without the need for understanding large numbers or even how many minutes are in an hour.

The following suggestions can help children understand and read analog clocks by focusing on the actions and functions of the minute and hour hands.

1. Discuss what happens to the big hand as the little hand goes from one hour to the next. When the big hand is at 12, the hour hand is pointing exactly at a number. If the hour hand

Figure 15.7

Approximate time with one-handed clocks.

"About 7 o'clock"

"A little bit past 9 o'clock"

"Halfway between 2 o'clock and 3 o'clock"

is about halfway between numbers, about where would the minute hand be? If the hour hand is a little past or before an hour (10 to 15 minutes), where would the minute hand be?

2. Move to working with a one-handed clock by removing the minute hand from a regular clock. Use lots of approximate language: "It's about 7 o'clock." "It's a little past 9 o'clock." "It's halfway between 2 o'clock and 3 o'clock" (see Figure 15.7).

3. Use two clocks, one with only an hour hand and one with two hands. Cover the two-handed clock. Periodically during the day, direct attention to the one-handed clock. Have children predict where the minute hand will be. Uncover the other clock and discuss.

4. After step 3 has begun, teach 5-minute intervals by counting by fives going around the clock (grade 2 CCSS-M). Instead of saying that the minute hand is "pointing at the 4," transition to the language "it is about 20 minutes after the hour." As skills develop, suggest that children always look first at the hour hand to learn approximately what time it is and then focus on the minute hand for precision.

5. Predict the reading on a digital clock when shown an analog clock, and set an analog clock when shown a digital clock.

6. Relate the time after the hour to the time before the next hour. This is helpful not only for telling time but also for number sense.

7. Finally, discuss the concept of A.M. and P.M.

The following activity assesses children's ability to read a clock.

◣ Activity 15.15

CCSS-M: 1.MD.B.3; 2.MD.C.7

One-Handed Clocks

 Prepare a page of Clock Faces (Blackline Master 31) by drawing an hour hand on each. Include placements that are approximately half past the hour, a quarter past the hour, a quarter until the hour, and some that are close to but not on the hour. For each clock face, the children's task is to write the digital time and draw the corresponding minute hand on the clock. If you have ELLs, note that telling time is done differently in different cultures. For example, in the Spanish language any time past 30 minutes is stated as the next hour minus the time until that hour. For example, 10:45 is thought of as 15 minutes before 11, or 11 minus a quarter. Be explicit that in English it can be said either way—"10:45" or "a quarter till 11."

technology ⏻
note

The "Time—Analog and Digital Clocks" applet at the National Library of Virtual Manipulatives allows children to change the time on an analog clock and see how it changes on the digital clock and vice versa. The "Time—Match Clocks" applet at the same website displays a time on the analog clock and children match that time on the digital clock. Times are also shown on the digital clock that children match using the analog clock.

After children learn how to read a clock, the following activity not only motivates them to think about telling time, but it also helps them to consider the relationship between analog clock reading and digital recording.

Activity 15.16

CCSS-M: 1.MD.B.3

Ready for the Bell

Give children a recording sheet with a set of **Clock Faces** (Black Line Master 31). Secretly set a timer to go off at the hour, half hour, or minute. When the bell rings, children should look up and record the time on the clock face and in numerals on the recording sheet. Although elapsed time is a third-grade topic in the *Common Core State Standards,* this activity provides opportunities for children to discuss the time between timer rings.

Money

Here is a list of the money ideas and skills typically required in the primary grades:

- Recognizing coins
- Identifying and using the value of coins
- Counting and comparing sets of coins
- Creating equivalent coin collections (same amounts, different coins)
- Selecting coins for a given amount
- Making change
- Solving word problems involving money (starting in second grade, CCSSO, 2010)

The following sections support the learning of these ideas and skills.

Recognizing Coins and Identifying Their Values

The names of our coins are conventions of our social system. Children learn these names the same way that they learn the names of any physical objects in their daily environment—through exposure and repetition.

The value of each coin is also a convention that children must simply be told. For these values to make sense, children must understand 5, 10, and 25 and think of these quantities without seeing countable objects. Where else do we say, "This is five," while pointing to a single item? A child who remains tied to counting objects by ones will be challenged to understand the values of coins. Lessons about coin values should focus on purchase power—a dime can buy *the same thing* that 10 pennies can buy.

Counting Sets of Coins

Naming the total value of a group of coins is the same as mentally adding their values. Second graders can be asked to do the mental mathematics required in counting a collection of different coins. Watch this video of an interview with **Edgar** who is thinking about a story problem involving money. Should the teacher ask other questions that link the amounts to the money, such as, "What is 100 cents also equal to?" in an effort to get the child to use money denominations such as one dollar or four quarters? Why is that flexibility important?

Children may sort their coins by value and start counting from the highest values, just as they often add or subtract the larger place values first. Or they may put coins together to make decade numbers, for example, adding a quarter and a nickel to make 30¢. With pennies aside, coins have the advantage of being in multiples of 5 and 10 and thereby lead to skip counting. The next activity helps prepare children for counting money.

 ## Activity 15.17

CCSS-M: 2.MD.C.8

Money Skip Counting

Explain to children that they will start skip counting by one number, and at your signal they will shift to a count by a different number. Use any two of these numbers: 100, 50, 25, 10, 5, 1. Say, you begin with 25 and 10, and write them on the board. Point to the larger number (25), and have children begin to skip count from that number. (Always start with the larger number.) After three or more counts, raise your hand to indicate a pause in the counting. Then point to the smaller number (10). Children continue the skip count from where they left off but now count by tens. If you have ELLs who are recent immigrants, invite them to share coins from their country and see how they compare to our coins. Children with disabilities may need to use a hundreds chart to help them with their skip counts.

 ## Formative Assessment Note

When a collection of coins is not arranged in descending order of values, children must first sort the collection. This is a skill based only on the ability to compare numbers and recognize the value of the coins. Check to see if children can put a string of numbers such as this in order from greatest to least: 5, 1, 5, 25, 10, 1, 25, 10. For a child experiencing difficulty with this task, try a collection with no duplicates. If there is still difficulty, the child may need more experiences with counting, the hundreds chart, and other concept-development activities for number sense and place value.

If the child can put the numeral string in order but cannot order a set of coins, the problem is most likely that the child has not learned the values of the coins.

Working with coins requires not only adding up the values but also first mentally giving each coin a value. Engage children in working with coins and developing addition concepts by having them add a mixed collection of coins.

Activity 15.18

CCSS-M: 2.MD.C.8

Coin-Number Addition

Show a small collection of coins not arranged in any order. Begin with only dimes and pennies. Then add some nickels and eventually quarters. Give children time to identify the coins and write down the corresponding numeric values of the coins (e.g., 5 for a nickel, 25 for a quarter). Have children share what they have written down to make sure everyone has identified the correct amounts.

Now the children's task is to add the numbers mentally. Do not suggest how they add the numbers or in what order because there is almost always more than one good way to do this. For example, rather than add from the largest values to the smallest—the typical way coins are taught in books—it is also reasonable to use the 5s to make tens or other methods. For this collection, note that it is easy to add 5 and 25, then 10, then 7 (the last 5 and two 1s). Discuss with children how they add each collection.

You can also pose story problems about money using the problem structures for addition and subtraction discussed in Chapter 9. Consider the following examples:

- Alexis has some coins. John gives her 1 dime and 2 pennies. Now Alexis has 36¢. What coins did Alexis have to begin with? (Joining: Start Unknown)
- Jay has 2 quarters and a dime. He needs 95¢ to buy a notebook. How much more money does Jay need? (Part–Part–Whole: Part Unknown)
- Andy has $11.65. He gave Kevin some money. Now Andy has $8.15. How much money did Andy give Kevin? (Separate: Change Unknown)
- Wendy has $2.67. That is $1.25 more than what Keith has. How much money does Keith have? (Comparison: Smaller Unknown)

As discussed in Chapter 9, changing the numbers and the location of the unknown will modify the level of difficulty.

Making Change

When you pay for something at a store using cash, you may give the clerk more money than the purchase price and expect to receive change back. Knowing how to make change is important for the clerk but also for the customers—so they can check to make sure they received the correct change!

Stop and Reflect

Before reading further, think about how you would make change from a hundred dollar bill for a purchase that cost $82.

You may have thought, I can start at 100, go back 10 to 90, then back 8 more to 82—so the change would be 10 + 8 or 18 dollars. You could also start at 100, go back 20 to 80, up 2 to 82, so that's 20 − 2 or 18. Or you may have thought to start at 82, go 8 more to 90 and then 10 more to 100—that's 8 + 10 or 18 dollars.

Making change is the same as finding a difference—specifically, a difference between the amount given to the clerk and the purchase price. We discussed a variety of strategies to find a difference in Chapters 9 and 12. One of those strategies, adding on or "think-addition," was used in the third strategy just described. Because making change is related to strategies based on number sense, children should have experiences with these strategies before they are asked to make change with money.

> 𝒬 **Teaching Tip**
>
> When introducing children to the process of making change, start with smaller values and connect the dime to the ten-frame.

The following activity builds from children's experiences using various strategies to find a difference.

Activity 15.19

CCSS-M: 2.MD.C.8

How Much Is the Change?

Write a target number on the board that is an amount of money that might be given to a store clerk for a purchase, most likely 25, 50, 75, or 100. To the left of this target, write a smaller starting number (the purchase price) and an arrow. Here are some examples:

$$13 \rightarrow 25 \qquad 56 \rightarrow 75 \qquad 29 \rightarrow 50$$

In creating the amounts for this activity, think in terms of purchases. If the target is 75, that means you gave the clerk 75¢. You would only do this for items costing more than 50¢. Similarly, for a target of 50, use numbers greater than 25. For a target of 100, any smaller number would be appropriate because you may have given the clerk a dollar bill.

Embed the numbers in story problems that describe making a purchase. Explain to the children that the first number written represents the amount of the purchase and the second number represents the amount of money given to the store clerk. The children's task is to find the difference (i.e., the change) using a strategy that they can explain. They may need to write down intermediate results. Discuss the solution methods used by different children.

When your children are ready, extend to target values greater than a dollar.

The next activity extends "How Much Is the Change?" and attempts to draw children's attention to the notion of using the fewest possible coins.

Activity 15.20

CCSS-M: 2.MD.C.8

The Fewest Coins

On the board, write start and target numbers as in "How Much Is the Change?" Then write on the board the values of the coins: 25, 10, 5, 1. Children must use only the numbers (i.e., coins) in the list to create the difference. As they use a number, they should write it down. Challenge children to try to use as few "coins" as possible or, in other words, as many of the larger numbers as possible. For example, if the target is 75 with a start of 58, they would write 1, 1, 10, 5. Have children discuss their solutions.

The Coin Box applet found at Illuminations on NCTM's website poses tasks that allow children to count coins, collect a given amount of money, exchange a given collection of coins for the fewest coins, and make change. There are two options to display coins—one that uses only the pictures of coins and another that places the coin onto a grid that indicates its value (e.g., a nickel is displayed on a 1 by 5 grid; a dime is displayed on a 2 by 5 grid). The National Library of Virtual Manipulatives applet called "Money" uses coins and bills. Children can count the money displayed, pay an exact amount, and make a dollar by dragging coins into a box. These applets are good tasks for math centers where children can practice skills related to counting money.

Other Measurable Attributes

Although children in grades preK–2 focus on measuring length, time, and money, they also need to engage in informal explorations with other measureable attributes, such as area, volume, and weight to prepare them for the more formal study of measuring these attributes that begins in third grade (CCSSO, 2010). Here we offer some ideas and activities for initial experiences with area, volume, and weight.

Area

Area is the measure of two-dimensional space inside a region. As with other attributes, children must first understand the attribute of area before measuring. Although there is no explicit mention of area in grades preK–2, children are expected to "Describe several measurable attributes of a single object" (CCSSO, 2010, p. 12) and to partition geometric shapes into equal shares. In addition, data from the 2011 NAEP suggest that fourth-grade students have an incomplete understanding of area, with only 24 percent able to find the area of a square given a perimeter of 12 units—even with a drawing of the square with tick marks around the sides. Instead, 44 percent merely counted the eight tick marks around the edge (National Center for Educational Statistics, 2014). Estimating and measuring area begins in third grade, as students connect to multiplication, and continue in grade 4 with finding the area of rectangles using formulas and real-world problems. Clearly, children in the earlier grades can and should explore the concept of area informally to lay a better foundation for later study.

Comparison Activities

Comparing area measures is more of a conceptual challenge than comparing length measures because areas come in a variety of shapes. Consequently, comparison activities with areas should help children distinguish between size (i.e., area) and shape, length, and other dimensions. A long, skinny rectangle may have less area than a triangle with shorter sides. Also important to understand is the idea that rearranging areas into different shapes does not affect the amount of area (although the perimeter can change). These ideas are especially difficult for young children to understand.

Direct comparison of two areas is frequently impossible except when the shapes involved have some common dimension or property. For example, two rectangles with the same width can be compared directly, as can any two circles. Comparison of these special shapes, however, does not challenge children to think deeply about the attribute of area. Instead, activities in which one area is rearranged (conservation of area) are suggested, like the next activity.

Activity 15.21

CCSS-M: K.MD.A.1; 1.G.A.3; 2.G.A.3

Two-Piece Shapes

Cut out a large number of rectangles with the same area (see **Rectangles of the Same Area** Activity Page) or use unruled 3 inch by 5 inch index cards. Each pair of children will need six rectangles. Have children fold and cut the rectangles on the diagonal, making two identical triangles. Next, have them rearrange the triangles into different shapes, including back into the original rectangle. (Having the original rectangle to compare to the other shapes helps children verify that the area remains the same.) The rule is that only sides of the same length can be matched up and must be matched exactly. Have children work in pairs to find all the shapes that can be made this way, gluing the triangles on paper as a record

(continued)

(see Figure 15.8). Discuss the area and shape of each figure. Ask, "Does one shape have a greater area than the rest? How do you know?" For children who struggle with comparing the areas, ask, "Did one shape take more paper to make?" Help children conclude that although each figure is a different shape, all the figures have the same *area*.

Figure 15.8

Different shapes, same area.

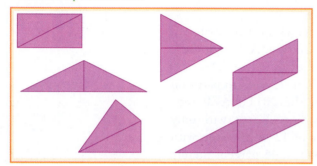

Tangrams, an ancient puzzle, can be used for the same purpose. The standard set of seven **Tangram Pieces** is cut from a square, as shown in Figure 15.9. The two small triangles can be used to make the parallelogram, the square, and the medium triangle. This permits a similar discussion about the pieces having the same area, but different shapes.

Figure 15.9

Tangrams provide an opportunity to investigate area concepts.

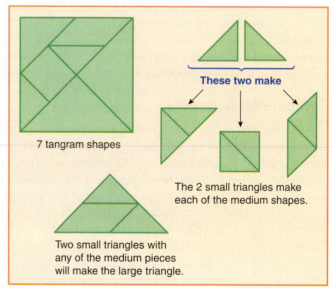

7 tangram shapes

These two make

The 2 small triangles make each of the medium shapes.

Two small triangles with any of the medium pieces will make the large triangle.

Activity 15.22

CCSS-M: K.MD.A.1; 1.G.A.3; 2.G.A.3

Tangram Areas

Give children outlines of several shapes made with **Tangram Pieces**, as in Figure 15.10. Ask groups to estimate which one they think has the largest (or smallest) area. Then let children use tangrams to decide which shapes are the same size, which are larger, and which are smaller. Ask children to justify their conclusions. Use the animal shapes from *Grandfather Tang's Story* (Tompert, 1997) to see if they have the same or different areas.

Figure 15.10

Compare the areas of shapes made of tangram pieces.

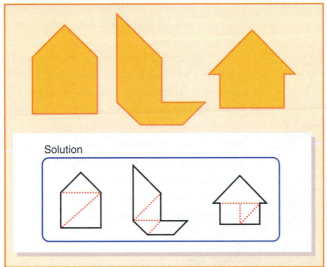

Using Physical Models of Area Units

Children need multiple opportunities to "cover the surface" of two-dimensional shapes to help develop their understanding of the attribute of area. Although squares are the most common area units, any tile that conveniently fills up a plane region can be used initially to explore the concept of area. Here are some suggestions for nonstandard area units:

- *Round counters, chips, or pennies.* It is not necessary that the area units fit with no gaps for early explorations.

- *Playing cards or small cardboard squares.* For relatively smaller areas, these area units work well and fit together with no gaps.

- *Sheets of newspaper or large cardboard squares.* These make excellent units for very large areas.

- *Pattern blocks.* The hexagon, trapezoid, blue rhombus, and triangle are easily compared to each other by laying one on top of the other.

In addition, standard units can be used:

- Color tiles (1-inch sides).
- White Cuisenaire rods or the unit cube from base-ten blocks (1-cm sides).

Figure 15.11

Measuring the area of a large shape with card stock squares.

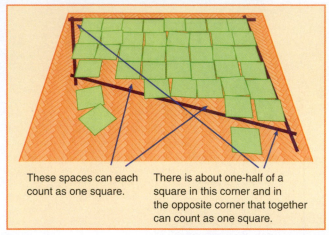

These spaces can each count as one square.

There is about one-half of a square in this corner and in the opposite corner that together can count as one square.

Children can use units to measure surfaces in the room such as desktops, bulletin boards, and books. Large regions can be outlined with masking tape on the floor. Small regions can be duplicated on paper so that children can work at stations.

In area measurements, there may be units that only partially fit. You may wish to begin with shapes in which complete units fit by building a shape with units and then drawing the outline. Once your children have experience covering regions with units and after they have learned to partition geometric shapes into equal shares, consider giving them a shape for which they have to consider partial units, as seen in Figure 15.11.

The following activity is a good way to see what ideas your children have about units of area.

◢ Activity 15.23

CCSS-M: K.MD.A.1; 1.G.A.3; 2.G.A.3

Fill and Compare

Draw two rectangles and a blob shape on a sheet of paper (or use the **Cover and Compare** Activity Page. Make it so that the three areas are not the same but with no area that is clearly largest or smallest. Ask children to estimate which shape has the smallest area and which shape has the largest area of the three shapes. After recording their estimate, they should use multiples of the same unit to fill in the shapes (e.g., color tiles, round counters). Alternatively, they can trace or glue the same two-dimensional unit on the shapes. Children should explain their strategy and justification in writing.

Your objective in the beginning is to develop the idea that area is measured by covering or tiling. Groups will likely find different measures for the same region. Discuss these differences with the children and point to the difficulties involved in making estimates around the edges. Avoid the idea that there is one "right" approach.

Volume and Capacity

Volume and *capacity* are both terms for measures of the "size" of three-dimensional regions. The term *capacity* is generally used to refer to the amount that a container will hold. Standard units of capacity include quarts, gallons, liters, and milliliters—units used for liquids as well as the containers that hold them. The term *volume* can be used to refer to the capacity of a container but is also used for the amount of space occupied by three-dimensional objects. Standard units of volume are expressed in terms of cubic length units, such as cubic inches or cubic centimeters. Although standard units for capacity and volume are beyond the expectations for the preK–2 grades, we list them here to further distinguish between volume and capacity.

Comparison Activities

The apparent volumes of solid objects are sometimes misleading, and a method of comparison is also very difficult, especially for primary grade children. So for the preK–2 grades, it is appropriate to focus on capacity. A simple method for comparing capacity is to fill one container with something and then pour the same amount into the comparison container.

Young children should have lots of experiences directly comparing the capacities of different containers as in the following activity.

Activity 15.24

CCSS-M: K.MD.A.2

Capacity Sort

Provide a variety of containers, with one marked as the "target." Ask children to sort the collection into those that hold more than, less than, or about the same amount as the target container. They are then to use the **Capacity Sort** recording sheet to circle the estimate of "holds more," "holds less," or "holds about the same." Provide a filler (such as beans, rice, or Styrofoam peanuts), scoops, and funnels. Working in pairs, have children measure and record results under "Actual Measure" on their recording sheet. Discuss what children noticed (e.g., that rounder/fatter shapes hold more).

Using Physical Models of Volume and Capacity Units

Two types of units can be used to measure volume and capacity: solid units and containers. Solid units are things like wooden cubes or tennis balls that can be used to fill the container being measured. The other unit model is a small container that is filled with liquid and poured repeatedly into the container being measured. The following examples are of units that you might want to collect.

- Plastic liquid medicine cups
- Plastic jars and containers of almost any size
- Wooden cubes or same-sized blocks of any shape
- Styrofoam packing peanuts (produces conceptual measures of volume despite not packing perfectly)

Remember your goal is to help children develop an understanding of the concept of capacity or volume. Children often think that a tall, narrow container holds more than a short, wide one because it is difficult for them to attend to two dimensions, the height and width. By having them explore capacity using a variety of containers, you can challenge this misconception. Try the following activity yourself as well as with children.

Activity 15.25

CCSS-M: K.MD.A.2

Which Silo Holds More?

Give pairs of children two sheets of equal-sized paper. With one sheet they make a tube shape (cylinder) by taping the two long edges together. They make a shorter, fatter cylinder from the other sheet by taping the short edges together. Then ask, "If these were two silos, would they hold the same amount, or would one hold more than the other?" To test the conjectures, use a filler such as rice or pasta. Place the skinny cylinder inside the fat one. Fill the inside tube and then lift it up, allowing the filler to empty into the fat cylinder.

You can also have children begin to use cups, pints, quarts, and gallon containers to help them begin to get a sense of their sizes. Having them use, for example, a measuring cup to fill a pint container or a pint container to fill a gallon container can help them begin to develop a sense of the relative sizes of customary units of capacity.

Weight and Mass

Weight is a measure of the pull or force of gravity on an object. *Mass* is the amount of matter in an object and a measure of the force needed to accelerate it. On the moon, where gravity is much less than on Earth, an object has a smaller weight than on Earth but the identical mass. For practical purposes, on Earth, the measures of mass and weight will be about the same. In this discussion, the terms *weight* and *mass* will be used interchangeably.

Although units of weight or mass appear in the expectations of the *Common Core State Standards* for third graders, it is good preparation for younger children to explore the attribute of weight using informal units.

Comparison Activities

Starting in kindergarten, children begin to explore the concept of heavier and lighter. The most conceptual way for children to compare the weights of two objects is to hold one in each hand, extend their arms, and experience the relative downward pull on each—effectively communicating to a preK–1 child what "heavier" or "weighs more" means. This personal experience can then be transferred to one of two basic types of scales—balances and spring scales.

When introducing children to a balance, have them estimate which of two objects is heavier by holding one in each hand. When they then place the objects in the two pans of the balance, the pan that goes down can be understood to hold the heavier object. If two objects are placed one at a time in a spring scale, the heavier object pulls the pan down farther. Both balances and spring scales have real value in the classroom. (Technically, spring scales measure weight and balance scales measure mass. Why?) With either scale, sorting and ordering tasks are possible with very young children.

Using Physical Models of Weight or Mass Units

Any collection of uniform objects with the same mass can serve as nonstandard weight units. For very light objects, large paper clips, wooden blocks, or plastic cubes work well. You can also use coins for weight units (e.g., U.S. nickels weigh 5 grams and pennies weigh 2.5 grams). Large metal washers found in hardware stores are effective for weighing slightly heavier objects. You will need to rely on standard weights to weigh things as heavy as a kilogram or more.

To measure the weight of objects you can use either a two-pan balance or a spring scale. With a balance scale, place an object in one pan and weights in the other pan until they balance. (Take the opportunity to make the connection to the equal sign, as discussed in Chapter 13, in which pan balances are used to think about creating equivalent quantities on each side.) With a spring scale, first place the object in the pan and mark the position of the pan on a piece of paper taped behind the pan. Remove the object and place just enough weights in the pan to pull it down to the same level. Discuss how equal weights will pull the spring with the same force.

Common Misconceptions with Measurement

This chapter began by highlighting that measurement is one of the most useful mathematics content strands because it is such a vital component in so many work- and life-related activities. Yet, measurement continues to be an area in which elementary school children in the United States consistently perform lower than the international average (Provasnik, 2012).

Table 15.2 provides a summary of the most common errors and misconceptions children will demonstrate with measurement, along with suggestions about how to help them work through these issues. Purposefully look for and target these common misconceptions that can interfere with your children's understanding of measurement concepts and skills.

Table 15.2. Common errors and misconceptions with measurement and how to help.

Misconception/Error	What It Looks Like	How to Help
1. When measuring an attribute (e.g., length, area, volume), the child places multiple individual units with gaps between the units or with some of the units overlapping; or the child has used unequal units.	Gaps between units and unequal units when measuring length: Overlap of units when measuring area:	• Ask the child to estimate the measure before measuring the object and explain why it is a reasonable estimate. • If the child uses unequal units, ask what the number refers to (e.g., the number of white Cuisenaire rods or brown Cuisenaire rods). • If the child overlaps length units, have the child use linking cubes to measure length. • If the child overlaps area units, have the child use a unit with some thickness that makes it difficult to overlap the pieces (e.g., plastic square tiles or pattern blocks).
2. Child counts the tick marks on a ruler rather than the spaces between the tick marks.	Child responds that the key is 6 inches long.	• Have the child use individual units to measure the object and compare the results. • Have the child place individual units along the ruler to emphasize the spaces are what he needs to count. • Have the child make his own ruler by connecting several individual units (see Activity 15.14).
3. Without attending to where an object is aligned on the left side of a ruler, the child reads the number on the ruler that aligns with the right most edge of the object.	Child responds that the car is 7 inches long.	• Ask the child to estimate the measure before measuring the object and explain why it is a reasonable estimate. • Have the child use individual units to measure the object and compare the results.
4. Child thinks that bigger units will result in a larger measure.	Child measures the length of an object using small paperclips as the unit. When asked to measure the same object using paperclips that are twice the size, the child estimates that the measure will be a larger number. Child measures the area of a rectangle using square tiles. When asked to measure the same rectangle using rectangular tiles that are clearly larger than the square tiles, the child thinks the measure will be a larger number.	• Give the child a lot of experiences measuring the same object's attribute with two different units whose sizes are extremely varied (say, where one of the larger units will cover several of the smaller units). Each time have the child predict how the measures will relate to the size of the units and discuss the results of the actual measures.

(continued)

Table 15.2. Common errors and misconceptions with measurement and how to help. (continued)

Misconception/Error	What It Looks Like	How to Help
5. Child thinks that a shape cut into parts and rearranged does not have the same area as the original shape.	Thinks the first shape has more area than the second shape.	• Have the child use 4 or 5 of the same kind of pattern block to create 3 to 4 different designs. Then have the child use one of the pattern blocks to iterate across each design, keeping count of how many are used in each design. • Have the child use the same set of pattern blocks to create 3 to 4 different designs. Then help the child trace around each design. Have them discuss how they can compare the areas of each. They may need to cut the pieces of one design to fit over another design to verify they have the same areas.
6. Child confuses the minute and hour hands on an analog clock, or reads the number closest to the hour hand whether correct or not.	When shown the time 6:45 on an analog clock, the child states one of the following times: 6:09 9:06 9:30 7:45	• Introduce the analog clock using only the hour hand (see Activity 15.15). • Have the child practice telling time with the Time applets on the National Library of Virtual Manipulatives website. • Ask the child to describe what happens to the hour hand as you move the minute hand on a geared clock. • Pair an analog clock with a digital clock so the child can check the times against each other.
7. Child thinks the size of a coin equates to its value.	The child thinks the dime is worth less than the penny and the nickel because it is smaller in size.	• Glue coins to linking cubes that represent their values or to a ten-frame filled to show the value of each coin. For example, glue a penny to a ten-frame with only one space filled; glue a nickel to a ten-frame with five spaces filled; and glue a dime to a ten-frame with ten spaces filled. • Have the child look closely at real coins, using a magnifying glass to see the details. Have the child write down 3 details about each coin that will help them distinguish between the coins. • Use real coins for counting activities.

16

Developing Geometric Reasoning and Concepts

BIG IDEAS

1 What makes shapes alike and different can be determined by an array of geometric properties (i.e., defining characteristics). Shapes can be classified into a hierarchy of categories according to the properties they share. For example, a square is like a rectangle because it has two pairs of parallel sides and four right angles; some rectangles are different from squares because they do not have four equal sides.

2 Shapes can be described in terms of their location in a plane or in space. Initially children use the words of everyday language such as *above, below, next to, in front of,* and *beside* to describe location and then later transition to simple coordinate systems to describe locations more precisely.

3 Shapes can be moved in a plane or in space without changing the shape's properties. These movements or transformations can be described in terms of translations (slides), reflections (flips), and rotations (turns).

4 Visualization involves being able to think about how two- and three-dimensional shapes look from different viewpoints and to mentally change the position and size of shapes.

Geometry is a "network of concepts, ways of reasoning, and representation systems" used to explore and analyze shape and space (Battista, 2007, p. 843). This critical area of mathematics appears in everything from global positioning systems to computer animation. The National Council of Teachers of Mathematics identifies geometry as the core of mathematics in the early years, alongside the strand of number (NCTM, 2000).

This sentiment is also seen in the *Curriculum Focal Points* (NCTM, 2006) in which geometry is included as one of three focal points in grades preK–1 and as a connection to the focal points in grade 2. The National Research Council (2009) in its publication *Mathematics Learning in Early Childhood* also supports an emphasis on geometry in the early grades. All of these directives are clear that geometry instruction in grades preK–2 should help children learn more about the world they live in and also play a significant role in supporting the development of number concepts.

The *Common Core State Standards* (CCSSO, 2010) and *Curriculum Focal Points* (National Council of Teachers of Mathematics, 2006) describe these expectations across the PreK–2 grades:

- In prekindergarten and kindergarten, children are expected to identify and describe various two- and three-dimensional shapes and describe their relative position using everyday language (e.g., *above*, *below*, *beside*). They should also draw and build shapes as well as compose larger shapes from smaller ones.

- In first grade, children should be able to distinguish between a shape's defining attributes (e.g., number of sides, closed) and irrelevant attributes (e.g., color, size, orientation). They also work on composing shapes to create new shapes and begin to decompose shapes into smaller shapes.

- Second graders are expected to be able to recognize and draw shapes given specific attributes (e.g., number of angles, equal length sides, "square" angles, and so on). They continue to work on decomposing shapes into smaller shapes.

Geometry Goals for Young Children

For too long, geometry curriculum emphasized the learning of terminology. Geometry is much more than vocabulary and naming shapes. First, it involves spatial sense. *Spatial sense* is an intuition about shapes and the relationships between shapes and is considered a core area of mathematical study in the early grades, like number (Sarama & Clements, 2009). Spatial sense includes the ability to mentally visualize objects and spatial relationships, including being able to turn things around in one's mind. It also includes familiarity with geometric descriptions of objects and position. You may have heard the adage that you either are or are not born with spatial sense. However, meaningful experiences with shape and spatial relationships, when provided consistently over time, can and do develop spatial sense (Sowder & Wearne, 2006). People with well-developed spatial sense appreciate geometric form in art, nature, and architecture and they use geometric ideas to describe and analyze their world.

Second, geometry has a number of significant content goals that apply to all grade levels. Let's look at four major geometry strands:

- *Shapes and Properties* includes a study of the properties of shapes in two and three dimensions, as well as a study of the relationships between properties.

- *Transformation* includes a study of translations, reflections, and rotations (slides, flips, and turns), the study of symmetries, and the concept of similarity.

- *Location* includes a study of ways to specify how objects are located in the plane or in space, such as coordinate geometry.

- *Visualization* includes recognizing shapes in the environment, seeing and using relationships between two- and three-dimensional objects, and being able to recognize, draw, and think about objects from different viewpoints.

This chapter is organized around these four strands. In the section for each strand, we begin with foundational experiences and move through more challenging experiences using van Hiele's levels of geometric thought as a guide. You will note that more attention is devoted to the shapes and properties strand to align with the emphasis identified in the *Common Core State Standards* for grades preK–2. However, you should also note that experiences targeted toward each of the strands have potential to enhance children's understanding in the other strands.

Developing Geometric Reasoning

All learners are capable of growing and developing the ability to think and reason in geometric contexts, but this ability requires ongoing and significant experiences across a developmental progression. Recently in mathematics education there has been an emphasis on using learning progressions and trajectories to help children move forward logically when learning different mathematics concepts and skills. Fortunately, in geometry such a progression has been well documented. The research of two Dutch educators, Pierre van Hiele and Dina van Hiele-Geldof, provides insight into the differences in geometric thinking through the descriptions of different levels of thought. The van Hiele theory (1984) significantly influences geometry curricula worldwide and can help all teachers understand developmentally appropriate next steps for their children's geometry instruction.

The van Hiele Levels of Geometric Thought

The van Hiele model is typically described as a five-level hierarchy of understanding spatial ideas (see Figure 16.1). Each level describes the thinking processes used in geometric contexts. Specifically, the levels describe what types of geometric ideas we think about (called *objects of thought*), how we think about those ideas, and what students can do (called *products of thought*). Clements and Battista (1992) proposed the existence of a level prior to the first level in the van Hiele model. We include this level because of its power to help you make sense of some of your young children's geometric reasoning (lower left in Figure 16.1); however, we have left this initial level unnumbered and maintained the original numbering of the van Hiele levels to be consistent with other resources and the other volumes in this series. In this volume, we will focus on Pre-recognition and Levels 0 and 1, as Levels 2, 3 and 4 are beyond the scope of this book.

Figure 16.1

The van Hiele theory of geometric thought, modified to include the prerecognition level.

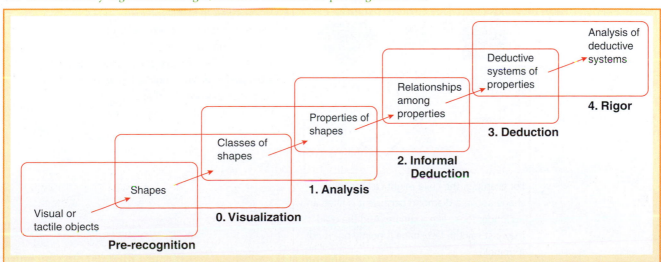

The van Hiele levels are developmental—learners of any age begin at the prerecognition level and progress to the next level through experiences with geometric ideas. Characteristics of the levels are provided in Table 16.1.

Table 16.1. Characteristics of the van Hiele levels.

Characteristic	Implication
1. Sequential	To arrive at any level above prerecognition, children must move through all prior levels. The products of thought at each level are the same as the objects of thought at the next level, as illustrated in Figure 16.1. The objects (ideas) must be created at one level so that relationships between these objects of thought can become the focus of the next level.
2. Developmental	When instruction or language is at a level higher than that of the children, children will be challenged to understand the concept being developed. A child can, for example, memorize a fact (such as all squares are rectangles) but not mentally construct the actual relationship of how the properties of a square and rectangle are related.
3. Age independent	A third grader or a high school student could be at level 0.
4. Experience dependent	Advancement through the levels requires geometric *experiences.* Children should explore, talk about, and interact with content at the next level while increasing experiences at their current level.

Table 16.2 provides a snapshot of the most common errors and misconceptions children will demonstrate with geometric thinking, along with suggestions about how to help them work through these issues. As you read through the chapter, look back at these common misconceptions and consider how particular activities can help mitigate these concerns and help promote your children's understanding of geometric concepts.

Table 16.2. Common errors and misconceptions in geometric reasoning and how to help.

Misconception/Error	What It Looks Like	How to Help
1. Child incorrectly identifies a shape due to nondefining characteristics such as orientation, size, color, and so on.	When a child sees shapes such as the following, he or she is unable to identify the shape or calls it by an incorrect name. For example, the child might call the third shape above a diamond because it is tilted and no longer looks like a square. And the child may just say the last shape is pointy but is not a triangle.	• Expose the child to a wide variety of examples of a given shape and ask the child to look for what they have in common. • Provide the child with quick and meaningful feedback when asked to identify shapes. • Use examples and nonexamples of shapes to focus on the defining attributes. • Carefully select posters, children literature, and examples to avoid using/displaying inaccurate or imprecise examples of shapes.

Table 16.2. Common errors and misconceptions in geometric reasoning and how to help.

Misconception/Error	What It Looks Like	How to Help
2. Child incorrectly identifies a 3-D shape by one of its faces.	Child calls a cube a square or a right rectangular prism a rectangle.	• Have the child build 3-D shapes by first constructing and naming the 2-D faces and then naming the 3-D shape. • Display in the classroom real 3-D shapes (as opposed to pictures) with their names. • Put a 3-D shape into a bag, box, or sock and ask the child to describe what they feel. When the child describes a face, show the 2-D face and ask whether this 2-D shape is what is in the bag. (See Activity 16.10 "Feeling It.")
3. When using a simple coordinate grid, the child incorrectly identifies the space as opposed to the intersection of the grid for location.	When asked to place a block on the location indicated by 3 right and 2 up, the child places the block in the space not on the intersection of the grid. 	• Use 2 pipe cleaners to help the child measure the horizontal and vertical distances. Where the two pipe cleaners overlap shows the child the point of location. • In Activity 16.24 "Hidden Positions," children place objects within the space and not on the grid. "Hidden Positions" is an early introductory activity to help children think about and practice location language (such as *above*, *below*, and so on). When transitioning to a simple grid (see Figure 16.21), emphasize the difference between the two formats. • Use a simple city map laid out on a grid to plan a trip. Point out that the grids represent the streets and the spaces represent buildings. Explain that because we travel along the streets, we will indicate our location along the grid lines.
4. Child is unable to identify an arrangement that looks different as congruent.	When finding all the ways to rearrange 3 right triangles, the child thinks the following designs are different because they look different because of their orientation. 	• Provide lots of experiences using and describing *slides*, *turns*, and *flips,* such as when putting together puzzles, making designs with pattern blocks, and investigating transformations on interactive applets (such as "Shape Tool" on NCTM's Illumination site). • When finding all the ways to rearrange, say, 3 right triangles, provide several copies of the right triangles. When children find one design, have them tape that design together. When they find another design, ask them to turn and flip their existing designs to see if this is a new (and different) design.
5. Child struggles with creating and/or moving mental images.	Child incorrectly describes shapes they cannot see or is unable to predict what a shape looks like after it has been flipped, turned, or slid. For example, the child is unable to predict what the Motion Flag below would look like if it is flipped over the indicated line segment. 	• Engage children in activities where they can check their predictions by manipulating physical or virtual materials. (See for example, Activities 16.20 "Motion Flag," 16.26 "Can You Remember?," and 16.28 "Notches and Holes.") • As children manipulate their materials, ask them to describe their movements. • Have children work on tangram puzzles as well as Mosaic Puzzles (see Activities 16.11 and 16.12).

Prerecognition

The objects of thought at this level are specific visible or tactile objects.

Children at this level are unable to identify and distinguish between many common shapes. They may notice only a subset of the visual characteristics of a shape, which results in an inability to distinguish between some shapes. For example, they may be able to distinguish between a circle and a square but not between a square and a triangle. Most prerecognition level children will know something about circles and squares but they tend to be less accurate identifying triangles and rectangles. Prerecognition children may identify any shape that has a prominent "point" as a triangle and any four-sided shape with long parallel sides as a rectangle (Clements & Sarama, 2000a).

The products of thought at the prerecognition level are shapes and what they "look like."

Standards for Mathematical Practice

> **6 Attend to precision.**

For prerecognition children, Clements and Sarama (2014) recommend activities in which examples and nonexamples that look alike are paired so as to focus attention on a shape's critical attributes. The next activity provides this kind of experience.

Activity 16.1

CCSS-M: K.G.A.2; K.G.B.4; 1.G.A.1

Tricky Shapes

Provide pairs of children with a worksheet that has several examples and nonexamples of a target shape (see Figure 16.2). (You can use these worksheets: **Tricky Shapes for Triangles** and **Tricky Shapes for Rectangles**.) They are to identify the examples and explain why they are like the given shape. They are also to describe why the nonexamples are not like the target shape. Facilitate a discussion with the whole class. Summarize by reviewing the relevant features of the target shape.

Level 0: Visualization

The objects of thought at level 0 are shapes and what they "look like."

Children at level 0 recognize and name figures based on global visual characteristics of the figure—using "vague holistic judgments" (Battista, p. 1, 2012) to justify their identifications. For example, a circle is defined by a level 0 child as a circle "because it looks like a loop" or a shape is a rectangle "because it looks like a door." Because appearance is dominant at this level, appearances can overpower a child's thinking about the properties of a shape. A level 0 thinker, for example, may see a square with sides that are not horizontal or vertical (it appears tilted) and believe it is a "diamond" (not a mathematical term) and no longer a square. Children at this level will sort and classify shapes based on their appearances—"I put these together because they are all pointy" (or "fat," "look like a house," "are dented in," and so on). Children are able to see how shapes are alike and different and as a result, they can create and begin to understand classifications of shapes.

Figure 16.2

"Tricky Shapes" uses examples and nonexamples that look alike to help children attend to critical attributes.

The products of thought at level 0 are classes or groupings of shapes that seem to be "alike."

The emphasis at level 0 is on shapes that children can observe, feel, build (compose), take apart (decompose), or work with in some manner. The general goal is to explore how shapes are alike and different and use these ideas to create classes of shapes (both physically and mentally). Some of these classes of shapes have names—rectangles, triangles, prisms, cylinders, and so on. Properties of shapes, such as parallel sides, symmetry, right angles, and so on, are included at this level but only in an informal, observational manner.

The following activity is a good representation of an experience for level 0 learners as it focuses on how shapes are alike and different.

 ## Activity 16.2

CCSS-M: K.G.B.4; 1.G.A.1; 2.G.A.1

Shape Sorts

Have children work in groups of four with a set of **2-D Shapes** (see Figure 16.3) on the following related activities, to be done in the order shown.

- Each child selects a shape. In turn, the children tell one or two things they find interesting about their shape.

- Children each randomly select two shapes and try to find something that is alike about their two shapes and something that is different.

- The group selects one target shape at random and places it in the center of the workspace. Their task is to find all other shapes that are like the target shape according to the same rule. For example, if they say, "This shape is like the target shape because it has a curved side and a straight side," then all other shapes that they put in the collection must have these properties. Figure 16.4 illustrates a few of the many possible ways a set might be sorted. Challenge children to do a second sort with the same target shape but using a different property.

- Do a "secret sort." You (or one of the children) create a small collection of about five shapes that fit a secret rule. Leave other shapes that belong in your set in the pile. Children try to find additional pieces that belong to the set and/or guess the secret rule.

Most of these activities can and should be done with three-dimensional shapes as well. See the **Expanded Lesson: Shape Sorts** for an enhanced version of this activity.

Figure 16.3

A collection of shapes for sorting.

These find-a-rule activities can elicit a wide variety of ideas as children examine the shapes. They may start describing the shapes with ideas such as "curvy" or "looks like a tree" rather than typical geometric properties. But as children notice more sophisticated properties you can attach appropriate names to them. For example, some children may notice that some shapes have corners "like a square" (explain that those are also called *right angles*) or that "these shapes are the same on both sides" (explain that we call that *symmetry*).

What makes this a level 0 activity is that children are operating on the shapes that they see in front of them and are beginning to see similarities and differences in shapes. By forming groups of shapes, they begin to imagine other shapes that are not present in the collection that belong to the groups they have identified.

Figure 16.4

By sorting shapes, children begin to recognize properties.

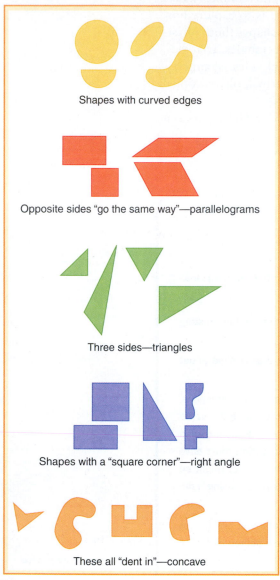

Shapes with curved edges

Opposite sides "go the same way"—parallelograms

Three sides—triangles

Shapes with a "square corner"—right angle

These all "dent in"—concave

Level 1: Analysis

The objects of thought at level 1 are classes of shapes rather than individual shapes.

Children at the analysis level are able to think about and identify shapes "by describing their parts and the spatial relationships between the parts" (Battista, p. 2, 2012). They are able to consider all shapes within a class rather than just the single shape on their desk. Instead of talking about *this* rectangle, they can talk about *all* rectangles. By focusing on a class of shapes, children are able to think about what makes a rectangle a rectangle (four sides, opposite sides parallel, opposite sides of the same length, four right angles, congruent diagonals, etc.). The irrelevant features (such as size or orientation) fade into the background, and children begin to understand that if a shape belongs to a particular class such as cubes, it has the corresponding properties of that class: "All cubes have six congruent faces, and each of those faces is a square." These properties were unspoken at level 0. Children operating at level 1 may be able to list all the properties of squares, rectangles, and parallelograms but may not see that these are subclasses of one another—that all squares are rectangles and all rectangles are parallelograms. In defining a shape, level 1 thinkers are likely to list as many properties of the shapes as they know.

The products of thought at level 1 are the properties of shapes.

Although level 1 children will continue to use physical models and drawings of shapes, they begin to see these individual shapes as representatives of classes of shapes. Their understanding of the properties of shapes, such as symmetry, perpendicular and parallel lines, and so on, continues to be refined. The identification of properties is an important cognitive activity (Yu, Barrett, & Presmeg, 2009).

In the following activity, level 1 children use the properties of shapes such as symmetry, angle classification (right, obtuse, acute), parallel and perpendicular, and the concept of congruent line segments and angles.

◣ ## Activity 16.3

CCSS-M: 2.G.A.1

Property Lists for Quadrilaterals

 Prepare handouts for **Parallelograms**, **Rhombuses**, **Rectangles**, **Squares** (see Figure 16.5). Assign groups of three or four children to work with one type of quadrilateral (for ELLs and children with disabilities, post labeled shapes as a reference). Ask children to list as many properties as they can that apply to all of the shapes on their sheet. They will need tools such as index cards (to check right angles, to compare side lengths, and to draw straight lines), mirrors (to check for symmetry), and tracing paper (for identifying angle congruence). Encourage children to use the words "at least" when describing how many of something; for example, "rectangles have at least two sides that are equal" because squares—included in the rectangles—have four.

Have children prepare their **Property Lists** under these headings: Sides, Angles, Diagonals, and Symmetries. Groups then share their lists with the class, and eventually a class list for each category of shape will be developed. For ELLs, placing emphasis on these words, having children say the words aloud, and having children point to the attribute on a shape as you say the word are ways to reinforce meaning and support their participation in discussions.

This activity may take two or three days. Share lists beginning with parallelograms, then rhombi, then rectangles, and finally squares. Have one group present its list. Then others who worked on the same shape should add to or subtract from it. The class must agree with everything that is put on the list. As new relationships come up in this presentation-and-discussion period, you can introduce proper terminology. For example, if an angle is larger than a right angle, then it is called *obtuse*. Other terms such as *acute, parallel,* and so on can be clarified as you help children write their descriptions.

Standards for Mathematical Practice

◀ **3** **Construct viable arguments and critique the reasoning of others.**

Figure 16.5

Shapes for "Property Lists for Quadrilaterals" activity.

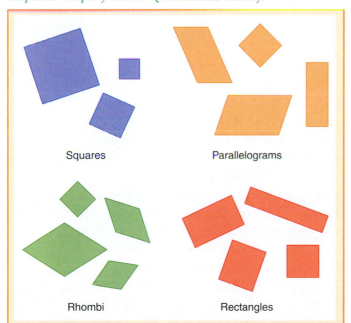

Squares   Parallelograms

Rhombi   Rectangles

Compare the last activity, "Property Lists for Quadrilaterals," with Activity 16.2, "Shape Sorts." In "Shape Sorts," the objects of children's thought are the very shapes that are in front of them. The results of that activity are collections or classifications of shapes. For young children, these classifications will be nonstandard groupings that make sense to the children—fat, tall, pointy, looks like a house, and so on. Soon they will also construct standard groupings that have standard names—squares, triangles, rectangles, prisms, and so on—as you supply the appropriate names as the collections are developed.

In "Property Lists for Quadrilaterals," the children only see a small collection of shapes at the top of their paper. However, the object of their thinking is the entire class of shapes for which these few are representative. In other words, children must assess whether the properties apply to all shapes in the category. In "Property Lists for Quadrilaterals" the object of thinking is the very type of thing (a class of shapes) that was the product of thinking in "Shape Sorts" at level 0.

Formative Assessment Note

How do you discover the van Hiele level of each child? Once you know, how will you select the right activities to match your children's levels? As you conduct an activity, listen to the types of observations that children make and record them on an **Observation Checklist**. Can they identify common shapes? Do they understand that shapes do not change when the orientation or size changes? Do they use properties in their descriptions and discussions of shapes? Can your children talk about shapes as classes? Do they refer, for example, to "rectangles" or do they base their discussion on a particular rectangle? Do they generalize that certain properties are attributable to a type of shape or simply the shape at hand? With careful observations such as these, you will soon be able to distinguish between the various levels.

Implications for Instruction

All teachers should be aware that the collection of geometric experiences they provide are the single most important factor in moving children up this developmental ladder to higher levels of geometric thought. The van Hiele theory and the developmental perspective of this book highlight the necessity of teaching at the child's level of thought. However, almost any activity can be modified to span two levels of thinking, helping children move from one level to the next.

As you choose activities for your children, keep in mind four features of effective geometry instruction for young children (Clements & Sarama, 2014):

- *Show and compare a variety of examples and nonexamples.* Have children compare examples and nonexamples that look alike using some nondefining feature to help children attend to a shape's relevant attributes.

- *Facilitate discussions about the properties of shapes.* When you encourage children to describe shapes, expect them to initially use visual descriptions (e.g., long, pointy, etc.) but then focus their attention on the relevant attributes (e.g., number of sides, sides of equal length) and help them develop essential language along the way.

- *Examine an array of shape classes that goes beyond the traditional.* Children in early childhood classrooms should experiment with and describe shapes beyond the typical circle, square, triangle, and rectangle. Their experiences should extend to semicircles, trapezoids, pentagons, hexagons, cubes, prisms, cones, and cylinders as well as different kinds of triangles and quadrilaterals and should include different orientations and sizes.

- *Challenge children with a wide range of geometric tasks at every level.* The use of physical materials, drawings, and computer models at every level of geometric thought is a must. Activities should also require and support children's reflection about the ideas they are learning.

Standards for Mathematical Practice

6 Attend to precision. ▶

Watch (https://www.youtube.com/watch?v=-v2D75Va_3Y) Douglas Clements talk about the issues with imprecision with many geometry activities found in the early grades and his recommendations for alternative activities.

Moving from Prerecognition to Level 0

Instructional considerations that support children transitioning from the prerecognition level to level 0 are as follows:

- *Provide opportunities for children to identify shapes in their classroom, school, and community.* However, be careful about using imprecise examples, as Doug Clements describes in the previous video.

- *Involve children in lots of experiences sorting shapes and describing why they believe a particular shape belongs to a group as well as why a particular shape does not belong.* Include a sufficient variety of examples of shapes so that irrelevant features (e.g., orientation, size, color) do not become important.

- *Engage children in ample opportunities to copy and build shapes using a wide variety of materials.* These activities should help children focus on the relevant and irrelevant attributes of shapes.

Moving from Level 0 to Level 1

Instructional considerations that support children moving from level 0 to level 1 are as follows:

- *Focus on the properties of figures rather than simple identification.* As new geometric concepts are learned, children should be challenged to use these attributes to classify shapes.

- *Challenge children to test ideas about shapes using a variety of examples from a particular category.* Say to them, "Let's see if that is true for other rectangles," or "Can you draw a triangle that does not have a right angle?" In general, question children to see whether observations made about a particular shape apply to other shapes of a similar kind.

- *Provide ample opportunities for children to draw, build, make, put together (compose), and take apart (decompose) shapes in both two and three dimensions.* These activities should be built around understanding and using specific characteristics or properties.

- *Apply ideas to entire classes of figures* (such as *all* rectangles, *all* prisms) *rather than to individual models.* For example, find ways to sort all possible triangles into groups. From these groups, define types of triangles.

The remainder of this chapter offers a sampling of activities organized around the four content strands found in the NCTM *Principles and Standards for School Mathematics*: Shapes and Properties, Transformations, Location, and Visualization. Understand that all of these subdivisions are quite fluid: the content areas overlap and build on each other. Activities found in one section may help develop geometric thinking in another content strand.

Shapes and Properties

This is the content area most often associated with geometry in preK through grade 8 classrooms. The early grades are the time when young children begin to "perceive, say, describe/discuss and construct objects in 2-D space" (National Research Council Committee, 2009, p. 177) but children need experience with a wide variety of both two- and three-dimensional shapes (Clements & Sarama, 2014). Triangles should be shown in more than just equilateral forms and not always with the vertex at the top. (If children say a triangle is upside down, it may be because they have rarely seen triangles illustrated differently.) Shapes should have curved sides, straight sides, and combinations of these. As children describe the shape or property, the terminology can be introduced.

The next activity can be modified to accommodate children at the prerecognition level, level 0, and level 1 by altering the object of the search. Here we focus on children at the prerecognition level.

Activity 16.4

CCSS-M: K.G.A.1; K.G.A.2; K.G.B. 4

Shape Show and Hunt

Use masking tape to create a large target shape that children can walk around on the community rug or floor. Ask children if they can name the shape or any attributes (such as straight or curved sides, number of sides, right angles, and so on). Make sure children, especially ELLs, understand the terms you use such as *square corners* and *right turns*. You can compare a square corner (right angle) to a capital "L" or the corner of a sheet of paper or an index card. You can also have the children draw the shape in the air or on paper. Then ask the children to find one or two items in the classroom, on the playground, or somewhere else at school that have this same shape or attribute. Take photos of the examples that children find so that they can be used later in the discussion. As children find their examples, ask them how they know it is like the target shape. Listen for how they describe their example. What are they focusing on? What words are they using? For children with disabilities, provide a cutout of the target shape that they can take with them as they search for an example.

In "Shape Show and Hunt," have children search for various shapes as well as properties of shapes. A shape hunt will be much more successful if you let children look for either one thing or for a specific list. Some examples that children can search for are: right angles ("square corners"); curved surfaces or curved lines; two or more shapes that can be put together to make another shape; circles inside each other (concentric); shapes with "dents" (concave) or without "dents" (convex); and solids that are like a box (prism), a cylinder, a pyramid, or a cone. *Cubes, Cones, Cylinders, and Spheres* (Hoban, 2000) shows photographs of three-dimensional shapes from everyday life that you can share with children.

The next activity gives children experience with a wide variety of two-dimensional shapes.

Activity 16.5

CCSS-M: K.G.A.2; K.G.B.4

Match It–Name It

Standards for Mathematical Practice

7 Look for and make use of structure.

Create a variety of familiar shapes from the assorted **2-D Shapes** Activity Page using card stock. Create multiples of the same shapes. Give each child different shapes from the set. Select a shape that matches one of the children's shapes. Ask the children to stand up if they think they have a shape that matches your shape. Have children (either those standing or others) explain how they know the shapes match and to name the shape if they can. Then have children try to find matches for their shapes with children sitting near them. Have children share their matches and encourage them to try to name the shapes.

Color Farm (Ehlert, 1990) and *Color Zoo* (Ehlert, 1989) are two visually motivating children's books you can use to engage children in thinking about shapes. Using cutout overlays of circles, rectangles, triangles, and other familiar shapes, images of either farm or zoo animals are created. The reader turns the page to remove a shape, transforming the image into a new animal. Because these books reinforce shapes, animals, and colors, they are great books for young learners, especially ELLs.

Young children also need experiences with three-dimensional shapes, as in the next activity which is adapted from Clements and Sarama (2000b).

Activity 16.6

CCSS-M: K.G.A.1; K.G.B.4; 1.G.A.2

Getting into Shape

After identifying and talking about the relevant attributes of a three-dimensional shape, have the children pretend they are inside of it. For example, after showing the children an oatmeal box (cylinder), tell them to pretend they are inside of the oatmeal box. Tell them to close their eyes and pretend to touch the walls of the cylinder. Ask them to describe the walls. Then have them pretend to trace the top of the cylinder and then the bottom of the cylinder with their finger. Ask, "What is the shape you traced?" (You can also have children draw the shape on paper.) The activity can be repeated with other 3-D shapes, such as a prism, where they feel and try to identify each face. Try to find large boxes or tubes for your children to get in so they can actually feel the inside and outside of the shapes.

The next activity helps to draw children's attention to the properties of shapes as children consider examples and nonexamples of shapes.

Activity 16.7

CCSS-M: K.G.A.1; K.G.A.2; K.G.B.4; 1.G.A.1; 2.G.A.1

Is It or Isn't It?

Draw an example of a two-dimensional shape on the board or projection unit. Ask children to name the shape and tell how they know. Draw another shape that is somehow different from the first shape—it could be another example of the shape or a nonexample that looks like the target shape and that children could mistake for the shape. For example, if the target shape is a triangle, display triangles that are "skinny" or oriented with the vertex pointing down. Or display a three-sided shape whose sides are not straight. You can also provide counterexamples such as a "triangle" musical instrument that has an open side. Have children identify and discuss the differences and whether those differences make the figure a nonexample. Summarize by highlighting the relevant features of the target shape.

The following activity requires children to think about the properties of target shapes so that they can then build them.

Activity 16.8

CCSS-M: K.G.B.5; 1.G.A.1; 2.G.A.1

Build It

Provide children with drawings of four or five varied examples of a target shape and plastic (flat) coffee stirrers cut to various lengths or a manipulative such as D-Stix. (D-Stix kits contain six to nine sticks of different lengths that can be used to make two- and three-dimensional shapes.) Children make the shapes by placing the stirrers on the drawings with the stirrers "connected" or touching at their endpoints. Have children name the shape and talk about the attributes. Challenge children to create examples of a target shape without having access to a drawing as a model.

Teaching Tip

Along the way, the names of any new shapes and their properties can be introduced and placed on the math word wall.

Clements and Sarama (2000a) describe how a kindergarten teacher challenged her children to create shapes with their bodies. Two children in the class created a rhombus by sitting on the floor facing each other with their legs spread and feet together. One child in the classroom suggested that if another child lay across their feet, they would have two triangles. See how creative your children can be!

Sorting and Classifying

As young children work at classification of shapes, be prepared for them to notice features that you do not consider to be "real" geometric attributes, such as "dented" or "looks like a rocket." Children at this level will also attribute to shapes ideas that are not part of the shape, such as "points up" or "has a side that is the same as the edge of the board."

For variety in two-dimensional shapes, use materials like a set of **2-D Assorted Shapes**. Make multiple copies so that groups of children can all work with the same shapes. Once you have your sets constructed, try Activity 16.2 "Shape Sorts." The secret sort in Activity 16.2 is one option for introducing a new property. For example, sort the shapes so that all have at least one right angle or "square corner." When children discover your rule, you have an opportunity to talk more about that property and name the property "right angle."

The following activity also uses the set of two-dimensional shapes to help children focus on properties of shapes.

 ## Activity 16.9

CCSS-M: 1.G.A.1; 2.G.A.1

What's My Shape?

 Cut out a double set of **2-D Assorted Shapes** on card stock. Glue each shape from one set inside a file folder to make "secret-shape" folders. The other set of shapes should be glued on cards and placed on the table for reference.

Designated one child in each group as the leader; he or she holds the secret-shape folder. The other children are to find the shape that matches the shape in the folder by asking only "yes" or "no" questions. The group can eliminate shapes (by turning over the cards) as they get answers about the properties that narrow down the possibilities. They are not allowed to point to a piece and ask, "Is it this one?" Rather, they must continue to ask questions about properties or characteristics that reduce the choices to one shape. The final shape card is checked against the one in the leader's folder. Provide a list of properties and characteristics (such as number of sides) to support the question asking of children with disabilities.

The difficulty of Activity 16.9 largely depends on the shape in the folder. The more shapes in the collection that share properties with the secret shape, the more difficult the task.

This activity can be adapted for three-dimensional shapes by using two sets of three-dimensional models. The leader can place the secret shape under a cloth or in a shoebox. Collections of 3-D shapes are available commercially, or you can collect real objects such as cans, boxes, balls, and Styrofoam shapes. Figure 16.6 illustrates some classifications of solids.

Figure 16.6

Early classifications of three-dimensional shapes.

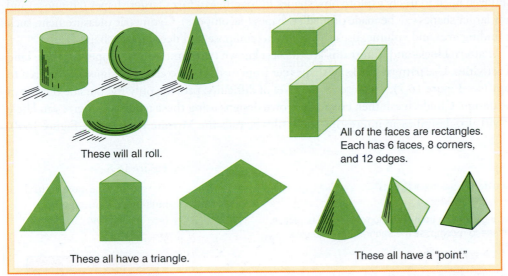

These will all roll.

All of the faces are rectangles. Each has 6 faces, 8 corners, and 12 edges.

These all have a triangle.

These all have a "point."

Formative Assessment Note

Using three-dimensional shapes, adapt Activity 16.2 "Shape Sorts" for a diagnostic interview. Make sure you have a collection of solids that has sufficient variation (curved surfaces, etc.).

The ways children describe these three-dimensional shapes provides good evidence of their level of thinking. The classifications made by level 0 thinkers are generally restricted to the shapes they have in front of them. Level 1 thinkers will begin to create categories based on properties, and their language will indicate that they know there are many more shapes in the group than those that are present. Children may say things such as, "These shapes have square corners sort of like rectangles," or "These look like boxes. All the boxes have square (rectangular) sides."

The next activity draws children's attention away from appearance to relevant properties by hiding the shapes from view.

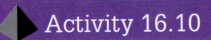

Activity 16.10

CCSS-M: K.G.B.4; 1.G.A.1; 2.G.A.1

Feeling It

You will need two sets of shapes, one that you will display and one that you will use to select a secret shape from. On one day, focus on two-dimensional shapes. On another day, use three-dimensional shapes. Give children time to explore the displayed shapes, asking them to run their fingers along the sides and around the corners (faces and edges for 3-D shapes). Secretly select one of the shapes from your set and place it in a box or a bag. Use a box with holes cut into the sides or a bag that has elastic around the top—or you could use a long sock. The idea is for children to be able to get their hands into the box, bag, or sock without being able to peek! Have the children try to guess what shape it is by feeling it. You can have one child feel the shape and describe its properties to others so that they can decide which of the displayed shapes it matches.

Composing and Decomposing Shapes

Children need to freely explore how shapes fit together to form larger shapes (compose) and how larger shapes can be made of smaller shapes (decompose). Geometric measurement, such as finding area and volume, uses this ability to compose and decompose shapes.

Pattern blocks and **Tangrams** are the best known two-dimensional shapes for these kind of activities. Use pattern blocks or shapes cut from card stock to create designs for children to copy (see Figure 16.7). To increase the level of difficulty, provide only the outside outline of the design. Children can then create their own designs using these materials. Pierre van Hiele (1999) also describes an interesting set of tiles he calls the **Mosaic Puzzle** (see Figure 16.8).

Figure 16.7

Assorted materials for composing and decomposing activities.

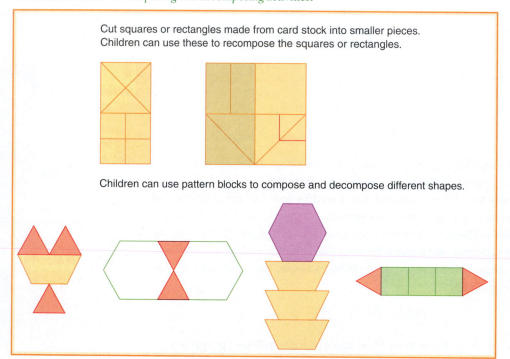

Cut squares or rectangles made from card stock into smaller pieces. Children can use these to recompose the squares or rectangles.

Children can use pattern blocks to compose and decompose different shapes.

Figure 16.8

The seven-piece mosaic puzzle is built on an isometric grid (van Hiele, 1999).

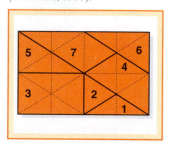

Standards for Mathematical Practice

> **1** Make sense of problem and persevere in solving them.

Activity 16.11

CCSS-M: K.G.B.6; 1.G.A.2; 2.G.A.1

Tangram Puzzles

Using a set of **Tangram Pieces**, have children explore the **Tangram Puzzles** Activity Page where they compose shapes to create a larger figure. Figure 16.9 shows tangram puzzles in increasing order of difficulty.

Activity 16.12

CCSS-M: K.G.B.6; 1.G.A.2; 2.G.A.1

Mosaic Puzzle

Give pairs of children a copy of the **Mosaic Puzzle** and have them use the **Mosaic Puzzle Questions** Activity Page to explore using what they know about a shape's properties to compose and decompose other shapes.

Figure 16.9
Four types of tangram puzzles illustrate a range of difficulty levels.

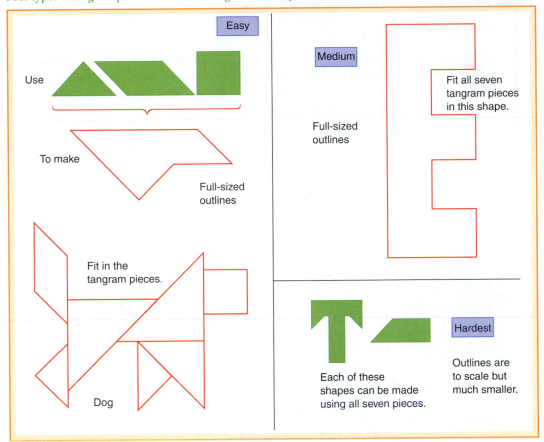

The value of the mosaic puzzle is that the set contains five different angles (which could lead to discussions about informal angle comparisons and groupings of angle measures such as right, acute, and obtuse).

🌿 Teaching Tip

Many pattern block designs and artwork created by children will have an element of symmetry in them. Although symmetry is not a core idea in the *Common Core State Standards* for grades K–2, you can use children's creations to introduce this idea informally.

"Patch Tool" at NCTM's Illuminations site is an interactive environment where children can compose shapes using different pattern blocks. It also provides five outlines of different designs where children have to decide which shapes are used to complete the designs. Also, the National Library of Virtual Manipulatives has a tangram applet with a set of fourteen puzzle figures that can be made using all seven of the pieces. The e-version of tangrams has the benefit of requiring the child to be much more deliberate in arranging the shapes because they have to anticipate how they will transform (e.g., flip, rotate) a given shape to make it fit.

The geoboard is one of the best devices for "constructing" two-dimensional shapes. Here are just a few of the many possible activities appropriate for thinking about composing and decomposing shapes using a geoboard.

Activity 16.13

CCSS-M: 1.G.A.2; 2.G.A.1

Geoboard Copy

Prepare **Geoboard Design Cards** (see Figure 16.10). Project the shapes onto a screen and have children copy them on geoboards (or **Geoboard Pattern (5 × 5)**, **Geoboard Pattern (10 × 10)**, and **Geoboard Recording Sheets**). Begin with designs using one band; then create more complex designs, including those that show a shape composed of smaller shapes. Discuss properties such as number of sides, parallel lines, or symmetry, depending on the grade level and readiness of your children. Children with disabilities may need to have a copy of the design card at their desk for closer reference.

Figure 16.10

Shapes on geoboards.

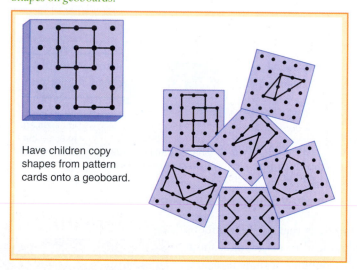

Have children copy shapes from pattern cards onto a geoboard.

🌿 *Teaching Tip*

Have lots of geoboards available in the classroom. It is better for two or three children to have 10 or 12 boards at a station than for each to have only one. That way, a variety of shapes can be made and compared before they are changed.

Teach children from the very beginning how to record their designs on geoboard recording sheets. To help children who struggle with this transfer, suggest that they first mark the dots for the corners of their shape ("second row, end peg"). With the corners identified, it is much easier for them to draw lines between the corners to make the shape. These drawings can be placed in groups for classification and discussion or sent home to families to showcase what children are learning.

The NCTM's Illuminations website offers interactive geoboard activities entitled "Making Triangles" and "Creating Polygons." Children can select and delete bands and select and delete vertices as they create triangles and other polygons.

 **Activity16.14**

CCSS-M: 1.G.A.2; 1.G.A.3;
2.G.A.1; 2.G.A.3

Decomposing on a Geoboard

Show children a shape from the **Decomposing Shapes** Activity Pages and ask them to copy it on their geoboards or **Geoboard Recording Sheets**. Then specify the number of smaller shapes they should decompose each large shape into, as in Figure 16.11. Also specify whether the smaller shapes are all to be congruent or simply of the same type. Alternatively, children can start with a smaller shape and duplicate the shape to create a larger shape (composing shapes).

Figure 16.11

Decomposing and composing shapes. Add special decompose conditions to make the activity challenging.

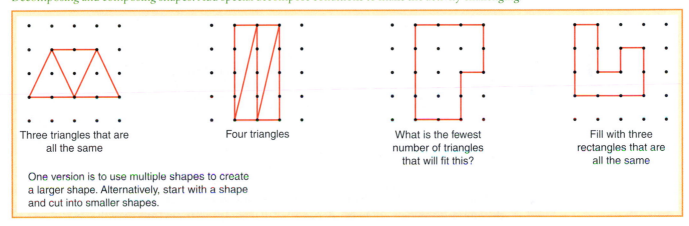

Three triangles that are all the same

Four triangles

What is the fewest number of triangles that will fit this?

Fill with three rectangles that are all the same

One version is to use multiple shapes to create a larger shape. Alternatively, start with a shape and cut into smaller shapes.

 **Teaching Tip**

On geoboard tasks, allow children to choose the tool (geoboard, grid paper, or dot paper) that best supports their thinking with a given problem.

The following activity provides children additional opportunities to decompose two-dimensional shapes.

 **Activity 16.15**

CCSS-M: 2.G.A.1

Two Shapes from One

 Provide children with a variety of cut-out shapes or use the **Two Shapes From One** Activity Page. Their task is to connect any two sides of the shape with a straight line, forming two shapes, and then they are to identify each shape using properties, such as the number of sides (see Figure 16.12). Challenge children to determine whether they can create two shapes with the same number of sides, more sides, or fewer sides than the original shape. Children with disabilities may find it challenging to see that the new shapes share one side and may miscount the number of sides of each. Allow them to cut out the new shapes if this is an issue.

Figure 16.12

Start with a shape and then draw a segment to divide the shape into two shapes.

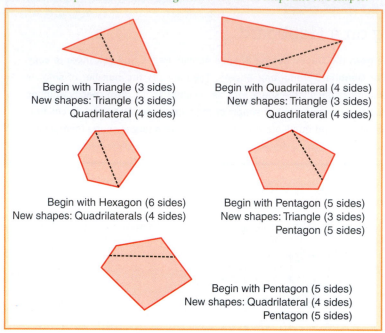

Begin with Triangle (3 sides)
New shapes: Triangle (3 sides)
Quadrilateral (4 sides)

Begin with Quadrilateral (4 sides)
New shapes: Triangle (3 sides)
Quadrilateral (4 sides)

Begin with Hexagon (6 sides)
New shapes: Quadrilaterals (4 sides)

Begin with Pentagon (5 sides)
New shapes: Triangle (3 sides)
Pentagon (5 sides)

Begin with Pentagon (5 sides)
New shapes: Quadrilateral (4 sides)
Pentagon (5 sides)

technology *note*

"Shape Cutter" at NCTM's Illuminations site is an applet where children can create and decompose a wide variety of shapes and then compose them into new shapes.

Categories of Two- and Three-Dimensional Shapes

As children's attention shifts to properties of shapes (moving to level 1 thinking), you will hear them use properties in their reasoning and discussions. Notice that the definitions of two- and three-dimensional shapes support the exploration of the relationships between shapes.

Two-Dimensional Shapes

Table 16.3 lists some important categories of two-dimensional shapes. Examples of these shapes can be found in Figure 16.13.

Table 16.3. Categories of two-dimensional shapes.

Shape	Description
Simple Closed Curves: Shapes that are closed by a curved line or by line-segments.	
Concave, convex	An intuitive definition of *concave* might be "having a dent in it." If a simple closed curve is not concave, it is *convex*.
Symmetrical, nonsymmetrical	Shapes that can be separated into two parts that are mirror images of each other are called *symmetrical*. Shapes may have one or more lines of symmetry. If a shape is not symmetrical, it is *nonsymmetrical*.
Regular	All sides and all angles are congruent.
Polygons	Simple closed curves with all straight sides.

Table 16.3.   Categories of two-dimensional shapes.

Shape	Description
Triangles: Polygons with exactly three sides.	
Classified by sides	
Equilateral	All sides are congruent.
Isosceles	At least two sides are congruent.
Scalene	No two sides are congruent.
Classified by angles	
Right	One angle is a right angle.
Acute	All angles are smaller than a right angle.
Obtuse	One angle is larger than a right angle.
Convex Quadrilaterals: Convex polygons with exactly four sides.	
Kite	Two opposing pairs of congruent adjacent sides.
Trapezoid*	At least one pair of parallel sides.
Isosceles trapezoid	A pair of opposite sides is congruent.
Parallelogram	Two pairs of parallel sides.
Rectangle	Parallelogram with a right angle.
Rhombus	Parallelogram with all sides congruent.
Square	Parallelogram with a right angle and all sides congruent.

*Some definitions of trapezoid specify *only one* pair of parallel sides, in which case parallelograms would not be trapezoids. The University of Chicago School Mathematics Project (UCSMP) uses the "at least one pair" definition, meaning that parallelograms and rectangles are trapezoids. Some regions mandate one definition over another, so consult your local curriculum (Manizade & Mason, 2014).

Figure 16.13

Classification of two-dimensional shapes.

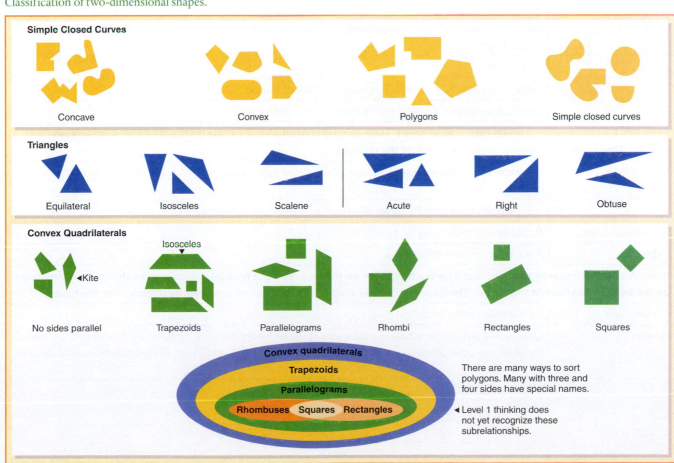

In the classification of quadrilaterals and parallelograms, some subsets overlap. For example, a square is a rectangle and a rhombus. All parallelograms are trapezoids, but not all trapezoids are parallelograms. Children often have difficulty seeing this type of subcategory. They may correctly list all the properties of a square, a rhombus, and a rectangle and still might identify a square as a "nonrhombus" or a "nonrectangle." To help children think about this relationship, suggest that a child can be on two different sports teams or belong to two different clubs. A square is an example of a quadrilateral that belongs to two other "clubs."

Three-Dimensional Shapes.

Important and interesting shapes and relationships also exist in three dimensions. Table 16.4 describes classifications of solids. Figure 16.14 shows examples of cylinders and prisms. Note that prisms are defined here as a special category of cylinder—a cylinder with a polygon for a base (Zwillinger, 2011). Figure 16.15 shows a comparable grouping of cones and pyramids.

Table 16.4. Categories of three-dimensional shapes.

Shape	Description
Sorted by Edges and Vertices	
Sphere and "egglike" shapes	Shapes with *no edges* and no *vertices* (corners). Shapes with *edges* but no *vertices* (e.g., a flying saucer). Shapes with *vertices* but no *edges* (e.g., a football).
Sorted by Faces and Surfaces	
Polyhedron	Shapes made of all faces (a face is a flat surface of a solid). If all surfaces are faces, all the edges will be straight lines.
	Some combination of faces and rounded surfaces (circular cylinders are examples, but this is not a definition of a cylinder).
	Shapes with curved surfaces.
	Shapes with and without edges and with and without vertices.
	Faces can be parallel. Parallel faces lie in places that never intersect.
Cylinder: Two congruent, parallel faces called bases. Lines joining corresponding points on the two bases are always parallel. These parallel lines are called *elements* of the cylinder.	
Right cylinder	A cylinder with elements perpendicular to the bases. A cylinder that is not a right cylinder is an oblique cylinder.
Prism	A cylinder with polygons for bases. All prisms are special cases of cylinders.
Rectangular prism	A cylinder with rectangles for bases.
Cube	A square prism with square sides.
Cone: A solid with exactly one face and a vertex that is not on the face. Straight lines (elements) can be drawn from any point on the edge of the base to the vertex. The base may be any shape at all. The vertex need not be directly over the base.	
Circular cone	Cone with a circular base.
Pyramid	Cone with a polygon for a base. All faces joining the vertex are triangles. Pyramids are named by the shape of the base: *triangular* pyramid, *square* pyramid, *octagonal* pyramid, and so on. All pyramids are special cases of cones.

Figure 16.14

Cylinders and prisms.

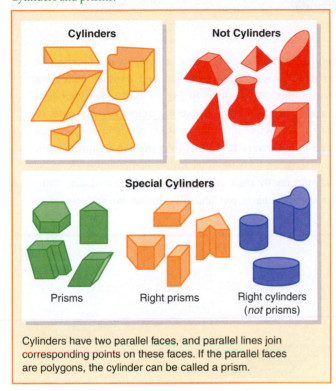

Cylinders have two parallel faces, and parallel lines join corresponding points on these faces. If the parallel faces are polygons, the cylinder can be called a prism.

Figure 16.15

Cones and pyramids.

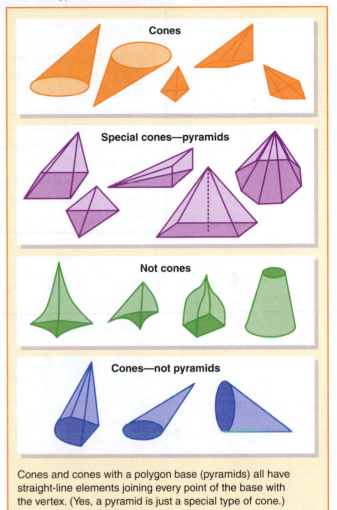

Cones and cones with a polygon base (pyramids) all have straight-line elements joining every point of the base with the vertex. (Yes, a pyramid is just a special type of cone.)

Some textbooks limit the definition of cylinders to just circular cylinders. These books do not have special names for other cylinders. Under that definition, the prism is not a special case of a cylinder. This points to the fact that definitions are conventions, and not all conventions are universally agreed upon.

At NCTM's Illuminations Activity called "Geometric Solids" children can explore a variety of geometric solids by rotating the solids and coloring and counting faces, edges, and vertices.

Applying Definitions and Categories.

Using these definitions and categories helps children focus more closely on the properties that make the shape what it is (not just that it looks like the others in the group). The next activity focuses children's attention on properties and provides a good way to introduce a category of shapes.

Activity 16.16

Mystery Definition

Standards for Mathematical Practice

6 Attend to precision.

Give children the **Mystery Definition** Activity Page, or project a collection of shapes that have one or more properties in common and another collection of shapes that do not have this commonality, such as in Figure 16.16. For your first collection be certain that you have allowed for all possible variables. For example, in Figure 16.16, a square is included in the set of rhombuses. Also, choose nonexamples to be as close to the examples as is necessary to help with a precise definition. The third or mixed set should also include those nonexamples with which children are most likely to be confused. Children should justify their choices in a class discussion. Note that the use of examples and nonexamples is particularly helpful for children with disabilities.

Figure 16.16

A mystery definition.

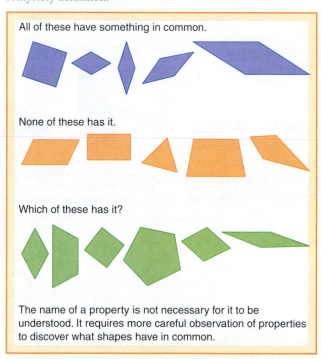

All of these have something in common.

None of these has it.

Which of these has it?

The name of a property is not necessary for it to be understood. It requires more careful observation of properties to discover what shapes have in common.

The value of the "Mystery Definition" activity is that children develop ideas and definitions based on their own concept development. After their definitions have been discussed, compared, and refined as needed, you can offer the conventional definition for the sake of clarity.

The next activity introduces children to the idea that there are different categories of triangles. It is not necessary that children in grades preK–2 know the different names (e.g., equilateral, isosceles, scalene), only that some shapes can be further categorized based on their properties.

Activity 16.17

CCSS-M: 2.G.A.1

Triangle Sort

Give teams of three to four children the **Assorted Triangles** Activity Pages which includes examples of right, acute, and obtuse triangles; examples of equilateral, isosceles, and scalene triangles; and triangles that represent every possible combination of these categories. Ask the teams to sort the entire collection of triangles into two or three groups so that no triangle belongs to two groups. Have them describe and discuss their groupings. If no group compared the length of sides or the size of the angles (i.e., congruent versus noncongruent) to form their groups, ask them to sort the entire collection by comparing the length of the sides (size of angles) within each triangle—delay giving these hints if you can. Again, no triangle should belong to two groups. When they complete this sort, have them describe and discuss their groupings. Provide appropriate terminology as ideas arise. For example, you can say, "A triangle that has all equal sides is a special triangle called an equilateral triangle." Add this new terminology and corresponding illustrations to the math word wall. For ELLs and other children who may struggle with vocabulary, focus on the specialized meaning of these new terms (such as contrasting "acute pain" and "acute angle"—acute can mean sharp or pointed) and root words (such as *equi-* meaning *equal* and *–lateral* meaning *side*). Extend the activity by repeating the process using quadrilaterals or a particular type of three-dimensional shape (e.g., cylinders or pyramids).

Construction Activities.

Building or drawing shapes is an important activity that requires children to pay attention to the properties and defining attributes of shapes (CCSSO, 2010). Young children should experience constructing two- and three-dimensional shapes using physical models.

For building two-dimensional models, use an activity like Activity 16.8, "Build It," but do not provide drawings as models for children. Challenge them to create two or more examples of a target shape and have them explain why their examples are like that shape. See whether others in the class agree with their explanations.

Building three-dimensional shapes is more difficult than building two-dimensional shapes. A variety of commercial materials permit fairly creative construction of geometric solids (e.g., Polydron and the Zome System). Alternatively, you can collect the following sets of building materials listed in the next activity.

Activity 16.18

CCSS-M: K.G.A.3; K.G.B.5; 1.G.A.2; 2.G.A.1

Constructing 3-D Shapes

Have children use one of the following sets of materials for construction:

- *Plastic coffee stirrers with modeling clay or twisted ties.* Plastic stirrers can be cut into different lengths and used to build the edges of the three-dimensional shape. To connect corners, use small balls of clay or insert twisted ties into the ends of the stirrers.

(continued)

- *Plastic drinking straws, pipe cleaners, and twist ties.* If you use drinking straws with flexible joints, cut the straws lengthwise from the top down to the flexible joint. These split ends can then be inserted into the uncut bottom ends of other straws, making a strong but flexible joint. Three or more straws are joined in this fashion to form two-dimensional polygons. Alternatively, you can use regular drinking straws, cut into various lengths, and insert two-inch lengths of pipe cleaner into the ends of the straws to form the corners/vertices. To make skeletal solids, use pipe cleaners or twist ties to join polygons side to side.

- *Rolled newspaper rods and tape.* Create superlarge skeletons using newspaper and masking tape or duct tape (see Figure 16.17).

With these homemade models, have children compare the strength and rigidity of triangular components with that of polygons with more than three sides. Point out that triangles are used in many bridges, in the long booms of construction cranes, in gates, and in the structural parts of buildings. Show children this **video (https://www.youtube.com/watch?v=k8hG3xJitAg)** of a math club project demonstrating how a bridge built from triangles is stronger than one built from squares.

Figure 16.17

Large skeletal structures can be built with tightly rolled newspaper.

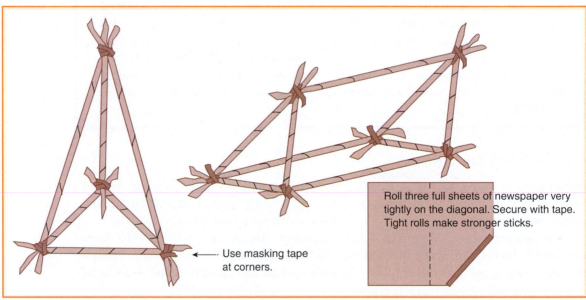

Roll three full sheets of newspaper very tightly on the diagonal. Secure with tape. Tight rolls make stronger sticks.

← Use masking tape at corners.

In the next activity, children are challenged to build two-dimensional shapes according to given properties.

Activity 16.19

CCSS-M: K.G.A.3; K.G.B.5;
1.G.A.2; 2.G.A.1

Can You Make It?

Create a collection of challenges. Each challenge describes one or more properties of a shape, and the challenge is to create a shape with these properties on a geoboard or using physical materials such as plastic (flat) coffee stirrers or straws cut to various lengths or a manipulative such as D-Stix. The list that follows is only a sample. Try combining two or more properties to create new challenges. Prompt children to create challenges that can be posted for others to make.

- A shape with only one square corner and four sides

- A shape with two square corners (or three, four, five, or six square corners)

- A shape with two pairs of parallel lines

- A shape with two pairs of parallel lines and no right angles

- A shape with one or two lines of symmetry (if your class has discussed symmetry)

You can also include impossible tasks, such as a four-sided shape with exactly three right angles. Also, note that a triangle with three congruent sides (equilateral) is not possible on a geoboard.

By recording the solutions to these challenges, there is the added bonus of identifying classes of shapes possessing certain properties.

Transformations

Transformations are changes in position or size of a shape. Usually, three transformations that describe changes in position are discussed at the PreK–2 level: *translations* (slides), *reflections* (flips), and *rotations* (turns). At the primary level, the terms *slide, flip,* and *turn* are adequate. Symmetry is included under the study of transformations due to its link to reflections. Although transformations as not explicitly listed in the *Common Core* standards for K–2, transformations are implicit as children are expected to consider shapes in different orientations.

Rigid Motions

Movements that do not change the size or shape of the object are called "rigid motions." Transformations at the Prek–2 level involve an introduction to the basic concepts of slides, flips, and turns that result in congruent shapes (see Figure 16.18). The goal is to help children recognize these transformations and to begin to explore their effects on simple shapes. Here are definitions of the rigid motions:

Slide: A slide (translation) moves an object along a *distance* and in a *direction*.

Flip: A flip (reflection) requires a *line of reflection*. The reflection is a transformation in which an object is flipped over the line of reflection.

Turn: A turn (rotation) requires a *center of rotation* (a point) and *a degree of rotation* (up to 360 degrees).

Clements and Sarama (2014) recommend having children use computer programs and applets to explore slides, flips, and turns of objects because children have to anticipate which rigid motion is needed for a target outcome and then purposefully select the screen tools to perform the rigid motion, which makes the motions more explicit to children. You can also draw children's attention to their intuitive use of rigid motions when they work on puzzles as they turn, flip, and slide pieces into place. Have them describe how they are moving the puzzle pieces to make them fit. Use these experiences to help young children reflect on how a shape does not change even as they change its position or orientation.

Flags can provide an interesting context for children to think about slides, turns, and flips because of how flags

Figure 16.18

Slide (translation), *flip* (reflection), *turn* (rotation).

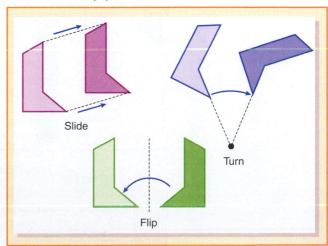

The NCTM's Illuminations applet called "Shape Tool" allow children to flip, slide, and rotate shapes to create various patterns and fill in designs, which informally introduce them to transformations.

move in the wind. Read to children a book about different flags or share pictures of flags used by different countries (e.g., *Flags of the World* by Selvie Bednar, 2009). Then use the following activity to explore these motions.

Activity 16.20

CCSS-M STANDARDS OF MATHEMATICAL PRACTICE: MP1; MP3; MP6; MP7

Motion Flag

Make copies of the first **Motion Flag** Activity Page and then copy the **Mirror Image** Activity Page on the back, as in Figure 16.19). You want the back image to match the front image when held to the light. Cut off the excess paper to leave a square. Alternatively, you can make the same design on squares of card stock using a marker. Give all children a two-sided Motion Flag. It might be helpful, especially for children with disabilities, to give children two Motion Flags each, one to leave in the original position and the other to manipulate.

Demonstrate each of the rigid motions. A slide is simply that—Motion Flag moves over a particular distance (such as 4 inches right and 2 inches down). Demonstrate turns, using only a clockwise motion. Similarly, demonstrate a horizontal flip (top goes to bottom) and a vertical flip (left goes to right). For all children, especially ELLs, ensure that these demonstrations include explicit practice with the vocabulary and that visuals are posted for reference. Practice by having children start with their Motion Flag in the same orientation. As you announce one of the moves, children slide, flip, or turn their Motion Flag accordingly.

Then display two Motion Flags side by side in any orientation. The task is to decide what motion or combination of motions will get the flag on the left to match the flag on the right. Children use their own flag to work out a solution. Test the solutions that children offer. If both flags are in the same position, call that a slide.

Once children understand how to use the Motion Flag, they can work in pairs. They begin with their Motion Flags in the same position. One child then changes his or her Motion Flag and challenges the other child to say what motion is required to make the two Motion Flags match. The solution is then tested and the roles reversed.

Figure 16.19

Motion Flag is used to show slides, flips, and turns.

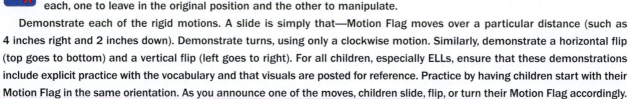

Stop and Reflect

Begin with the **Motion Flag** in the left position shown in Figure 16.19. What rigid motions are required to get the Motion Flag in the position on the right in Figure 16.19? Will it take one move or more than one move (transformation)? Try to find all the positions that require two moves. Are there any positions that require more than two moves?

At first, children might be confused when they can't get their Motion Flag into the new position with one transformation. This creates an excellent problem—but don't be too quick to suggest that it may take two moves. There are often numerous ways to get the flag to the new position.

Line Symmetry

Transformations for Prek–2 children should involve the initial development of line symmetry. If a shape can be folded on a line so that the two halves match exactly, then it is said to have *line symmetry* (sometimes called *reflectional* or *mirror symmetry*). Notice that the fold line is actually a line of *reflection*—the portion of the shape on one side of the line is reflected onto the other side, demonstrating the connection between line symmetry and transformations (flips).

One way to introduce line symmetry is to show examples and nonexamples using an all-of-these/none-of-these approach, as in Figure 16.16. Here's another possibility:

Fold a sheet of paper in half and cut out a shape of your choosing along the fold. Open the paper and describe what you notice.

Another approach to introduce line symmetry is to use mirrors. When you place a mirror on a picture or design so that the mirror is perpendicular to the table, you see a shape with symmetry when you look in the mirror. Have children create designs with mirror images, as in the following activity.

Activity 16.21

CCSS-M STANDARDS OF MATHEMATICAL PRACTICE: MP3; MP6; MP7

Pattern Block Mirror Symmetry

 Give children a plain sheet of paper with a straight line through the middle. Ask them to use no more than six to eight pattern blocks to make a design completely on one side of the line that touches the line in some way. When the one side is finished, children try to make the mirror image of their design on the other side of the line. After the design is complete, have children place the mirror on the line and look into it from the side of the original design to check their work. With the mirror in place they should see exactly the same image as they see when they raise the mirror. For children with disabilities, make sure the line of reflection is vertical with the design to the left and to the right of the line. The task is harder when the line is oriented horizontally or diagonally. You can also challenge children to make designs with more than one line of symmetry.

Children often refer to the ideas of symmetry when working with pattern blocks and other designs. They may observe, "I can fold my butterfly drawing and it matches!" or "This side of my pattern block design matches the other side." Capitalize on these opportunities to discuss the idea of symmetry so your children have a strong foundation for more formal study that will come in later grades.

Location

In preK and kindergarten, children learn about everyday positional descriptions—*above, below, beside, in front of, behind,* and *next to* (CCSSO, 2010). These "place learnings" (Clements & Sarama, 2014) are useful for helping children begin to specify locations. However, helping children refine the way they reason and communicate about direction, distance, and location enhances spatial understandings. Geometry, measurement, and algebra are all supported by the use of a grid system with numbers or coordinates attached that can specify the location. Children at the primary level can begin to think in terms of a grid system to identify location in preparation for more sophisticated ways of reasoning about location.

As children learn to use language to describe an object's relative position in space they also need opportunities in which they have to pay attention to the space around them and how it is organized. Using and building simple maps can help children become more aware of their environment and how they navigate through it (e.g., Clements & Sarama, 2014). Children develop the ability to navigate by first paying attention to landmarks in their environment (Clements, 1999). In the next activity children use a simple map that includes landmarks to locate hidden objects.

Activity 16.22

CCSS-M: K.G.A.1

Playground Scavengers

Prepare some simple maps of your playground area that identify some big landmarks and different paths through the playground area. Give different groups of children different maps. Children will use their map to move from one location to another to find a hidden treasure. On each map, highlight the starting point and the ending point and draw a path along the route you want children to take.

After children have some experience using simple maps, having them create their own maps will help them not only notice landmarks but also how those landmarks are positioned in the environment as they are challenged to identify a path that connects these landmarks.

Activity 16.23

CCSS-M: K.G.A.1

Making Maps

Identify landmarks in your classroom that children can use in their design of a classroom map showing a path from one landmark to another. For example, children can create a map between the block area and the sink. Mark the path first with masking tape and have children walk along the path, drawing their attention to objects they pass along the way. (These objects are other landmarks that they could include on their maps.) After they create their map, they can walk along the path again and add additional landmarks to their maps to improve the detail and usefulness of their maps.

The maps young children create can vary greatly due to individual children's drawing skills. You do not want children to get bogged down in providing a lot of detail in representing landmarks, so explicitly demonstrate what you mean by simple drawings of landmarks. Alternatively, you can provide cutout pictures of the landmarks that they can glue to their maps so they can attend more to the positions of the landmarks in relation to each other and the path.

When children are able to attend to and describe landmarks in the space around them, it is time to help them see the value of having a way to specify location without pointing or identifying specific landmarks. The next activity can serve as a readiness task for coordinates as children refine their ways of describing location.

Standards for Mathematical Practice

4 Model with mathematics.

Activity 16.24   CCSS-M: K.G.A.1

Hidden Positions

 Give each child a **Hidden Positions Gameboard**. Two children sit with a "screen" separating their desktop space so that neither child can see the other's grid (see Figure 16.20). Each child has four different pattern blocks. The first player places a block on four different sections of the grid. He then tells the other player where to put blocks on her grid to match his own. When all four pieces are positioned, the two grids are checked to see if they are alike. Then the players switch roles. Model the game once by taking the part of the first child. Use words such as *top row, middle row, last row, above, below, next to,* and *beside.* Children can play in pairs as a station activity. For children with disabilities, consider starting with just one shape, then move to two shapes, and so on. For children ready for a greater challenge, increase the size of the grid up to 6 × 6. As the grid size increases, notice how the need for a system of labeling positions increases.

As children begin to see the need to label positions (possibly because they have played "Hidden Positions" with an extended grid), they can begin to use simple coordinates to describe positions. Use a **Simple Coordinate Grid** like the one shown in Figure 16.21 and explain how to use two numbers to designate an intersection point on the grid. The first number tells how far to move to the right. The second number tells how far to move up. Initially use the words along with the numbers: "right 3 and up 0." Be sure to include 0 in your introduction. Then select a point on the grid and have children decide what two numbers name that point. If your point is at (2,4) and children incorrectly say "four, two," then simply indicate where the point is that they named.

The next activity explores the notion of different paths on a grid.

Figure 16.21

A simple coordinate grid. The X is at (3,2) and the O is at (1,3). Use the grid to play "Three in a Row" (like Tic-Tac-Toe). Put marks on intersections, not spaces.

Figure 16.20

The "Hidden Positions" game.

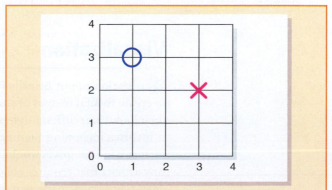

Activity 16.25

CCSS-M: K.G.A.1

Paths

On a sheet of **2-Centimeter Grid Paper** (see Blackline Master 5), mark two different points A and B as shown in Figure 16.22. Using a projection unit or floor tiles, demonstrate how to describe a path from A to B. For the points in the figure, one path is "up 5 and right 6." Another path might be "right 2, up 3, right 4, up 2." Count the length of each path. As long as you always move toward the target point (in this case either right or up), the path lengths will always be the same. Here they are 11 units long. Children draw three paths on their papers from A to B using different-colored crayons. For each path they write directions that describe their paths. Ask the children, "What is the greatest number of turns that you can make in your path? What is the smallest number? Where would A and B have to be in order to get there with no turns?" For children who need a challenge, add a coordinate system on the grid and have them describe their paths using coordinates. For example, $(1,2) \rightarrow (3,2) \rightarrow (3,5) \rightarrow (7,5) \rightarrow (7,7)$.

The "Hiding Lady Bug" applet on NCTM's Illuminations website is similar to "Paths" but offers some additional challenges. Children move a ladybug by listing directions that will hide a ladybug beneath a leaf. When the directions are complete, the ladybug is set in motion to follow them. The ladybug can also be directed to draw shapes such as a rectangle or to travel through mazes. Creating directions and predicting their outcome will help children develop ideas about navigation and location as they hone their visualization skills.

Figure 16.22

Different paths from A to B on a grid.

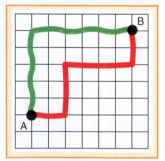

Once a coordinate system has been introduced, children may want to use it in a simple game similar to the commercial game called "Battleship." Each player has a grid similar to the one in Figure 16.21. Players secretly put their initials on five intersections of their own grid. You can use a context to make the game more motivating. For example, these locations could indicate the location of hidden treasures. Then, with the grids kept separate as in "Hidden Positions," the players take turns trying to locate the other player's hidden treasures by naming a point on the grid using coordinates. The other player indicates if the guess was a hit or a miss. When a player scores a hit, he or she gets another turn. Each player keeps track of where he or she has guessed locations, recording an "X" for a hit and a "0" for a miss. The game ends when one player has found all of the other player's hidden treasures.

Visualization

Visualization might be called "geometry done with the mind's eye." It involves being able to create mental images of shapes and then turn them around mentally, thinking about how they look from different viewpoints and predicting the results of various transformations. It involves imagining the impact of certain actions on two- and three-dimensional shapes, such as what the parts would look like if you cut a shape in half or rotated it a quarter turn. Any activity that requires children to think about, manipulate, or transform a shape mentally or to represent a shape as it is seen visually will contribute to the development of children's visualization skills.

Two-Dimensional Imagery

Children at the prerecognition level may notice only a subset of the visual characteristics of a shape, which results in an inability to distinguish between some shapes. Therefore, visualization activities for this level will have children trying to attend to the details of images. The following activity is based on an idea from NCTM's *Principles and Standards for Mathematics* (National Council of Teachers of Mathematics, 2000).

 Activity 16.26

CCSS-M: K.G.B.4; 1.G.A.2; 2.G.A.1

Can You Remember?

 Display one of the simple **Sketches of Figures** (see Figure 16.23) for about 5 seconds. Then have children attempt to reproduce it on their own. Show the same figure again for a few seconds and allow children to modify their drawings. Repeat with additional figures.

Have a class discussion where children are asked to describe how they thought about the figure or give examples of attributes of the figure that helped them remember what they saw. As children learn to verbally describe what they see, their visual memory will improve. Support children with disabilities by having them identify the displayed figure from a set of figures that look similar.

Standards for Mathematical Practice

◀ **7 Look for and make use of structure.**

Figure 16.23

Examples to use in the "Can You Remember?" activity.

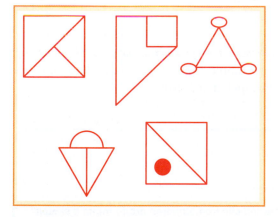

Finding out how many different shapes can be made with a given number of simple tiles requires that children mentally flip and turn shapes in their minds and find ways to decide whether they have found them all. That is the focus of the next activity.

 Activity 16.27

CCSS-M: 1.G.A.2; 2.G.A.1

Pentominoes

A pentomino is a shape formed by joining five squares where each square must have at least one side in common with another. Provide children with five square tiles and a sheet of **1-Centimeter Grid Paper** for recording. Challenge them to see how many different pentomino shapes they can find. Shapes that are flips or turns of other shapes are not considered different. Do not tell children how many pentomino shapes there are. Good discussions will come from deciding whether some shapes are really different and if all shapes have been found.

**Standards for
Mathematical Practice**

1 **Make sense
of problems and
persevere in
solving them.** ▶

Once children have decided that there are just 12 pentominoes (see Figure 16.24), the 12 pieces can be put on card stock and then be used in a variety of activities, such as the following.

- Use each of the 12 shapes as a tessellation tile and create a tessellation design.
- Try to fit all 12 pieces into an 8 by 8 square, a 6 by 10 rectangle, or a 5 by 12 rectangle
- Examine each of the 12 pentominoes and decide which ones will fold up to make an open box. For those that are "box makers," which square is the bottom of the box?

Another good challenge for children is exploring the number of shapes that can be made from four (45-degree) right triangles (i.e., halves of squares) (see Figure 16.25), where sides that touch must be the same length. How many of each of these "ominoes" do you think there are?

Figure 16.24

There are 12 different pentomino shapes.

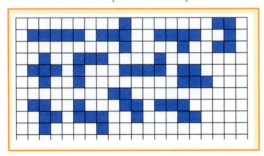

Figure 16.25

Find all the possible shapes made from four right triangles.

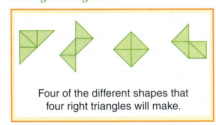

Four of the different shapes that
four right triangles will make.

Based on an idea found in the NCTM's *Principles and Standards for School Mathematics* for prek–2 geometry, the next activity is a great example of how you can ask children to use their "mind's eye" to predict the outcome of manipulating a shape.

 ## Activity 16.28

CCSS-M: K.G.B.1; 1.G.A.2; 2.G.A.1

Notches and Holes

Fold a sheet of paper in half and open it, showing children. Children are to make a sketch of the paper when it is opened, showing a line for the fold. Then display the folded paper on a projection unit and cut notches in one or two sides and/or cut off one or two corners. You can also use a paper punch to make a hole. While still folded, display the paper showing the notches and holes. The folded edge should be to the left (see Figure 16.26). Children are challenged to draw the notches and holes where they think they will appear when you open the paper.

Figure 16.26

An example for the "Notches and Holes" activity.

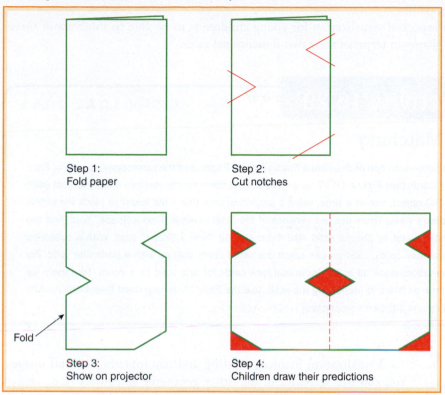

Step 1:
Fold paper

Step 2:
Cut notches

Fold

Step 3:
Show on projector

Step 4:
Children draw their predictions

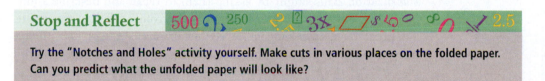

Stop and Reflect

Try the "Notches and Holes" activity yourself. Make cuts in various places on the folded paper. Can you predict what the unfolded paper will look like?

The activity "Notches and Holes" can be modified for use with children who are at any level of geometric thought. To introduce this activity, begin with only one fold and only one cut. Adding additional cuts and additional folds increases the challenge. Predicting the result helps build visualization skills and is also very motivating!

Three-Dimensional Imagery

Visualization skills in three-dimensions can also be developed through the map-building activities that are used to help children learn about location. Consider the following task that you can pose just after your class returns to the classroom from another location in the building:

Imagine that we are walking back to our classroom from the gym. What are some of the landmarks that we pass along the way?

After children have had time to visualize the path between the gym and their classroom, make a list of the landmarks that children thought of and take it with the class the next time you walk that path.

Another aspect of visualization for young children is to be able to think about three-dimensional shapes in terms of their two-dimensional faces.

Activity 16.29

CCSS-M: 1.G.A.2; 2.G.A.1

Face Matching

Provide children with one of the **Find a Shape** Activity Pages and the corresponding sets of **Face Matching Cards** (see Figure 16.27 for an example). (Alternatively, you can simply project each face of a 3-D object, one at a time, using a projection unit. Use a file folder to block the object from children's view.) There are two versions of the task: Given a "Find a Shape" card, find the corresponding solid, or given a solid, find the matching "Find a Shape" card. With a collection of individual face cards, children can select the set of cards that go with a particular solid. For another variation, stack all of the individual face cards for one solid face down. Turn them up one at a time as clues to identifying the solid. Use the **Face Matching Card Questions** Activity Page and collect children's responses.

Figure 16.27

Matching face cards with three-dimensional shapes.

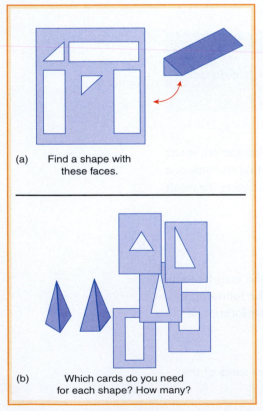

(a) Find a shape with these faces.

(b) Which cards do you need for each shape? How many?

Visualization involves creating and manipulating mental images. You can use activities in the other geometry categories (e.g., shapes and properties, transformation, location) to help children improve their visualization skills simply by asking them to recall and describe a hidden shape, describe how a shape would look from a different viewpoint, and predict what will happen before they manipulate (e.g., decompose, compose, flip, slide, turn) shapes. Look for those opportunities as you plan lessons and as you interact with your children.

17

Helping Children Use Data

BIG IDEAS

1 Statistics is a different field of study from mathematics; although mathematical concepts are used in statistics, statistics is primarily concerned with analysis of data and the resulting practical implications.

2 Doing statistics involves a four-step process: formulating questions, collecting data, analyzing data, and interpreting results.

3 Data are gathered and organized in order to answer questions about the population from which the data come. Data, always from a sample of the population, are used to make inferences about the population.

4 Different types of graphs and other data representations provide different information about the data and, hence, the population from which the data were taken. The choice of graphical representation can affect how well the data are understood.

5 Classification is fundamental to data analysis and is how young children begin their work in statistical analysis. A collection of objects with various attributes can be classified or sorted in different ways. A single object can belong to more than one class.

6 The shape of the data can provide a "big picture" of the data, as opposed to thinking of the data as a collection of numbers. Graphs can provide a sense of the shape of the data, including how spread out or clustered the data are.

Graphs and statistics bombard the public in areas such as advertising, opinion polls, population trends, health risks, and progress of children in schools. We hear that the average amount of rainfall this summer is more than it was last summer or that the average American household consists of 2.54 people. In April 2016 the median price of a new home was $321,100, and the mean was $379,800. Knowing these statistics should raise an array of questions: How were these data gathered? What was the purpose? What does it mean to have an average of 2.54 people? Why are the median and the mean for home sales so different, and which one makes more sense for communicating about the prices of homes?

Statistical literacy is critical to understanding the world around us, essential for engaged citizenship, and vital for developing the ability to question information presented in the media (Shaughnessy, 2007). Misuse of statistics occurs even in trustworthy sources such as newspapers, where graphs are often designed to exaggerate a finding. Therefore, it is crucial to prepare statistically literate students who understand the basic concepts of statistics and who are able to ascertain the trustworthiness of what they see or read in newspapers, magazines, and on internet sites. Children at the preK–2 level can begin developing this understanding. The *Common Core State Standards for Mathematics* (CCSSO, 2010) and the *Curriculum Focal Points* (National Council of Teachers of Mathematics, 2006) indicate that preK–K children should learn how data can be categorized while first and second graders should collect, organize, represent, and interpret data using picture and bar graphs. Second graders extend their work to generating and representing measurement data on line plots. The focus of learning at these and every grade level should be on ways to use, present, and interpret data in the context of real questions.

What Does It Mean to Do Statistics?

Doing statistics is, in fact, a different process from doing mathematics—a notion that has recently received much attention in standards documents and research (Burrill & Elliott, 2006; Franklin et al., 2005; Shaughnessy, 2003). As Richard Scheaffer (2006), past president of the American Statistics Association, notes,

> Mathematics is about numbers and their operations, generalizations and abstractions; it is about spatial configurations and their measurement, transformations, and abstractions. . . . Statistics is also about numbers—but numbers in context: these are called data. Statistics is about variables and cases, distribution and variation, purposeful design or studies, and the role of randomness in the design of studies, and the interpretation of results. (pp. 310–311)

Students need to be statistically literate so they can make meaningful interpretations of the world. This section describes some of the big ideas and essential knowledge regarding statistics and explains the general process of doing statistics.

Is It Statistics or Mathematics?

Statistics and mathematics are two different fields; however, statistical questions are often asked in assessments with questions that are mathematical in nature rather than statistical. The harm in this is that children are not focusing on statistical reasoning, as shown by the following exemplars from Scheaffer (2006).

So, which of these problems involves statistical reasoning? Both? Neither? As explained by Schaeffer, only the second one is statistical in nature. The first requires computing with multiplication or using the formula for averages and working backward—which is

1. The average weight of 50 prize-winning tomatoes is 2.36 pounds. What is the combined weight, in pounds, of these 50 tomatoes? (NAEP sample question)
   a. 0.0472   b. 11.8   c. 52.36   d. 59   e. 118

2. Table 17.1 gives the times each girl has recorded for seven trials of the 100-meter dash this year. Only one girl may compete in the upcoming track meet. Which girl would you select for the meet and why?

Stop and Reflect 500 ⌒, 250 ☙ ⸮ 3✗ ▱ 8 ⌐5 ° ∞⌒ ⟋ 2.5

Before reading further, label each of the preceding questions as "doing mathematics" or "doing statistics."

Table 17.1. Race time for three runners.

Runner	Race						
	1	2	3	4	5	6	7
Suzie	15.2	14.8	15.0	14.7	14.3	14.5	14.5
Tanisha	15.8	15.7	15.4	15.0	14.8	14.6	14.5
Dara	15.6	15.5	14.8	15.1	14.5	14.7	14.5

mathematical thinking, not statistical thinking. The second question is statistical in nature because the situation requires analysis—graphs or averages might be used to determine a solution. The mathematics here is basic; the focus is on statistics. In particular, notice that the context is central to responding to the second question, which is an indication that it is statistical reasoning.

In statistics, the context is essential to analyzing and interpreting the data (Franklin & Garfield, 2006; Franklin et al., 2005; Langrall, Nisbet, Mooney, & Jansem, 2011; Scheaffer, 2006). Looking at the spread, or shape, of data and considering the meaning of unusual data points (outliers) are determined based on the context.

The Shape of Data

A big conceptual idea in data analysis can be referred to as the shape of data: a sense of how data are spread out or clustered, what characteristics about the data set as a whole can be described, and what the data tell us in a global way about the population from which they are taken. Graphs, such as bar graphs and line plots, can illustrate the distributions (shape) of data (Kader & Jacobbe, 2013). In the early grades, the shape of data can be discussed informally by looking at almost any graph. Figure 17.1 shows six different line plots, each showing a different shape to the data. Although the line plot in Figure 17.1(a) is not exactly symmetrical, meaning the left side of the graph looks just like the right side, we would still describe it as symmetrical because we are describing the shape of the data in a general sense. In Figure 17.1(c), we could say that the values cluster between 10 and 20, inclusive, and that 10 is the peak (mode), meaning it is the most frequently occurring value.

Whenever there are two or more graphs of the same type (such as picture, bar, line plot), it is worth talking with children about the overall look of the graphs—how they are alike and how they are different—to help the children focus more on each data set as a whole. Consider, for example, the two graphs in Figure 17.2, showing data that have been gathered from a class of 25 children. In Our Favorite Spring Colors graph, although there is a most

Figure 17.1

Line plots showing different distributions (shapes) of data.

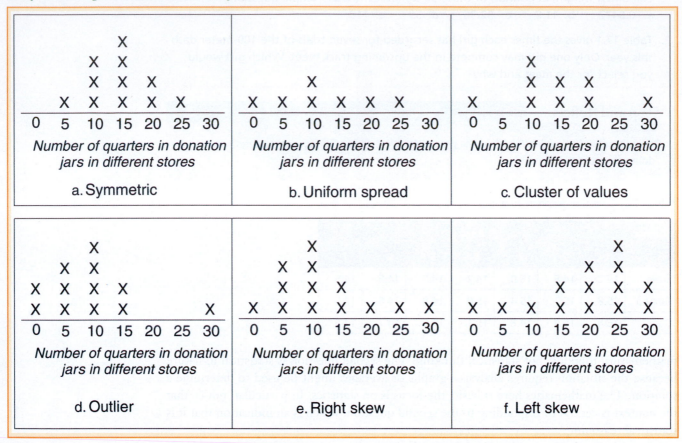

Teaching Tip

When looking at graphs, young children tend to focus on a single data point, like their own. Lay sheer material, such as a curtain, over the data display so that children can still see the shape of the data but not individual pieces of data.

favored color, the data are essentially distributed equally or uniformly. In Our Favorite Sports graph, two sports received most of the votes from the class and the remainder of the class is somewhat spread among the other three categories.

Different graphing techniques or types of graphs can provide a different snapshot of the data as a whole. For example, bar graphs and circle graphs (percentage graphs) each show how the data cluster in different categories. The circle graph focuses more on the relative values of this clustering, whereas the bar graph adds a dimension of quantity. The choice of which and how many categories to use in these graphs will result in different pictures of the shape of the data.

The Process of Doing Statistics

Just as learning addition involves much more than the procedure for combining, doing statistics is much more than being able to create a bar graph or line plot. To *meaningfully* engage children in learning and doing statistics, they should be involved in the full process, from asking and defining questions to collecting and analyzing data to interpreting results. This chapter is organized around this process, which is presented in Figure 17.3.

Table 17.2 provides a snapshot of the most common errors and misconceptions children will demonstrate with statistical thinking, along with suggestions about how to help them work through these issues. As you read through the chapter, look back at these common misconceptions and consider how particular activities and the questions you ask can help mitigate these concerns and help promote your children's ability to do statistics.

Figure 17.2

The shapes of the data in these two bar graphs are quite different.

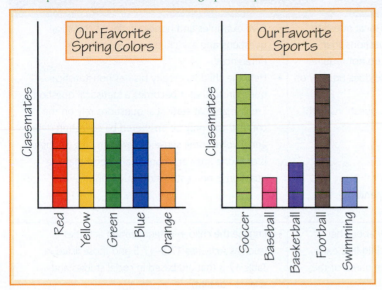

Figure 17.3

Process of doing statistics.

1. Develop Statistical Questions
   - Use interesting, relevant questions for the students to explore
   - Engage students in generating questions that can be answered using statistics
   - Focus on questions that include variability
   - Consider what data will answer the question:
     – Include questions that generate numerical data
     – Include data that can be gathered within the classroom or school
2. Gather and Organize Data
   - Decide who will be asked the question(s) or what source(s) will be used for gathering data
   - Outline a plan for collecting the data
   - Choose the best way to record the data
   - Carry out the data collection plan
3. Choose a Data Analysis Plan
   - Decide which representation will best tell the story related to your question(s)
   - Prepare those data displays (by hand or using technology)
   - Select ways to interpret the data (combining or comparing)
   - Carry out the analysis plan
4. Interpret the Findings
   - Use representations from #3 to answer the question(s) from #1
   - Look at the shape of the data if in a graphical representation
   - Explore questions such as:
     – What does our data tell us about our class? And, what doesn't it tell us?
     – What might we infer?
     – What new questions might we have?
   - Look for factual information as well as inferences that go beyond the data

Table 17.2. Common errors and misconceptions in doing statistics and how to help.

Misconception/Error	What It Looks Like	How to Help
1. Child asks mathematical questions and not statistical questions for *driving questions*.	When asked to generate a statistical question (*driving question*), child asks questions that only involve computations and do not require predictions or interpretation and does not rely on the context. For example, the child suggests questions such as these: • How old is my dog? • How many days are in April? • How long is the playground? • How much time did Avery spend on homework last night?	• Give examples and nonexamples of statistical questions and ask children to identify the differences. • Help the child to modify his/her nonstatistical question so that it becomes a statistical question. • Emphasize that statistical questions rely on the context, can only be answered by collecting data, and involve some sense of variability (i.e., if there is only one answer, chances are good that the question is not a statistical question).
2. When organizing data, the child simply lists the data and does not use categories.	After the child collects data, say about her classmates' favorite book, the child lists each classmate's name along with the name of the favorite book.	• Engage the child in categorization activities (such as Activities 17.3–17.5 and those listed in Table 17.3 that are based in social studies and science content). • Have the child compare her list of data to a list that has been categorized. Ask the child to try to articulate the difference between the two ways.
3. Child sorts objects based on one rule and ignores additional rules.	The child is asked to sort attribute materials using the rule "small triangles." He includes large triangles in the group because he is focused only on the attribute of the shape being a triangle.	• Initially use sorting materials that have explicit attributes that are easily identifiable (such as attribute blocks, pattern blocks, teddy bear counters). Once the child demonstrates success with sorting, you can use sorting materials whose attributes are more difficult to describe (such as shoes and seashells). • Reduce the attribute materials to a set that differs only on two attributes and have the child do several sorts. Increase the number of attributes as the child demonstrates successful sorts. • As the child participates in daily cleanup routines, have the child describe to you why he is returning certain materials to particular bins. • Have the child identify the sorting rules to ensure he understands which attributes to track on.
4. When looking at a graph, the child focuses only on single data points instead of looking at the data set as a whole.	When asked to describe something about the class graph that shows the ways children travel to school, the child explains, "That's my sticky note there! I ride the bus."	• Focus discussions on the shape of the entire data set. • To help children look at the data set as a whole, have them compare the shapes of two picture graphs, two bar graphs, or two line plots. • If you have children draw a picture or write their names on sticky notes and then place those onto graphs, after an initial discussion, replace those sticky notes with blank ones so the children no longer see their particular data. • Lay sheer material, such as a sheer curtain, over the data display so that children can still see the shape of the data but not individual pieces of data.

Formulating Questions

Statistics is about more than making graphs and analyzing data. It includes both asking and answering questions about our world. Data collection then has a purpose—to answer questions. Hourigan and Leavy (2015/2016) call these *driving questions* because they motivate involvement in the processes of doing statistics. The analysis of the data should add information about some aspect of our world related to the questions we are asking. Political pollsters, advertising agencies, market researchers, census takers, wildlife managers, and hosts of others engage in this process of gathering data to answer questions and make informed decisions.

Children, even young children, should have opportunities to generate their own questions, decide on appropriate data to help answer these questions, and determine methods of collecting data (CCSSO, 2010; NCTM, 2000). The children's book *The Best Vacation Ever* (Murphy, 1997) is about a little girl who gathers data from her family about what is important to them to help decide where the family would have the best vacation. This book, appropriate for first or second grade, nicely introduces the concept of gathering data to answer a question.

Whether the question is teacher initiated or student initiated, children should engage in conversations about how well-defined the question is. For example, if the teacher asks, "How many brothers and sisters do you have?" there may be a need to discuss half siblings. If children want to know how many shoes each classmate owns, questions may arise as to whether they should count bedroom slippers and flip-flops.

When children formulate the questions, the data they gather become more meaningful. How they organize the data and the techniques for analyzing them have a purpose. Often questions will come naturally in the course of a class discussion or from questions arising in other content areas. The next two sections suggest many ideas.

Questions about "Me and My Classmates"

Young children want to learn about each other, their families and pets, measures such as arm span or time to get to school, their likes and dislikes, and so on. At the preK–2 level, the easiest questions to deal with are those that can be answered by each class member contributing one piece of data. Here are a few ideas:

- *Favorites:* TV shows, games, movies, ice cream, video games, fruit, seasons of the year, colors, sports, sports teams (when there are many possibilities, start by restricting the number of choices)
- *Numbers:* Number of pets, siblings, or letters in name; hours watching TV, hours of sleep; time spent on the computer; bedtime
- *Measures:* Height, arm span, length of foot, long-jump distance, seconds to run around the swing set on the playground, minutes spent traveling to school, daily temperature, shadow length

These questions are good to get children started, but consider how to expand these questions by thinking how the information might be used to make decisions. For example, when thinking about about children's favorite ice cream, you might ask, "Which three ice cream flavors should we buy for a future celebration?" Or when asking about children's favorite books, you could ask, "Which types of books should the school library buy?"

Questions beyond Self and Classmates

The questions in the previous section are designed for children to contribute data about themselves. These questions can be expanded by asking, "How would our data compare to another class?" For example, do other second-grade children spend the same amount of time

 **Teaching Tip**

If your children have "buddies" in the upper grades, they can collect data from their buddies.

watching TV or like the same foods as they do? How much taller are children in the next grade or two grades ahead of them? Comparisons can also be made between your own class and selected groups of adults to which the children have access, such as parents or faculty. Comparison questions are a good way to help children focus on the data they have collected and the variability within that data (Russell, 2006).

To further expand your children's perspective, you might explore ways that your class can compare themselves or their data with similar classes in other places in the state, other states, or perhaps even in a foreign country. This can open up not just a source of interesting data but also a way for your children to see beyond their own localities, as is done in the next activity.

 ## Activity 17.1

CCSS-M: 2.MD.D.10

Who Is in Our Village?

The picture books *If America Were a Village: A Book about the People of the United States* (Smith, 2009) and *If the World Were a Village: A Book about the World's People* (Smith, 2011) provide an excellent opportunity to compare class data or school data to the wider population in the United States and in the world, respectively. Each book explores relative wealth, culture, language, and other influences, providing the statistics in the adapted case of the country (or the world) being a village of 100 people. Read the books in their entirety or select several excerpts for comparisons to the class. Ask children if they think data from our class (or school) will be similar to the data in the book for particular topics. Gather and compare class data to data for the United States and/or for the world. Then ask children what else they think might be interesting data about our country or our world that could be added to the pages of these books.

The local newspaper can suggest all sorts of data-related questions. For example, how many advertisements are included in the newspaper on different days of the week? How many sports stories are about different types of sports (e.g., basketball, football, swimming, etc.)? How many pages is the local paper each day of the week?

Science, of course, is about inquiry and is full of measurements and therefore provides excellent opportunities for interdisciplinary learning experiences. For example, consider this short list of ideas:

- How many plastic bottles or aluminum cans are placed in the school's recycling bins over a given week?
- How many times do different types of balls bounce when each is dropped from the same height?
- How many days does it take for different types of bean, squash, and pea seeds to germinate when kept in moist paper towels?
- Which brand of bubble gum will give you the largest bubble?
- Do some liquids expand more than others when frozen?
- Does a plant grow faster when watered with water, soda, or milk?

Before going on a field trip children can develop questions that are used to gather data on the trip (Mokros & Wright, 2009). For example, when visiting a zoo, children might look for the number of animals that are smaller than a small dog, like a Jack Russell terrier, or how many animals are larger than a large dog, like a golden retriever. (Make sure that the animals or objects chosen are ones that all the children are familiar with!) Other questions might be:

- How many animals have wings and how many don't?
- Are there more animals with fur than not?
- How many animals have no legs, two legs, four legs, or more legs?
- How many animals move around in various ways (e.g., fly, slither, crawl on four legs, walk on two legs, etc.)?

You can work with zoo personnel before going on the trip to identify possible topics to share with children to help them develop questions that they are curious about.

Discussions about communities provide a good way to integrate social studies and mathematics. As you study the community in which children live, many questions arise, as seen in the next activity.

 Activity 17.2   CCSS-M: 1.MD.C.4; 2.MD.D10

What Can We Learn about Our Community?

This activity plays out over several days. First, ask children to turn in a note card with three statistical questions they would like to investigate during the year. This could be assigned as homework, with children's families helping to brainstorm ideas. Collect these ideas. When you have time to start the investigation, take one question from the set. As a class, refine the question to one that can be answered using statistics. Examples of questions include:

- How many different kinds of restaurants or stores are in our community (fast food restaurants versus "sit down" restaurants; Italian, Mexican, or American; convenience stores, grocery stores, clothing stores, variety stores)?
- How many responses are made by local firefighters each month? How many different types of responses are made by local firefighters each month (fire, medical, hazardous, public service)? (Data can usually be found on websites of local institutions.)
- How many state and local government officials do voters elect?

Discuss ways to gather the data. Set up a plan and deadline for gathering the data. When children bring in the data, encourage them to select and use data displays (e.g., bar graph, line plot, etc.). Invite children to share. Return to the question and ask, "What does our data tell us about _____?" Consider how the different data displays communicate the answer to this question. See Expanded Lesson: Using Data to Answer a Question for a full lesson around this activity.

Children will need help in designing questions that can be answered using statistics. These are questions that include variability and for which data can be gathered. Providing examples and nonexamples can help children, in particular those with disabilities, focus on the elements of an appropriate statistical question. For example, in the questions below, some can be answered using statistics and some cannot.

1. How much change do I have in my pocket?
2. What is the typical amount of loose change a person carries in their pocket?
3. What cereal is most healthy?
4. What reasons do people use in selecting gum (e.g., taste, cost, bubble-making quality, long lasting, good breath)?

5. How long do different kinds of gum keep their flavor?
6. Which store has the best prices?
7. Where will you buy shampoo?

Questions 1, 3, and 7 are *not* statistical in nature. Question 3 could be adapted to a statistical question with a more specific focus on what is meant by healthy. Similarly, question 7 is very broad and will need to be focused in order to collect the data needed to answer it. Facilitating discussions with children about examples and nonexamples as well as questions they develop improves their ability to generate appropriate statistical questions.

Data Collection

There are two main types of data—*categorical* and *numerical*. Categorical data (as the name implies) are data grouped by labels (categories) such as favorite after-school activity, colors of cars in the school parking lot, and the most popular name for the class guinea pig. Categorical data are ordered arbitrarily—in other words, the bars in a bar graph could be put in any arrangement. Numerical data, on the other hand, count things or measures on a continuous scale. Numerical data are ordered numerically—for example on a number line—and can include fractions or decimals. This kind of data includes how many miles to school, the temperature in your town over a one-week period, or the weight of children's backpacks.

Teaching Tip

When children initially collect data through observations or surveys, limit the number of possible choices to choose from.

Collecting Data

Gathering data is not easy for children, especially young children. How to collect good data is an important (and sometimes skipped) part of the discussion as children learn statistics. Consider the following scenario that addresses the importance of having these much-needed discussions. A teacher asked her first graders to gather data on "Are you 6?" After hearing the prompt, 18 eager children began asking others in the class if they were 6 and tallying yes or no responses. The problem? They had no idea whom they had asked more than once or whom they had not asked at all. This provided an excellent entry into a discussion about how statisticians gather data. Carolyn Cook, a kindergarten teacher, asked her children to help think of an organized way they could gather data from their classmates about their favorite flavors of ice cream. These kindergartners decided a class list would help them keep track of who had been asked and what their response had been (see Figure 17.4) (Cook, 2008).

Children may start to collect data by counting objects or by hand raising, then move to using a ballot or survey with a limited number of response options and finally using a ballot or survey with unlimited response options (Hudson, Shupe, Vasquez, & Miller, 2008). Data can also be collected through observation. This creates a shared context for children in that they all will be a part of observing phenomena. For example, set up a bird feeder outside the classroom window and collect data at different times during the day to count the number or type of birds that visit the feeder. Children can also collect observational data on field trips (Mokros & Wright, 2009) and at evening or weekend activities with their families.

Using Existing Data Sources

Data do not always have to be collected by surveys or observations; existing data abound in various places, such as the following print resources and data on the internet.

Print Resources

Newspapers, almanacs, sports record books, maps, and various government publications are sources of data that may be used to answer children's questions.

Children's literature is also an excellent and engaging resource. Children can tally words in a repeating verse like "Hickory, Dickory, Dock" (Niezgoda & Moyer-Packenham, 2005). Similarly, books like *Goodnight Moon* (Brown, 2005) and *Green Eggs and Ham* (Seuss, 1960) have many repeated words or phrases.

Web Resources

The internet provides seemingly endless data that are often accessed by simply typing the related question into a search. Children may be interested in facts about another country as a result of a social studies unit or a country in the news. Olympic records in various events over the years or data related to environmental issues are other examples of topics around which children's questions may be formulated. For these and hundreds of other questions, data can be found on the Web. Following are a few websites with a lot of interesting data.

- **NCTM Illuminations State Data Map** is a source that displays state data on population, land area, political representation, gasoline use, and more.
- **The Official Olympic Records** contains all Olympic records, providing information about the games and events, such as the medalists in every Olympic event since Athens 1896.
- **Internet Movie Database** offers information about movies of all genres.
- **Google Earth** allows you to take a virtual trip to explore cities and regions in any place in the world—even children's hometown—where they can make interesting comparisons.

Figure 17.4

Kindergartners collect data on favorite ice cream flavors, tally the data, and create a horizontal bar graph.

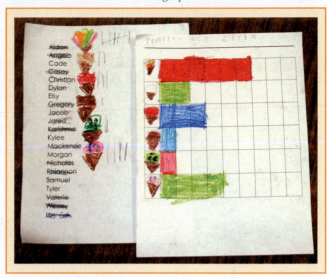

Source: Cook, C. D. (2008). "I Scream, You Scream: Data Analysis with Kindergartners." Teaching Children Mathematics, 14(9), p. 539. Reprinted with permission. Copyright © 2008 by the National Council of Teachers of Mathematics. All rights reserved.

Data Analysis: Classification

Data analysis begins with organizing the data in a meaningful way, using techniques such as sorting or graphing, with the resulting visual providing a snapshot of the data. The data are then analyzed with the goal in mind of how the information answers the questions that started the statistical inquiry and provided the purpose for collecting the data.

Classification involves making decisions about how to categorize things, a basic activity that is fundamental to data analysis. In order to answer the questions being asked, decisions need to be made regarding how to represent and categorize the data that have been gathered. Young children initially might simply put the data in one list and not use categories to organize the data (Clements & Sarama, 2009). For example, if children are asked to represent the class data about how children arrived at school, some children may simply list each child and their response. Therefore, discussions are necessary about how things might be categorized and how some categorizations might be more helpful than others in answering the questions being asked.

Curriculum Focal Points (National Council of Teachers of Mathematics, 2006) and the *Common Core State Standards* (CCSSO, 2010) identify classification by attributes as a topic for preK–K children. Children's literature can offer a perfect lead-in to sorting activities. For example, *Frog and Toad are Friends* (Lobel, 1970) is a classic story about friends who help search for Frog's missing button. Whenever Frog's friends ask, "Is this your button?" Frog responds (with a touch of frustration), "No, that is not my button! That button is ____, but my button was ____." Children can use Frog's descriptions to sort a collection of buttons. One pre-K teacher used the children's book *Whose Shoes? A Shoe for Every Job* (Swinburne, 2011) to create a context for children to categorize their shoes. (Watch this **video (https://www.youtube.com/watch?v=ezaUlqc_xzw&list=PLRY-hkA40X06NRPAADyqsG-FWoNwfU3Sq&index=2**) of these young learners deciding on categories for their shoes.) Attribute activities, the topic of the next section, are another way to provide opportunities for children to think about classification. Attribute materials are explicitly designed to develop flexible reasoning about the characteristics of data.

Classifications Using Attribute Materials

Attribute materials can be any set of objects that lend themselves to being sorted and classified in different ways—for example, seashells, leaves, children's shoes, or the children themselves. The *attributes* are the ways that the materials can be sorted. For example, hair color, height, and gender are attributes of children. Each attribute has a number of different *values*: for example, blond, brown, or red (for the attribute of hair color); tall or short (for height); male or female (for gender). Commercially available attribute blocks come in sets of 60 pieces, with each piece having four attributes: color (red, yellow, blue), shape (circle, triangle, rectangle, square, hexagon), size (big, little), and thickness (thick, thin). The specific values, number of values, or number of attributes that a set may have is not important.

Initially, attribute activities are best done by sitting in a large circle on the floor where all children can see and have access to the materials to be sorted. The following activity is a simple Venn diagram activity that preK–1 children will enjoy.

Standards for Mathematical Practice

> **7 Look for and make use of structure.**

◣ ◥ **Activity 17.3**   CCSS-M: K.MD.3; 1.MD.C.4

What about "Both"?

Give children two large loops of string and attribute blocks. Direct them to put all the red pieces inside one string and all triangles inside the other. Let the children try to resolve the difficulty of what to do with the red triangles. When the notion of overlapping the strings to create an area common to both loops is clear, more challenging activities can be explored. It will be helpful, especially for children with disabilities, to place labels on each loop of the string.

In addition to attribute blocks, you can use Woozle Cards (see Figure 17.5). To make the cards, copy the **Woozle Cards** Activity Page on white cardstock. Color all the Woozles on one page the same color, then another page in another color, etc., to have color as an attribute for sorting Woozles. Select two attributes (e.g., shape and number of dots) and follow the same steps described for the attribute blocks.

As shown in Figure 17.6, the labels need not be restricted to single attributes. If a piece does not fit in any region, it is placed outside of all the loops.

Figure 17.5

Sample set of Woozle cards and list of attributes.

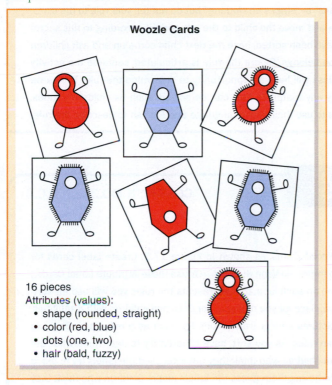

Woozle Cards

16 pieces
Attributes (values):
• shape (rounded, straight)
• color (red, blue)
• dots (one, two)
• hair (bald, fuzzy)

Figure 17.6

A Venn diagram activity with attribute pieces. A rule is written on a label card for each Venn diagram circle.

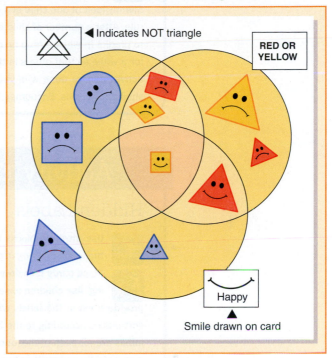

◀ Indicates NOT triangle

RED OR YELLOW

Happy
▲
Smile drawn on card

technology note

Digital versions of attribute blocks can be found by visiting the National Library of Virtual Manipulatives (NLVM) or Glencoe's Virtual Manipulative website. The NLVM applet provides several classification problems for children to do. They are shown a set of blocks inside a loop having the same shape, size, or color. Their task is to drag inside the loop other blocks that belong according to the target attribute.

As children progress, make sure to introduce labels for negative attributes such as "not red" or "not small." Also important is the eventual use of *and* and *or* connectives to form two-value rules such as "red and square" and "big or happy." This use of *and*, *or*, and *not* significantly widens children's classification schemes.

An engaging and challenging activity is to infer how things have been classified when the loops are not labeled. The following activities require children to make and test conjectures about how things are being classified.

Standards for Mathematical Practice

1 Make sense of problems and persevere in solving them.

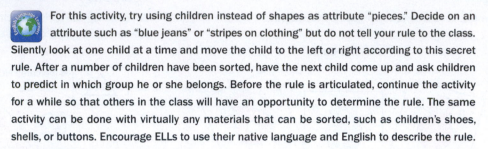

Activity 17.4

CCSS-M: K.MD.3; 1.MD.C4

Guess My Rule

 For this activity, try using children instead of shapes as attribute "pieces." Decide on an attribute such as "blue jeans" or "stripes on clothing" but do not tell your rule to the class. Silently look at one child at a time and move the child to the left or right according to this secret rule. After a number of children have been sorted, have the next child come up and ask children to predict in which group he or she belongs. Before the rule is articulated, continue the activity for a while so that others in the class will have an opportunity to determine the rule. The same activity can be done with virtually any materials that can be sorted, such as children's shoes, shells, or buttons. Encourage ELLs to use their native language and English to describe the rule.

Activity 17.5

CCSS-M: K.MD.3; 1.MD.C4

Hidden Labels

 Use attribute blocks or Woozle Cards, as shown in Figure 17.5. Create label cards for the loops of string used to make the Venn diagram. (Or use these Attribute Label Cards.)

 Place cards face down, one on each loop, that represents the rules you will use for sorting. Ask children to select a piece for you to place. For ELLs and children with disabilities, provide a list of the labels with pictures and/or translations for each as a reference. Begin to sort pieces according to the hidden rules. As you sort, have children try to determine what the labels are for each of the loops. Let children who think they have guessed the labels try to place a piece in the proper loop but avoid having them guess the labels aloud. Children who think they know the labels can be asked to "play teacher" and respond to the guesses of others. Point out that one way to test an idea about the labels is to select a piece that you think might go in a particular section. Wait to turn the label cards up until most children have figured out the rule.

Figure 17.7

Guess the rule that was used to sort these bugs.

Classifications Using Content Areas

"Guess My Rule" and "Hidden Labels" can and should be repeated with real-world materials connected to other content areas and to children's experiences. For example, if you are doing a unit on wildlife in the backyard, you can use pictures of creatures (see Figure 17.7) to sort by relevant attributes and have children guess the sorting rule. To connect reading and data, children can sort and analyze data within a book (e.g., kinds of animals, shapes, locations). Children can also keep track of the kinds of books they read as a class (by topic area) or the number of times different words are used in a story. Children can bring in things they can recycle and these objects can be sorted by type (English, 2013). Table 17.3 lists additional ideas that can be used for classification activities related to social studies and science. Using ideas related to content and the real world helps children understand that data analysis is useful as well as engaging!

Table 17.3. Classification ideas related to social studies and science.

Social Studies	Science
• Places in the United States and outside the United States • Country or state of origin of classmates • Past, present, and future events • Goods (such as, bread, milk, apples, pants, socks, shoes) and services (such as, waiting tables at a restaurant, mowing yards, repairing cars) • Continents and oceans • U.S. presidents according to the state where they were born • Availability of items (scarce, average, abundant) • Jobs in the local community • Climates in the United States	• Sensory descriptors for items (hard/soft, rough/smooth, cold/warm, loud/quiet, sweet/sour/bitter/salty, high/low, and bright/dull) • Relative size or weight of a collection of objects (big/little, large/small, heavy/light, wide/thin, long/short) • Position of objects found in the classroom (over/under, in/out, above/below, left/right) • Speed (fast/slow) of different animals (ants, turtles, snakes, cheetahs) or types of transportation (car, bicycle, airplane, walking) • Materials or objects that float or sink in water • Weather observations (sunny, cloudy, raining, snowing) • Substances that will or will not dissolve in water • Characteristics of plants (edible/nonedible, flowering/nonflowering, evergreen/deciduous) • Physical characteristics of animals (body coverings or methods of movement) • Other characteristics of animals (wild/tame, water homes/land homes, hibernate/do not hibernate, migrate/do not migrate, camouflage/no camouflage)

 ## Formative Assessment Note

The ability to classify is an important skill for early data analysis. You can assess your children's classification skills by observing them in small groups and listening to children as they participate in full-class discussions. Require children to explain their reasoning for placement of items. Here are some suggestions for what to listen and look for:

- After gathering data, do children use categories to sort the data or do they just list the information (e.g., list each child in the class and their favorite ice cream)?

- Are children able to place items into categories once the categories have been identified? Do they use valid reasons for placing items in a category?

- Do children contribute to ideas for classification schemes?

- Do children understand that different classification schemes will result in a different organization of the items being sorted? For example, children's names may be sorted by number of letters, and they can also be sorted by which part of the alphabet they begin with—first half or second half. These two schemes would result in different classifications.

- Do children correctly use an overlapping category—items that belong to two different groups at the same time?

- Can children correctly use the logical connectors *and* and *or* and the adjective *not* when creating classifications?

Data Analysis: Graphical Representations

Graphs summarize the data that were collected, providing a visual image of the data that cannot be captured in other forms. In the CCSS-M (2010), representing and interpreting data begins in grade 1, but preK–K children first experience a form of graphical representation when they use loops to categorize attribute materials. PreK–2 classes can "graph" data about themselves by placing information in loops with labels. A graph of "Our Pets" might consist of a picture of each child's pet or favorite stuffed animal (in lieu of a pet) that can be affixed to a wall display showing how the pets were classified.

How data are organized should be directly related to the question that caused you to collect the data in the first place. For example, suppose that children want to know how many pockets they have on their clothing (Russell, 2006). Data collection involves each child in the room counting his or her pockets.

> ### Stop and Reflect
>
> 500 📝 250 ⟨⟩ ⟨?⟩ 3x ▱ ⟨⟩5° ∞ 0 ⟍ 2.5
>
> If your second-grade class had collected these data, what methods might you suggest they use for organizing and graphing them? Is one of these ideas better than others for answering the question about how many pockets?

Different classifications would produce different graphs. A bar graph made with one bar for every child will certainly tell how many pockets each child has. However, is it the best way to answer the question? If the data were categorized by number of pockets, then a graph showing the number of children with no pockets, one pocket, two pockets, three pockets, and so on will easily show which number of pockets is most common and how the number of pockets varies across the class.

Creating Graphs

Children should be involved in deciding how they want to represent their data. However, for children with little experience with the various methods of picturing data, you will need to introduce options. Graph the data using these options and facilitate a discussion with the class to decide which method might be best and why.

Creating graphs requires care and precision, including determining appropriate scale and labels, so that an audience is able to see at a glance the summary of the data gathered for a particular question. Once children have made the graph, the most important activity is discussing the meanings of various parts of the representation and what it tells people who see it. Analyzing data that are numerical (number of pockets) as opposed to categorical (color of socks) is an added challenge for children as they struggle to make sense of the graphs (Russell, 2006). If, for example, the graph has three stickers above the five, children may think that five people have three pockets or three people have five pockets (see Figure 17.8). Children should be challenged to determine how this issue can be remedied.

Often, young children have difficulty distinguishing between the data and the larger event from which the data were collected. They think of the data as triggers or "pointers" to the event, not as specific information about the event (Konold, Higgins, Russell, & Khalil, 2004). For example, instead of recognizing that more children in the class have two pockets than five pockets, they may describe how they can put their lunch money in their front pocket or that they counted their pockets by twos. Focusing on the meaning of the symbols used in a graphical representation of the data as

Standards for Mathematical Practice

6 Attend to precision. ▶

Standards for Mathematical Practice

1 Make sense of problems and persevere in solving them. ▶

Figure 17.8

Looking at the "5" column, does this graph mean that five people have three pockets or three people have five pockets?

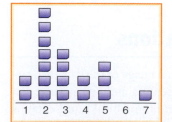

well as having children make comparisons between different groups (e.g., How many pockets do fifth graders have?) can help make the intent of the graph more salient for children (Russell, 2006).

The value of having children construct their own graphs is not so much that they learn the techniques as that they are personally invested in the data and that they learn how a graph conveys information. What we should *not* do is only concentrate on the details of graph construction. Your objectives should also focus on the issues of analysis and communication.

Children should construct graphs or charts by hand and with technology. Use the time saved by technology to focus on discussions about the information provided by each graph. The Data Grapher on NCTM's Illuminations website provides tools to create pictographs and bar graphs.

Analyzing Graphs

Once a graph has been constructed, engage the class in a discussion of what information the graph tells or conveys—this is the analysis. Questioning and assessment should focus on how effectively the graph communicates the findings of the data gathered. For example, ask, "What can you tell about our class by looking at this graph of the number of books read in one week?" Graphs convey factual information (e.g., there is a wide variability in the number of books first graders read in one week) and also provide opportunities to make inferences that are not directly observable in the graph (e.g., most first graders read between five and seven books in one week). Discussions about graphs that children have created help them analyze and interpret other graphs and charts that they see in newspapers and on TV. For example, you can select simple graphs from newspapers or websites and ask children "What can you learn from this graph?" "What do you not know that you wish you knew?" These questions help children focus on what different graphs can and cannot illustrate.

The difference between *actual facts* and the *inferences that go beyond the data* is an important idea in data analysis. Children can examine graphs found in newspapers or magazines and discuss the facts in the graphs and the message that may have been intended by the person who made the graph. Children's conceptual ability to analyze data and draw conclusions and interpretations is often weak (Tarr & Shaughnessy, 2007); discussing and analyzing data is a way to support this higher-level thinking skill.

Graphs for PreK–2 Children

The following progression for introducing different kinds of graphs in grades preK–2 is recommended based on research findings (Friel, Curcio, and Bright, 2001):

1. Object graphs
2. Picture graphs
3. Line plots
4. Bar graphs

All of these types of graphs help children focus on the count or frequency for each value along the vertical scale. However, at first glance, this progression does not follow the one recommended in the *Common Core State Standards* (CCSSO, 2010) and the *Curriculum*

Focal Points (National Council of Teachers of Mathematics, 2006) because line plots appear after bar graphs in both of these documents—very likely because object, picture, and bar graphs all deal with categorical data while line plots are for numerical data. The recommended progression above moves from graphs where each piece of data is evident (object graphs, picture graphs, and line plots) to bar graphs where the individual data values seem to disappear—at least from the perspective of a child. We recommend having children work simultaneously with both line plots and bar graphs with explicit individual data rather than having children avoid asking questions that require numerical data (and a line plot). This way children can ask interesting questions that may require either categorical or numerical data to answer.

Object Graphs

An object graph uses the actual objects being graphed. Examples include types of shoes, favorite fruit, and shapes of buttons. A large graph mat with square grids can be used on the floor to display the objects in an organized manner. (You can use a plastic shower liner for the mat and electrical tape to create the grids.) Each item is placed in a square so that comparisons and counts are easily made. Notice that an object graph is a small step from sorting. If real objects are sorted into groups, those groups can be lined up for comparison—an object graph! This **video (https://www.youtube.com/watch?v=4SIY1-idRqY &list=PLRY-hkA40X06NRPAADyqsG-FWoNwfU3Sq&index=3)** demonstrates how a teacher introduces an object graph to help preschoolers organize their shoes to better answer their questions.

Picture Graphs

Picture graphs (also called pictographs) move up a level of abstraction by using a drawing or picture of some sort that represents what is being graphed. The picture can represent one piece of data or it can represent a designated quantity. For example, a picture of a book can be assigned to mean five books in a graph of how many books were read each day of the week. When children view the graph and see four books for Monday, they skip count to determine that twenty books were read on Monday. This **video (https://www.youtube .com/watch?annotation_id=annotation_1611844189&fea ture=iv&index=4&list=PLRY-hkA40X06NRPAADyqsG-FWoNwfU3Sq&src_vid=4SIY1-idRqY&v=Z6ZnsCZJSzQ)** demonstrates how preschoolers are able to transition from object graphs to picture graphs.

Teaching Tip

Pictographs are a great way to connect to skip counting and early experiences with multiplication.

Children can make their own drawings for picture graphs; however, if you find this too time consuming, there are various ways to make picture graphs easier to create, and thereby keep the focus on the meaning of the graph rather than the creation of it. Some suggestions are to use stickers, clip art (copied repeatedly on a page that can then be cut out), or shapes cut out with a die-cut.

Bar Graphs

After object and picture graphs, bar graphs are among the first ways used to group and present data with children in grades preK–2. To help transition from object and picture graphs to bar graphs, have children use something to represent the pieces of data or the things being counted. An easy idea is to use Post-It notes to represent the individual pieces of data. These can be stuck directly to the board or to a chart and rearranged if needed. To help children keep their notes in line you may wish to use a gridded chart similar to the graph mat described in the section on object graphs. Figure 17.9 illustrates a few ideas that can be used to make a graph quickly with the whole class.

Figure 17.9

Some ideas for quick graphs that can be used again and again.

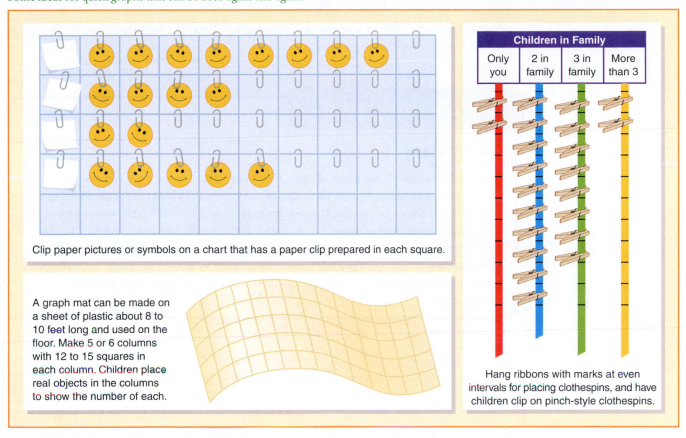

Clip paper pictures or symbols on a chart that has a paper clip prepared in each square.

A graph mat can be made on a sheet of plastic about 8 to 10 feet long and used on the floor. Make 5 or 6 columns with 12 to 15 squares in each column. Children place real objects in the columns to show the number of each.

Children in Family			
Only you	2 in family	3 in family	More than 3

Hang ribbons with marks at even intervals for placing clothespins, and have children clip on pinch-style clothespins.

For preK–2 children, it is reasonable to have between two to six different bars in a graph. Initially bar graphs should be made with each bar consisting of countable parts so that the individual pieces of data do not seem to disappear. The Post-it notes in the next activity, "Picture Graphs to Bar Graphs," serve this purpose.

Activity 17.6

CCSS-M: 1.MD.C.4; 2.MD.D.10

Picture Graphs to Bar Graphs

Determine a question that lends itself to pre-set categories and is of interest to children (e.g., favorite sport, ice cream, pet type). Ask children to draw a picture to represent their category (say, the ball that goes with their favorite sport) on a sticky note, place their sticky note in a "row" on the white board (or wall) so that there is a little space between them. Invite children to make observations about their picture graph. Discuss with the class how they might make a bar graph to illustrate their data. Move the sticky notes so there is no space between them and they look like a bar. Discuss ways to know how long the bar is and add a scale next to the bars to show the height (or length) of each bar.

Standards for Mathematical Practice

◀ **2** **Reason abstractly and quantitatively.**

The next transition is to begin using rectangular bars as seen in traditional bar graphs. Initially, you can have children shade each bar with alternating colors to keep individual pieces of data visible. Friel, Curcio, and Bright (2001) also recommend using grid lines to help children read the counts or frequencies and label the bars with numerical values.

Bar graphs can also be a source for creating put-together, take-apart, and comparison word problems.

Activity 17.7

CCSS-M: 2.MD.D.10

Story Bars

Have children make a bar graph of some data using linking cubes. Choose a situation with 5 or 6 bars with no more than 10 or 12 cubes in each. For example, the graph in Figure 17.10 shows prices for six toys. The task for children is to use the graph itself to create at least two story problems about the toy prices. For example, one problem might be "How much more money does the doll cost than the football?" Another problem could be "If you had $20, which toys could you buy? How much change would you get back?" Children can swap their story problems with a partner or you can pose some of their problems to the entire class.

technology note

The Bar Chart applet at the National Library of Virtual Manipulatives website allows children to create bar graphs of 3 to 12 columns with 5 to 20 rows of data each. Each piece of data is its own block in the bar so that individual data are visible. A numerical scale is shown along the vertical scale to help read the frequency for each category.

Figure 17.10

Using bar graphs to create story problems.

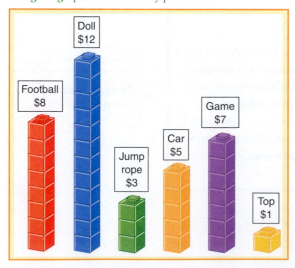

Line Plots

Object, picture, and bar graphs are useful for illustrating categorical data, for example, favorite colors or TV shows. When data are numerical (i.e., grouped along a continuous scale), they should be ordered along a number line.

Line plots, introduced in the CCSS-M standards in grade 2 using whole-number units (CCSSO, 2010) are counts of things along a numeric scale. To make a line plot, a number line is drawn and an X is made above the corresponding value on the line for every corresponding data element (in middle school and beyond the X is replaced by dots and the graph is then called a *dot plot*). (Watch this **video** (**https://www.youtube.com/watch?v=mHCBtKFhV8M**) about making line plots.) One advantage of a line plot is that every piece of data is shown on the graph, making it is a very easy type of graph for children to make. A line plot is essentially a bar graph arranged along a numerical scale with a potential bar for every indicated whole-number value on the horizontal scale. An example of a line plot is shown in Figure 17.11.

Figure 17.11

A line plot of the number of carrots in snack bags.

Number of carrots in snack bags

> ### 🌱 *Teaching Tip*
>
> **A common error that children make, especially when using technology to create graphs, is to use a line graph instead of a line plot. In line graphs we assume that the points on the line between the identified values are feasible values (e.g., those temperatures were passed through on the way from one identified value to the next). Data used with line plots are not continuous in that sense.**

To introduce line plots in a concrete manner, relate them to picture graphs, but use a numeric scale rather than a categorical scale, as done in the next activity. Having children be "in the graph" is also an important experience that will enable them to better understand the more abstract graphical representation.

Activity 17.8   CCSS-M: 1.MD.C.4; 2.MD.D.10

Stand by Me

Use masking tape to mark a line on the floor of the classroom or gymnasium and label it with numbers ranging from 2 minutes to 20 minutes (or whatever is appropriate for your children). Have children write on a Post-It note how many minutes it takes them to travel to school. By groups, ask children to stand on the location above that number in a line. Encourage peers to confirm their neighbors are standing in the correct place. Then ask children to leave their Post-it note at the number where they are standing and sit down. Recreate the line plot on an interactive white board or use the Post-it notes to recreate the line plot above a line drawn on the board. (Label the line with the same numbers as the masking tape line, e.g., 2 minutes to 20 minutes.) Have children create the line plot on their own paper. Ask children questions about their data (e.g., how many more or less in one category than another). As a summary, ask children to write one observation about the data. ELLs and children with disabilities will benefit from one sentence starters such as, "I notice that _____ children travel _____ minutes."

Line plots, because of the numerical scale, can be used to show measurements. Second graders are expected to generate measurements of objects to the nearest whole unit (CCSSO, 2010). They might measure to the nearest inch and plot, for example, their foot length, their cubit (length of forearm from elbow to finger tips), the height of their desk, and so on. Data can also be gathered from plants growing, time passing, or weather, as in the next activity.

Activity 17.9   CCSS-M: 2.MD.D.9

Storm Plotter

Create a class line plot with the horizontal scale labeled in whole number units and chart the amount of rain (or snow) that falls with each storm (install a rain gauge or access the

(continued)

information online). Place the data from each storm on the line plot. This can be done all year and color-coded by month. As more data is gathered, you can ask, "What do we notice about rain fall in our area?" Focus on variability—how does the storm total in October compare to the total in February? If you don't want to take months gathering data, instead look up the rain/snow fall in various cities/towns after a storm has passed through and use that to create a storm plot.

Interpreting Results

Interpretation is the fourth step in the process of doing statistics. As seen in the sample test items shown at the beginning of the chapter, sometimes questions focus on mathematical ideas rather than statistical ideas. Although it can be helpful to ask mathematical questions, when your learning objectives are related to doing statistics, it is essential to ask questions that are statistical in nature. That means the questions focus on the context of the situation, asking what can be learned or inferred from the data.

The emphasis of the questions in this phase is to get children to notice differences in the data and provide possible reasons for those differences (Franklin & Mewborn, 2008). You can start by engaging the class in a discussion of what information the graph shows or conveys. "What can you tell about our class by looking at this shoe graph?" Graphs convey factual information (e.g., more people wear sneakers than any other kind of shoe) and also provide opportunities to make inferences that are not directly observable in the graph (e.g., kids in this class do not like to wear leather shoes). Hourigan and Leavy (2015/2016) identified three different levels of questions you can ask to help children interpret and reason with data displayed in graphs:

- *Level 1 Questions: Reading the data* directly from the graph. For example, you could ask, "Which kind of shoe appears the most? Which appears the least? How many sneakers are there? Did any types of shoes appear the same number of times?

- *Level 2 Questions: Reading between the data*, which requires combining the data in some way and involves some interpretation. For example, you could ask, "How many more sneakers are there than boots? How many shoes are there in our graph? What are the two most popular kinds of shoes and how do you know?

- *Level 3 Questions: Reading beyond the data*, which involves making predictions or inferences from the data. For example, you could ask. "If someone else had collected this data and we did not know when, could we tell what time of year the data was collected? What kind of shoe would you expect most children to come to school tomorrow wearing?

These questions increase in their difficulty across the three levels, with Level 3 type questions being challenging for young children. But this is a skill that can and should be developed, even with preK–2 children. Using *driving questions* (Houligan & Leavy, 2015/206) that the children are interested in can help with their motivation to engage in thinking about questions from all three levels.

When asked about graphs, young children tend to initially focus on individual pieces of data in a data display and not on the data as a whole (Clements & Sarama, 2009). So when asked to describe something about a graph, they may state, "There I am! I ride the bus to school." The idea is to help children consider the data set as a whole. One way to accomplish this is to draw their attention on the *shape of data:* a sense of how the data are spread or grouped. Are the data spread out uniformly? Symmetrically? Are the data clustered? Are there data points that are very different from most of the other data (outliers)? When data are depicted on a number line, such as on a line plot, the idea of data being spread out or grouped together also takes on a numeric meaning. For example, in a measure of the heights of boys and girls in inches, we might notice that the girls' heights are spread over a wider range than the boys' heights. The boys' heights may cluster more around a particular height.

Remember the goal is to keep the focus on statistical thinking. Here are some recommended questions to get you started on having meaningful discussions about interpreting data (Franklin et al., 2005; Friel, O'Conner, & Mamer, 2006; Russell, 2006; Shaughnessy, 2006). (Think about how these questions relate to the three levels of questions identified by Hourigan and Leavy (2015/2016)):

- What do the numbers tell us about our class (or another class)?
- If we asked another class the same questions, how would that data look? What if we asked a larger group, how would the data look?
- How do the numbers in this graph *compare* to this graph?
- Where are the data "clustering"? Where are the data located that are *not* in the cluster?
- What does the graph *not* tell us?
- What new questions arise from these data?
- What is the maker of the graph trying to tell us?

Standards for Mathematical Practice

3 **Reason abstractly and quantitatively.**

These prompts apply across many data displays. Reflecting on and responding to questions such as these certainly should be a major focus of your instruction. Consider it the *after* phase of your lesson, although some of these questions will be integrated in the *during* phase as well.

Our world is inundated with data. It is essential that we prepare our children to be literate about what can be interpreted from data and what cannot be interpreted from data. It is not too early to start this preparation in grades preK–2.

Appendix A

Common Core State Standards

Standards for Mathematical Practice

The Standards for Mathematical Practice describe varieties of expertise that mathematics educators at all levels should seek to develop in their students. These practices rest on important "processes and proficiencies" with long-standing importance in mathematics education. The first of these are the NCTM process standards of problem solving, reasoning and proof, communication, representation, and connections. The second are the strands of mathematical proficiency specified in the National Research Council's report *Adding It Up:* adaptive reasoning, strategic competence, conceptual understanding (comprehension of mathematical concepts, operations and relations), procedural fluency (skill in carrying out procedures flexibly, accurately, efficiently and appropriately), and productive disposition (habitual inclination to see mathematics as sensible, useful, and worthwhile, coupled with a belief in diligence and one's own efficacy).

Source: Common Core State Standards for Mathematics was developed by the Council of Chief State School Officers. Copies may be downloaded at http://www.ccsso.org/.

1   Make sense of problems and persevere in solving them.

Mathematically proficient students start by explaining to themselves the meaning of a problem and looking for entry points to its solution. They analyze givens, constraints, relationships, and goals. They make conjectures about the form and meaning of the solution and plan a solution pathway rather than simply jumping into a solution attempt. They consider analogous problems, and try special cases and simpler forms of the original problem in order to gain insight into its solution. They monitor and evaluate their progress and change course if necessary. Older students might, depending on the context of the problem, transform algebraic expressions or change the viewing window on their graphing calculator to get the information they need. Mathematically proficient students can explain correspondences between equations, verbal descriptions, tables, and graphs or draw diagrams of important features and relationships, graph data, and search for regularity or trends. Younger students might rely on using concrete objects or pictures to help conceptualize and solve a problem. Mathematically proficient students check their answers to problems using a different method, and they continually ask themselves, "Does this make sense?" They can understand the approaches of others to solving complex problems and identify correspondences between different approaches.

2   Reason abstractly and quantitatively.

Mathematically proficient students make sense of quantities and their relationships in problem situations. They bring two complementary abilities to bear on problems involving quantitative relationships: the ability to *decontextualize*—to abstract a given situation and represent it symbolically and manipulate the representing symbols as if they have a life of their own, without necessarily attending to their referents—and the ability to *contextualize*, to pause as needed during the manipulation process in order to probe into the referents for the symbols involved. Quantitative reasoning entails habits of creating a coherent representation of the problem at hand; considering the units involved; attending to the meaning of quantities, not just how to compute them; and knowing and flexibly using different properties of operations and objects.

3   Construct viable arguments and critique the reasoning of others.

Mathematically proficient students understand and use stated assumptions, definitions, and previously established results in constructing arguments. They make conjectures and build a logical progression of statements to explore the truth of their conjectures. They are able to analyze situations by breaking them into cases, and can recognize and use counterexamples. They justify their conclusions, communicate them to others, and respond to the arguments of others. They reason inductively about data, making plausible arguments that take into account the context from which the data arose.

Mathematically proficient students are also able to compare the effectiveness of two plausible arguments, distinguish correct logic or reasoning from that which is flawed, and—if there is a flaw in an argument—explain what it is. Elementary students can construct arguments using concrete referents such as objects, drawings, diagrams, and actions. Such arguments can make sense and be correct, even though they are not generalized or made formal until later grades. Later, students learn to determine domains to which an argument applies. Students at all grades can listen or read the arguments of others, decide whether they make sense, and ask useful questions to clarify or improve the arguments.

4 Model with mathematics.

Mathematically proficient students can apply the mathematics they know to solve problems arising in everyday life, society, and the workplace. In early grades, this might be as simple as writing an addition equation to describe a situation. In middle grades, a student might apply proportional reasoning to plan a school event or analyze a problem in the community. By high school, a student might use geometry to solve a design problem or use a function to describe how one quantity of interest depends on another. Mathematically proficient students who can apply what they know are comfortable making assumptions and approximations to simplify a complicated situation, realizing that these may need revision later. They are able to identify important quantities in a practical situation and map their relationships using such tools as diagrams, two-way tables, graphs, flowcharts, and formulas. They can analyze those relationships mathematically to draw conclusions. They routinely interpret their mathematical results in the context of the situation and reflect on whether the results make sense, possibly improving the model if it has not served its purpose.

5 Use appropriate tools strategically.

Mathematically proficient students consider the available tools when solving a mathematical problem. These tools might include pencil and paper, concrete models, a ruler, a protractor, a calculator, a spreadsheet, a computer algebra system, a statistical package, or dynamic geometry software. Proficient students are sufficiently familiar with tools appropriate for their grade or course to make sound decisions about when each of these tools might be helpful, recognizing both the insight to be gained and their limitations. For example, mathematically proficient high school students analyze graphs of functions and solutions generated using a graphing calculator. They detect possible errors by strategically using estimation and other mathematical knowledge. When making mathematical models, they know that technology can enable them to visualize the results of varying assumptions, explore consequences, and compare predictions with data. Mathematically proficient students at various grade levels are able to identify relevant external mathematical resources, such as digital content located on a website, and use them to pose or solve problems. They are able to use technological tools to explore and deepen their understanding of concepts.

6 Attend to precision.

Mathematically proficient students try to communicate precisely to others. They try to use clear definitions in discussion with others and in their own reasoning. They state the meaning of the symbols they choose, including using the equal sign consistently and appropriately. They are careful about specifying units of measure, and labeling axes to clarify the correspondence with quantities in a problem. They calculate accurately and efficiently, express numerical answers with a degree of precision appropriate for the problem context. In the elementary grades, students give carefully formulated explanations to each other. By the time they reach high school they have learned to examine claims and make explicit use of definitions.

7 Look for and make use of structure.

Mathematically proficient students look closely to discern a pattern or structure. Young students, for example, might notice that three and seven more is the same amount as seven and three more, or they may sort a collection of shapes according to how many sides the shapes have. Later, students will see 7×8 equals the well remembered $7 \times 5 + 7 \times 3$, in preparation for learning about the distributive property. In the expression $x^2 + 9x + 14$, older students can see the 14 as 2×7 and the 9 as $2 + 7$. They recognize the significance of an existing line in a geometric figure and can use the strategy of drawing an auxiliary line for solving problems. They also can step back for an overview and shift perspective. They can see complicated things, such as some algebraic expressions, as single objects or as being composed of several objects. For example, they can see $5 - 3(x - y)^2$ as 5 minus a positive number times a square and use that to realize that its value cannot be more than 5 for any real numbers x and y.

8 Look for and express regularity in repeated reasoning.

Mathematically proficient students notice if calculations are repeated, and look both for general methods and for shortcuts. Upper elementary students might notice when dividing 25 by 11 that they are repeating the same calculations over and over again, and conclude they have a repeating decimal. By paying attention to the calculation of slope as they repeatedly check whether points are on the line through $(1, 2)$ with slope 3, middle school students might abstract the equation $(y - 2)/(x - 1) = 3$. Noticing the regularity in the way terms cancel when expanding $(x - 1)(x + 1)$, $(x - 1)(x^2 + x + 1)$, and $(x - 1)(x^3 + x^2 + x + 1)$ might lead them to the general formula for the sum of a geometric series. As they work to solve a problem, mathematically proficient students maintain oversight of the process, while attending to the details. They continually evaluate the reasonableness of their intermediate results.

Connecting the Standards for Mathematical Practice to the Standards for Mathematical Content

The Standards for Mathematical Practice describe ways in which developing student practitioners of the discipline of mathematics increasingly ought to engage with the subject matter as they grow in mathematical maturity and expertise throughout the elementary, middle, and high school years. Designers of curricula, assessments, and professional development should all attend to the need to connect the mathematical practices to mathematical content in mathematics instruction.

The Standards for Mathematical Content are a balanced combination of procedure and understanding. Expectations that begin with the word "understand" are often especially good opportunities to connect the practices to the content. Students who lack understanding of a topic may rely on procedures too heavily. Without a flexible base from which to work, they may be less likely to consider analogous problems, represent problems coherently, justify conclusions, apply the mathematics to practical situations, use technology mindfully to work with the mathematics, explain the mathematics accurately to other students, step back for an overview, or deviate from a known procedure to find a shortcut. In short, a lack of understanding effectively prevents a student from engaging in the mathematical practices.

In this respect, those content standards which set an expectation of understanding are potential "points of intersection" between the Standards for Mathematical Content and the Standards for Mathematical Practice. These points of intersection are intended to be weighted toward central and generative concepts in the school mathematics curriculum that most merit the time, resources, innovative energies, and focus necessary to qualitatively improve the curriculum, instruction, assessment, professional development, and student achievement in mathematics.

Appendix B

Common Core State Standards

Grades K–2 Critical Content Areas and Overviews

CCSS Mathematics | Grade Kindergarten Critical Areas

In Kindergarten, instructional time should focus on two critical areas:

1. representing and comparing whole numbers, initially with sets of objects; and

2. describing shapes and space.

Source: Common Core State Standards for Mathematics was developed by the Council of Chief State School Officers. Copies may be downloaded at http://www.ccsso.org/.

More learning time in Kindergarten should be devoted to number than to other topics.

1. *Students use numbers, including written numerals, to represent quantities and to solve quantitative problems, such as counting objects in a set; counting out a given number of objects; comparing sets or numerals; and modeling simple joining and separating situations with sets of objects, or eventually with equations such as $5 + 2 = 7$ and $7 - 2 = 5$.* (Kindergarten students should see addition and subtraction equations, and student writing of equations in kindergarten is encouraged, but it is not required.) Students choose, combine, and apply effective strategies for answering quantitative questions, including quickly recognizing the cardinalities of small sets of objects, counting and producing sets of given sizes, counting the number of objects in combined sets, or counting the number of objects that remain in a set after some are taken away.

2. *Students describe their physical world using geometric ideas (e.g., shape, orientation, spatial relations) and vocabulary.* They identify, name, and describe basic two-dimensional shapes, such as squares, triangles, circles, rectangles, and hexagons, presented in a variety of ways (e.g., with different sizes and orientations), as well as three-dimensional shapes such as cubes, cones, cylinders, and spheres. They use basic shapes and spatial reasoning to model objects in their environment and to construct more complex shapes.

Grade K Overview

Counting and Cardinality

- Know number names and the count sequence.
- Count to tell the number of objects.
- Compare numbers.

Operations and Algebraic Thinking

- Understand addition as putting together and adding to, and understand subtraction as taking apart and taking from.

Number and Operations in Base-Ten

- Work with numbers 11–19 to gain foundations for place value.

Measurement and Data

- Describe and compare measurable attributes.
- Classify objects and count the number of objects in each category.

Geometry

- Identify and describe shapes.
- Analyze, compare, create, and compose shapes.

CCSS Mathematics | Grade 1 Critical Areas

In Grade 1, instructional time should focus on four critical areas:

1. developing understanding of addition, subtraction, and strategies for addition and subtraction within 20;

2. developing understanding of whole number relationships and place value, including grouping in tens and ones;

3. developing understanding of linear measurement and measuring lengths as iterating length units; and

4. reasoning about attributes of, and composing and decomposing, geometric shapes.

1. ***Students develop strategies for adding and subtracting whole numbers based on their prior work with small numbers.*** They use a variety of models, including discrete objects and length-based models (e.g., cubes connected to form lengths), to model add-to, take-from, put-together, take-apart, and compare situations to develop meaning for the operations of addition and subtraction, and to develop strategies to solve arithmetic problems with these operations. Students understand connections between counting and addition and subtraction (e.g., adding two is the same as counting on two). They use properties of addition to add whole numbers and to create and use increasingly sophisticated strategies based on these properties (e.g., "making tens") to solve addition and subtraction problems within 20. By comparing a variety of solution strategies, students build their understanding of the relationship between addition and subtraction.

2. ***Students develop, discuss, and use efficient, accurate, and generalizable methods to add within 100 and subtract multiples of 10.*** They compare whole numbers (at least to 100) to develop understanding of and solve problems involving their relative sizes. They think of whole numbers between 10 and 100 in terms of tens and ones (especially recognizing the numbers 11 to 19 as composed of a ten and some ones). Through activities that build number sense, they understand the order of the counting numbers and their relative magnitudes.

3. ***Students develop an understanding of the meaning and processes of measurement, including underlying concepts such as iterating (the mental activity of building up the length of an object with equal-sized units) and the transitivity principle for indirect measurement.***[1]

4. ***Students compose and decompose plane or solid figures (e.g., put two triangles together to make a quadrilateral) and build understanding of part-whole relationships as well as the properties of the original and composite shapes.*** As they combine shapes, they recognize them from different perspectives and orientations, describe their geometric attributes, and determine how they are alike and different, to develop the background for measurement and for initial understandings of properties such as congruence and symmetry.

---

[1]Students should apply the principle of transitivity of measurement to make indirect comparisons, but they need not use this technical term.

Grade 1 Overview

Operations and Algebraic Thinking

- Represent and solve problems involving addition and subtraction.
- Understand and apply properties of operations and the relationship between addition and subtraction.
- Add and subtract within 20.
- Work with addition and subtraction equations.

Number and Operations in Base-Ten

- Extend the counting sequence.
- Understand place value.
- Use place value understanding and properties of operations to add and subtract.

Measurement and Data

- Measure lengths indirectly and by iterating length units.
- Tell and write time.
- Represent and interpret data.

Geometry

- Reason with shapes and their attributes.

CCSS Mathematics | Grade 2 Critical Areas

In Grade 2, instructional time should focus on four critical areas:

1. extending understanding of base-ten notation;
2. building fluency with addition and subtraction;
3. using standard units of measure; and
4. describing and analyzing shapes.

1. *Students extend their understanding of the base-ten system.*   This includes ideas of counting in fives, tens, and multiples of hundreds, tens, and ones, as well as number relationships involving these units, including comparing. Students understand multidigit numbers (up to 1000) written in base-ten notation, recognizing that the digits in each place represent amounts of thousands, hundreds, tens, or ones (e.g., 853 is 8 hundreds + 5 tens + 3 ones).

2. *Students use their understanding of addition to develop fluency with addition and subtraction within 100.*   They solve problems within 1000 by applying their understanding of models for addition and subtraction, and they develop, discuss, and use efficient, accurate, and generalizable methods to compute sums and differences of whole numbers in base-ten notation, using their understanding of place value and the properties of operations. They select and accurately apply methods that are appropriate for the context and the numbers involved to mentally calculate sums and differences for numbers with only tens or only hundreds.

3. *Students recognize the need for standard units of measure (centimeter and inch) and they use rulers and other measurement tools with the understanding that linear measure involves an iteration of units.* They recognize that the smaller the unit, the more iterations they need to cover a given length.

4. *Students describe and analyze shapes by examining their sides and angles. Students investigate, describe, and reason about decomposing and combining shapes to make other shapes.* Through building, drawing, and analyzing two- and three-dimensional shapes, students develop a foundation for understanding area, volume, congruence, similarity, and symmetry in later grades.

Grade 2 Overview

Operations and Algebraic Thinking

- Represent and solve problems involving addition and subtraction.
- Add and subtract within 20.
- Work with equal groups of objects to gain foundations for multiplication.

Number and Operations in Base-Ten

- Understand place value.
- Use place value understanding and properties of operations to add and subtract.

Measurement and Data

- Measure and estimate lengths in standard units.
- Relate addition and subtraction to length.
- Work with time and money.
- Represent and interpret data.

Geometry

- Reason with shapes and their attributes.

Appendix C

Mathematics Teaching Practices

NCTM Principles to Action (2014)

Establish mathematics goals to focus learning.

Effective teaching of mathematics establishes clear goals for the mathematics that students are learning, situates goals within learning progressions, and uses the goals to guide instructional decisions.

Source: Republished with permission of National Council for Teachers of Mathematics (NCTM), from NCTM Mathematics Teaching Practices from Principles to Actions © 2014; permission conveyed through Copyright Clearance Center, Inc.

Implement tasks that promote reasoning and problem solving.

Effective teaching of mathematics engages students in solving and discussing tasks that promote mathematical reasoning and problem solving and allow multiple entry points and varied solution strategies.

Use and connect mathematical representations.

Effective teaching of mathematics engages students in making connections among mathematical representations to deepen understanding of mathematics concepts and procedures and as tools for problem solving.

Facilitate meaningful mathematical discourse.

Effective teaching of mathematics facilitates discourse among students to build shared understanding of mathematical ideas by analyzing and comparing student approaches and arguments.

Pose purposeful questions.

Effective teaching of mathematics uses purposeful questions to assess and advance students' reasoning and sense making about important mathematical ideas and relationships.

Build procedural fluency from conceptual understanding.

Effective teaching of mathematics builds fluency with procedures on a foundation of conceptual understanding so that students, over time, become skillful in using procedures flexibly as they solve contextual and mathematical problems.

Support productive struggle in learning mathematics.

Effective teaching of mathematics consistently provides students, individually and collectively, with opportunities and supports to engage in productive struggle as they grapple with mathematical ideas and relationships.

Elicit and use evidence of student thinking.

Effective teaching of mathematics uses evidence of student thinking to assess progress toward mathematical understanding and to adjust instruction continually in ways that support and extend learning.

Appendix D

Activities at a Glance

Volume I

This table lists the named and numbered activities in Part 2 of the book. In addition to providing an easy way to find an activity, the table provides the mathematics content for each activity stated as succinctly as possible, as well as the related *Common Core State Standards*. Remember though, this is a book about teaching mathematics, not a book of activities. Every activity should be seen as an integral part of the text that surround it. It is extremely important not to take any activity as a suggestion for instruction without reading the full text in which it is embedded.

Chapter 8 Developing early number concepts and number sense.

Activity		Mathematical Content	CCSS-M	Page
8.1	Counting Up and Back	Practice skill of counting forward and backward	K.CC.A.1; K.CC.A.2	115
8.2	Line Them Up!*	Practice number sequences and the use of the number line	K.CC.A.1; K.CC.A.2; K.CC.A.3	116
8.3	Number Necklaces*	Practice number matching and develop basic addition	K.CC.A.3	116
8.4	Counting Moose Tracks*	Develop one-to-one correspondence and cardinality	K.CC.B.4.A	117
8.5	Egg Carton Counting	Develop one-to-one correspondence and cardinality	K.CC.B.4.A	117
8.6	Seashell Counts*	Develop one-to-one correspondence and cardinality	K.CC.B.4.A	117
8.7	Fill the Tower*	Develop one-to-one correspondence	K.CC.B.5	118
8.8	Number Tubs	Develop counting skills and the need for number names	K.CC.B.4; K.CC.B.5; K.CC.A.3	119
8.9	The Find!*	Develop the idea of cardinality	K.CC.B.4; K.CC.B.5	120
8.10	Learning Patterns	Develop instant recognition of an amount arranged in dot patterns	K.CC.B.4	121
8.11	Dot Plate Flash	Practice recognition of amounts without counting	K.CC.B.4a, b	121
8.12	Counting On with Counters	Practice counting on	K.CC.A.2; K.CC.B.5	123
8.13	Real Counting On*	Practice counting on to tell all	K.OA.A.1; 1.OA.B.5	123
8.14	Make Sets of More/Less/Same*	Develop relational concept of more/less/same	K.CC.C.6	124
8.15	Find the Same Amount*	Identify sets with more/less/same	K.CC.A.3; K.CC.C.6	124
8.16	More, Less, or the Same*	Develop concept of one more, two more, one less, two less, zero	K.CC.A.3; K.CC.C.6; K.O.A.A.1	125
8.17	One/Two Less and More Dominoes*	Develop concept of one more, two more, one less, two less	K.OA.A.2; K.CC.A.3; K.CC.B.4c; 1.OA.C.5	127
8.18	Make a Two-More-Than Set*	Develop concept of one more, two more, one less, two less	K.OA.A.2; 1.OA.C.5	127
8.19	A Two-More-Than Machine	Practice with one more, two more, one less, two less relationships	1.OA.C.5	127
8.20	Five-Frame Tell-About*	Develop benchmark of 5 for numbers to 10	K.CC.C.7; K.OA.A.5	128
8.21	Number Medley*	Develop benchmarks of 5 and 10 for numbers to 10	K.CC.C.6; K.CC.C.7	129
8.22	Ten-Frame Flash*	Practice benchmarks of 5 and 10 for numbers to 10	K.CC.B.5	130
8.23	Build It in Parts*	Practice part–whole concepts using manipulatives	K.OA.A.3; 1.OA.C.6	131
8.24	Show Me the Parts!	Practice part–whole concepts with fingers	K.OA.A.3; 1.OA.C.6	133
8.25	Covered Parts	Develop missing-part concepts	K.OA.A.2	133
8.26	Missing-Part Cards*	Practice missing-part concepts	K.OA.A4	134
8.27	I Wish I Had*	Practice missing-part concepts	K.OA.A.1; K.OA.A.2; K.OA.A.3	134
8.28	Number Sandwiches*	Practice missing-part concepts	K.OA.A.2; 1.OA.C.6	135
8.29	Ten and Some More	Develop concept of teen numbers	K.NBT.A.1	137
8.30	Build the Number with Cards*	Practice part–whole concepts with different representations	K.NBT.A.1; 1.NBT.B.2; 2.NBT.A.1	138

* Activity titles with an asterisk include a downloadable Activity Page, Expanded Lesson, or Blackline Master.

Activity		Mathematical Content	CCSS-M	Page
8.31	More and Less Extended	Extend one more, two more, one less, two less relationships to teen numbers	K.CC.C.6; K.NBT.A.1	138
8.32	Patterns on a Hundreds Chart	Explore patterns in numbers to 100	K.CC.A.1; K.CC.A.2; 1.NBT.A.1; 1.NBT.C.5; 2.NBT.A.2	139
8.33	Missing Numbers*	Practice sequence of numbers to 100	K.CC.A.1; K.CC.A.2; 1.NBT.A.1; 1.NBT.C.5; 2.NBT.A.2	140
8.34	Add a Unit to Your Number	Connect number to real world measures	K.MD.A.1; 1.MD.B.3; 2.MD.A.3	142
8.35	Is It Reasonable?	Connect number to real world measures	K.MD.A.1; 1.MD.A.2; 2.MD.A.3	142

Chapter 9   Developing meanings for the operations.

Activity		Mathematical Content	CCSS-M	Page
9.1	Build It in Parts Equations	Practice part–whole concepts with representations and symbols	1.OA.A.1; 2.OA.A.1	156
9.2	True or False?	Develop the meaning of the equal sign	1.OA.D.7	156
9.3	Guinea Pigs in Cages*	Develop strategies for exploring both addends unknown problems	K.OA.A.3; 1.OA.A.1; 1.OA.B.4	158
9.4	Up and Down the Number Line	Practice using units on a number line	K.OA.A.2; 1.OA.A.1; 1.OA.A.2; 2.OA.A.1	159
9.5	Missing-Part Subtraction	Develop subtraction as a name for a missing part	K.OA.A.2; 1.OA.A.1; 1.OA.A.2; 2.OA.A.1	160
9.6	More Than Two Addends	Practice adding more than two addends	1.OA.B.2	162
9.7	Snack Time Sharing	Develop fair sharing/partition division	K.CC.B.4; K.CC.B.5; K.CC.C.6; 1.OA.A.1; 2.OA.C.4	166
9.8	Quick! How Many Are There?	Develop skip counting through subitizing	K.CC.B.5; 1.OA.C.5; 2.NBT.A.2; 2.OA.C.4	169
9.9	Divide and Conquer!*	Develop fair sharing/partition division and repeated subtraction/measurement division	2.OA.C.4	170

Chapter 10   Helping children master the basic facts.

Activity		Mathematical Content	CCSS-M	Page
10.1	If You Didn't Know	Use known basic facts to determine unknown facts	1.OA.C.6; 2.OA.B.2	187
10.2	How Many Feet in the Bed?	Practice facts for +2 and −2	1.OA.A.1; 1.OA.C.6; 2.OA.B.2	188
10.3	One More Than and Two More Than with Dice and Spinners*	Practice addition facts for +1 and +2	1.OA.C.5; 1.OA.C.6; 2.OA.B.2	188

(continued)

* Activity titles with an asterisk include a downloadable Activity Page, Expanded Lesson, or Blackline Master.

Chapter 10 Helping children master the basic facts. (*continued*)

Activity		Mathematical Content	CCSS-M	Page
10.4	What's Alike? Zero Facts	Develop understanding of adding zero	1.OA.C.5; 1.OA.B.3; 1.OA.C.6; 2.OA.B.2	189
10.5	Double Magic*	Practice addition double facts	1.OA.C.5; 1.OA.B.3; 1.OA.C.6; 2.OA.B.2	190
10.6	Calculator Doubles	Practice addition doubles facts	1.OA.C.5; 1.OA.B.3; 1.OA.C.6; 2.OA.B.2	190
10.7	How Many More to Equal 10?	Develop and practice number combinations that make 10	1.OA.B.4; 1.OA.C.6; 2.OA.B.2	191
10.8	Move It, Move It*	Develop Making 10 strategy	1.OA.B.3; 1.OA.C.6; 2.OA.B.2	192
10.9	Frames and Facts*	Practice Making 10 strategy	1.OA.B.3; 1.OA.C.6; 2.OA.B.2	192
10.10	Flash*	Practice using 5 and 10 as anchors	1.OA.B.3; 1.OA.C.5; 1.OA.C.6; 2.OA.B.2	193
10.11	On the Double!	Practice near doubles addition facts	1.OA.B.3; 1.OA.C.6; 2.OA.B.2	193
10.12	Apples in a Tree*	Practice subtraction to 20	1.OA.B.4; 1.OA.C.6; 2.OA.B.2	195
10.13	Apples in Two Trees	Develop missing-value concept, relating addition to subtraction	1.OA.B.3; 1.OA.B.4; 1.OA.C.6; 2.OA.B.2	196
10.14	Clock Facts	Develop 5-minute intervals on the clock as a strategy for fives multiplication facts	2.NBT.A.2	198
10.15	Salute!	Identify the missing addend	1.OA.B.4; 1.OA.C.6; 2.OA.B.2	199
10.16	What's under My Thumb?	Connect addition and subtraction facts	1.OA.B.4; 1.OA.C.6; 2.OA.B.2	199
10.17	Bowl-a-Fact*	Practice creating equations in addition and subtraction	2.OA.B.2	201

Chapter 11 Developing whole-number place-value concepts.

Activity		Mathematical Content	CCSS-M	Page
11.1	Counting in Groups	Develop concept of groups of 10 as an efficient method of counting	K.NBT.A.1; 1.NBT.B.2a	214
11.2	Groups of Ten*	Develop concept of groups of 10 as a method of counting	K.NBT.A.1; 1.NBT.B.2a; 1.NBT.B.2b; 1.NBT.B.2c	214
11.3	Estimating Groups of Tens and Ones*	Develop the concept of two-digit numbers as ten and some more	K.NBT.A.1; 1.NBT.B.2a; 1.NBT.B.2b	216
11.4	Too Many Tens	Estimate and group quantities into hundreds, tens, and ones	2.NBT.A.1	217
11.5	Can You Make the Link?	Develop alternative groupings of ten to represent a number	1.NBT.B.2; 1.NBT.C.5	217
11.6	Three Other Ways	Develop alternative groupings of tens and hundreds to represent a number	2.NBT.A.1; 2.NBT.A.3; K.CC.B.5	218

* Activity titles with an asterisk include a downloadable Activity Page, Expanded Lesson, or Blackline Master.

Activity		Mathematical Content	CCSS-M	Page
11.7	Base-Ten Riddles*	Develop alternative groupings of tens and hundreds to represent a number	1.NBT.A.1; 2.NBT.A.1; 2.NBT.A.3	218
11.8	Counting Rows of Ten*	Develop and connect three oral counting strategies	1.NBT.B.2c	219
11.9	Counting with Base-Ten Models	Develop and connect three oral counting strategies	1.NBT.B.2; 1.NBT.C.5	220
11.10	Tens and Ones with Fingers	Develop and connect three oral counting strategies	1.NBT.B.2a; 1.NBT.B.2b; 1.NBT.B.2c	220
11.11	Say It/Display It	Connect oral and symbolic names for numbers to physical representations	2.NBT.A.1a; 2.NBT.A.1b; 2.NBT.A.3	223
11.12	Digit Change	Apply place value concepts to symbolic representations	1.NBT.B.2; 1.NBT.C.5; 1.NBT.C.6; 2.NBT.A.1; 2.NBT.A.3; 2.NBT.B.5; 2.NBT.B.8	223
11.13	Finding Neighbors on the Hundreds Chart*	Explore patterns in numbers to 100	CCSS-M: K.CC.A.1; K.NBT.A.1; 1.NBT.A.1; 1.NBT.B.2; 1.NBT.C.5	227
11.14	The Hundreds Chart with Models*	Develop concepts of 1 more/less and 10 more/less for two digit numbers	K.CC.A.1; K.NBT.A.1; 1.NBT.A.1; 1.NBT.B.2; 1.NBT.C.5	227
11.15	The Thousands Chart*	Extend patterns for 1 to 100 to patterns to 1000	2.NBT.A.1; 2.NBT.A.2; 2.NBT.A.3; 2.NBT.B.8	228
11.16	Who Am I?	Develop relative magnitude of numbers to 100	1.NBT.A.1; 1.NBT.B.2; 1.NBT.B.3; 2.NBT.A.1; 2.NBT.A.2; 2.NBT.A.4	228
11.17	Who Could They Be?	Develop relative magnitude of numbers to 100	1.NBT.A.1; 1.NBT.B.2; 1.NBT.B.3; 2.NBT.A.1; 2.NBT.A.2; 2.NBT.A.4	229
11.18	Close, Far, and in Between	Explore relative differences between multidigit numbers	1.NBT.A.1; 1.NBT.B.2; 1.NBT.B.3; 2.NBT.A.1; 2.NBT.A.2; 2.NBT.A.4	229
11.19	50 and Some More	Develop 50 as a benchmark part of numbers between 50 and 100	1.NBT.B.4	230
11.20	The Other Part of 100*	Develop missing-part strategies with a whole of 100	1.NBT.B.4; 2.NBT.B.5	231
11.21	Compatible Pairs	Explore addition combinations that make multiples of 10 or 100	2.NBT.B.5	231
11.22	Calculator Challenge Counting	Develop mental addition strategies through skip counting	1.NBT.C.5	232
11.23	Wipe Out!	Reinforce place value understanding while practicing addition and subtraction of multidigit numbers	2.NBT.A.1; 2.NBT.B.5; 2.NBT.B.7	232
11.24	Numbers, Squares, Lines, and Dots*	Develop invented strategies for addition and subtraction	2.NBT.B.7	233
11.25	Hundreds Chart Addition*	Practice adding two or three digit numbers	2.NBT.B.5	234
11.26	How Much Between?*	Develop strategies to find the difference	2.NBT.B.5	234

* Activity titles with an asterisk include a downloadable Activity Page, Expanded Lesson, or Blackline Master.

Chapter 12 Building strategies for whole-number computation.

Activity		Mathematical Content	CCSS-M	Page
12.1	Little Ten-Frame Sums*	Develop invented strategies for addition	2.NBT.B.5	240
12.2	Exploring Subtraction Strategies*	Practice solving word problems with two-digit numbers	2.OA.A1	249
12.3	Crossing a Decade*	Extend the Making 10 strategy to two-digit numbers	1.NBT.C.4; 2.OA.A.2	250
12.4	I Am . . . , Who Is . . .?*	Practice mental math with addition and subtraction of decade numbers	1.NBT.C.4; 1.NBT.C.5; 1.NBT.C.6	251
12.5	Just Adjust It	Practice using algebraic thinking to adjust numbers to make addition easier	1.NBT.C.4; 2.NBT.B.5; 2.NBT.B.9	252
12.6	Odd or Even?*	Develop patterns when adding two-digit numbers	2.OA.C.3	253
12.7	How Far to My Number?*	Develop missing part strategies (such as *adding on*) for subtraction	2.NBT.B.5; 2.NBT.B.9	255
12.8	Tricky Trading*	Explore regrouping across zero	2.NBT.B.7; 2.NBT.B.9	260
12.9	Pick Your Strategy	Determine which strategy is most useful to add or subtract depending on the numbers involved	1.NBT.C.4; 2.NBT.B.5; 2.NBT.B.6; 2.NBT.B.7; 2.NBT.B.9	261
12.10	Is It Over or Under?	Develop strategies to make computational estimations	2.NBT.B.5; 2.MD.A.3; 2.MD.C.7	264
12.11	Round Up?	Develop strategies to round numbers to the nearest ten or hundred	2.NBT.B.5	265
12.12	Box Math*	Practice computation and estimation through problem solving	2.NBT.B.5	267

Chapter 13 Promoting algebraic reasoning.

Activity		Mathematical Content	CCSS-M	Page
13.1	One Up and One Down with Addition*	Develop an understanding of how complementary changes in two addends leave the sum unchanged	K.OA.A.3; 1.OA.D.7; 1.OA.C.6 ; 2.OA.B.2	272
13.2	Diagonal Sums*	Explore place-value relationships and generalize patterns	1.NBT.C.4; 2.NBT.B.9	274
13.3	Ten and Then Some*	Develop ideas about equivalence	1.OA.C.6; 1.OA.D.7; 2.OA.B.2	277
13.4	Different but the Same	Develop ideas about equivalence	1.OA.C.6; 1.OA.D.7; 2.OA.B.2	278
13.5	Seesaw Comparisons	Develop the concept of the equal sign as a balance	1.OA.D.7; 2.NBT.A.4	278
13.6	What Do You Know about the Shapes?	Develop an understanding of the equal sign	K.MD.A.2; 1.OA.D.7; 2.NBT.A.4	279
13.7	Tilt or Balance?	Develop an understanding of the equal sign and the less than and greater than symbols	1.NBT.C.4; 2.NBT.A.4; 2.NBT.B.7	280
13.8	True or False Equations	Explore the meaning of the equal sign	1.OA.B.3; 1.OA.D.7; 1.NBT.B.4; 2.NBT.B.5	282
13.9	What's Missing?	Explore the meaning of the equal sign	1.OA.D.7; 1.OA.D.8; 2.OA.A.1	282

* Activity titles with an asterisk include a downloadable Activity Page, Expanded Lesson, or Blackline Master.

Activity		Mathematical Content	CCSS-M	Page
13.10	Make a Statement!*	Create equivalent expressions	1.OA.D.7; 1.OA.D.8; 2.OA.A.1	284
13.11	Toys, Toys, Toys	Explore variables in a context	1.OA.A.1; 1.OA.C.6; 2.OA.A.1	286
13.12	Five Ways to Zero	Apply properties, such as identify for addition, to create equations	1.OA.B.3; 1.OA.C.6; 1.OA.D.7; 2.OA.B.2	289
13.13	Fair Shares for Two	Develop a concept of even and odd numbers based on fair sharing	1.OA.B.3; 2.OA.C.3; 2.NBT.B.5	291
13.14	Bumps or No Bumps*	Develop a concept of even and odd numbers based on doubles or multiples of 2	1.OA.B.3; 2.OA.C.3; 2.NBT.B.5	291
13.15	Broken Calculator: Can You Fix It?	Explore properties of odd and even numbers	1.OA.B.3; 2.OA.C.3; 2.NBT.B.5	292
13.16	Convince Me Conjectures*	Make and test generalizations about whole number operations and properties	1.OA.B.3; 2.NBT.B.9	293
13.17	Can You Match It?	Distinguish between the structure of a repeat pattern and its representation	K.MD.B.3; K.G.A.1; K.G.B.4; 1.G.A.2	295
13.18	Same Pattern, Different Stuff	Distinguish between the structure of a repeat pattern and its representation	K.MD.B.3; K.G.A.1; K.G.B.4; 1.G.A.2	296
13.19	Predict Down the Line	Explore the structure of repeating patterns analytically	K.MD.B.3; K.G.A.1; K.G.B.4; 1.G.A.2; 2.OA.C.3	297
13.20	What Is My Rule?	Develop functional relationships from patterns	1.OA.C.6; 2.OA.B.2; 2.OA.C.4	299
13.21	What's Next and Why?	Explore relationships in number patterns	1.OA.C.6; 1.NBT.C.4; 2.OA.B.2; 2.NBT.A.2; 2.NBT.B.5	300
13.22	Calculator Skip Counting*	Explore patterns in skip counts	1.NBT.C.5; 2.NBT.A.2	300

Chapter 14   Exploring early fraction concepts.

Activity		Mathematical Content	CCSS-M	Page
14.1	Halves or Not Halves?*	Develop an understanding of fractional parts	1.G.A.3; 2.G.A.3	308
14.2	Size and Shape Check*	Examine the concept that fractional parts do not have to be the same shape to be the same size	2.G.A.3	309
14.3	Different Shapes for Fair Shares*	Develop an understanding of fractional parts	1.G.A.3; 2.G.A.3	309
14.4	Paper Strip to Number Line*	Extending an understanding of fractional parts to a number line	1.G.A.3; 2.G.A.3	311
14.5	Sets in Equal Shares*	Develop an understanding of fractional parts using fair sharing with set models	1.G.A.3; 2.G.A.3	312
14.6	Cut Me a Fair Share!*	Use partitioning to create equal shares	1.G.A.3; 2.G.A.3	315
14.7	How Much Did She Share?	Develop an understanding of equal parts in fractions	1.G.A.3; 2.G.A.3	319

(*continued*)

* Activity titles with an asterisk include a downloadable Activity Page, Expanded Lesson, or Blackline Master.

Chapter 14 Exploring early fraction concepts. (*continued*)

Activity		Mathematical Content	CCSS-M	Page
14.8	More, Less, or Equal to One Whole	Develop an understanding of fractional parts	1.G.A.3; 2.G.A.3	321
14.9	Playground Fractions*	Develop concept of equal shares using an area model	1.G.A.3; 2.G.A.3	322
14.10	Pattern Block Creatures	Develop an understanding of fractional parts, in particular focusing on the size of fractional parts as opposed to the number of pieces or partitions	1.G.A.3; 2.G.A.3	322
14.11	Cut Them Up Again!	Explore different ways to partition a quantity into equal parts	1.G.A.3; 2.G.A.3	324
14.12	Keeping It Fair	Explore fraction equivalence	1.G.A.3; 2.G.A.3	325
14.13	Who Is Winning?	Develop fraction concepts using a linear model	1.G.A.3; 2.G.A.3	325

Chapter 15 Building measurement concepts.

Activity		Mathematical Content	CCSS-M	Page
15.1	About One Unit*	Develop familiarity with standard units (any attribute)	1.MD.A.2; 2.MD.A.1; 2.MD.A.3	335
15.2	Familiar References	Explore a variety of real world benchmarks or references for standard units	1.MD.A.2; 2.MD.A.1	336
15.3	Personal Benchmarks	Explore useful benchmarks using body lengths	2.MD.A.1	337
15.4	Guess the Unit*	Develop the concept of various units of measure	2.MD.A.3	337
15.5	Estimation Quickie	Practice estimating measures of different attributes	K.MD.A.1; K.MD.A.2; 1.MD.A.1; 1.MD.A.2; 2.MD.A.3	340
15.6	Estimation Scavenger Hunt*	Practice measurement estimation in real contexts	1.MD.A.2; 2.MD.A.1; 2.MD.A.3	341
15.7	Longer, Shorter, Same	Explore the concept of length through direct comparisons	K.MD.A.2; 1.MD.A.1; 2.MD.A.3	342
15.8	Length (or Unit) Hunt	Explore the concept of length through direct comparisons; develop familiarity with a standard unit	K.MD.A.2; 1.MD.A.1; 1.MD.A.2; 2.MD.A.3	342
15.9	Will It Fit?	Explore the concept of length through indirect comparisons	1.MD.A.1; 2.MD.A.3; 2.MD.A.4	342
15.10	Crooked Paths*	Develop concept of length along paths that are not straight	1.MD.A.1; 2.MD.A.3; 2.MD.A.4	343
15.11	How Long Is the Teacher?	Develop methods for measuring length	1.MD.A.2; 2.MD.A.1; 2.MD.A.2; 2.MD.A.3	344
15.12	Estimate and Measure*	Develop an understanding of length measurement	1.MD.A.2; 2.MD.A.1; 2.MD.A.3	344
15.13	Changing Units*	Explore the inverse relationship between unit size and measure	2.MD.A.2; 2.MD.A.3	345
15.14	Make Your Own Ruler	Develop an understanding of rulers by making a ruler	1.MD.A.2; 2.MD.A.1; 2.MD.A.3	347
15.15	One-Handed Clocks*	Develop an understanding of the hour hand in reading a clock	1.MD.B.3; 2.MD.C.7	350
15.16	Ready for the Bell*	Practice reading a clock and develop an understanding of the relationship between an analog clock and a digital clock	1.MD.B.3	351

* Activity titles with an asterisk include a downloadable Activity Page, Expanded Lesson, or Blackline Master.

Activity		Mathematical Content	CCSS-M	Page
15.17	Money Skip Counting	Practice skip counting in amounts related to coin values	2.MD.C.8	352
15.18	Coin-Number Addition	Develop skill in counting money	2.MD.C.8	352
15.19	How Much Is the Change?	Practice finding differences in amounts related to coin values	2.MD.C.8	354
15.20	The Fewest Coins	Develop skill in finding differences with money	2.MD.C.8	354
15.21	Two-Piece Shapes*	Develop an understanding of area; equivalent areas with different shapes	K.MD.A.1; 1.G.A.3; 2.G.A.3	355
15.22	Tangram Areas*	Develop the concept of area	K.MD.A.1; 1.G.A.3; 2.G.A.3	356
15.23	Fill and Compare*	Develop an understanding of units to measure area	K.MD.A.1; 1.G.A.3; 2.G.A.3	358
15.24	Capacity Sort*	Develop the concept of capacity	K.MD.A.2	359
15.25	Which Silo Holds More?	Explore volume of cylinders with non standard units	K.MD.A.2	359

Chapter 16 Developing geometric reasoning and concepts.

Activity		Mathematical Content	CCSS-M	Page
16.1	Tricky Shapes*	Attend to relevant properties of shapes	K.G.A.2; K.G.B.4; 1.G.A.1	368
16.2	Shape Sorts*	Develop ways that two-dimensional shapes are alike and different	CCSS-M: K.G.B.4; 1.G.A.1; 2.G.A.1	369
16.3	Property Lists for Quadrilaterals*	Explore properties attributable to special classes of quadrilaterals	2.G.A.1	370
16.4	Shape Show and Hunt	Attend to relevant properties of shapes in the real world environment	K.G.A.1; K.G.A.2; K.G.B. 4	374
16.5	Match It–Name It*	Attend to relevant properties of shapes	K.G.A.2; K.G.B.4	374
16.6	Getting into Shape	Attend to relevant properties of three-dimensional shapes	K.G.A.1; K.G.B.4; 1.G.A.2	375
16.7	Is It or Isn't It?	Attend to relevant properties of shapes	K.G.A.1; K.G.A.2; K.G.B.4; 1.G.A.1; 2.G.A.1	375
16.8	Build It	Attend to relevant properties of shapes by building shapes	K.G.B.5; 1.G.A.1; 2.G.A.1	375
16.9	What's My Shape?*	Develop oral descriptions of shapes based on properties	1.G.A.1; 2.G.A.1	376
16.10	Feeling It	Attend to relevant properties of shapes by touching objects	K.G.B.4; 1.G.A.1; 2.G.A.1	377
16.11	Tangram Puzzles*	Practice composing shapes	K.G.B.6; 1.G.A.2; 2.G.A.1	378
16.12	Mosaic Puzzle*	Explore properties of two-dimensional shapes and compose and decompose shapes	K.G.B.6; 1.G.A.2; 2.G.A.1	378
16.13	Geoboard Copy*	Practice representation of shapes	1.G.A.2; 2.G.A.1	380
16.14	Decomposing on a Geoboard*	Explore ways to compose and decompose shapes	1.G.A.2; 1.G.A.3; 2.G.A.1; 2.G.A.3	381
16.15	Two Shapes from One*	Explore ways to decompose shapes	2.G.A.1	381
16.16	Mystery Definition*	Develop defining properties of special classes of shapes	1.G.A.1; 2.G.A.1	386
16.17	Triangle Sort*	Develop defining properties of triangles	2.G.A.1	387

(continued)

* Activity titles with an asterisk include a downloadable Activity Page, Expanded Lesson, or Blackline Master.

Chapter 16 Developing geometric reasoning and concepts. (*continued*)

Activity		Mathematical Content	CCSS-M	Page
16.18	Constructing 3-D Shapes	Explore how two-dimensional faces fit together to create three-dimensional shapes	K.G.A.3; K.G.B.5; 1.G.A.2; 2.G.A.1	387
16.19	Can You Make It?	Explore ways to build shapes from properties	K.G.A.3; K.G.B.5; 1.G.A.2; 2.G.A.1	388
16.20	Motion Flag*	Develop the concepts of slides, flips, and turns	CCSS-M STANDARDS OF MATHEMATICAL PRACTICE: MP1 MP3 MP6 MP7	390
16.21	Pattern Block Mirror Symmetry	Develop the concept of line symmetry	CCSS-M STANDARDS OF MATHEMATICAL PRACTICE: MP3 MP6 MP7	391
16.22	Playground Scavengers	Explore location in the real world environment	K.G.A.1	392
16.23	Making Maps	Develop an understanding of location in the real world environment	K.G.A.1	392
16.24	Hidden Positions*	Develop a readiness for coordinates	K.G.A.1	393
16.25	Paths*	Explore location on a coordinate grid	K.G.A.1	394
16.26	Can You Remember?*	Develop early spatial visualization skills and visual memory	K.G.B.4; 1.G.A.2; 2.G.A.1	395
16.27	Pentominoes*	Develop early spatial visualization skills	1.G.A.2; 2.G.A.1	395
16.28	Notches and Holes	Develop spatial visualization skills	K.G.B.1; 1.G.A.2; 2.G.A.1	396
16.29	Face Matching*	Connect two-dimensional and three-dimensional shapes	1.G.A.2; 2.G.A.1	398

Chapter 17 Helping children use data.

Activity		Mathematical Content	CCSS-M	Page
17.1	Who Is in Our Village?	Gather and analyze data about members of the class	2.MD.D.10	406
17.2	What Can We Learn about Our Community?*	Generate questions about the community, gather data, and analyze it	1.MD.C.4; 2.MD.D10	407
17.3	What about "Both"?*	Explore attributes of shapes using a Venn diagram	K.MD.3; 1.MD.C.4	410
17.4	Guess My Rule	Develop the concept of classification	K.MD.3; 1.MD.C.4	412
17.5	Hidden Labels*	Develop the concept of classification	K.MD.3; 1.MD.C.4	412
17.6	Picture Graphs to Bar Graphs	Explore a bar diagram as a way to organize data	1.MD.C.4; 2.MD.D.10	417
17.7	Story Bars	Use a bar diagram to display and analyze data	2.MD.D.10	418
17.8	Stand by Me	Explore a line plot as a way to organize and analyze data	1.MD.C.4; 2.MD.D.10	419
17.9	Storm Plotter	Use a bar diagram to display and analyze data	2.MD.D.9	419

* Activity titles with an asterisk include a downloadable Activity Page, Expanded Lesson, or Blackline Master.

Appendix E

Guide to Blackline Masters

This Appendix has images of all 33 Blackline Masters (BLM) that you and your children will find useful to engage in many math activities. You can create full-sized masters from these images, print them from point of use pop-ups throughout the text or from the contents listing in the navigation bar of your eText.

Blackline Master	Number
0.5-Centimeter Grid Paper	7
10 × 10 Grids	25
10 × 10 Multiplication Array	16
10,000 Grid Paper	19
1-Centimeter Dot Paper	8
1-Centimeter Grid Paper	6
1-Centimeter Isometric Dot Paper	10
1-Centimeter Square/Diagonal Grid Paper	11
2-Centimeter Isometric Grid Paper	9
2-Centimeter Grid Paper	5
Addition and Subtraction Recording Sheets	20
Base-Ten Grid Paper	18
Base-Ten Materials	32
Blank Hundreds Chart	2
Clock Faces	31
Coordinate Grid—4 Quadrants	23
Coordinate Grid—Quadrant I	22
Degrees and Wedges	30

Blackline Master	Number
Double Ten-Frame	15
Five-Frame	12
Four Small Hundreds Charts	4
Geoboard Pattern (10 by 10)	28
Geoboard Pattern (5 by 5)	26
Geoboard Recording Sheets (10 by 10)	29
Geoboard Recording Sheets (5 by 5)	27
Hundreds Chart	3
Multiplication and Division Recording Sheets	21
Number Cards 0-10	1
Observation Checklist	33
Place-Value Mat (with Ten-Frames)	17
Rational Number Wheel	24
Ten-Frame (Horizontal)	14
Ten-Frame	13

Suggestions for Use and Construction of Materials Card Stock Materials

Card Stock Materials

A good way to have many materials made quickly and easily for children is to have them duplicated on card stock, laminated, and then cut into smaller pieces if desired. Once cut, materials are best kept in clear freezer bags with zip-type closures. Punch a hole near the top of the bag so that you do not store air.

The following list is a suggestion for materials that can be made from card stock using the masters in this section. Quantity suggestions are also given.

Five-Frames and Ten-Frames—12–14

Five-frames and ten-frames are best duplicated on light-colored card stock. Do not laminate; if you do, the mats will curl and counters will slide around.

10 × 10 Multiplication Array—16

Make one per child in any color. Lamination is suggested. Provide each child with an L-shaped piece of card stock to frame the array.

Base-Ten Materials—32

Run copies on white card stock. One sheet will make 4 hundreds and 10 tens or 4 hundreds and 100 ones. Cut into pieces with a paper cutter. It is recommended that you not laminate the base-ten pieces. A kit consisting of 10 hundreds, 30 tens, and 30 ones is adequate for each child or pair of children.

Place-Value Mat (with Ten-Frames)—17

Mats can be duplicated on any pastel card stock. It is recommended that you not laminate these because they tend to curl and counters slide around. Make one for every child.

Rational Number Wheel—24

These disks should be made on card stock. Duplicate the master on two contrasting colors. Laminate and cut the circles and also the slot on the dotted line. Make a set for each child.

Many masters lend themselves to demonstration purposes. The 10×10 array, the blank hundreds board, and the large geoboard are examples. The place-value mat can be used with strips and squares or with counters and cups directly on the document camera. The missing-part blank and the record blanks for the four algorithms are pages that you may wish to write on as a demonstration.

The 10,000 grid is the easiest way there is to show 10,000 or to model four-place decimal numbers.

The degrees and wedges page is the very best way to illustrate what a degree is and also to help explain protractors.

All of the line and dot grids are useful for modeling. You may find it a good idea to have several copies of each easily available.

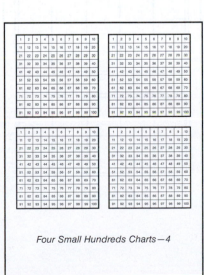

Number Cards 0–10—1

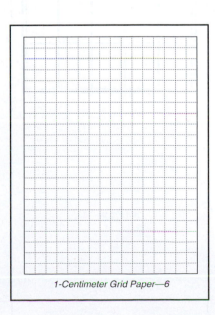

Blank Hundreds Chart—2

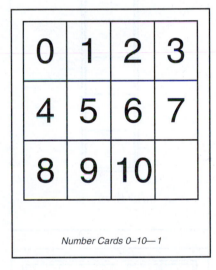

Hundreds Chart—3

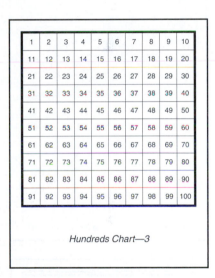

Four Small Hundreds Charts—4

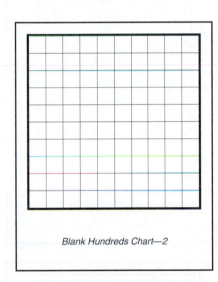

2-Centimeter Grid Paper—5

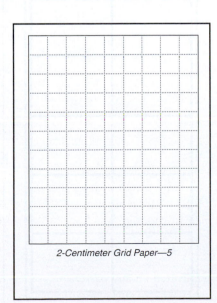

1-Centimeter Grid Paper—6

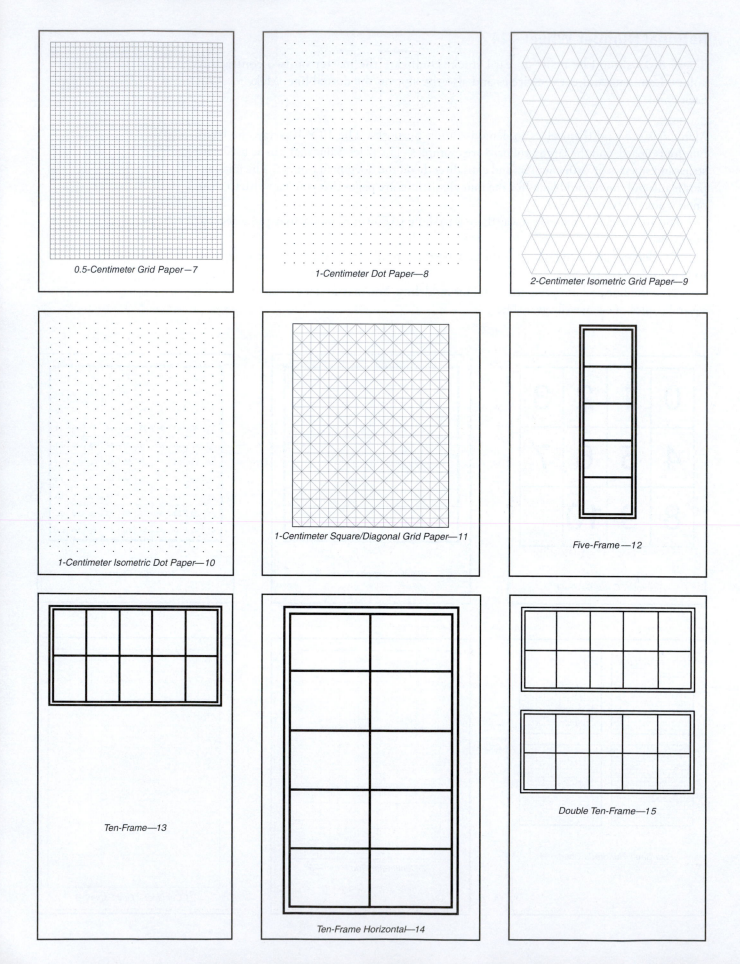

0.5-Centimeter Grid Paper—7

1-Centimeter Dot Paper—8

2-Centimeter Isometric Grid Paper—9

1-Centimeter Isometric Dot Paper—10

1-Centimeter Square/Diagonal Grid Paper—11

Five-Frame—12

Ten-Frame—13

Ten-Frame Horizontal—14

Double Ten-Frame—15

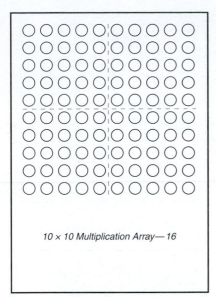

10 × 10 Multiplication Array—16

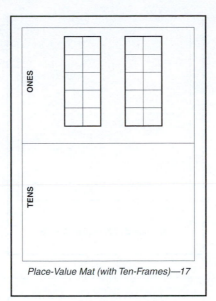

Place-Value Mat (with Ten-Frames)—17

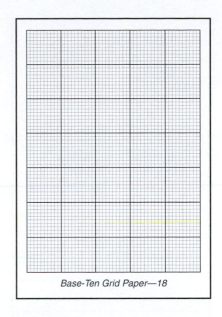

Base-Ten Grid Paper—18

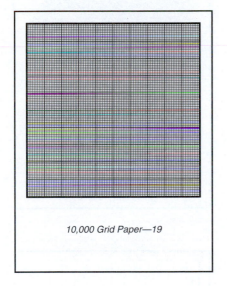

10,000 Grid Paper—19

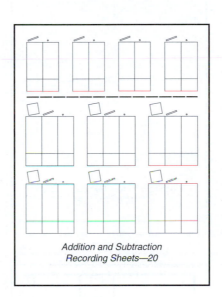

*Addition and Subtraction
Recording Sheets—20*

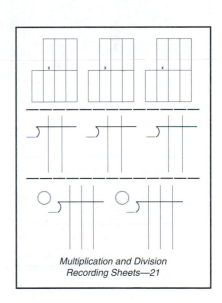

*Multiplication and Division
Recording Sheets—21*

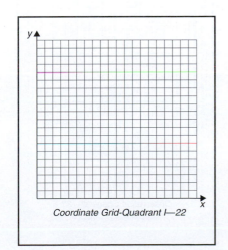

Coordinate Grid-Quadrant I—22

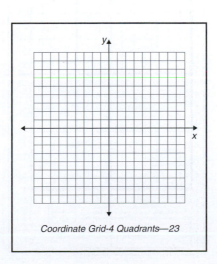

Coordinate Grid-4 Quadrants—23

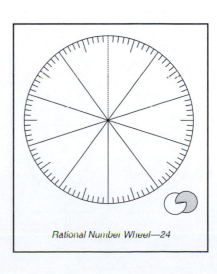

Rational Number Wheel—24

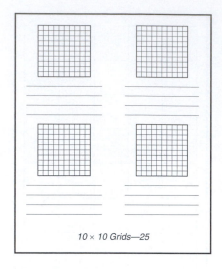

10 × 10 Grids—25

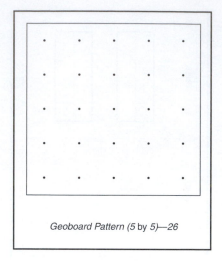

Geoboard Pattern (5 by 5)—26

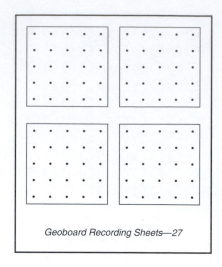

Geoboard Recording Sheets—27

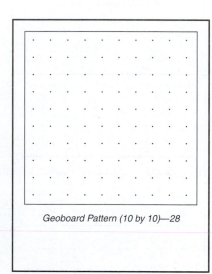

Geoboard Pattern (10 by 10)—28

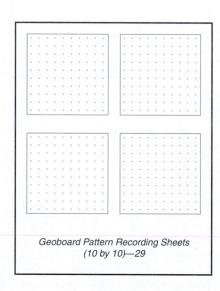

*Geoboard Pattern Recording Sheets
(10 by 10)—29*

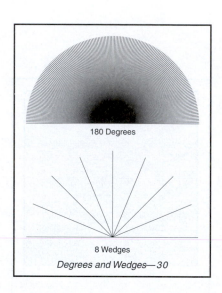

180 Degrees

8 Wedges

Degrees and Wedges—30

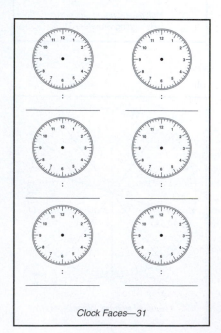

Clock Faces—31

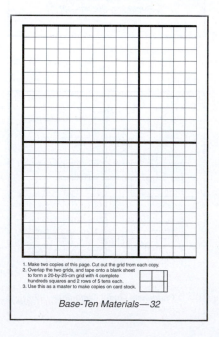

1. Make two copies of this page. Cut out the grid from each copy.
2. Overlap the two grids, and tape onto a blank sheet to form a 20-by-25-cm grid with 4 complete hundreds squares and 2 rows of 5 tens each.
3. Use this as a master to make copies on card stock.

Base-Ten Materials—32

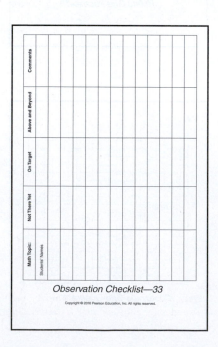

Observation Checklist—33

References

Chapter 1

Ambrose, R. (2002). Are we overemphasizing manipulatives in the primary grades to the detriment of girls? *Teaching Children Mathematics, 9*(1), 16–21.

Bleiler, S., Baxter, W., Stephens, C., & Barlow, A. (2015). Constructing meaning: Standards for mathematical practice. *Teaching Children Mathematics, 21*(6), 336–344.

Council of Chief State School Officers. (2010). *Common Core State Standards*. Washington, DC.

Claessens, A., Duncan, G., & Engel, M. (2009). Kindergarten skills and fifth-grade achievement: Evidence from the ECLS-K. *Economics of Education Review, 28*, 415–427.

Friedman, T. (2007). *The world is flat 3.0: A brief history of the twenty-first century*. New York: Picador.

National Council of Teachers of Mathematics. (2000). *Principles and standards for school mathematics*. Reston, VA: Author.

National Council of Teachers of Mathematics. (2006). *Curriculum focal points for prekindergarten through grade 8 mathematics: A quest for coherence*. Reston, VA: Author.

National Council of Teachers of Mathematics. (2014) *Principles and actions: Ensuring mathematical success for all*. Reston, VA: NCTM.

National Research Council. (2001). *Adding it up: Helping children learn mathematics*. J. Kilpatrick, J. Swafford, & B. Findell (Eds.). Washington, DC: National Academies Press.

Norton, A., & D'Ambrosio, B. S. (2008). ZPC and ZPD: Zones of teaching and learning. *Journal for Research in Mathematics Education, 39*(3), 220–246.

Piaget, J. (1976). *The child's conception of the world*. Totowa, NJ: Littlefield, Adams.

Schoenfeld, A. H., Floden, R. E., & the Algebra Teaching Study and Mathematics Assessment Project. (2014). *An introduction to the TRU Math Dimensions*. Berkeley and E. Lansing, MI: Graduate School of Education, University of California, Berkeley & College of Education, Michigan State University. Retrieved from: http://ats.berkeley.edu/tools.html and/or http://map.mathshell.org/materials/pd.php.

Skemp, R. (1978). Relational understanding and instrumental understanding. *Arithmetic Teacher, 26*(3), 9–15.

Steen, L. A. (Ed.). (1997). *Why numbers count: Quantitative literacy for tomorrow's America*. New York: The College Board.

von Glasersfeld, E. (1995). *Radical constructivism: A way of knowing and learning*. London: Falmer Press.

Vygotsky, L. S. (1978). *Mind and society*. Cambridge, MA: Harvard University Press.

Watts, T., Duncan, G., Siegler, R., & Davis-Kean, P. (2014). What's past is prologue: Relations between early mathematics knowledge and high school achievement. *Educational Researcher, 43*(7), 352–360.

Wiggins, G., & McTighe, J. (2005). *Understanding by design* (2nd ed.). Alexandria, VA: Association for Supervision and Curriculum Development.

Wood, T., & Turner Vorbeck, T. (2001). Extending the conception of mathematics teaching. In T. Wood, B. S. Nelson, & J. Warfield (Eds.), *Beyond classical pedagogy: Teaching elementary school mathematics* (pp. 185–208). Mahwah, NJ: Lawrence Erlbaum.

Chapter 2

Anderson, L.W., & Krathwohl, D. R. (Eds.) (2001). *A taxonomy for learning, teaching, and assessing: A revision of Bloom's Taxonomy of educational objectives: Complete Edition*. New York: Addison Wesley, Longman.

Ball, D. L. (1992). Magical hopes: Manipulatives and the reform of math education. *American Educator, 16*(2), 14–18, 46–47.

Boaler, J. (2016). *Mathematical mindsets*. San Francisco: Jossey-Bass.

Boaler, J. (2013). Ability and mathematics: The mindset revolution that is reshaping education. *FORUM, 55*(1), 143-152.

Bray, W. S. (2013). How to leverage the potential of mathematical errors. *Teaching Children Mathematics, 19*(7), 425–431.

Breyfogle, M., & Williams, L. (2008/2009). Designing and implementing worthwhile tasks. *Teaching Children Mathematics, 15*(5), 276–280.

Carter, S. (2008). Disequilibrium and questioning in the primary classroom: Establishing routines that help students learn. *Teaching Children Mathematics, 15*(3), 134–137.

Council of Chief State School Officers. (2010). *Common Core State Standards*. Washington, DC.

Chapin, S., O'Connor, C., & Anderson, N. (2009). *Classroom discussions: Using math talk to help students learn* (2nd ed.). Sausalito, CA: Math Solutions.

Clement, L. (2004). A model for understanding, using, and connecting representations. *Teaching Children Mathematics*, 11(2), 97–102.

Davis, B., Sumara, D., & Luce-Kapler, R. (2008). *Engaging minds: Changing teaching in complex times*. New York: Routledge.

Dweck, C. (2006). *Mindset: The new psychology of success*. New York: Random House.

Dweck, C. (2014, November). *The power of believing you can improve*. [Video File]. Retrieved from https://www.ted.com/talks/carol_dweck_the_power_of_believing_that_you_can_improve?language=en.

Fosnot, C. T., & Dolk, M. (2001). *Young mathematicians at work: Constructing number sense, addition, and subtraction*. Portsmouth, NH: Heinemann.

Green, E. (2014, February). Why do Americans stink at math? *New York Times Magazine*. Retrieved from http://www.nytimes.com/2014/07/27/magazine/why-do-americans-stink-at-math.html?_r=0

Green, E. (2015). *Building a better teacher: How teaching works*. New York: W.W. Norton.

Herbel-Eisenmann, B. A., & Breyfogle, M. L. (2005). Questioning our patterns of questioning. *Mathematics Teaching in the Middle School*, 10(9), 484–489.

Hiebert, J., Carpenter, T. P., Fennema, E., Fuson, K., Wearne, D., Murray, H., Olivier, A., & Human, P. (1997). *Making sense: Teaching and learning mathematics with understanding*. Portsmouth, NH: Heinemann.

Hiebert, J., & Grouws, D. A. (2007). The effects of classroom mathematics teaching on students' learning. In F. K. Lester (Ed.), *Second handbook of research on mathematics teaching and learning* (pp. 371–404). Charlotte, NC: Information Age Publishing.

Hong, L. (1993). *Two of everything: A Chinese folktale*. New York: Albert Whitman.

Humphreys, C., & Parker, R. (2015). *Making number talks matter*. Portland, ME: Stenhouse.

Hunt, A., Nipper, K., & Nash, L. (2011). Virtual vs. concrete manipulatives in mathematics teacher education: Is one type more effective than the other? *Current Issues in Middle Level Education*, 16(2), 1-6

Jacobs, V. R., & Ambrose, R. C. (2008). Making the most of story problems. *Teaching Children Mathematics*, 15(5), 260–266.

Jacobs, V. R., Lamb, L. L. C., & Philipp, R. A. (2010). Professional noticing of children's mathematical thinking. *Journal for Research in Mathematics Education*, 41(2), 169–202.

Jacobs, V. R., Martin, H. A., Ambrose, R. C., and Philipp, R. A. (2014). Warning signs! *Teaching Children Mathematics* 21(2), 107–113.

Kilic, H., Cross, D. I., Ersoz, F. A., Mewborn, D. S., Swanagan, D., & Kim, J. (2010). Techniques for small-group discourse. *Teaching Children Mathematics*, 16(6), 350–357.

Lesh, R. A., Cramer, K., Doerr, H., Post, T., & Zawojewski, J. (2003). Model development sequences. In R. A. Lesh & H. Doerr (Eds.), *Beyond constructivism: A models and modeling perspective on mathematics teaching, learning, and problem solving* (pp. 35–58). Mahwah, NJ: Lawrence Erlbaum.

Lim, K. H. (2014). Error-eliciting problems: Fostering understanding and thinking. *Mathematics Teaching in the Middle School*, 20(2), 106–114.

McCoy, A., Barnett, J., & Combs, E. (2013). *High-yield routines: Grades K-8*. Reston, VA: NCTM.

Moschkovich, J. N. (1998). Supporting the participation of English language learners in mathematical discussions. *For the Learning of Mathematics*, 19(1), 11–19.

Murrey, D. L. (2008). Differentiating instruction in mathematics for the English language learner. *Mathematics Teaching in the Middle School*, 14(3), 146–153.

National Council of Teachers of Mathematics. (2014). *Principles to Actions: Ensuring Mathematical Success of All*. Reston, VA: NCTM.

Parrish, S. (2011). Number talks build numerical reasoning. *Teaching Children Mathematics*, 18(3), 198–206.

Parrish, S. (2014). *Number talks: Helping children develop mental math and computation strategies, grades K-5*. Sausalito, CA: Math Solutions.

Pesek, D., & Kirshner, D. (2002). Interference of instrumental instruction in subsequent relational learning. In J. Sowder & B. P. Schappelle (Eds.), *Lessons learned from research* (pp. 101–107). Reston, VA: National Council of Teachers of Mathematics.

Philipp, R., & Vincent, C. (2003). Reflecting on learning fractions without understanding. *OnMath*, 2(7).

Rasmussen, C., Yackel, E., & King, K. (2003). Social and sociomathematical norms in the mathematics classroom. In H. L. Schoen & R. I. Charles (Eds.), *Teaching mathematics through problem solving: Grades 6–12* (pp. 143–154). Reston, VA: National Council of Teachers of Mathematics.

Simpson, A., Mokalled, S., Ellenburg, L., & Che, S. M. (2014/2015). A tool for rethinking questioning. *Mathematics Teaching in the Middle School*, 20(5), 294–302.

Smith, M., Hughes, E., Engle, R., & Stein, M. (2009). Orchestrating discussions. *Mathematics Teaching in the Middle School*, 14(9), 548–556.

Smith, M. S., & Stein, M. K. (1998). Selecting and creating mathematical tasks: From research to practice. *Mathematics Teaching in the Middle School*, 3(5), 344–350.

Smith, M. S., & Stein, M. K. (2011). *5 Practices for orchestrating productive mathematics discussions*. Thousand Oaks, CA: Corwin Press.

Stein, M. K., & Bovalino, J. W. (2001). Manipulatives: One piece of the puzzle. *Teaching Children Mathematics*, 6(6), 356–359.

Stephan, M., & Whitenack, J. (2003). Establishing classroom social and sociomathematical norms for problem solving. In F. K. Lester, Jr., & R. I. Charles (Eds.), *Teaching mathematics through problem solving: Grades pre-K–6* (pp. 149–162). Reston, VA: National Council of Teachers of Mathematics.

Suh, J. M. (2007a). Developing "algebra-'rithmetic" in the elementary grades. *Teaching Children Mathematics*, 14(4), 246–253.

Suh, J. M. (2007b). Tying it all together: Building mathematics proficiency for all students. *Teaching Children Mathematics*, 14(3), 163–169.

Thompson, P. W. (1994). Concrete materials and teaching for mathematical understanding. *Arithmetic Teacher*, 41(9), 556–558.

Utah State University. (2016). *National Library of Virtual Manipulatives*. Retrieved October 1, 2016 from http://nlvm.usu.edu.

Wagganer, E. L. (2015). Creating math talk communities. *Teaching Children Mathematics* 22(4), 248–254.

Wallace, A. (2007). Anticipating student responses to improve problem solving. *Mathematics Teaching in the Middle School*, 12(9), 504–511.

Wickett, M., Kharas, K., & Burns, M. (2002). *Lessons for algebraic thinking*. Sausalito, CA: Math Solutions Publications.

Wiggins, G. (2013, May 5). Letter to the Editor. *New York Times*, p. 2.

Wood, T., Williams, G., & McNeal, B. (2006). Children's mathematical thinking in different classroom cultures. *Journal for Research in Mathematics Education, 37*(3), 222–255.

Yackel, E., & Cobb, P. (1996). Sociomathematical norms, argumentation, and autonomy in mathematics. *Journal for Research in Mathematics Education, 27*(4), 458–477.

Chapter 3

Association of Mathematics Teacher Educators, & National Council of Supervisors of Mathematics. (n.d.). *Improving student achievement in mathematics through formative assessment in instruction*. Joint position paper, http://amte.net/sites/default/files/overview_amte_ncsm_position_paper_formative_assessment.pdf.

Bray, W., & Santagata, R. (2014). Making mathematical errors: Springboards for learning. In Karp & A. Roth McDuffie (Eds.), *Using research to improve instruction* (pp. 239–248). Reston, VA: NCTM.

Casa, T. M., Firmender, J. M., Cahill, J., Cardetti, F., Choppin, J. M., Cohen, J., Zawodniak, R. (2016). Types of and purposes for elementary mathematical writing: Taskforce recommendations. Retrieved from http://mathwriting.education.uconn.edu.

Council of Chief State School Officers. (2010). *Common Core State Standards*. Washington, DC.

Daro, P., Mosher, F., & Corcoran, T. (2011). *Learning trajectories in mathematics: A foundation for standards, curriculum assessment and instruction*. Philadelphia, PA: Consortium for Policy Research in Education.

Fennell, F., Kobett, B., & Wray, J. A. (2015). Classroom-based formative assessments—Guiding teaching and learning. *Teaching Children Mathematics, 21*(6), 325-327.

Frayer, D. A., Fredrick, W. C., & Klausmeier, H. J. (April 1969). *A schema for testing the level of concept mastery* (Working Paper No. 16), University of Wisconsin Center for Educational Research.

Hattie, J. (2009). *Visible learning: A synthesis of over analyses relating to achievement*. New York, NY: Routledge.

Hattie, J. (2015). *The effective use of testing: What the research says*. *Education Week*, October 28.

Jacob, V. R., Lamb, L., & Philipp, R. A. (2010). Professional noticing of children's mathematical thinking. *Journal for Research in Mathematics Education 41*(2), 169–202.

Lepak, J. (2014). Enhancing students' written mathematical arguments. *Mathematics Teaching in the Middle School 20*(4), 212–219.

National Council of Teachers of Mathematics. (2014). *Principles to Action: Ensuring Mathematical Success of All*. Reston, VA: NCTM.

National Governors Association & Council of Chief State School Officers. (2010, June). *Common Core State Standards Initiative*. Retrieved from www.corestandards.org.

Nyquist, J. B. (2003). *The benefits of reconstruing feedback as a larger system of formative assessment: A metaanalysis*. Unpublished master's thesis. Vanderbilt University, Nashville, TN.

Parker, R., & Breyfogle, L. (2011). Learning to write about mathematics. *Teaching Children Mathematics, 18*(2), 90–99.

Petit, M., & Bouck, M. (2015). The essence of formative assessment in practice: Classroom examples. *NCSM Journal of Mathematics Education Leadership, 16*(1), 19–27.

Philipp, R., Cabral, C., & Schappell, B. (2012). *IMAP integrating mathematics and pedagogy*. New York, NY: Pearson.

Popham, W. J. (2008). *Transformative assessment*. Alexandria, VA: Association for Supervision and Curriculum Development.

Rigelman, N., & Petrick, K. (2014). Student mathematicians developed through formative assessment cycles. In K. Karp & A. Roth McDuffie, *Annual Perspectives in Mathematics Education: Using Research to Improve Instruction*. Reston, VA: NCTM.

Simpson, A., Mokalled, S, Ellenburg, L. A., & Che, S. M. (2014/2015). A tool for rethinking teachers' questioning. *Mathematics Teaching in the Middle School, 20*(45), 294–302.

Smith, M. S., & Stein, M. K. (2011). *5 Practices for orchestrating productive mathematics discussions*. Thousand Oaks, CA: Corwin Press.

Stephan, M., McManus, G., & Dehlinger, R. (2014). Using research to inform formative assessment techniques. In K. Karp & A. Roth McDuffie (Eds.), *Annual Perspectives in Mathematics Education: Using Research to Improve Instruction*. (pp. 229–238). Reston, VA: NCTM.

Stiggins, R. (2009). Assessment for learning in upper elementary grades. *Phi Delta Kappan, 90*(6), 419–421.

Webb, N. L. (2002, April). An analysis of the alignment between mathematics standards and assessments for three states. In *Annual Meeting of the American Educational Research Association, New Orleans, LA*.

Wiliam, D. (2007). Content then process: Teacher learning communities in the service of formative assessment. In D. B. Reeves (Ed.), *Ahead of the curve: The power of assessment to transform teaching and learning* (pp. 183–204). Bloomington, IN: Solution Tree.

Wiliam, D. (2010). Practical techniques for formative assessment. Presentation given in Boras, Sweden, September 2010. Retrieved June 11, 2011, from www.slideshare.net/BLoPP/dylanwiliambors-2010.

Wiliam, D., & Leahy, S. (2015). *Embedding formative assessment: Practical techniques for K-12 classrooms*. West Palm Beach, FL: Learning Sciences International.

Wilson, L. D., & Kenney, P. A. (2003). Classroom and large-scale assessment. In J. Kilpatrick, W. G. Martin, & D. Schifter (Eds.), *A research companion to Principles and Standards for School Mathematics* (pp. 53–67). Reston, VA: NCTM.

Chapter 4

Bray, W. S. (2009). The power of choice. *Teaching Children Mathematics, 16*(3), 178–184.

Cassone, J. D. (2009). Differentiating mathematics by using task difficulty. In D. Y. White & J. S. Spitzer (Eds.), *Mathematics for every student: Responding to diversity, grades Pre-K–5* (pp. 89–98). Reston, VA: National Council of Teachers of Mathematics.

Council of Chief State School Officers. (2010). *Common Core State Standards*. Washington, DC.

Gilbert, M. C., & Musu, L. E. (2008). Using TARGETTS to create learning environments that support mathematical understanding and adaptive motivation. *Teaching Children Mathematics, 15*(3), 138–143.

Kingore, B. (2006, Winter). Tiered instruction: Beginning the process. *Teaching for High Potential*, 5–6.

Murray, M., & Jorgensen, J. (2007). *The differentiated math classroom: A guide for teachers, K–8.* Portsmouth, NH: Heinemann.

National Council of Teachers of Mathematics. (2000). *Principles and standards for school mathematics.* Reston, VA: Author.

Nebesniak, A. L., & Heaton, R. M. (2010). Student confidence & student involvement. *Mathematics Teaching in the Middle School, 16*(2), 97–103.

Rasmussen, C., Yackel, E., & King, K. (2003). Social and sociomathematical norms in the mathematics classroom. In H. L. Schoen & R. I. Charles (Eds.), *Teaching mathematics through problem solving: Grades 6–12* (pp. 143–154). Reston, VA: National Council of Teachers of Mathematics.

Skemp, R. (1978). Relational understanding and instrumental understanding. *Arithmetic Teacher, 26*(3), 9–15.

Small, M. (2012). *Good questions: Great ways to differentiate mathematics instruction.* Reston, VA: NCTM.

Sullivan, P., & Lilburn, P. (2002). *Good questions for math teaching: Why ask them and what to ask, K–6.* Sausalito, CA: Math Solutions.

Sousa, D., & Tomlinson, C. (2011). *Differentiation and the brain: How neuroscience supports the learner-friendly classroom.* Bloomington, IN: Solution Tree Press.

Tomlinson, C. (1999). Mapping a route towards differentiated instruction. *Educational Leadership, 57*(1), 12–16.

Tomlinson, C. (2003). *Fulfilling the promise of the differentiated classroom: Strategies and tools for responsive teaching.* Alexandria. VA: Association of Supervision and Curriculum Development.

Chapter 5

Aguirre, J. M., & del Rosario Zavala, M. (2013). Making culturally responsive mathematics teaching explicit: a lesson analysis tool. *Pedagogies: An International Journal, 8*(2), 163–190.

Annie E. Casey Foundation. (2014). *Kids count: 2014 data book.* Baltimore, MD: Author. Retrieved May 17, 2016 from http://www.aecf.org/m/resourcedoc/aecf-2014kidscountdatabook-2014.pdf.

Averill, R., Anderson, D., Easton, H., Te Maro, P., Smith, D., & Hynds, A. (2009). Culturally responsive teaching of mathematics: Three models from linked studies. *Journal for Research in Mathematics Education, 40*(2), 157–186.

Baker, S., Lesaux, N., Jayanthi, M., Dimino, J., Proctor, C. P., Morris, J., Gersten, R., Haymond, K., Kieffer, M. J., Linan-Thompson, S., & Newman-Gonchar, R. (2014). *Teaching academic content and literacy to English learners in elementary and middle school* (NCEE 2014-4012). Washington, DC: National Center for Education Evaluation and Regional Assistance (NCEE), Institute of Education Sciences, U.S. Department of Education. Retrieved from the NCEE website: http://ies.ed.gov/ncee/wwc/publications_reviews.aspx.

Boaler, J. (2008, April). Promoting "relational equity" and high mathematics achievement through an innovative mixed ability approach. *British Educational Research Journal, 34,* 167–194.

Boaler, J., & Staples, M. E. (2014). "Creating mathematical futures through an equitable teaching approach: The case of Railside School. In N. S. Nasir, C. Cabano, B. Shreve, E. Woodbury, & N. Louie (Eds.), *Mathematics for equity: A framework for successful practice.* New York: Teachers College Press.

Council of Chief State School Officers. (2010). *Common Core State Standards.* Washington, DC.

Council of Chief State School Officers. (2011). *Application of Common Core State Standards for English language learners.* Washington, DC.

Celedon-Pattichis, S. (2009). What does that mean? Drawing on Latino and Latina students' language and culture to make mathematical meaning. In M. W. Ellis (Ed.), *Responding to diversity: Grades 6–8* (pp. 59–74). Reston, VA: National Council of Teachers of Mathematics.

Celedon-Pattichis, S., & Ramirez, N. G. (2012). *Beyond good teaching: Advancing mathematics education for ELLs.* Reston, VA: NCTM.

Chval, K. B., & Pinnow, R. (2010). Preservice teachers' assumptions about Latino/a English language learners. *Journal of Teaching for Excellence and Equity in Mathemaitcs, 2*(1), 6–12.

Cirillo, M., Steele, M., Otten, S., Herbel Eisenmann, B. A., McAneny, K., & Riser, J. Q. (2014). Teacher discourse moves: Supporting productive and powerful discourse. In K. Karp & A. Roth McDuffie (Eds.), *Annual perspectives in mathematics education 2014: Using research to improve instruction* (pp. 141–150). Reston, VA: NCTM.

Choppin, J. (2014). Situating expansions of students' explanations in discourse contexts. In K. Karp & A. Roth McDuffie (Eds.), *Annual perspectives in mathematics education 2014: Using research to improve instruction* (pp. 119–128) Reston, VA: NCTM.

Chao, T., Murray, E., & Gutierrez, R. (2014). *NCTM research brief: What are classroom practices that support equity-based mathematics teaching?* Retrieved from http://www.nctm.org/Research-and-Advocacy/research-brief-and-clips/Classroom-Practices-That-Support-Equity-Based-Mathematics-Teaching/.

Cobb, P., Gresalfi, M., & Hodge, L. (2009). An interpretative scheme for analyzing the identities that students develop in mathematics classrooms. *Journal for Research in Mathematics Education, 40*(1), 40–68.

Cummins, J. (1994). Primary language instruction and the education of language minority students. In C. F. Leyba (Ed.), *Schooling and language minority students: A theoretical framework* (pp. 3–46). Los Angeles: California State University, National Evaluation, Dissemination and Assessment Center.

Drake, C., Land, T. J., Bartell, T. G., Aguirre, J. M., Foote, M. Q., McDuffie, A. R., & Turner, E. E. (2015). Three strategies for opening curriculum spaces. *Teaching Children Mathematics, 21*(6), 346–353.

Dunleavy, T. K. (2015). Delegating mathematical authority as a means to strive toward equity. *Journal of Urban Mathematics Education, 8*(1), 62–82.

Echevarria, J., Vogt, M. E., & Short, D. (2008). *Making content comprehensible for English learners: The SIOP model* (3rd ed.). Boston, MA: Allyn & Bacon.

Echevarria, J. J., Vogt, M. J., & Short, D. J. (2012). *Making content comprehensible for English Learners: The SIOP model* (4th Ed.). New York: Pearson.

Fernandez, A., Anhalt, C., & Civil, M. (2009). Mathematical interviews to assess Latino students. *Teaching Children Mathematics, 16*(3), 162–169.

Garrison, L. (1997). Making the NCTM's Standards work for emergent English speakers. *Teaching Children Mathematics, 4*(3), 132–138.

Gomez, C. L. (2010). Teaching with cognates. *Teaching Children Mathematics, 16*(8), 470–474.

Gresalfi, M. S., & Cobb, P. (2006). Cultivating students' discipline-specific dispositions as a critical goal for pedagogy and equity. *Pedagogies: An International Journal, 1*(1), 49–57.

Gutierrez, R. (2015). HOLA: Hunt for opportunities–learn–act. *Mathematics Teacher, 109*(4), 270–277.

Gutierrez, R. (2009). Embracing the inherent tensions in teaching mathematics from an equity stance. *Democracy and Education, 18*(3), 9–16.

Haas, E., & Gort, M. (2009). Demanding more: Legal standards and best practices for English language learners. *Bilingual Research Journal, 32*, 115–135.

Janzen, J. (2008). Teaching English language learners in the content areas. *Review of Educational Research, 78*(4), 1010–1038.

Kena, G., Musu-Gillette, L., Robinson, J., Wang, X., Rathbun, A., Zhang, J., Wilkinson-Flicker, S., Barmer, A., and Dunlop Velez, E. (2015). *The Condition of Education 2015* (NCES 2015-144). U.S. Department of Education, National Center for Education Statistics. Washington, DC. Retrieved May 17, 2016 from http://nces.ed.gov/pubsearch.

Kersaint, G., Thompson, D. R., & Petkova, M. (2009). *Teaching mathematics to English language learners*. New York, NY: Routledge.

Khisty, L. L. (1997). Making mathematics accessible to Latino students: Rethinking instructional practice. In M. Kenney & J. Trentacosta (Eds.), *Multicultural and gender equity in the mathematics classroom: The gift of diversity* (pp. 92–101). Reston, VA: National Council of Teachers of Mathematics.

Kisker, E. E., Lipka, J., Adams, B. L., Rickard, A., Andrew-Ihrke, D., Yanez, E. E., & Millard, A. (2012). The potential of a culturally based supplemental mathematics curriculum to improve the mathematics performance of Alaska native and other students. *Journal for Research in Mathematics Education, 43*(1), 75–113.

Livers, S. D., & Bay-Williams, J. M. (2014). Timing vocabulary support: Constructing (not Obstructing) Meaning. *Mathematics Teaching in the Middle School, 10*(3), 153–159.

Mathis, S. B. (1986). *The hundred penny box*. New York, NY: Puffin Books.

Maldonado, L. A., Turner, E. E., Dominguez, H., & Empson, S. B. (2009). English language learning from, and contributing to, mathematical discussions. In D. Y. White & J. S. Spitzer (Eds.), *Responding to diversity: Grades pre-K-5* (pp. 7–22). Reston, VA: NCTM.

Moll, L. C., Amanti, C., Neff, D., & Gonzalez, N. (1992). Funds of knowledge for teaching: Using a qualitative approach to connect homes and classrooms. *Qualitative Issues in Educational Research, 31*(2), 132-141.

Moschkovich, J. (2009). *NCTM research brief: Using two languages when learning mathematics: How can research help us understand mathematics learners who use two languages?* Reston, VA: National Council of Teachers of Mathematics.

Myller, R. (1991). *How big is a foot?* South Holland, IL: Yearling Books. National Center for Educational Statistics. (2014). *NAEP questions tool*. Retrieved from http://nces.ed.gov/nationsreportcard/itmrlsx/landing.aspx.

NCTM (2014). *Access and Equity in Mathematics Education: A Position of the National Council of Teachers of Mathematics.* Retrieved May 27, 2016 from http://www.nctm.org/uploadedFiles/Standards_and_Positions/Position_Statements/Access_and_Equity.pdf.

Nasir, N. S., Cabana, C., Shreve, B., Woodbury, E., & Louie, N. (Eds.) *Mathematics for Equity: A Framework for Successful Practice.* New York: Teachers College Press.

National Research Council. (2001). *Adding it up: Helping children learn mathematics.* J. Kilpatrick, J. Swafford, & B. Findell (Eds.).Washington, DC: National Academies Press.

Neumann, M. D. (2005). Freedom quilts: Mathematics on the Underground Railroad. *Teaching Children Mathematics, 11*(6), 316–321.

Perkins, I., & Flores, A. (2002). Mathematical notations and procedures of recent immigrant students. *Teaching Children Mathematics, 7*(6), 346–351.

Robinson, J. P. (2010). The effects of test translation on young English learners' mathematics performance. *Educational Researcher, 39*(8), 582–590.

Secada, W. G. (1983). *The educational background of limited-English proficient students: Implications for the arithmetic classroom.* Arlington Heights, IL: Bilingual Education Service Center. (ERIC Document Reproduction Service No. ED 237318)

Setati, M. (2005). Teaching mathematics in a primary multilingual classroom. *Journal for Research in Mathematics Education, 36*(5), 447–466.

Shein, P. P. (2012). Seeing with two eyes: A teacher's use of gestures in questioning and revoicing to engage English language learners in the repair of mathematical errors. *Journal for Research in Mathematics Education, 43*(2), 182–222.

Simic-Muller, K. (2015). Social justice and proportional reasoning. *Mathematics teaching in the middle school, 21*(3), 162–168.

Tomaz, V. S., & David, M. M. (2015). How students' everyday situations modify classroom mathematical activity: The case of water consumption. *Journal for Research in Mathematics Education, 46*(4), 455–496.

Turner, E. E., Celedón-Pattichis, S., Marshall, M., & Tennison, A. (2009). "Fijense amorcitos, les voy a contra una historia": The power of story to support solving and discussing mathematical problems among Latino and Latina kindergarten students. In D. Y. White & J. S. Spitzer (Eds.), *Responding to diversity: Grades pre-K–5* (pp. 23–42). Reston, VA: National Council of Teachers of Mathematics.

Vollmer, G. (2000). Praise and stigma: Teachers' constructions of the typical ESL student. *Journal of Intercultural Studies, 21*(1), 53–66.

Wager, A. (2012). Incorporating out-of-school mathematics: From cultural context to embedded practice. *Journal of Mathematics Teacher Education, 15*(1), 9–23.

Whiteford, T. (2009/2010). Is mathematics a universal language? *Teaching Children Mathematics, 16*(5), 276–283.

Yoon, B. (2008). Uninvited guests: The influence of teachers' roles and pedagogies on the positioning of English language learners in the classroom. *American Educational Research Journal, 45*, 495–522.

Zike, D. (n.d.). *Dinah Zike's teaching mathematics with foldables.* Columbus, OH: Glencoe McGraw-Hill.

Chapter 6

Assouline, S. G., & Lupkowski-Shoplik, A. (2011). *Developing math talent: A comprehensive guide to math education for gifted students in elementary and middle school* (2nd ed.). Waco, TX: Prufrock Press.

Baroody, A. J. (2011). Learning: A framework. In F. Fennell (Ed.), *Achieving fluency: Special education and mathematics,* (pp. 15–58). Reston, VA: NCTM.

Berch, D. B., & Mazzocco, M. M. M. (Eds.). (2007). *Why is math so hard for some children? The nature and origins of mathematical learning difficulties and disabilities.* Baltimore, MD: Brookes.

Bruner, J. S., & Kenney, H. J. (1965). Representation and mathematics learning. *Monographs of the Society for Research in Child Development, 30*(1), 50–59.

Bush, S., Karp, K., & Nadler, J. (2015). Artist? Mathematician? Developing both enhances learning! *Teaching Children Mathematics, 22*(2), 61–63.

Council of Chief State School Officers. (2010). *Common Core State Standards.* Washington, DC.

Center for Applied Special Technology (CAST) (n.d.). Retrieved October 1, 2016 from http://www.cast.org

Flores, M., Hinton, V., & Strozier, S. (2014). Teaching subtraction and multiplication with regrouping using the concrete-representational-abstract sequence and strategic instruction model. *Learning Disabilities Research and Practice, 29*(2), 75–88.

Dobbins, A., Gagnon, J. C., & Ulrich, T. (2014). Teaching geometry to students with math difficulties using graduated and peer-mediated instruction in a response-to-intervention model. *Preventing School Failure: Alternative Education for Children and Youth, 58*(1), 17–25.

Fuchs, L. S., & Fuchs, D. (2001). Principles for the prevention and intervention of mathematics difficulties. *Learning Disabilities Research and Practice, 16*(2), 85–95.

Gagnon, J., & Maccini, P. (2001). Preparing students with disabilities for algebra. *Teaching Exceptional Children, 34*(1), 8–15.

Gavin, M. K., & Sheffield, L. J. (2010). Using curriculum to develop mathematical promise in the middle grades. In M. Saul, S. Assouline, & L. J. Sheffield (Eds.), *The peak in the middle: Developing mathematically gifted students in the middle grades,* (pp. 51–76). Reston, VA: NCTM, National Association of Gifted Children, & National Middle School Association.

Griffin, C. C., Jossi, M. H., & van Garderen, D. (2014). Effective mathematics instruction in inclusive schools. In J. McLeskey, N. L. Waldron, F. Spooner, & B. Algozzine (Eds.), *Handbook of effective inclusive schools: Research and practice,* (pp. 261–274). New York: Routledge.

Heddens, J. (1964). *Today's mathematics: A guide to concepts and methods in elementary school mathematics.* Chicago, IL: Science Research Associates.

Hodges, T. E., Rose, T. D., & Hicks, A. D. (2013). Interviews as RtI Tools. *Teaching Children Mathematics, 19*(1), 30–37.

Hunter, A. E., Bush, S. B., & Karp, K. (2014). Systematic interventions for teaching ratios. *Mathematics Teaching in the Middle School, 19*(6), 360–367.

Johnsen, S. K., Ryser, G. R., & Assouline, S. G. (2014). *A teacher's guide to using the Common Core State Standards with mathematically gifted and advanced learners.* Waco, TX: Prufrock Press.

Karp, K., & Howell, P. (2004). Building responsibility for learning in students with special needs. *Teaching Children Mathematics, 11*(3), 118–126.

Lewis, K. (2014). Difference not deficit: Reconceptualizing mathematical learning disabilities. *Journal for Research in Mathematics Education, 45*(3), 351–396.

Mack, N. K. (2011). Enriching number knowledge. *Teaching Children Mathematics, 18*(2), 101–109.

Mancl, D. B., Miller, S. P., & Kennedy, M. (2012). Using the concrete-representational-abstract sequence with integrated strategy instruction to teach subtraction with regrouping to students with learning disabilities. *Learning Disabilities Research and Practice, 27*(4), 152–166.

Mazzocco, M. M. M., Devlin, K. T., & McKenney, S. J. (2008). Is it a fact? Timed arithmetic performance of children with mathematical learning disabilities (MLD) varies as a function of how MLD is defined. *Developmental Neuropsychology, 33*(3), 318–344.

McMaster, K. L., & Fuchs, D. (2016). Classwide intervention using peer-assisted learning strategies. In, S. Jimerson, M. Burns, & A. Van Der Heyden (Eds.) *Handbook of response to intervention* (pp. 253–268). New York: Springer.

Miller, S. P., & Kaffar, B. J. (2011). Developing addition with regrouping competence among second graders with mathematics difficulties. *Investigations in Mathematics Learning, 4*(1), 24–49.

NCTM (National Council of Teachers of Mathematics). (2007b). *Research brief: Effective strategies for teaching students with difficulties in mathematics.* Retrieved from www.nctm.org/news/content.aspx?id=8452.

NCTM (National Council of Teachers of Mathematics). (2011b, July). *Position statement on interventions.* Reston, VA: NCTM.

NCTM (National Council of Teachers of Mathematics). (2014). *Position statement on access and equity in mathematics education.* Reston, VA: NCTM.

Rakow, S. (2013). Helping gifted learners soar. *Educational Leadership, 69*(5), 34–40.

Read, J. (2014). Who rises to the top? *Peabody Reflector, 83*(1), 19–22.

Reis, S., & Renzulli, J. S. (2005). *Curriculum compacting: An easy start to differentiating for high potential students.* Waco, TX: Prufrock Press.

Rotigel, J., & Fellow, S. (2005). Mathematically gifted students: How can we meet their needs? *Gifted Child Today, 27*(4), 46–65.

Sadler, P., & Tai, R. (2007). The two pillars supporting college science. *Science, 317*(5837), 457–458.

Sheffield, L. J. (Ed.). (1999). *Developing mathematically promising students.* Reston, VA: National Council of Teachers of Mathematics.

Storeygard, J. (2010). *My kids can: Making math accessible to all learners K–5.* Portsmouth, NH: Heinemann.

Torgesen, J. K. (2002). The prevention of reading difficulties. *Journal of School Psychology, 40*(1), 7–26.

Van Tassel-Baska, J., & Brown, E. F. (2007). Toward best practice An analysis of the efficacy of curriculum models in gifted education. *Gifted Child Quarterly, 51*(4), 342–358.

Ysseldyke, J. (2002). Response to "Learning disabilities: Historical perspectives." In R. Bradley, L. Danielson, & D. Hallahan (Eds.), *Identification of learning disabilities: Research to practice,* (pp. 89–98). Mahwah, NJ: Erlbaum.

Woodward, J. (2006). Developing automaticity in multiplication facts: Integrating strategy instruction with timed practice drills. *Learning Disability Quarterly, 29*(4), 269–89.

Chapter 7

Aspiazu, G. G., Bauer, S. C., & Spillett, M. D. (1998). Improving the academic performance of Hispanic youth: A community education model. *Bilingual Research Journal, 22*(2), 1–20.

Barnard, W. M. (2004). Parent involvement in elementary school and educational attainment. *Children and Youth Services Review, 26*(1), 39–62.

Bay-Williams, J. M., & Meyer, M. R. (2003). What parents want to know about standards-based mathematics curricula. *Principal Leadership, 3*(7), 54–60.

Bay, J. M., Reys, B. J., & Reys, R. E. (1999). The top 10 elements that must be in place to implement standards-based mathematics curricula. *Phi Delta Kappan, 80*(7), 503–506.

Boaler, J. (2009). *What's math got to do with it? How parents and teachers can help children learn to love their least favorite subject.* New York: Penguin Books.

Britt, B. A. (2015). *Mastering basic math skills: Games for third through fifth grade.* Reston, VA: NCTM.

Council of Chief State School Officers. (2010). *Common Core State Standards.* Washington, DC.

CCSSI. (n.d.) Myths and Facts. Accessed June 2, 2016 at http://www.corestandards.org/about-the-standards/myths-vs-facts/.

Civil, M., & Menéndez, J. M. (2010). *NCTM research brief: Involving Latino and Latina parents in their children's mathematics education.* Retrieved from www.nctm.org/uploadedFiles/Research_News_and_advocacy/Research/Clips_and_Briefs/Research_brief_17-civil.pdf.

Civil, M., & Planas, N. (2010). Latino/a immigrant parents' voices in mathematics education. In E. L. Grigorenko & R. Takanishi (Eds.), *Immigration, diversity, and education (pp. 130–150).* New York, NY: Routledge.

Cooper, H. (2007). The battle over homework: *Common ground for administrators, teachers, and parents* (3rd ed.). Thousand Oaks, CA: Corwin Press.

Else-Quest, N. M., Hyde, J. S., & Hejmadi, A. (2008). Mother and child emotions during mathematics homework. *Mathematical Thinking and Learning, 10,* 5–35.

Ernst, K., & Ryan, S. (2014). *Success from the start: Your first years teaching elementary school.* Reston, VA: NCTM.

Henderson, A. T., Mapp, K. L., Jordan, C., Orozco, E., Averett, A., Donnelly, D., Buttram, J., Wood, L., Fowler, M., & Myers, M. (2002). *A new wave of evidence: The impact of school, family, and community connections on student achievement.* Austin, TX: Southwest Education Development Laboratory.

Hiebert, J., & Grouws, D. A. (2007). The effects of classroom mathematics teaching on students' learning. In F. K. Lester (Ed.), *Second handbook of research on mathematics teaching and learning* (pp. 371–404). Charlotte, NC: Information Age Publishing.

Hildebrandt, M. E., Biglan, B., & Budd, L (2013). Let's take a road trip. *Teaching Children Mathematics, 19*(9), 548–553.

Jaschik, S. (2014). Evolving ACT. *Inside Higher Ed.* Accessed June 2, 2016 at https://www.insidehighered.com/news/2014/06/06/act-unveils-changes-reporting-and-some-parts-its-test.

Kliman, M. (1999). Beyond helping with homework: Parents and children doing mathematics at home. *Teaching Children Mathematics, 6*(3), 140–146.

Knapp, A. K., Jefferson, V M., & Landers, R. (2013). Learning together. *Teaching Children Mathematics, 19*(7), 432–439.

Lee, J., & Bowen, N. K. (2006). Parent involvement, cultural capital, and the achievement gap among elementary school children. *American Educational Research Journal, 43*(2), 193–218.

Legnard, D., & Austin, S. (2014). The math promise: Celebrating at home and school. *Teaching Children Mathematics, 21*(3), 178–184.

McNeil, N. M., Fyfe, E. R., Petersen, L. A., Dunwiddie, A. E., & Brletic-Shipley, H. (2011). Benefits of practicing 4 = 2 + 2: Nontraditional problem formats facilitate children's understanding of mathematical equivalence. *Child Development, 82*(5), 1620–1633.

Meyer, M., & Arbaugh, F. (2008). Professional development for administrators: What they need to know to support curriculum adoption and implementation. In M. Meyer, C. Langrall, F. Arbaugh, D. Webb, & M. Hoover (Eds.), *A decade of middle school mathematics curriculum implementation: Lessons learned from the Show-Me Project* (pp. 201–210). Charlotte, NC: Information Age Publishing.

Mistretta, R. M. (2013). "We *do* care," say parents. *Teaching Children Mathematics, 19*(9), 572–580.

Patall, E. A., Cooper, H., & Robinson, J. C. (2008). Parent involvement in homework: A research synthesis. *Review of Educational Research, 78*(4), 1039–1101.

Peterson's. (2015). *A Brief History of the SAT and How It Changes.* Accessed June 2, 2016 https://www.petersons.com/college-search/sat-scores-changes-test.aspx.

Rodríguez-Brown, F. V. (2010). Latino families: Culture and schooling. In E. G. Murillo, Jr., S. A. Villenas, R. T. Galván, J. S. Muñoz, C. Martínez, & M. Machado-Casas (Eds.), *Handbook of Latinos and education: Theory* (pp. 350–360). New York, NY: Routledge.

Seeley, C. L. (2009). *Faster isn't smarter: Messages about math, teaching, and learning in the 21st century.* Sausalito, CA: Math Solutions.

Whitenack, J. W., Cavey, L. O., & Henney, C. (2015). *It's elementary: A parent's guide to K-5 mathematics.* Reston, VA: NCTM.

Wieman, R., & Arbaugh, F. (2014). Making homework more meaningful. *Mathematics Teaching in the Middle School, 20*(3), 160–165.

Chapter 8

Baer, E. (1990). *This is the way we go to school.* New York: Scholastic.

Baroody, A. J. (1987). *Children's mathematical thinking: A developmental framework for preschool, primary, and special education teachers.* New York: Teachers College Press.

Baroody, A. J., Li, X., & Lai, M. L. (2008). Toddlers' spontaneous attention to number. *Mathematics Thinking and Learning, 10,* 1–31.

Council of Chief State School Officers. (2010). *Common Core State Standards.* Washington, DC.

Clements, D., Baroody, A., & Sarama, J. (2013). *Background research on early mathematics.* Background Research for the National Governor's Association (NGA) Center Project on Early Mathematics. Washington, DC: NGA.

Clements, D., & Sarama, J. (2014). *Learning and teaching early math: The learning trajectories approach* (2nd ed.). New York: Routledge.

Dale, P. (2007). *Ten in the bed.* Somerville, MA: Candlewick Press.

Ethridge, E. A., & King, J. R. (2005). Calendar math in preschool and primary classrooms: Questioning the curriculum. *Early Childhood Education Journal, 32*(5), 291–296.

Fosnot, C. T., & Dolk, M. (2001). *Young mathematicians at work: Constructing multiplication and division.* Portsmouth, NH: Heinemann.

Hamre, B. K., Downer, J. T., Kilday, C. R., & McGuire, P. (2008). *Effective teaching practices for early childhood mathematics.* White paper prepared for the National Research Council. Washington, DC.

Henkes, K. (2008). *Chrysanthemum.* New York, NY: HarperCollins.

Himmelman, J. (2010). *Ten little hot dogs.* Tarrytown, NY: Pinwheel Books.

Howden, H. (1989). Teaching number sense. *Arithmetic Teacher, 36*(6), 6–11.

Jordan, N. C., Kaplan, D., Locuniak, M. N., & Ramineni, C. (2007). Predicting first grade math achievement from developmental number sense trajectories. *Learning Disabilities Research & Practice, 22*(1), 36–46.

Kaplan, R. (2000). *The nothing that is: A natural history of zero.* New York: Oxford University Press.

Litwin, E. (2012). *Pete the cat and his four groovy buttons.* New York: HarperCollins.

Locuniak, M. N., & Jordan, N. C. (2008). Using kindergarten number sense to predict calculation fluency in second grade. *Journal of Learning Disabilities, 41*(5), 451–459.

Mazzocco, M. M. M., & Thompson, R. E. (2005). Kindergarten predictors of math learning disability. *Learning Disabilities Research & Practice, 20*(3), 142–155.

Metzger, S. (2008). *We're going on a leaf hunt.* New York, NY: Cartwheel Books.

Murphy, S. (2003). *3 little firefighters.* New York: HarperCollins.

NCTM (National Council of Teachers of Mathematics). (2000). *Principles and standards for school mathematics.* Reston, VA: NCTM.

National Council of Teachers of Mathematics. (2006). *Curriculum focal points for prekindergarten through grade 8 mathematics: A quest for coherence.* Reston, VA: Author.

National Research Council Committee. (2009). *Mathematics learning in early childhood: Paths toward excellence and equity.* Washington, DC: National Academies Press.

Park, J. & Brannon, E. (2013). Training the approximate number system improves math proficiency. *Psychological Science, 24*(10), 2013–2019.

Slobodkina, E. (1938). *Caps for sale.* New York: Scholastic Books.

Stoeke, J. M. (1999). *Hide and seek.* New York: Dutton Juvenile Books.

Watts, T., Duncan, G., Siegler, R., & Davis-Kean, P. (2014). What's past is prologue: Relations between early mathematics knowledge and high school achievement. *Educational Researcher, 43*(7), 352–360.

Wilson, K. (2006). *Moose tracks!* New York: Margaret K. McElderry.

Wright, R., Martland, J., Stafford, A., & Stanger, G. (2008). *Teaching number: Advancing children's skills and strategies.* London, UK: Sage.

Chapter 9

Baroody, A. J., Wilkins, J. L., & Tiilikainen, S. H. (2003). The development of children's understanding of additive commutativity: From protoquantitive concept to general concept? In A. J. Baroody & A. Dowker (Eds.), *The development of arithmetic concepts and skills* (pp. 127–160). Mahwah, NJ: Erlbaum.

Blote, A., Lieffering, L., & Ouwehand, K. (2006). The development of many-to-one counting in 4-year-old children. *Cognitive Development, 21*(3), 332–348.

Carpenter, T. P., Fennema, E., Franke, M. L., Levi, L., & Empson, S. B. (2014). Children's mathematics: *Cognitively guided instruction* (2nd ed.). Portsmouth, NH: Heinemann.

Council of Chief State School Officers. (2010). *Common Core State Standards.* Washington, DC.

Christelow, E. (2004). *Five little monkeys play hide-and-seek.* New York, NY: Clarion.

Clement, L., & Bernhard, J. (2005). A problem-solving alternative to using key words. Mathematics *Teaching in the Middle School, 10*(7), 360–365.

Clements, D. H., & Sarama, J. (2007). Early childhood mathematics learning. In F. K. Lester, Jr. (Ed.), *Second handbook on mathematics teaching and learning* (pp. 461–555). Charlotte, NC: Information Age Publishing.

Clements, D. H., & Sarama, J. (2009). *Learning and teaching early math: The learning trajectories approach.* New York, NY: Routledge.

Crespo, S., & Kyriakides, A. (2007). To draw or not to draw: Exploring children's drawings for solving mathematics problems. *Teaching Children Mathematics, 14*(2), 118–125.

Cuyler, M. (2010). *Guinea pigs add up.* New York: Walker.

Dougherty, B., Flores, A., Louis, E., & Sophian, C. (2010). *Developing essential understanding of number and numeration for teaching mathematics in prekindergarten–grade 2.* Reston, VA: National Council of Teachers of Mathematics.

Drake, J., & Barlow, A. (2007). Assessing students' level of understanding multiplication through problem writing. *Teaching Children Mathematics, 14*(5), 272–277.

Drescher, D. (2008). *What's hiding in there?* Edinburgh, Scotland: Floris.

Fagnant, A., & Vlassis, J. (2013). Schematic representations in arithmetical problem solving: Analysis of their impact on grade 4 students. *Education Studies in Mathematics, 84*, 149–168. doi:10.1007/s10649-013-9476-4.

Fosnot, C. T., & Dolk, M. (2001). *Young mathematicians at work: Constructing number sense, addition, and subtraction.* Portsmouth, NH: Heinemann.

Fuchs, L. S., Fuchs, D., Prentice, K., Hamlett, C. L., Finelli, R., & Courey, S. J. (2004). Enhancing mathematical problem solving among third-grade students with schema-based instruction. *Journal of Educational Psychology, 96*(4), 635–647.

Gutstein, E., & Romberg, T. A. (1995). Teaching children to add and subtract. *Journal of Mathematical Behavior, 14*, 283–324.

Huinker, D. (1994, April). Multi-step word problems: A strategy for empowering students. *Presented at the annual meeting of the National Council of Teachers of Mathematics*, Indianapolis, IN.

Knuth, E. J., Stephens, A. C., McNeil, N. M., & Alibali, M. W. (2006). Does understanding the equal sign matter? Evidence from solving equations. *Journal for Research in Mathematics Education, 37*(4), 297–312.

McElligott, M. (2007). *Bean thirteen.* New York: Putnam Juvenile.

Murata, A. (2008). Mathematics teaching and learning as a mediating process: The case of tape diagrams. *Mathematical Thinking and Learning, 10*, 374–406.

National Research Council Committee. (2009). *Mathematics learning in early childhood: Paths toward excellence and equity.* Washington, DC: The National Academies Press.

Overdeck, L. (2013). *Bedtime math.* New York: Feiwel and Friends.

Pinczes, E. (1999). *One hundred hungry ants.* New York, NY: Houghton Mifflin.

Pinczes, E. (2002). *Remainder of one*. New York, NY: Houghton Mifflin.

Roberts, S. (2003). Snack math: Young children explore division. *Teaching Children Mathematics, 9*(5), 258–261.

Ruschak, L., & Carter, D. (1990). *Snack attack: A tasty pop-up book*. New York, NY: Simon & Schuster.

Schifter, D., Bastable, V., & Russell, S. J. (1999). *Making meaning for operations: Facilitator's guide* (Developing mathematical ideas: Number and operations, part 2). Parsippany, NJ: Dale Seymour.

Schifter, D. (2001). Learning to see the invisible: What skills and knowledge are needed to engage with students' mathematical ideas? In T. Wood, B. S. Nelson, and J. Warfield (Eds.), *Beyond classical pedagogy: Teaching elementary school mathematics* (pp. 109–134). Mahwah, NJ: Lawrence Erlbaum.

Schwartz, S. (2013). *Implementing the Common Core State Standards through mathematical problem solving kindergarten–grade 2*. Reston, VA: NCTM.

Sowder, L. (1988). Children's solutions of story problems. *Journal of Mathematical Behavior, 7*(3), 227–238.

Sulentic-Dowell, M. M., Beal, G., & Capraro, R. (2006). How do literacy experiences affect the teaching propensities of elementary pre-service teachers? *Journal of Reading Psychology, 27*(2–3), 235–255.

Shield, M. & Swinson, K. (1996). The link sheet: A communication aid for clarifying and developing mathematical ideas and processes. In P. C. Elliott & M. J. Kenney (Eds.) *Communication in Mathematics, K-12 and Beyond*. (pp. 35-39). Reston, VA: NCTM.

Verschaffel, L., Greer, B., & De Corte, E. (2007). Whole number concepts and operations. In F. Lester (Ed.), *Second handbook of research on mathematics teaching and learning* (pp. 557–628). Reston, VA: National Council of Teachers of Mathematics.

Whitin, P., & Whitin, D. (2008). Learning to solve problems in the primary grades. *Teaching Children Mathematics, 14*(7), 426–432.

Xin, Y. P., Jitendra, A. K., & Deatline-Buchman, A. D. (2005). Effects of mathematical word problem-solving instruction on middle school students with learning problems. *Journal of Special Education, 39*(3), 181–192.

Chapter 10

Anno, M. (1982). *Anno's Counting House*. New York: Philomel Books.

Ashcraft, M. H., & Christy, K. S. (1995). The frequency of arithmetic facts in elementary texts: Addition and multiplication in grades 1–6. *Journal for Research in Mathematics Education, 26*, 396–421.

Baroody, A. J. (1985). Mastery of the basic number combinations: Internalization of relationships or facts? *Journal for Research in Mathematics Education, 16*(2), 83–98.

Baroody, A. J. (2003). The development of adaptive expertise and flexibility: The integration of conceptual and procedural knowledge. In A. J. Baroody & A. Dowker (Eds.), *The development of arithmetic concepts and skills: Constructing adaptive expertise* (pp. 1–34). Mahwah, NJ: Erlbaum.

Baroody, A. J. (2006). Why children have difficulties mastering the basic number combinations and how to help them. *Teaching Children Mathematics, 13*(1), 22–31.

Baroody, A. J., Bajwa, N. P., & Eiland, M. (2009). Why can't Johnny remember the basic facts? *Developmental Disabilities Research Reviews, 15*, 69–79.

Bay-Williams, J. M., & Kling, G. (2014). Enriching addition and subtraction fact mastery through games. *Teaching Children Mathematics, 21*(4), 239–247.

Bley, N. S., & Thornton, C. A. (1995). *Teaching mathematics to students with learning disabilities* (3rd ed.). Austin, TX: Pro-Ed.

Boaler, J. (2012, July 3). Timed tests and the development of math anxiety. *Education Week*. Retrieved from http://www.edweek.org/ew/articles/2012/07/03/36boaler.h31.html.

Boaler, J. (2014). Research suggests that timed tests cause math anxiety. *Teaching Children Mathematics, 20*(8), 469–474.

Boaler, J. (2015a, January 28). *Fluency without fear*. Retrieved from https://www.youcubed.org/fluency-without-fear/.

Boaler, J. (2015b). *What's math got to do with it?* New York: Penguin.

Boaler, J. (2016). *Mathematical mindsets*. San Francisco, CA: Jossey-Bass.

Brownell, W., & Chazal, C. (1935). The effects of premature drill in third grade arithmetic. *Journal of Educational Research, 29*(1), 17 28.

Council of Chief State School Officers. (2010). *Common Core State Standards*. Washington, DC.

Forbringer, L., & Fahsl, A. J. (2010). Differentiating practice to help students master basic facts. In D. Y. White & J. S. Spitzer (Eds.), *Responding to diversity: Grades pre-K–5* (pp. 7–22). Reston, VA: National Council of Teachers of Mathematics.

Fuson, K. C. (1984). More complexities in subtraction. *Journal for Research in Mathematics Education, 15*(3), 214–225.

Fuson, K. C., & Kwon, Y. (1992). Korean children's single-digit addition and subtraction: Numbers structured by ten. *Journal for Research in Mathematics Education, 23*(2), 148–165.

Gravemeijer, K., & van Galen, F. (2003). Facts and algorithms as products of students' own mathematical activity. In J. Kilpatrick, W. G. Martin, & D. Schifter (Eds.), *A research companion to Principles and Standards for School Mathematics* (pp. 114–122). Reston, VA: National Council of Teachers of Mathematics.

Godfrey, C. & Stone, J. (2013). Mastering fact fluency: Are they game? *Teaching Children Mathematics, 20*(2), 96–101.

Gray, E., & Tall, D. (1994). Duality, ambiguity, and flexibility: A "proceptual" view of simple arithmetic. *Journal for Research in Mathematics Education, 25*(2), 116–140.

Hamm, D. (1994). *How many feet in the bed?* New York, NY: Simon and Schuster.

Heege, H. T. (1985). The acquisition of basic multiplication skills. *Educational Studies in Mathematics, 16*(4): 375–388.

Henry, V. J., & Brown, R. S. (2008). First-grade basic facts: An investigation into teaching and learning of an accelerated, highdemand memorization standard. *Journal for Research in Mathematics Education, 39*(2), 153–183.

Hong, L. (1993). *Two of everything*. Morton Grove, IL: Albert Whitman & Company.

Kamii, C. K., & Anderson, C. (2003). Multiplication games: How we made and used them. *Teaching Children Mathematics, 10*(3), 135–141.

Kling, G. (2011). Fluency with basic addition. *Teaching Children Mathematics, 18*(2), 80–88.

Kling, G., & Bay-Williams, J. M. (2014). Assessing basic fact fluency. *Teaching Children Mathematics, 20*(8), 488–497.

Kubler, A. (2001). *There were ten in the bed*. Swindon, UK: Child's Play.

Lewis, T. (2005). Facts + fun = fluency. *Teaching Children Mathematics, 12*(1), 8–11.

Mazzocco, M. M. M., Devlin, K. T., & McKenney, S. J. (2008). Is it a fact? Timed arithmetic performance of children with mathematical learning disabilities (MLD) varies as a function of how MLD is defined. *Developmental Neuropsychology, 33*(3), 318–344.

National Research Council. (2001). Adding it up: *Helping children learn mathematics*. J. Kilpatrick, J. Swafford, & B. Findell (Eds.).Washington, DC: National Academies Press.

NCTM (National Council of Teachers of Mathematics). (2006). *Curriculum focal points for prekindergarten through grade 8 mathematics: A quest for coherence*. Reston, VA: NCTM.

Ramirez, G., Gunderson, E. A., Levine, S. C., & Beilock, S. L. (2013). Math anxiety, working memory, and math achievement in early elementary school. *Journal of Cognition and Development, 14*(2), 187–202.

Rathmell, E. C., Leutzinger, L. P., & Gabriele, A. (2000). *Thinking with numbers*. Cedar Falls, IA: Thinking with Numbers.

Richardson, K. (2002). *Assessing math concepts: Hiding assessment*. Bellingham, WA: Mathematical Perspectives.

Sarama, J., & Clements, D. H. (2009). *Early childhood mathematics education research: Learning trajectories for young children*. New York, NY: Routledge.

Shoecraft, P. (1982). Bowl-A-Fact: A game for reviewing the number facts. *Arithmetic Teacher, 29*(8), 24–25.

Toft, K. M., & Sheather, A. (1998). *One less fish*. Watertown, MA: Charlesbridge.

Verschaffel, L., Greer, B., & De Corte, E. (2007). Whole number concepts and operations. In F. Lester (Ed.), *Second handbook of research on mathematics teaching and learning* (pp. 557–628). Reston, VA: National Council of Teachers of Mathematics.

Wallace, A. H., & Gurganus, S. P. (2005). Teaching for mastery of multiplication. *Teaching Children Mathematics, 12*(1), 26–33.

Watanabe, T. (2006). The teaching and learning of fractions: A Japanese perspective. *Teaching Children Mathematics, 12*(7), 368–374.

Chapter 11

Burris, J. (2013). Virtual place value. *Teaching Children Mathematics, 20*(4), 228–236.

Byrge, L., Smith, L. B., & Mix, K. (2013). Beginnings of place value: How preschoolers write three-digit numbers. *Child Development 85*(2), 437–443.

Cuyler, M. (2005). *100th day worries*. New York: Simon & Schuster.

Council of Chief State School Officers. (2010). *Common Core State Standards*. Washington, DC.

Dougherty, B., Flores, A., Louis, E., & Sophian, C. (2010). *Developing essential understanding of number and numeration for teaching mathematics in prekindergarten–grade 2*. Reston, VA: National Council of Teachers of Mathematics.

Fuson, K. C. (2006). Research on whole number addition and subtraction. In D. Grouws (Ed.), *Handbook of research on mathematics teaching and learning* (pp. 243–275). Charlotte, NC: Information Age Publishing.

Kamii, C. K. (1985). *Young children reinvent arithmetic*. New York: Teachers College Press.

Labinowicz, E. (1985). *Learning from children: New beginnings for teaching numerical thinking*. Menlo Park, CA: AWL Supplemental.

Murphy, S. (2004). *Earth day, hooray!* New York: HarperCollins.

National Council of Teachers of Mathematics. (2000). *Principles and standards for school mathematics*. Reston, VA: Author.

Ross, S. H. (1986). *The development of children's place-value Numeration concepts in grades two through five*. Presented at the annual meeting of the American Educational Research Association, San Francisco, CA.

Ross, S. H. (1989). Parts, wholes, and place value: A developmental perspective. *Arithmetic Teacher, 36*(6), 47–51.

Ross, S. R. (2002). Place value: Problem solving and written assessment. *Teaching Children Mathematics, 8*(7), 419–423.

Thaler, M. (2014) *The 100th day of school from the black lagoon*. New York: Scholastic.

Wright, R., Martland, J., & Stafford, A. (2008). *Early numeracy: Assessment for teaching and intervention*. London: Sage.

Chapter 12

Barker, L. (2009). Ten is the magic number! *Teaching Children Mathematics, 15*(6), 336–345.

Bowen, A. (2006). *The great math tattle battle*. Park Ridge, IL: Albert Whitman.

Caldwell, J., Kobett, B., & Karp, K. (2014). *Essential understanding of addition and subtraction in practice, grades K–2*. Reston, VA: NCTM.

Carpenter, T. P., Franke, M. L., Jacobs, V. R., Fennema, E., & Empson, S. B. (1998). A longitudinal study of invention and understanding in children's multidigit addition and subtraction. *Journal for Research in Mathematics Education, 29*(1), 3–20.

Coates, G. D., & Thompson, V. (2003). *Family Math II: Achieving success in mathematics*. Berkeley, CA: EQUALS Lawrence Hall of Science.

Cobb, P., & Merkel, G. (1989). Thinking strategies: Teaching arithmetic through problem solving. In P. Trafton (Ed.), *New directions for elementary school mathematics: 1989 yearbook* (pp. 70–81). Reston, VA: National Council of Teachers of Mathematics.

Council of Chief State School Officers. (2010). *Common Core State Standards*. Washington, DC.

Fleischman, H. L., Hopstock, P. J., Pelczar, M. P., & Shelley, B. E. (2010). *Highlights from PISA 2009: Performance of U.S. 15-yearold students in reading, mathematics, and science literacy in an international context* (NCES 2011–004). Washington, DC: U.S. Government Printing Office.

Fuson, K. C. (2003). Developing mathematical power in whole number operations. In J. Kilpatrick, W. G. Martin, & D. Schifter (Eds.), *A research companion to Principles and Standards in School Mathematics* (pp. 68–94). Reston, VA: National Council of Teachers of Mathematics.

Gravemeijer, K., & van Galen, F. (2003). Facts and algorithms as products of students' own mathematical activity. In J. Kilpatrick, W. G. Martin, & D. Schifter (Eds.), *A research companion to Principles and Standards for School Mathematics* (pp. 114–122). Reston, VA: National Council of Teachers of Mathematics.

Hiebert, J., & Grouws, D. A. (2007). The effects of classroom mathematics teaching on students' learning. In F. K. Lester (Ed.), *Second handbook of research on mathematics teaching and learning* (pp. 371–404). Charlotte, NC: Information Age Publishing.

Humphreys, C., & Parker, R. (2015). *Making number talks matter.* Portland, ME: Stenhouse Publishers.

Kamii, C. K. (1985). Young children reinvent arithmetic. New York, NY: Teachers College Press.

Kamii, C. K., & Dominick, A. (1998). The harmful effects of algorithms in grades 1–4. In L. J. Morrow (Ed.), *The teaching and learning of algorithms in school mathematics* (pp. 130–140). Reston, VA: National Council of Teachers of Mathematics.

Kamii, C. K., & Joseph, L. (1988). Teaching place value and double-column addition. *Arithmetic Teacher, 35*(6), 48–52.

Keiser, J. M. (2010). Shifting our computational focus. *Mathematics Teaching in the Middle School, 16*(4), 216–223.

Klein, A. S., Beishuizen, M., & Treffers, A. (2002). The empty number line in Dutch second grade. In J. Sowder & B. Schapelle (Eds.), *Lessons learned from research* (pp. 41–44). Reston, VA: National Council of Teachers of Mathematics.

Lynch, K., & Star, J. (2014). Views of struggling students on instruction incorporating multiple strategies in algebra I: An exploratory study. *Journal for Research in Mathematics Education, 45*(1), 6–18.

Madell, R. (1985). Children's natural processes. *Arithmetic Teacher, 32*(7), 20–22.

NCTM (National Council of Teachers of Mathematics). (2014). *Position statement on access and equity in mathematics education.* Reston, VA: NCTM.

National Research Council. (2001). *Adding it up: Helping children learn mathematics.* J. Kilpatrick, J. Swafford, & B. Findell (Eds.). Washington, DC: National Academies Press.

Peltenburg, M., van den Heuvel-Panhuizen, M., & Robitzsch, A. (2012). Special education students' use of indirect addition in solving subtraction problems up to 100: A proof of the didactical potential of an ignored procedure. *Educational Studies in Mathematics, 79*(3), 351–369.

Perkins, I., & Flores, A. (2002). Mathematical notations and procedures of recent immigrant students. *Mathematics Teaching in the Middle School, 7*(6), 346–351.

Reinhart, S. (2000). Never say anything a kid can say. *Mathematics Teaching in the Middle School, 5*(8), 478–483.

Rittle-Johnson, B., Star, J. R., & Durkin, K. (2010, April). Developing procedural flexibility: When should multiple solution methods be introduced? *Paper presented at the Annual Conference of the American Educational Research Association,* Denver, CO.

Siegler, R. S., & Booth, J. L. (2005). Development of numerical estimation: A review. In J. I. D. Campbell (Ed.), *Handbook of mathematical cognition* (pp. 197–212). New York: New York Psychology Press.

Torbeyns, J., De Smedt, B., Ghesquiere, P., & Verschaffel, L. (2009). Acquisition and use of shortcut strategies by traditionally schooled children. *Educational Studies in Mathematics, 71,* 1–17.

Verschaffel, L., Greer, B., & De Corte, E. (2007). Whole number concepts and operations. In F. Lester (Ed.), *Second handbook of research on mathematics teaching and learning* (pp. 557–628). Reston, VA: National Council of Teachers of Mathematics.

Wright, R., Martland, J., Stafford, A., & Stanger, G. (2008). *Teaching number: Advancing children's skills and strategies.* London: Sage.

Chapter 13

Ball, D. L., & Bass, H. (2003). Making mathematics reasonable in school. In J. Kilpatrick, W. G. Martin, & D. Schifter (Eds.), *A research companion to Principles and Standards for School Mathematics* (pp. 27–44). Reston, VA: National Council of Teachers of Mathematics.

Bezuszka, S. J., & Kenney, M. J. (2008). The three R's: Recursive thinking, recursion, and recursive formulas. In C. E. Greenes & R. Rubenstein (Eds.), *Algebra and algebraic thinking in school mathematics: 70th NCTM yearbook* (pp. 81–97). Reston, VA: NCTM.

Blanton, M. L. (2008). *Algebra in the elementary classroom: Transforming thinking, transforming practice.* Portsmouth, NH: Heinemann.

Blanton, M., Levi, L., Crites, T. W., & Dougherty, B. J. (2011). *Developing essential understanding of algebraic thinking for teaching mathematics in grades 3–5. Essential Understanding Series.* Reston, VA: NCTM.

Carpenter, T. P., Franke, M. L., & Levi, L. (2003). *Thinking mathematically: Integrating arithmetic and algebra in elementary school.* Portsmouth, NH: Heinemann.

Carraher, D. W., & Schliemann, A. D. (2007). Early algebra and algebraic reasoning. In F. Lester (Ed.), *Second handbook of research on mathematics teaching and learning: A project of the National Council of Teachers of Mathematics* (Vol. II, pp. 609–705). Charlotte, NC: Information Age Publishing.

Council of Chief State School Officers. (2010). *Common Core State Standards.* Washington, DC.

Falkner, K. P., Levi, L., & Carpenter, T. P. (1999). Children's understanding of equality: A foundation for algebra. *Teaching Children Mathematics, 6*(4), 232–236.

Fisher, E., Roy, G., & Reeves, C. (2013). The functionator 3000: Transforming numbers and children. *Teaching children mathematics 29*(4), 254–260.

Fosnot, C. (2007). *The sleepover.* Portsmouth, NH: Heinemann.

Fosnot, C. T., & Jacob, B. (2010). *Young mathematicians at work: Constructing algebra.* Reston, VA: NCTM.

Harris, T. (2000). *Pattern fish.* Minneapolis, MN: Milbrook Press.

Hong, L. (1993). *Two of everything.* Morton Grove, IL: Albert Whitman & Company.

Humphreys, C., & Parker, R. (2015). *Making number talks matter.* Portland, ME: Stenhouse Publishers.

Kaput, J. J. (2008). What is algebra? What is algebraic reasoning? In J. J. Kaput, D. W. Carraher, & M. L. Blanton (Eds.), *Algebra in the early grades.* Reston, VA: National Council of Teachers of Mathematics.

Kieran, C. (2007). Learning and teaching algebra at the middle school through college levels. In F. K. Lester (Ed.), *Second handbook of research on mathematics teaching and learning* (pp. 707–762). Charlotte, NC: Information Age.

Knuth, E. J., Alibali, M. W., McNeil, N. M., Weinberg, A., & Stephens, A. C. (2011). Middle school students' understanding of core algebraic concepts: Equivalence & variable. *Early Algebraization,* 259–276.

Knuth, E. J., Stephens, A. C., McNeil, N. M., & Alibali, M. W. (2006). Does understanding the equal sign matter? Evidence from solving equations. *Journal for Research in Mathematics Education, 37*(4), 297–312.

Kroll, V. (2005). *Equal shmequal.* Watertown, MA: Charlesbridge Publishing.

Liu, N., & Fosnot, C. (2007). *The Double-Decker Bus.* Portsmouth, NH: Heinemann.

Maida, P. (2004). Using algebra without realizing it. *Mathematics Teaching in the Middle School, 9*(9), 484–488.

Mann, R. L. (2004). Balancing act: The truth behind the equals sign. *Teaching Children Mathematics, 11*(2), 65–69.

McNamara, J. C. (2010). Two of everything. *Teaching Children Mathematics, 17*(3), 132–136.

McNeil, N. (2014). A change-resistance account of children's difficulties understanding mathematical equivalence. *Child Development Perspectives, 8*(1), 42-47.

McNeil, N. M., & Alibali, M. W. (2005). Knowledge change as a function of mathematics experience: All contexts are not created equal. *Journal of Cognition and Development, 6*, 285–306.

McNeil, N. M., Grandau, L., Knuth, E. J., Alibali, M. W., Stephens, A. C., Hattikudur, S., & Krill, D. E. (2006). Middle school students' understanding of the equal sign: The books they read can't help. *Cognition & Instruction, 24*(3), 367–385.

Molina, M., & Ambrose, R. C. (2006). Fostering relational thinking while negotiating the meaning of the equals sign. *Teaching Children Mathematics, 13*(2), 111–117.

National Council of Teachers of Mathematics. (2006). *Curriculum focal points for prekindergarten through grade 8 mathematics: A quest for coherence*. Reston, VA: Author.

Numeroff, L. (1985). *If you give a mouse a cookie*. New York, NY: Harper Collins.

RAND Mathematics Study Panel. (2003). *Mathematical proficiency for all students: Toward a strategic research and development program in mathematics education* (Issue 1643). Santa Monica, CA: Rand Corporation.

Russell, S., Schifter, D., & Bastable, V. (2011). *Connecting arithmetic to algebra: Strategies for building algebraic thinking in the elementary grades*. Portsmouth, NH: Heinemann.

Schifter, D. (1999). Reasoning about operations: Early algebraic thinking, grades K through 6. In L. Stiff & F. Curcio (Eds.), *Developing mathematical reasoning in grades K–12* (pp. 62–81). Reston, VA: National Council of Teachers of Mathematics.

Schifter, D., Monk, G. S., Russell, S. J., & Bastable, V. (2007). Early algebra: What does understanding the laws of arithmetic mean in the elementary grades? In J. Kaput, D. Carraher, & M. Blanton (Eds.), *Algebra in the early grades*. Mahwah, NJ: Lawrence Erlbaum.

Schifter, D., Russell, S., & Bastable, V. (2009). Early algebra to reach the range of learners. *Teaching Children Mathematics, 16*(4), 230–237.

Sharratt, N. (1996). *My mom and dad make me laugh*. Somerville, MA: Candlewick.

Stephens, A. C., Knuth, E. J., Blanton, M. L., Isler, I., Gardiner, A. M., & Marum, T. (2013). Equation structure and the meaning of the equal sign: The impact of task selection in eliciting elementary students' understandings. *The Journal of Mathematical Behavior, 32*, 173–182.

Warren, E., & Cooper, T. J. (2008). Patterns that support early algebraic thinking in elementary school. In C. E. Greenes & R. Rubenstein (Eds.), *Algebra and algebraic thinking in school mathematics: 70th NCTM yearbook* (pp. 113–126). Reston, VA: National Council of Teachers of Mathematics.

Chapter 14

Bailey, D. H., Hoard, M. K., Nugent, L., & Geary, D. C. (2012). Competence with fractions predicts gains in mathematics achievement. *Journal of Experimental Child Psychology, 113*, 447–455.

Bay-Williams, J. M., & Martinie, S. L. (2003). Thinking rationally about number in the middle school. *Mathematics Teaching in the Middle School, 8*(6), 282–287.

Booth, J., & Siegler, R. (2008). Numerical magnitude representations influence arithmetic learning. *Child Development, 79*(4), 1016–1031.

Brown, G., & Quinn, R. J. (2007). Investigating the relationship between fraction proficiency and success in algebra. *Australian Mathematics Teacher, 63*(4), 8–15.

Council of Chief State School Officers. (2010). *Common Core State Standards*. Washington, DC.

Champion, J., & Wheeler, A. (2014). Revisit pattern blocks to develop rational number sense. *Mathematics Teaching in the Middle School, 19*(6), 337–343.

Clarke, D., Roche, A., & Mitchell, A. (2008). 10 practical tips for making fractions come alive and make sense. *Mathematics Teaching in the Middle School, 13*(7), 373–380.

Cramer, K., & Henry, A. (2002). Using manipulative models to build number sense for addition of fractions. In B. Litwiller (Ed.), *Making sense of fractions, ratios, and proportions* (pp. 41–48). Reston, VA: National Council of Teachers of Mathematics.

Cramer, K., & Whitney, S. (2010). Learning rational number concepts and skills in elementary school classrooms. In D. V. Lambdin & F. K. Lester, Jr. (Eds.), *Teaching and learning mathematics: Translating research for elementary school teachers* (pp. 15–22). Reston, VA: NCTM.

Cramer, K., Wyberg, T., & Leavitt, S. (2008). The role of representations in fraction addition and subtraction. *Mathematics Teaching in the Middle School, 13*(8), 490–496.

Cwikla, J. (2014). Can kindergartners do fractions? *Teaching Children Mathematics, 20*(6), 354–364.

Ellington, A. J., & Whitenack, J. W. (2010). Fractions and the funky cookie. *Teaching Children Mathematics, 16*(9), 532–539.

Empson, S. (2002). Organizing diversity in early fraction thinking. In B. Litwiller (Ed.), *Making sense of fractions, ratios, and proportions* (pp. 29–40). Reston, VA: National Council of Teachers of Mathematics.

Empson, S., & Levi, L. (2011). *Extending children's mathematics: Fractions and decimals*. Portsmouth, NH: Heinemann.

Fosnot, C. T., & Dolk, M. (2001). *Young mathematicians at work: Constructing number sense, addition, and subtraction*. Portsmouth, NH: Heinemann.

Hackenberg, A. J. (2007). Units coordination and the construction of improper fractions: A revision of the splitting hypothesis. *The Journal of Mathematical Behavior, 26*(1), 27–47.

Hodges, T. E., Cady, J., & Collins, R. L. (2008). Fraction representation: The not-so-common denominator among textbooks. *Mathematics Teaching in the Middle School, 14*(2), 78–84.

Hutchins, P. (1986). *The doorbell rang*. New York, NY: Greenwillow Books.

Lamon, S. J. (2012). *Teaching fractions and ratios for understanding: Essential content knowledge and instructional strategies* (3rd ed.). New York, NY: Taylor & Francis Group.

Mack, N. K. (2001). Building on informal knowledge through instruction in a complex content domain: Partitioning, units, and understanding multiplication of fractions. *Journal for Research in Mathematics Education, 32*, 267–295.

Moyer-Packenham, P. S., Ulmer, L. A., & Anderson, K. L. (2012). Examining pictorial models and virtual manipulatives for third-grade fraction instruction. *Journal of Interactive Online Learning, 11*(3), 103–120.

NCTM (National Council of Teachers of Mathematics). (2006). *Curriculum focal points for prekindergarten through grade 8 mathematics: A quest for coherence*. Reston, VA: NCTM.

National Mathematics Advisory Panel. (2008). *Foundations for success*. Jessup, MD: U.S. Department of Education.

Olive, J. (2002). Bridging the gap: Using interactive computer tools to build fraction schemes. *Teaching Children Mathematics, 8*(6), 356–61.

Olive, J., & Vomvoridi, E. (2006). Making sense of instruction on fractions when a student lacks necessary fractional schemes: The case of Tim. *Journal of Mathematical Behavior, 25*(1), 18–45.

Petit, M., Laird, R. E., & Marsden, E. L. (2010). *A focus on fractions: Bringing research to the classroom*. New York, NY: Taylor & Francis.

Petit, M., Laird, R. E., Marsden, E. L., & Ebby, C. (2016). *A focus on fractions: Bringing research to the classroom* (2nd ed.). New York: Taylor & Francis.

Post, T. R., Wachsmuth, I., Lesh, R. A., & Behr, M. J. (1985). Order and equivalence of rational numbers: A cognitive analysis. *Journal for Research in Mathematics Education, 16*(1), 18–36.

Pothier, Y., & Sawada, D. (1990). Partitioning: An approach to fractions. *Arithmetic Teacher, 38*(4), 12–17.

Roddick, C., & Silvas-Centeno, C. (2007). Developing understanding of fractions through pattern blocks and fair trade. *Teaching Children Mathematics, 14*(3), 140–145.

Russell, S. J., & Economopoulos, K. (2008*). Investigations in number, data, and space*. New York: Pearson.

Siebert, D., & Gaskin, N. (2006). Creating, naming, and justifying fractions. *Teaching Children Mathematics, 12*(8), 394–400.

Siegler, R. S., Carpenter, T., Fennell, F., Geary, D., Lewis, J., Okamoto, Y., et al. (2010). *Developing effective fractions instruction for kindergarten through 8th grade: A practice guide* (NCEE 2010- 4039). Retrieved from www.whatworks.ed.gov/publications/practiceguides.

Siegler, R. S., & Ramani, G. B. (2009). Playing linear number board games—but not circular ones—improves low-income preschoolers' numerical understanding. *Journal of Educational Psychology, 101*, 545–560.

Sowder, J. T., & Wearne, D. (2006). What do we know about eighth-grade student achievement? *Mathematics Teaching in the Middle School, 11*(6), 285–293.

Steffe, L. P., & Olive, J. (Eds.) (2010). *Children's fractional knowledge*. New York: Springer.

Streefland, L. (Ed.). (1991). *Fractions in realistic mathematics education: A paradigm of developmental research*. Boston, MA: Kluwer Academic Publishers.

Thompson, P. W., & Saldanha, L. A. (2003). Fractions and multiplicative reasoning. In J. Kilpatrick, W. G. Martin, & D. Schifter (Eds.), *A research companion to principles and standards for school mathematics*, (95–113). Reston, VA: National Council of Teachers of Mathematics.

Tzur, R. (1999). An integrated study of children's construction of improper fractions and the teacher's role in promoting learning. *Journal for Research in Mathematics Education, 30*, 390–416.

Watanabe, T. (2007). Initial treatment of fractions in Japanese textbooks. *Focus on Learning Problems in Mathematics, 29*(2), 41–60.

Wearne, D., & Kouba, V. L. (2000). Rational numbers. In E. A. Silver & P. A. Kenney (Eds.), *Results from the seventh mathematics assessment of the National Assessment of Educational Progress* (pp. 163–191). Reston, VA: NCTM.

Williams, L. (2008). Tiering and scaffolding: Two strategies for providing access to important mathematics. *Teaching Children Mathematics, 14*(6), 324–330.

Zhang, X., Clements, M. A., & Ellerton, N. F. (2015). Engaging students with multiple models of fractions. *Teaching Children Mathematics, 22*(3), 138–147.

Chapter 15

Battista, M. (2012). *Cognition-based assessment and teaching of geometric measurement: Building on students' reasoning*. Portsmouth, NH: Heinemann.

Blume, G., Galindo, E., & Walcott, C. (2007). Performance in measurement and geometry from the viewpoint of Principles and Standards for School Mathematics. In P. Kloosterman & F. Lester, Jr. (Eds.), *Results and interpretations of the 2003 mathematics assessment of the National Assessment of Educational Progress* (pp. 95–138). Reston, VA: National Council of Teachers of Mathematics.

Dietiker, L., Gonulates, F., Figueras, J., & Smith, J. P. (2010, April). *Weak attention to unit iteration in U.S. elementary curriculum materials*. Presentation at the annual conference of the American Educational Research Association, Denver, CO.

Council of Chief State School Officers. (2010). *Common Core State Standards*. Washington, DC.

Clements, D. H., & Sarama, J. (2009). *Learning and teaching early math: The learning trajectories approach*. New York, NY: Routledge.

Curry, M., Mitchelmore, M., & Outhred, L. (2006). Development of children's understanding of length, area, and volume measurement principles. In J. Novotna, H. Moraova, M. Kratka, & N. Stehlikova (Eds.), *Proceedings for 30th Conference of the International Group for the Psychology of Mathematics Education, Vol. 2*, pp. 377–384.

Hightower, S. (1997). *Twelve snails to one lizard: A tale of mischief and measurement*. New York: Simon & Schuster.

Jenkins, S. (2011a). *Actual size*. Boston, MA: Houghton Mifflin.

Jenkins, S. (2011b). *Just a second*. New York, NY: Houghton Mifflin.

Joram, E. (2003). Benchmarks as tools for developing measurement sense. In D. H. Clements (Ed.), *Learning and teaching measurement* (pp. 57–67). Reston, VA: NCTM.

Kloosterman, P., Rutledge, Z., & Kenney, P. (2009). Exploring the results of the NAEP: 1980s to the present. *Mathematics Teaching in the Middle School, 14*(6), 357–365.

Leedy, L. (2000). *Measuring Penny*. New York, NY: Henry Holt and Company.

Myller, R. (1991). *How big is a foot?* South Holland, IL: Yearling Books. National Center for Educational Statistics. (2014). *NAEP questions tool*. Retrieved from http://nces.ed.gov/nationsreportcard/itmrlsx/landing.aspx.

National Council of Teachers of Mathematics. (2003). *Navigating through measurement in prekindergarten–grade 2*. Reston, VA: Author.

NCTM (National Council of Teachers of Mathematics). (2006). *Curriculum focal points for prekindergarten through grade 8 mathematics: A quest for coherence*. Reston, VA: NCTM.

NCTM (National Council of Teachers of Mathematics). (2009). *Focus in high school mathematics: Reasoning and sense making*. Reston, VA: NCTM.

National Council of Teachers of Mathematics. (2011b, March). *Position statement on the metric system*. Retrieved from www.nctm.org/about/content.aspx?id=29000.

National Research Council Committee. (2009). *Mathematics learning in early childhood: Paths toward excellence and equity*. Washington, DC: National Academies Press.

Provasnik, S., Kastberg, D., Ferraro, D., Lemanski, N., Roey, S., and Jenkins, F. (2012). *Highlights from TIMSS 2011: Mathematics and Science Achievement of U.S. Fourth- and Eighth-Grade Students in an International Context* (NCES 2013-009). National Center for Education Statistics, Institute of Education Sciences, U.S. Department of Education. Washington, DC.

Thompson, T. D., & Preston, R. V. (2004). Measurement in the middle grades: Insights from NAEP and TIMSS. *Mathematics Teaching in the Middle School, 9*(9), 514–519.

Tompert, A. (1997). *Grandfather Tang's story*. New York: Dragonfly Books.

Towers, J., & Hunter, K. (2010). An ecological reading of mathematical language in a grade 3 classroom: A case of learning and teaching measurement estimation. *The Journal of Mathematical Behavior, 29,* 25–40.

Chapter 16

Battista, M. T. (2007). The development of geometric and spatial thinking. In F. Lester (Ed.), *Second handbook of research on mathematics teaching and learning* (pp. 843–908). Reston, VA: NCTM.

Battista, M. (2012). *Cognition-based assessment and teaching of geometric shapes: Building on students' reasoning.* Portsmouth, NH: Heinemann.

Bednar, S. (2009). *Flags of the world.* New York, NY: Abrams Books.

Clements, D. (1999). Geometric and spatial thinking in young children. In J. Copely (Ed.), *Mathematics in the early years* (pp. 66–79). Reston, VA: National Council of Teachers of Mathematics.

Clements, D. H., & Battista, M. T. (1992). Geometry and spatial reasoning. In D. A. Grouws (Ed.), *Handbook of research on mathematics teaching and learning* (pp. 420–464). Old Tappan, NJ: Macmillan.

Clements, D. H., & Sarama, J. (2000a). Young children's ideas about geometric shapes. *Teaching Children Mathematics, 6*(8), 482–488.

Clements, D. H., & Sarama, J. (2000b). The earliest geometry. *Teaching Children Mathematics, 7*(2), 82–86.

Clements, D., & Sarama, J. (2014). *Learning and teaching early math: The learning trajectories approach* (2nd ed.). New York: Routledge.

Council of Chief State School Officers. (2010). *Common Core State Standards.* Washington, DC.

Ehlert, L. (1989). *Color zoo.* New York: HarperCollins.

Ehlert, L. (1990). *Color farm.* New York: HarperCollins.

Hoban, T. (2000). *Cubes, cones, cylinders and shapes.* New York: Greenwillow.

National Center for Educational Statistics. (2014). *NAEP questions tool.* Retrieved from http://nces.ed.gov/nationsreportcard/itmrlsx/landing.aspx.

National Council of Teachers of Mathematics. (2000). *Principles and standards for school mathematics.* Reston, VA: Author.

NCTM (National Council of Teachers of Mathematics). (2006). *Curriculum focal points for prekindergarten through grade 8 mathematics: A quest for coherence.* Reston, VA: NCTM.

National Research Council Committee. (2009). *Mathematics learning in early childhood: Paths toward excellence and equity.* Washington, DC: National Academies Press.

Sarama, J., & Clements, D. H. (2009). *Early childhood mathematics education research: Learning trajectories for young children.* New York, NY: Routledge.

Sowder, J. T., & Wearne, D. (2006). What do we know about eighth-grade student achievement? *Mathematics Teaching in the Middle School, 11*(6), 285–293.

Tompert, A. (1997). *Grandfather Tang's story.* New York: Dragonfly Books.

van Hiele, P. M. (1984). A child's thought and geometry. In Geddes, D., Fuys, D. & Tischler, R. (Eds.). *English Translation of Selected Writings of Dina van Hiele-Geldof and Pierre M. van Hiele,* Washington, DC: National Science Foundation.

van Hiele, P. M. (1999). Developing geometric thinking through activities that begin with play. *Teaching Children Mathematics, 5*(6), 310–316.

Yu, P., Barrett, J., & Presmeg, N. (2009). Prototypes and categorical reasoning: A perspective to explain how children learn about interactive geometry objects. In T. Craine & R. Rubenstein (Eds.) *Understanding geometry for a changing world.* Reston, VA: NCTM.

Zwillinger, D. (Ed.) (2011). *Standard mathematical tables and formulae* (32nd ed.). Boca Raton, FL: CRC Press.

Chapter 17

Brown, M. (2005). *Goodnight moon.* New York, NY: Harper Collins.

Burrill, G. F., & Elliot, P. (2006). *Thinking and reasoning with data and chance: 68th NCTM yearbook.* Reston, VA: NCTM.

Council of Chief State School Officers. (2010). *Common Core State Standards.* Washington, DC.

Clements, D. H., & Sarama, J. (2009). *Learning and teaching early math: The learning trajectories approach.* New York, NY: Routledge.

Cook, C. D. (2008). I scream, you scream: Data analysis with kindergartners. *Teaching Children Mathematics, 14*(9), 538–540.

English, L. (2013). Surviving an avalanche of data. *Teaching Children Mathematics, 19*(6), 364–372.

Franklin, C. A., & Garfield, J. B. (2006). The GAISE Project: Developing statistics education guidelines for grades PreK–12 and college courses. In G. F. Burrill & P. C. Elliott (Eds.), *Thinking and reasoning with data and chance: 68th NCTM yearbook* (pp. 345–376). Reston, VA: NCTM.

Franklin, C. A., Kader, G., Mewborn, D., Moreno, J., Peck, R., Perry, M., & Scheaffer, R. (2005). *Guidelines for assessment and instruction in statistics education (GAISE) report.* Alexandria, VA: American Statistical Association.

Franklin, C. A., & Mewborn, D. S. (2008). Statistics in the elementary grades: Exploring distribution of data. *Teaching Children Mathematics, 15*(1), 10–16.

Friel, S. N., Curcio, F. R., & Bright, G. W. (2001). Making sense of graphs: Critical factors influencing comprehension and instructional implications. *Journal for Research in Mathematics Education, 32,* 124–158.

Friel, S. N., O'Conner, W., & Mamer, J. D. (2006). More than "mean median mode" and a bar graph: What's needed to have a statistical conversation? In G. F. Burrill & P. C. Elliott (Eds.), *Thinking and reasoning about data and chance: 68th NCTM yearbook* (pp. 117–138). Reston, VA: National Council of Teachers of Mathematics.

Hourigan, M., & Leavy, A. (2015/2016). Practical problems: Using literature to teach statistics. *Teaching Children Mathematics, 22*(5), 282–291.

Hudson, P. J., Shupe, M., Vasquez, E., & Miller, S. P. (2008). Teaching data analysis to elementary students with mild disabilities. *TEACHING Exceptional Children Plus, 4*(3), Article 5. Retrieved June 7, 2016 from http://escholarship.bc.edu/education/tecplus/vol4/iss3/art5.

Kader, G. D., & Jacobbe, T. (2013). *Developing essential understanding of statistics for teaching mathematics in grades 6–8.* Reston, VA: NCTM.

Konold, C., Higgins, T., Russell, S., & Khalil, K. (2004). *Data seen through different lenses.* Amherst, MA: University of Massachusetts. Retrieved from www.srri.umass.edu/publications/konold-2004dst.

Langrall, C., Nisbet, S., Mooney, E., & Jansem, S. (2011). The role of context expertise when comparing data. *Mathematical Thinking and Learning, 13*, 47–67.

Lobel, A. (1970). *Frog and Toad are friends.* New York: HarperCollins.

Mokros, J., & Wright, T. (2009). Zoos, aquariums, and expanding students' data literacy. *Teaching Children Mathematics, 15*(9), 524–530.

Murphy, S. (1997). *The best vacation ever.* New York: HarperCollins.

National Council of Teachers of Mathematics. (2000). *Principles and standards for school mathematics.* Reston, VA: Author.

National Council of Teachers of Mathematics. (2006). *Curriculum focal points for prekindergarten through grade 8 mathematics: A quest for coherence.* Reston, VA: Author.

Niezgoda, D. A., & Moyer-Packenham, P. S. (2005). Hickory, dickory, dock: Navigating through data analysis. *Teaching Children Mathematics, 11*(6), 292–300.

Russell, S. J. (2006). What does it mean that "5 has a lot"? From the world to data and back. In G. F. Burrill & P. C. Elliott (Eds.), *Thinking and reasoning about data and chance: 68th NCTM yearbook* (pp. 17–30). Reston VA: National Council of Teachers of Mathematics.

Shaughnessy, J. M. (2003). Research on students' understanding of probability. In J. Kilpatrick, W. G. Martin, & D. Schifter (Eds.), *A research companion to Principles and Standards for School Mathematics* (pp. 216–226). Reston, VA: NCTM.

Shaughnessy, J. M. (2006). Research on students' understanding of some big concepts in statistics. In G. F. Burrill & P. C. Elliott (Eds.), *Thinking and reasoning about data and chance: 68th NCTM yearbook* (pp. 77–98). Reston, VA: National Council of Teachers of Mathematics.

Shaughnessy, J. M. (2007). Research on statistics learning and reasoning. In F. Lester, Jr. (Ed.), *Second handbook of research on mathematics teaching and learning* (pp. 957–1010). Reston, VA: National Council of Teachers of Mathematics.

Scheaffer, R. L. (2006). Statistics and mathematics: On making a happy marriage. In G. F. Burrill & P. C. Elliott (Eds.), *Thinking and reasoning about data and chance: 68th NCTM yearbook* (pp. 309–322). Reston, VA: National Council of Teachers of Mathematics.

Seuss, Dr. (1960). *Green eggs and ham.* New York, NY: Random House.

Smith, D. (2009). *If America were a village: A book about the people of the United States.* Tonawanda, NY: Kids Can Press.

Smith, D. (2011). *If the world were a village: A book about the world's people* (2nd ed.). Tonawanda, NY: Kids Can Press.

Swinburne, S. (2011). *Whose shoes? A shoe for every job.* Honesdale, PA: Boyds Mill Press.

Tarr, J. E., & Shaughnessy, J. M. (2007). *Data and chance. Results from the 2003 National Assessment of Educational Process.* Reston, VA: NCTM.

Index